Amish D

Jacob's Da

Coll

7 books in one

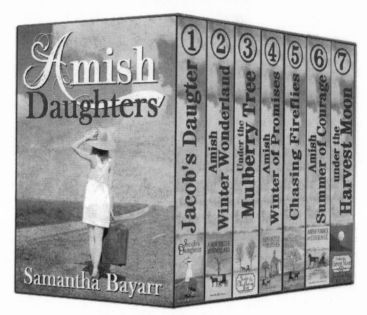

Samantha Bayarr

TABLE OF CONTENTS

Jacob's Daughter
BOOK 1

Samantha Jillian Bayarr

Copyright © 2011 by Samantha Jillian Bayarr

CHAPTER 1

"I'm what?"

"You heard me, Abby. Now hurry up and put this dress over your head before we miss our bus."

Lizzie Barlow stood her ground. She could feel no sympathy for her daughter at the moment. They had to get on that bus to Indiana, and there was no time for the temper-tantrums of a ten-year-old to complicate their already life-threatening situation.

"I'm not Amish! You take that back!"

Lizzie pursed her lips. "Actually, Abby, you *are* Amish because *I'm* Amish."

Abby placed her hands on her hips in defiance.

"I'm not Amish! Why do I have to dress like them?"

Lizzie shushed her daughter, who was practically screaming.

She stamped her feet. "I want to go home right now!"

Lizzie firmly grasped her daughter by her arms and forced her to look at her. "We don't live there anymore. We have to go to Indiana. We'll make a new life there, and you'll love it so much you'll never want to leave."

Tears pooled in Abby's eyes. "If it's so great in Indiana, then why did you leave?"

The question pricked Lizzie's heart, and she was growing impatient with her daughter.

"It's complicated, Abby."

"Is it because of my father?"

Tears streamed down her cheeks, and Lizzie bit her lower lip to keep from giving in to her child's whims.

"We are *not* having this conversation right now. We're running out of time. Get dressed and we can talk once we arrive safely in Indiana."

"Why do we have to wear these awful clothes, Mom?"

Lizzie looked in the faded mirror in the bathroom of the bus depot, trying to wipe the remaining makeup from her face. "They aren't awful. And we're wearing them so

Eddie's friends won't notice us if they should come looking."

"But I wanna wear my Hello Kitty shirt!"

Lizzie sighed. "Please don't make this harder than it already is, Abby. Slip this dress over your head, and hurry before we miss the bus."

She'd begun making the Amish dresses secretly, being careful to hide them from Eddie, Abby's drug-addicted father, so they would have them for their escape. Finding out he was Abby's father only three months ago, he'd threatened Lizzie that he'd kill her and take Abby if she wouldn't give him large sums of money to pay off his debt and support his drug habit. Lizzie didn't intend to stick around long enough to find out how much worse the situation with him would get. For weeks, she'd planned her escape from Eddie's threats, until the day he was found dead from a drug-induced, car accident that totaled Lizzie's car.

Dating him only two short weeks when she was still only seventeen, Lizzie tried to convince herself he was "the one" when they'd met, but she knew deep down she needed to end it with him so they could keep the passion between them respectable because he was a pushy *Englischer*. Sadly, she knew she could never really love him as much as a person ought to in order to take their relationship to the next level. She'd given her heart to only one man in her life, and she knew she could never feel that way for another. But when Eddie took advantage of her, she was left pregnant and ran from him.

Despite changing her name, Eddie still managed to locate her. And that's when the threats began. He demanded money from her to keep quiet about being Abby's father, and started threatening her when she wouldn't give him any more. Trying to spare her daughter from knowing the ugly truth of how she came into the world, she gave in to Eddie's threats until she just couldn't take it anymore.

Lizzie didn't make much money as a pharmacy technician, and when Eddie learned of her employment after coming into the pharmacy to try to redeem an illegal prescription for pain meds, he tried to force her to steal prescription medications for him. Out of fear of what he might do, she'd promised him she would do it, even though she had never stolen anything in her life, and she wasn't about to start. She'd managed to keep him at bay for a couple of days by telling him she hadn't found a way around the cameras in the pharmacy, but when he began showing up at her job, threatening her and her fellow employees, Lizzie was fired. It was too late for her to wish she'd moved farther away from him than the next small town over.

That same day, Eddie stormed out of the pharmacy in a rage of anger, and then totaled her car that he'd been *borrowing* by running it into the side of a tree, ending his battle with drugs—and his life.

Lizzie hadn't even cried. It wasn't that she was heartless, or didn't care that he'd died—she'd done her crying ten years earlier when she decided to leave him after he violated her. In truth, it was over between them the day that he drugged her and stole her innocence.

Still, she could feel little more than relief that her nightmare with him would be put to rest along with his remains. Though Eddie's pain and suffering was ended, her anger over the mountain of debt she was left with due to his reckless behavior had all but destroyed her. Not to mention the threats from the men who wanted her only child in exchange for a debt she didn't owe.

Because she'd let her car insurance policy lapse to give money to Eddie, she was stuck with a car that was no longer drivable, but was still responsible for the payment. And when those thugs started threatening her over the money that Eddie had borrowed from them and for drugs he had never paid for, Lizzie knew it was time to leave this life of debt and pain behind—for Abby's sake—and for her own peace of mind. Her mistakes in judgment had caused her ten-year-old daughter more harm than she was capable of understanding at her young age, and Lizzie knew what she had to do; it was time for her to face the sins of her past, and suffer the consequences to spare Abby from being caught in the middle of her poor choices any longer.

Losing her job, her car, and the threats from the drug-dealers all in a week's time was too much for Lizzie to handle. She'd seen the men before, and even witnessed them roughing Eddie up one night outside of her small, rented house. That's when she heard him promise them Lizzie could get them drugs. And that's when she decided the only way to get away from the thugs that were threatening her was to continue her original plan and find a place to hide from Eddie's mistakes; a place no one would ever think to look for her.

The Amish community.

No one knew of Lizzie's past—not even her own daughter. Given the nature of the events that prompted her to flee from the only way of life she'd ever known, she determined over the years to keep her past hidden, and had even practiced continuously to lose her German accent, and pattern her life after the *Englisch*. She determined, however, to maintain the teachings of her upbringing–even if only in secret. So far, she'd managed to keep her past hidden all these years, and now she was about to walk right back into it with Abby in tow.

Lizzie pulled the plain shoes and stockings from the backpack where she'd kept them hidden for weeks, and handed a pair to her daughter. "Put these on. We have to hurry and pin your hair up in the back."

Abby was busy texting her friends, probably telling them how unfair her only parent was being at the moment, and Lizzie knew it was going to be an even bigger argument when she broke the news to her daughter that the phone would soon be turned off due to non-payment. She reminded herself that it was for the best, since she wouldn't take any chances that Eddie's drug-dealing friends could use the device to track them down. She would have to wait for a while to get a new phone; necessities were the only thing they had money for until Lizzie could find a new job.

She would also worry about getting a cheap car once they got to Indiana; she would use a portion of the money she'd gotten from selling all of their things on Craig's List.

She would need a car to look for work so she could find a small house to rent for her and Abby to start over.

Lizzie pulled her hair up and twisted it at the base of her neck, pinning it in place. She placed a prayer *kapp* over her head and handed the other one to Abby.

"Where did you get these weird hats?"

"They're called *prayer kapps*, and I made them."

"How do you know how to make this stuff?"

"YouTube has a video for everything; you know that." She wasn't exactly lying. YouTube did have a how-to video for practically everything, but Lizzie already knew how to make the *prayer kapps*, but she wasn't ready to tell Abby the entire story of her past just yet. She would save it for when they were far enough away from Ohio that she could relax enough to tell her everything.

When they were completely dressed in their disguises, Lizzie took one last look in the mirror. She never intended to wear Plain clothing again—let alone to walk back into Amish territory, but it was out of necessity that she would brave this move.

Without makeup, Lizzie thought she looked well beyond the twenty-eight years that she was, and getting pregnant at seventeen had not helped matters. It was more likely that all the hardship of the past years had aged her. Deep down, she knew some fresh air and a good dose of home-cooking was all it would take, and she'd be good as new.

As they exited the bus depot restroom, Lizzie looked over her shoulder to make sure no one had followed her and Abby. Just a few more minutes and they would be on the bus and on their way to Indiana where Eddie's *friends* would never suspect to look for them.

She *had* to go back home.

It was her only chance of escaping from her life with Eddie for good. Lizzie's own mother had died when she was Abby's age, and if her father had known about Abby, he would have shunned her. It was probably the best thing for her at the time to assume she'd been shunned, since it forced her to grow up and go to college. But even her education couldn't save her now from the damage Eddie had done.

They boarded the bus, but only when it pulled away from the depot, did Lizzie begin to relax a little. Their immediate future was unsure, but her destination for now, was the Miller Bed and Breakfast just off County Road 27, near the home where she grew up.

CHAPTER 2

Jacob Yoder tossed the basin full of water out the barn door, and put a hand to his freshly shaved chin. His skin felt funny after having worn the beard for the past ten years, but it was time to end his mourning period for Nellie. They'd been married only ten months before she died, and Jacob had suffered more with the guilt that he'd married her on the rebound, than with the pain of losing a wife that was dear to him. His guilt only magnified when she died giving birth to his son, Caleb. She was a good woman and did not deserve the fate she'd been dealt when she married him. The only good thing to come from their marriage was Caleb, and it was time for Jacob to try to put the sins of his past behind him—for Caleb's sake. He would no longer hold onto the past or wish for what could have been; he would honor his wife's memory and do right by their son.

He married Nellie when he was just eighteen years old, even though he was still in love with Lizzie. He and Lizzie had been best friends since they were ten years old. Her father had refused to allow her to court like other girls her age. So they did what most of the Amish teenagers did at the time, and saw each other secretly. Being the only daughter of Hiram Miller, Lizzie's activities were constantly monitored by her two older brothers, especially after her *mamm* had died from complications after miscarrying a child that came along unexpectedly when Lizzie was only ten years old.

Despite the strict ties on Lizzie, she and Jacob still managed to sneak in some time together, until her *bruder*, David, caught them and reported back to her father. From that day on, they were forbidden to see each other again. Because of the risk of seeing each other and getting caught, Jacob longed for the day she would turn eighteen and marry him. But when her brother, David came to him with the news that she no longer wanted to see him, he was devastated.

One month later, Jacob began to court Nellie, and Lizzie ran off with some *Englisch* friends. It had broken his heart to learn that she'd left Indiana after sending word with her brother, David that she no longer wanted to see him just a few short weeks before, but his future with Nellie was already set in motion. If only she'd had the guts to say it to his face, he might have had the chance to talk her out of her decision.

Jacob pushed the memories away, putting them back where he'd kept them for the past ten years—locked away in his numb heart, where he refused to let himself feel them. Lizzie was his past, and he needed to stop thinking about her. He had several acres of corn that needed to be harvested, and a young son that was itching to learn to be just like his *daed*. Jacob had spent too many years thinking that the sins of his past were responsible for his wife's death. But now, he was determined to put all of it behind him and be the best father the boy could have.

Caleb wandered sleepily into the barn, the sun barely up. He took a step back at the sight of Jacob standing before him—beardless. "*Daed,* is that you?"

"*Jah,* I shaved my *baard.*"

It was an outward sign to end his mourning period, but it wouldn't quiet the guilt that had eaten away at him for so many years. That was something he would have to work on to get rid of—for Caleb's sake.

Caleb thought about it for a minute and then looked to the ground. "Does this mean you will be getting married again? When Jonah Beiler's *daed* shaved his *baard*, he got married, and now Jonah has a new *mamm.*"

Jacob put a hand on top of his son's head and gave his thick, blonde hair a shake. "You're not getting a new *mamm,* and I'm not getting married."

Caleb smiled up at Jacob. "It wouldn't be so bad having a *mamm.*"

Jacob sighed. He didn't intend to get married again, despite the fact that there were presently two women his age in the community who never married. He'd gone to school with both of them as a young boy, but had never had any other contact with them since. They'd attended church services and community outings, but Jacob never paid them any mind because he had no reason to consider them for anything other than part of a working community—no matter how much prompting he'd had from friends and family to take a second look at them.

Jacob's only focus now would be his son and his farm. If the sudden change in weather would be any indication of the winter ahead of them, he would need to bring in his crop in record time. He knew the task would easily be accomplished with the help of his family and neighbors. He was happy that Caleb was taking an active interest in the harvest, and Jacob was determined to teach him to be a good farmer. Though he didn't want to add to the chores the boy already did, he knew that he needed the experience if he was to take over his father's land one day.

Knowing the single women of the community would attend the harvest, Jacob was suddenly wary of his decision to shave off his beard so soon. It had been a shield for Jacob for the past ten years, and now the entire community would think he was in the market for a wife—especially with wedding season upon them. Panic filled him, and he whispered a short prayer while Caleb ran off to feed the chickens.

Just as he ended his prayer, Jacob could hear the clip-clop of the horses pulling buggies full of the *menner* who were traveling up the lane to begin the harvest. Soon, the day would be underway, and the men would bring in the crops while the women prepared food and visited.

Jacob put a hand to his chin and rubbed at the bare skin. It was too late to rethink his decision, but it wasn't too late to guard his heart against any of the women who would show an interest in him. He would have to keep his eyes toward the ground when the food was served, and he would keep his company contained to that of the men in the community. Even though he'd been a widower for ten years, there had been room in his heart for only one woman, and he had never found room for any other—not even for his own wife.

CHAPTER 3

Lizzie stepped off the bus in Elkhart, Indiana, feeling full of hope for the first time in months. Though she knew it would be a challenge to be in her old stomping ground after so many years, she was excited to see her Aunt Bess again. It wouldn't be the same as seeing her *daed* or her brothers, but with her aunt running the B&B, it would be easier to blend in since she catered to the *Englisch*. She wondered if her aunt would accept her as an *Englischer* after all these years, but the phone conversations they'd had recently gave Lizzie hope that she would be able to make the transition easier for Abby. Not only would it be easier for her to have help from a family member, but she looked forward to introducing her daughter to her aunt, and finally telling Abby of her family history.

The only thing that made her nervous about her decision to go back home, was the possibility of running into Jacob Yoder. Surely he was married by now with several children, and she wasn't certain how that would make her feel. Probably jealousy would surface, along with resentment that her daughter would not be able to benefit from having a *daed* of her own. Lizzie would never dream of calling him out after all this time. After all, she's the one that left and never told him where she was going. But she was just a young girl, and he'd made it plenty clear to her that he wanted nothing more to do with her. Being the coward that he was, he'd passed the message along with her older brother, David. If he'd had the courage to face her, she would have told him she loved him, but it was all in the past, and she didn't intend on socializing with the community who had likely shunned her, so it wouldn't be an issue to avoid Jacob and his family.

Abby watched the landscaping go by from the window of the cab. She was angry with her mom, who hadn't explained much to her about why they were running away from the only life Abby had ever known. She'd treated her like a baby when she'd asked her mom questions about Eddie. Despite Lizzie's efforts to sugar-coat the truth, and let Abby think he was just an old friend who had problems, she saw right through her mom's stories to protect her from the truth. She knew there was more to the story than what she'd been told, but all she cared about was that he seemed to be the reason they left Ohio, and that didn't make any sense to her since the man was dead.

Abby didn't like feeling like her mom was lying to her. She'd overheard enough heated conversations between her mom and Eddie to know something bad was going on. During Red Ribbon week at school, Abby had learned all about the ways drugs can destroy lives, and it seemed Eddie was now a cliché of an example to her. Unfortunately, nothing in the lectures in school could have prepared her for the way that destruction would affect her own life.

Abby reached into her back pack for her cell phone; at least she could find comfort in her friends. She texted out a message to her best friend, Rachel, and then pushed send. She held her phone up hoping to get a better signal so it would send since it didn't seem to be working. She looked closely when the text failed, noting that she had several bars. She tried to resend, and became frustrated when it wouldn't work. Pushing in Rachel's number, she held it to her ear and listened to the rings until an automated message answered her call. She held the phone out to look at the face, thinking she'd punched the wrong number. Hanging up, she tried it again. The same message came up.

She pushed the phone toward Lizzie, who was lost in her own thoughts. "There's something wrong with my phone. I can't call Rachel!"

Lizzie pulled the phone to her ear and listened to the message. "I haven't paid the bill, Abby, I'm sorry."

Abby pushed the phone back toward her mother when she tried to give it back to her. "Can't you pay the bill so I can talk to Rachel? If I can't talk to her, I won't be able to get through this vacation."

Lizzie put the phone down on the seat between them and turned to her daughter. "I'll get us new phones when we settle in Indiana and I get a job. Until then, I'm afraid you're going to have to be without communication with your friends. And this isn't a vacation. We aren't going back to Ohio."

Abby snatched the phone up from the seat of the cab, and shot a look at Lizzie that alarmed her. "What do mean we aren't going back? All my friends are there! I don't want a new phone; I want you to turn this one back on so I can call Rachel. Please, Mom!"

Lizzie gazed at the prying eyes of the cab driver in the rearview mirror. "We can talk about this when we get to the Bed & Breakfast."

Abby crossed her arms in defiance. "My life is going to be ruined unless you turn my phone back on!"

Lizzie looked at her sternly. "I'm not turning it back on, so drop it, Abby."

Abby rolled down the window of the cab and tossed the phone out the window, watching it bounce along the road while the cab sped away from it. Lizzie didn't even notice; she was too wrapped up in what she was going to say to her *aenti* when they arrived at the Bed & Breakfast.

Abby turned her face back toward the window, watching the farms go by slowly. She didn't see any malls or schools, or even a McDonald's anywhere. What was she going to do so far away from everything and everyone she cared about? Her mother rattled on about how good the move would be for them, and that she had a surprise for Abby, but she didn't care. She was wearing an itchy dress that she'd surely be teased for if her friends could see her, and she couldn't see past the miles of farmland and endless ribbons of road that led her further away from her life.

CHAPTER 4

Caleb sat under a tree with a plate of fried chicken that Miriam Graber handed to him, and now she was talking his ear off about how much help he'd been all day to his *daed*. He ignored her, realizing that the sudden attention had to do with the conversations he'd overheard the women discussing that involved his *daed*, and his newly shaven face, leaving them hoping he was thinking of taking a wife. Martha Schrock was busy trying to hand him a plate piled high with cakes and pastries, asking if he would take it to his *daed*, when Caleb noticed the beardless man ducking behind a tree near the pond. He watched his *daed* for several minutes before deciding to walk down to the pond and see why he was hiding from these women who were eager to be his new *mamm*.

Caleb picked up a rock and tossed it sideways toward the pond just like Jacob had shown him the previous summer. He watched in awe as it skipped across the glassy surface several times before sinking to the bottom. "Look, *Daed*, I did it just like ya showed me!"

Jacob placed a hand on his son's shoulder, feeling a little bit of pride as he watched the rings slowly disappear on the sparkling water. He couldn't help himself when it came to Caleb, but it humbled him to know that the boy looked up to him so much. Twinges of guilt tried to ruin the moment with thoughts that Nellie would never see her son do any of the simple things that Jacob sometimes took for granted. He'd seen his son soaking up the attention of Miriam and Martha, who would each probably make fine *mamm's* for his son, and he felt selfish for denying him the one thing that was within his power to give. He would never be able to give him his real *mamm*, but he could give the boy what he craved...a new *mamm*. He'd been selfish with his son long enough and maybe it was time to revisit the idea of taking a wife—for Caleb's sake.

"I saw you talking to Miss Martha and Miss Miriam. I'm guessing you think that either of them would make a fine *mamm* for you."

Jacob's heart did a summersault in his chest at the thought of it. He suddenly felt well beyond the twenty-eight years that he was. He felt he was much too young to be a widower, and considering a second marriage with a woman who would most like want her own *kind* in addition to raising Caleb. Was he ready to start all over again with a baby with Caleb being ten years old? Was he really ready to marry just for the sake of giving Caleb a *mamm?* Maybe not, but perhaps it would make up for the sins of his past.

Caleb looked up at his *daed* and studied him for a moment. "I heard the women talking about the fact you shaved off your *baard*. They think you want to get married." He continued to study Jacob. "Is it true?"

Jacob took in a lung-full of fresh air and then let it out. "If you're wanting a *mamm,* I'd be willing to take it under consideration."

Caleb shook his head disappointedly. "It would be nice to have a *mamm.* And a *bruder."*

Jacob choked down his son's bold statement.

"Maybe you're putting the cart before the horse, Caleb. I haven't even asked either of them if I could call on them properly. It's a process that takes time."

He hoped the statement would satisfy the lad until he could think of a way out of the mess, but by the expression on Caleb's face, this wasn't going to be easy.

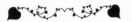

Lizzie shook as she stepped out of the cab. The driver was already at the trunk retrieving their small suitcases, but Lizzie's feet felt heavy as she heaved her backpack over her shoulder and tried to step toward the front walk of the B&B. She took note that the oversized home had been recently painted, and four freshly painted rocking chairs graced the front porch that was surrounded by flowering plants in a myriad of colors. She could hear ducks on the pond quacking happily. Oh how she'd missed that sound. And the smell of the water floating gently on the breeze. The only thing that would make this moment less stressful was a tall glass of lemonade and a trip back in time. She glanced over at Abby feeling guilty for thinking such a selfish thought. But she was nervous about being so near her *daed*—even if she wouldn't be seeing him.

Aunt Bess came running out the front door, her apron flying in the breeze as she planted herself in front of Lizzie. "*Wie gehts,* Elizabeth? I've missed you so much!"

Bess hugged Lizzie so hard she nearly took her breath away. Her aunt smelled of fresh-baked bread and smoked ham, no doubt from preparing for their visit. Lizzie felt the warmth of the older woman's embrace, feeling like she was finally home.

Aunt Bess pulled away and examined Abby. "Who is this precious child with such a long face?"

"This is my daughter, Abby."

The word felt strange coming from Lizzie's lips, and Abby looked at her quizzically. She knew she would have a lot of explaining to do, but not yet. She wanted to settle in first, and *then* break the news to Abby that they were here for good—with Lizzie's family. She hoped to be able to see her father and younger brother, Seth, but she was sure she had been shunned at some point over the last eleven years since she'd turned her back on Amish soil.

Her aunt pulled Lizzie close again and whispered in her ear. "I see by your garb that you're planning on re-joining the community, *jah?*"

Lizzie swallowed hard. "*Nee.* I made the dresses and *kapps* as a disguise. I'll explain everything later."

Aunt Bess pulled away from Lizzie, her smile unfading, and picked up their suitcases and headed inside the B&B. Lizzie looked at Abby, who was wearing a scowl deep enough to cause concern, but it wasn't something that could be helped at the moment. Lizzie wondered how long the child would remain silent, but giving her the cold shoulder for the time being was probably best until she could explain everything to her *aenti* without Abby blurting out the wrong thing.

CHAPTER 5

Jacob had managed to carefully avoid Martha and Miriam the remainder of the work day, despite their many attempts at cornering him and offering to feed him their cooking. As his neighbors left his stretch of land, he thanked God that at least Caleb had given up his quest for a new *mamm* for the time being. Tomorrow would be a new day to fight the battle, but he hoped that Caleb would be too distracted with helping the *menner* with the harvest to pester him anymore.

By the end of the week, they would be at the Beiler farm for the barn-raising, and Jacob worried that being around Jonah would only remind him of his desire for a new family just like his. Jacob thought that perhaps he should consider taking in an older widow to cook and clean to give Caleb a break from his cooking, and the chore of housecleaning they shared along with the chores of running the farm. Maybe then Caleb would give up his quest for a new *mamm,* and Jacob wouldn't have to worry about becoming involved in another loveless marriage. It wasn't that Jacob was against marriage; he had never gotten over his first love and didn't want to repeat the mistake he'd made in marrying Nellie.

Jacob laid his weary head on his pillow, willing the memories of Lizzie to leave him. Why was he still thinking of her after all these years? And with his wife being dead for ten years, he should be thinking of her, instead of the one that got away almost eleven years ago.

Over the years, he'd continuously thought that if he could have seen Lizzie one last time—or even been able to say goodbye, that it would be easier for him to deal with, than the reality of never seeing her again, and always wondering what had become of her. Even her own family had not heard from her in the eleven years since her disappearance. Because there was no word from her, there had never been a formal shunning; the community and Jacob had feared she was dead.

Lizzie tucked Abby into the thick quilt of the room at the far end of the B&B that Aunt Bess set aside for visiting families. Lizzie didn't mind sharing the room with her daughter, but she wasn't sure Abby was too happy about it.

"How long are we staying here? Don't get me wrong—I like your Aunt Bess, but she dresses in the same strange clothes you made us wear to get here. Are you going to make me wear those clothes while we're here?"

Lizzie sighed. She knew Abby would be full of questions, but she just needed a good night's rest before she tackled her daughter's protest over their living situation and her curiosity about the family she was meeting for the first time.

"How about we take a walk down to the pond after breakfast and I'll tell you everything. But right now, I think we should get some sleep. It's been a really long day."

Abby crossed her arms and looked away. "But I don't want to have a talk tomorrow. I want to go home. I want to sleep in my own bed and watch TV. I didn't see a single TV in this house!"

Lizzie turned her daughter's chin toward her and looked her in the eye. "You know I had to sell everything to come here. And the house belongs to the landlord. I'm sorry, but you will have to get used to living here—at least until we can get our own place again. As far as TV goes, you're going to have to live without it for now. Amish don't watch TV."

"That's just wrong, Mother!"

Lizzie snuffed out the light that rested on the table between the two beds and crawled beneath the warm, homemade quilt. The bedding smelled like it had been dried outside on the clothesline in the sunshine.

Oh how Lizzie had missed that smell...

Lizzie opened her eyes at first light. She could hear the ducks quacking outside the open window. Her aunt was more than likely at the pond's edge with her toes dipped in the water, throwing bread to the ducks. Forcing herself from the cocoon of quilts, Lizzie followed the smell of fresh-brewed coffee to the kitchen.

Aunt Bess entered in through the back door and set an empty bread basket on the table. "I knew you'd wake up when you smelled the *kaffi* brewing."

Lizzie smiled. "Actually it was the furiously hungry ducks that stirred me this morning, but I slept like a *boppli.* I haven't slept that soundly in some time."

Her aunt smiled. "Are ya ready to tell me why you're here? And without a *mann* or a *vadder* for the child?"

"I don't have a husband, and her *vadder* is gone."

Aunt Bess put a hand under Lizzie's chin, forcing her to look into her eyes. "You're too young to be without a husband. There are several widowers in the community, but the only one your age is Jacob Yoder. I know the two of you were in love when you were *kinner,* perhaps you could get to know him again. He owns the farm and all the land on the other side of pond, just down the lane."

Her aunt pointed in the direction of his farm, but Lizzie had let her vision blur at the mention of Jacob. The thought of him married broke her heart all over again. Had he married Nellie Fisher after she left the community? She knew she had no right to be upset that Jacob had taken a wife, but she'd always hoped he would marry *her* someday.

CHAPTER 6

Abby sat on the landing of the stairs listening to her mother and great aunt talk. She knew better than to eavesdrop, but the mention of the name Jacob Yoder pricked her ears. It was the name listed on her birth certificate as her father. And now Aunt Bess was saying he lived on the other side of the pond. She wondered why her mother was keeping her father from her if he was this close to them. She was certain her mother would say she had "grown-up" reasons for not telling her, but Abby didn't care—she was still mad at her mother for letting her cell phone—the only avenue to the outside world, get turned off and refusing to pay the bill.

Abby continued to listen as her great aunt explained to her mother that Jacob had been married, and how his wife had died giving birth to his son, Caleb, who was just a few months younger than Abby. Was it possible that Caleb was her brother? Did she even want a brother? A sister most certainly, but a brother?

Abby went back upstairs, determined to pack her small suitcase and leave this backward home. Her mother had lied to her about a lot of things, and she was now more angry than ever. She didn't want to be Amish for a single minute longer. She was certain that her brother had a TV, and probably video games. But most of all, she hoped her dad would have a cell phone she could use to call Rachel.

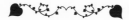

Abby had managed to slip out the front door of the B&B without her mother or great aunt noticing her. Aunt Bess was in the middle of offering her mother a job to clean the upstairs rooms of the B&B since the older woman suffered from swollen knees and it hurt her back to climb the stairs and stoop to clean. Her mother eagerly accepted, leaving Abby as the last one to be informed she was planning on staying in the area for an extended period of time, which only added fuel to Abby's already full plate of anger for her mother at the present time.

Pulling on her straw hat to shield her eyes from the sun, Abby walked slowly down the long, country road to the other side of the pond, where she was certain life would be much easier for her.

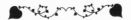

Caleb scattered feed for the chickens as he watched the barefoot *Englischer* walk down the lane toward their farm. Who was she, and why was she walking toward him with a funny look on her face? He watched with a laugh in his heart when she struggled to keep the oversized straw hat from blowing off her head in the breeze. She seemed to look lost as she looked around her, and then set her eyes back on Caleb. Walking up the long path toward his home, he noticed a sense of determination in her that he'd never seen before. She didn't look much older than he was, but the suitcase she toted carelessly at her side suggested she thought she was old enough to be on her own.

As she approached Caleb, she examined him from head to toe, and then let her eyes wander to the surrounding farm.

Caleb stepped in her path. "Are you lost or running away?"

Abby stopped scanning the property and set her eyes on Caleb. "Both. Do you know where I can find Jacob Yoder?"

Caleb pointed behind him. "He's in the barn. What do ya want with him?"

Abby set her jaw upward. "That's private."

Caleb watched the girl walk toward the barn and disappear in the shadow of the open doorway.

Abby walked cautiously toward the barn and entered through the open door. She hoped she wasn't in the wrong place, assuming the young farm-hand had steered her in the right direction. As she approached a man mucking out one of the horse stalls, she examined him from the short distance that separated them. On his head was a straw hat like the young boy was wearing, and his clothing was the same style, but he didn't have the beard she'd witnessed the Amish men his age wearing when she and her mother rode through town yesterday in their cab ride to the B&B.

Taking a brave step forward, Abby cleared her throat to get the man's attention. He looked up and leaned against his pitchfork. "Excuse me, Sir. Can you tell me where I can find Jacob Yoder?"

Jacob stepped out of the stall and set aside the pitch fork to close part of the distance between them. "I am Jacob Yoder. Who might you be?"

Jacob took another step forward.

"I'm Lizzie's daughter."

Jacob pulled of his hat and blew out a heavy sigh. "Lizzie Miller?"

Abby set her suitcase down and moved toward the horse that seemed anxious for her attention. "That was her name when she was younger, but she changed it when she left home. At least that's what she told me, but she's been keeping some secrets from me my whole life that I'm just now finding out—like where my father was all this time."

Jacob looked into the girl's eyes. He could see Lizzie in them, and it scared him that she could look just like her mother did when they had attended school together.

"I'm not sure how I can help you. What is your name?"

Abby reached up and touched the horse nickering for attention on his soft nose. "My name is Abby, and my birth certificate says Jacob Yoder is my father. When I heard my mom and Aunt Bess talking this morning about you living here, I decided to come here and let you be a father to me. I'm mad at her for lying to me, and I don't want to go back there. She is expecting me to be Amish just because she is." Abby fanned out the skirt of her white sundress. "I like wearing my own dresses, not the itchy Amish ones that she made us wear when we came here so Eddie's thugs wouldn't find us."

Jacob looked behind him at the milking stool and collapsed onto it before he lost his balance. He knew he hadn't fathered Lizzie's child since they had never been intimate, but he wondered why she would name him as father on the girl's birth certificate. He couldn't think straight. "Who is Eddie? And why are his *thugs* looking for you? Are you and your *mamm* in some sort of danger?"

Abby continued to stroke the horse on the nose.

"Eddie is this mean guy that used to come over and hit my mom and make her give him money, but he's dead now. He crashed mom's car. But now his thugs came over and told mom to give them the money Eddie owed them. That's why we dressed in the Amish clothes to come here and hide from those men. They had a gun."

Jacob took in a deep breath, trying to digest the little girl's ramblings. He wasn't so sheltered that he didn't know what the word *thug* meant. He also knew the danger of having unsavory characters looking for Lizzie and this child—the child who seemed to think he was her *daed*.

CHAPTER 7

Bess poured a third cup of coffee, emptying the pot. "Should I brew another pot of *kaffi?*"

Lizzie shook her head. "I'm good. If I drink any more I won't sleep later."

Bess sat down across from Lizzie and stared into her cup. "Do ya plan on going home, Elizabeth?"

"Do ya mean to see my *daed* and *bruder?*"

"*Jah.* You haven't been shunned. It's not too late."

Lizzie stood and began to pace the small kitchen, despite her aunt's prodding to sit back down. "Ya don't understand. I won't be welcomed back into the community. Mine would be considered the longest running *rumspringa* in the history of this community. Besides, you're forgetting I had a child out of wedlock."

Bess stood beside her and placed loving arms around her. "If ya confess all that to the Bishop, he will baptize you. *Gott* himself doesn't hold that against you; how can the elders hold it against you that Eddie drugged you and compromised you? And now he's *dot,* so in the eyes of the elders, they may consider you a widow."

Lizzie sighed. "I think you're giving them more credit than what they're due. The elders and the Bishop will not be so quick to overlook my transgressions."

"Then give a general confession, and the rest will be our little secret—and between you and *Gott,* of course."

Lizzie hugged her aunt, grateful for her discretion. But there was just a little bit more to her story that she needed to reveal.

"When I found out I was pregnant, I moved to a small, unincorporated community in Ohio named Barlow. I chose the community because it reminded me a little of the Amish community. Once I settled in, I legally changed my name to Lizzie Barlow."

Bess crinkled her brow. "What was the significance of the name?"

"I chose the name Lizzie because that's what Jacob always called me, and I was still very much in love with him at the time."

The confession brought tears to Lizzie's eyes. Though the mere thought of Jacob filled her with regret, she knew if she hadn't left, she wouldn't have Abby. Besides, she would never have been able to bear watching Jacob court and marry Nellie Fisher if she'd stayed. Her life had not been easy since she left home, but maybe that was all about to change.

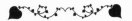

Jacob stood on wobbly legs. He had no idea how he would explain to this child he wasn't her father, but the worry on the forefront was Lizzie. He was already way behind in his chores, and would need to complete them before he could take Abby back. It didn't seem likely that he would be able to convince her to go back on her own, and he worried that Lizzie would be frantic over her disappearance—especially given the story that she'd relayed to him about the danger they may be in. But the truth of the matter was that he didn't have a phone to call her at the B&B, and a small part of him hoped Lizzie herself would show up on his property to claim her daughter. Though he was eager to see her again, he was more than a little disturbed by Lizzie's actions. They had put him in quite the predicament.

Jacob faced Abby and cleared his throat as if the act could somehow give him the words to say to her. "My son Caleb is in the yard feeding the chickens, but I can assume he's moved on to the pigs by this time. Would you like to go out and help him so I can get a few things finished here, and then we can sit in the house and maybe have some lunch before we go have a talk with your *mamm*—I mean your mom?"

Abby took a small leap backward and squealed, leaving Jacob searching for a snake or a spider. "I don't want to go back. She's trying to make me Amish and I don't like it."

Jacob chuckled. "I'm Amish, Abby."

Abby's eyes filled with tears. "Then it's true. I'm Amish and there's nothing I can do about it."

"Being Amish is a very *gut* thing, not a bad thing. Didn't your *madder* tell you that?"

"You mean my *mother?*"

Jacob nodded.

"She never told me we were Amish before yesterday. And she didn't tell me anything about *you*. When I saw my birth certificate, I asked her about the name, and she just said that was the name of my real father. Every time I tried to ask her anything about you, she would turn all sad, and sometimes she'd cry. So I stopped asking her."

Jacob's heart sank. How could he tell Abby the truth when she'd been told he was her *vadder?* This was Lizzie's mess, and she would have to be the one to get herself out of it.

Abby looked up at Jacob, tears streaming down her face. "How come you never came looking for me?"

Jacob searched for the right words. "I'm sorry you're upset Abby, but I didn't know anything about you either until you showed up here on my farm."

Abby cried harder. "But you're my father, you should have known about me!"

Jacob looked up when movement in the doorway caught his eye. Caleb entered the barn, and circled Abby.

"Is she my *schweschder?*"

Jacob stood between them. "This is not your business, Caleb."

He ignored his father. "Is your *mamm dot* too?"

Abby crossed her arms. "Will you guys speak English around me, cuz I don't understand your language."

Jacob felt distraught over Abby's lack of knowledge of her heritage. "Didn't your *mamm* teach you the Amish language?"

"I already told you. She told me yesterday she was Amish, and that I am too. She's never talked like that, but I heard her say some funny words to her Aunt Bess."

"My son wanted to know if your mom was still alive."

Abby turned to Caleb. "She's very much alive. Why would you ask me such a thing?"

Caleb's gaze fell to the ground. "Because my *mamm* is not. She died when she was birthing me."

Abby gulped.

Caleb looked at his *daed* with hopeful eyes. "If she's my *schweschder,* does that mean her *mamm* will want to be my new *mamm?"*

Jacob looked at his son sternly. "*Halten* Caleb."

Abby's eyes grew wide. "He wants my mom to be *his* mom?"

Jacob ignored her question. "Caleb, take Abby into the *haus* and get her some lemonade, and then get back to your chores. When I finish in the barn, I'll hitch up the buggy, and we will take you back so I can have a grownup talk with your mom."

Both children obeyed Jacob's orders, and skipped up to the house, leaving him with a lot of conflicting thoughts.

CHAPTER 8

Lizzie yawned and leaned back in her chair to get a better look at the kitchen clock. "I should go check on Abby. If I let her sleep any longer, she'll be wired the rest of the day. And I won't be able to get her to sit still long enough to talk to her about everything."

Dragging her feet up the stairs, Lizzie felt the weight of her day already slowing her down. She was not looking forward to having to explain everything to her daughter, who was already starting to rebel against her. If she wasn't careful, she would drive her child away even further, but if she continued to sugar-coat the truth, she would never have her daughter's respect.

Lizzie opened the door to the room they shared and noticed Abby's bed was empty. Scanning the room, she immediately noticed Abby's small suitcase was no longer on the floor in a disheveled mess where she'd left it. Knowing she'd warned her daughter to put it away in the morning or forfeit her breakfast, she peeked into the closet to see if it was tossed carelessly in there or if she'd closed it and put it away neatly like she was asked to do. Alarmed by the empty space were her daughter's suitcase should be, Lizzie's heart skipped a beat. Immediately dropping to the floor, she pulled up the dust-ruffle to search for it under the bed.

It wasn't there.

Lizzie threw back the covers of Abby's bed, but still, nothing.

There was no trace of Abby left in the room.

Lizzie's heart slammed against her ribcage as she practically flew down the stairs to the kitchen. Out of breath, she found her aunt still sitting at the table savoring her last cup of coffee.

"Abby's gone!"

Bess pushed the chair behind her, stepping forward to steady Lizzie. "Sit down and take a deep breath and define *gone*."

Lizzie allowed the woman to guide her into the chair she'd been comfortable in just moments ago. "She's not upstairs. Her suitcase is gone. We *have* to go look for her."

Bess straightened her apron and held a hand across her ample breast. "She's on foot, so she couldn't have gotten far. Let me call the surrounding people with phones in their barns and ask them to start searching for her. Your *daed* is the furthest out on the main road…is it okay if I call him?"

Lizzie didn't have to think about it. "Yes! Call him—but don't tell him details—only that the daughter of a guest is missing—please, *aenti*—I don't want him to find out about his *kinskind* in this way."

Bess nodded while Lizzie ran out to the barn to begin hitching the horse to her aunt's buggy. She was confident she remembered how to hitch up a horse, but more than that, she needed something to keep her hands busy while Aunt Bess made the phone calls. She wouldn't allow herself to think beyond her daughter's obvious reasons for running off. She'd lied to her about a lot of things, and she understood the child's tantrum. But with danger lurking over their heads because of Eddie, she feared for her daughter's safety more than ever. Trying desperately to think logically, she knew they had gotten far enough away, and in a remote enough place that it was highly unlikely that the thugs would be able to track her down, but she knew that even as cautious as she was about leaving no trail, they could still find her.

Grateful that the gelding was patient with her nervous fumbling of the harnesses, Lizzie was able to hitch the horse fairly quickly. Just as she finished, her aunt was out the door, draping a shawl over her shoulders, and hoisting herself into the buggy. Lizzie climbed up beside her and took the reins, and slapped them gently against the gelding.

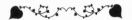

Jacob worked quickly, knowing that every minute that Abby remained on his farm was another minute that Lizzie would be worried about her daughter. Unfortunately, it just couldn't be helped. He had a cow to milk and animals to feed before he could take her back. The rest of his chores could wait until later, but the animals couldn't wait for their grain.

His mind drifted to his younger days when he was courting Lizzie. He remembered how angry and hurt he was that she'd sent her eldest brother, David, to break off their relationship as if it had meant nothing to her. He'd intended to marry her—to have a family with her, and grow old with her. And now she comes back to the community with another man's *kind*, trying to claim he'd fathered her. He would be excommunicated from the community if the elders were to discover this, and it would ruin his reputation as a trusted member of the community.

A small part of him wanted to hold onto the memory of Lizzie when she was young and innocent of the ways of the *Englischers,* but that was next to impossible with evidence to the contrary that had invaded his own home.

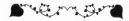

In the house, Abby was amazed by the things Caleb continued to point out that *their* dad had made. Every piece of furniture was carved to perfection. And the solid wood banister on the stairway tempted Abby to slide down it. It was a fine house indeed, and Abby hadn't even noticed the lack of televisions or other electronic equipment.

The "tour" was contained to the downstairs rooms, but Abby's favorite room was a sun porch with a fireplace and two cozy rocking chairs. Her mom used to rock her when she was younger, but they had been forced to part with the one piece of furniture with any sentimental value when her mother decided to move them here. A renewed sense of anger welled up in Abby, but she quickly pushed it aside, realizing she was beginning to miss her mom.

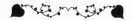

Lizzie steered the gelding toward the main road, lost in her thoughts. Too many emotions attacked her at the moment, and she feared she would not be able to contain her composure much longer. She chided herself for thinking that coming to the Amish community would solve her problems. But running away seemed to be what she did best. And now, it seemed, she'd passed that trait onto her only child. Abby had left willingly—packed her suitcase and left. She wondered if this is how her *daed* had felt when she ran away from home nearly eleven years ago. Lizzie feared for Abby, who was much younger than she had been when she left. She wasn't capable of taking care of herself in dangerous situations. Although, to be honest, she hadn't been either, or she wouldn't even have had Abby in the first place.

Lizzie pushed aside thoughts of the past. She had to find her daughter, and even the fear of seeing her *daed* and *brieder* for the first time in eleven years couldn't compare to the fear she held for her child.

CHAPTER 9

Lizzie wrung her hands while her aunt prepared coffee and sliced cake for the neighbors who had already arrived back at the B&B empty-handed. Though the original plan was for everyone to meet back at the B&B at noon whether they'd found her or not, Lizzie wasn't certain she could wait even another minute.

"We have to call the police, Aunt Bess!"

Bess steered her to an empty chair. "You know better than anyone that the police will not consider her missing for another few hours. And we still have people out looking. There are three, including your *daed* who have not yet reported back here. We'll wait a few more minutes on them before we make the call. It's nearly noon. I know it's tough, but give it until your *daed* arrives."

Tears welled up in Lizzie's eyes threatening to spill over, but she swallowed them down, determined to brave this out for Abby's sake. She offered up a plea to God, asking for forgiveness for her past mistakes, asking that He not hold it against Abby for the way she came into this world. Guilt consumed her, despite every effort to let God heal her of her past transgressions. At the moment, she didn't feel very forgivable.

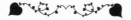

Jacob assisted Abby onto the front bench of the buggy alongside him and Caleb. The *kind* was fascinated by the mode of transportation, exclaiming she felt like she'd stepped into the pages of a fairytale. He imagined what it would be like to be Abby's *daed*. He'd wanted a daughter, but he never got that opportunity since his wife died. The fact remained; Abby was not his *kind,* and he needed to return her to Lizzie. The very thought of Lizzie heated his face. Was it possible he still had feelings for her?

Hiram Miller pulled into the yard of the B&B, his son, Seth, seated next to him. Seth jumped from the buggy the moment he saw Lizzie and ran to her, pulling her into his arms.

"We thought you were *dot.*"

Lizzie wriggled from his strong arms. "I'm still very much alive! You're all grown up, little *bruder.*"

He ruffled Lizzie's hair. "I'm taller than you are now, so you can't tease me anymore."

Lizzie smiled at her younger sibling until her *daed* stepped into her line of vision, a stern look on his face.

"Does your presence here mean you've finally put your *rumspringa* behind you, and you're ready to fully embrace our faith?"

Lizzie lowered her gaze in respect. "*Jah.*"

"*Das gut.* When we find the missing *kind* I will fetch the Bishop and we will get you baptized at once."

Lizzie kept her eyes downcast. "*Daed,* the missing *kind* is my *dochder* and she's your *kinskind.*"

Before he could say a word, another buggy pulled into the yard and Abby jumped out, rushing to Lizzie's side. "I'm so sorry, Mom. I didn't mean to run off. But I found my dad!"

No sooner had she said it, than a handsome man with familiar, blue-green eyes stood before them holding Abby's suitcase out to her. She looked at the boy-turned-man, the very one she used to love. The boyish glint in his eyes was replaced by small crow's feet in the corners. The sides of his sandy brown hair were peppered with a little gray. But his chin was clean-shaven. If it was possible, he was even more handsome than she'd thought when they were teenagers. He was no longer a skinny teenager, but a well-built man who still made her heart flutter.

Abby slipped her hand in Jacob's. "See Mom, I found my father."

Lizzie looked into Jacob's face, her heart slamming against her chest wall at her daughter's blunt words.

Hiram Miller pushed between them. "Is this true, Jacob? Did you *vadder* this *kind?"*

Jacob swallowed. "Maybe we should all go inside and have a talk about this."

Hiram pursed his lips. "There is nothing to talk about. Seth, go fetch the Bishop. Tell him we will be needing him for a confession and a *hochzich*. Elizabeth, you get into a blue dress, and get out of those *Englisch* clothes at once."

Lizzie stomped her foot. "*Daed,* you can't make me marry this man! I don't even know him anymore."

Hiram narrowed his eyes at Lizzie. "You knew him well enough to have a *boppli*. I knew I should have taken sooner measures to separate the two of you instead waiting like a fool, thinking I could trust either of you."

His harsh words rang in Lizzie's and Jacob's ears, causing them to look at one another with grief.

"*Ach, y*ou're the one that broke us apart all those years ago? David told me Lizzie—Elizabeth—didn't wish to see me anymore."

The sound of her name on Jacob's lips sent a wave of heat through her belly. He was the only one that had called her Lizzie. What once had been a term of endearment had become her permanent legal name. And now her father was ruining every memory she had of Jacob and trying to force them to marry over a mistake she had made in placing Jacob's name on Abby's birth certificate as a measure to keep her safe from Eddie.

"*Daed,* did you tell my *bruder* to lie to me about Jacob not wanting to see me anymore?"

Hiram narrowed his eyes. "I was doing what was best for you, but it seems that you allowed Jacob to disgrace you and compromise you before I could end it."

"But I didn't..."

"Silence *dochder.* If you want to remain in this community you will marry Jacob and make this right. "

Hiram turned to Jacob, who was looking into the hopeful eyes of his own son. "What have you to say for your actions? To *vadder* two *kinner* so close in age—it's disgraceful. And marrying another after the way you behaved with my *dochder*. You should have married my *dochder,* but instead you married poor Nellie Fisher and planted your seed with her too! Have you no shame?"

As shocked as he was by Hiram Miller's accusations, Jacob knew that to deny the claim would be to risk being shunned, especially if his name really was on the child's birth certificate. The community would have no reason to doubt Lizzie's word or her honor. Yes, an admission would be a way to give Caleb the new *mamm* that he desired, but above all, he didn't want to be the reason Lizzie left the community a second time since they'd not had any closure the first time. And here she was standing before him now, looking more lovely than he ever imagined.

"Forgive me, Hiram. I will marry Elizabeth and make this right."

Lizzie couldn't believe what she was hearing. "But Jacob, you can't…"

Hiram stepped between them. "When Seth returns with the Bishop we will have *two* confessions and a wedding."

Lizzie couldn't look at Jacob. She was so embarrassed. Abby clung to her side, and Caleb stepped forward and slipped his hand in hers.

"I'm Caleb. I'm *froh* you will be my new *mamm.*"

His statement nearly broke her heart, and from the look on Jacob's downcast face, it had affected him the same way. Lizzie couldn't help but smile back at Caleb, his innocent eyes gleaming.

CHAPTER 10

Lizzie had very little recollection of what happened for the next few hours while she was coerced into a confession, baptized, and finally married. Thankfully, she'd remembered her aunt's advice regarding a general confession. She knew that the way Abby was brought into this world was against the ways of the people, and God's *word*, so she felt relief that she was finally rid of the burden she'd carried for the past eleven years. Abby had given her a little grief when she was dressing in the blue dress that her aunt had loaned her, but she quickly calmed down when she realized she would finally have the dad she had wanted her entire ten years.

Before Lizzie realized, her *daed* and *aenti* were hugging her and welcoming her back into the community. She couldn't help but weep happy tears that her *daed* and brothers were back in her life. And she had a husband, which would finally allow her to hold her head up. But her heart quickened at the thought of being married to a man she once loved as a young girl, but who was now a stranger to her in every way. Even at their ceremony there was no exchange of a kiss between them. She knew she could learn to love him again; she already respected him for not shaming her in front of her family, and was grateful he'd taken the blame away from her. She would have a lifetime with him to try to make up for the position she'd put him in, and hoped he would eventually forgive her.

Jacob watched Lizzie as she pasted on a smile from ear to ear while her family welcomed her back into the community, and he told himself he'd done the right thing. For him, Caleb, and for Lizzie and Abby. Having a wife would be good for him. He had to admit that he was nervous about her expectations, and wasn't sure he was immediately ready to fulfill any obligations other than provider. It would take him a while to let go of the irritation he felt over being forced into a marriage that he would have preferred to decide for himself. She was beautiful, and he was certainly attracted to her, but she had been living among the *Englisch* for the past ten-plus years, and he had no idea what kind of person she'd become. Only the fact that she'd accepted the baptism, had he felt comfortable enough to have her as his son's *mamm.*

He continued to watch her as she made her way through the friends and family that had been present after arriving for the earlier search of Abby. Since they had remained for the wedding, he felt obligated to greet them and accept their well-wishes along-side his wife, but he couldn't help but be mesmerized by this woman who was now his wife, and yet a stranger in every way.

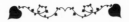

Caleb led Abby out to the barn to play with the kittens that Aunt Bess had told them about. Abby was unsure of her new role as big sister, and wasn't sure she could get used to the way they talked. But she was happiest about having a new dad, and a little brother was a small price to pay for that. She only hoped he wasn't whiny or needy the way her friend's siblings had been when she visited them.

"Is your *aenti* going to let us take one of the kittens home with us?"

"What do you mean *home?* I live here now."

"You will move into our *haus* now since your *mamm* married my *daed*—our *daed.*"

"I don't think we're moving in your house."

"When my friend's *daed* married his new *mamm,* she moved in their house with them."

"If I move in with you do I get my own horse?"

"If you ask *daed* he will get you one. I have my own horse, and chickens, and a milking cow."

"I don't want any of that—just a horse. And one of these cute little kittens."

Caleb picked up a black kitten with white paws. "I want this one."

Abby snuggled up to two of them who purred and nuzzled her neck. "I want them all."

"We might be able to convince *daed* to let us each have one if we tell him they'll be good mousers."

"No! I don't want them catching mice. That's terrible and I won't let my kitten kill cute little mice."

"*Daed* will be more agreeable if we tell him we want them to catch the mice in the barn. They can become a problem when they get into the sacks of grain we use to feed the animals."

"I guess you're right, but I don't like the idea of it. Do you really think mom and dad will let us keep them?"

Caleb chuckled. "All we have to do is put on our sad face and *daed* will give in."

Caleb demonstrated his best sad face, and the two of them giggled. Abby thought that maybe having a little brother wouldn't be so bad after all.

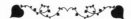

Lizzie was so happy to be back with her *daed* and her younger brother, Seth, that she had let go of the anger she had felt before the wedding. She would have to find a way to put aside the past, and move beyond the fact that her *daed* and brother, David, had been the reason she and Jacob had been torn apart all those years ago. And though it still pricked her conscious, she reminded herself she would not have Abby if not for her family's actions.

Now, she would have to adjust to raising Nellie's child as well as her own, and she would do her best to honor her deceased friend by raising her son with the same love she showed her own daughter.

Seth approached Lizzie as Abby wandered into the yard toting a rambunctious kitten in her arms. He knelt down beside her. "I'm your *Onkel* Seth."

Abby searched his smile for a moment, and then leaned in to whisper in his ear. "Then will you help me convince my mom to let me have this kitten to take to our new house?"

Seth winked at Abby. "I'll try, but my *schweschder*—sister can be pretty stubborn. But for my new niece, I will try my best." He patted Abby's head that had been neatly tucked under a prayer *kapp,* and stood to meet Lizzie's scrutiny.

Lizzie whispered to Seth. "I should probably ask Jacob before I give her an answer. He's my husband now."

Seth nodded before giving her a hug. "I'm happy you're home again. You'll see, this will be a *gut* life for you."

Lizzie knew he was right. So why did she feel such a nervous feeling in her gut? For one thing, she wasn't sure how the sleeping arrangements would work in Jacob's home, and she wondered what Jacob would expect of her tonight as far as wifely duties.

CHAPTER 11

"But I don't like this room, mom! I miss my Hello Kitty posters and my stuffed animals. Can I at least get a new bedspread? This old quilt looks itchy."

Lizzie tried to be patient with her daughter, but her tantrums would not fare well with her new husband. He would expect order and harmony under his roof, and it was up to Lizzie to rear Abby in the humble ways of the Amish, and to help rid her of her pride. She'd tried to raise her with the basic values she was instilled with, but she had to admit that raising her *Englisch* had spoiled her.

"This is a nice room, Abby. I'm counting on you to accept this room as it is. And tomorrow we will begin to make you a few new dresses. You cannot wear your jeans or shorts anymore."

"If I'd known having a new dad would be so tough I would have kept my mouth shut. It's my fault your dad made you marry him, isn't it?"

Lizzie couldn't lay such a burden on her *dochder*. It was her own fault. Her deception had caused the chain of events that forced her into a marriage with Jacob.

"Of course it's not your fault. The decision for us to be a family was a good one. It will be good for us, you'll see."

Abby stifled a yawn. "Why was your dad so angry with you?"

"Because I hadn't been a good daughter. Because I ran away like you did today. I never told him he had a granddaughter and that was wrong for me to keep you apart from my family. And I'm so happy you're back safe and sound."

Lizzie stroked the purring kitten's fur that was curled up on Abby's bed. "Get some rest. Soon it will be morning, and you have a lot to learn about being part of an Amish family."

Abby folded her arms. "That sounds like you're gonna give me chores. Caleb told me you would."

"It won't be much different from the cooking and cleaning I've already taught you—except it will be done without the use of some of the modern conveniences we're used to, so it takes a little longer."

Abby turned her back. "That sounds like chores to me."

Lizzie bent down and kissed her daughter, and tucked the quilt around her. After putting out the lamp at her bedside table, she closed the door gently behind her, believing she could already hear Abby snoring lightly. It had been a long day for all of them.

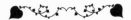

Jacob finished nighttime prayers with Caleb, wondering if he should have included Abby. But knowing there would be plenty of time for that once she became better acquainted with the schedule he and Caleb were already used to, it would get easier to incorporate time with his new daughter. He didn't want to exclude her, but he didn't want to push Amish ways on her too quickly for fear she would rebel, and that could be cause for discord in the house— something he'd like to keep under control.

As he left Caleb's room, he could hear Lizzie conversing quietly with Abby and decided to go to his own room and clear out some space for his new *fraa*. He felt suddenly strange at the thought of sharing his marriage bed with another woman, and wondered how Lizzie would react.

A gentle knock at the door startled him. When he opened the door, Lizzie stood with downcast eyes, her hands twisting the corner of her apron. Jacob's thoughts flashed to a time when he had no trouble pulling her into his arms, but those days had passed, and now he felt unsure of himself.

"*Kume*. This is to be your room too. I made some room in the bureau for your things, and there is a separate set of pegs on the far wall where you can hang your dresses and aprons." Jacob pointed, but Lizzie didn't follow his hand gesture—her eyes remained downcast, and she hadn't even stepped one foot inside the room. Part of him felt sorry for her, but the other part of him was still irritated about being forced into a marriage with her before he was ready make that decision for himself. He would have to put it behind him if he was to keep peace under his roof.

"I can give you some privacy while you ready yourself for the night. I think I'd like a fresh glass of milk and another piece of the cake your *aenti* sent home with us. Would you like some too? I can bring it up here on a tray if you'd like."

Lizzie shook her head, but didn't say a word. She was already nervous enough without trying to eat something this late at night. A blush rose to her face as he brushed by her to get through the door. Knowing she didn't have much time before he would return, she closed the door after he walked toward the stairs, and picked up her suitcase from the floor and placed it on the bed. As she pushed open the lid and rifled through her things, she realized she had nothing that was considered proper to sleep in. The only thing she had was a summer nightie that would be considered immodest by her new husband. Spotting a plaid robe on Jacob's row of pegs across the room, she knew she would be able to pass for proper attire if she wore the robe over her nightgown. The last thing she wanted to do was to begin her new marriage with a lack of propriety. The least she felt she could do for Jacob after he rescued her from shame, would be to honor him in every way. Not only had he married her despite a misunderstanding, but he was giving her and her daughter a roof over their heads, and had agreed to take on the role of father to Abby, though he wasn't even her real father.

CHAPTER 12

Jacob lifted his knuckles to the door and knocked lightly. He felt funny knocking on his own bedroom door, but he wanted to be considerate of his new bride. When he didn't hear a response, he entered the room cautiously, relieved to see Lizzie standing at the window, unaware he'd stepped inside. As he closed the door, he cleared his throat discretely, but was unable to prevent Lizzie from being startled by his sudden presence. Immediately he noticed she was wearing his robe, even though the lamp had been turned down and he could only see her by the pale moonlight entering through the sheer curtain on the window.

He pointed to the bed. "Are you ready to turn in?"

She looked toward the bed, avoiding eye-contact with him. "Honestly, I don't mean any disrespect, but I don't feel comfortable sleeping in the same bed you slept in with your previous *fraa*. I don't mind sleeping on the floor if you have extra quilts."

Jacob gathered the quilts and pillows from the bed. "I understand. I didn't have time to take care of it given the urgency of our wedding, but I will go into to town tomorrow and purchase a new bed."

Lizzie kept her head down while she took the offered bedding. "Thank you, Jacob. Perhaps when you return we can sit down and talk a little. I *am* very sorry for the predicament I placed you in."

Jacob put up a hand to stop her. "We will have plenty of time to discuss things later. I suggest we get some sleep. The sun comes up mighty early and there is much to be done."

Jacob left the room, and she could hear him opening a door down the hall as she arranged the bedding on the floor at the foot of the bed near the bureau. Just as she rested her head on the feather pillow, Jacob entered the room with two more quilts and a pillow. He let them drop to the floor near Lizzie and knelt down to prepare a bed for himself next to her.

Lizzie popped her head up off her pillow and looked him in the eye for the first time since earlier that afternoon before he'd agreed to marry her at her *daed's* insistence. "What are you doing? I agreed to sleep on the floor. You are welcome to sleep on the bed. There is no reason we should both sleep on the floor."

Jacob finished spreading out the quilts and lay down next to her. "I can't sleep in the bed if you are sleeping on the floor. It would not be honorable of me. You are my *fraa*, and I will sleep here with you until I can purchase a marriage bed that is new to both of us."

Lizzie pursed her lips, not knowing whether to be irritated with the man, or to fall in love with him all over again for being such a gentleman. But since he had placed his quilts nearly two feet from hers, and had bundled himself in a separate quilt, she could assume with great relief that nothing was expected of her tonight. Feeling anxious over when or if they would consummate their marriage Lizzie was irritated for a whole new reason. How was she ever to get any sleep between the uncomfortable floor that already hurt her back, and the uncomfortable silence that had fallen between her and her new husband?

Lizzie woke to the sound of a rooster crowing, and lingered in the quilts just for a moment before opening her eyes. If she concentrated hard enough she could trick herself into believing she was a young girl again back on her *daed's* farm, and the nightmare of having to marry Jacob had not taken place. She opened her eyes to reality, and her back felt the strain of sleeping on the hardwood floor. She turned over slowly, her back cracking a little. Neither Jacob, nor his quilts rested beside her any longer. Her head shot up, knowing he would expect a meal after his morning chores, and she wasn't ready to disappoint the man so soon.

After throwing on the work dress that her *aenti* had given her that no longer fit the aging woman, she neatly folded the quilts and placed them on the end of the bed, and then went down the hall to wake up Abby. She feared it would be a struggle to get her daughter out of bed and into the dress she'd made for her, but she was prepared to do battle with her for the sake of keeping her vows to Jacob in being his helpmate. She would have to curtail Abby's outspoken nature in order that she not become a bad influence on Caleb. She knew she had been too liberal with Abby, and she would not be immediately open to change.

Lizzie knocked on Abby's door before entering, but to her surprise, she was already awake. "I'm so glad you're up. That makes my job a little easier this morning."

Abby yawned. "I might be awake, but I'm not ready to get up. It wasn't such a good idea to let my kitten sleep with me. He kept me awake by pawing at my hair most of the night. And now I'm too tired to get up. Can't you take the kitten and feed him for me and let me sleep a little longer? The sun is barely up."

Lizzie pulled the quilt from Abby. "No ma'am. You need to feed him yourself. You're the one that wanted the responsibility of the kitten, so you will be the one to feed him. Maybe we can make a little bed on the floor for him tonight so you can get some sleep."

"Do I have to wear that dumb dress, or can I wear my jeans?"

Lizzie pulled the dress off the hook and handed it to Abby. "We already discussed this. I know this is a lot of change in just a few days, but you will get used to it. Hurry up and dress, I'm sure Caleb could use some help feeding the chickens."

Abby folded her arms. "You said I had to feed Mr. Whiskers. You didn't say anything about having to feed chickens too!"

Lizzie ran her hand down the kitten's back. "Is that what you've named him?"

Abby grinned. "I think it's a good name since he has such long white whiskers."

Lizzie giggled at the kitten. "He does need to grow into those whiskers!"

Abby pulled the quilt back over her. "Just five more minutes to play with Mr. Whiskers, please? Then I'll help Caleb with whatever you want."

Lizzie couldn't deny her daughter another few minutes of play-time with her new kitten. Especially after she'd agreed to help her new brother as soon as she got up. Lizzie had already put her through so much in the last two days, she was happy Abby was being as agreeable as she was—but she was certain her mood was up only because of the kitten. And Lizzie was prepared to use it as long as it would last.

CHAPTER 13

Jacob yawned and stretched his aching back from sleeping on the floor. After getting very little sleep, he decided to get up and get an early start to his day so he could make time to go into town and purchase a new mattress for his bed so he and Lizzie would be able to sleep comfortably. But it wasn't just the hardwood floor against his back that had kept him awake. He'd wanted to pull Lizzie into his arms and hold her. Sleeping so close to her had stirred feelings in him that he thought to be long-since gone along with his youth. He'd watched her sleep for most of the night; he was in awe of her beauty, and felt disbelief that she was his wife.

When he finished with the animals, he went for the long-handled razor out of habit, but decided to shave anyway. He knew that he was married now, and would be expected to grow the beard. But he and Lizzie had not had a proper courting period, and he wanted to remain clean shaven until they consummated the marriage. The very thought of it brought heat to his face, and caused his heart to pound heavily in his chest.

He allowed the razor to glide down his chiseled jawline. Not paying any attention to what he was doing, he nicked his jaw. Too distracted to care that he was bleeding, he let his thoughts drift back to Lizzie as he continued to shave. Another nick to the other side didn't bring him from his stupor. He hadn't thought about how he was going to feel with her in his house. Wasn't this what he'd wanted since his youth? He'd let his thoughts be consumed with her to the point of confession to the Bishop just after his Nellie had passed. Though he hadn't confessed the entire truth, the guilt that he felt for not giving himself fully to the woman he'd married was his disgrace—the disgrace that would cause him to grieve for his wife well beyond the normal mourning period. It's what had closed him off from the idea of marrying again. But here he was, married to the one woman who had claimed his heart so many years ago, and it frightened him beyond anything he could imagine.

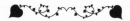

Lizzie set aside the blueberry muffins she'd baked from dried blueberries she'd found in the pantry. While they cooled, she drained the last of the bacon from the pan and scooped the scrambled eggs from the larger skillet. She was grateful that Jacob had installed a gas stove in his home, making food preparation easier for her. She would have struggled to prepare food on a wood-burning stove like she'd grown up using. As a young girl, she'd burned a lot of things before getting the hang of it, and she knew each stove was different, and she'd have had a tough time making a *gut* first impression on her new husband if she'd burned his first meal.

Her heart quickened at the thought of Jacob as her husband, and wondered if she would ever be able to fully look him in the eye. One thing was certain; she would beg his forgiveness and confess everything to him when they spoke later today as he'd promised. Amish did not divorce but in very rare occasions, but she didn't fear that. She feared a lifetime with a man who would not be able to forgive her for forcing him into a marriage that he didn't ask for. But she was determined to spend her lifetime making it up to him, and doing her best to prevent him from regretting his decision to go along with the marriage.

Distracted by her own thoughts of the man she'd yearned for since her youth, she burned the back of her hand on the edge of the stove as she pulled the second batch of muffins from the oven. She immediately dropped the pan on the stove and let out a whine.

Jacob entered in through the kitchen door and spotted Lizzie's clumsiness with the pan and went to her aid when he realized she'd burned her hand.

He drew her hand into his, examining the redness that was already forming a small white blister. He steered her over toward the sink and turned on the cold faucet, pushing her hand under the water. She continued to whine a little, but hadn't looked up at him. When she did, she gasped at the sight of blood dripping down both sides of his chin.

"What on earth happened to you? You're bleeding!"

He shook off her worry. "I cut myself shaving."

Lizzie's heart did a flip-flop in her chest. If he'd shaved, did that mean he hadn't taken their marriage seriously? As a married Amish man, he was to grow out his beard. Had he changed his mind overnight, and had intentions to go to the Bishop and have the marriage annulled? Lizzie's heart ached as he held her hand under the stream of water from the kitchen faucet. His nearness made her desire him even more, but she quickly hardened her heart against the fearful thought that she might not be married to him much longer. Pulling her hand away, she ushered him to the table and wrapped her hand in a water-drenched tea-towel.

Jacob noticed the sudden stiffness in Lizzie's body-language, and her sudden urgency for him to let go of her hand. Had he pushed her too far by taking her hand into his? He wondered why she suddenly pulled her hand away. Did she think it too forward even for them as a married couple? He'd enjoyed the softness of her skin, but he feared she may not want him to be a husband to her in every way. Was she with the *Englisch* so long that her heart had forgotten the gentleness of Amish love? He feared the meal she'd made for him was only a gesture to appease him and go through the motions of her wifely duties. As he searched her averting gaze, he wondered if she regretted marrying him, and had intent to confess the entire truth to the Bishop, and then ask for an annulment.

Feeling discouraged, he sat down at the head of the table and waited for her to sit beside him. When she did, he bowed his head for the silent prayer.

Dear Gott, denki for this wonderful bounty of food my new fraa has prepared for my familye. I ask you to bless our marriage even though we did not enter into it with pure hearts. I will honor her as I said in my vows, and will love her as you intended. Please do not put doubt in our minds for this marriage, but give us the strength to endure whatever trials you put before us as atonement for our sinful actions.

CHAPTER 14

Abby felt jealousy rise up in her at the sight of Jacob walking into the barn with Caleb hoisted on his shoulder. She stood up from playing with the kittens and walked toward Caleb's horse. She reached up and caressed his soft nose, her back to her dad and brother. Anger finally claimed her as she listened to them converse and joke with each other.

Abby whirled around to meet her dad's eye. "When can I have my own horse? Caleb said you would buy me one."

Jacob tried not to let her tone alert him, but spoke calmly in response. "We can go to the auction on Saturday if you'd like, and you can pick one out then. But you must spend the week learning from Caleb how to care for a horse. If you're ready by Saturday, then we will go in search of a gentle horse that I will teach you how to break."

Abby scrunched up her face. "What do ya mean "break"? Will I have to hurt it? Cuz my mom says we should always be kind to animals."

Jacob chuckled at Abby's naïve approach to farm life, and wondered if a week would be enough time to teach her all there was to know about caring for a horse.

"To break a horse means to train it. And no, it won't hurt the horse. It is not the Amish way to hurt any animal, so your *mamm* was correct in her instruction."

"How long do I have to wait for my new cell phone? My friends are probably worried about me by now since they haven't heard from me for three days."

Jacob feared a conversation with his new daughter about the use of phones and television, and other *Englisch* devices. "The Amish don't use phones except in emergency situations. Some members of the community have phones in their barns, but I don't. I thought your *mamm* explained to you about that."

Abby crossed her arms. "When my phone got shut off cuz she wouldn't pay the bill, she said I could get a new phone once we settled in Indiana. Are you telling me you aren't gonna let me have one?"

Jacob tried to choose his words carefully, so as not to alienate Abby. "When you enter your *rumspringa* you may choose to get a phone. But for now, we will have no more talk of it."

"I thought having a father was going to be fun. You could at least *try* to spoil me!" Abby stormed off, tears spilling from her porcelain cheeks.

If this is one my trials, Gott, then I accept it with a willing spirit. But please bless me with the strength to endure the kind's wrath, and bless me with the words to break her like the wild horse that the Englisch ways have implanted themselves in her spirit.

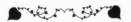

Lizzie set herself to making beds after doing the noon dishes. Jacob had excused himself after the noon meal to go into town, and she hoped he still intended to fulfill his promise to purchase a new bed even though he hadn't mentioned it specifically. Caleb stayed behind to work with

Abby in the barn—something about teaching her how to care for the horse. Lizzie was too preoccupied to pay any attention, and wasn't concerned unless they were getting into trouble, which she didn't think they would do since Caleb seemed to be a well-behaved child.

Noting the house could use a good sweeping with the broom, and the rugs looked like they desperately needed to be hung on the clothesline so she could smack the dirt off of them, Lizzie made use of the time that Jacob was gone to surprise him with a clean home when he returned. A small part of her felt a little strange cleaning another woman's home, but it was her home now and she would take pride in keeping it clean. It was the way of the Amish that she automatically took over the duties as the new wife, but it didn't keep the little butterflies from fluttering in her stomach for fear that she may move something that was sacred memorabilia of Nellie's.

She and Nellie had been friends before she left the community, so why did she feel jealousy over the woman even though she was deceased? Perhaps because the woman had been the first to love Jacob, while she'd lost her virtue after Eddie had spiked her drink, and had no recollection of the act. The thought of it made her shutter. And even though she'd never had relations again with any man, she hoped Jacob wouldn't view her as damaged goods.

Her *daed* assumed Jacob had been the one to compromise her virtue and that was how Abby had come into the world—she'd been violated, but it was a hazy memory at best. She couldn't help but wonder what Jacob must think about her to accuse him of being the one doing the violating—but that sort of thing was not in his nature, even if she'd been the type of girl to provoke such an action from him. He was a good man, and she felt fortunate that he'd taken the blame for her mistake.

If only she knew the real reason why...

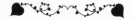

Jacob was happy that he'd been able to convince the manager of the mattress store to deliver the new bed this afternoon. He wasn't happy it had cost him an extra fifty dollars to convince the man, but he didn't think he could endure sleeping on the floor another night. And he wasn't about to begin his marriage on a sour note by sleeping in the bed he'd shared with Nellie in order to preserve his own sleep and aching back. It was better this way. So why did he feel so funny about his purchase?

His heart quickened at the thought of sleeping so near Lizzie, and wondered if she would expect him to fulfill his husbandly duties to her right away. Normally, time spent directly after a wedding in the community was spent visiting family, but given the abruptness of their wedding, and the fact they had two children to think about, visiting was not going to be a part of their initial acquaintance with one another as a couple. He was grateful for that much, as he wasn't looking forward to the dinner with Lizzie's family on Saturday. He was also happy this upcoming Sunday was an off-Sunday for the community, and he would not have to face the Bishop or the Elders of the church for another ten days when the next church service would take place.

At least the time at home with his new family would afford him a chance to try to make amends with Lizzie and Abby, who seemed to have a rebellious streak most likely from spending so much time with the *Englisch*. He wondered how the *kind* would be during a Sunday service, and if it would be a struggle to get Abby to accept the faith of the community. He prayed that things would go smoothly and the natural course of getting to know each other would fall into place as though they'd always been a family. Though he knew his reasons for the marriage were to preserve both of their honors in the community, he still couldn't help but feel anxious over his hasty decision to marry Lizzie, and wondered if it would last.

CHAPTER 15

By the time Jacob returned home that evening, it was dusk, and Lizzie had been keeping the evening meal warm and the children occupied—especially Abby, who didn't understand why they had to wait for Jacob so she could eat. Abby wasn't used to being on a schedule or having to wait for family to sit and have a meal together. In a lot of ways, Lizzie regretted not being a little more strict with her daughter. It would have made the transition into the Amish community and lifestyle more pleasant. She knew it was her own fault the *kind* was whining, and hoped it wasn't too late to train her to the strict ways she would now have to live by.

Lizzie looked out the kitchen window at her husband as he greeted a delivery truck in the driveway. Two young men exited the plain white truck and began to unload a mattress and box-spring from the back. Lizzie's heart skipped a beat. Jacob had done as he'd promised, and they could begin their marriage with a bed of their own. She was delighted when the delivery men took away the old bed, but she hoped Jacob, who'd remained expressionless when they removed them, was not experiencing it as a loss. His lack of beard had been an outward sign that his mourning period had ended even though very few widowed Amish men shaved, but she still felt unsure of his feelings, and knew that only time would tell how he was dealing with it.

When all the excitement had passed, and the delivery men had left, Lizzie pulled the evening meal back out of the oven where it had been warming for nearly an hour and set it on the table. It was getting late, and though she was very tired, she was suddenly very wary of bedtime.

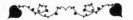

Lizzie made the new bed with the linens and quilt that her aunt had given her for her wedding dowry. And since the bedding store had thrown in two new pillows with the purchase, they would have a fresh new start to their life together. Most traces of Nellie had been removed from the house many years ago as far as Lizzie could see, or maybe it was possible that since they had only been married for ten months before she passed that she hadn't had enough time to make her mark on the home in the way that years of marriage would have done. Either way, Lizzie intended to make her mark on the home starting with the linens; she intended to make the bedroom a place they could eventually connect—at least she hoped so.

Jacob walked in the room and grabbed the other side of the sheet and tucked it into the corner. "I put the *kinner* to bed, but your *dochder* asked if you would tuck her in."

Lizzie looked at him as he grabbed the other side of the quilt and helped, then fitted a pillow case to the other pillow and set it on the bed. It was the first time she'd really looked him over since they'd married the day before. His eyes were kind, but held a hint of apprehension in their reflection. He smiled, and then pushed down his suspenders and pulled his blue dress shirt over his head exposing his muscular flesh. His abs were so defined, Lizzie wondered if he spent his days working out at a gym. She felt heat rising up her neck until it reached her cheeks. Her gaze fell a little wondering if he intended to undress fully in front of her. The smirk on his face showed that he did if she didn't vacate the room or turn around.

She cleared her throat. "I think I'll go tuck Abby in and read her a story. I'll be back in a few minutes."

She quickly exited the room before she was tempted to stare at Jacob any longer. She knew he was her husband, and she was allowed to see him without his clothing, but she wasn't sure she was ready for that yet. Her one-time, short-lived experience with the opposite sex had not prepared her for what would certainly be an inevitable part of their marriage. Jacob had been married long enough to gain some experience, and she worried she would be clumsy and inadequately prepared. There was also the possibility of becoming pregnant again since her first and only experience had brought Abby into her life. Was she prepared for another child? Did she even want anymore? Did Jacob? Amish didn't use birth-control, so she would have to discuss the possibility of children with him—perhaps before they decided to consummate the marriage.

Perhaps some prayer would be in order as well.

Jacob couldn't help but smile when Lizzie exited the room so hastily. He knew it wasn't right to infuriate his new bride, but he reveled in the blush that had claimed her cheeks. He didn't intend to torture her with teasing, but he didn't mind making her squirm a little for forcing him into marrying her. But he had to admit, he could have done worse if he'd picked his own wife. He'd already noticed she didn't appear to have cut her hair the way most Amish girls do when they go out to live among the *Englisch,* and Abby had the same long, light brown hair and blue eyes as her mother. It would be tough to keep to himself physically since he was very attracted to Lizzie, but he needed to be sure she was committed to the marriage for the right reasons before he would consider consummating.

Lizzie took her time with Abby, talking to her about school. She wasn't happy about the school being so small, but she was happy to hear she wouldn't be expected to go until the harvest was brought in which would amount to at least another month. Until then, Caleb would work with *their* father, and Abby would work alongside her at the B&B making beds and doing dishes. Abby groaned at the thought of doing chores, but she also knew it would be another opportunity to sample more of the cookies, pies and pastries

Aunt Bess kept on hand for her guests. Abby was intrigued with the baked goods, and wanted to learn to make them herself.

When Lizzie returned to the room she now shared with Jacob, she was happy that the lamps had been turned down, and he seemed to be sleeping. She sank to the corner of the room and dressed in her nightie as discretely as she could, and then slipped carefully under the quilt.

Jacob turned to her. "I purchased some fabric when I was in town so you could sew some dresses and night clothes for you and Abby. I also got you a treadle sewing machine and placed it in the front room just before I came up here for the evening."

Well there it was—open confirmation of his disapproval. Lizzie's heart slammed against her ribcage.

"*Denki,*" she said quietly before rolling over and closing her eyes against the tears that were pushing a lump into her throat.

It probably would have been more obvious if he'd just come right out and said he's ashamed of the way I dress! But at least he got me a sewing machine!

CHAPTER 16

Lizzie woke with a stiff neck from sleeping rigidly to avoid accidentally bumping Jacob during the night. When she turned over in the bed, he was already gone and the sheet was cold, indicating he'd been up for some time. She lay there for a minute, wondering if there would ever be a time when he would linger under the quilt and hold her before getting up for the day. She pushed the silly, romantic notion aside, feeling defeated by their present living situation. They were going through the motions of marriage, but had no closeness or intimacy as would be the norm for a newly married couple.

She forced herself out from under the warm quilt and set her feet on the chilly wood floor. The rain she'd heard several hours ago had no-doubt cooled the temperature, but she hoped it would warm soon. Her *daed* had promised that he would give her the contents of her things they'd stored away in the barn after she'd left, and she hoped her cloak and aprons would still fit her. She didn't expect her dresses to still fit since she'd been a scrawny teenager, and her figure had grown womanly curves at her hips and bust when she had Abby.

As she dressed for the day in the work dress her *aenti* had given her, she made mental note of the chores she would have to complete before leaving for the B&B at one o'clock. Check-out time was at noon, and Aunt Bess served a noon meal before the guests left, so Lizzie could begin cleaning the rooms, and then wash the noon dishes. She was happy that Jacob hadn't objected to her obligation to her aunt, but she was happier she'd have money to contribute for the household expenses, especially since Jacob had married her and was now responsible for her as her provider. Knowing that she could help eased some of the guilt over pushing him into the responsibility.

Another silent breakfast ensued between Lizzie and Jacob, while the children filled the air with chatter over the ducks in the pond and the changing leaves on the trees. Lizzie was grateful for the innocent conversation of the children, because it allowed her to study her husband's reaction to her daughter. His responses to their questions were gentle and attentive, and he smiled often. Lizzie's heart beat rapidly in her chest thinking about what a kind and loving man he was. It was those very same traits that made her fall in love with him when they were young.

Jacob didn't like the silence between him and Lizzie, but he was grateful for the children to fill the gap between them. He'd caught her watching him several times throughout the morning meal, but didn't know how to incorporate her in the conversation. They'd conversed through the children, and he admired the gentleness in her tone when she spoke to them. Her smile was genuine when she addressed their constant questions, and he liked the way her dimples lit up her face. He'd fallen in love with that dimpled smile when they were young, so why was he having so much trouble connecting her to that girl now? Was his heart still so reserved from the heartache of her leaving him then? He tried reasoning with himself that the thought was unsubstantiated, but maybe he needed to address the subject of forgiveness a little more closely during his prayer time.

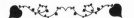

The sun rested high above their heads as Lizzie and Abby walked the mile from their new home to the B&B. The last of the season's blackbirds flitted in the colorful trees overhead, which provided a canopy of shade for part of the journey. Jacob and Caleb had long-since traveled to neighboring farms to help bring in the harvest. Being at the Hockstetler farm, Jacob had boasted about the large pumpkin crop, and promised to bring a few home with him for pies. Lizzie hoped there would be enough for her to can some so they would have use of the pumpkin for Christmas pies in addition to the apples she planned on canning from the two apple trees she'd noticed on the other side of the barn. She hoped her skills as a homemaker would prove to Jacob she was capable of being a good Amish *fraa.*

Abby picked up a rock in the dirt road and tossed it ahead of them for the third time. "Do I have to start calling you *mamm* like Caleb does?"

The question caught Lizzie off guard, but she was glad Abby brought up the subject. "I would like it if you could learn the language of the Amish people. I feel bad that I never taught you before now. It was wrong of me to keep your heritage from you; I should have been teaching you from the beginning."

"Why did you run away from my father? Did you hate him?"

Lizzie's heart nearly fell to her shoes. "No, Abby. I loved him very much, but I didn't think he loved me back. I acted in haste and didn't think things through. I'm grateful for the time I spent away from the Amish community because it taught me a valuable lesson."

Abby picked up the rock again when they came upon it in the road. After tossing it again, she looked up at Lizzie and squinted her eyes against the sun. "Am I supposed to be learning a lesson by giving up my life in Ohio to stay here?"

Lizzie swallowed hard, choosing her words carefully. "Remember a few days ago how afraid you were to get on the bus to come here? I told you that you would learn to love it here. I'm hoping that's what you'll learn by being here. The Amish are a gentle people—not at all like the troublesome people we've encountered in the past few months."

"You mean that Eddie guy? Who was he anyway, and why did I hear him say he was going to take me away from you?"

Lizzie felt her knees buckle at the question, and she slowed her pace to keep her balance. "He was a bad man that thought he could force me to give him money to pay for his mistakes. I met him just after I left home. I was a stupid kid back then, and I didn't make good decisions about who I made friends with. I'm glad that part of my life is over, and I'm glad to be back with people who really love me."

"Like Jacob—my dad?"

Lizzie smiled nervously at Abby's question, but she was too young to understand the circumstances of her mother's marriage. Lizzie hoped in time Jacob would forgive her and learn to love her, but she knew that despite her relationship with him, he would be a *gut vadder* to Abby, and that was all that mattered to her at the moment.

CHAPTER 17

Though Lizzie missed her work as a pharmacy technician, she discovered that she enjoyed working alongside Abby at the B&B even more. Lizzie was proud of her for being so much help with very little complaining. Her day would have dragged by if her daughter would have rebelled against the work that needed to be done. She discovered after the first guest room that Abby preferred to do the dusting and sweeping with the broom over the making of the beds. In her defense, she did not have long enough arms to spread the linens across the mattresses.

Lizzie giggled at her first attempt, and wondered if it was too late in life to begin training Abby in the Amish ways in order to make them stay with her into her adulthood. Visions of her *rumspringa* made Lizzie shudder at the thought of her little Abby running off the way she had. It made her think of her *daed,* and she wondered if he would ever feel he could trust her again.

After three steady hours of work making certain each room was prepared for new guests that would arrive shortly, and for those that had stayed on at the B&B, Lizzie took pride in the ache that had crept into the small of her back, knowing she'd earned it for the hard work that made her feel at home.

When they returned to the farm, Abby ran down to the pond where Caleb was chasing the ducks. It made Lizzie giggle to watch him running after them, their feathers flying and squawking so loudly she wondered if they were enjoying the game or in fear for their lives. With the children occupied, she thought she might take a few minutes before she needed to prepare the evening meal to try to talk to her new husband. As she entered the double doors that hung open, she heard whistling from the other side of the horse stalls and followed the sound of the familiar hymn.

Lizzie stopped in her tracks when she spotted Jacob leaning over a wash stand on a table. His back turned away from her, she stood and watched him shave, admiring the muscles that chiseled out his bare back. She crept a little closer, hoping she wouldn't startle him for fear he would cut his chin the way he had the day before. Curious as to why he continued to shave, she felt irritation rise up in her. As a married man, he should not be shaving. But would she complain, knowing she liked his clean-shaven look? But what would the community think if he should continue to shave instead of growing a beard? Would they question the legitimacy of their marriage?

Before she could reason with her questions, Jacob turned to face her. "You don't have to sneak up on me. If you want to watch me shave, you're more than welcome to."

Lizzie's face turned a deep shade of red. Was he trying to provoke her? "I wasn't trying to sneak up on you; I just didn't want to startle you. I didn't want you cutting your throat open."

He set the towel down and turned around, his suspenders dangling at his sides, and his well-muscled chest and abdomen enticed her. She wondered if he was intentionally teasing her, and the smirk on his face indicated he probably was. She could feel the heat rising up to her cheeks, and her voice was shaky when she tried to speak. "I was hoping we could spend a minute talking before I went in and cooked the evening meal. I didn't mean to interrupt you."

His smile deepened, exposing the tiny lines that had formed on his manly face. She studied him for a moment, realizing how handsome he'd become in the past ten years. He took a step toward her, his eyes fixed on hers, and stood close enough that she could smell the flecks of shaving soap that clung to his face. She wanted to reach out and touch him, but she didn't want to break the spell that lingered between them.

"*Mamm,* Abby needs you!"

Caleb's sudden burst startled Lizzie, and the way he addressed her almost seemed foreign.

She turned her head from Jacob, breaking the spell. "Is she hurt?"

"She got too close to the duck nest in the reeds and her foot is stuck."

All three of them ran to the edge of the pond, where Abby whined, her arm outstretched toward the duck nest.

She looked up into Jacob's face, who was wading in the water to get to her. "I can't reach the babies, Dad, and I want one."

Jacob reached down and untangled her foot, scooping her up in his arms. "Those babies have to stay with their *mudder,* just like you have to stay with yours. You could have drowned, Abby. Promise me you won't go out that far among the reeds ever again."

She leaned his head against his shoulder and he hugged her tight until he reached the grassy edge of the pond. "I won't. I promise."

Lizzie felt a tear glide down her cheek. She was happy that the two had bonded over such a simple thing, and Abby hadn't talked back. But most endearing was the gentleness with which Jacob had spoken to her daughter. He was truly a loving man, and she couldn't have asked God Himself for a better man to be her husband and the father of her child.

After Abby was all dried, she ran downstairs to help Lizzie prepare the evening meal. She rolled out dough for biscuits, and used an upside down glass to cut the circles of dough.

"How come you never asked me to help you cook before? I like cooking."

Surprised to hear such a statement from Abby, she smiled happily. "I guess we just never had the time to make big meals."

"But we did more work today than I've ever seen you do, and we still had time to cook breakfast and now dinner."

Lizzie picked up the baking pan full of freshly cut biscuits and placed them in the oven. "Things are different here. You work hard, but everything you do is for your family—to feed them and care for their needs."

"I'm not happy about not being able to watch TV, but there's so much more to do here, I didn't even miss it today."

Lizzie smiled knowingly, wondering why she'd ever left the community.

CHAPTER 18

Lizzie could barely keep her eyes open as she finished the last stitch on her new nightgown. Everyone had been asleep for at least two hours, but she'd wanted to finish it before retiring. She didn't want to cause anymore discomfort to her husband by wearing the summery nightie anymore for fear that it appeared too worldly for an appropriate Amish *fraa* to wear. Not to mention the scowl on his face when he went for his robe and saw that she was still wearing it. She supposed he was set in his ways, and having her invade his space would take some getting used to, but that didn't stop her from thinking it a little funny that he was so territorial.

Creeping up the stairs as quietly as she could, she forgot which one of the stairs squeaked until it was too late. She remained still for a moment, listening to be sure she hadn't disturbed anyone in the house. When all remained quiet, she proceeded to her room and slipped beneath the quilt.

Jacob rolled over toward her, and before she could put her back to him, his arm slipped across her stomach, his head resting on her shoulder. Panic pushed her heart rate to its limits, and she wondered if she could roll away from him without waking him. If he woke up, it would be awkward, and might give him ammunition to tease her later. He nestled his head a little, leaving her wondering if he was connecting with her on a subconscious level, or if he was merely used to roaming around an empty bed and had no idea he was cuddling her. Either way, she didn't dare move for fear of disturbing him. She closed her eyes, and tried to calm her heart rate, but she couldn't breathe. She took a few deep breaths, feeling like she wasn't getting enough air; she had to roll over on her side before she hyperventilated so much she passed out.

With one smooth roll, she was on her side with her back to him. No sooner had she settled in position and caught her breath, than Jacob moved closer to her, pulling her into a spooning position with the strong arm that still circled her waist. His warm breath on the back of her neck tickled her spine, and she had to admit she didn't mind the closeness of her husband. She'd spent many a lonely night lying awake over her adult years wishing for a moment like this with a husband, and now she was experiencing it. It was nice, even if Jacob wasn't aware of what he was doing.

In the morning, Jacob was missing from the bed as he had the previous mornings. She had no idea what time he got up every day, but it was obviously what he was used to doing. She wondered if he'd woken while he was still cuddling her, or if he was completely unaware of the contact that had taken place overnight. Her heart fluttered at the thought of it. Dressing quickly, she ran down the stairs to prepare a big morning meal, knowing the cold weather would drive up her husband's appetite. She'd felt a closeness with him last night, and she would do whatever it took to make the marriage right, even if all she could do was cook and clean for him for the time being, but she would do it as any good Amish *fraa* would.

When everyone was seated at the table for breakfast, Jacob bowed his head for the silent prayer. Abby bowed her head, and Lizzie was delighted that she seemed eager to participate in some of the simple traditions already.

Jacob went for his second helping of pancakes and looked over at Lizzie with a smile. "We will be going to the Beiler's today for the barn-raising. I'd like it if you and Abby would join me and Caleb. Your help will be needed with the preparation of meals and cleanup."

Lizzie's heart skipped a beat at the invitation, and she accepted with a nod. It was normal for the wives to accompany their husbands during working bees, and this would be their first as a married couple. She hoped it meant he was beginning to accept her as his wife, and that he intended to portray that to the community. But the fact remained that he was still shaving his beard and they'd been married for four days already.

Jacob turned to Abby. "Do you think you're ready to go to auction tomorrow and pick out a pony?"

Abby nearly jumped out of her seat. "Do you mean it, Dad?"

He smiled at Lizzie, and then looked back at Abby whose eyes were wide as saucers. "Caleb says you've been a good student to his instruction on how to care for the horses. I think we can get you your own horse so you can learn to ride too."

Abby leaped from her chair and swung her arms around Jacob's neck. "Thank you, Dad. I promise I'll take real good care of it. You won't have to yell at me or anything!"

Jacob sent a confused look to Lizzie at Abby's statement. She hoped he didn't think she had yelled at Abby in the past. Her punishment of the child had consisted of a time-out chair, and she herself wondered if Abby had perhaps been scolded inappropriately at the public school. Shrugging it off for now, she lifted herself from her chair and asked Abby to help with the dishes. If they were to get an early start to the barn-raising, Lizzie would need to hurry with the necessary chores and put together some food to take along to share with the community.

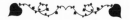

Lizzie's stomach filled with butterflies as the gentle rocking of the buggy bumped her into Jacob repeatedly. Abby and Caleb sat in the back chattering non-stop about the puppies at the Beiler farm with which Caleb was certain Jacob would permit him to bring one of them home with them at the end of the day. Lizzie was too preoccupied with thoughts of Jacob being so near, and nervousness over her first community appearance as Jacob's wife. She knew the women would accept her, and she probably knew a lot of them already from school, but it was going to be awkward as they tested her for signs that she had become too *Englisch* while she had been away from the community.

CHAPTER 19

From the look of the crowd that had already gathered at the Beiler farm, they were late, even though it was only seven o'clock. The sun had not been up for long, but the neighbors seemed eager to get the barn-raising underway. Jonah and Rebecca Beiler greeted them with their *mamm,* Martha, when they pulled into the yard that was already crowded with buggies and plenty of children running around.

Before taking his horse to the large area of shade trees with the other horses, Jacob made a few introductions. "This is my *fraa,* Elizabeth, and my *dochder,* Abby."

Lizzie held a hand out to Martha, trying to place her. She was slightly in shock at hearing Jacob refer to Abby as his daughter. It was something that would take some getting used to, but she supposed now was as good a time as any to establish their place.

"*Wie gehts,* Elizabeth?"

"Please, call me Lizzie."

Martha nodded acceptance of the nickname, and directed them toward a group of women from the community already preparing a feast big enough to feed two communities. "*Kume,* join us while we prepare meals for our *familye.*"

Abby clung to Lizzie's side despite the promptings from Caleb, Rebecca and Jonah to play a quick game of tag before they would be expected to cart tools and supplies to their *daeds* during the building process. Lizzie preferred to have Abby at her side; if nothing else, she was a shield for the prying questions she was sure to endure throughout the day from the other women. She noticed her own *daed* and *bruder* were not in attendance, but she'd heard from Aunt Bess that his own farm was a struggle for him since he'd aged in recent years. Seth would be needed to help at home with their *daed* until he would take a wife, but Lizzie had the feeling he would stay on even after he was married. It was the Amish way, and she chided herself for not staying to keep house for him in her *mamm's* absence.

As the day wore on, Lizzie relaxed more with the women, and even accepted an invitation to a quilting bee the following week to begin the wedding dowries for the young girls in the community who would be marrying in the upcoming wedding season, which was nearly upon them.

Abby and Caleb were asleep by the time they reached home that night. Caleb woke up enough to walk into the house, but Abby was so worn out, Jacob picked her up and took her up to her room. Lizzie followed, watching as her husband placed a gentle kiss on Abby's forehead after tucking her under the quilts.

Jacob moved past her as he exited Abby's room. "I have to unhitch the horse. I'll be in when I've given him a good rubdown."

Lizzie hunched her shoulders thinking she could use a good rubdown herself. She was tired and ached all over. She could only imagine how much more Jacob must be sore from the hard day he'd put in. They'd managed to get the frame and the roof finished. The interior work would be up to Adam Beiler and his son, Jonah, who was a year older than Abby.

Lizzie readied herself for bed, and then went downstairs to make a fresh pot of coffee for Jacob. A chill had blown in from the north earlier in the afternoon, and the ride home in the dark had chilled her to the bone; she could only imagine how cold Jacob was up on the roof for so many hours, unprotected from the strong gusts of wind.

Just as she had finished pouring herself a cup, the door flew open with a cold rush of air. Jacob entered shivering, and she handed him the cup she'd meant for herself. He sat at the table and wrapped both hands around the steaming cup, and sipped it. Lizzie poured another cup and sat beside him.

"*Denki* for the *kaffi*. It's gotten pretty cold in the last couple of hours. I was hoping the weather would hold out until we could finish the harvest."

Lizzie looked up into his blue-green eyes, afraid to say what was on her mind, but they hadn't talked about anything personal yet, and she was beginning to worry they would always have a very formal marriage that centered around the children, and community obligations. Did he really see her as his wife and Abby as his daughter, or was he doing what was expected of him in order to maintain his position in the community?

Jacob cleared his throat. "I'd like to take you for a buggy ride tomorrow evening after we return from the auction."

Lizzie's heart rate sped up at the thought of it. She wasn't going to argue if he was reaching out to her, but buggy rides were for courting and they were not courting— they were married. It suddenly dawned on her why he was shaving—he intended to court her. Excitement rose in the depths of her belly over his offer.

"That would be lovely. I'd like that."

Lovely? Did she just say the word *lovely* to Jacob?

He nodded and rose from his chair and rinsed his coffee cup at the sink, and then left the room. She heard the squeak of the steps, and decided it was best if she stayed downstairs and took care of the pot of coffee before going up—she would give him time to fall asleep before retiring for the evening.

CHAPTER 20

Lizzie woke up with Jacob's arm laying across her waist, his ankle crossing hers, and his head wedged in the crook of her neck. She chided herself for drinking that second cup of coffee because she had to use the bathroom, and Jacob had her trapped beneath him. If she moved, she would surely wake him, but she was close to wetting the bed if she didn't break free from him. She tried rolling over on her side the way she had the night before, but he pulled her closer just like he had before. The only thing she could do was to risk disturbing him before her bladder burst.

With one quick movement, she slid to the edge of the bed and stood up. Looking back, he seemed undisturbed, and Lizzie let out a sigh of relief before tip-toeing out of the room. When she returned, she tried slipping back under the quilt without shivering, but the house was a little chilly.

"Is everything alright?" Jacob whispered in a raspy voice.

Her back was to him, but she was worried that he'd be upset with her for waking him. "I'm fine. I'm sorry for disturbing you."

"You shouldn't drink *kaffi* so close to bedtime. You're shivering. *Kume,* let me warm you up." He pulled her close, wrapping his strong arms around her.

Lizzie couldn't help but smile at his invitation. She scooted back toward him and allowed him to cradle her in the warmth of his body. Nothing more was said between them, but Lizzie suddenly felt protected and safe for the first time in years.

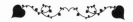

At the auction, Jacob hoisted Caleb and Abby on each of his broad shoulders so they could get a better look at the horses they considered bidding on. Jacob had allowed Abby to choose three, and they now waited for the best price. Satisfied with the price he'd bid on the solid white gelding, Jacob waited for a counter-bid, but there was none. Abby ran happily to claim her prize while Jacob paid the auctioneer, and Lizzie delighted in watching the father-daughter interaction between Jacob and Abby.

After he willingly cuddled her last night, she was looking at him a little differently—almost with love. She had to admit that being in his arms had stirred some unresolved feelings of the past, and she wondered if he felt it too as he looked back at her with a wide grin spread across his lips. She could get lost in that smile if she wasn't careful. Before she knew his intentions for their marriage, she would keep a lock on her heart. She felt suddenly very fragile and exposed, not wanting to be hurt again where Jacob was concerned.

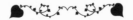

Jacob felt like a teenager again as he smiled at Lizzie. It was almost as if no time had passed, and they were young again, and ready to explore where their future could take them. But as Caleb and Abby crowded around his sides, the new horse tagging along, reality set in, and he realized his obligation to his family needed a stronger base than a teenage crush. He may not have asked for this family, but it was his responsibility now, and he would find a way to keep his feelings in check until he could establish where Lizzie's loyalties stood before giving his heart so freely again. He hadn't stopped loving her. That was obvious to him when he took her in his arms the night before. But unless she intended to return those feelings, he would remain reserved for the sake of his obligation.

Abby whined all the way home, complaining the jostling of the buggy was making her feel sick. When they finally pulled into the yard, Jacob instructed Caleb to tie up the buggy and lead the new horse into the barn so he could take Abby to her bed. No sooner had he picked her up out of the buggy when she let loose the contents of her stomach down his shirt. Lizzie rushed to his aid apologetically, but he whisked Abby into the house. Lizzie grabbed towels from the mud room off the kitchen and wet them in the sink, hoping she could catch most of the mess before it made a trail to Abby's room.

Jacob placed Abby gently in her bed and removed her shoes. Smoothing back her hair, he whispered something Lizzie couldn't make out, but it caused the corners of her daughter's lips to turn up slightly. It was tough for Lizzie to allow Jacob to take control over her daughter, but it was a nice change from the burden she'd shouldered alone for the past ten years.

Jacob squeezed Abby's hand. "You get some rest after your *mamm* puts some dry clothes on you. Caleb and I will tend to your horse and you can visit with him in the morning before service."

She nodded; her smile fading as he left the room.

CHAPTER 21

Even though Lizzie was a little sad she and Jacob had missed out on their chance to take a buggy ride, she was too tired by the time she settled Abby down and got her back to sleep. Though she was certain Abby suffered only from a case of motion-sickness, she wouldn't take the chance that it was more and leave her just to spend some time courting her husband. The thought of it made her giggle. She was certain it was the first time that a husband and wife would spend the beginning of their marriage courting one another, but she hoped they would get another chance soon.

With the stress of a full day ahead of them, Lizzie turned in before Jacob came in from tending to the horses. She was nearly asleep when she felt him slip under the quilt and move in close to her.

"I'm sorry I was too tired to make you *kaffi.*" Lizzie mumbled.

He nuzzled her neck and kissed her lightly. "I think we had a full day, and we could both use some rest."

He kissed her again, sending shivers down her spine. She wanted to turn and kiss him full on the mouth, but she feared rejection if he considered her too forward from living among the *Englisch* too long. As tough as it was, she would wait for him to make the advances. Even as slow as they came, she was satisfied for now knowing he desired to have some closeness with her. On the other hand, what if he wanted to consummate their marriage, and she kept her back to him sending him the signal she was uninterested? She turned slightly to see if he would make another advance, but to her dismay, he was already asleep.

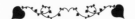

Jacob had a tough time keeping his mind on the church service that morning. He couldn't believe he'd been bold enough to kiss the back of Lizzie's neck twice last night, but he knew his defenses were down because of being over-tired. He knew she was tired too, but she hadn't pushed him away. In fact, she had moved closer to him each night. Maybe it was time for him to come clean about the real reason he'd married her. As much as he'd tried to reason with himself at the time, it wasn't because Caleb needed a new *mamm,* or to spare his reputation in the community; it was because he'd never gotten over her. She was his first love, and he couldn't help but feel that the circle of life had brought them back together. He no longer carried the guilt over Nellie's passing; he knew it wasn't his fault, and there was nothing he could have done to prevent it from happening. It was God's will.

Before he realized, they had gotten through their first service as a family, and every time he looked back at Abby, she seemed to be content. Lizzie had even smiled at him from the other side of the room where she sat with his new daughter. He'd whispered a silent prayer of thanks for Abby, knowing that if not for her, he wouldn't be married to Lizzie. Thinking about it though, he knew he needed to find out from her once and for all why she'd placed his name on Abby's *Englisch* birth certificate. He guessed there were several things they needed to work out before they could move forward into a relationship. There could be no secrets between them—even the one he'd harbored for the past ten years.

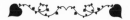

"Your dad is my grandpa, right?" Abby was asking from the back of the buggy on the way to her father's farm.

"Yes, Abby." Lizzie's voice cracked at the admission. In all the time she'd been away, she never once gave thought to what her own father was missing out on by not knowing about Abby. She was, after all, his first grandchild, and she'd denied them both the opportunity to be a family. Guilt made her heart flutter, and she wondered if the strictness in her father's tone would carry over to the dinner they were about to encounter at his house. She hadn't intended to disappoint her father, or stain her mother's memory, but that's how it looked in the eyes of her father, and she hoped marrying Jacob and joining the church would eventually make things right between them. She knew that a good start would be to teach Abby all she could about the Amish, and to make sure she even learned the language.

Lizzie stiffened her shoulders as they entered her father's house, determined that no matter what he said to her, or no matter how disapproving his tone, she would be respectful and show Abby a good example of how to properly yield to the authority of a parent.

Her older brother, David, and his wife, Leah, had not yet arrived with her nephew. To her surprise, her father and younger brother, Seth, greeted her with open arms and smiles. Was it because she was married? Or did they do it out of respect for Jacob only? At the moment, she didn't care; she was home, and this was the happiest she'd been in a long time.

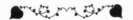

Abby already saw the advantages to having a grandpa—*Grossdaddi*—as he'd taught her to say. Seeing the never-ending smile spread across her mom's—*mamm's*—lips was enough to make any child's heart sing. She watched her *mamm* most of the afternoon, and realized she'd never seen her so happy—*froh*. Her new *Onkel* Seth, and her new *bruder*, Caleb, had spent a good part of the afternoon teaching her a few simple words that would make things easier to understand when eavesdropping on adult conversation—something Seth and Caleb both admitted to enjoying. She was just happy because her mother was happy, and she discovered that having a big family to care about you was more important than having a cell phone or TV—especially now that she had a new *daed*.

CHAPTER 22

Lizzie felt the awkwardness drift away between her and her *daed* the moment he handed her the quilt that her *mamm* had made for her tenth birthday. She'd never gotten the chance to give it to her since she passed away two months before. It was something Lizzie had never known about—until now.

Tears welled up in her eyes at the beautiful, intricate stitching her *mamm* was known for. Her quilts had been the best in the community, and all the women were in awe of her detailed quilts and her eye for matching and arranging the colors and patterns.

"Why didn't you give this to me sooner, *Daed?*"

Hiram cleared his throat. "It was in the attic in a trunk that I just couldn't bring myself to going through until a few years ago. I knew she'd made it for you, but I couldn't look at her things after she died, so I packed them all in the trunk and put them in the attic. He handed her a brown paper bag that was folded at the top.

"I found this in the trunk too. I'd forgotten about it until I went in search of things you might want now that you're married. It's the quilt she started making for the *boppli* before she…well, I thought you might want to finish it and use it when you and Jacob expand your *familye* and have your next *boppli.*"

Her heart skipped a beat at the thought of carrying Jacob's child.

Hiram urged her to take the bag, despite her hesitation.

Lizzie opened the bag, a lump forming in her throat as she pulled out the yellow baby quilt that was nearly finished. Her hands shook as she turned it over, examining each stitch. She held it to her cheek, believing she could almost smell her *mamm* in the folds of the fabric.

"*Denki*. I only hope I can make my stitches as evenly as *mamm's*. She was the best quilter in this community—that's a lot to live up to."

Hiram put his arm across her shoulder. "I have faith in you."

Those few simple words and the affection from her father was all she needed to tell her she was forgiven.

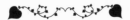

The entire ride home, Lizzie's thoughts were occupied with visions of what a new *boppli* would mean to her *daed*. It was clear to her from their conversation that he'd felt cheated out of the joy of helping to raise Abby. He seemed proud to be a *grossdaddi*, and Lizzie did not want to disappoint him further by letting on that she and Jacob had not yet had the opportunity to even create a *boppli*.

Jacob startled her by placing his hand on top of hers. "You seem preoccupied. Did you have an unpleasant conversation with your *daed*?"

"*Nee*. In fact, it was a very good talk. He gave me the quilt my *mamm* was making for the *boppli* she was having before she..."

Jacob squeezed her hand. "That's something very special. I noticed the large quilt on the top of the boxes your *daed* helped me put in the back of the buggy. Is that the one? It's very nice."

Lizzie couldn't help leaning her head on his shoulder for comfort. He put his arm around her to steady her shaking.

"She made that one for my tenth birthday, but she never got the chance to give it to me. She was gone a few months before. The trunk he gave me contains a lot of her things she used in the kitchen, and even some of her personal things. He thought I could use them now that I'm married."

Jacob tightened his grip across her shoulders, holding the reins with his left hand. "You can make it your home by putting your *mamm's* things anywhere you want. I want you and Abby to feel at home there, and I want you to do whatever you need to in order to be comfortable."

Lizzie cuddled in closer to him. "*Denki.* That means a lot to me."

Jacob smiled at her. "I have an idea."

He pulled the buggy into the drive of the B&B instead of continuing on to their farm. "Do you think your *aenti* would agree to stay with the *kinner* for an hour so we can take that buggy ride we missed out on?"

He assisted her down. "I don't see why not. She hasn't seen Abby in a couple of days, and she was going to teach her how to make a snitz pie."

It didn't matter to Lizzie that she was already exhausted from the long day at church, and then the dinner with her family, what mattered was that she was finally going to get the chance to have a *gut* talk with her husband.

CHAPTER 23

Jacob steered the buggy down the ribbon of road, keeping his eye on the large harvest moon that illuminated their path with a romantic, amber glow. Lizzie leaned against him, making it tough for him to break the silence with their long-overdue talk about the circumstances that brought them together as a married couple.

"I'm only curious about one thing. Why did you name me as Abby's *vadder?*"

Lizzie straightened, and Jacob wished he hadn't been so blunt. He enjoyed having her so close to him, but now it was evident that her defenses were up, and he feared they would remain distant until the matter was resolved.

"I was very emotional at the time of her birth because of the circumstances that brought her into existence in the first place. I was alone and scared, and without a midwife, I gave birth in a hospital. They required the legal document, and I was afraid that with such a document as public record of her birth that Eddie, her real father, would take her from me if he knew the truth."

Jacob slowed the horse, looking for a spot to pull over on the side of the dirt road. He didn't want to continue on endlessly because of the late hour, and be too far away from home to pick up the *kinner* at a reasonable time, and he knew his horse could probably use a break.

"You weren't married to him?"

He wasn't trying to embarrass her, but he could tell by the look on her face that he'd done just that. He immediately regretted the question.

"No. I was out with him the last night I saw him, and he said he needed to stop at a friend's house before we went to dinner. We never made it to the restaurant. He and his friends offered me a glass of water, and I took it never dreaming they would put drugs in it, but they did. The last thing I remembered was Eddie taking me home and putting me in my bed because I was too dizzy to walk. When I woke up the next morning, I was *naked* and all alone."

Tears welled up in her eyes, and Jacob pulled her into his arms, kissing the top of her hair. "I'm so sorry he violated you in that way."

She'd made her peace with what had happened, including her decision to keep Abby in spite of how she was conceived. But that didn't mean she would ever forget the fear and hurt she felt—not to mention the shame.

Jacob lifted her chin and looked into her moist eyes as if he'd read her thoughts. "It's *his* shame, *not* yours."

She cleared her throat. "I know that now, but after what happened, I didn't think I could ever come home. When I learned I was pregnant, I moved to another town and changed my name legally. That's why my last name is Barlow. I didn't want to bring shame on my family. I led people to believe my *husband* was deceased, and I became *Englisch* to the world around me. After a few years, it came naturally."

"That doesn't explain why you named me as her *vadder.*"

Lizzie sniffed back the tears that threatened to spill, her heart racing at the confession she was about to make.

"I was still very much in love with you. I hadn't gotten over you, and since I couldn't make up a name or put Eddie's name as her father, I named you. I know I acted like a silly, immature girl by doing such a thing, but I just wasn't thinking straight at the time."

Jacob's mind was reeling, and his heart was beating so hard, he worried it would shoot out of his chest.

"If it's confessing we're doing, I have one of my own."

"What could a *gut* man like you have to confess?"

He hesitated for a moment, as if to gather his thoughts. "When you left the community, I was so devastated I tried to drown my sorrow by courting Nellie Fisher. I knew it was wrong to lead her on when I didn't feel the same, but I thought I could force myself to have a life with her—that I would learn to love her in time. She was a good woman and she deserved better than the small part of my heart, but I never got over you either. You were my first love—the only one I could ever give my heart to."

She looked up at him, disbelief in her eyes.

He ignored the shock on her face and continued before he lost his nerve. "When she died giving birth to Caleb, I was riddled with such guilt that I could barely function. My own *mamm* had to come in and help me care for him because I was no *gut* to him in the state I was in. My *familye* assumed I was grieving, but I couldn't tell them the truth. I only just told the Bishop before we were married. It was a burden that had plagued me until just a week ago before you came back to the community when I decided to shave and force myself to let go of the past. Telling the Bishop was the final step in putting my shame behind me and allowing *Gott* to forgive me."

Lizzie couldn't believe her ears. After all this time, he'd been hurting just as much as she had. "Thank you for being so honest with me, Jacob."

He picked up the reins. "We should probably head back to pick up the *kinner*. Your *aenti* is probably getting worried, and tomorrow is a long work day."

Lizzie thought about the wash she'd have to do at the B&B after doing her own family's wash, and realized it was best they go home even though she wasn't ready.

Jacob steered the buggy back toward home. "How did you manage on your own among the *Englisch* for so long?"

"I went to a trade-school after passing the GED test and became a pharmacy technician. It was good work until Eddie caught up to me. There was no denying she was his child—they look too much alike. He threatened to tell her, and take her from me if I didn't give him money for drugs. His friends even threatened to kill me if I didn't help him. But he died in a car crash a few weeks ago, and I'm sure his friends have forgotten all about me by now."

Jacob pulled her close with one arm, afraid if he let go of her, something would happen to her. He hoped she was right about the men giving up their quest for money for a dead man's debt, but he would willingly pay any amount to keep his *fraa* and *dochder* safe. It didn't matter that Abby was not his flesh and blood, and he would not shame Lizzie further by denying what the community believed about his part in conceiving her. As far as he was concerned, Abby was his *dochder* in every way that counted. He was proud of his decision to claim her as his *dochder,* for he already loved her as if she was.

CHAPTER 24

Lizzie woke up, surprised that Jacob was still cuddling her close to him. She nudged him slightly since she could see just enough in the dimly lit room to know the sun would be fully up soon. He groaned slightly, pulling her closer still. She didn't want to leave his arms, but they both had a lot of work to do without many hours of daylight to complete since the days had grown shorter.

"Stay with me just a few minutes longer." He whispered in her ear sending shivers of desire through her.

If she had her way, they wouldn't get up at all, but she was having a tough time grasping his sudden urge to lounge. Every day since they'd been married, he'd been up hours before her, yet today, he was willing to linger. Was he overtired and worn out from his added responsibility, or did he simply want to cuddle her? Either way, she wouldn't argue for long, even though she knew the delay would prolong her workday. She snuggled him, knowing the time spent with him would be worth every agonizing minute her day would extend by for staying with him.

Jacob was very aware of the desire he was invoking in her. He couldn't help feeling it himself. But he knew there was no time for the kind of closeness he desired with her, and he wasn't sure if she was ready for that yet. Not wanting to push her too far, he didn't dare kiss her, despite the magnetic pull he felt from her to do so. He wasn't sure he would be able to stop at kissing if they started anything, and there was no time for that now, no matter how much he desired to become one with her. They had a full day of work ahead of them, but that didn't stop him from wanting to hold her just a little longer.

Lizzie had to be strong for both of them. "If I stay too long, I'll want to stay longer and longer still. If we don't get up now I'm afraid we'll stay here all day."

His eyes opened slightly and he smiled at her.

"Would that be such a bad thing?"

At first thought, it wouldn't but... "We have obligations, Jacob. Not just to each other, but to the *kinner* and the community. I'm expected to help my *aenti* with Monday wash, and I believe you and Caleb are expected at the Belier's to finish the inside of the barn."

He leaned up and kissed her forehead. "You're right. I don't want you thinking I'm not a responsible man."

She tousled his curly brown hair. "I have the utmost admiration for you. After what you did for me and Abby, I could never see you as irresponsible."

He smiled at her, feeling his heart tug away with her as she lifted herself from the bed.

He was falling in love with her all over again.

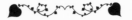

Lizzie couldn't keep her mind on task. Her arms went through the motions, hanging the linens on the clothesline at the B&B, but a soft blush covered her cheeks from thinking of Jacob and his desire for her. It was the same desire she felt for him, but was afraid to admit even to herself. Happiness had been a long time in coming to her, and she still feared it would leave her if she blinked too long. Abby's presence was the only thing that kept her grounded.

"Will we get home in time for *daed* to show me how to harness Snowball?"

Lizzie looked at the sun that rested high above their heads. "We have two more loads of linens to finish, and then we can go home. If we hurry and clean the last room we should be home with enough time for you to spend about thirty minutes before dinner."

"I don't have to help you cook?"

Lizzie smiled. "I think I can do without your help just this once."

Abby rushed at Lizzie with a hearty hug, and then went back to work hanging towels on the clothesline.

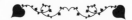

Lizzie pulled the last piece of fried chicken from the iron skillet and placed it on the linen-clad platter. She covered it to keep it warm while she checked on her biscuits. Seeing they still had a couple of minutes, she set the table and went out to ring the bell to alert Jacob the meal was ready.

Jacob, Caleb and Abby came rushing in the door, laughing at something. It startled Lizzie, causing her to knock her hand against the hot stove when she took the biscuits out of the oven. "Oh, not again!"

Before she realized, Jacob was at her side, pulling her hand under the cold-running water in the sink. He put his arm around her and kissed her lightly on the cheek.

"I'm sorry for startling you again."

"It isn't your fault. I knew you were coming in, I just had my mind on other things."

Jacob looked her in the eye and smiled. "I've had a tough time keeping my mind on my work too."

She smiled back, losing herself in his dimples.

"I'd like it if we could take another buggy ride tomorrow night. Do you think you could arrange with Aunt Bess to stay with the *kinner?*"

"I'll ask her in the morning when I go over to clean the B&B. It'll be a short day tomorrow since she only has two guests."

Jacob's face lit up. "*Gut.* I was hoping to have some time to help Abby with Snowball. Caleb and I don't have anywhere to be tomorrow, so we will be here when you return. I'd like it if I could spend the afternoon working with her and the horse. The sooner we break him, the sooner she'll be able to ride him."

Lizzie turned off the water, satisfied she'd left her hand under the cool tap long enough. "That would make her happy. All she talks about all day is how much she wants to ride that horse. I think she'd sleep in the barn with him if we let her."

Jacob beamed at his daughter, and Lizzie loved him all the more for it.

CHAPTER 25

Lizzie was excited to hear that her aunt would watch the children so she and Jacob could take a buggy ride after the evening meal. She hoped tonight would be the night he would kiss her. As much as she tried to keep her mind on her work, she couldn't help but let her mind slip back to thoughts of Jacob. But she had work to do or she would never get home to him.

Watching Abby dust the furniture and fluff the pillows, she admired how much she fit into the Amish lifestyle so quickly, right down to the purple dress with the black apron she now wore. Since they'd gotten Snowball, she hadn't mentioned cell phones, computers or TV even once, and Lizzie wondered if her adaptation to her surroundings would stay with her.

"Are you happy now that you have a father?"

Abby looked up from her work, surprised at the question. "I thought I would miss my cell phone and TV, but I'm having a lot more fun here. And I have to admit that having a dad—*daed*—is really nice. You were right. I do love it here because everyone is nice. And I even have a few friends—Annie and Rebecca."

"Do you want to know the nice thing about your friend Annie? She's also your new cousin."

"It is nice to have a big family now. I was always lonely when it was just you and me for a family, but now I have a *daed,* and a *bruder, onkels,* and even a *grossdaddi.*"

Lizzie's eyes misted over, knowing she'd made the right decision for her daughter.

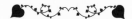

Lizzie watched from the fence post as Abby took her first ride on Snowball. He'd been gentle enough that Jacob felt he was ready for a rider—especially since the auctioneer claimed he'd been saddled before. Jacob was grateful that the previous owner of the seven-year-old gelding had broken him in and appeared to have treated him well, creating a gentle animal fit for his daughter.

Abby felt very comfortable on Snowball, as though she was meant for horseback riding. She felt like the luckiest girl in the world to have such a nice new *daed* to get her a horse of her own. She knew her friend, Rachel, would be envious of such a gift, and she intended to write to her— snail-mail, of course, just as soon she got the chance. Her *mamm* had tried to explain to her how much more satisfying getting a real letter in the mail can be, but she was still a little unsure of it. The important thing, though, was that she would help her to keep in contact with her best friend.

Jacob continued to walk beside Snowball, ensuring Abby's safety since the horse was new to her. "You're doing a *gut* job of learning. Snowball seems to have been made just for you."

Abby leaned in and stroked Snowball's silky neck.

"Can I braid his mane with red ribbons and put jingle bells around his neck for Christmas?"

Jacob laughed heartily. "That sounds like a *gut* idea. If we get him trained in time, we can have him pull the sleigh."

Abby's eyes grew wide. "You have a sleigh?"

Jacob smiled at her excitement. "*Jah.* We take the sleigh to visit neighbors at Christmas. It goes easier in the snow than the buggy."

Abby giggled, delighting Jacob.

"I can't wait for it to snow!"

Jacob could see that raising a *dochder* was going to be a lot different than raising Caleb—especially since she'd been raised as an *Englischer*. He might have missed her first steps, and other firsts in her young life, but he knew there were plenty of "firsts" ahead of them to look forward to as a *familye*—including her first sleigh ride.

And he could hardly wait.

CHAPTER 26

Jacob was eager to get his wife home after their buggy ride—especially since Aunt Bess offered to keep the children overnight. He had to admit that he was nervous to be alone with Lizzie, even though they'd slept in the same bed together since their marriage. But this was different. They would have no responsibilities except to each other for the entire night. But first, he would enjoy the remainder of their buggy ride together by the light of the harvest moon.

Lizzie reached for Jacob's hand and leaned into his shoulder. She didn't mind the chill in the air; her thoughts of Jacob were keeping her cheeks pretty heated. The quilt that spread across their laps was the very quilt her *mamm* had made for her. She wanted to use it once before giving it to Abby for her bed. It was made for her at Abby's same age, and Lizzie felt it important that she have something from the *grossmammi* she would never get to meet.

Jacob clenched her cold fingers in his. "Are you warm enough?"

"I'm a little cold, but I'd like to stop for a minute alongside the road to gaze at the stars if that's alright with you."

"*Jah.*" Jacob pulled the buggy to the side of the dirt road and gazed upward. "The sky is full of stars tonight."

Lizzie nuzzled in a little closer, and Jacob put his arm around her.

"I really missed the stars living in the city. The view out here is so bright, whereas the stars are hard to see against the city lights."

Lizzie tilted her head up. "There must be a billion of them out tonight."

Jacob watched her as she smiled at the stars. She was so beautiful against the moonlight, he wondered if it was too soon to kiss her. He loved her more than he ever thought he could, and didn't think he could stand to wait even another moment for her full lips to touch his.

She turned to him then. "Are you still angry with me?"

Jacob's heart caught in throat. He wasn't expecting such a question. "Why would I be angry with you?"

"Because you were forced to marry me!"

Jacob pulled both of her hands in his and turned to face her. "No one forced me. I did it willingly. At first I thought it was to keep from being excommunicated. But when I saw how much you and Abby needed me I realized that maybe Caleb and I needed you too."

Lizzie swallowed the lump that tried to invade her throat. "How do we make this work when it really seems like we used each other to stay in the community?"

Jacob pulled her close enough to smell the flowery fragrance of her hair. "Because I never stopped loving you! And it took being forced into a marriage to make me realize it."

Lizzie giggled. "So you admit to being forced to marrying me?"

"Yes! But that doesn't mean I'm not happy with the decision."

Lizzie looked him in the eye, noticing for the first time just how handsome he really was. She'd not been able to really look at him since they'd been married, and she realized she was happy too.

Jacob cupped her cold cheeks in his warm hands and pulled her close, placing his lips on hers. Leaning into his advances, she tasted his sweet kisses, feeling like they were drips of honey on her tongue.

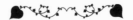

Lizzie slipped under the quilt and waited for Jacob to finish taking care of the horse and buggy. She put her fingers to her lips, remembering the way Jacob's lips felt when they'd touched hers. They'd shared one kiss when they were younger, but it was nothing like the passionate kiss they'd just shared only a few minutes ago.

Jacob entered the bedroom, causing Lizzie's pulse to race. It made her so nervous she jumped from the bed and stood in front of the window. Jacob stood behind her, folding his arms around her.

"Is something wrong?"

Everything is right for the first time in a very long time. So why am I so afraid?

She turned around swiftly and looked him in the eye, her mouth slightly agape as though she wanted to say something and forgot midsentence. He dragged his fingers through her long, brown hair and lowered his mouth to hers. Love surged through him as he drew her so close he could barely breathe, but he feared he would lose his breath altogether if he let her slip from his grasp. She welcomed the kiss as his mouth swept over hers with sweet desperation. She knew that desperation well; it had been building in her soul for the past ten years, and escalated during the week while she waited for him to claim her as his. She stumbled backward, pulling him toward the bed where she could give herself to him with reckless abandon. Jacob was her one true love, and she would have him forever this time around.

CHAPTER 27

One year later…

"I can't do this anymore, Jacob. You're going to have to ask someone else!"

Jacob smoothed Lizzie's damp hair from her face, and watched the midwife's face for the signal.

"One more push, Lizzie. Just one more, I promise."

Exhausted, Lizzie pushed once more, feeling the pressure of her baby's head emerging. She hadn't struggled this much giving birth to Abby. Was something wrong?

"Stop pushing for a minute and let me ease out the shoulders. This one looks like he's built like his *daed.*"

Jacob squeezed Lizzie's hand and whispered in her ear to distract her from pushing for a minute.

"I've never been more in love with you than right now, Lizzie."

Lizzie giggled, tears streaming down her cheeks when her baby emerged. He was beautiful, with a full head of curly brown hair like Jacob's. The midwife wiped his face and handed him to Lizzie for examination.

He was perfect in every way.

Suddenly, another contraction assailed Lizzie, causing her to let out a scream. Jacob lifted the baby from her arms and stood up, fear directed at the midwife.

"I think we have another *boppli* trying to make its way into your *familye.*"

Lizzie pushed herself up on her elbows. "What do you mean another one? You only heard one heartbeat!"

"Sometimes these things get missed. Get ready to push so we can deliver this little one."

Lizzie laid back, a thousand thoughts whirling in her head, but all she had time to concentrate on were the contractions causing her to push another baby from her. One good push and the next one was born, screaming loudly.

Lizzie held her arms out for her new daughter.

The midwife listened to Lizzie's abdomen through the stethoscope. "That was the last one, I promise!"

Lizzie smiled at Jacob, who held his son, while she held his daughter—his real daughter. Lizzie had to admit she'd been a little afraid this day would come. She'd been hoping for a boy her entire pregnancy, concerned that Abby would no longer feel like Jacob's daughter if he had one of his own. But here she was, faced with reality, and wondered how her husband was feeling.

When the midwife finished with Lizzie, she took newborn Samuel from Jacob's arms and went across the room to clean him up while Lizzie and Jacob picked out a name for their daughter.

"What do you think of the name Rachel? That was my *mamm's* name."

Jacob kissed Lizzie gently. "I think it's a perfect name."

Lifting her chin gently, he kissed her again. "Is something troubling you?"

Lizzie chose her words carefully. "I wonder what you're thinking now that I've truly given you a *dochder.*"

Jacob smoothed back Lizzie's hair and kissed her on the forehead. "I'll always cherish Abby, and I couldn't love her any more if she was my own flesh and blood. I'm sure you feel the same for Caleb."

Lizzie frowned. "You're right. I do. But Abby isn't your real *dochder*, and this *boppli* is your flesh and blood."

Jacob smiled. "You gave me a *dochder* when I married you, and I gave you a son. Now we've been blessed with another one of each, and for that, I will always love you."

"I love you too, Jacob."

Lizzie and Jacob couldn't stop smiling. They each now held a newborn—their children—made from their love.

**PLEASE CONTINUE READING...
BOOK TWO in this series is on the next page...
Amish Winter Wonderland

Amish Winter Wonderland
Book 2

Samantha Jillian Bayarr

CHAPTER 1

"Do you even *like* boys?"

Lillian Stoltzfus didn't like the tone her younger sister, Hannah, was using—or her implications.

"That isn't funny. Of course I like boys! They just don't like me!"

Hannah held up her hand apologetically. "I didn't mean that the way it sounded. But you have to admit that it appears you *want* to be a spinster."

"That's a mean thing to say, Hannah"

"Maybe you need to make yourself a little more available to the *menner* when we have working bees. You have a lot to offer a husband since you have your own bakery that *daed* built for you. It's on your own land and everything. What man wouldn't want you for his *fraa—wife?*"

Lillian sighed. "You know he only built the bakery on the land adjoining our farm so he could keep an eye on me—that, and the fact he only had *dochdern—daughters.* We both know if he'd had the son he wanted, I probably wouldn't have any of it. He's saving that land to sell to a potential suitor for me! But that's exactly the problem, I'm afraid. The *menner* in this community don't seem to want a strong, independent woman for a *fraa. "*

Hannah pinched her brow against the hazy October sun as they hung the last of the wash on the clothes line. Being the last day in October, it was already nearly too chilly to hang wash on the line, but the two of them made the decision, despite the fact their fingers were so cold, they could barely grasp the wet clothes.

Hannah winked at her. "Don't get discouraged. You aren't going to end up becoming a spinster if I can help it."

Lillian picked up the wicker hamper and walked toward the house. "Of course I will—especially since I'm about to turn twenty-five. But at least with my baking business, I won't be a burden to *mamm* and *daed.*"

"You're forgetting one thing. There *is* one man in the community still unmarried who's about your age."

Lillian stopped in her tracks. "If you're going to try to sell me on Seth Miller again, it won't work! He's five years older than me. It's obvious he doesn't want a *fraa,* or he'd already have one. Besides, he's way too quiet. He never talks to me when he comes into the bakery—ever. I take that as a sign he just isn't interested in me."

If the truth be told, Lillian had been interested in him for the past year, ever since he started coming into the bakery on a regular basis. But though he would sometimes linger, he never said very much, especially nothing that would give her the impression he liked her. She was hopelessly infatuated with him, and it frustrated her that she was alone in her feelings. She couldn't even be sure she could consider Seth a friend because friends usually talked more than the two of them did.

Hannah pushed out her lower lip. "Or he's just shy. Lillian, you're much prettier than I am. How could he *not* want you for his *fraa?* A man would have to be blind not to see how perfect you are."

Lillian turned her back on her *schweschder—sister.* "Don't insult me, Hannah. We both know you inherited *mamm's* beauty. And no man is that shy. I think he has too much responsibility to his *daed.* Maybe that's why his *schweschder* ran away all those years ago—because of Hiram Miller's strict parenting."

Hannah stayed on her heels. "I'm not going to criticize the man's parenting, but I'll agree he does seem to work poor Seth to the bone. His loyalty to his *daed* is honorable—that's a *gut* quality in a man. As far as you not being pretty, maybe if Seth saw you in something other than work dresses, he might take notice. Every time he comes into the bakery, your hair is always messy, and you're wearing flour-covered work dresses, and your underarms are sweaty. You might as well wear *Daed's* trousers and suspenders for all the feminine quality you display."

Lillian turned sharply to confront her younger sibling. "That's because I'm always working! Maybe if you worked as hard as I do you'd understand that. Seth has seen me at the church services in my Sunday dress, and he doesn't take notice. What have you to say about that?"

"I'd say I'm going to make you a new dress! You haven't made a new dress in at least two years, and you wear the same dull, worn out brown dress every service. You would look nice in a blue. Maybe that would attract his attention. And the blue would go nicely with your eyes."

Lillian pursed her lips. "Such talk of vanity. You better not let *daed* hear you talking like that or he will make you have a meeting with Bishop Troyer."

Hannah waved a careless hand at her. "I'll begin your dress today after I go into town with *daed*. I will get the most beautiful blue material for a dress, and you can wear it to the singing on Saturday."

Lillian continued on her path to the kitchen door. "I have never attended a singing, and I have no intention of attending one now. I'm too old."

"You are not too old. I want you to come to the singing with me and Jonathon Graber. I'll have him bring his cousin, Henry, and we'll make Seth jealous."

"First of all, Seth will likely not attend the singing because he's older than I am—he's thirty! Second, Henry is barely twenty, so I'm way too old for him. And third—when did you start dating Jonathon?"

Hannah smiled. "We've been sneaking around for months, and you would know that if you didn't work all the time."

Lillian narrowed her eyes. "You think I want to work so much? I didn't ask for that bakery—let's not forget that."

"You don't have to take it out on me. But promise you won't tell *daed* about Jonathon; I don't want him interfering."

"So my little *boppli schweschder* is to be married before me. I'm going to be the last one to be married in the community—if I'm lucky enough to marry at all!"

Seth entered the small baking house nestled on the main road at the far edge of the Stoltzfus farm, and spotted Lillian immediately. His heart thumped in his chest, and heat crawled up his neck when her blue eyes pierced his. She was waiting on an *Englisch* woman, but she paused to look at him at the sound of the bells on the door that jingled his presence. He hated those bells that caught him unaware every time he entered the small bakery, forgetting to avert his eyes in time to avoid eye-contact with Lillian. It caught him off guard every time, but yet for some reason, he couldn't pull his eyes away from her.

He tried not to stare as she pushed stray, dark blonde tendrils behind her ear with the back of her flour-covered hand. A light dusting of sheen illuminated her cheeks, indicating she'd been hard at work preparing his special order—the same order he picked up every Monday and every Thursday for the past year. He'd come in every week, and still he found it difficult to converse with Lillian, though he'd been hopelessly infatuated with her for some time. If not for all the work he did around the farm, his waistline would be a tell-tale sign of his feelings for Lillian.

At twenty-nine, he'd missed his chance to court in his teenage years and his twenties due to extra responsibilities on his *daed's* farm. And now, he felt socially awkward from lack of experience at a time when he'd felt more confident, but his youthful bravery had faltered with time. He had no hope for a suitable mate, feeling he'd become set in his ways and wouldn't know how to act even if the situation presented itself. Working long hours on the farm, sometimes alone, had rendered him speechless in Lillian's presence, lest he open his mouth and make a fool of himself by tripping over his words.

No, it was best to keep as quiet as possible around her, and not risk gazing upon her beautiful face too long. Though he knew it was pointless to hope for a life with her, it didn't stop him from wanting to take her for a buggy ride.

Lillian tried not to let her voice falter as Seth stepped forward to pick up his order. She'd added a couple of pumpkin muffins to his regular order, and now she wished she hadn't done it. It was a bold move on her part, but she had to do something to get his attention once for all. Though she now second-guessed her assertiveness, it was too late to remove them from the closed box. He'd think it un-Christian of her if she removed items from his box after he'd already paid. She'd put them in as a gift, and there was no taking them back. Thankfully, he wouldn't discover them until he reached home.

It was all Hannah's fault for planting ideas in her head about Seth, and making her think she had a chance with him. And now she was trying to win his attention with baked goods? Heat crept up her cheeks as she felt like a fool for thinking Seth would show an interest in her over a couple of pumpkin muffins. He'd been ordering from her bakery since she opened it last year, and he'd never offered her any indication he was interested in anything beyond the pies and pastries she baked for him and his *daed* every week. But it was Seth's loyalty to his *daed* that kept him from having a life of his own, and that didn't give Lillian confidence that she could ever win his heart—not that she was sure if she even wanted to. To open herself up to him could mean heartache, and she wasn't sure she could risk it.

What she still couldn't figure out was why Seth's silence irritated her so much today. Perhaps the surprise in his box of baked goods would spark a conversation from his all-business tone when he came back in on Thursday.

She could only hope…

CHAPTER 2

Hiram Miller sat down with his cup of *kaffi—coffee* and a pumpkin muffin from the bakery. He wondered why Seth had gotten the extra goody, but as he bit into the moist treat, he had no complaints.

Seth came in from the morning milking and stared at the confection in his *daed's* hand. "Where did that come from?"

Hiram held up the muffin for inspection. "It was in the box you got from the bakery. Didn't you check the order yesterday when you got it?"

Seth went to the box that rested on the counter, and saw the other muffin and reached inside to retrieve it. "I didn't think to check it. Miss Stoltzfus has never gotten our order wrong. Maybe she was having a sale, or they're day-old and she was giving them away. But in case it was a mistake, I'll make up the difference when I go back on Thursday."

Hiram chuckled. "I'm sure she'll appreciate that. In the meantime, I'm going to enjoy this muffin. No sense in letting it go to waste."

Seth poured himself a cup of coffee and joined his *daed* at the table and decided he would do the same. One bite of the delicious muffin sent his senses straight to Heaven. Not only was Lillian beautiful, she could bake like an angel. He looked across the table at his *daed,* who sat silent, and wondered what it would be like to have Lillian sitting across the table from him chattering in her pleasant, joyful tone with him. He was lonely, and he had been for a long time. Was it too late to hope he could ever win her heart? One thing he was sure of; it would never happen if he couldn't get up enough courage to talk to her.

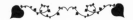

"Hold still or I'm going to stick you with a pin."

Lillian fidgeted on purpose. She didn't want to be on display in front of her *mamm* and *daed* while Hannah measured the bottom of her new dress for the hem.

"I'm being as still as I can, but you've had me standing on this chair so long I'm getting dizzy."

Hannah looked up at her and scoffed. "That's a fib, Lillian, and you know it. Confess right now!"

Lillian narrowed her eyes, and crossed her arms. "I will do no such thing. You're making me feel uncomfortable with all this attention. I don't need a new dress."

Beth Stoltzfus looked up from her mending and admired the blue dress on her daughter. "Yes you do. And that color is perfect for you. I get tired of seeing you in the same dull brown and gray dresses all the time. The brighter color will do you some *gut*."

Lillian's cheeks heated. "But *mamm*, this is the color for marrying. And it's November now. I don't want to wear this color during wedding season. The entire community will believe I am fishing for a husband!"

Thankfully, her *daed* hadn't looked up from his reading with her comment.

Her *mamm* tipped her head. "I could see them thinking that. But since when do you let gossip control what you do? It makes me *froh—happy* to know that I have a *dochder* who is strong enough to withstand the pressures of the rest of the youth."

Lillian conceded. There was nothing to gain from openly disagreeing with her *mamm,* and Hannah was determined to make her social life her personal responsibility until her match-making efforts were successful. Perhaps when she failed and Seth failed to show interest in her, Hannah would eventually give up. If not, she was in for a long winter.

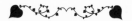

Lillian looked at the time, noting that Seth was later than usual in picking up his order—not that she was keeping track of him or anything. But he was a creature of habit, and he was never this late, and there was no sign of him. She stared out the bakery window, wondering what could be keeping him, as she dialed the phone to her *daed's* barn.

He picked up on the fourth ring. "Efram Stoltzfus here."

Lillian cleared her throat. "*Daed,* would you mind hitching the small buggy for me so I can make a delivery?"

"If it's far I can drive you. It will be dark soon."

Lillian could feel the blush creeping up her cheeks. She didn't want her *daed* tagging along, and having Seth think she was a *boppli—baby.*

"No. it's just down the road to the Miller's. They never picked up their order and I don't want it to turn stale."

"I should have it ready by the time you walk down to the barn." He hung up without another word.

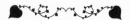

Lillian felt her nerves jangle as she drove the small buggy down the lane toward Seth's farm. She wasn't sure if she hoped he was there or not, but she had to admit she was a little concerned about why he hadn't shown up for his order. As she pulled into the yard, she spotted Hiram Miller mending a section of fence near the barn.

He tipped his hat when she exited the buggy, the box of baked goods in her hands. "Evening, Miss Stoltzfus."

"*Gut* evening, Mr. Miller. When I closed the bakery, I realized Seth had not yet picked up your order. I hope you don't mind I brought it over, but I didn't want it to get stale, and I figured you would want the pie for your evening meal."

He took the box from her. "*Denki.* Seth had to go over and help his *schweschder,* Lizzie and her husband. I expect him back any time if you'd like to wait for him."

Hiram smiled knowingly, making Lillian worry that he could read her anxiousness in knowing Seth's whereabouts.

She shrugged. "I don't need to see him for anything. He can settle his bill when I see him on Tuesday. Have a *gut* night, Mr. Miller."

He tipped his hat again, the corners of his mouth forming a smile. Lillian could feel the heat reaching her cheeks, and she bolted away without another word. Did he know how she felt about his son? She prayed Seth wouldn't think she was being too forward by bringing his order to his *haus—house.*

CHAPTER 3

Seth had to admit he was more than a little curious when he saw that Lillian had dropped off his bakery order—especially since she'd included two pumpkin muffins again. He wasn't certain why she'd done it a second time when he hadn't even paid her for the first batch. His palate wasn't going to complain, but if she was going to insist on increasing his order, the amount of money he would owe her would increase each week. Not to mention his waistline. He was growing out of his clothes as it was, and his older sister, Lizzie, was no longer able to make him new shirts since her recent pregnancy had confined her to bed rest most of the day after an early false labor scare.

He wished he would have the time to stop in and settle his bill with her, but that would not be possible to do until Tuesday when he picked up his regular order. As much as he wanted to see her, he was needed to help Jacob since Lizzie was unable to, and his nephew, Caleb, still had a cast on his arm from falling from the loft in the barn. His niece, Abby offered to help, but she just wasn't strong enough to help dig the posts for the new fence, and she was needed to help Lizzie with the twins and the housework.

Lillian had begun to creep into his thoughts a lot lately, and he wondered if he would be able to contain his emotions much longer without bursting forth with the truth to the next person he spoke to. He was bubbling with new energy that was powered by his long-standing crush on the baker of sweet confections that made his mouth water as much as it did when he thought about kissing her.

Hiram sat at the kitchen table, feeling guilty over every bite he sank his teeth into of the delicious pumpkin muffin Miss Stoltzfus had brought over the night before—for Seth—not for *him*. He'd noticed the blush that heated her cheeks at the mention of his son, and he hadn't missed the look of disappointment on Seth's face when he learned she'd stopped by the house while he was gone.

He'd selfishly expected Seth to take care of things when Lizzie ran off. But the man knew that it was his fault just as much as the fact that Seth was nearly thirty years old without a *fraa* or *kinner* of his own. Why hadn't he seen it before now the way his son longed for Miss Stoltzfus? Had he really been so wrapped up in the needs of his own farm that he would deny another one of his *kinner* the happiness they deserved? He had to do something—but what?

Hiram said a silent prayer, asking *Gott*—God to forgive him for being so selfish with his children, and to help him find a way to help Seth. When he was finished, Seth entered the kitchen and peeked in the pink box from the bakery. He sat down across from his *daed,* cup of coffee in one hand, the muffin in the other. Hiram watched his son look at the muffin with a hazy, far-off look in his eyes, and wondered if he was going to eat it, or stare at it the entire morning.

Hiram cleared his throat. "I thought we could ride out to the *Das Dutchman Essenhaus* for your birthday tomorrow."

Seth put the muffin down. "What about Lizzie? She would be heartbroken if we didn't come to her *haus.* Since she's unable to get around, I thought it would be nice if we went over there. Abby promised to bake me a cake!"

Hiram smiled. "Well if my *granddochder*—granddaughter is making a cake, how can we go anywhere else?"

He silently thanked God for the little girl he'd known nothing about until five years ago when his own daughter had returned home. He only wished his Marian was still alive to see the *grandkinner* grow up. He watched Seth savoring his muffin, realizing he'd allowed his own loneliness over his wife's death to interfere with raising his children. He'd driven Lizzie away after tearing her apart from Jacob, and now he'd done the same thing to Seth. It was his fault Seth was a single man, and he aimed to remedy that.

"Could you run an errand for me today and run the new harnesses over to Efram Stoltzfus? I figured since you have to help Jacob finish the fencing you could stop by there first since he's right across the road from your *schweschder's haus.*"

Seth's heart raced at the possibility of running into Lillian when he dropped off the buggy harnesses for her *daed.* But then he realized she might not be there, but at her bakery instead. Perhaps it would give him the opportunity to settle his bill.

CHAPTER 4

Lillian swung the broom one more time, trying to encourage her chickens from the bare trees. They had begun nesting in the trees since she hadn't taken the time to clip their wings last week, and they were way overdue for the task. Behind her, she heard a buggy approaching, but she didn't have time to stop what she was doing to socialize with whoever was paying a visit—especially since whoever it was would be there to see her *daed.*

Swinging the broom in a wider arc, she smacked the branches just below the nesting chickens, but they wouldn't budge.

"That's no way to get a chicken out of a tree," a voice behind her said with a chuckle.

Without turning around, she realized she recognized the voice as belonging to Seth. What was he doing here? She took another swing with the broom, ignoring his mocking laughter.

Before she realized, he was behind her and grabbed the broom from her.

"Give that back!"

He smiled and looked toward the chickens, his cheeks turning pink. "Why are you wasting your time bothering them? They look comfortable up there."

Lillian turned toward him, hands on her hips.

"They're up there because I got too busy at the bakery last week and didn't have time to clip their wings. They just discovered they can fly, and if I don't get them down and get their wings clipped I will lose the eggs, and I need them for my baking."

He laughed more heartily. She'd never remembered hearing him laugh before. He had a nice laugh—even though he was laughing at *her.*

"If you want to get them down, sprinkle some feed in the grass. When they're distracted, you can grab onto them."

Why hadn't she thought of that? He must think her a fool to let a couple of chickens get the better of her. And why was he suddenly talking to her?

She looked at him as though it was the first time she was seeing him—really seeing him. His skin still held a little color from a summer in the sun, and she could see the strength of his muscles beneath his shirt that he had long-since grown out of. The shadow of whiskers on his chin defined his chiseled jaw, his cheekbones prominent above the dimples that deepened when he smiled. His hazel eyes were kind, his dark blonde hair wind-blown to the side after his hat blew to the ground.

He picked up his hat, his gaze set on her. "I'd be more than happy to help you clip the wings if you get some feed from the barn to bring them down out of the tree."

Lillian stepped away from him without saying a word, and was back in no time at all with a scoopful of chicken feed. Seth watched her as she scattered the feed along the grass, thinking how beautiful she looked against the cold, November sun. Why hadn't he noticed before now just how truly beautiful she was? She stirred in him a desire to break away from his father's farm and begin a family of his own—with Lillian. But would she have him?

Lillian giggled as she watched Seth calling to the chickens, trying to coax them from the branches of the tree. When he finally got the last one down, he picked up the pair of cutting shears from the tree stump where Lillian had left them. He picked up one of the hens without effort and began clipping her wings.

Lillian picked up another hen, set her on the tree stump, and held her hand out to Seth for the cutting shears.

"I know you didn't come all the way over here to clip my chicken's wings."

Seth's face heated. "I don't mind helping. But I did bring your *daed's* new harnesses. My *daed* finished them early and asked if I'd bring them over since I was going to my *schweschder's haus* across the road from you."

"*Denki.* He's in the barn. I'm sure he will be happy to have them early."

Seth paused. "Are you sure I can't help you finish up with the chickens?"

She smiled at him warmly. "These are the last of them. I can finish quickly and then I have to gather the eggs and get to the bakery. I'm a little behind in getting my bread orders in the oven."

Seth ignored her and held out the wing of the hen she was holding in place, and he began to snip the edge of the wing.

Lillian wondered why he continued to help despite her polite protest, but she welcomed the help. It would help her get to the bakery that much sooner. And she had to admit having Seth talk to her was a lot nicer than having him ignore her.

Seth looked up at her as she shivered from a cold gust of wind. He pulled off his jacket and draped it across her shoulders before she realized what he was doing.

She looked into his kind eyes. "*Denki.* I left my jacket in the *haus.* I didn't think it would take me this long to take care of my hens. And I certainly didn't think it was going to be this cold today."

Seth looked up at the gray clouds rolling in.

"Looks like we might get our first snow of the season."

As if cued by God, Lillian watched in awe as snowflakes began to float down from the heavens.

Seth stood back and admired Lillian as she twirled in the sea of snowflakes. They melted on his warm cheeks, as he thought that this was the most time he'd ever spent with her—and he was actually talking to her without stammering. Maybe he *could* ask her to take a buggy ride with him. Maybe not yet, but hopefully soon.

CHAPTER 5

Lillian walked toward the barn with Seth's coat, but she couldn't help lifting the collar to her face. She breathed in the smell of fresh mowed hay, smoked wood and homemade peppermint soap. She could get lost in that smell if she wasn't careful—lost in the thought of a man who might never be hers.

Seth looked up at Lillian as she entered the barn, her cheeks pink from the cold air that blew in alongside her. She held out his coat to him with downcast eyes, and he wondered if her sudden shyness was due to her *daed,* who stood only a few feet away from them.

"*Denki* for letting me use your coat. I hope you weren't too cold."

"*Nee,* I was warm in the barn. Do you need a ride to the bakery? I know it's just up the road, but I'm heading out now and could drop you off on my way. It's getting pretty cold with the snow blowing."

Lillian lowered her gaze again. "*Denki,* but I enjoy the walk. It gives me energy to start my day."

Seth watched her walk away, then waved goodbye to Efram. As he stepped toward the opening of the barn, he pulled up his collar against the wind that would assail him when he made his exit. As the collar brushed his cheek, he smelled sugar and cinnamon with a hint of lavender soap— the same scents he'd enjoyed while being near Lillian when they clipped the chicken's wings. He felt a renewed sense of hope as he reflected on their time together. Although it was short, it amazed him that he could so easily converse with her. She was easy on the eyes and easy to get along with, and she smelled heavenly.

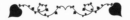

The scent of peppermint lingered in Lillian's memory as she milled about the kitchen of her bakery. while she packaged the last of the whoopie pies, she looked out at the long line of customers waiting for them, and felt a sense of relief at her decision to spend the morning baking a half dozen batches more than she usually did. It was her busy season, and if she couldn't stay on top of the demand, she would be swimming in late orders like she did her first season.

Pushing aside thoughts of Seth, Lillian served a constant stream of customers until closing time. She hadn't even had time to sit down for more than five minutes before packs of *English* customers entered her bakery looking for a taste of Amish culture. In the winter months, the majority of her customers consisted of *Englischers,* because it was easier for them to get to her than some of her regular Amish customers across Elkhart County. Though some were only a few miles away, navigating a buggy in the winter was difficult and often too dangerous, so most of the community contained their driving for necessities only, and usually kept to the back roads.

Lillian put the last of the baking utensils into the large, stainless steel sink when she heard the bells chime on the door. She chided herself for forgetting to lock the door and place the *Closed* sign in the window. She had nothing else to sell. Walking out to the lobby, her heart caught in her throat at the sight of Seth standing patiently with his hat in his hands. It wasn't his usual day to come into the bakery, but she was delighted at seeing him twice in one day.

Seth looked into her eyes and smiled. "When I saw you earlier, I was so distracted by helping you with the chickens that I forgot to settle my bill for the order you dropped off with my *daed* yesterday."

If the truth be told, he was too distracted by her nearness to think about paying her what he owed.

Lillian smiled shyly, heat rising to her cheeks.

"*Denki,* but you didn't need to make an extra trip just to pay your bill. I knew you'd pay it when you came in next week."

He stepped forward and shoved the money into her hand. His hand seemed to linger on hers, or maybe it was her imagination, but for that few seconds, her blood boiled at his heated touch. She tucked the money into her apron pocket and cast her eyes down to hide her flushed face.

"It was no trouble at all. I was at my *schweschder's haus* helping Jacob fix their fence. We should be done with it some time tomorrow. And just in time before this snow begins to stick."

Lillian looked out the large window of the bakery at the snowflakes, temporarily mesmerized by the enchantment of their swirling. Winter would be her favorite season if not for the fact that it was also wedding season in the community. And the wedding invitations were lining up nearly every week for the next five weeks. She'd hoped this would be her year, but another season was upon them, and she would not be making any announcements of her own *again.*

CHAPTER 6

Seth rode past the bakery on his way to Lizzie's house, and breathed in the smells of the breads and pastries. Lillian was probably hard at work preparing for the many customers of *Englischers,* whose cars he noticed parked in the roped-off span of grass that served as a parking lot. His mouth watered at the delectable aroma, and wished he had the nerve to stop in at the noon hour and sample some of the confections. He had a pretty big sweet tooth, but his cravings had recently turned more toward the baker than for the baked goods.

He pulled into Lizzie's yard, his stomach still growling. His niece, Abby, was at the wood pile gathering a few freshly chopped pieces for the wood stove. She dropped what was in her arms and ran to meet him.

"*Gudemariye, Onkel* Seth. Happy Birthday!"

He jumped down from the buggy and hugged her.

"*Denki,* Abby. Is your *daed* in the barn?"

"*Jah,* he's getting the posts ready for the fence work. I'll let *mamm* know you're here."

Seth gave her another quick hug. "You tell her to stay in the *haus* where it's warm. I'll be in to see her in a few minutes after I let Caleb and your *daed* know I'm here."

He watched her bound into the house, and remembered back when her pigtails would fly when she ran. Now, at fifteen, she wore her hair pinned beneath her *kapp*, and he realized his brother-in-law would have to start watching the boys around her soon. He envied Jacob for having a family—something he feared he may never have. But then his thoughts returned to Lillian. Maybe it was time he asked for that buggy ride. He was thirty years old today, and he wasn't going to waste another day that he could spend with Lillian. He wanted a family, and he prayed Lillian did too.

Lillian turned over the sign that hung from the bakery door to show that she was closed for the day. She was exhausted, but she still had at least an hour's worth of dishes to do before she could leave. Feeling overwhelmed, she considered filling the large, stainless steel sink and letting them soak overnight. But tomorrow was Sunday, and the bakery was closed, and she would be getting up early for church. It had already been a long day, and she felt like she'd inhaled at least a pound of flour over the course of the day, and probably an equal amount of powdered sugar.

She entered the kitchen with a sigh, and noticed an unclaimed order sitting on the counter. Searching through her daily tickets, she realized she'd packed one box too many of the whoopie pies she'd baked. Knowing they would not keep until Monday, she wished she'd given them away. But she still could. Seth's sister, Lizzie, lived across from the bakery, and she could take them there if she left now. Not wanting to interrupt their evening meal, she decided to leave the dishes and take the treat to Lizzie for her *kinner*. She could come back after a quick visit, and then finish the dishes before going home.

Lillian walked across the busy road holding the box of pies close to guard them against the blowing snow. Her coat was pulled tight, but the wind was determined to get in. Halfway down the long driveway, she wondered if this had been such a *gut* idea, but she had never really reached out to Lizzie despite the fact they'd been neighbors for just over five years. They'd mingled at social gatherings, but she wouldn't classify her as a close friend.

Fear crept into her mind when she noticed Seth's buggy on the side of the house, and she hoped he wouldn't see her visit as presumptuous. It was too late to turn around and go back to the bakery, Lizzie's daughter, Abby, had already seen her.

Lillian greeted her at the wood pile. "*Gut* evening, Abby. I had some left over whoopie pies and I thought your *mamm* would like them for the *kinner*."

"*Denki*. Please *kume* inside and warm up for a minute before you go back. You look like you're frozen to the bone."

Lillian's heart pounded loudly in her ears. She hoped Seth would be in the barn and not in the house. She couldn't turn down an offer of hospitality, but she wasn't sure she wanted to run into Seth either. The sun was sinking quickly, and she didn't want to walk the long lane in dim light without a lantern, but her cold toes and fingers won the internal argument.

"*Denki.* I would like to warm up for a minute, but I have a lot of dishes still waiting for me at the bakery that I must get to before I go home for the day."

Lillian followed Abby into the warm house, her increasing heart rate already warming her.

CHAPTER 7

Abby flung open the oven and sighed dramatically. "My cake is burned! I don't have time to make another one."

Lillian rushed to her side and took the smoking cake pans out of the oven. "Maybe we can fix it. It only looks like it got the edges. Get me a couple of plates and I'll turn them over to see how bad the bottoms are."

Abby handed Lillian two round plates—one for each layer. Turning each of them over carefully, the two of them surveyed the damage.

Abby settled into a chair, holding the back of her hand to her forehead. "I was so afraid I'd burned *Onkel* Seth's birthday cake."

Lillian's heart did a flip flop. "It's your *Onkel* Seth's birthday?"

Abby smiled. "*Jah.* Will you please stay for a few more minutes and help me with the frosting? *Onkel* Seth has said many times how *gut* the frosting on your cakes is. Will you teach me your secret?"

Lillian didn't want to overstay her welcome, and it was beginning to get dark. Knowing the Yoder's had a phone in their barn, she decided to phone her *daed* when she finished and ask him to pick her up.

"Do you have cream and cardamom?"

Abby scrunched up her face. "Why do we need cream and cardamom?"

Lillian smiled mischievously. "Those are my secret ingredients. But don't tell anyone or they won't buy my cakes anymore."

The two of them laughed as Abby got out the butter and powdered sugar, along with the secret ingredients. Lillian set the cakes on the window sill and cracked the window just a little to allow the layers to cool. Then they busied themselves mixing up the ingredients into a rich, whipped frosting.

Lillian heard stomping of feet near the kitchen door, and she knew Seth and Jacob were there. They entered the large kitchen, knocking the snow from their work boots, and brushing off fresh snowfall from their coats.

"*Onkel* Seth! You're not supposed to see your cake yet. Go see *mamm.* She was asking for you—something about taking a measurement."

Lillian giggled quietly, knowing that Abby had just given away Seth's gift from his sister, but she was happy he would be vacating the kitchen since her heated cheeks were sure to give away her feelings about seeing him.

Seth turned back before leaving them, flashing a quizzical look in Lillian's direction.

Abby pointed to Lillian. "She was kind enough to drop off left over whoopie pies from the bakery, and then I had a cake disaster, so she offered to help. *Onkel* Seth, will you give her a ride home when we finish? "

Lillian's blush turned to fire on her cheeks at the bold request from Abby. She held her hand up in rebuttal. "I can call my *daed* from the phone in the barn and ask him to pick me up. I'll be out of your way in just a few minutes."

Lizzie waddled into the room holding a hand over her swelling abdomen. "Please stay for the meal, Lillian. Then Seth can take you to your *haus* when we finish."

It wasn't like her family would be expecting her for the evening meal. She always stayed late at the bakery on Saturday evenings to do extra cleaning before leaving it vacant until Monday morning. How could she say no to Lizzie's hospitality? She would welcome the chance to get to know her better—if she could keep her mind off Seth for that long.

❦❦❦❦❦

After the meal, and the birthday gathering Lillian hadn't planned on attending, she helped Abby wash the dishes while Lizzie sat at the kitchen table with her knitting.

Lizzie poured herself a second cup of coffee from the pot that sat on the table. "*Denki* for helping Abby with the cake. That frosting was the best I've ever tasted."

Lillian turned around. "It's my *grossmammi's* recipe."

Lizzie's look softened into a warm smile. "I'm sure you probably have other things to do this evening. You don't have to stay and help with the dishes."

Lillian smiled back. "I don't mind. It's the least I can do since you shared your meal with me. The only thing I have waiting for me is a pile of dishes at the bakery— nothing fun. I enjoyed myself tonight. *Denki* for your hospitality."

Lizzie and Abby looked at each other knowingly.

"May I go back to the bakery with Lillian and help her with the dishes, *mamm?"*

"I was about to suggest that very thing."

Lillian put the last plate into the rinse water.

"*Denki,* but I can do them."

Lizzie put down her knitting. "Lillian, you have been a big help tonight. I will get my *bruder* to take you both to the bakery where you can wash those dishes twice as fast with an assistant, and then Seth can bring Abby back home."

"*Denki,* that's very kind."

Lillian felt flutters of nerves in her stomach at the thought of a buggy ride with Seth—even if they wouldn't be alone.

CHAPTER 8

Seth had hoped he would get the chance to ask Lillian for a buggy ride before he lost his nerve, but with his niece along, he couldn't ask her. He felt butterflies in his stomach as he steered the mare down the snow covered lane to the bakery with Lillian beside him. If not for Abby chattering constantly in the back of the buggy, he'd have felt like he was on a real date with Lillian. As he listened to the two them converse, he realized neither of them had said a word to him the entire trip. Was it possible that Lillian wasn't interested in him? Maybe he would have to wait to see if she showed an interest in him before being hasty enough to ask her to take a buggy ride. He wasn't fond of rejection, and he didn't want to risk his heart being broken if she didn't feel the same about him as he already felt about her.

Lillian found it hard to concentrate on the constant questions about baking that Abby kept shooting her way. Her mind was on the man sitting next to her in the buggy. He was quiet—a little too quiet. Shouldn't he feel at ease with his niece along with them? Or was it possible that he had no interest in her, and his earlier kindness was just because of the Amish ways? She hoped it wasn't out of community obligation that he'd helped her with the chickens. If the truth be told, she was happy that she'd been invited to share Seth's birthday celebration with him and his family. She wondered what it would be like to be part of Seth's family as be his wife. A deep blush settled on her face, and she was glad for the cold weather to disguise her pink cheeks as being from the outside temperature, rather than from her intimate thoughts of Seth.

Abby marveled at the quaint bakery that Lillian owned and ran. She loved to bake, but wasn't very *gut*. In fact, she was clumsy in the kitchen. Since her own *mamm* didn't have a *mamm* after age ten, neither of them had gotten the benefit of learning proper baking skills—something that is handed down from mother to daughter.

Abby pushed up her long sleeves as Lillian refreshed the water in the large sink. "Would you teach me how to bake the way you do? I would like to learn, but my *Aenti* Bess is too busy with the bed & breakfast, and my *mamm* never learned."

Lillian smiled, an idea sparking in her mind. "I could use some help in the morning preparing orders and helping customers. If your *mamm* could spare you for about three hours a day, you can help me and I will teach you as we work. I'd pay you a wage, of course."

Abby's eyes grew wide. "A job? I would like that. I'm sure *Mamm* would let me come to the bakery after I'm done dropping off the twins at school. I would have to leave every day in time to pick them up from school at noon."

Seth walked into the room, rolling up his sleeves.

"I'm not very *gut* at the washing, but I can help dry."

Abby and Lillian giggled.

"You really want to help, *Onkel* Seth? I thought you hated doing dishes?"

Seth nudged her. "Only because you like to have soap fights. Then my sister gets after me, while you just stand there looking innocent and let me take all the blame."

Abby laughed. "Don't listen to him, Lillian, that only happened once, and we both got yelled at."

Lillian scooped up soap bubbles from the sink and tossed them playfully at Seth and Abby. "*Halten argumentierung,* or we will never get this done!"

Abby and Seth looked at each other mischievously, and then each grabbed a handful of soap and splattered Lillian, which caused her to burst into laughter.

"That hardly seems fair, two against one!"

Seth laughed at her.

Abby then grabbed a handful and pitched it at her uncle.

Lillian did the same, and before they knew it, there was an all-out soap-suds fight going on—girls against Seth. Lillian laughed so hard, tears were coming to her eyes. The floor was covered in soapy water, and the sink was nearly empty of the fresh water Lillian had run. Their clothes were splotched with suds; Lillian's hair was soaked to her scalp.

Seth broke off the laughter. "I better get a mop. Where do you keep it?"

Lillian forced herself to be serious. "It's around the corner near the back door."

Lillian had enjoyed the playful banter, but it was time to get the mess cleaned up or she was never going to get home, and she didn't want her *daed* to worry and come looking for her—that could be cause for embarrassment in front of Seth. She remembered the words of her sister, and knew that if she was lucky enough to date Seth, she would keep it quiet the way Hannah and Jonathon had. She'd been told by a few of her friends when they were younger that dating in the community is always kept secret until the couple is ready to publish their wedding. She certainly didn't want her *daed* to find out about her new *friendship* with Seth—even if that's all the further it ever went.

CHAPTER 9

Lillian waved to Seth and Abby, who'd taken her place in the front seat of the buggy, as they turned around to leave. Her heart fluttered at the thought of seeing Seth again in the morning. He'd actually said he looked forward to seeing her at the meal after church. She hoped Hannah had enough time to finish her new dress so she could wear it to the service, but even if she didn't, she would consider wearing one of Hannah's dresses so she wouldn't appear tired in the same brown dress she usually wore. Her cheeks heated, and she knew that if her *daed* had any idea of the way she was thinking, he'd give her a scolding and probably take her straight to the Bishop for a lecture on being prideful. At the moment, she didn't care—she wanted to look nice to catch Seth's eye.

Seth's heart sunk as he waved goodbye to Lillian. Snowflakes fell on her cheeks, warming them and making her look like an angel. Part of him wanted to draw her into his arms and warm her. She was so beautiful he wondered why he hadn't seen it before. Why did she have to be so beautiful? As he moved the buggy forward, he was tempted to look back to see her one last time, but he knew better than to give in to the temptation. Thankfully, Abby had already begun with her teenage chatter.

"*Onkel* Seth, are you going to ask Miss Lillian for a buggy ride?"

Seth's heart skipped a beat. "What would make you ask me a question like that?"

Abby giggled. "Because I see the way the two of you look at each other when you think no one is looking."

"And how is that, Miss busy-body?"

Abby continued to giggle. "You look at her like you're smitten with her, and she looks at you the same way."

Seth thought about it for a minute. Was it possible that what Abby was saying was true? Did Lillian have an interest in him after all?

"You must be mistaken, Abby. You're young and may not understand grownup expressions."

"I'm not a baby, *Onkel* Seth. And let's not forget I grew up among the *Englischers* for the first ten years of my life. That makes me a little more grown up than the other girls my age in the community."

Seth furrowed his brow. "I suppose you're right. But do you really think she is interested in me?"

Abby didn't have to think about it. "I'm a girl—I know these things."

"If you're wrong, then I'd be left heartbroken and looking like a fool."

Abby cupped her arm in his. "*Onkel* Seth, no one would ever accuse you of being a fool. You're too kind for that."

Seth steered the horse to the side door of his sister's house. "Thanks for the insight, but you know I have too much responsibility to my *daed* to worry about taking Lillian for a buggy ride. Be sure and tell your *daed* I'll be by first thing in the morning to help him set up the benches for the service."

She kissed him on the cheek before jumping down from the buggy. "I will. Happy birthday, *Onkel* Seth. I hope you'll change your mind and talk to Lillian after services tomorrow at the meal."

Seth scrunched up his face, feeling defeated at the thought of trying to work up enough nerve to ask her to take a buggy ride with him. He was better in group situations—especially when it came to conversing with females. He'd never had the time to date, and he wasn't sure he could do it now.

Besides, his loyalties were with his *daed,* and taking care of him was second nature to him. He was getting on in years, and there was no way his *daed* could shoulder the responsibilities of the farm alone. Seth had all but taken over the harness-making business since his *daed* was only able to make one piece per week lately. His arthritis prevented him from cutting the leather, and even sewing had become more difficult. His *daed* was his responsibility, and he knew he had no business wishing for a life with Lillian when he couldn't give her the attention she deserved. Maybe it was best if he didn't see her any more than was necessary. He already liked her too much, and didn't want to give her the wrong impression—that could only lead to heartbreak for both of them. He would have to put a stop to any further misguiding on his part where she was concerned. It saddened him that there could never be anything between them. He wished things could be different, but he just didn't see how.

CHAPTER 10

Lillian's stomach was in knots as her family rode to the church services. She was grateful for the new snow that had blown into Elkhart County overnight, knowing she could keep her coat on during services. She regretted letting Hannah talk her into the blue dress, and hoped Seth wouldn't find it presumptuous to wear the color during wedding season. She didn't want Seth to think she was hinting around at an invitation as a suitor. And she certainly didn't want the other women in the district to view her as desperate to land a husband—even if she did feel that way all of a sudden.

Hannah nudged her and leaned in to whisper so their parents wouldn't overhear their conversation.

"Why are you scowling? You should feel happy in your new dress. Seth will be sure to notice you now."

Lillian's scowl deepened. "That's exactly what I'm afraid of. I shouldn't have worn this color during wedding season. I appreciate you making the dress for me, but I don't want Seth thinking I'm baiting him."

"You aren't baiting him—I am!"

Lillian's face grew pale. "What?"

"Oh dear *schweschder,* stop worrying. I made the dress for your own *gut.*"

Lillian suddenly felt sick. "Why did you do that? You could have made any other color than blue. I can't go into the service like this. The women will talk about me behind my back. You know how some of them like to gossip."

Hannah smiled. "Of course they're going to talk. And we want them to."

Lillian's eyes widened at her sister's madness. "Why on earth would I want the women in the community to talk about me behind my back?"

Hannah winked at her. "Because it will stir things up a bit and it will surely get back to Seth through his *schweschder.*"

Lillian was shaking. "Why would I want gossip about me wearing this dress to get back to Seth? Are you trying to cause me grief?"

Hannah put her arm around Lillian. "Even if he notices you on his own, he's a man and may not put it together. But with the help of a little bit of talk circulating, he will hear that you have hinted at wanting a suitor."

Lillian pulled away from Hannah. "I'm not going to let you make me into the subject of gossip. I will leave my coat on the entire day if I have to, but no one will see what I'm wearing. If I'd known this was your plan, I wouldn't have agreed to let you make this dress for me. I won't let you embarrass me."

"I'm sorry. I wasn't trying to embarrass you. I was just trying to give Seth a shove in the right direction."

Lillian pursed her lips. "Who says I want Seth to notice me?"

"The look on your pale face does. Just admit that you like him."

Lillian crossed her arms. "I won't do any such thing, or you might just go so far as to tell him. Then if he isn't interested in me, I will look like a fool."

Hannah's look softened. "He won't think you're a fool. He'll be flattered by your interest in him."

"I'm not going to push him into noticing me. It isn't proper."

Hannah's eyes narrowed. "What isn't proper my dear *schweschder,* is becoming a spinster when there is a perfectly *gut* man available. It's not your fault he's so shy, and you shouldn't have to pay for his shyness."

Lillian thought about what Hannah was saying. In a lot of ways she was right. But their *daed* would say they were wrong, and would probably scold them severely for plotting such trickery against a man.

Lillian was grateful the deep snow had slowed their travel, and they were a few minutes late to the service that had begun without them. She kept her head down as she slipped onto the end of the bench beside Hannah. Seth was more than likely near the front of the room since the service was at his sister's house, and he was usually one of the first to volunteer to help set up the benches.

No sooner had she felt at ease with the thought of Seth being far enough away from her that he wouldn't notice her attire, than he walked in, quietly stomping the snow from his boots. She couldn't help but look his way as he sat on the bench directly across from her. They were so close they could have reached out and touched hands. Thankfully, Seth pushed his nose in his Bible and didn't look her way.

Seth regretted sitting across from Lillian the moment he sat down. He could have gone back outside and continued to tend the horses, but he was cold and didn't want to disturb anyone by getting up and leaving after he'd just sat down. Instead, he buried his face in his Bible, trying desperately not to look in Lillian's direction. Unfortunately, he just couldn't help but slight his eyes toward the bottom hem of a blue dress that hung just below the hem of her long black coat.

Why was she wearing a blue dress? She always wore a brown dress—not that he'd been keeping track. With wedding season upon them, it was unusual to see her in the very color for marrying. Had she become betrothed and he wasn't aware of it? The very thought of it made his stomach queasy—not that he had any right to lay claim on her. But he knew there weren't any single men in the community her age, which meant she would have had to choose from younger men or the few widowers who were nearly old enough to be her grandfathers.

Seth looked up, scanning the room for any of the single young men to see if he could catch any of them making eyes at her during the service, as was often done. None looked her way, even after several minutes. A sinking thought suddenly occurred to him. Had he somehow given her the wrong impression over the past few days, and she wore that dress as a hint to him that she needed a husband? If that was the case, he knew he had to avoid her more than ever.

Putting his concentration on the church service, Seth closed his eyes hoping to put Lillian out of his thoughts. Was it possible to ignore her, when he was so aware of her presence, it warmed him from head to toe? He could smell the lavender soap she used—the same scent that tickled his senses when he'd helped her get the chickens out of the tree. He'd enjoyed the calming scent again last night as he drove her home from the bakery. It drove him mad with the desire to hold her in his arms.

Unable to stand it any longer, Seth opened his eyes and looked over at Lillian. Their eyes met, and her smile warmed his heart. He smiled back at her. He couldn't help it. Her smile was so inviting, and her lips so tempting, he found his gaze wandering to them like a moth to a flame. He wanted to kiss her, to hold her, and to tell her just how he felt about her. But he couldn't. It wouldn't be fair to her. He would only disappoint her when he wasn't able to follow through and have a normal relationship with her. His life was too full of responsibility, and there was no room for Lillian.

Seth looked away and hung his head in defeat. If he couldn't control his desire for Lillian it would destroy him. He certainly couldn't smile at her again, or she might get the wrong idea, and he wouldn't risk hurting her.

CHAPTER 11

Lillian thought her heart would pound its way out of her ribcage when Seth smiled at her. But when he looked away just as quickly, and ignored her for the remainder of the service, she had to wonder what had prompted the shift in his behavior. He'd been very kind to her recently, and now he almost seemed to be avoiding her. With the meal underway, she'd been so busy serving that she hadn't noticed where Seth had gone.

Lizzie approached her. "Aren't you too warm with your coat on, Lillian?"

If the truth be told, she was starting to sweat, but she couldn't take the coat off. "I'm fine. I just haven't gotten used to the cold yet this season."

Lizzie moved in closer to whisper in her ear. "I have another dress you can borrow. You can go upstairs and no one will notice."

Lillian could feel the blood draining from her face. If Lizzie had seen the dress, then Seth probably had seen it too. "Hannah made the dress, and I didn't want to insult her by not wearing it, but I regretted putting it on as soon as we were on our way here this morning."

Lizzie smiled warmly, making Lillian feel more at ease.

"*Denki.* I would like to change into *any* other color than this blue. It's embarrassing."

Lizzie looped her arm in Lillian's. "There isn't any reason to be embarrassed. But I'll admit, I was a little shocked to see you wear that color—because you're single, I mean."

Lillian sighed. It was all she could do to keep the tears that stung her eyes from falling. "You're right about that. I see married women wearing this color all the time. I do hope no one saw the dress."

Lizzie offered a sympathetic smile. "I don't mean to alarm you, but I think my *bruder* saw it. The look on his face was like that of a ghost."

Lillian could no longer hold the tears at bay. They rushed down her cheeks like a dripping rain gutter. "He's the last person I wanted to see me in this dress."

No sooner had the words left her lips, than regret began to fill her nervous stomach. "I didn't mean that the way it sounded."

Lizzie pulled her close and patted her back for a moment. "Of course you did. I saw the way the two of you looked at each other through the meal last night. You like him, and he likes you too. But with my *bruder,* he will be a tough one to break. He's like a stubborn horse that bucks and won't let anyone saddle him. He feels a deep sense of responsibility to my *daed.* I did too at first, but it made me bitter toward him. That's why I left when I was younger— and ended up getting myself into some trouble with the *Englisch.* Seth and I had to take care of my *daed* once my *mamm* died. David and Daniel were already married and each had *kinner* of their own by that time, so the responsibility was left to me and Seth. I was a coward and left because I didn't want to keep *haus* for my *daed.* When I found out my *daed* sabotaged my relationship with Jacob when we were younger, it was hard not to see him as anything but a harsh and selfish man. He's been lost without my *mamm,* and he's getting older. He hasn't been able to care for the farm on his own for a lot of years. Seth was the responsible one and stayed to care for him—still is. Because of this, he's never allowed himself to get too close to any of the women in the community because of his loyalty, but maybe you can change that. I've seen the way he looks at you. Maybe if he could find a woman who would stand by him and help care for my *daed,* then he would break down the barrier he's put up and let someone in his heart— someone like you."

Lillian sniffled. "I do like him, but I don't think he feels the same. He's never really talked to me until recently. And today he's ignored me—except for…"

Lizzie searched Lillian's far-off expression.

"Except for what?"

Lillian smiled at the memory of Seth's warm smile during church services. "He smiled at me today, and it felt like a genuine smile of interest. But then his expression changed and he didn't look my way again the entire morning. As soon as the service was over, he jumped from his seat and practically ran outside. I haven't seen him since."

Lizzie giggled. "He sent Abby after a plate of food for him. She took it out to the barn. She mumbled something about him being too busy to get it himself. I didn't think anything of it at the time, but it makes sense now. Let's get you into this dress and meet me downstairs when you're changed. We'll take desert out to the barn and he can see that you aren't wearing the blue dress anymore. Maybe that will ease his mind a little."

"*Denki* for your help. I'll be sure to return the dress later this week after I wash it."

Lizzie waved a hand toward her. "You will do no such thing. I made this dress just before I discovered I was pregnant with the twins. I've never been able to fit into it, so it's just been sitting here gathering dust. You keep it. It was meant to be worn, and I know you will get a lot of use from it."

Lillian took the purple dress from Lizzie, feeling grateful for her new friend's generosity.

CHAPTER 12

Seth felt like a coward for hiding out in the barn, but the sight of Lillian in the blue dress was giving him a nervous stomach. Just why, he couldn't figure out, but he suspected it had something to do with the feelings he had toward her. There had been a girl or two who had caught his eye when he was much younger, but none that could make his insides heat up the way they did when he set his eyes on Lillian. She had a generous spirit that enhanced her beauty, making her the most beautiful woman he'd ever seen. And for that reason alone, he couldn't continue to look upon her beauty and wish for something that could never be. His duty was to his *daed,* and until the man took his last breath, he would honor him and care for him the way he'd learned was his responsibility from the teachings at the Sunday services.

Still, he couldn't help but wish things could be different for him. But wishing wouldn't bring his *mamm* back, or make his *daed* a younger, stronger man. It was best for everyone if he stayed out in the barn until everyone had left for the day. After, he could help Jacob load up the benches and put their furniture back in the house. With no one but the horses to keep him company, he felt lonely. Even the *menner* could be heard in the main part of the barn having happy conversation. He could join them instead of hiding out in the loft, but he wasn't up for any conversation at the moment. He was more comfortable sulking and feeling sorry for himself for now.

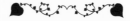

Lillian was relieved that no one except Hannah noticed she had changed her dress. Grabbing her arm and pulling her aside, Hannah furrowed her brow, showing impatience with her.

"Why did you change? I made that dress so you could catch Seth's eye, and now you've ruined everything by changing before he could see how nice you look in it."

Lillian bit her tongue, holding back the harsh words she wanted to say. Instead she pasted a smile on her face and spoke as gently as she could to her sister.

"He saw me, and that's why no one knows where he is. According to Lizzie, he had Abby bring him a plate of food out in the barn so he wouldn't have to come in the *haus.*"

Hannah raised an eyebrow. "Is that who gave you the dress? Getting chummy with his *schweschder* will help you catch him."

Lillian yanked her arm away from Hannah. "I'm not getting chummy with her to catch Seth. And who says I want to "catch" him anyway? If he doesn't like me of his own accord, then I don't want him."

Hannah laughed. "You do too, or you wouldn't have changed. You're trying to impress him by wearing this purple dress—another color you never wear."

Lillian was fuming, but trying very hard not to yell at her younger sister. "Why do you always think you're right about everything?"

Hannah pressed her hands on her hips. "Why do you always play the martyr? You don't have to fill the shoes of our dead *bruder.*"

Lillian's face turned ashen. "How do you know about the *boppli?*"

"I found his things in the attic, and I've heard *mamm* crying over him every year on his birthday."

Lillian sat in a chair, feeling like she'd had the wind knocked out of her. "I always thought I carried that burden all by myself of not being the son *daed* wanted. I've been trying so hard to make up for it by accepting the land he gave me and working the bakery. I know it wasn't the business he would've made if I was a *buwe—boy*, but he pushed it on me when I didn't want it. I love the bakery, I really do. But sometimes I wish he wouldn't have given it to me the way he did."

Hannah smoothed back Lillian's hair that had come unpinned from her *kapp*. "Why do you think I act like a tomboy all the time and help *daed* in the barn? It's the only way I can get any real attention from him."

Lillian laughed. "I thought you did it just to make me mad."

Hannah smiled and leaned her head on Lillian's shoulder. "I do it for that reason too."

They both laughed.

Hannah looked serious suddenly. "I guess that's why I've been pushing you to get married. Because I was jealous of the attention you get from *daed*. I didn't want that to continue once I wasn't living there anymore if I should get married before you did. I'm sorry for being so pushy about Seth. Give him time. He does like you—I can see it in his eyes. But he's a man you will have to have patience with. He has his own problems with his own *daed.*"

Lillian hugged her sister. "That's what Lizzie was explaining to me when she gave me the dress. I like her. I don't know why we were never friends before this."

Hannah nudged Lillian. "Because you're jealous of every married woman in the community."

Lillian frowned. "I suppose you're right. I probably shouldn't be like that since they're *all* married now, and I've run out of friends."

Hannah nudged her again. "You'll always have me, dear *schweschder.*"

Lillian smiled, feeling lighter after confessing her deepest burdens to her sister. It helped that Hannah understood since she was feeling some of the same pressures and insecurities concerning their *daed's* love. If only she could figure out how to help Seth overcome his own burdens.

CHAPTER 13

Lillian shook as she followed Lizzie out to the barn with a tray full of desert for the *menner*. She wasn't sure if she was shivering from the cold, or shaking for fear of encountering Seth, but she suspected it was a little of both. Now that she felt vulnerable in Lizzie's purple dress, she wished she'd taken the time to put her coat back on. Now Seth would see that she'd changed her dress, and she feared he would think she was fickle. But it was too late to worry about it, so she kept her gaze lowered, hoping she wouldn't have to make eye-contact with him.

As she handed out the last of the pie to the men, Lillian breathed a sigh of relief that Seth didn't seem to be in the barn any longer. Hoping to slip out unnoticed, she walked under the loft, where straw floated down into her hair. Shielding her eyes, she noticed a pair of boots dangling from the loft above. She recognized those boots—they were the same pair of boots she'd spent the entire service staring at. They belonged to Seth.

Moving out from directly under the shower of falling straw, she looked up at Seth, who appeared to be hiding out from the rest of the men. Lizzie approached her and took her empty tray. She handed her the last slice of pie from her own tray. "Will you please take this up to my *bruder?* I'm afraid I can't climb the ladder to the loft in my condition."

Lillian's first thought was that Seth could come down from the loft to get his own pie if he wanted any, but she nodded a reluctant agreement to take the pie to him. After Lizzie exited the barn, Lillian climbed the ladder with one arm, the other cradling the pie. When she was high enough that Seth noticed her, he reached up and took the pie and grabbed her free hand to help pull her onto the loft.

"Lizzie must have sent you up here, *jah?"*

"Nee, I offered." Lillian didn't want him thinking she'd been forced to take him the pie. She hoped the gesture would soften him a bit toward her.

Seth took a healthy bite of the pie and swallowed it almost whole. "This must be one of your pies. I can tell the difference."

Lillian laughed at him. "How can you tell? You didn't even take the time to chew before you swallowed it."

Seth's face turned pink. "Normally I savor your pie, but I wasn't going to take a chance at letting it linger in my mouth long if it wasn't yours. Especially if it was one that Abby made. Don't tell her I said this, but I'm happy you're going to take the time to teach her how to bake, because her cooking scares me. Now that Lizzie is far into her confinement, Abby has been taking over the cooking, and taking my Saturday night meals here with my *familye* has been leaving me feeling hungry when I go home since I can't stomach my niece's cooking."

Lillian laughed. "I can probably teach her a few basic meals too—so you won't have to go home hungry anymore."

Seth nodded sheepishly. "*Denki.* I'm sure her *daed* would be happy about that too. She does pretty well when Lizzie's right there to guide her, but she can't always sit with her since she needs to spend a lot of her time resting now."

"Maybe I can write down some simple recipes for her to follow, and when she masters those, we can work on some of the more complicated things. Didn't Lizzie take the time to teach her when she was young?"

"When they were living among the *Englisch,* she didn't have time to teach her since she was a working, single mother. And since they've been back here, Abby only wanted to bake, but she just hasn't gotten the feel for it yet. She still has a few years before she will have to do the cooking for a *familye* of her own."

"I guess I was lucky that my *mamm* was able to teach me at a young age. I think it's easier to grasp when you're younger, than to try to learn once you get older."

Lillian watched him savor the last bite of her shoofly pie, and leaned in to take the plate from him. His hand brushed against hers as the plate switched hands, and his face was close to hers. They both paused, Lillian feeling a twinge of electrical energy pass between them. "I suppose I should get back in the *haus* to help with the dishes before I go home."

He smiled warmly. "*Denki* for the *gut* pie."

She smiled back, but started down the ladder before she gave in to the temptation to kiss him.

CHAPTER 14

"Did you spill something on your new dress?"

"*Nee,* I didn't spill anything on it *mamm.* I just couldn't wear that blue this time of year. It's fine for the younger girls like Abby, or even the women who are already married. But after some thought, I realized it made me look desperate."

Her *mamm* pushed back the stray tendrils that had fallen from her *kapp.* "Such prideful thoughts from the youth these days. You are way past your days of *rumspringa.*"

Lillian cast her eyes downward. "I know *mamm.* I'm sorry, but I just couldn't let Seth see me in that dress. I don't want him thinking I want to trap him into marriage."

Her *mamm* pulled her close. "So that's what this is about? Why didn't you tell me you were interested in Seth Miller?"

Lillian cuddled in close to her *mamm.* "Because that is not the sort of thing you tell your *mamm.*"

"I'm glad you told me. If it be *Gotte's wille,* then Seth will like you no matter what color dress you wear."

Lillian sighed and buried her head in her *mamm's* shoulder. "I hope you're right."

Lillian whispered a silent prayer, asking God to bless her with a husband. Since she'd never thought it was possible, she'd never asked for such a thing. Her prayers were always unselfish, but this time, she would make an exception and pray for something her own heart desired.

A fresh blanket of snow covered the narrow path Lillian walked to get to the bakery. She could have taken the long drive that her *daed* had probably had a chance to sprinkle with salt to melt the snow, but she knew it would take her twice as long, rather than crunching through the snow on the path. Her boots kept her feet from touching the snow, but the cold cut right through her black bonnet no matter how low she kept her head. The large oak trees provided a great deal of shelter from the wind that swirled the snow into a fine dust against the sunlight peeking up over the horizon. The weight of the snow on the branches created a canopy overhead, and provided an insulated calm from noises of the busy street only a few yards from her.

When she was younger, she loved to play in the snow no matter how cold it was. But now it seemed to lose some of its appeal. Lost in thought, she didn't see the snowball before it plunged into her arm. Lillian whipped her head around in the direction the assault had come from just in time to see Hannah duck behind one of the many trees that lined the path. Scooping up a handful of the damp snow, she tossed it toward the tree and hit it dead-center. The impact sprayed snow on Hannah's coat, causing Lillian to let out a chuckle.

The look on Hannah's face let Lillian know she was in for a snowball war. She scrambled to form as many snowballs as she could, making sure she stayed behind the shelter of the trees. When she was satisfied she had enough ammunition to keep Hannah at bay for a few minutes, she poked her head from around the tree intending to fire the first snowball, when she was hit hard in the shoulder. The snowball splattered over her face and hair, chilling her to the bone, but she was determined not to let her little sister win this battle.

When she picked up the last of her snowballs, she was hit from two different directions. She searched the wooded area for the third person, but didn't see anyone. Tossing her last snowball in the direction of the mystery player, she heard a squeal. Abby stuck her arms out from around both sides of the tree in surrender.

"Don't fire, I'm unarmed."

Lillian scooped up enough snow to form a few more snowballs, tossing one in Abby's general direction, not intending to hit her with it. "I don't believe you. You hit me pretty hard, so now it's your turn to suffer the consequences."

Abby squealed again. "I promise I won't fire anymore, just don't get me."

Just as Lillian was about to throw the snowball at Abby, despite her plea, she was hit from behind between her shoulder blades. Turning around quickly to see her assailant, Seth stood behind her wearing a big smile, a snowball in each hand. Lillian quickly threw both snowballs in her hands, but she wasn't fast enough. She was hit in both shoulders by Seth's perfect aim.

She quickly threw her hands up in surrender. "I surrender. I give up."

Seth tossed the snowball lightly, letting it hit the tree next to her. "You could have hit me with that, and I surrendered."

Seth laughed. "I was trying to hit the tree—not you."

"I don't believe you." Lillian bent down to scoop up more of the snow.

Seth did the same, and the two began to fire continuous snowballs at each other until Lillian accidently hit Seth on the top of his head and knocked off his hat. He threw himself to the ground pretending he was badly hurt, but he was laughing so hard Lillian didn't take him seriously. By that time, Abby and Hannah had gathered around him and watched as he flapped his arms and legs in an arc to form the perfect snow-angel.

Lillian stepped forward, hands on her hips. "Do you surrender?"

Seth held up his hands. "Okay, I surrender. No more. I'm soaked to the skin and I have to go help Jacob."

Lillian picked up his hat and handed it to him.

"Why are you here?"

"I gave Abby a ride up the lane to the bakery so she wouldn't have to walk in the deep snow, but you weren't there yet. So we started walking up the trail, and that's when we saw the two of you plotting against each other with the snowballs, so we decided to join in. But I surrender, I promise."

Lillian laughed and they all joined in. She brushed the snow off her coat, and they walked the rest of the way to the bakery. Lillian thanked Seth for bringing Abby, and she watched him steer the horse across the street where he disappeared beyond the snow-covered trees that lined the lane to Lizzie's house.

CHAPTER 15

Lillian had so many things to prepare for the day ahead, and she was grateful for having two helpers this morning. It was unusual for Hannah to help her, but she figured with Abby there to help, her sister offered in order that she wouldn't appear selfish. No matter what the reason, her morning help allowed her the luxury to daydream just a bit. She'd enjoyed seeing the playful side of Seth during their snowball fight, and she even saw a hint of a competitive opponent. Being very competitive herself, it was a quality she readily admired in him.

For whatever reason, he seemed to suddenly be everywhere she was. She suspected that her new connection to Abby and Lizzie was going to bring them together even more. But what if she didn't want to be thrown in with him? What if she only welcomed the idea because it would seem he was the last man available for her? Did she really want him just because there was no one else for her? Did he want her for the same reason? She had grown to like him over the past year, but was it only infatuation, or something deeper? Had God brought them together, or was it something simpler?

While the first batch of whoopie pies baked, Lillian showed Abby how to make the filling. Hannah unfolded and assembled the pink, cardboard boxes and stacked them in the corner so they could be filled once things were underway. Next she brewed a fresh pot of coffee and set out the creamer, sugar, and stirring straws for customers.

Lillian had an order for a four-tier cake for an *Englisch* wedding. She'd taken a trip to town and purchased a magazine that boasted many wedding cake ideas. She'd practiced for many weeks, and now her self-taught talents would pay off with her first order. If she did a *gut* job, she would soon get more orders. But it was unusual for the *Englisch* to have weddings this time of the year. She planned on making one for her sister, and her cousin, Annie, when they got married, so she hoped it would be something she could do as a contribution to the weddings in the community.

Still, she wished it was she that was getting married this season, the same she had for the past few years. But it would seem that it just wasn't her time yet. Even if she and Seth decided to pursue a relationship, there wouldn't be any proposal from him until next season. As hard as she tried, she couldn't keep her mind on the weddings of her family and neighbors, while pushing her own desires for the same down where they wouldn't make her show her jealousy.

Abby spread the filling over the whoopie pie halves like Lillian instructed, carefully measuring each portion. "Are you going to the skating party on Saturday at Goose Pond?"

Lillian looked at her quizzically. "That skating party is for the youth, not for me. I'm too old."

Abby smiled. "You can be a chaperone. *Onkel* Seth is chaperoning."

Lillian's heart fluttered at the thought of seeing Seth at a social function. "I don't know if I should."

Hannah stepped into the back of the kitchen. "I think you should go, Lillian. You enjoy skating. It's one of your favorite things to do in winter. You're a much better skater than I am."

Lillian shook her head. "I didn't skate even once last season. I've probably forgotten how."

Hannah laughed at her. "That's *narrish—foolish.* Skating is like riding a bike; you never forget how."

Lillian raised an eyebrow. "Skating on ice requires a lot more skill than riding a bike."

Hannah nudged her ribs "Then you're afraid of making a fool of yourself in front of Seth."

"*Nee.* "I'm afraid I'll be clumsy and fall. I'm getting older and could break my leg."

Abby shook her head and giggled. "You talk like you're as old as my *grossdaddi.*"

Lillian sighed. "Okay, I'll go. But going as a chaperone makes me feel old."

"I could ask *Onkel* Seth if he'll escort you."

Lillian looked at the innocent look on Abby's face.

"*Nee.* That would embarrass me even more."

Abby smiled. "If you go with my *Onkel* Seth it will be more like a date and less like chaperoning."

Lillian's face turned deep red. "He hasn't invited me!"

Abby snickered. "I'll tell him to invite you."

Lillian threw her hands up. "*Nee!* I mean—I appreciate your willingness to help, Abby, but sometimes grownups have to do things on their own."

"Grownups make things more difficult than they ought to," Abby grumbled.

Lillian tried to calm her nerves. "That may be true, but if your *Onkel* Seth is going to escort me anywhere, I'd like it to be his idea, and not because he was prompted to do so."

Abby's expression turned to sulking. "Yes ma'am."

Lillian looked at the clock on the wall. "It's ten o'clock, time to open the bakery. Let's get the last of these whoopie pies in the boxes, and then we'll start on the cookies. I usually bake those until just after the lunch hour. That usually holds me over for the day. Tomorrow we will bake snitz pies and shoofly pies in the morning. Wednesday and Friday are cake days."

Abby shook her head as she worked to fill the pink boxes with whoopie pies. "That seems like a schedule I can remember easily."

Lillian smiled as she turned over the sign on the door indicating they were open. She already had three customers pulling into the parking area.

CHAPTER 16

Hiram looked out the kitchen window at the snow as he dipped his hand in the pink cake box to retrieve a pastry. He smiled at the new flurries, knowing he would be able to send Seth over to help Lizzie with getting the *kinner* to school and Abby to the bakery. His new quest to keep throwing Seth together with Lillian was working—and would continue so long as it kept snowing as much as it had been the past week. Hiram only had a few outstanding orders for leather harnesses, so Seth was needed to help his sister and brother-in-law. At least that's what Hiram had led him to believe.

Jacob spent his free time repairing buggies for the folks in the community, and he had more work than he could handle alone, so Seth was sent by to help pick up the slack. Taking the *kinner* to school and Abby to the bakery was an added bonus in Hiram's plan. With Abby's help, he'd managed to convince Seth to chaperone the skating party. Now all he had to do was drop a few hints that he should escort Lillian.

Seth hurried in through the kitchen door, stomping the snow from his work boots. "I can't believe how much snow is coming down."

Hiram tried to contain a smile. "I guess you'll have to go get Abby and the *kinner* again today before you help Jacob with the buggy repair."

He hung up his wet coat on a peg near the wood stove to dry. "Are you sure you don't need any help today?"

"*Nee.* I have one order to fill today. I think my hands will hold out that long. Besides, your *schweschder's familye* needs your help more than I do right now."

He looked at the expression on his *daed's* face, who almost seemed to be smiling—something he rarely did. "Are you up to something, *Daed?*"

Hiram dipped the plain donut in his coffee. "I was thinking you should take Lillian Stoltzfus to the skating party on Saturday. Since you'll both be chaperones, I think it would be proper if you would escort her."

Seth nearly choked on the bite of coffee cake he'd put in his mouth. "You're not suggesting I take her on a date, are you?"

Hiram bit his lip so he wouldn't smile. "*Nee.* I think you should be neighborly and escort her so she doesn't have to attend alone, that's all."

Seth cradled a warm mug of coffee between his hands, studying his *daed's* mischievous expression. "I'll ask her if she needs an escort when I pick up Abby in a few hours."

Hiram nodded and smiled at his son. He felt he owed his son so much more than what he was trying to do now, and hoped it would somehow make up for years of neglecting his son's needs to be sure his own needs were met first.

Seth wondered what his *daed* was up to. The man had rarely shown an interest in his needs. But suddenly he was showing signs of charity and kindness. Was he ill? Or worse, could the old man be dying? He'd noticed his *daed* taking naps in the afternoon for several months, and he was getting thin. Was it possible that he knew he wasn't going to be around much longer, and wished Seth to be married?

"Have you been to see Doctor Davis lately?"

"*Nee.* You know I don't see any reason to see the doc unless I'm ailing, which I'm not. I'm fit as a mule."

"And stubborn like one. Maybe you should pay him a visit. Or I could see if he'd come by and give you a once-over just to make sure. You seem a little thin, and the dark circles under your eyes are getting bigger."

"We don't need to be wasting the doc's time for the likes of me. What I have, there's no cure for. It's just old age catching up with me."

"I don't like hearing you talk like that, *Daed.* I don't know what I'd do if anything happened to you if I could have prevented it by insisting you see the doc."

Hiram hung his head in shame. "If it weren't for me, you would probably have a *fraa* and *kinner.*"

"Is that what this is about? You think I need to escort Lillian because you think I'm going to marry her?"

"I'm ashamed to admit that I've stood in the way of the happiness of my own *kinner* for my own selfishness. That's why your *schweschder* ran away, and you are still single. If I hadn't forced my obligations on you, you'd probably be married with *kinner* of your own. I'm sorry that I've relied on you so much. I'm sorry that I never allowed you any free time to do what you wanted to do with your life."

Seth placed his hand over his *daed's.* "I've stayed here to help you of my own free will. I don't hold any of that against you. I know you had a hard time when you lost *mamm.*"

"You and Lizzie lost her too, and I didn't make things easy for you. Please forgive me."

Seth swallowed the lump that formed in his throat.

"I forgive you *daed,* but there's nothing to forgive. You have always loved us and have been a *gut* provider."

"But I wasn't always fair in the way I treated either of you, and for that, I'm sorry. I need to make amends with Lizzie too—for the way I had your *bruder,* David, break them up."

Seth patted his *daed* on the shoulder. "We both know you love us, and that's all that matters. I've always been curious why you broke them up. You don't have to tell me, but it might make you feel better to get it off your conscience."

Hiram poured himself another cup of coffee and then sat back down with a loud sigh. "My biggest fault is that I acted selfishly. When your *mamm* died, I was so afraid of losing you too, that I held on too tightly. When Lizzie started getting serious with Jacob, I knew it would only be a matter of time before he married her, and then he would take her away from me. When she ran off, you were the only one I had left, and I guess I leaned on you too much."

Seth pushed at the uneaten coffee cake on his plate with his fork. "Lizzie has been back with us for over five years, and yet I've continued to stay here with you. You didn't force me to. I guess I've been a little afraid to venture out on my own. I've thought about dating over the years, but I'm afraid of rejection. I like Lillian, but what if she doesn't like me?"

Hiram's look softened. "Why wouldn't she like you? You're a kind man with faith stronger than any man I've seen."

Seth shook his head. "That isn't always enough."

"Why wouldn't it be enough? Faith is the most important thing in any marriage. Without *Gott,* a man's life is nothing."

Seth cast his eyes downward. "I have no way to support her. You need the money from your harness business, and I don't have any money to buy any land."

Hiram chuckled. "Don't you know that Efram will let you work off the land adjacent to his farm if you marry his *dochder?* Miss Lillian has her bakery on that very property."

Seth bit into his bottom lip, feeling frustration well up in him. "I will not let Lillian support me. I have to be able to be a *gut* provider for her and our *kinner.*"

Hiram placed a hand on his son's arm. "You have handcrafted every piece of furniture in this *haus,* and even made pieces for your *bruder* and *schweschder.* I think you could sell your furniture at the flea market in Shipshewana."

Seth couldn't believe what he was hearing. It had been his heart's desire to make the furniture as more than a hobby. He loved working on his own creations, and if he did this, it could afford him the opportunity to have a life with Lillian that he so desired. Seth thought about it for a few minutes while he finished his coffee cake. If he wanted to win Lillian's hand, he had to get started on his new business.

"*Denki, Daed.* I'll get started on it right away."

CHAPTER 17

"*Ach,* I'm so excited for you. Do *Mamm* and *Daed* know you plan on publishing your wedding at the next Sunday service?"

Lillian admired the dreamy look in Hannah's eyes as she spoke of her plans. "It's supposed to be a surprise, so don't tell either of them. Although I think they suspect since I planted a few extra rows of celery in the kitchen garden over the summer. *Mamm* makes mention of the celery smell in the root cellar every time she goes in there. I laugh it off and say I spilled the seeds over the ground when I was planting."

They both giggled mischievously.

"And that satisfies her question? She must suspect something."

"I'm sure she does, but she wouldn't spoil it for me."

Lillian hugged Hannah, but she couldn't help but feel a little twinge of jealousy mixed with happiness. Just because Seth had begun to talk to her didn't mean he was interested in keeping her from becoming a spinster. She wished he'd come into the bakery this morning when he picked up Abby, but he seemed to be in a hurry. Maybe Abby would tell her why in the morning, but for now, she helped Hannah make the beds with clean linens so they could go to sleep. Lillian was tired from a long day at the bakery, but she wondered if she would be able to keep her mind off Seth long enough to get any rest.

Seth waited at the lumber yard for his order, while he thought about the items he would start making. He knew from visiting the flea market that no one else was selling pie cupboards or rocking chairs, and those were his specialties. He mentally calculated how long it would take him to earn the kind of money he needed in order to purchase the land from Ezra so he could marry Lillian. He quickly became discouraged when he realized it would take him until he was forty years old to make a serious dent against the worth of the land.

Seth was so deep in thought that he didn't see his brother, David, approach him. David patted him on the back, causing Seth to jump nearly a foot to the left.

"Is something wrong little *bruder?*"

Seth cleared his throat. "I guess you're going to find out anyway, so I might as well tell you. I'm making furniture to earn money so I can start to date Lillian Stoltzfus."

David chuckled. "It's about time you decide to date her. She's perfect for you."

Seth kicked at the snow. "I'm not sure it's going to make a difference. I can't rely on winter sales since I'll have to rent space indoors to sell my furniture, and that will seriously cut into my profits."

David clapped a hand on Seth's shoulder. "You're thinking on too small of a scale. Have you tried the furniture consignment stores and the Country Store downtown? They sell homemade items. We could also put an advertisement in the newspaper directing people to the flea market so you'll raise more interest. With Christmas coming soon, you might get a lot more sales if you try those things."

Seth's heart lightened at the thought of having more orders than he could fill. "*Denki* for the *gut* ideas. Is there any chance I could get you to help me with the first set of furniture. I'm sure I could get Jacob to help too since we just finished his last buggy repair, as long as he doesn't have any more repairs come in."

"Of course you can count on me for help. I have to get some nails, but I'll see you at first light tomorrow."

"*Denki.*"

David started to walk away, but Seth stopped him.

"Can I ask you a question about *Daed?*"

David put up a hand to stop him. "Yes, I've noticed he's not looking well. He seems tired—and—old."

"I was going to say the same thing. When I mentioned to him that he should see the doc, he refused. It's making me a little nervous.*"

David creased his brow. "He and Doc have been friends for a lot of years. I'll stop by his farm on the way home and see if he'll pay *Daed* a friendly visit. If anyone can get him to open up about his health, it's Dr. Davis."

"What if it's something serious?"

David clapped a hand on Seth's shoulder. "Let's not borrow trouble by putting the cart before the horse."

Seth couldn't help but worry. It's all he'd done since his *mamm* died. He stood there for a minute, realizing that for the first time, he was able to admit he'd stayed by his *daed's* side all these years out of fear. When his *mamm* died, David was already grown and had a wife and a baby on the way. Lizzie was too young to be keeping house, but she and Seth had grown up very quickly with the added responsibilities suddenly expected of them.

It was all Seth could do to keep from getting choked up. His face felt hot, despite the snowflakes melting on his red cheeks. At a time when the community was busy preparing for a fresh new start with the abundance of weddings and Christmas just around the corner, Seth felt suddenly alone—like an orphan.

Dear Gott, am I to spend the rest of my life alone? I'm not ready for You to take my daed to be with You. I wasn't ready when You took my mamm.

Seth tipped his head toward the heavens and closed his eyes against the snowfall. The world around him was blanketed in a cocoon of white, muffling the sounds of life that threatened his moment of silence with *Der Herr*.

CHAPTER 18

Lillian clucked at her mare, who seemed to be pulling the buggy at a snail's pace. She could tell the roads were getting slick with the snowfall, and was grateful she took the smaller buggy. It would be lighter and easier for Nutmeg to pull if the snow got any thicker on the roads.

Out of the corner of her eye, she noticed Seth standing very statuesque in the snow. As the buggy rolled by the lumber yard, she admired the peaceful expression that swathed his face in a wintery glimmer that made her think he'd never looked more handsome.

Steering Nutmeg to the parking lot of Fork's General Store, she sat for just a minute, unsure if she should approach Seth and interrupt what seemed to be a moment of solace he richly savored.

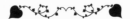

The scent of lavender fingered its way into Seth's thoughts. The snow continued to fall, but the overwhelming floral aroma pricked his senses like none other. That heavenly scent could only mean one thing.

Lillian.

He didn't dare open his eyes, deciding the possibility of her standing near enough for him to inhale her lavender soap was more enticing than the reality that he was more than likely standing alone in the snow.

Then he felt her.

She laid a gentle hand across his arm. "Seth, are you alright?"

Her voice was angelic, and her touch, even through his jacket, was enough to bring heat to his cold cheeks. He slowly opened his eyes and met hers as she smiled sweetly at him.

He cleared his throat and straightened his spine.

"I hope I didn't alert you. I was just enjoying the snow and having a little talk with *Gott.*"

Lillian smiled brightly, noting her reflection in the hazel-blue of his eyes. "I was on my way into Fork's and noticed how peaceful you looked. I wasn't sure if you realized how long you were standing here. By the look of the layer of snow on your coat, I'd say a long while. I didn't want you to catch a cold."

Seth couldn't help but smile at the thought of her worrying about his well-being. He hadn't realized how much he craved such a thing until this moment. He knew Lizzie worried about him, but having Lillian worrying over him seemed somehow different. Pleasantly different.

"I hear from Abby you'll be chaperoning the ice-skating party tomorrow."

"*Jah.* I'm tagging along with Hannah and her new beau."

Seth wished she hadn't said that before he'd had a chance to ask if he could escort her, but it was too late to ask now. If he pressed the issue, he might appear desperate, and he didn't want to seem weak. Women folk liked strong, decisive men—men who were leaders in every way.

"I hope you'll save me a turn around the pond."

Lillian smiled. "*Jah,* I will do that"

Seth could feel heat rushing to his cheeks "I better check to see what's taking my order so long."

"Are you doing a big building project in the winter?"

"*Nee.* I'm starting my own business. I'm building pie cabinets and rocking chairs to sell at the auction and The Country Store downtown in Goshen."

"Miriam Hochstetler sells homemade soap to that store. That would be a good place to sell. They get a lot of business from the *Englisch.* Did you make the pie cupboard in Lizzie's kitchen?"

"*Jah.* I made the rocking chairs on the front porch too."

Lillian's eyes grew wide. "They're all so lovely."

Seth smiled happily that she'd noticed his workmanship. "*Denki.*"

Lillian had an idea pop into her head so fast she wouldn't miss the opportunity that had fallen into her lap.

"Will you be making other types of furniture as well? Because I could use two small tables and a few chairs for the lobby of my bakery so my customers can sit with a cup of coffee and a pastry while they wait for their order. Such a thing could help increase my profits."

A light went on in Seth's head. If he helped her by making furniture for her, it could still afford him the opportunity to spend time with her. "I'd be more than happy to do that for you. It can be my first official order."

Lillian beamed with delight. "That would be wonderful. How long will it take for you to make them?"

"I can have designs drawn up early next week. If you stop by in the afternoon on Wednesday I can show them to you. I've set up a workshop inside the barn."

"I can do that. I'll also see you tomorrow night at the skating party. Don't forget to bring your lantern."

Seth raised an eyebrow. "A lantern?"

"*Jah.* Haven't you ever attended a skating party? Everyone brings a lantern and sets it around the edge of the pond so you can see where you're skating."

Seth shook his head as if he knew. He'd never been to a skating party even though he was quite an accomplished skater. He didn't want to remind her of what she probably already knew. He was not a socialite, having never attended a youth singing or any of the other outings he should have taken advantage of in his younger days during the *rumspringa* he never had.

Lillian was relieved when Seth nodded without saying a word about her obvious lack of knowledge of how parties are conducted among the youth. Who was she trying to fool anyway? By choice she'd never had the desire to attend any of the youth outings, and had never had the desire to experience the days of *rumspringa.* She was truly naïve in every way that dealt with social functions, but she hoped Seth had not recalled having never seen her among the hopefuls waiting for a proper courtship. He didn't need to know that Hannah had told her about the lanterns. She hoped when he saw how well she could skate, he would think she was a regular social butterfly.

CHAPTER 19

Lillian closed the bakery earlier than usual, as she had no other orders, and closing early was normal during the winter hours. She was excited to go to the skating party even though she hadn't ever attended a youth outing. But she was going as a chaperone, and so was Seth. It almost made her feel old to think of herself as a chaperone to the youth. With her twenty-fifth birthday being Monday, she was feeling older than ever. Her *mamm* had laughed the day before when she'd voiced her concerns, and told her she was too young to be thinking she was old. But to be her age and unmarried—well, she was old in that sense.

Pushing the negative thoughts from her mind, she determined she would have a *gut* time at the party. She imagined having Seth's strong arms about her waist as they skated around the pond in the moonlight. Surely it would be a romantic night for the two of them, and might initiate a courtship between them. With that thought in mind, Lillian hustled through the dishes and wiped down the counters, not wanting to leave anything that would attract mice looking for a meal and a warm place to set up house.

By the time she arrived home for the evening meal, her toes were already feeling rather cold. While Hannah set the table, Lillian took a minute to warm her feet near the wood stove that heated their house. She listened to her *mamm* and sister converse happily, while Hannah avoided questions of the seriousness of her relationship with Jonathon. She wished she could have the same closeness that Hannah had with their *mamm,* but she knew she had arrived too close to the death of their older brother for her *mamm's* pain to have gone away when she was born.

Pushing even more negative ideas from her thoughts, she whispered a silent prayer to keep her mind on the things that bring happiness, rather than the pain of the past. She also said a quick prayer for the safety of all who would attend the skating party. Remembering the chatter over last year's party when some of the youth had engaged in horse-play that had resulted in one of them breaking an arm, she determined that nothing of that sort would happen while she was chaperoning.

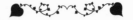

Lillian lifted the deep purple dress that Lizzie had given her and slipped it over her head. She heard the clip-clop of horse's hooves on the long drive to their house, and knew that Jonathon had come to pick the two of them up for the party. She felt funny being a third wheel to her sister's date, but Hannah had insisted she go with them. And since Seth never asked to escort her, she had conceded.

A knock sounded at the door, and Hannah poked her head inside. "Are you ready? They're here."

Lillian stopped pushing the pins into her *kapp.*

"They?"

Hannah shook her head casually. "Jonathon and Henry. Let's go. I don't want them to wait on us."

Lillian crossed her arms. "I'm not going!"

Hannah stepped inside the room and closed the door behind her. "What do you mean you aren't going? They're here waiting on us."

"Why did you set this up? I told you I didn't want to go with Henry. He's too young for me, and I promised Seth I would skate with him. He's going to think Henry is my date."

"Henry is going to make Seth jealous, remember? I did this for your own good."

Lillian fought back tears. "Like the blue dress was for my own good? That was an embarrassing disaster. I do not want to go with Henry."

Hannah smiled mischievously. "The situation with the dress turned out alright. You got that purple dress as a result, and it looks beautiful on you."

Lillian pursed her lips. "Don't flatter me with your prideful talk. I do not want to go with Henry and that's final. I will have *Daed* hitch up the buggy for me, and I'll drive myself."

Hannah tried to put on her best smile. "*Daed* just left with the small buggy. You'll never get Nutmeg to pull the larger one in this deep snow, and my horse is too uncontrollable to pull a buggy. You'll go with us and I'll sit in the back with you."

Feeling the situation was hopeless, she once again conceded to her sister's devious plans. She didn't want to stay behind since she'd promised Seth she'd skate with him. This was the only way of getting there, and she would suffer through it for the sake of seeing Seth. She would make sure all conversation with Henry was causal, and she would keep her distance from him to be sure he wouldn't get the wrong idea.

When they went outside to the buggy, Henry was gentleman enough to assist Lillian into the back, but then he climbed in beside her. Her heart nearly stopped as she glared at Hannah, who was already climbing up into the front of the buggy beside her betrothed.

Henry turned to her. "I'm honored you agreed to accompany me tonight."

How could she explain to him that she hadn't agreed to allow him to escort her at all? That it had been her sneaky sister who'd set the whole thing up. She couldn't be cruel to the poor boy, but he was, after all just a nineteen-year-old boy. Lillian glared at Hannah, who ignored her as she snuggled in close to Jonathon. Henry offered her half of the quilt for her lap, but she refused in spite of the cold wind that whistled into the buggy. She wasn't about to give him any reason to think she wanted to snuggle up to him.

CHAPTER 20

By the time they reached Goose Pond, Lillian was shivering so much her teeth had begun to chatter. She allowed Henry to help her out of the back of the buggy to avoid slipping on the icy path while scanning the area for Seth. When her eyes met his, Henry still had ahold of her hand from assisting her out of the buggy. Lillian quickly snatched her hand away, but Seth had already seen all he needed to see to know Henry had escorted her.

Anger pushed at Lillian's heart as she grabbed her lantern and her skates and walked over to the pond, leaving Henry to run on her heels to keep up. If not for the anger clouding her mind, she would have been able to enjoy the warm glow of the lanterns lining the pond's edge, and the light snow that floated from the sky above like feathers. Large tree trunks had been placed along the ends to serve as seating, and Lillian sat on the end to put on her skates. Though she didn't feel like skating anymore, she reminded herself she was there to chaperone, and she would do just that.

Henry straddled the tree trunk close to Lillian and began to lace up his skates. She didn't like his closeness, especially since Seth seemed to be watching them. Henry made small talk with her about the ice and helping her light her lantern, but she didn't want to encourage him. Before she realized, Henry was helping her to her feet and pulling her onto the ice. He laughed, not realizing she wasn't enjoying his playfulness. He was very handsome, and Lillian couldn't understand why he hadn't found anyone to settle down with yet. Not that she was interested in him because of his looks.

As far as she was concerned, her heart already belonged to Seth.

But Seth was ignoring her at the moment. And who could blame him?

Seth skated alone on the outer edge of the pond, thinking to himself that he wished he'd never agreed to chaperone the skating party. He felt humiliated at the thought of his earlier daydreams of skating romantically with Lillian. It was obvious that she'd been escorted by Henry Graber. He didn't know much about the lad, except that he, himself, was more than ten years older than the young man. He felt suddenly very old—too old to be skating among the youth. But he was a chaperone tonight, which made him feel that much older.

Abby bumped into Seth. "Aren't you going to skate with Lillian?"

Seth hung his head. "She's here with Henry Graber. He escorted her; I can't just take his date from him."

Abby smiled. "Sure you can. She doesn't look like she's having a very good time with him. She almost looks like she's trying to skate away from him. What I don't understand is why she didn't mention Henry escorting her. She told me she was going with Hannah and Jonathon."

"Maybe she didn't want me to know about it. But she promised me a skate around the pond when I saw her yesterday. She seemed genuinely happy about the idea. Maybe I was wrong."

Abby smiled. "There's only one way to find out."

As Lillian and Henry were skating by, Abby shoved Seth into them. Henry broke free from Lillian to keep from falling, but she began to fall until Seth reach out a hand and steadied her. It irritated him that Henry skated away to save himself, but that didn't matter now. He was holding Lillian, and she was smiling for the first time tonight.

"Are you hurt?"

She smoothed the flap of her coat. "*Nee,* I'm fine."

"I'm sorry I'm so clumsy. I didn't mean to scare off your date."

Lillian flashed him a confused look. "Henry's not my date. He rode with my sister and me, but he didn't escort me."

Now it was Seth's turn to smile. "I have to admit, I'm happy to hear that. May I skate with you?"

She tightened her grip on his arm that she hadn't yet let go of. "I thought you'd never ask."

Seth whisked her across the ice as though they were made to skate together. She felt comfortable in his arms, and he now wished the night would never end.

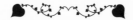

Henry stood on the outside edge of the pond fuming. But when he caught sight of Abby skating alone, he knew the best way to seek vengeance against Seth for stealing Lillian away was to skate with his young niece. Pushing off with one foot, he skated fast to catch up with Abby. He held his arm out to her and she took it with a smile.

"You're Abby, *jah?*"

"*Jah.* And you're Henry? I thought you were Lillian's date."

"*Nee.* I came here with my cousin, Jonathon and his betrothed."

Abby looked at him whimsically. "Hannah and Jonathon are to be married?"

"*Jah.* The Bishop will publish their wedding at next week's service. How about you? Do you have a beau?"

Abby giggled. "*Nee.* My *daed* says I'm too young."

Henry smiled. "How old are you?"

Abby slowed a little so she could skate at the same pace as Henry. "I'm fifteen."

Henry pulled her toward the opening of the dead brush around the edge of the pond so they could step off the ice. "So you've entered your *rumspringa* years."

Abby shook her head. "My *daed* says I'm not allowed to have a *rumspringa* either, even though he told me I could have one when I first met him."

"Wait a minute. You're the girl that moved here a few years ago when you found your real *daed?*"

"*Jah.* My *mamm* and I lived in Ohio before we moved here."

Henry motioned for them to sit on the edge of one of the logs that surrounded the fire pit so they could warm up a bit and talk more.

"Was it fun living among the *Englisch?*"

Abby shrugged. "I thought it was before I moved here. But my *familye* is here, and the life is simpler. Quieter. Less troublesome, and I prefer that to the *Englisch* ways."

Henry gazed into the fire, mesmerized by the flames licking the logs. "Not me. I have a friend who is *Englisch,* and I've been thinking of going to stay with him and starting a life for myself among the *Englisch.* There isn't anything here for me except farming, and I'm not very *gut* at being a farmer."

Abby rolled her sore ankles, rotating them clockwise and then counter-clockwise. "What would you do there with no *familye* to support you?"

Henry sat up straight. "I'll have to get a job. Don't you ever miss it? Being in the *Englisch* world?"

Abby giggled. "*Nee.* We live in the same world as the *Englisch,* but I can see how you might see it that way."

Abby stared into the fire, holding up her bare hands to warm them. She had thought about returning to Ohio, and what, if anything might be there for her. Maybe just a few childhood memories, but none of that was worth leaving her family.

CHAPTER 21

Seth was so preoccupied with his skating partner, and the easy conversation he was having with her, that he hadn't noticed Abby sitting with Henry. Now he watched them every time he and Lillian rounded the curve in the pond. He took note when they sat around the fire pit in the open field outside the edge of the pond. Henry was far too old for Abby to be getting caught up in his false charms, but she was laughing like the young school-girl that she was.

Lillian nudged Seth with her hip, nearly sending him into the brush that bordered the edge of the pond.

"Are you worried about Abby?"

"*Jah.* I don't like her talking to Henry. He's much too old for her."

Lillian smiled at his protective nature, and wondered if he would be that protective over his own daughter someday. Her thoughts made her blush, but her cheeks were most likely already pink from the cold. Still, she turned her face instinctively to hide her intimate thoughts.

"You shouldn't worry about Abby. She's a tough girl. I think she can take care of herself. Besides, they're only talking."

"I hope you're right. Something about him just doesn't feel right to me."

Lillian giggled. "You're only saying that because you thought he was my date for the evening."

Seth smiled. "I just wanted to make sure I could skate with you, that's all."

Why was he so afraid to admit how he felt about her? She'd just given him the perfect opportunity, and he didn't take it. Was he really that afraid of rejection?

"Would you like to go sit down by the fire? You're shivering."

She had to admit she was chilled to the bone, but she was also enjoying the quietness of the pond since most everyone had stopped skating to warm up around the fire. With only the sound of their blades scraping the ice, and Seth's melodic voice chattering away as if they'd been friends their entire lives, she wasn't ready to trade this for warmth among the crowd.

Seth looked over and noticed Abby and Henry walking away from the rest of the youth to a secluded area near the Miller's barn.

"I'm sorry, Lillian, but I should probably check on Abby. She's going off alone with Henry, and I don't think that's wise."

Reluctantly, Lillian agreed. He undid the laces of his skates quickly, and shoved his feet into his boots, and then ran toward the Miller's barn.

Lillian opted to sit near the fire and warm herself while Seth dealt with his niece alone. She sat down on one of the logs where she'd left her boots. Pulling off her skates, she paused to hold her feet up toward the fire for a few minutes. Before she realized, she heard shouting. It sounded like Seth and Henry were yelling at one another. She pushed her feet in the boots and stood up in time to see Seth and Henry rolling on the ground in the distance.

Were they fighting?

Seth approached Abby and Henry cautiously, hoping to avoid embarrassing his young niece. "What are the two of you doing out here away from the rest of the youth?"

Abby held a hand to her chest. "*Onkel* Seth you startled me."

Henry grabbed for Abby's hand. "We weren't doing anything wrong. We were just following a rabbit and her *boppli.*"

Seth stood his ground. "That may be so, but it appears as though you were trying to lure my niece into a dark corner for unsavory things. Even if you weren't, being in this position could soil her reputation."

Abby held tight to Henry's hand. "I'm not a *boppli* anymore, *Onkel* Seth."

Henry grinned eagerly. "You heard her. She's capable of making her own decisions. Run along and leave us alone."

Seth took a step toward Abby. "You go back to the rest of the youth right now. Henry is too old for you. He's nearly five years older than you, and that's too much."

Abby let go of Henry's hand, placing her fists on her hips. "You're five years older than Lillian and you think it's okay to date *her*."

Seth's patience was wearing thin. "We are both adults. You are not an adult, but Henry is, so that makes it wrong."

Henry took a step forward. "You mean to tell me you've had a thing for Lillian this whole time? Why did she agree to come here with me tonight if you two are dating?"

Seth scolded Abby again and told her to go back and sit with the other girls.

Then he turned to Henry. "My relationship with Lillian is none of your business."

Henry took a step forward, getting closer than Seth felt comfortable with. "It's my business if she's a tease. She comes here with me, and then ends up with you? Maybe she isn't such a nice girl after all."

Seth ground his teeth against the accusation. "I don't think you should say things that could hurt a woman's reputation like that."

Henry laughed coarsely. "Did she tell you she was kissing me in the back of the buggy on the way over here tonight?"

Abby gasped at his statement.

Seth took a threatening step closer to Henry. "I don't believe you."

Henry smiled devilishly. "I was doing her a favor since she's probably going to end up a spinster."

Seth could feel the anger rising up in him. "So now you aim to destroy the reputation of two girls? You're a liar, and I'm going to give you one more chance to tell the truth."

Henry poked Seth in the chest with his right index finger. "I did kiss her, and she enjoyed every minute of it! I guess that makes her mine. But you can have her back if you don't mind having a soiled *fraa.*"

Seth wanted to shove him away. "Someone should teach you a lesson, but you aren't worth my time. You're a disgusting liar, and I aim to tell the Bishop of your actions."

Henry stepped closer into Seth's personal space.

"When you talk to the Bishop, make sure you tell him that I hit you, too."

Dumbfounded by such a ridiculous statement, Seth didn't see Henry's fist come at him until it was too late. Pain shot through his jawbone and he barely had time to register the taste of blood in his mouth before another blow connected to the side of his face. Something in Seth made him react—maybe adrenaline—maybe pent up anger over years of being overly submissive to his *daed's* stern upbringing, or even the deep sadness of never getting over his *mamm's* death. But whatever it was, it made him want to hit Henry. Before he realized, the two of them were on the ground, rolling around and punching one another until Jonathon pulled his cousin away from the fight.

Seth scrambled to his feet, blood filling his mouth. He spat on the ground, leaving a red stain in the fresh snow. Wiping the side of his cheek, he stepped away from the crowd and over to Abby. "I'm sorry," he whispered.

"I'm not! You should have hit him a few more times."

Seth placed a hand on her shoulder. "That's enough. We're peaceful people. That fight should never have happened."

"But *Onkel* Seth, you were only defending yourself after he hit you. And someone needed to teach him he can't go around telling lies about Lillian. Sometimes it's necessary to fight back. I don't blame you for that, and neither will *Gott.*"

"The Bishop will surely hear of this and I could be disciplined harshly."

Lillian rushed to his side. "Are you alright? That cut on your cheek might need stitches."

He wasn't ready to face Lillian just yet. He needed to sort out his feelings about what Henry had said. It was very likely that the young man had lied about kissing her in the back of the buggy, but what if he hadn't lied? What if there was some truth to his statements? Was Lillian that kind of woman?

Lillian reached up to touch the side of his face, but he jerked away from her before her hand could make contact with him.

"I'm sorry; I was only going to move your hair aside to get a better look at the cut on your cheek. I didn't mean to worry you."

Seth didn't know how to react to her concern over his injuries. But why hadn't she asked what they were fighting about? Did she already know? Or was she innocent in all of this, and her concern for his well-being was sincere? He couldn't think straight at the moment. He needed to go home, and to pray the Bishop wouldn't demand he be shunned for his actions.

CHAPTER 22

Lillian stood in the snow, wondering what had just happened. She didn't understand why Seth would fight with Henry, and what was even more confusing was his reaction to her when she tried to get a look at his injury. He'd backed away from her like she was contagious with influenza. She struggled to find a reason for his change in attitude toward her, but no matter what she thought of, none of it made any sense. One minute they were on the ice talking and laughing, getting along almost as if he was her beau. And the next minute he was fighting like a violent man. She'd never seen anything in Seth that would make her think he was violent. So what had caused him to physically fight Henry?

Lillian hadn't seen who started the fight, but it apparently changed Seth in a way she wasn't sure she liked. She hadn't known too much about Seth personally until recently, but she'd always thought of him with respect. He was a kind man, not at all like the man she'd witnessed walking away from a brutal fight just moments ago. What had pushed him to the point that he would turn into the type of man who would hit another? She sighed. Perhaps if this was the type of behavior he was capable of, she was glad she found out before her heart became too invested in him.

Seth went straight to the barn when he reached his farm. He'd warned Abby not to tell his sister about the fight until he had a chance to sort it out and go to the Bishop. He wasn't sure if what he'd done required a confession, but he knew Abby would back up his story about Henry initiating the physical confrontation.

His mind wandered to Lillian and the shame he felt so deeply, he couldn't even allow her to console him after the fight. He knew she was only trying to be the kind and loving woman he'd grown to love, but his actions were shameful. Now he just couldn't face her. Why hadn't he just walked away? Abby had commended his defense of her honor and that of Lillian's honor, but he didn't feel very honorable. He was a peaceful man, but something inside him raged—something he'd been holding in for a long time.

After washing the blood from his face, he headed toward the house, intending to go straight to bed. When he walked into the kitchen, his *daed* sat at the table, his fingers laced around a steaming mug of coffee.

"When I heard the buggy pull into the yard, I put on a pot of *kaffi*. Thought you could use something to warm you up, but by the look of your face, I'd say you need more than *kaffi*."

Seth sat down after pouring himself a mug of coffee. His *daed* looked pale, and he wondered why he was still awake at this late hour. He was glad he was still awake because he needed to talk this out before it ate away at him.

Seth sighed heavily. "I really messed things up, *daed*. I let a hot-tempered young man get to me. He swung the first couple of punches, but after that, I hit him back."

Hiram tried not to pass judgment on his son, who was obviously remorseful for his actions. "What started the fight?"

Seth hung his head in shame. "He was trying to lure Abby away from the group, and then he made inappropriate comments that could soil Lillian's reputation."

Hiram cleared his throat. "I can understand you wanting to protect your niece, but what on earth could he have possibly said about Lillian that would cause you to react so negatively?"

Seth looked his *daed* in the eye. "He claims that she was kissing him in the back of Jonathon's buggy."

"Do you think there's any truth to his statements?"

Seth pushed the mental image from his thoughts.

"I don't know. I hope not, but I can't be certain."

Hiram leaned forward in his chair. "Did you ask her?"

"*Nee.* I couldn't face her after what I'd done. She knew about the fight, but didn't know why, and I wasn't going to tell her the horrible things he said about her."

Hiram placed a shaky hand over Seth's. "If he tried to compromise her, the Bishop should know about it."

"I skated with her part of the night, and she didn't seem like a woman who'd been compromised. But Henry said he she kissed him back when he kissed her. What if she did? And then she spent the rest of the evening with me. What kind of a woman does a thing like that?"

Hiram removed his hand, and cradled his coffee cup.

"I'm ashamed to hear you say such a thing about Lillian. She's a respectable young woman, not the sort to engage in such sinful actions. And a woman of that character doesn't suddenly get the reputation for such things at her age. I think you need to have a talk with Lillian and get her side of the story. She deserves that much from you. I can see how much you love her; don't make the mistake of losing her over this."

He knew his *daed* was right, but he wasn't able to process his next move at the moment. He dragged himself up the stairs to his bed, but sleep eluded him. Instead, he found solace in a much-needed chat with God.

CHAPTER 23

Lillian woke from a fitful dream that replayed the fight between Seth and Henry. Her wind-up alarm clock beside her bed told her it was only four-thirty in the morning. Too early to get up, but too late to go back to sleep. She'd stayed home from visiting with her family the day before, but she couldn't do that this morning. She had bread to bake and whoopie pie orders to fill—and a student to teach. She wasn't looking forward to facing Abby, and she hoped Seth wouldn't bring her to the bakery the way he had the previous week.

Lillian pushed herself from her warm bed and pulled her robe tightly around her waist. At least she could make the coffee for *mamm*. When she entered the kitchen, Hannah had already put the coffee pot on to brew.

Lillian wasn't ready to talk to her sister. She was angry, but she couldn't avoid her altogether since they both still lived at home. She tried to go about her business as she readied pans and set the table in preparation for breakfast. She went for her heavy, wool cloak by the door, but Hannah stopped her short.

"I already gathered the eggs."

Lillian moved about in silence, heating up the oven so she could make fresh muffins for her family.

Hannah shifted in her chair. "How long are you going to go without speaking to me? You didn't say a word to me on the way home from the skating party, and you didn't come out of your room until after we left to go visiting yesterday."

They'd been brought up to remain quiet rather than speak harshly to one another, and Lillian didn't feel she could utter a word to Hannah without some measure of harshness toward her. If her sister hadn't insisted on dragging her into another one of her schemes, the previous week would have gone smoothly, and Seth would probably be her beau by now. But instead, she wasn't speaking to Hannah, and she wasn't sure if she would ever get the chance to have another conversation with Seth as long as they lived.

Lillian mixed together a quick batter for cinnamon muffins, determined to ignore Hannah's childish pleadings. She said a quick prayer in her head to keep from saying something she might regret later, but Hannah's words added to the anger that roiled inside her.

Finally, she could take it no longer. "You made Seth jealous. Your plan worked—better than any of us could have imagined. Are you happy now? Or will you continue to hurt others with your schemes?"

Hannah whispered so low, it was almost inaudible.

"I never meant for anyone to get hurt—especially not my dear *schweschder*. I'm sorry. Will you ever be able to forgive me?"

Lillian poured the last of the batter into the second muffin tin before putting them in the oven. She didn't dare speak, for fear she would declare aloud a refusal to forgive Hannah. She wanted to forgive her more than anything, but she couldn't get the image of Seth's bloody face out of her head. What should have been a magical night for her and Seth, turned out to be a nightmare because of Hannah's foolishness.

Before walking upstairs, Lillian turned to Hannah.

"I will forgive you, but I need some time to work through my anger. I hope you'll understand."

Lillian didn't wait for an answer. She'd said all she could. Now all she wanted to do was go to the bakery—her only escape at the moment.

Seth pulled up to the bakery to drop off Abby. As she stepped down from the buggy, he handed her a large spice box he'd had in the back. "Please give this to Lillian, and tell her I wish her a happy birthday."

Abby pushed the box back toward him. "Tell her yourself, *Onkel* Seth. She isn't going to know you care about her if you don't give her this gift in person."

Seth sighed. "I won't be ready to see her until after I go to the Bishop and talk to him. I'm just not ready to face her, and I'm not even sure she'll want to see me. But I still want her to know I care. So, please Abby, give her the box. I'm hoping the contents will let her know what she means to me."

Abby reluctantly took the box after seeing the torment in her uncle's eyes. Somehow she had to help make this right between the two of them. She felt responsible for walking off with Henry at the skating party. If she hadn't been so careless, her uncle wouldn't have confronted Henry to salvage her reputation. It was her responsibility to keep her reputation intact by doing as it says in the Bible, and avoiding the appearance of wrong-doing, but she hadn't done that. She trudged inside the warm bakery, meeting Lillian with a smile.

She held out a small package to Lillian wrapped in plain brown paper, with a bow made from raffia.

"Happy birthday!"

Lillian took the package, surprised that her apprentice had remembered her birthday. *"Denki."*

She untied the raffia and un-wrapped the paper. Inside was a large, quilted square in the wedding ring pattern. She looked at Abby with obvious confusion. "I think it's beautiful. Did you sew this?"

Abby beamed with delight. *"Jah. Mamm* showed me how to do it. I spent the week making it. Do you like it?"

Lillian paused. "I do like it, but I don't understand why you would start me off on a marriage quilt when I'm not even betrothed."

Abby smiled angelically and hooked her arm in Lillian's as they walked into the kitchen. "I'm hoping that will change very soon."

Lillian didn't dare hope for such a thing anymore, but she didn't want to hurt the young girl's feelings. "I'll tuck it away in my dowry for the future."

Then Abby handed her the spice box Seth had given her. "This is from *Onkel* Seth. He wanted to give it to you himself, but he's on his way to see the Bishop. He told me to wish you a happy birthday."

Setting Abby's gift on the counter, Lillian took the box and smiled weakly. She was unsure of how to feel about Seth ever since the fight on Saturday. She prayed the Bishop would help him without enforcing a shunning against him.

Abby waved a hand in front of Lillian. "You seem like you're far away in your thoughts."

Lillian smiled sadly. "I'm sorry. I was just thinking..."

"Lillian, I promised *Onkel* Seth I wouldn't talk about what happened on Saturday, but there's something I think you should know. Henry hit my *onkel* twice in the face before he defended himself. He didn't start the fight—Henry did."

Lillian sighed. "I'm sure you're right, but we can't condone violence in our community. The Bishop will do what's right for your *onkel* and for the community."

"But you don't understand! *Onkel* Seth was defending *you!*"

Lillian gasped. "Me! How was he defending me?"

Abby's gaze fell. "Henry told *Onkel* Seth that you two were kissing in the back of Jonathon's buggy on the way over to the skating party. Please tell me it isn't true!"

Lillian couldn't breathe. She set the spice box on the counter and went to the sink and turned on the faucet. She splashed cold water on her face, fighting the tears that tightened in her throat.

Abby rushed to her side. "I didn't mean to upset you. Maybe I should have listened to *Onkel* Seth and kept my mouth shut."

Lillian took the linen towel Abby handed to her and wiped her face. "I'm glad you told me. Except now I know it's my fault Seth was hurt."

Abby laid a hand over Lillian's shoulder. "It isn't your fault at all. It's Henry's fault for lying. He *was* lying, wasn't he?"

"Of course Henry lied. I could never kiss a man I don't love. But your *Onkel* Seth didn't believe him—did he?"

Abby shook her head frantically. "*Nee.* He defended you, didn't he? But he didn't really say, come to think of it."

"Well he shouldn't have defended himself against such lies. Henry's kind isn't worth the fight."

Tears rushed to Lillian's eyes and threatened to spill over. Now she had yet another reason to feel angry. If she saw Henry anytime soon, she'd slap him across his face for telling such lies—lies that could ruin her reputation. Lies that could cause Seth not to trust her. Now more than ever she feared losing ground with him. What if a small part of him believed Henry's lies? Then neither Seth, nor any man in the community would court her. She'd be destined to marry Henry or become a spinster.

Does that fool have any idea the damage his lies could cost me?

CHAPTER 24

Seth took a deep breath before knocking on Bishop Troyer's door.

Mrs. Troyer opened the door with a smile.

"*Kume.* I'll tell the Bishop you're here."

Seth fidgeted, choosing to stand rather than taking the chair Mrs. Troyer offered. Was it too late to change his mind about his inevitable confession? His hands shook as he waited for the Bishop to meet him in the small sitting room. He just wanted this to be over, and to get through it without being shunned.

Bishop Troyer entered the room with a welcoming smile. Seth knew the Bishop was a fair man, but that didn't keep him from feeling like he could throw up his breakfast.

This time, he took the chair offered to him, fearing his shaky legs would give out on him.

The aging man eased himself onto the sofa. "I suspect you're here to make a confession. But let me save you the trouble. There isn't much that gets by me in my own community, and I already had several visits from some of the youth that attended the skating party on Saturday night. You may not know this, but this isn't the first scuffle Henry Graber has been into. I've warned his folks that since he's past his *rumspringa*, he could be excommunicated for his behavior. They have assured me the boy will be disciplined. As for the accusations against Lillian Stoltzfus, I haven't spoken to the boy yet, but I imagine you can count on getting a visit from him with an explanation. I fully expect a public apology at Sunday's service."

Seth shifted uneasily in the chair. He was relieved that he wouldn't be shunned for his part in the fight, but he had another issue that needed dealing with—his anger.

Seth cleared his throat. "There's still something I have weighing on my mind. After the fight, all I could think about was being angry with my *mamm* for dying and leaving me at such a young age, and having resentment toward my *daed* for leaning on me so much when I was too young to handle the responsibility."

Bishop Troyer nodded his head knowingly. "Those feelings are natural, and I'm surprised they haven't come out sooner. I spoke with your *schweschder* quite in length about the same issues when she returned to the community. Your *daed* should have leaned more on the community during his hardship. It would have saved him the heartache of losing his *dochder* to the *Englisch,* but he didn't. I've discussed this with him recently. He loves both of you, and you should make an effort to forgive him—and your *mamm.*"

Seth nodded. There wasn't much else to be said. But the Bishop's word hit a nerve. If his *daed* had been confessing to this man, he might have even more reason to be concerned about his *daed's* health.

Seth waved to the Bishop and his wife as he drove his buggy out onto the main road. Part of him wanted to go straight to the bakery and see Lillian, but he figured she might still want some distance from him after the way he acted. Mostly, he wanted to go home and have a nice long talk with his *daed.*

Lillian walked home from the bakery just before dusk. It had been a long day, and she was emotionally and physically drained. Her *daed* hadn't had a chance to shovel the path from the bakery to the house, so she was grateful she'd had the sense to wear her boots as she trudged through the deep snow. Mesmerized by the crunching and squeaking of the snow beneath her feet, she almost missed the rattle that came from the spice box she cradled in her arms. Though she'd been curious the entire day as to what was inside the gift from Seth, she'd been grateful the bakery had been too busy for her open it. Opening the box could either confirm Seth believed her, and he loved her. Or it could break her heart. Either way, she wasn't ready to let go of the hope she desperately held onto.

Pausing for a minute on the path, Lillian listened to the coo of a snowy owl nesting in the tree above her head. His yellow eyes glowed, and his head tipped to one side as if to greet her. Lillian admired his beauty, while she whispered a prayer of thanks to God for placing such an elegant creature in her path to remind her of His grace. She needed to stop feeling sorry for herself and forgive her sister.

She even needed to forgive Henry for the things he said about her, and for hitting Seth.

When she reached the yard, Hannah was near the large oak tree talking to Jonathon. Hannah saw her and rushed to her side, pulling Lillian into her arms. "*Ach,* dear *schweschder,* Jonathon just told me about Henry's accusations against you. I'm so sorry. I know you weren't kissing him in the back of the buggy. But even if I hadn't been there, I would never believe such lies about you. I'm so sorry I made you ride with him."

Lillian hugged her sister tightly. "*Denki.* I'm sorry too. I didn't mean to have an unforgiving heart toward you."

Hannah giggled. "I knew you would come around. I wasn't worried. But now that I know what he said, I must go to Bishop Troyer and tell him the truth so he can discipline Henry."

"*Denki.*"

"Where did you get the spice box?"

Lillian smiled shyly, heat rising in her cheeks. "It was a gift from Seth."

"Jonathon and I will go to the Bishop now so no more time is lost. I'll be back in time for your birthday dinner."

Lillian's heart felt lighter than it had in the past two days. She held fast to the spice box, feeling as though she was ready to face the contents—good or bad.

CHAPTER 25

Jonathon and Hannah drove up the lane that led to Henry's house. Never had Jonathon been more ashamed of his cousin than now. He'd overlooked the problems he'd had recently, writing them off as youthful mischief, but tarnishing a woman's reputation and hitting a man who would defend her was more than Jonathon could excuse. Their plan was to confront Henry before going to the Bishop in case they had anything to confess from their unexpected visit to Jonathon's cousin.

To the side of the barn, Henry was busy chopping wood atop a large tree stump. He stopped what he was doing and swung the ax to rest in the stump. He greeted his visitors with a forlorn expression, and with much hesitation.

When he approached the buggy, he cast his eyes downward. "I've been to the Bishop this afternoon, and I confessed everything to him. I'm sorry for the trouble I've caused your *schweschder*. I plan to make my peace with her, and I pray she can find it in her heart to forgive me. I'll make sure Seth knows the truth too so he'll never have to wonder if his *fraa* has been soiled by the likes of me."

Hannah did a double-take of Henry's words in her mind. "Seth and Lillian are not married. Why would you say such a strange thing?"

Henry looked Hannah in the eye. "Because I could see how much he loved her when he defended her honor. I'm sorry it took me so long to see it. I guess I acted like that because I was jealous."

Hannah felt the heat of shame creep up her neck. She'd set out to make Seth jealous, and it ended up being Henry that was driven to jealousy. "I'm sorry for trying to pair the two of you when I knew how she felt about Seth. She's tried to hide her feelings from me for a long time, but I know my *schweschder* better than she knows herself sometimes. I'm sorry for putting you in the middle of my schemes. I never thought it would cause so much harm."

Henry smiled. "In a way I'm glad the whole thing happened. If not for facing excommunication, I wouldn't have taken such a soulful look at my life. After talking to the Bishop, I've decided to take the baptism."

Jonathon clapped a hand on Henry's shoulder.

"That's *gut* news, cousin. I'm happy you've decided to stay in the community. If not, you would have been missed."

"You're not ashamed to call me cousin?"

Jonathon smiled. "*Nee.* I'm proud to call you cousin. But if you have any more troubles, ask me for help. I'll be there for you. That's what *familye* does."

"*Denki* for being so lenient with me."

Jonathon helped Hannah back into the buggy. She needed to get home for her sister's birthday party, and she had an even better gift of this unexpected visit to give than what she'd made for her.

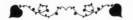

Seth toyed with the idea of going to see Lillian for her birthday, but after Abby gave him the news that she hadn't opened his gift, he figured he'd give her some more time before he tried to talk to her. He was grateful she'd accepted the gift rather than turning it away as he'd feared she might. Right now, though, he would work on making the first of four chairs for the lobby of her bakery. He still held out hope that she'd come by to see his work on Wednesday. Until then, he would carve the chairs with all the love he held in his heart for her. It no longer mattered what happened or didn't happen with Henry. He loved her, and he was determined to put this matter behind him.

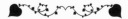

Lillian placed the spice box on her bed and sat beside it. Fear and excitement gripped her, playing tug-of-war with her heart. She loved Seth, but if the contents of the box proved nothing more than a gift of friendship it could crush her. Reaching a shaky hand toward the box, she said a quick prayer for strength. A note lay just inside the box atop a fold of blue material, the same color as the dress Hannah had made for her. Lillian's heart skipped a beat at the sight of it, but she picked up the note nonetheless.

She was almost too afraid to open the note.

Dear Lillian,

It is difficult for me to express my deepest regret over the events that took place on Saturday night, but you have to know I would do it all over again for the sake of defending your honor.

Please accept this gift as a token of my sincere friendship, with the hope you'll give me the chance to prove my worth to you.

The spice box belonged to my mamm, and the contents are the treasures I've been collecting since her passing. I pray that over time, you will add to these treasures and return it to me some day.

Seth

Tears welled up in Lillian's throat at the gift Seth had given her. She didn't even need to look at the contents of the box to know he'd given her his heart and was asking for hers in return. Excitement rose in her stomach like butterflies. Was it possible that she and Seth could make a life together? She would find out on Wednesday when she paid him a visit to thank him for the gift and to check on her furniture order. But for now, she couldn't wait to get a look at what was underneath the blue fabric.

She lifted the delicate material, realizing it was an old-fashioned handkerchief with embroidered roses on it. With its silky crochet border, it was the most exquisite handkerchief she'd ever seen. Setting it aside, she dove into the contents that mostly appeared to be a collection of boyhood treasures. There was everything from a buffalo-head nickel, to snowflake cutouts and dried flowers, a cracked robin's egg to acorns, small pinecones, and a heart-shaped rock.

But then a particular item caught her eye. In the midst of all the tiny keepsakes was a feather—a feather Lillian knew could have only come from one of her own chickens. She was the only one in the whole community to raise white bantam chickens. Her *daed* had questioned her when she'd ordered them from the feed store in Middlebury. She'd wanted them because their feathers were just like goose down, and she had told her *daed* all those years ago she was going to make a bundle of money making feather pillows. Lillian giggled at the thought of it. She'd only made enough pillows to satisfy her own family before she tired of the laborious work she'd put into those few pillows.

Lillian held the fresh white plume against her cheek and closed her eyes. "Seth must have slipped this feather in his pocket the day he helped me clip their wings," she said aloud.

Tears streamed down her face at the declaration of love wrapped up into that one little feather. How long had Seth loved her and kept it to himself? She knew she'd kept quiet about her feelings for him for nearly a year already. Had it really been that long? Why had she wasted so much time? Time that she could have spent with him. If she'd only said something to him—anything—they might be married now and expecting a *boppli.*

The very thought of carrying Seth's *boppli* brought heat to her cheeks, and a fire to her belly. She continued to daydream of a life with Seth until her *mamm* called her downstairs for the evening meal.

CHAPTER 26

Before Lillian realized, it was Wednesday, and she was on her way to Seth's house to examine the furniture plans Seth would have ready for her. Yesterday had been so busy at the bakery she scarcely had a free minute to sit down and rest her aching feet. Seth had dropped Abby off in the morning, but hadn't picked her up in the afternoon. He warned her ahead of time that he would be too busy that afternoon to get her, so she was on her own, having to leave the bakery early to get her twin siblings from school.

Lillian had waved to him through the front window of the bakery when he'd dropped off Abby, but neither of them had time to visit. This would be the first time she would be able to see him since she'd received his birthday gift for her. She was both excited and nervous to see him, especially since they had a lot to talk about. Lillian wondered if they would be able to have an easy conversation the way they had on Saturday night before the fight broke out. She'd enjoyed that magical time with him, and hoped they could get that back.

When Lillian pulled into the yard in front of Seth's house, she parked her buggy so that Nutmeg was under the pole barn and out of the wind. She stepped down and made sure there was fresh water in the trough before heading toward the barn. She stopped short when she noticed his *daed* sitting on the back stoop without a jacket. He shivered against the snow flurries swirling around him. Lillian rushed to the older man's side. "What are you doing sitting out here in the cold? Are you hurt?"

Hiram took the hand Lillian offered to him. "*Nee,* I got a little disoriented and my head hurts. I should probably go in the *haus* before I catch cold."

Lillian walked into the house with Hiram on her arm. One quick survey of the kitchen proved it was in need of cleaning. "*Kume,* sit while I make a fresh pot of *kaffi.* Have you had anything to eat today?"

Hiram shook his head. "I haven't had anything since the noon meal. With Seth busy working on his new business, I think he forgot about me this evening. He's been burning the oil out of every lantern in the *haus* working late hours on his furniture."

Lillian couldn't help but feel somewhat responsible for Seth falling behind with the house and care for his *daed.* She knew he was probably trying to get her order done quickly, so she would just have to help him. She set about the kitchen, getting a sink full of soapy water ready to soak the dishes while she began preparations for a meal. Grateful she'd brought muffins and biscuits for the two of them, she decided to serve them with the meal. A quick survey of the staples in the kitchen proved to be a little scarce, but she could fry up some potato wedges and ham steaks. It would be quick, and she could wash the dishes while the potatoes cooked.

Setting her mind to task, Lillian made light work of cleaning the kitchen and preparing a quick meal.

Hiram reached for the coffee pot to freshen his cup while he waited for Lillian to finish with the cooking.

"You should sit and rest, Mr. Miller. I can get that for you."

Hiram smiled as he sank back into his chair.

"You're going to spoil me. My son is a lucky man to have you."

Lillian blushed at his statement. She and Seth hadn't made any kind of plans yet; was it possible that his *daed* knew something she didn't know? She quickly finished the dishes before putting the ham steaks in the skillet to fry. It was an easy kitchen to work in, and she wondered what it would be like if she and Seth were to marry and this would be her kitchen. Heat rose up her neck until it reached her cheeks. Thankfully, her back was turned to Seth's *daed*.

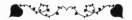

Seth hadn't realized how late it had gotten. He was so engrossed in his work, and enjoying every minute of it, that he hadn't noticed when it became dark outside of the warmth of the barn. It had been hours since he'd seen his *daed*, and he wondered how he was handling the extra workload in the house. It was ironic that their roles had changed so quickly, but Seth was happier with this arrangement. He was happier working and letting his *daed* retire from his work as a harness maker. Seth still intended to fill the few orders that would come in from time to time, but his sole focus would now be on building his furniture business.

Seth stretched his sore back muscles and set his tools down. He'd finished the first of the four chairs Lillian had ordered from him. He looked at his pocket watch, wondering why she hadn't shown up as planned. She was supposed to approve the designs for her order, and it was nearly too late for a social call. He'd even missed his evening meal, and hoped his *daed* had saved him a plate of whatever it was he'd made.

Pulling on his coat, he turned off the gas lanterns and threw open the large barn door and stepped outside, cold air assaulting his nostrils. Thick snowfall made him duck his head as he pushed up the collar of his jacket to shield the wind against his face. He closed the barn door and set the latch, making note that he would need to repair the loose hardware before winter winds tore the door from its hinges. Nearing the house, Seth noticed Lillian's buggy and wondered why she hadn't come to the barn to see her order.

When he entered the mudroom, Seth could smell ham and potatoes. Had his *daed* invited Lillian to eat with him? After he finished hanging up his coat and hat, he turned the corner into the kitchen, surprised to see his *daed* sitting at the table while Lillian served him a plate of food. She turned around, her angelic face glistening from the heat of the stove.

"I was beginning to wonder if I was going to have to pry you from the barn to eat."

She smiled sweetly as she set a full plate of food at the place across from his *daed*.

Hiram looked at him with sunken eyes. "Sit down Seth. And Lillian please join us."

Lillian hesitated, looking to Seth for approval. He didn't say a word, but merely nodded for her to sit and share the meal with them—a meal she had obviously prepared. A quick survey of the clean kitchen suggested she may have taken care of that too.

Embarrassment suddenly consumed him, making it difficult to swallow the lightly seasoned potatoes. He didn't want her thinking she needed to clean up after him. If they were married, that would be a different story, but they weren't, and he felt she'd overstepped her boundaries.

Shame soon replaced Seth's feelings of embarrassment. His *daed* was his responsibility, not Lillian's. And he'd made a fair deal with his *daed* about the house-work falling on his shoulders now so he could work and provide for the aging man. If he needed to hire help for his *daed,* he would do that, but he didn't want Lillian cleaning up after him. It just didn't feel right.

Intending to speak to Lillian after the meal, he tried his best to engage in the small talk between her and his *daed*. How could he be so delighted to see her, and be so furious with her at the same time?

CHAPTER 27

A knock at the door startled Seth, who had been deep in thought. Rising from his chair, he gazed upon Lillian who was carrying on a light conversation with his *daed,* oblivious to the visitor who had interrupted their meal.

Seth opened the door, shocked and disturbed to see Henry standing on his back stoop, hat in hand.

Henry cleared his throat. "I know I'm the last person you want to see, but I came to speak my peace. I'd like to apologize."

Seth gritted his teeth. "I believe Lillian is the one you should be apologizing to."

He opened the door all the way and invited Henry inside. "She's in the kitchen. You can go on in and tell her what you came here to say."

Seth had conflicting thoughts at the moment. He would deal with the meal and dish-washing situation after they finished eating. But for now, he would make sure Lillian's honor and reputation were protected. Following Henry into the kitchen, Seth caught sight of the look of melancholy on Lillian's face. It was amazing how fast she went from smiling to frowning when she saw Henry.

Lillian dabbed at her mouth with the linen napkin from her lap and looked at Seth with fearful eyes.

"Henry has something he wants to say to you." Seth gestured for Henry to begin, but hadn't offered him to sit with them. Normally if folks dropped in during meal times, they would always get an invitation, but Seth wasn't in an inviting mood at the moment.

Henry gripped his hat nervously and cleared his throat. "I came to tell Seth I was sorry for starting a fight, but I also want to say I'm sorry for the lies I told about you. The last thing I want to do is soil your reputation, and stand in the way of you marrying a man who will respect you for the kind person you are."

Lillian knew she needed to forgive him, but she felt embarrassed in front of Seth and his *daed.*

Hiram looked up from his plate. "I think what you did was unforgivable. You should be horse-whipped."

Lillian gasped at his comment. Though part of her agreed with him, she would never voice it out loud. "*Denki* for the apology. I'm sure it took great courage to come here and speak to us."

Henry turned to Seth. "I want you to know, I never kissed Lillian. I lied because I was jealous of you. You're a lucky man to have such a *gut* woman to love you."

Lillian's heart slammed against her ribcage. Why would he say such a thing? What if Seth doesn't feel the same way?

Seth nodded, the corners of his mouth turning up.

"I think any man would be lucky to have her love him."

Lillian let go of the breath she'd been holding in. Although he hadn't agreed with Henry, at least he hadn't openly rejected her. She stood abruptly and started clearing the table, knowing she needed to keep her hands busy.

Seth stood there and watched Lillian taking charge and cleaning up his kitchen for the second time today. He was stunned that she would be so gutsy as to take charge of a house that wasn't hers. Was she doing it because she found his domestic skills lacking? Or was she simply being kind and helpful? Her attitude didn't appear condescending in any way, but that didn't mean she wasn't harboring loathsome feelings toward him or feeling obligated because of his incompetence. Whatever it was, he didn't like it, and he intended to speak to her about it before she left.

Seth walked Henry out to his buggy. After a short conversation, which Seth had missed most of because he wasn't really listening, he waved goodbye to Henry. The young man was the least of Seth's troubles. Until he could sort out how he would handle the fact that Lillian was inside his kitchen cleaning it, he would get her horse ready for the trip home.

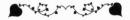

Lillian dried the last plate and wiped out the iron skillet, putting it back in the cabinet where she'd gotten it. Hiram was snoring lightly from his chair in the sitting room, and she found it comforting. It amazed her how comfortable she felt in Seth's house.

CHAPTER 28

Lillian took one last look at the kitchen before getting her coat from the mudroom. As she lifted it from its hook, she wondered if it could ever be *her* hook—if she could find her place here in this house with Seth. She knew if she married him, it would be with the added responsibility of taking care of his *daed.* But she would gladly take on the extra workload if it meant she didn't have to be lonely anymore. She'd longed for Seth for nearly a year, and now, it seemed, she was closer than ever to seeing that dream come to pass.

Exiting the house, she felt a little sad that her time there would soon be over—for now, anyway. She found Seth in the barn smoothing stain on a beautifully handcrafted chair that she hoped was for her. Lillian pointed to the chair. "Is that for me?"

Seth beamed with happiness over his work. "*Jah.* If you don't like this one, I can make another, but I thought this style would go nicely in your bakery."

Lillian smiled. "*Nee.* Don't change it, I like this one. God has really blessed you with a gift. It's wonderful. "

She was leaning so close that Seth wanted to kiss her. He cleared his throat and backed up, reminding himself he needed to discuss the issue of boundaries. Mesmerized by her facial expression as she studied the plans for the tables, he lost his train of thought.

Lillian let out a little yelp. "*Ach,* I think I got a splinter from your work table. It stings."

Seth took her hand to examine her index finger. "*Jah,* I see it. Looks pretty deep. But not to worry, I'm an expert at getting splinters out since I get them so often."

He reached up and grabbed a box off the shelf above his head. Pulling out tweezers and strips of cheese cloth, he turned up the lantern that sat on his work bench and held her hand under the light for a better look. When he neared her finger with the tweezers, she flinched.

Seth looked into her doe-eyes. Was it possible that he could love her as much as he did when they hadn't even had one buggy ride together yet?

"I'm not going to hurt you. Relax your hand. It will make things easier."

"For who?" she squealed.

Seth couldn't help but smile. "For both of us."

He tried to maneuver the splinter from her finger, but he may have lodged it deeper. Pulling a needle and thread and a small bottle of rubbing alcohol from the box, he sterilized the needle and set to work trying to remove it.

"Now hold still. I might have to dig just a little to get the last of it."

Lillian jerked her hand from his grasp. "It will work its way out on its own sooner or later."

Seth looked at her sternly. "And in the meantime, it will get infected."

"I don't want you to hurt me."

Seth pulled her hand into his, holding it gently. "I could never hurt you."

They both just sat there for a moment, until Seth couldn't stand it any longer. He let go of her hand and cupped her face in his hands, drawing her to him. Adrenaline coursed through him like an electric current when his lips touched hers. The more he kissed her, the more he wanted from her. She was intoxicating like raw honey, and her mouth tasted sweet. He was dizzy with passion for this woman, but he pulled himself away from her before things went any further. He had the rest of his life to explore the depth of his love for her, but for now, he had a splinter to remove.

CHAPTER 29

Seth sat at the table enjoying one of the zucchini muffins Lillian had brought to them the night before. After their kiss, he decided to pick his battles with her rather than risk losing her over an argument about her helping him. His *daed,* who was really to blame for his embarrassment over the dirty kitchen, sat across from him watching him devour his breakfast.

"Lillian never did tell me why she was here yesterday. I was so busy enjoying her company and her help that I never asked her. Does her visit mean the two of you are finally courting?"

Seth let out a heavy sigh. "Since you brought up the subject of her helping here yesterday, can you please tell me why she was serving you food when I came in the *haus* last night? By the sparkle in this kitchen, I can tell you didn't clean it, and the food was too tasty for you to have prepared it. How could you embarrass me like that, *daed?*"

"You think I let her wash the dishes and cook our meal because I was trying to embarrass you? I thank God that she came along when she did, because if she hadn't, I might have frozen to death before you left the barn. I got dizzy and slipped on the stoop. There's no telling how long I sat out there in the cold before she brought me into the *haus* and put some hot *kaffi* in me. I'm not well, son. I've known for some time now, since my outing with Doctor Davis over the summer. I'm getting progressively worse, and it's probably going to get worse as time goes by. I didn't want to tell you like this, but I know you've noticed changes in me lately."

Seth raked his fingers through his thick hair. "What is wrong with you? Can it be fixed?"

Hiram tried to paste a smile on his face. "It doesn't matter. When God decides it's my time, then that's the final word. I've made my peace with it, and I think you should too. None of us knows when it's our time, but I happen to know mine is sooner than yours."

Tears welled up in Seth's eyes. "Is there anything the doc can do?"

"He mentioned aggressive medicines, but it would only buy me a few more months, and I would be too sick and too weak to enjoy the time I have left."

Seth was almost afraid to speak the words, but he had to know what he was dealing with. "Did he say how long you have?"

"Maybe another year. And I'd like to see you and Lillian get married, so don't waste any more time with her. I want to have *grandkinner* from the two of you, so make your move, Son. You'd be a fool to let her slip away."

All the anger over Lillian's help now pointed to himself for being so petty. To let his pride get in the way of the woman he loved would be pure foolishness.

"I won't *Daed.* I promise."

Seth picked up Lillian for their first official date. She chose to go sledding at Bonnyville Mill, but he didn't care where they went as long as they were together. She'd brought an extra quilt and a thermos full of hot cocoa so they would stay warm. Seth put her long sled into the back of the buggy, and they were off on their first outing together.

When they arrived at the park, Seth was surprised and happy that there were only a few kids sledding. He looked forward to a quiet afternoon with Lillian in the snow. Lillian, it seemed had a different idea. She picked up a handful of snow and tossed it at him playfully.

"Are you sure you want to challenge me? Remember I won the last snowball fight."

Lillian laughed at him. "You didn't win. I did."

"I know one thing I'll bet I'm better at than you are."

Lillian laughed again even harder. "I doubt that."

"I happen to be the best at making snowmen."

Lillian hooked her arm in Seth's and pointed to a stretch of undisturbed snow near a patch of pine trees. "If we build him together, I'll bet he'll be even better."

Seth agreed, and they each started a small snowball, rolling them along the ground until they increased in size. Seth stopped and watched Lillian for a minute, noting that every other roll, she'd turn the ball of snow to make the packing on of snow more even.

What a smart idea.

He mirrored her technique, and before long they had the bottom and the middle. Seth looked around the base of the trees for items they could use to bring the snowman to life while Lillian rolled the top piece that would be his head.

With rocks to form his mouth, nose and eyes, Seth stood back to observe their handiwork. "He's missing something—don't you think so?"

Lillian tipped Seth's hat off his head and placed it on their snowman.

Seth put his hand under his chin thoughtfully. "He looks kind of like Bishop Troyer. What do you think?"

Lillian laughed. "You're right, he does."

Seth pulled Lillian's hands in his. "Do you think he'll marry us?"

Lillian nearly lost her breath at his question.

"What?"

Seth knelt down before her. "Lillian, I've loved you for a very long time, and was too much of a coward to tell you. But I promise you that if you marry me, I'll spend the rest of my life making up for lost time with you. I need you in my life to keep me grounded. You make me happy, and I can't imagine my life without you."

Lillian couldn't believe what she was hearing. She'd longed for this moment for so long, and now that it was happening, she was having a tough time believing it.

Happy tears welled up in her eyes as she threw her arms around his neck. "I love you, Seth Miller. Yes I will marry you."

CHAPTER 30

Lillian rushed into the house after Seth dropped her off. She couldn't wait to tell Hannah about the proposal. Almost before she finished her story, the two of them were crying happy tears, and Hannah insisted they have a double wedding. That was only three weeks away, but she would discuss it with Seth, knowing he would think it was a *gut* idea. They'd already been in love for so long that waiting would just be cruel.

On Christmas day, members of the community gathered in the garden of the Miller Bed & Breakfast for the double wedding ceremony. A light snow fluttered down from the heavens just for them, it would seem, and Lillian was so nervous she could barely contain herself. Deciding to wear the dress that Hannah had made for her so she could catch Seth's attention, they'd made a sheer white apron to go over the top of it that matched the one Hannah wore.

As they stood before the Bishop waiting for the blessing of the marriage, Lillian looked over at Seth who was grinning from one ear to the other.

I'm the luckiest woman in the world. Denki, Gott for blessing me with more than I could have ever asked for.

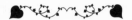

When the last of the wedding guests left the B&B, Seth took his bride upstairs to the room they would stay in for the night. He sat on the bed and pulled Lillian toward him, pressing his lips gently against hers. She leaned into the kiss with a sense of urgency that made Seth eager for her, but they had the rest of their lives to be together, and he intended to take his time learning everything about her. For now, he had a gift for her—a gift that he felt would help them begin their lives together.

Reaching in his pocket, he pulled out a tiny object and stopped kissing her long enough to slip it into her hand.

Lillian turned the rock over in her hand a few times, and chuckled to herself knowingly.

"What is this for?"

She knew what it was, but she wanted to hear him say it.

Seth smiled. "It's the first keepsake for the spice box—something to begin earmarking our life together. It's one of the rocks from our snowman."

Lillian couldn't help but laugh as she pulled out a similar rock from the fold of her wedding dress. "I have one too, and I'd almost forgotten about it. I took the poor snowman's nose when you weren't looking."

Seth laughed. "If that isn't the best sign that you were meant to be my *fraa,* I don't know what is."

He kissed her again, letting his lips trail to her ear.

"I have a feeling we're going to need a bigger box for our mementos."

Lillian let the rocks slip from her hands and leaned into her husband's kiss. She couldn't have agreed with Seth more, but for some things, Lillian doubted she would need a keepsake box to remember them. She would keep each moment of their love tucked away in her heart for always.

THE END

NORWEGIAN SUGAR COOKIES
(Cookie and frosting recipes were handed down to me from my grandmother)

<u>INGREDIENTS</u>
1 cup real butter, softened
1 ½ cups sugar
½ cup powdered sugar
2 eggs
½ tsp. vanilla
½ tsp. almond extract
½ tsp. ground nutmeg
½ tsp. salt
1 tbsp. baking powder
1 tsp. cream of tartar
¼ cup heavy cream
5 cups sifted flour

Mix together butter, sugar and eggs. Add vanilla, almond extract and cream. In a separate bowl, mix dry ingredients. Fold in flour mixture slowly until well blended. Flatten dough between two pieces of parchment paper and place in refrigerator for two hours. Roll our chilled dough to desired thickness and cut shapes with cookie cutters. Bake at 350 degrees for 6-10 minutes, or until golden around the edges, depending on the thickness. Cool, then, frost and decorate.

FROSTING
¼ cup butter
½ tsp. vanilla
2-3 tbsp. cardamom (to taste)
¼ cup heavy cream
4 cups powdered sugar

Under the Mulberry Tree
Book 3

Samantha Jillian Bayarr

CHAPTER 1

"What do you mean he's not my real father?"

Abby was shaking, while aiming imaginary daggers at her *mamm.*

Lizzie reached out to her daughter, but when Abby flinched away, she slowly retracted her hand.

Abby stood up from the porch swing abruptly and stood near the railing. A slight wind blew stray hairs from beneath her prayer *kapp,* which she angrily pushed behind her ear. The warm October sun shone brightly on her cheeks, heating her almost to agitation, but she wouldn't turn to face her *mamm.*

Abby picked at splattered vegetables on her apron, silence weighing heavily between her and her *mamm.* If only she hadn't confided in her *mamm* about the teasing from her peers about Jonah Beiler, whom she just realized was not really her cousin.

They'd spent most of the day at a canning bee, and the *menner* had been there to help bring in the bushels of fruits and vegetables for canning. At the noon meal, she'd sat with the youth until her cousin, Jonah, decided to tell the others about their beautiful, forbidden kiss under the mulberry tree in the school yard. No one had seen them do it, and they'd made a pact that it would never happen again. But there he sat, betraying her confidence.

Before she realized, everyone was calling them *kissing cousins.* Abby couldn't take it anymore and left the Miller's house. When her *mamm* caught up to her later at home, Abby had no choice but to tell her about what happened, but denied the kiss ever happened. If only it had been that easy for her or her *mamm* to tell the truth. Then none of this would have mattered. Her love for Jonah would not have felt like a sin, and her peers would never have teased her since she and Jonah were not blood-related after all.

Abby swung around angrily. "How could you have lied to me my entire life? I'm almost twenty years old; you could have told me a long time ago and spared me and everyone else a lot of trouble. Does *Daed*...I mean, *Jacob,* know about this, or did you lie to him too?"

Lizzie sighed. "Yes, he knows, Abby, but you have to understand *why* I lied."

"There is *never* any reason to tell a lie this big! Who is it *Mother?* Who is my real father? And why have you kept him from me all these years?"

Lizzie tried to remain calm. "Do you remember why we moved here?"

Abby rolled her eyes. "Of course I do. Because that guy Eddie was after us...oh heavens no...*please* tell me my real father is *not* Eddie the drug addict!"

Lizzie's face drained of all color except for the blazing red of her cheeks. "I'm sorry, Abby, but it's true."

Abby couldn't breathe. Her whole life had been a lie. She was the child of a drug addict—a man who was dead. Tears pooled in her eyes as she stared down the long drive that led to the main road. The wind blew orange and red leaves across the lawn. Even they had purpose. As for her, she no longer had a father.

Abby brushed past her *mamm* and into the house. She took the stairs two at a time until she reached the top.

In her room, she pushed on her heavy bureau, determined to block the door that had no lock. The feet of the large piece of furniture dug into the hardwood floor, but she finally wedged it in front of the door. Then she threw herself onto her bed, and began to sob into the quilt she and her *mamm* had made together.

A light knock sounded at the door.

Abby turned slightly. "Go away *mother.* I'll never believe another word that comes from your mouth!"

Abby quieted her sobbing long enough to listen to the fading footfalls of her *mamm,* letting her know that she'd given up the fight.

She slid down from the bed onto the floor, where she retrieved the small suitcase from under her bed that she'd brought with her when she and her *mamm* had come to the community. Tossing it up on the bed, she filled it with her few belongings, including the two thousand dollars she'd saved from working for her aunt Lillian at the bakery. Picking up the packed suitcase, Abby crossed the room and pushed open her window and tossed the suitcase out the window, watching mindlessly as it hit the front lawn below.

Pushing the bureau back in the corner of her room, she ran down the stairs and out the front door, her *mamm* fast on her heels.

"Abby, *kume* sit back and down and talk to me."

Abby turned; her face flush. "I don't want to hear another word that comes from your mouth ever again. I'm leaving here and never coming back. There is nothing for me here but a life full of lies. "

Her last words to her *mamm* had stung them both that day, and Abby had not been able to remove them, or the look on her *mamm's* face from her memory since the day she spoke them five long years before.

CHAPTER 2

FIVE YEARS LATER...

Stepping off the bus, Abby wondered if she'd really gotten all the rebellion out of her system after spending the last five years among the *Englischers,* and if she was really ready to return home and make amends with her *mamm.* Her *mamm's* reaction to her return would determine if she was truly ready to be baptized into the church and make a life for herself in the Amish community.

Now, at nearly twenty-five years old, she knew it would be tough to go back, and the possibility of running into Jonah Beiler after all this time would be even tougher. Over the years, she'd had time to get over his admission about kissing her under the mulberry tree, but the embarrassment had made her swear off boys forever.

Jonah had made a career out of teasing her, and up until the point where he told everyone about the their shared kiss, the worst thing he'd ever said about her was that she'd kissed a frog down at Goose Pond when she hadn't. She was sure Jonah had no idea the impact his lie that day would have on her entire life, but that didn't make it any easier to forgive him. Jonah was three years older than Abby, and she felt he should know better than to do such a thing. Even now, she feared they would forever be branded as *kissing cousins.*

Jonah had been a thorn in her side from the moment they'd first met—always teasing her and getting her into trouble. But as the years passed, they became closer. And when Abby turned eighteen, their relationship changed entirely. They started to develop feelings for each other that others might consider an unholy crush. It wasn't until she went home and complained to her *mamm* about the youth teasing her, that she discovered the truth. The full impact of her *mamm*'s lie had changed her entire life.

But that was in the past, and she was prepared to make amends with everyone—even Jonah. As for his sister, Becca, she'd missed her wedding to Levi Graber. Abby and Becca had been best friends, in addition to their supposed blood-relation to one another. There was a lot of lost time she needed to make up for with her friend, and she hoped the time had not caused a break in their friendship.

There were a number of different reasons Abby left that day, her *mamm's* lies being at the top of that list. If the truth be told, the idea had been building in Abby ever since she and her *mamm* had first stepped foot onto Amish soil. She'd been trying to break free, always feeling a nagging in the back of her mind that she didn't fit in. When she discovered why, suddenly everything made perfect sense. The breaking point for Abby began with her love for Jonah Beiler, and ended with her *mamm's* lies. Those lies had torn her away from the only father she'd ever known, and from Jonah, who could have been her husband had she known it was not a sin to love him.

Her decision to leave the community stemmed more from her desire to escape the life she'd felt trapped in for the previous nine years. She loved her parents, but when she discovered that Jacob Yoder was not her real father, she no longer needed an excuse to leave; it was already well-formed in her mind. She'd felt betrayed by her *mamm*, and she pitied Jacob for accepting the responsibility of raising her when he knew he couldn't possibly be her real father. Finding out she was really half *Englisch* was enough to make her want to revisit her past.

The fight between her and her *mamm* escalated to beyond reason and had prompted her to do the very same thing her *mamm* had done when she was about the same age—run.

But here she was, about to walk back into the Amish community that had claimed her childhood. The only difference between her return and that of her *mamm*, was that she wasn't toting a child along with her.

After leaving home, she'd gone back to the same small town where she'd spent the first ten years of her life, and had worked at The Brick Oven, a large bakery in the historic district downtown. Having developed a love and obvious talent for creating Amish pastries and pies that drew in customers for miles, Abby's confections kept the bakery from going under in a weak economy. She hadn't planned on returning to Ohio, but she'd missed the friends she'd left behind as a child, and wanted to revisit the childhood memories. But they hadn't quite turned out to be what she'd remembered them to be.

The home they'd lived in was now run-down and in a bad part of town. Maybe it had always been that way, but she'd thought things differently as a child. She hadn't even meant to stay for so long in the battered town, but when she landed the job at the bakery, time stood still. For the first time, she felt she had something that was hers alone. Then she reunited with her best friend, Rachel. They'd become roommates and had a lot of fun together—in the beginning.

When Rachel began to bring home boyfriends to spend the night, Abby pulled away from her and began working more hours at the bakery, much to her employer's delight. She loved making Amish treats that customers would line up out the door just to get a taste of. There were always several standing orders every day from her regular customers who had come to depend on her sweet creations to keep them satisfied.

But when the letter came from *Onkel* Seth explaining the hardship he and *Aenti* Lillian had endured, she couldn't turn down his plea asking for help with the bakery. At that point, Abby knew it was time go home to her *familye* in Indiana; no matter how much she dreaded facing her *mamm,* she couldn't pass up the opportunity to go home to the Amish community where she knew in her heart, she belonged.

While in Ohio, she'd managed to find Eddie's older sister, and his parents. It was nice to find family she hadn't known she had, but it just wasn't the same. True, she'd adapted to life in the Amish community and had accepted

Jacob as her *daed,* but having blood relatives in Ohio seemed to make a difference—in the beginning. Still, she felt alone there, and lacked a true sense of belonging. The only place she'd felt completely accepted was at home in Indiana with her *mamm* and Jacob—her *daed.*

CHAPTER 3

Abby felt overwhelmed as she pulled her suitcase behind her across the bus depot—until her eyes locked onto the last person she expected to see.

"*Daed.* I'm so glad to see you.*"*

Abby threw her arms around the aging man, a sense of home claiming her emotions.

"I'll always be your *daed,"* Jacob whispered.

Abby pulled away, wishing she'd worn the plain dress she'd left home in, instead of the *Englisch* clothing. She wrapped her coat around her, trying to hide her attire as she searched her *daed's* face for acceptance. Abby felt he looked older than she'd remembered, and his eyes held sadness behind the smile he so desperately clung to. His hair and beard had thinned, and both were peppered with more gray than the last time she'd seen him. She suddenly felt responsible for the crease in his brow that suggested more worry than she cared to see, but his welcoming nature would never let her take the blame. Still, she felt suddenly very selfish for leaving without telling him goodbye when she'd run off five years ago.

"I'm so sorry I left, *Daed.* How's *Mamm?"*

His smile widened. "She's eager to see you. Let's get you home where you belong."

Home. Could it really be that easy?

Jacob picked up his daughter's *Englisch* suitcase, looking past the blue jeans and form-fitting shirt she wore, and tossed it in the back of the buggy.

At least she hasn't cut her hair.

Abby climbed into the buggy feeling a little strange sitting next to her *daed,* as it was apparent to anyone looking at him that he was Amish. She, for all anyone knew, was an *Englischer.* Her feelings were conflicted at the moment, but she intended to honor her parents by dressing Amish while back at home. The problem was, she didn't *feel* very Amish at the moment. Before she left the community, she'd stopped questioning who she was, but when her *mamm* told her the truth about Jacob, she suddenly felt lost in her place in the community and didn't feel she could stay there. But could she go home now and put it all behind her? She wasn't sure of much at the moment, except she wanted to try—for the sake of her family.

They rode in silence, leaving too much time for thoughts of regret to seep into Abby's mind. She had tried to push back the guilt about running from her family for nearly five years, and now it was rushing back in a sea of bad memories and last words. She and her *mamm* had written to each other over the years, but they'd managed to avoid talking about that final day when everything escalated

She knew now what she didn't know then—that her *mamm's* lies were only to protect her from a dangerous man who had less paternal love for her than the ground she walked on. God's green earth was far kinder to her than her biological father had been capable of, and she felt bad that it had taken her so long to realize it. The land and the community that resided in it were all that she needed.

Her family had taught her to appreciate that such simple things were the very core of who she was, and trying to find herself among the *Englisch* would never fill her heart the way home could.

Abby knew she had a lot of fences to mend, and she had to start with the man sitting quietly beside her, who was more of a father to her than she felt she deserved at the moment.

"I was surprised to see you at the bus depot— especially after I never even said "goodbye" to you when I left. I'm sorry for acting so immature. I love you, *Daed.* I hope you know that."

Jacob clicked at the mare, steering her off the main road. "Abby, there's no reason to bring up the past when it's been forgiven. You're home now, and that's all that matters."

Abby shifted nervously in her seat. "I want you to know that I'm home to stay."

Jacob kept his eyes on the road. "I'm glad to hear that. So you'll be taking the baptism then?"

She didn't need to wait for her *mamm's* approval of her return. Having her *dead* pick her up was confirmation enough for Abby. "*Jah.* I'd like to go see Bishop Troyer first thing tomorrow morning. Will you drive me?"

The corners of Jacob's mouth turned up into a smile. "I think that's a *gut* idea, but let's get you home first; your *mamm* has been waiting a long time to see you."

The mare increased speed as they pulled onto the long drive to the house. The horse knew she was home, even if Abby didn't. Despite the familiar row of snow-laden oak trees lining the lane, and the icy pond, it was difficult for Abby's heart to accept. Anticipation and dread filled her entire being at the thought of seeing her *mamm* again.

CHAPTER 4

Abby stepped down from buggy in front of the house, and stood there while Jacob put away the horse. She willed her feet to move, but she couldn't get them past the freshly shoveled walkway that led to the snow-covered porch. Abby listened to the wind push at the porch swing, weighed down with snow, the rusted chain squeaking in protest. Remembering how the sound used to comfort her, she shuffled her feet toward the steps, hoping her wobbly legs would support her effort to reach the front door.

The familiar sound of the door hinge made her look up in time to meet her *mamm's* soulful eyes. Her *mamm* knew the difficulty Abby faced without even having to say a word. She, herself, was the prodigal son in female form, and she, too, had come home looking for redemption.

Tears pooled in Lizzie's eyes and her heart beat out of sync at the sight of her daughter. Despite the *Englisch* clothes, and the long hair cascading from beneath her pink, knitted hat, Lizzie could still see her daughter beneath all of it.

She didn't wait for an invitation. She hurried down the porch steps and pulled Abby close, taking in the smell of her grown up child. How she'd missed that smell of baking spices that had clung to Abby from the day she'd made her first snitz pie. It was the scent only a mother could love, and she'd longed for it for too long.

Abby succumbed to her *mamm's* embrace that felt like a cool breeze on a hot day, quenching a need that brought relief to her very soul. All thoughts of the past dwindled away in that one embrace, leaving her wondering why she'd ever left home in the first place. She felt suddenly very safe and protected, like a baby chick under its momma's wing. It was a feeling she never wanted to lose again.

"I missed you so much, *Mamm.* I'm so sorry for leaving the way I did. Please forgive me for breaking your heart."

Lizzie kissed her daughter's hair. "I'm the one who needs forgiveness. I promise I will never tell another lie as long as I live."

Abby sighed, her warm breath creating a vapor into the cold air. "Let's go inside where it's warm. I could use a cup of your hot cocoa with a dollop of whipped cream and cinnamon on top."

Lizzie smiled. "That's a *gut* idea. And we'll make some for your *daed*—I mean, Jacob."

Abby turned to her *mamm,* a serious expression clouding her face. "He's my *daed.*"

Lizzie's eyes moistened with tears again. "You know he loves you like you were his own *dochder.*"

Abby nodded. "I *am* his *dochder.* I know that now.*"

Nothing more needed to be said about it. They both knew where the other stood on the matter, and for once, they both agreed.

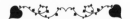

Abby ran a hand along the handmade quilt she and her *mamm* had made at one of the quilting bees when they'd first arrived in the community fifteen years ago. She recalled the feel of the gathering that had welcomed them, and worked hard to provide her *mamm* with a belated wedding dowry after she'd married Jacob—her *daed.* Funny how that word no longer felt foreign to her the way it had for so long after she'd run off.

Abby examined more closely the squares of fabric she'd stitched, noting the difference in the quality versus that of her *mamm.* Remembering the stories told to her about her *grossmammi* attending quilting bees with her *mamm* at the same age brought a lump to her throat. There were many times over the past five years that Abby had wished she'd taken the quilt with her. None of that mattered now. She was finally home to stay.

Hoisting her suitcase up onto her childhood bed, she determined to unpack only the necessities and leave the rest in there. She would store it under the bed until she could figure out what to do with the *Englisch* clothes it contained. From a set of hooks near the door, she lifted a purple dress. The material was freshly ironed, and it smelled of winter air. She was certain her *mamm* had hung it on the outside line in anticipation of her homecoming. She always loved the smell of clothes drying outside—even in winter, and her *mamm* had made it even more welcoming.

Pulling the freshly laundered dress over her head, she was reminded of the first time she put on a plain dress. She had made such a fuss with her *mamm* that day, fighting with her and complaining. She wondered if it would have made a difference if she'd learned the truth back then. It was very possible that they would have never come to live in the community, and she would never have known Jacob as the loving *daed* that he is. Abby had been the most unfair to him when she'd left home, and her siblings—especially Caleb, had taken her sudden disappearance very hard.

After stuffing the suitcase under the bed, Abby walked toward the door to exit the room. The tell-tale squeak of the loose floorboard caused her heart to quicken. Pausing, she toyed with her emotions over the contents of the small space beneath the floorboard that held her hidden treasures away from the rest of the world. Unable to resist a small peek, she knelt down and pulled back the braided rug. Sticking her finger into the small knothole, she yanked on the resistant board until it gave way. She sat on her haunches and stared into the rectangular opening for the longest time, savoring the contents as if they were relished jewels.

Blowing the dust from the opening, she lifted the Hello Kitty shirt from its neatly folded state and held it up for examination. Her *mamm's* cell phone lay at the bottom as evidence of a lie that Abby had told regarding its whereabouts. The items were, at the age of ten, her last links to the *Englisch* world she'd left behind. The only value they held now was to serve as proof of a life better left behind.

CHAPTER 5

In the kitchen, Abby found her only sister, Rachel, helping her *mamm* with the evening meal. At nearly fifteen, it was apparent that Rachel was a lot more comfortable in the kitchen than Abby had been at that age. Awkwardness claimed Abby as she looked for an opportunity to blend with her *mamm's* and Rachel's routine. Taking a deep breath, Abby stepped in and pulled the dishes from the shelf to set the table. She knew if she didn't take charge of the situation, her younger sibling would never respect her, and would more than likely treat her as an outsider.

"*Denki, Mamm,* for washing my dresses and hanging them outside to dry. They smell like home. "

Lizzie smiled at her daughter. "I wanted you to feel at home."

Abby looked at her *mamm* thoughtfully. "I do. How are *Onkel* Seth and *Aenti* Lillian? I'm eager to see them Sunday at church service."

Lizzie's eyes showed stress at the mention of her brother and his *wife*. "They weren't in attendance at the service two weeks ago, and when we tried to visit, Lillian wouldn't get out of bed to greet us. She didn't even want to attend the *boppli's* funeral, but my *bruder* enforced it. Did your *onkel* tell you they had to do emergency surgery at the hospital to remove her uterus? She nearly bled to death, and my *bruder* would have been burying her too. The *boppli* was stillborn; there was nothing they could do to save him."

Tears choked Abby. Her uncle hadn't said any of that in his brief letter to her—but how could he? No wonder he needed someone to take over the bakery.

"Can we try to visit Sunday after the service?"

Lizzie forced a smile. "We can always try. I'm sure she'd be happy to see you."

Abby breathed a silent prayer for her *aenti*. She felt guilty for not being there for her in her time of need. Lillian was one more person with whom Abby had a lot of making up to do.

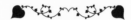

Jonah pushed open the large, double doors of the oversized barn in which he built buggies. The cold night air welcomed him after a long day of work, and his empty stomach alerted him he'd missed another meal. He looked toward the end of his property where the Miller's bakery sat closed, just as it had for over a month. When Seth had told him he'd sent for Abby's return so she could run the bakery in his *fraa's* absence, Jonah had mixed feelings about the situation. Though his stomach would be happy to have fresh baked goods from the bakery, he was a little more than apprehensive about seeing Abby again.

Jonah made his way through the deep snow to the small house he'd built on the property he'd acquired a year ago from Efram Stoltzfus. Since Lillian and Seth had set up house at Hiram Miller's farm after they married, Jonah had been able to purchase all but the small lot where Lillian's bakery had stood. Jonah was happy to purchase the land, as he wanted to expand on his buggy making business. After his *daed's* death, Jonah gave the house to his newlywed sister since they'd wanted a bigger place to raise a family. The vacant land Jonah purchased had originally been for Lillian's dowry, but Seth's unwillingness to leave his *daed* had turned into an opportunity for Jonah.

Come Monday, Jonah knew he would have to be on his guard around Abby, fearing his sinful feelings for his cousin would return. After Abby had left the community, he'd had to confess to the Bishop and take the sole responsibility for their error in judgment regarding the forbidden kiss.

Though Jonah knew his sweet tooth would probably draw him to the bakery again, he would need to keep his distance from Abby, especially with how vulnerable he'd felt when he learned of her return to the community.

He'd felt responsible for her hasty departure, despite her *mamm* telling him it was something Abby just needed to get "out of her system". He couldn't help but wonder if her reaction to breaking her trust that last day he'd seen her had everything to do with her decision to leave. Despite all the praying and confessing to God over his love for Abby, he felt the worst over hurting her with his foolish betrayal.

Jonah was determined to keep his feelings in check, and to make sure he didn't hurt Abby again—even if that meant staying away from the bakery. It would be tough to do since the bakery sat at the edge of his property, and he would have to drive by whenever he went anywhere. He couldn't avoid her indefinitely—not that he wanted to.

Abby cuddled up in the warm quilt that smelled like winter sunshine. She was exhausted, but sleep eluded her. She would be baptized tomorrow, putting to rest the *Englisch* part of her. Having spent the past five years among the *Englisch,* she knew there was nothing there for her. Despite having Eddie's family; her true family bonds were here in the Amish community. The odds of finding a suitable mate in either community were against her, but she was determined to devote herself to family.

A light knock interrupted her reverie.

"Are you awake?" Rachel's whisper was barely audible, but the quietness of the house allowed her voice to permeate the barrier between them.

Abby sat up, noting the bright moonlight streaming in through her window. *"Jah. Kume."*

Rachel opened the door slowly, and stood quietly in the doorway. Abby patted the edge of her bed, beckoning her sister to sit with her. With downcast eyes, Rachel walked timidly toward the bed and lowered herself cautiously to the edge.

Abby slipped the corner of quilt around the shivering child. "It's very cold tonight, *jah?*"

Rachel leaned back and cradled the spare pillow under her arm, leaning on one elbow to face Abby.

"I'm glad you're home because now I will have someone to tell all my secrets to."

Shocked at the strange turnaround in her sister's attitude, Abby leaned on her elbow facing Rachel, eager to listen to all she had to say.

CHAPTER 6

Despite the cold snow blowing into the buggy, Abby's hands and neck were on fire and damp with sweat. Was it too late to rethink the decision to get baptized? She'd prayed about it late into the night after Rachel had finally gone back to her own bed. Her sister's words kept ringing in her ears, leaving her wondering what the community would think of her return. Her brother, Caleb, still hadn't spoken a word to her, but thanks to Rachel's secrets, Abby knew why.

It was no secret to Abby that Caleb was bothered by her hasty departure, and her return that echoed the same. But nothing had prepared her to hear from Rachel that Caleb had tried to convince her family to shun her after she'd left the community.

The few letters she'd received from her *mamm* while she was away had hinted that Caleb had not approved of her actions. Since no one else was home the day she left, Lizzie had kept the truth from the rest of the family, confiding only in her husband, who knew the circumstances. Abby would have preferred the truth to be out in the open, but it wasn't her story to tell—it was her parent's story.

Another thought pricked Abby's heart. How was she to fully confess to the Bishop and accept her baptism if she wasn't able to explain her extended absence from the community without betraying her *mamm?* She couldn't. The only way to handle it was to take full responsibility for leaving, and keep her *mamm's* lie out of it. It wasn't her lie to tell, and it would have no bearing on her confession. In her heart, this was what she wanted to do more than anything—to be baptized and remain in the community. Being free from her *mamm's* secrets and lies would make it a lot easier.

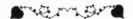

At dinner, Abby was surprised when Caleb asked her to get him another slice of pie. She wasn't sure if it was for the sake of the familt that he'd spoken, or because she had received the baptism, but she was about to find out.

Caleb pushed his chair back from the table and locked his eyes on Abby. "May I have a word with you out in the barn?"

Abby looked to her *mamm* with pleading eyes.

Lizzie shooed her *dochder* with her hand. "Go on now and talk to your *bruder* while I take care of the dishes."

For the first time in five years, it hit her that Caleb wasn't her brother after all, and it felt foreign to hear her *mamm* say it. She paused, but when her *mamm* reminded her to put on her coat, she snapped out of her conflicting thoughts.

Caleb turned on the gas lights that hung from the rafters of barn, and closed the door against the snow.

"I brought you out here because I didn't think Rachel and Samuel needed to hear what I wanted to say to you."

Abby looked at him sternly. "Rachel told me you wanted the *familye* to shun me after I left five years ago."

Caleb busied himself by picking up a broom and sweeping the already clean floor between the stalls. "If you hadn't taken the baptism today, I would have insisted on it. When you first came to live with us, I was too young to understand the impact it would have in my life to have an *Englischer* as a *schweschder"*

Does he know we're not related?

"At the time, all I cared about was having a new *mamm,* and I admit, she's been very *gut* to me and to my *daed.* But if you are going to reside here, you need to get rid of the *Englisch* clothes and the *Englisch* ways. Put it all behind you because I don't want you to influence our *bruder* and *schweschder* negatively."

Abby put her hands on her hips. "The last time I checked , *Daed* was the head of this *familye,* not you. And this is *my familye* too, not just yours."

"For the last five years you have not shown that they're your *familye.* What of that?"

Abby started to walk away and then turned abruptly. "I don't have to put up with you talking to me. You aren't even…"

Abby bit her tongue. She couldn't finish her sentence without exposing her parent's lies to Caleb, who seemed oblivious to the truth. He wasn't her brother, but she wouldn't hurt him with the truth, no matter how unfair he was being toward her.

"We're grown up now, Abby, and we're going to have to learn to treat each other as adults. We only had a few years together as children, and now we must put our grownup troubles behind us for the sake of the *familye."*

Abby swallowed the tears that tried to make their way from her throat to her eyes. She wasn't the only one that

had been hurt by the lie that her *mamm* and *daed* had chosen
to keep hidden.

"I'm here to stay, dear *bruder*. I'm sorry if my
actions hurt you or the rest of the *familye*. I won't give you
any cause for concern. My loyalties are to this *familye* from
here on out."

Caleb's look softened. He reached for Abby, and she
allowed him to tuck her under the comfort of his arm as they
walked out of the barn. "I missed you, Abby."

CHAPTER 7

Abby looked out her bedroom window at the fresh
blanket of snow that covered the ground, and caused a white
shadow to form along the tree branches. From this view,
with the sun barely peeking over the horizon, her world
seemed serene and without problems. She silently thanked
God for the chance to make a fresh start in the community,
and for the strength to overcome her fears of attending her
first church service.

Abby chose a dark pink dress for the service. Though
she knew she needed to put aside any residual feelings she

may have for Jonah, she couldn't help but wonder if he'd thought of her over the past five years. It was foolish for her to hope that they could ever have a future together, given that the entire community, including Jonah, believed them to be first cousins. She was determined to keep busy with the bakery—anything to take her mind off Jonah. That wouldn't be an easy task. After all, a girl never forgets her first love— she carries it with her all her life.

If it be Your wille, Gotte, please bless me with a husband. Please help me to forget Jonah.

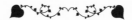

Jonah fidgeted with his hat as he walked into the Graber home just before the service began. Deciding he didn't want the temptation to see Abby during the service, he took a seat on the end of the front bench.

Within minutes, Caleb pushed his way onto the bench next to him. "Why are you sitting way up here this morning?"

Jonah cleared his throat. "Just felt like a change is all."

Caleb nudged him. "You know Abby's back."

"*Jah,* I heard. You never mentioned she was coming back. Didn't you know either?"

Caleb picked up the *Ausbund* from the bench beside him and opened it to the first hymn. "*Jah,* I knew about it, but I didn't say anything because I didn't think she would really come back, much less get baptized yesterday."

Jonah raised an eyebrow. "She was baptized yesterday?"

"*Jah,* I was surprised too. But if she intended to live in our *haus,* she needed to make her commitment to *Gott* and the community."

The singing of the hymn began, and Jonah found it hard to concentrate enough to sing along. Since Abby had taken the baptism, that would mean she would remain in the community. How was he going to avoid her? Did he even feel the same for her?

It doesn't matter. My love for her is forbidden. Please Gott, help me to forget Abby, and send me a fraa.

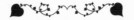

As the service neared its end, Abby left her seat beside Rachel and went into the kitchen to help the women set out the food for the shared meal. She'd noticed her brother sitting with a handsome man at the front of the room, and hoped he would introduce her. Knowing the man was single from his lack of a beard, she hoped to make a good impression in case he wasn't betrothed. Maybe there was hope for her to find a husband in the community after all.

Before long, Abby was so busy serving the *menner,* that she didn't notice Caleb when he walked up in front of her. Her brother's friend had her back to them, but when he turned around, Abby nearly dropped the plate of food she had extended to Caleb.

It was Jonah—no mistake about it.

Abby allowed herself to peruse his physique, noting that he'd outgrown his skinny youth. He was now slim, but strong; the outline of his chest and arms showed muscle that he never had before. She liked it. When she finally gazed into his eyes, her pulse raced, as she lost herself in their blue depths, just as she had many times as a teenager. She wanted to throw her arms around him and tell him how much she'd missed him, but she couldn't. Giddiness rushed through her as he smiled at her.

Jonah's eyes darted nervously between Caleb and Abby, who seemed to be shocked to see him. But when his eyes locked with hers, he saw a familiarity that made him swoon all over again. If it was possible, she was more beautiful than he'd remembered. Her hazel eyes were welcoming, her milky skin accented by the flattering blush of her cheeks. More than ever, he wanted to pull her into his arms and declare his love for her, but it was forbidden. There was no denying he still loved her, but he had to keep it buried, for the community would not allow a marriage between first cousins any more than the *Englischers* would.

Abby shook herself from her reverie. "Jonah, it's so *gut* to see you again."

Jonah nodded nervously. "*Jah.* It's been a long time—five years?"

Abby cast her eyes downward. "*Jah.* It's been too long. But I'm back now—to stay. I was baptized yesterday."

Jonah wasn't sure if he was happy about that or not. "*Jah,* your *bruder* told me. *Das gut.* Welcome back, cousin."

The words stung Abby. She wanted to scream out that she wasn't his cousin—that she loved him—still. Timidity and propriety were taught among the community, but she almost didn't care if she broke the rules. She wanted Jonah to know they weren't cousins. But she couldn't do that without dishonoring her *mamm* and *daed.*

"*Denki,* Cousin." Abby nearly choked on the words, but they needed to be said. For the sake of having them sink in, if for nothing else.

CHAPTER 8

Jacob pulled the family buggy into his brother-in law's yard. After assisting Lizzie out of the buggy, he offered the same to his *kinner,* but they all bound out like white rabbits hopping in the deep snow. All except for Abby, who lingered in the back, seemingly lost in thought.

Jacob reached for her. "Abby, *kume.* I thought you were eager to see your *Onkel* Seth and *Aenti* Lillian."

Abby looked at her *daed* quizzically. How long had she been sitting there daydreaming of Jonah? Was it possible her *daed* could tell what she was thinking about?

Abby dipped her head, hoping he wouldn't see her flaming cheeks, and took the hand he extended to her. Pushing the lap quilt aside, she stepped from the buggy into the deep snow, wishing she'd worn her boots instead of her brown loafers. She had decided on them when they left the house a few hours ago, thinking they would look nicer with her dress. Now, she was paying for such thoughts of vanity with cold, wet feet.

Inside, Seth scrambled to push open the draperies on the windows to let the bright sun into the rooms that seemed lifeless and unkempt. Abby ignored the sullenness of her uncle's face as she threw herself into his waiting arms.

"I've missed you so much, little Abbster, and so has your *aenti.* "

Seth put her down.

"How is she, *Onkel* Seth? The truth."

Seth hesitated.

"I'm no longer a young child. I'm all grown up as you can see, and I need to see *Aenti* Lillian. Where is she?"

Her *onkel* looked worn out and defeated, but he pointed toward the back of the house. "She's in bed. She won't leave the room, and cradles the *boppli's* blanket like he's still alive."

Seth choked back tears.

Lizzie stood at her daughter's side. "Maybe you should leave her alone. She needs time to heal."

"Please, *Onkel* Seth. I feel terrible enough for not being here when it happened." Abby lowered her voice almost to a whisper. "But I would never be able to live with myself if I didn't at least *try* to reach out to her."

Seth nodded his consent, and Abby didn't give him a chance to change his mind. She practically ran to the room where her aunt had holed up in since her baby's unexpected death.

Abby knocked lightly on the door, but she didn't get an answer. Opening the door cautiously, she searched the darkened room for signs of her aunt. A noise from the corner of the room brought Abby's eyes into focus on her aunt, who rocked in a chair mindlessly, a blank expression spread across her face. Abby walked softly toward her, careful not to startle the woman. She placed her hand carefully across her aunt's arm, speaking her name quietly.

Lillian looked up at her with swollen, red-rimmed eyes. Abby knelt down beside her just in time to embrace her as she collapsed in her arms. Abby rocked the crying woman as she hummed softly the same German lullaby her *mamm* had hummed to her well into her teens. It was the only thing Abby's *mamm* had remembered from her own *mamm* before she'd passed, and it was the only thing Abby knew to do to comfort her aunt.

Abby eyed the empty cradle in the opposite corner of the room, and wondered why her uncle had not removed such a grave reminder of their loss and packed it out of sight. She would have to broach the subject lightly to avoid upsetting him more than he already was. It broke Abby's heart that her aunt and uncle had lost their only child. Knowing they could never have any of their own had to be even more devastating. It was something Abby could only imagine, but from Lillian's sobbing, she was beginning to feel the strain of it right along with her.

After a while, Lillian's sobs turned to sniffles, and then began to subside altogether. "Every time I feel like I can't cry anymore, it seems I have more to get out. I'm sorry for losing control like that."

Abby felt badly for her. "Don't apologize, *Aenti.* Crying is *Gott's* gift to us. It allows us to release our sorrows to Him."

Lillian looked at her niece seriously. "*Gott* didn't save my *boppli.* Why?"

"None of us knows what *Gotte's Wille* is for our lives. But if we seek Him in our time of need, He will reveal His plan to us. Have you prayed about this yet, *Aenti?*"

Lillian pushed herself back into the rocking chair and held the small quilt to her face. "What's the point? My *boppli* is gone, and I can't have any more because of the surgery."

Abby moved in closer to her *aenti.* "Have you considered adopting a *boppli?* The woman who owns the bakery I worked for in Ohio has a teenage *dochder* who is pregnant. She is looking for a *familye* to adopt her *boppli.*"

At Abby's suggestion, Lillian's expression changed. "That won't bring back my *boppli.* I'm tired. Can you please go now? I need to lie down."

Abby stood, feeling worse than when she'd first seen her *aenti.* "I'm sorry if I upset you. But please think about what I said."

Lillian shooed her with her hand as she shuffled toward the bed and collapsed onto it. "Please close the door when you leave. And don't let anyone else in here. I'm too tired to visit."

Abby swallowed the lump in her throat and left the room, feeling as though she'd done more than damage to her poor aunt instead of helping as she'd intended to do.

CHAPTER 9

"What did you say to her to upset her so much, Abby?"

Abby sighed helplessly. "I might have suggested she consider adopting a *boppli*. I told her about my old boss's *dochder* who is pregnant and looking for a *familye* to adopt her *boppli*. After I said it, she asked me to leave. I'm really sorry, *Onkel* Seth. I didn't mean to make things worse."

Abby was practically in tears, but her uncle didn't look displeased with her admission.

"Is there any way you could arrange for us to meet this young girl?"

Abby was confused. "But *Aenti* just told me she wanted me to leave her alone. I don't think she'll accept a *boppli* that isn't her own."

Seth fought back tears. "She's so hurt right now; she doesn't know what she wants. But there isn't any harm in meeting with the pregnant teenager. Will you see if you can arrange it?"

Her uncle's enthusiasm gave Abby hope. "Of course. I'll call her just before I open the bakery in the morning. Are you sure this won't upset *Aenti* Lillian?"

"I can't be certain of anything anymore. But it doesn't hurt to explore another chance to have a *familye* with Lillian."

Abby hoped she hadn't started something that would cause her aunt more pain. The last thing she wanted to do was pour salt on the poor woman's wounds.

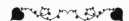

Abby scraped the last bit of pink frosting from the bottom of the mixing bowl and smeared it across the heart-shaped sugar cookie. She put it with the others so the frosting could set before she boxed them for potential orders throughout the day. Melanie, her old boss, at the Brick Oven Bakery in Ohio had shown her how to make the cinnamon-candy cookies for Valentine's Day the previous year. The cookies were a big item with the *Englischers,* and Abby hoped it might help bring in some new business to Lillian's small bakery.

The jingling of the bells on the front door alerted her to an early customer, but she hadn't yet turned the sign over to reveal she was open for business yet. Abby wondered who might be venturing out at such an hour. Poking her head around the corner of the kitchen, Abby spotted Becca, Jonah's sister, and her childhood friend.

A very pregnant Becca greeted her with a welcoming smile. "*Gudemariye,* cousin. My *bruder* told me I could find you here. I've missed you."

Abby pasted on a smile for her friend, even though to hear Becca call her "cousin" was irritating enough to prickle her nerves. But it wasn't like she could tell even her best friend the secret that put an end to their friendship when she left. "I missed you too, but I was afraid you wouldn't want to see me after hearing the rumors about your *bruder* and me."

Becca waved a casual hand at Abby. "That was a long time ago. But I always knew you were a different sort from the first time I met you. It didn't surprise me when I learned what happened between the two of you. I could see the way the two of you looked at each other. But I hope now that you're older and wiser that all that foolishness is behind you. After all, you left my *bruder* to confess to the Bishop alone. He took full responsibility for what happened. The Bishop told him he should have known better since he was older, but I'm just not sure my *bruder* saw it that way."

Abby couldn't deny the truth about the kiss to Becca. Her friend knew her better than that. But she had no idea what Jonah had gone through when she left. It had never dawned on her that he would have to face a confession alone. She felt terrible about it, but there was nothing to be done about it now except apologize to him.

"I never meant to cause more trouble when I left, but at the time, I thought running from my problems was my only solution. I'm sorry I hurt you in the process."

Becca picked up one of the cookies and bit into it.

"This is very tasty, cousin. I must have a box of these."

Abby cringed at the word "cousin" again. Would she ever be able to get past this? Or was she doomed to be forced to live with her *mamm's* lies for the rest of her life?

"When is the *boppli* to arrive? Is it your first?"

Becca rolled a hand over her swelling abdomen lovingly. "*Jah*, it's my first *boppli.* And he or she is due any day."

Abby felt a twinge of concern. "Should you be out on such a day if you're that close to the end of your confinement?"

Becca hugged Abby. "You will see some day when you have your own *boppli,* and you will want the distraction of visiting to keep you busy while you wait. The last few days have been the hardest for me to sit still knowing I am to be a *mamm* soon."

Abby didn't think she would ever be so lucky as to have her own *boppli* since the man she loved could never be her husband. She found envy creeping into her mind, and she pushed it back and smiled for the sake of her friend.

After boxing up a fresh batch of cookies for Becca, she bid her farewell, and happily sent her on her way. It wasn't that she didn't want to visit with her friend; she guessed that she needed to ease herself into her past relationships, or her nerves would not be able to withstand the added pressures she was already under with her family. One good thing that would come from helping her aunt, would be that she would have less time to think about Jonah.

Jonah practically had to sit on his hands the entire day to keep from walking down to the bakery. The heavenly smells drifting on the gentle breeze was not enough to satisfy him. Not to mention his craving for looking into Abby's warm hazel eyes. Feelings of guilt soon replaced the warm thoughts of Abby, and he found himself reaching out to *Gott* like never before.

If it's a sin to love Abby, Gott, then why won't you take away these strong feelings I have for her? I surrender my wille to You, dear Gott.

Despite his prayers, the urgency to see Abby still remained deep-seated in his heart. Deciding to take a walk in the early evening air to clear his mind, he pulled his coat from the peg near the door of the barn and shoved his hat on his head before walking out into the snow.

Light snow swirled around like mosquitoes in July, the sun dipping toward the horizon. Jonah searched his mind for any scenario where he and Abby could have a normal life together as his feet crunched in the snow, but a solution eluded him. He walked with no real direction in mind, but before he realized, he faced the set of mulberry trees near the school yard. Pacing between them was Abby, who seemed to be talking to herself. Unsure of whether he should approach her, he stood back and watched her verbal struggle, wishing he could hear what she was saying.

CHAPTER 10

Abby paced back and forth between the mulberry trees—the very spot where she and Jonah had shared their one and only special kiss. She called out to God, begging him for a way out of this mess. For a way that she and Jonah could share more than stolen glances and forbidden kisses. With her *mamm's* lie hanging over their heads, they would never be permitted to marry, and she would never live in sin with him just for a chance to be with him. But how could she tell Jonah the truth without soiling her *mamm's* honor and reputation with the community. Not to mention what the exposed lie would do to her *daed.*

Gott, please send me a sign that you will make this right for us. I surrender my wille to You.

Abby looked up at the increasing flurries that swirled about her. Snowflakes caught on her cheeks and melted, leaving a light mist behind. As she turned toward the school house, she noticed Jonah leaning up against the building watching her. She stopped in her tracks, and waited as he slowly made his way over to her.

Jonah looked into her eyes, thinking how beautiful she looked with the snow fluttering around her and moving wisps of her auburn hair loose from her *kapp.* "What are you doing out here so late? You look cold."

Abby tipped her chin toward him, admiring his slight smile. "I should ask you the same thing."

Jonah shuffled his feet in the snow, wishing his toes would warm up. "I needed to take a walk. Clear my head of a few things."

"Becca came into the bakery this morning. She didn't stay long. But I had a lot of work to get done to prepare for my first day back. I was grateful to have a steady stream of customers today."

Jonah nodded politely. He didn't want to talk about the bakery. He wanted to know why she left. He wanted answers to questions he'd been asking himself repeatedly for the past five years. He'd missed her.

Abby pulled her knitted scarf around her head and neck to shield it from the increasing snow. "Your *schweschder* told me you had to confess to the Bishop after I left the community. I'm sorry I left you to endure that alone. I never meant to hurt you Jonah, but you shouldn't have publically exposed our sin the way you did."

Jonah kicked at the snow. "I never meant to hurt you either Abby, but I couldn't deny my love for you any longer. I acted like a foolish boy. I'm not even sure we should be alone now."

Jonah closed the distance between them, and Abby stood her ground. "I've missed you Abby. So much it hurts."

Abby closed her eyes as he brushed his warm cheek against hers. She wanted him to kiss her again. To kiss her like he didn't care about the consequences of the community—or the world, for that matter. What she couldn't understand was why he was so willing to risk everything to be near her when he didn't know they weren't cousins.

Abby took a step back. "We can't do this again, Jonah. We have to keep our relationship proper. If we don't, we risk excommunication."

Jonah moved in closer to her again. "It's been five long years, and I've prayed until there were no more words, begging *Gott* to make me stop loving you. Seeing you again has only made those feelings stronger. Wrong or not, I can't help how I feel."

"Your love is not wrong, Jonah." The words came out in a whisper.

Abby found it difficult to breathe around the lump in her throat. Swallowing down the tears, she asked God for the courage to walk away from Jonah. As hard as she tried, her feet wouldn't move. Instead, she tipped her heard toward Jonah's, allowing him to press his warm lips against hers ever so softly. Her breaths came in shallow puffs as she leaned into his kiss with the sort of passion she'd seen *Englischers* display when she lived in Ohio.

Abby could not deny her love for Jonah, but she couldn't betray her *mamm* at the same time. She was torn between the truth and a lie that had ruined her life in more ways than she cared to acknowledge.

Jonah suddenly pulled away. "I can't do this to you, Abby. I must do right by you this time."

Abby caught her breath. "But Jonah, you don't understand. There's something you don't know. It doesn't have to be like this. I can make it right. Just give me some time."

"Abby, no amount of time is going to change things. We could sneak around like we did before and hope we don't get caught, but what would that prove? We can't marry, which means I can't be with you the way I want to—the way I've longed to be with you for a very long time."

Tears fell down Abby's cold cheeks, worrying her they would freeze. "Jonah, I love you. I've always loved you, and I can't make it stop no matter how much I've begged *Gott* to take away the love I have for you. But I know a way we can be together. You have to trust me and give me some time."

"Abby you don't understand how guilty I feel for loving you—how guilty I've felt all these years. I don't understand why I love you differently than my other cousins. Maybe it's because I never even met you until I was thirteen years old. I know we didn't grow up together, and we've never had a traditional cousin-to-cousin relationship, but that's no excuse for way I've acted out my feelings for you. Or for the way I've jeopardized your standing in the community."

Tears pooled in Jonah's eyes. It broke Abby's heart to see him like this. Couldn't she just tell him the truth now and take care of it later with her parents? Or would the truth backfire on her and make things worse?

Jonah pressed a lingering kiss on her forehead. "I will always love you, but we can't be together. Deep down we both know it. If even *Gott* can't change the fact that we are cousins, then what hope is there?"

Jonah turned on his heel and walked away. Abby called after him, but he walked more swiftly and never turned around. Abby fell to her knees in the deep snow, sobbing uncontrollably.

Gott, please give me the strength to confront my mamm and daed. Bring the truth to light, and bless Jonah and me with a love that honors You.

CHAPTER 11

Abby had to stay focused on her Uncle Seth and Aunt Lillian, and that meant putting her own problems aside for the day. She would deal with her *mamm* later. But for now, she had to help *Aenti* Bess ready the rooms at the B&B for the arrival of Melanie and her daughter, Ellie, tomorrow. Abby was already exhausted from a full day at the bakery, but she had promised her family that she would help make this visit go as smoothly as possible.

She feared her uncle had gotten his hopes up about the possibility of adopting Ellie's baby. And it was through no fault of her own that Abby felt responsible for the whole thing. Because of this, she'd worked hard for the past two days arranging everything from having a taxi pick Melanie and Ellie up at the train station, to arranging three rooms at the B&B for the two women and the adoption attorney—just in case.

She'd even pushed aside her own prayers to talk to God about bringing these two women together for the sake of the baby's well-being. She couldn't imagine the hurt that her aunt was feeling because of her loss. But if it was even a tiny bit as much as the hurt she felt for the loss of Jonah, she didn't know how her aunt was able to bear it.

Bess surveyed the neatness of the last room Abby cleaned. "You're a lot better at this than you were when you were a child. If not for the girl I have working here, there's no way I could keep this place open. I'm thankful you were able to help me this week while she's taking her trip to see her *familye*. What do say we get some hot *kaffi* in you before you head home in the cold?"

Abby pushed stray hairs behind her ear. "That sounds *gut*. Some *kaffi* will keep me awake until my slow mare trots home."

Abby collapsed into the first chair at the small table in the kitchen. They had already cleaned the dining room for the guests, and the kitchen table was more for family anyway.

Aenti Bess pushed a mug of hot coffee in front of Abby, who looked like she could fall asleep in it. "What's with the long face? If this adoption is troubling you, let it go and let *Gott* have control of it. You've done all you can; the rest is up to Him."

Abby sipped her coffee slowly, hoping for a little more time to think before she blurted out what was really on her mind.

Aenti Bess winked at her. "This is about a *mann*, isn't it? Perhaps a certain forbidden love that's gotten your feathers so ruffled?"

Abby swallowed hard the hot liquid, hoping it would keep her from speaking her mind.

Bess cleared her throat. "You know it wasn't that long ago that I had a similar conversation with your *mamm* at this very table. She was still so much in love with your *daed*. But she'd run off to Ohio, same as you did. While she was gone, your *daed* married her best friend. She didn't think your *daed* would ever take her back—especially since she had you. But when you ran off and went in search of Jacob, nothing else mattered to her except finding you. And when your *daed* showed up with you and everyone thought Jacob was your *daed,* he didn't deny it. He let the lie go to protect you and your *mamm.* He did the honorable thing by marrying your *mamm* that day."

Abby let a fresh tear fall unchecked. "I don't understand why he did that. And I certainly don't understand why they led me to believe he was my *daed* all those years."

Bess took her hands in hers. "They did it to protect you in case the *menner* that were after your biological father for his debt would ever come looking for you. It was to protect you."

"But I've been in Ohio for the past five years and no one came after me. Maybe there was no real danger. Or they didn't recognize me when I went there because I'd grown up. I don't know what to think. But what I do know is that lie has hurt me in a lot of ways. It's prevented me from having a life with Jonah."

Bess leaned back in her chair and crossed her arms over her ample bosom. "You have to decide if you will honor your *mamm* and *daed* as it says in the Bible, or if you will choose your own path. If you choose your own path, you will have to leave the community. And since you were just baptized a few days ago, are you prepared to leave again? Search your heart, and seek *Gott* for the answers."

Abby leaned her head down and cupped her chin with her hands. She rested her elbows on the table to support her head that threatened to slip off her tired shoulders from lack of sleep. "I've prayed so much I'm certain *Gott* is tired of hearing the same thing from me."

Bess slurped the bottom of her coffee. "Then change your prayers. Whenever I don't get an answer, I change my prayers to reflect another person's needs, rather than my own. When our prayers are selfish and greedy, *Gott* has a way of making us wait for an answer until we pray for His *wille* and not our own."

Abby sat up straight. "You think I should be praying for *Mamm?* She's the cause of all this. She's the one that lied—not me. It's really hard to keep from being angry with her."

"But you were baptized. Did you confess the kiss you shared with Jonah to the Bishop before your baptism?"

Abby stood up and poured another cup of coffee.

"No. I didn't feel the need to confess the kiss because it wasn't a sin. Jonah and I are *not* cousins."

Bess held her cup out to Abby for a refill. "The point is, Abby, that the community views you as cousins. And unless your *mamm* and *daed* go to the Bishop and confess the lie, you will not be able to be with Jonah. So you might consider changing your prayers."

Abby finally got the point. It didn't help that she was emotionally and physically drained. But her *aenti* was painfully right about one thing—she could never ask her *mamm* to confess. She could only pray about it, and hope God would change her *mamm's* heart.

CHAPTER 12

Jonah paced back and forth alongside the bakery, wondering if he should go inside and talk to Abby. It had been two days since they shared the kiss under the mulberry tree, and he needed to convince her to go with him to the Bishop to confess. He'd nearly driven himself mad with worry that someone might have seen them. If that was the case, it would only be a matter of time before they were excommunicated. It was still early, and the bakery probably wouldn't be open for at least another hour, but he could smell something so *gut,* his mouth was watering. Grabbing the door handle before he lost his nerve, he swung it open, the bells jingling his presence.

Abby poked her head around the corner of the kitchen, chiding herself for forgetting to lock door behind her yet again. She wasn't ready for customers yet. When she caught sight of Jonah, her heart did a somersault.

Jonah quickly pulled his hat off his head and held it in front of him as he walked toward Abby. "I think we should talk about what happened the other night. It seems history is repeating itself, and if we don't get it under control, we'll both be excommunicated. I'm a buggy maker, and I can't make a living outside the community. *Englischers* don't have a need for buggies, and I don't know the first thing about fixing their fancy cars. My place is in the community, and I don't want to risk losing that."

Abby continued to cut heart shapes in the cookie dough and place them on the baking sheet. "I agree with you about not being able to make a living among the *Englisch,* but I won't confess to something I'm not sorry for."

Jonah grabbed one of the heart-shaped cookies with pink frosting and shoved a bite of it in his mouth to keep his hands occupied. "Don't worry, I'll pay for this," he said around the cookie in his mouth.

Abby turned to him playfully. "You better."

Her smile melted his heart. He set his hat and the cookie on the counter and pulled Abby into his arms. He kissed the top of her hair that smelled like sugar cookies, moving his lips to her forehead, and then down her cheek.

"*Gott* help me, Abby, I love you, and I don't know how to stop."

Abby didn't try to resist Jonah's advances. She wanted him to hold her and never let her go. Tilting her head until her lips met his, she tasted the sweet frosting from the cookie. The sweetness of his mouth somehow tasted better than the cookie, and she continued to kiss him with a hunger for it.

But once again, Jonah pushed her away from him.

"Abby, we can't do this every time we see each other. I've written my *onkel* in Florida about the possibility of going to live there in his community. I was undecided, but it's obvious we can't stay in this community together and keep a level of propriety in our relationship. It's probably better if I leave after I confess to the Bishop next Saturday. I guess it's better if we say our goodbyes now."

Abby fell back against the counter, feeling as though she'd had the wind knocked out of her. Tears welled up in her eyes as she looked at Jonah. The front of his coat was covered in flour from her apron, his eyes cast to the floor. She couldn't tell him the truth now; it would seem like a desperate attempt to keep him here. But she couldn't just stand by and let him leave before she had a chance to fix the situation either.

"Jonah, please don't leave. I told you I can fix this. I can't tell you how, but I'm going to very soon if you'll just trust me."

"I can't stay here near you when all I want to do is hold you and kiss you. It's not right, Abby, and I won't sneak around like a sinner waiting to get caught. You need to move on with your life. I'll always love you, but I have to go. Goodbye Abby." His voice was weak and tearful.

Before Abby could say another word, he placed a dollar on the counter, picked up his hat and walked briskly toward the door.

Abby struggled to move her feet and find her voice, but she was filled with too much trepidation to function. She tried calling after him, but it was too late.

The door closed and he was gone.

Anger filled Abby, and she grabbed several of the heart-shaped cookies in both hands and smashed them against the opposite wall. She wished she'd never come back to the community.

Lizzie followed the sound of soft crying that led to Abby's bedroom door. Lifting her hand to knock, she paused, wondering if talking to her daughter would do either of them any good. Abby had gone straight to her room after coming home early from the bakery, and she didn't even come down for the evening meal. Lizzie knew what was troubling her daughter, and it was *her* fault.

Dear Gott, give me the strength to do the right thing where Abby is concerned. Bless me with the courage to do the right thing. Show me how to make things right for her and Jonah.

CHAPTER 13

At two o'clock, Abby turned the *Closed* sign over on the door of the bakery and locked the door. She had planned to meet Melanie for a late lunch at the B&B while her *aenti* and *onkel* met with Ellie about the adoption. It was hard to feel excited about seeing her old boss and friend, but she had to push her feelings about Jonah aside for the time-being and put her trust in God to make things right. That wasn't an easy task either, given the fact that Jonah planned to leave the community in only a few days.

As Abby stacked the last of the pans in the deep sink to soak while she tidied up the rest of the kitchen for the day, she heard the jingle of bells on the front door. She froze in place for a minute, trying to remember if she'd locked the door. She was sure she had. The only other person who had a key was Lillian.

Abby grabbed a broom from the corner and walked slowly around the corner to the dining room of the bakery.

Lillian held up her hands in mock defense. "It's just me; put the broom down!"

Abby looked at the broom, which she still held above her head like a baseball bat, and smiled as she lowered it. "Sorry. I guess I'm a little jumpy. Why aren't you at the B&B? Where's *Onkel* Seth?"

Lillian looked at her with tearful eyes. "I told him I'd meet him there. But the truth is, I'm not sure I can go."

Abby took Lillian's hands in hers. "No one is forcing you to go, *Aenti*. And just because you meet her doesn't mean you're obligated to adopt the *boppli.*"

Lillian rested her head on Abby's shoulder. "I think your *onkel* will be disappointed in me if I don't go along with this."

Abby smoothed her *aenti's* hair. "That doesn't sound like *Onkel*. I think he just wants you to be happy is all."

Lillian pulled away from Abby and wiped her eyes.

"Enough about me. Tell me what's gotten you so down."

Abby had hoped her mood had not been so obvious, but she wasn't about to unload her problems on her *aenti* when the woman was still mourning the loss of her *boppli.*

"It's nothing I can't work out easily."

Lillian raised an eyebrow. "Does this have anything to do with Jonah packing up his things and closing down his business? I heard he's leaving for Florida next week."

Abby tried to contain her emotions. "I don't want to talk about it, *Aenti.*"

"Does Jonah know you two are not cousins?"

Abby felt the shock of her *aenti's* statement like a strong, winter wind. "Jonah doesn't know, but how did *you* know we aren't cousins?"

"I've suspected for a while, Abby, but that doesn't matter. What matters is how you're going to handle the situation."

Abby threw her hands up in defeat. "There's nothing I can do. If I tell Jonah the truth, I'll be betraying my *mamm.* But if I stand by and do nothing, he's going to leave. I don't want him to leave. I love him so much it hurts."

"Does he love you?"

Abby fought back tears. "Yes. He told me he still loves me, and he's leaving because he thinks that our love is a sin."

"Abby, you can't let him think he's a sinner. You have to tell him the truth or he'll never trust you. You're not being fair to him—or to yourself."

"But if I expose the truth, it won't be fair to my *mamm.* No matter what I do, someone is going to be hurt."

Lillian shook her head with disgust. "Only *Gott* can show you what is the right path to take, but I think you need to have a talk with your *mamm.* Maybe she will fix it."

Abby could see that *Aenti* Lillian focusing on *her* problems instead of her own was a good distraction for her *aenti.*

"Will you help me talk to my *mamm?*"

Lillian smiled weakly. "Of course I will. I'll do anything to help you. And if I help you, it might take my mind off my own troubles."

Abby smiled. "Funny, but I was thinking the same thing about you."

Lillian hugged her niece again. "Why don't we help each other? Maybe together we can figure everything out."

"That sounds like a *gut* idea."

Lillian moved over to the sink full of dirty cake pans and pie tins. "Why don't we start with these dishes, and then you can give me a ride over to the B&B so I can meet with Ellie."

Abby didn't waste any time at all. She picked up an extra apron and tossed it to her *aenti,* and the two of them made light work of dishes.

Everything wasn't settled yet, but Abby felt better about Jonah. Finally, she had someone on *her* side. Someone to help her figure out what would be the right thing to do. Maybe, just maybe she could keep Jonah from leaving. But was it too soon to hope that they could have a future together?

CHAPTER 14

Jonah rushed through his day, trying to finish the last two buggies he'd been making to fill his existing orders. He'd turned down four orders for new buggies in the past two days, and he hoped he wouldn't regret it. He knew he could use a little extra money to relocate to Florida, but if he stayed to make four more buggies, it would be Spring before he was able to leave the community. And that would mean more chances that he'd fall back into sinful desires for Abby, which would, in turn, lead to being excommunicated. Then he wouldn't have anywhere to go after his *onkel* in Florida heard of his actions. No, it was best to finish what he'd started, and leave as planned.

For the past few days, Jonah had rehearsed what he'd say to the Bishop when he went to confess. He was sure the Bishop would demand discipline, but would probably wave it in lieu of his departure from the community. Jonah wished it could be another way, but he didn't see how. But what was it Abby had said about trusting her? Did he dare hope there was a way out of having to confess to something he wasn't sorry for? And was it too much to hope that God would bring a miracle to their lives? After all the praying he'd done, he could only hope.

Kneeling down, Jonah double-checked the rear wheel to be sure it would not come loose from the axle. Distracted by his thoughts, Jonah didn't notice the buggy door slipping from the clutches of the vice above his head before it was too late. He knew better than to leave the door teetering on top of the buggy while he jostled the carriage, but it was too late to rethink his error in judgment. Pain seared through his skull as the heavy wooden frame of the door fell from the roof of the buggy and connected with his head.

Taking a deep breath, Jonah pushed to his feet, feeling a sudden need for fresh air. He staggered out of the barn and into the snow-filled yard, feeling as though his wobbly legs couldn't carry him any further. The corners of his vision began to turn dark, but as hard as he fought to keep focus, it was no use. Coldness assaulted him as the darkness engulfed him.

Abby boxed the last of the heart-shaped, frosted sugar cookies and set them aside for Jonah. She hoped that the distraction of the cookies would give her enough time to talk him into changing his mind about leaving the community.

When she was satisfied with the cleanliness of the bakery, she turned off the lights and locked the door behind her. Pulling her scarf tightly to shield her face from the wind, Abby headed up the long drive toward Jonah's barn at the other end of the property. Knowing it would be dark soon, she hoped her visit would also gain an offer from Jonah to drive her home after they talked.

As she neared the curve of the drive, just beyond the large oak trees that stood like sentinels at either side of the footpath, she noticed Jonah exiting the barn. Happy to see him, she picked up her pace a little. She waved, but he didn't seem to notice her. His gait seemed off balance, and bright red smeared his blonde hair like paint from a barn. But how would he have gotten paint in his hair, and where had it come from?

Was it blood?

Abby dropped the box of cookies and ran the rest of the way toward Jonah, but she did not reach him in time. She watched helplessly as he collapsed face-down into the snow. Her feet struggled to gain any headway on the icy path. When she reached him, his face was half-buried in the snow, his body too calm. She dropped to her knees and began to push frantically at the snow, fearing it prevented him from breathing. A low groan escaped his blue lips. A good sign.

"Jonah, can you hear me?"

Abby jiggled him. "Jonah, please; open your eyes."

Abby pushed with all her strength to roll Jonah onto his back, hoping to get a better look at his injury. Pulling a handkerchief from the pocket of her coat, she gently mopped at the icy blood that dripped down his forehead. She looked around, knowing there was no one within shouting distance to help her, and decided she would have to drag him into the barn alone. She needed to get him out of the cold wind and warmed up so he didn't go into shock. She also knew Jonah had a phone in the barn for his business. She hoped he hadn't disconnected it in preparation for leaving.

Abby's legs felt weak, her breathing ragged from a combination of being cold and fearing for Jonah's safety. But she was determined to get him inside the shelter of the barn no matter what it took.

Gott, please give me the strength to move Jonah into the safety of the barn, and please don't let him die.

Crouching behind him, she looped her arms under his armpits, heaving him a step at a time until he lay just inside the barn. Grabbing a wool blanket that hung over the horse stall, she tucked it around Jonah, and then she wriggled out of her coat and placed it under his head. When she moved his head, he groaned again, and it was a sound Abby was happy to hear. She'd been happier if he'd opened his eyes. She prayed it would happen soon.

When Jonah was settled comfortably, Abby stood, picked up the phone, and held it to her ear, relieved to hear a dial tone. But who should she call? Every minute care was delayed; Jonah was losing blood from the deep gash in the side of his head. She dialed Dr. Davis's house first, hoping he would advise her. After what seemed like an eternity on the line with the doctor's wife, she learned he was at the B&B checking on Ellie. She hung up and dialed her *aenti* Bess, happy that the doctor was there. She knew the trip to Jonah's place would only take the doctor a few minutes to reach them instead of nearly an hour form his own farm.

Tears welled up in her eyes as she waited for the doctor to come to the phone. Jonah seemed lifeless as he lay on the floor of the barn, and that frightened her.

"This is Dr. Davis."

"This is Abby Yoder. I'm at Jonah Beiler's *haus*. He passed out and he has a deep cut on his head. It's bleeding a lot. I don't know what to do."

"Is he awake?"

"No! He's breathing, but the cut won't stop bleeding."

"I need you to apply pressure to the wound, and try to wake him up. I'll be there in just a few minutes."

"Please hurry!"

Abby hung up the phone and rushed to Jonah's side, praying the doctor would make it in time to mend him.

CHAPTER 15

Jonah moved in and out of consciousness, trying desperately to cling to Abby's angelic voice. She was praying in between crying and whispering declarations of love in his ear. Did he know why she was crying? Was he dreaming? He wished he could open his eyes and comfort her, but the pain in his head kept him from reaching out. The pressure in his head caused him to groan.

"Stay with me, Jonah. Please don't leave me. I love you."

Her voice was like butterflies fluttering above his head, but he was too cold for that to be the case. Maybe it was more like snowflakes. Jonah shivered and groaned from the pain.

"Jonah please wake up. I need you to know how much I love you."

Jonah tried to open his mouth to say it back to her, but he just couldn't form the words. He felt her love in the warm clutches of her hand on his. Was she really next to him, holding his hand? He could feel her warm breath in his ear, and smelled the baking spices he always enjoyed whenever she was near. A muffled noise that sounded like the door to his barn opening startled him out of his reverie. Then there was another voice—a male. The voice was familiar, but he struggled to place it. Abby was telling the man he'd gotten hurt. It was Doctor Davis.

Jonah suddenly remembered the buggy door falling on his head. The last thing he remembered was trying to get a little fresh air. Was he bleeding? A vague memory plagued him of feeling blood dripping down his face before seeing it land in the snow at his feet—just before he fell. And now he could hear Doctor Davis asking Abby to help him clean his head wound. Is that why his head hurt so much? Had the door cut open his head when it landed on him?

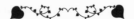

Abby watched Doctor Davis sponge a cleansing solution over the wound on Jonah's head while she tried not to become squeamish. "Is he going to need stitches?"

"I'm afraid so. He'll also need to be monitored for the next twenty-four hours. If he doesn't wake up, he could slip into a coma. The fact that he's groaning means that he can feel some of the pain, and hopefully that's enough to keep him out of danger. I'll let him sleep until I'm done stitching him up since I don't have any Novocain to numb him."

Abby gasped. "Does that mean he's going to feel it when you stitch him up?"

"It's possible, but he probably won't remember it when he wakes up."

Abby hated the thought of Jonah being able to feel the doctor stitching up his wound, but she knew it couldn't be avoided. If he didn't get the bleeding under control soon, it could put him at further risk.

When the doctor tied the last stitch, he reached into his bag and retrieved smelling salts. "You might want to take a step back. I've seen patients flail around when this stuff is placed under their nose."

Abby did as she was instructed, hoping it would work to wake Jonah without startling him.

Please, Gott, let him wake up.

It took a minute, but Jonah soon stirred. He groaned as his eyelids fluttered. His hand reached toward the wound on his head, but the doctor stopped him from touching the stitches.

"Hold on Jonah, I need to bandage your head to keep infection out. Lie still for just another minute."

The sound of Jonah's phone ringing startled Abby. She looked to him. "Should I answer that?"

Doctor Davis nodded and chuckled. "It could be someone looking for me since my services seem to be much needed today."

Abby answered it. "This is Abby Yoder."

"This is Levi Graber. Your *aenti* at the B&B told me Doctor Davis went over there because Jonah is injured. Is everything alright?"

Abby wasn't sure how much she should tell Levi, fearing it might worry Becca unnecessarily. "He got a few stitches in his head, but he's talking to the doctor now. How is Becca?"

"That's the reason I'm calling. Becca is in labor. We need the doctor over here as soon as possible."

"Hold on a minute." Abby put her hand over the receiver and told Doctor Davis what was going on.

Jonah struggled. "I need to get up. I have to go to my *schweschder*."

Doctor Davis put a firm hand on Jonah's shoulder.

"You won't be going anywhere for a few days, so be still while I bandage you up." He looked to Abby. "Ask Levi how far apart the contractions are."

After talking with Levi another minute, Abby put her hand back over the receiver of the phone. "He said about thirty minutes apart."

"Tell Levi I'll be there in about an hour. It sounds like she has a while to go yet."

Abby relayed the doctor's message to Levi, and told him to send her love to Becca, and for her not to worry because her brother was in good hands.

Jonah groaned again. "How bad is it, Doc?"

The doctor looked at him over the glasses that rested low on his nose. "Thirty-seven stitches. And on top of that, you have a concussion. You'll be off your feet for at least three days. That is if we can keep this cut from getting infected."

Jonah tried to smile, but winced from the pain.

"Thirty-seven, huh? That's ten more than my knee when I was twelve, remember?"

Doctor Davis chuckled. "I see your memory is intact. That's a good sign. But you'll still have to be watched. I imagine since your sister seems to be in labor, and you don't have any other family here, you could probably talk your cousin here into staying with you for a couple of days. She's the one that found you. She's an excellent nurse-maid. You're lucky she found you as quickly as she did, or things might have been worse."

Abby blushed at the thought of staying with Jonah. She knew her parents would never allow her to stay with Jonah without a chaperone, but she couldn't let him down. Caleb would not be able to take time from work to stay with him, and that left only her. She knew it would mean closing the bakery for a few days, but maybe this was all part of God's plan. She hoped Lillian would agree to go back to the bakery in her absence, knowing her aunt would heal faster with the bakery to tend to. And Jonah would heal faster with Abby to tend to his care. After all, the doctor himself had suggested it, but perhaps if Rachel came along, her parents would permit it.

CHAPTER 16

"I'm a grown woman, and capable of making my own choices, *Mamm*. I'm going to stay with Jonah while he heals, and I'll bring Rachel with me as a chaperone. You might be able to get in the way of my marrying Jonah, but I cannot let you prevent me from making certain he survives this crisis."

Her *mamm* sank onto the bed while Abby packed a few of her belongings. "I didn't know you wanted to marry him, Abby. Why didn't you tell me things were so serious between the two of you?"

Abby pursed her lips. She did not want to have this conversation now. She needed to hurry back to Jonah and relieve Doctor Davis so he could get over to Becca's house to deliver her baby.

"It doesn't matter, because we can never be together since the community thinks we're cousins. Do you have any idea how guilty Jonah feels for loving me the way he does? He thinks he's a sinner! And I can't do anything to make him stop from feeling that way unless I betray your honor."

Abby began to cry. "I will never love another *mann* the way I love Jonah, so I'm destined to become a spinster. So I'll be a burden on *Daed* for the rest of my life—or the rest of his, whichever ends first. But I'm certain it will be me because I'll probably die from a broken heart before old age can claim me."

Lizzie tried to comfort her daughter, but there were no words that would undo the damage her lies had caused. How had she missed the new developments in their relationship since Abby had returned? What could she do to make up for the damage? Could she possibly go to the Bishop and confess? Was it too late to salvage things for Abby and Jonah?

"I'm sorry, Abby. I never meant for you to be hurt in any of this."

"Well I am hurt, *Mamm*. And Jonah and I continue to be hurt. The only thing that will fix this is having the truth out in the open to the Bishop and the entire community."

There. She'd said it. She wasn't proud of her disrespectful suggestion, but she couldn't hold it in any longer.

Lizzie hung her head. "I'm not sure I can do that, Abby. It might make things worse—especially for your *daed.*"

Abby gathered her things in her arms and placed them in her childhood suitcase. "He isn't my *daed*. My *father* is a dead drug-dealer. Say it *mother*. I want to hear you say it out loud to me. You couldn't even say it five years ago when I found out the truth. I'm still surprised you admitted it to me at all. Why did you? It would have been better if I'd never known. At least that way I wouldn't know there was nothing keeping me from marrying Jonah."

"I'm sorry, Abby."

"Sorry doesn't fix this mess. Sorry doesn't allow me and Jonah to marry. Sorry won't mend my broken heart."

Abby picked up her things and went to the door.

"Are you going to let Rachel go with me?"

Lizzie nodded her consent, tears filling her eyes when Abby walked away without saying another word.

Abby left word with *Aenti* Bess to have her Aunt Lillian stop by Jonah's house after she and Uncle Seth left the B&B so she could let her know she wouldn't be able to work at the bakery for a few days. She hated to let Lillian down after she'd promised to work for her, but it had already been closed more than a month before she'd returned from Ohio.

After settling herself and Rachel into the room Jonah assigned to them, the two of them busied themselves in the kitchen preparing a light meal for Jonah. The doctor had suggested a diet consisting of mostly liquids until tomorrow. Abby found ingredients to make chicken soup and biscuits with honey. Feeling comfortable in Jonah's modest house, Abby wondered what it would be like if she was able to live there with him as his wife.

Please Gott, make a way for Jonah and me to be married. I want to be his fraa more than anything.

Abby carried a tray to Jonah's room and knocked lightly on the door. It hadn't been easy helping the doctor get Jonah up the stairs, especially since he had to stop frequently to quell dizziness and nausea. But Jonah had stubbornly insisted he be able to convalesce in his own bed. She didn't blame him. He would never have been comfortable on the sofa downstairs, and he would probably not be a cooperative patient without proper rest.

At Jonah's groan, Abby entered the room cautiously. Setting the tray at the end of the bed, she blushed at the sight of him lying helplessly in the bed built for two. The doctor had removed Jonah's blood-stained shirt, and he lay there with his torso exposed. Abby admired his muscular build, noting that he was no longer the young boy she'd fallen in love with as a teenager. Thankful his eyes were closed so he couldn't see the deep blush that painted her cheeks with fire, she continued to admire him until he cleared his throat. The noise startled her, bringing more heat to her already pink cheeks.

Abby straightened, rethinking her decision to stay with Jonah. If not for her *mamm's* lies, she would already be his wife, and she would be able to lie next to him and cradle him in her arms. She had to keep a clear head or she was going to fall into temptation, and she didn't want that any more than Jonah would.

Seeing that his eyes were now wide open, she motioned to the tray at the foot of the bed. "Can you sit up for a few minutes and eat a little something? I made you some chicken soup and biscuits."

Jonah tried to smile, but couldn't manage it with the amount of pain he was in. "Smells *gut*. I can try. Can you push the extra pillow behind me?"

Abby reached for the pillow, wishing she'd walked over to the opposite side of the bed to get it. With her hand on the pillow, her face was close to Jonah's—too close. He looked at her with hopeful eyes, and she knew he wanted to kiss her just as much as she wanted to be kissed. He reached for her, but the pain in his head won. He winced, and Abby picked up the pillow and readied it behind him while he attempted to straighten himself in the bed.

"I hate that you went to all this trouble for me. I'm not sure I can stomach anything beyond the broth in the soup."

Abby smiled. "Not to worry. Rachel is downstairs eating your portion, and will probably devour my portion as well if I don't return soon."

Abby held the bowl up for him while he painstakingly took hold of the spoon and attempted to bring it to his mouth. "I don't know why I feel so weak. Maybe it's because this headache hasn't subsided. The doc gave me something for it, but it hasn't helped yet."

Abby smiled. "The doctor said you would feel weak and groggy for a few days. You lost quite a lot of blood and you have a concussion. I can help you; that's what I'm here for."

Abby lifted a spoonful of broth to his full lips, wishing she could kiss them just one last time.

Who was she trying to fool?

There was no way she could live without this man, and she had a plan to make sure she wouldn't have to. When he was well, she intended to tell him the truth about everything—no matter the consequences.

CHAPTER 17

Abby pushed the button on her wind-up alarm beside the large bed she shared with Rachel, and pushed herself from the warmth of the quilt. Holding up the face of the clock toward the moonlight, she noted the time, and reset the alarm for six o'clock. She'd been in to wake Jonah every two hours as the doctor ordered to be sure he didn't slip into a coma, and to check the dressing for signs of bleeding.

Exhausted, she forced her feet down the hall to Jonah's room. She hated to wake him again, but no matter how cruel it seemed, it was necessary. Each time, she'd knock lightly, get no answer, and then enter his room anyway. The first time, she'd felt shy, but now that it was four o'clock in the morning, she was ready to get it over with and get a little more sleep before having to start her busy day.

Abby crept into the room, letting the moonlight guide her to Jonah's side. The quilt had slipped to his waist, and she watched the gentle rise and fall of his diaphragm for a minute, admiring his well-formed abdominal muscles. As she reached for the edge of the quilt to cover him, her hand grazed his heated skin. He was too warm. Placing the back of her hand under his chin and across his forehead, she realized he was burning up with fever.

Abby grabbed the battery-operated thermometer from the bedside table that Doctor Davis had left for her, and tucked it under his arm. She held it there for several minutes. Jonah groaned and tried to wriggle free from the light pressure she placed on his shoulder to hold the thermometer in place.

"Jonah, can you wake up? I need you to open your eyes for me for just a minute if you can."

Jonah moved and groaned. "I'm cold."

Abby pulled the thermometer from his armpit and shined the doctor's flashlight on it to read it. Abby became alarmed when she saw it was 102.8 degrees.

"Jonah, you have a fever." Her voice seemed suddenly loud in the quietness of the night.

"I'm cold," Jonah mumbled again.

Abby pulled up the quilt and tucked it under his chin, but she needed to do something to bring his fever down. Then she remembered her *daed* packing snow around her when she had a bad case of the flu that first winter she'd come to live in the community.

Abby placed a hand on Jonah's shoulder and let him know she'd be back in a minute.

He didn't respond.

Racing down the stairs to the kitchen, Abby searched the cupboards for something large enough to put snow into. Finding a large canning pot that had most likely belonged to his *mamm,* Abby held it close to her as she pushed her feet into her boots that she'd left by the back door, and then slipped her arms into her coat.

The moon shone bright against the white snow, illuminating the quiet yard. Packing as much snow as she could into the oversized pot, she lifted it, surprised at how heavy it was. Realizing it was going to take several trips to get as much snow as she needed to pack around Jonah to cool him, she considered waking Rachel to help, but figured it would probably take more time than doing the job herself.

By the time Abby reached Jonah's room with the fifth pot of snow, she was so out of breath, she feared she would not be able to continue, but she was determined get as much as possible. But even after she finished, she would have to mop up the trail of slush she'd left from the back door to Jonah's room by leaving her boots on during each trip. She could have removed them, but time was crucial, and she didn't mind mopping up the mess later. She was, however, grateful Jonah's floors were all wood and linoleum between the back door and his bedroom.

Packing the last bit of snow over the section of quilt that was tucked closely around his neck, she noted that some of the snow had already melted and was soaking through the quilt. She felt bad for Jonah as she watched him shiver, his teeth chattering almost non-stop.

Abby feared for Jonah more, as it was obvious infection had set in the wound as the doctor had warned. She kissed his warm forehead, tears pooling in her eyes.

Please Gott, save Jonah's life, and spare him from any more pain.

CHAPTER 18

Promptly at seven o'clock, Doctor Davis arrived as promised. It had been a long night for Abby, and she'd just poured a third cup of coffee when the aging doctor tapped lightly on the back door.

Abby opened the door.

"How's the patient this morning?"

"I've had him packed in snow for the last few hours, and the fever is starting to come down."

Abby had finally had to wake Rachel to help her, as the snow was melting almost as quickly as she could get it to him. With the two of them working, they'd been able to keep a constant packing of fresh snow for the past few hours. The continuous running up and down the stairs had all but worn Abby out. Rachel was back in bed, and she didn't have the heart to disturb her. Abby figured with the doctor there, she might as well let Rachel sleep for an hour.

"I brought some medicine to bring down the fever, and I'll have to ride into town and pick up some antibiotics for him." He followed Abby to Jonah's room.

"How's Becca? The *boppli?*"

"A healthy boy. Named him Adam. Becca is worn out, but in good health. She was anxious to be here with her brother, but I told her not to worry, that he was in good care with his cousins. She seemed a little concerned about that, but I told her not to worry because you're very capable of taking care of him."

Abby knew why Becca was concerned about her staying with her brother after the conversation they'd had the day before at the bakery. But she couldn't worry about that now. She'd made sure she brought Rachel with her to establish a sense of propriety, even if it may appear not to be enough. Her only concern for the time being was nursing Jonah back to health.

Under the wet quilt, Jonah shivered and groaned.

"Doctor, will you get him up and help him change into some dry clothes? I need to put dry linens on the bed."

Abby left the room to get dry bedding, which she'd noticed in the bureau of the room she shared with her sister. When she returned, she knocked to see if the doctor was finished helping Jonah change. When she entered, Doctor Davis was helping Jonah get into a fresh night shirt. Abby averted her eyes, fearing she would blush at the sight of his bare chest. She went straight to the bed and began to change the linens. She hurried when she heard Jonah groaning from the pain.

"I need to get back to bed; I feel pretty dizzy. Is that normal, Doc?"

Doctor Davis tucked himself under Jonah's arm and walked him back to his freshly made bed. "It might take about a week for the dizziness to go away. I'll give you some more pain medication, and hopefully that will help you sleep. Rest is what you need now to recover. I'm going to pick up some antibiotics this morning, and I'll be back as soon as I can. In the meantime, it looks like your nurse here is doing a fine job of putting you on the road to recovery."

Jonah managed a weak smile for Abby, and her heart did a somersault behind her ribcage. Almost immediately, Jonah fell back asleep, so Abby walked Doctor Davis out of the room and paused for a minute in the kitchen.

"Is he out of the woods yet? Or is he still at risk because of the infection?"

Concern furrowed the doctor's brow. "I'm not going to lie to you, Abby; he still has a long recovery ahead of him. It might take days for the antibiotics to make him well enough to get out of bed for longer than a few minutes. He's lucky to have such a caring *cousin.*"

Abby's pulse raced. There was something in the way Doctor Davis said that word that alerted her. "You *know* that Jonah and I aren't cousins?"

The man flashed a hesitant look. "Your folks told me several years ago when you had a really bad case of the flu. They thought it might be important for me to put it in the medical records in case it was ever needed. I wasn't sure if you knew, or I wouldn't have suggested you stay here with Jonah."

Abby was a little upset. "How many other people in the community know?"

"As far as I know, I'm the only one. I don't believe the Bishop knows. And judging by the way Jonah acts around you, I'm guessing he doesn't know either. I can tell he loves you, but he carries a sorrowful look that reveals his broken heart. I know the two of you have a history; I'm glad you have Rachel here with you."

"I plan on telling Jonah the truth as soon as he's well enough to handle it. I can't let him leave the community because he can't bear to be around me."

The doctor placed a hand on Abby's shoulder. "Do you think that's wise to expose your folk's confidence like that? That also might have a negative impact on the way the community views you for staying here with him. Just because my wife and I are *Englisch,* doesn't mean I don't adhere to the rules of the community, and I'm certain they would frown upon such a thing. "

Abby's eyes began to tear up and her throat constricted. ""I'm not too concerned what the community thinks of me at the moment. All I care about is helping Jonah get back on his feet. I love him and I want to marry him, but I can't do that if the Bishop believes us to be first cousins. This secret has gone on long enough. I no longer need protection from my *real* father since he's been dead for fifteen years. The truth will save Jonah and me a lot of hurt."

The doctor pulled on his heavy coat. "There doesn't seem to be an easy way out of this situation. Even if the truth comes out, people in the community might be reluctant to see you and Jonah as anything other than cousins. I know you didn't come to the community until you were older, but that doesn't mean they aren't used to the idea of you being cousins. It might take folks a lot longer to come around to the truth if it should be known to them."

"I know there will be consequences no matter what happens, but I can't keep letting Jonah think his love for me is a sin. That's why he's planning on leaving,"

"I don't think he should think about traveling for at least two weeks. I'd like him to stick around until his stitches are ready to come out, but that will be up to him."

Abby was relieved to hear that she had a little extra time to sort things out, even though she felt bad that Jonah's accident was the reason.

CHAPTER 19

Abby placed a cool rag on Jonah's forehead, allowing her hands to linger on his warm skin. He was still fighting the fever and was due for another dose of medicine, but she hated to keep disturbing him. He'd only gone to sleep about an hour before, after a fitful afternoon of trying to withstand the pain of his headache. The pain meds were barely taking the edge off, but Jonah had refused anything stronger, claiming he preferred to stay as alert as possible. She didn't blame him for that, except she suspected it was so he could take advantage of the little bit of time they had left together before he left the community.

Abby planned on telling him the truth at some point in the next two days, since he wouldn't need her to stay with him any longer than that. Rachel had originally viewed their stay as a vacation from her regular chores at home, but she'd soon found out she'd traded one set of chores for another. And with Abby relying on her so heavily, Rachel had voiced her resistance on more than one occasion already.

Jonah stirred, the corners of his mouth struggling to form a weak smile. Abby appreciated the effort, smiling back fully. "You feel up to swallowing a few pills? It's time for your medicine. Doctor Davis was here while you were sleeping and brought the antibiotics. And since you feel warm again, you need to take another dose of the Tylenol to bring your fever down."

Jonah tried to sit up a little, but struggled against the pain. "I can't believe how much my head hurts. Maybe I need some fresh air."

"I'm not sure it's wise to go outside, but I can open the window if you think you can handle the cold. It's snowing again."

"*Denki.* I'd like it if you'd open the window. You can always get me an extra quilt if I get too cold."

Abby smiled. She was enjoying taking care of Jonah, and it made her happy that he was depending on her. She couldn't help but wish things could be different for the two of them. That they could have a normal relationship—one that wouldn't bring shame to her *mamm* and *daed.*

Abby poured the pills into Jonah's hand, and then gave him a glass of water. It saddened her to see the strain it caused him to swallow three little pills, but she prayed they would be swift to bring healing to his body. When he handed her back the glass, she placed it on the bedside table, and then started to leave his side, but he set his hand on hers.

"Wait. Don't go."

Abby smiled at his neediness. "I'm just going over to open the window for you."

His hand lingered on hers. "Make sure you come back over here when you're done. I want to talk to you."

Abby shook her head firmly. "There will plenty of time to talk in a few days once you begin to recover. You need your rest—doctor's orders."

"The doc isn't here. And maybe this can't wait."

Abby placed her hands on her hips. "Just because Doctor Davis isn't here to tell you what to do doesn't mean I'm going to let you go against his orders. This accident has caused me to do a lot of thinking. I've never been as afraid as I was when I thought I could lose you. So I'm going to make certain that you follow the doctor's orders."

"By the way, how's my *schweschder?"*

Abby turned around and smiled. "She had a healthy *buwe.* His name is Adam."

"That was my *daed's* name. He would have been so happy to have *grandkinner* named after him. I miss him and my *mamm* so much."

"I don't imagine it's easy to have both your parents gone. Your *daed* was a *gut* man. I'm sure he's looking down from heaven with a smile for little Adam."

Jonah held a weak hand out to her. After opening the window, she moved to the side of the bed and put her hand in his. He pulled gently on her hand until she sat on the edge of the bed next to him. Her cheeks heated as her thigh brushed against his even though a thick quilt separated them.

"Abby, I want to apologize for putting your honor in jeopardy. The other day when I saw you by the mulberry tree—our tree, all those feelings from the past came rushing back to me."

Abby interrupted him. "Jonah, I don't think we should be discussing this right now. You might not know what you're saying because of the fever."

Jonah pushed her hand to his forehead. "I think my fever broke about ten minutes ago. I'm fine. I'm not going to break if you talk to me. I really need to get this out in the open."

Abby pulled her hand back from his face, which was cool to the touch. "You have five minutes to say what you have to, and then you're going to rest."

Jonah tried to smile, and Abby could tell he was already worn out, but she would indulge him for a few minutes.

"What I was trying to say is that I'm sorry for treating you disrespectfully. I should never have put either of us in that situation."

Abby put her hand on his. "You weren't disrespectful. I encouraged the attention because I love you."

"I love you too, Abby, but we both need to face the truth."

Abby jumped from the edge of the bed. "The truth is…" She stood by the window, unable to finish her sentence.

Jonah patted the edge of the bed. "*Kume,* sit back down and talk to me about this without getting upset."

Reluctantly turning around to face him, Abby swallowed the tears that threatened to spill. Jonah patted the bed again, motioning her with his eyes to sit.

Jonah looked at her sorrowfully. "I don't want to hurt you anymore than I already have. I should have never let our relationship get this far out of hand. All it's done is hurt both of us. I don't want you to be hurt anymore. The sooner we face the truth, the better it will be for both of us. And the truth is, we can never marry because we're cousins."

Abby placed another hand on Jonah's head to be sure his fever had truly broken. She didn't want him to misunderstand what she was about to say.

"The truth is that we are *not* cousins at all."

Jonah turned pale. "Abby that's not funny. You shouldn't joke about that. How do you figure we aren't cousins?"

Abby took a deep breath and held it for a minute. When she let it out with a whoosh, all her anxiety went with it. "We aren't cousins because Jacob Yoder is not my real *daed.* My real *daed* is an *Englischer* named Eddie Monroe."

Jonah sat up suddenly, ignoring the intense pain in his head. "What are you saying? That you've known all this time we weren't cousins, and you let me suffer through the agony of wanting you and thinking I could never have you?"

"I left the community when I found out five years ago. When I came home, I thought it was over between us, so I didn't say anything. But when I talked to you the other day, I realized we both still had strong feelings for each other, and I prayed about it for the right way to handle the situation. I didn't mean for you to be hurt by any of this, but I didn't want to tell you that the reason we couldn't be together was because of a lie my own *mamm* had told. I felt like I was betraying both of you."

Jonah held her hand tightly. "Go with me to Florida. We can be together there."

Abby couldn't answer him. She'd run away once already and that didn't solve the problem. But she had to admit, the chance to marry Jonah held more weight with her emotions at the moment.

The sound of breaking dishes from outside the bedroom door caused Abby to jump from the edge of Jonah's bed.

CHAPTER 20

Rachel stood outside Jonah's door holding his breakfast tray, waiting for a break in Abby's conversation with their cousin so she wouldn't interrupt. But when she heard her sister say they didn't share the same *daed,* she felt like she couldn't breathe. And when she heard her cousin ask Abby to run away with him to Florida, Rachel had heard enough and threw the breakfast tray to floor, storming down the hall to pack her things. She was angry and had to get away from Abby. She wouldn't stick around and watch her sister hurt her or the rest of the family by selfishly running away again. She had to get home—to get her *mamm* to fix things somehow.

When Abby reached the doorway to Jonah's room, she found a tray on the floor, a ceramic bowl full of oatmeal had split down the middle; oatmeal spilling from the gap. A puddle of orange juice glittered with bits of the broken glass spread across the middle of the path between her and her sister, who'd ducked inside the spare room and slammed the door shut.

Abby's heart pounded in perfect rhythm to the sound of horses hooves coming from outside. Jonah had a visitor. Scrambling to pick up the mess, Abby wondered just how much of her conversation with Jonah that her sister had overheard. Perhaps staying here had not been her best idea yet, but Abby didn't trust herself anymore to make the right decision about this situation. How could she leave here with Jonah and try to have a normal life with him when this mess would forever be held over their heads? But on the other hand; how could she possibly turn down his offer?

Abby mopped up the spilled juice with the linen napkin. She could hear the kitchen door swing open and a voice call out. It was Caleb.

"We're up here," Abby called out. "Will you grab the broom near the door and bring it up to me?"

Caleb was soon up the stairs, broom in hand.

"What happened here?"

Abby grabbed the broom from him and began to clear the broken glass from the hallway. "Rachel dropped the tray. I'll have it cleaned up in no time."

From down the hall, the door to the spare room swung open forcefully, and Rachel stepped into the hallway, tears staining her red-rimmed eyes. "Why don't you tell him the truth? You and I both know I threw that tray down on purpose."

Caleb walked toward his distraught, younger sister. "Why would you do such a thing?"

Rachel leered at Abby. "I'd tell you to ask your *schweschder,* except she isn't your *schweschder."*

Caleb's eyes widened as he turned to Abby. "What is she saying?"

Tears filled Abby's eyes, and she found it difficult to breathe. "Rachel, I'm sorry. I never meant for you to find out this way. I'm still your *schweschder."*

Rachel stormed down the hall toward them. "You're *half* right about that because you and I are only related by *mamm;* you and Caleb aren't related at all. And neither are you and Jonah. I guess that's why you're planning on running off to Florida with him."

Abby couldn't face the looks from both of her siblings that seemed to cut right through her. She let the broom drop to the floor and ran down the stairs. Caleb called after her, but she grabbed her coat and ran out of Jonah's house.

Caleb stepped over the mess of dishes and food that still littered the hallway, and turned to Rachel. "Get yours and Abby's things together. I'll be taking you home."

Rachel did as she was told.

Caleb walked into his cousin's room and closed the door. He crossed over to the bed and looked Jonah in the eye for several minutes before composing his emotions enough to speak. "Are you planning on running off to Florida with Abby?"

Jonah felt vulnerable lying flat on his back, and tried to push himself up on his elbows. When he'd managed to position himself so he could lean his back against the headboard of the bed, he closed his eyes momentarily until the severe pounding in his head let up a little. "I asked her to go with me. I'd like to marry her. I love her. I always have. And now that she told me we aren't really cousins after all, I won't let anything stop me from having the life I've dreamed of having with her for several years now."

Shivering, Caleb crossed to the open window and closed it. "What makes her think she isn't related to you or to me?"

Jonah winced against the pain in his head, and ignored the dizziness he felt from sitting upright. "She told me her real *daed* is an *Englischer* named Eddie Monroe. You don't share the same *daed* or *mamm* the way you thought you did. After your *daed* married Abby's *mamm,* you became siblings my marriage only. Since I'm *your* cousin, I'm not hers. Which means she and I are free to marry."

Caleb collapsed into a chair in the corner of Jonah's room. If what his cousin was saying had any truth to it; that meant his *daed* had been lying to him for the past fifteen years. Unless *he* didn't know the truth either. Was it possible he only *thought* he was Abby's *daed* all these years, and his *mamm*—Abby's *mamm,* had lied to all of them?

Caleb turned to Jonah. "How long has Abby known?"

"She found out five years ago. That's why she left the community."

It was obvious to Caleb that he'd misjudged Abby. It was Abby's *mamm* he needed to confront.

CHAPTER 21

Abby wandered around in the snow, the wind stinging her cheeks with tiny ice crystals. Before she realized, she found herself standing before the set of mulberry trees beside the school house. Funny how she always ended up here—where it all started.

Lowering herself onto the snow-covered swing that hung from one of the trees, Abby was reminded that there were no students in attendance. They'd been out of school for the past few days after the teacher, Nettie Graber, had fallen on the icy steps and broken her right leg and her left arm. The replacement, Nettie's niece, Katie, was due in from Nappanee next week.

Abby relished the solitude, but wished for Jonah to be by her side. She struggled to understand how things could have gotten so far out of control, but this was a perfect example of how one little lie could hurt so many people. This was too big for her to continue to push aside. She wasn't even sure how she would have the strength of spirit to forgive her *mamm.* She thought she had forgiven her, but new pain and anger plagued her, leaving her wondering if she'd ever be able to get past this hurt.

The look in Caleb's eyes were of judgment—for her—even though Abby was just as much a victim of the aftermath of the lie as he and Rachel were. Did he blame her for what her *mamm* had done? As the sound of a buggy neared, she looked up, noting that it was her *Onkel* Seth. She ran to the road to greet him.

Seth signaled the mare to stop when Abby approached. "You look frozen to the bone. What are you doing out here? You must have three inches of snow in your hair." he reached down and assisted her into the buggy and handed her a lap quilt. Despite being out of the wind, Abby continued to shiver, her teeth chattering so much she couldn't speak.

Seth clicked to mare, and they began to move slowly along the slushy road. "From the look of you, I'd guess you could use someone to talk to. I was on my way over to Jonah's place so I could talk to you about something, but I don't want to add to your burdens."

Abby pulled the other lap quilt around her shoulders. "I could actually use the distraction. Maybe if I can help someone else solve their troubles, it might take my mind off of my own."

Seth smiled. "Fair enough. Do you want me to drop you back at Jonah's?"

Abby shook her head. "Caleb and Rachel are there now. Take me to the bakery. Maybe I could help *Aenti* Lillian for a while."

"That's kind of what I wanted to talk to you about. Lillian won't go back to the bakery. We've been to the B&B the past three days and she refuses to meet Ellie. I'm worried the girl is going to go back to Ohio and change her mind about letting us adopt her *boppli.*"

"I'm not going to tell you that worry is a sin because I'm guilty of doing an awful lot of worrying myself lately. But it seems to me that if you want *Aenti* to do anything, you have to let it be *her* idea. Or at least let her *think* that it's her idea."

Seth steered the horse toward the bakery. "I'm not sure I follow that line of thinking."

"Well you know the expression, *you can lead a horse to water, but you can't make him drink?* It's sort of the same principle. When you go to the B&B, don't ask her visit with Ellie. Wait for her to decide on her own. As for the bakery, you'll have to bring her, but not ask her to bake anything. If you bring her for a visit with me, she'll naturally pitch in to help, and it will be *her* idea, not because either of us has asked her to do it."

Seth set the break. "That makes sense. Will you be here for a while? I'd like to bring her by today. It's still early enough that the two of you could have a pretty productive day. I could have her here in less than thirty minutes. What you do think?"

Abby stepped out of her *onkel's* buggy. "I think that's a *gut* idea. Tell her I need someone to talk to; that will get her here. And *Gott* knows I need to talk."

"I'll be back with her as soon as I can."

"Denki, Onkel Seth."

Abby turned to leave, but swung back around. "One more thing...maybe *Aenti* Lillian needs a simple reminder of why you married her in the first place."

Seth smiled. *"Denki,* Abby. I know just the thing."

Abby watched him drive off, and then turned toward Jonah's house. Noting that Caleb's buggy was still there, she knew Jonah was in capable hands for the time being. And knowing her brother would not leave his cousin alone in his weakened state, Abby let herself into the bakery, grateful she'd had the key in her coat pocket.

Tying on a clean apron, Abby was eager to have something to occupy her hands and her mind. Before long, she was humming her favorite hymn, and mixing enough batter for several tins of cinnamon muffins. She intended to send some home with Caleb, and some with her *aenti.*

But given the circumstances, there was no way Caleb would tolerate her staying with Jonah—not even with a chaperone. She wouldn't abandon Jonah in his time of need, even if it meant having to speak to the Bishop. She guessed that her brother was making arrangements to stay overnight with Jonah, and Abby would be agreeable with that, as long as no one stood in the way of her spending the day with him. She would get her *aenti* to come back to the bakery for a few days, until Jonah was back on his feet again.

But there was still the matter of Jonah's question.

CHAPTER 22

By the time Lillian was dropped off at the bakery, she was nearly frantic with worry for Abby. The way her husband described finding her crying in the school yard was enough to break her heart for her niece. She had an idea Abby's troubles involved Jonah in some capacity, and she was just the person to help.

Her husband promised to come back in two hours to pick her up after he went into town for a few supplies. Lillian was looking forward to a nice talk with Abby, but more than that, she was eager to be at the bakery again. Truth be told, she missed it. The feel of flour between her fingers, the smell of freshly baked bread. She was so happy that for the first time in nearly two months her husband hadn't tried to convince her to go back to the bakery, she found herself wanting to be there more than ever.

Walking inside, the jingling of the bells on the door alerted her niece, who was hard at work, that she'd come to help her. Grabbing an apron from a peg on the back wall of the kitchen, Lillian felt ready to dive into baking.

"I'd say by the amount of things you're preparing, you're either planning on opening the bakery for the day, or this problem of yours is bigger than I can help you with."

Abby looked up her with sad eyes. "Maybe a little of both."

Lillian grabbed a section of bread dough and began to knead. "How's Jonah? He must be feeling a lot better if you're here instead of at his *haus.*"

Abby sighed. "Caleb and Rachel are with him. They're both upset with me. I've really made a mess of things."

Lillian covered her bread dough with cheesecloth and set it aside. "Tell me what happened."

"I told Jonah the truth about us not being real cousins, and he asked me to go to Florida with him. I'm not sure I can do that, even though it's probably the only chance we'll have of leading a normal life together."

Lillian gave an encouraging smile. "Is that what you want to do?"

Abby pulled a tray of heart-shaped cookies from the oven. "I'll miss my *familye*—especially Rachel. She's the only *schweschder* I have. When I first came back, she was distant and didn't trust me. Now she trusted me and I let her down again. She was standing outside of Jonah's door and heard our conversation. She's upset that he asked me to go to Florida with him."

"What about Caleb? What did he say about it?"

"*Ach, Aenti,* Rachel had already told him before I had a chance to explain it to him. You should have seen the look on his face. He blames me for what my *mamm* did. I don't want him to have anger and unforgiveness for me or for my *mamm.* I remember when we first met how much he wanted a new *mamm.* He was so happy that we'd joined him and his *daed* to make a *familye.* But now I think he wishes we hadn't."

Lillian hugged Abby, who'd begun to cry. "Don't say such things. It might take a little time for the shock of it to sink in, but he'll remember the love he has for both of you. Caleb hasn't forgotten what it felt like to lose his own *mamm,* and how excited he was when your *mamm* became his *mamm* too. Just give it some time."

Abby wiped her tears with the edge of her apron. "I don't think I have much time left. Jonah is planning to leave in just a few days. If I don't go with him, I fear I may never see him again."

Lillian grabbed the bowl of pink icing and began to spread it on the cooled cookies. "Have you talked to your *mamm* yet?"

Abby placed another batch of heart-shaped cookies into the oven. "I gave her a chance to do the right thing and she said she couldn't do it. She isn't going to go to the Bishop, so I guess I have no other choice but to go to Florida with Jonah."

Lillian choked up at the thought of it. "If you leave, I'll miss you, and so will your *familye*. I know how much your *mamm* missed you when you left five years ago. She cried a lot. She put up a brave front, but I could see the sadness in her eyes."

"I know how much it hurt her, so why doesn't that make her want to do whatever it takes to make this right? Why do you suppose she won't go to the Bishop? She mentioned it might be worse for my *daed* if she did that. Do you think Jacob could be excommunicated for this?"

Lillian bit into one of the heart-shaped cookies. "These are so *gut*. You've made a lot of progress with your baking skills."

Setting the cookie down, Lillian chose her words carefully. "Bishop Troyer is a very understanding and lenient *mann,* but your *daed* is the head of the *familye,* and that means it's his responsibility to uphold the bylaws of the community. What your *mamm* did, well...he went along with it, and that could mean strict discipline for him."

Abby swallowed a lump in her throat. "He's been a *gut daed* to me. Better than my real *daed* could have ever been. I don't want him to be hurt in all of this. I think he was just trying to be honorable and do what was right in the situation. My *mamm* is the one that put Jacob's name on my birth certificate. She's the one that didn't speak up and tell the truth from the very beginning. I know she was only trying to protect me, but her decision has hurt me more than it could have ever protected me."

The jingling of the bells on the front door moved the two of them out of the kitchen. Rachel stood at the doorway with her eyes cast downward.

"Caleb sent me down here to get you and bring you back to Jonah's *haus.*"

"How did he know I was here?"

"He could smell the cookies. He said to bring some with you."

Abby smiled. That was a *gut* sign. If he wanted cookies, that meant he was ready to talk to her. If only she could say the same for Rachel.

CHAPTER 23

Abby didn't waste any time gathering a dozen cookies and putting them into a box to take with her to Jonah's house.

"I hate to leave you here all alone, *Aenti.*"

Lillian shooed her with her hand. "Being here was just what I needed to feel better. It might take some time for me to get back to my old routine, but I feel ready to try. Besides, your *Onkel* Seth will be back here in about an hour to pick me up. I think we might have to go around the community and gift some of these cookies and muffins and bread, but I'm alright with that. Go and talk to your *bruder,* and try to reconnect with Rachel. She needs her big *schweschder* right now. She's at that delicate age where she's working on becoming an adult, and she really needs you."

Abby hugged her *aenti.* "I know. She's the biggest reason I don't want to leave. I never had an older *schweschder.* You were the closest thing I had to that, and I'll never forget how much it meant to me to have you around. I can't take that away from her."

Lillian smiled. "Now you're thinking straight. Pray some more about this. *Gott* will make things right. Maybe not in the way you see it, but in the way that's best for everyone."

Abby gathered the cookies and muffins and headed out into the snow toward Jonah's house, hope filling her that God would make things right.

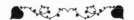

Lillian pulled the last of the loaves of fresh bread out of the oven and set them aside to cool. She'd finished most of the cleanup, and wrapped most of the loaves of bread. She'd heard a buggy pull into the parking lot a few minutes before, and tried to hurry so she wouldn't make her husband wait. Just a few more dishes, and she would be done. If she knew her husband, he was probably talking to the horse rather than coming inside and talking to the women-folk. He had no idea Abby had left, but Lillian giggled at the thought of her husband talking to the horse anyway. A little cold weather and snow wouldn't hurt him. Besides, she only had about ten minutes worth of work to finish. She knew if he got cold enough, he'd come in and stand by the stove to warm up. In the meantime, she had bread pans to wash.

Seth knew his wife would stay and talk even after she heard his buggy pull into the lot behind the bakery. She knew him well enough to know he'd choose talking to his horse over being a third party to women's conversation. This, he knew, would afford him the time to set up the surprise he had for her, hoping to break through her shell of sadness. Thankful for the continuous snow, Seth set to work on the bottom of the snowman. He hoped he'd have enough time to finish it before Lillian came outside, but she knew he'd go inside the bakery to get her if he got too cold.

The snow was packing very nicely, making quick work of the bottom portion. Next, he rolled the middle, making sure it was smaller, but not so large that he wouldn't be able to lift it onto the bottom. Seth pushed the large bottom portion so it was centered with the large window in the front of the bakery. Next, he pushed the middle up onto the base, and quickly rolled a head for it. Plopping the head on top, he was satisfied with the height.

Almost as tall as me.

Pulling the stones from his pocket, he pushed them into the head to make eyes. He hoped Lillian would know that the stones came from the keepsake spice box he'd given her five years ago for her birthday. He hoped this gesture would remind his wife of how much he loved and cherished her.

Locating a couple of fallen twigs from the large maple tree in the lot, Seth pushed them into the sides of the middle for arms. Next he snapped off a few smaller branches and broke them into short pieces to make a large smile on the snowman.

When he was satisfied the snowman was finished, he stood proudly beside him and waited patiently for Lillian to exit the bakery.

Lillian took the baked goods out the back door of the bakery and placed them in the back of the buggy. Seth was nowhere around. Wondering if he'd gone in the front door, which would have been unlocked, she went back inside to check for him and make sure she locked the front door before leaving. Once inside, she called out her husband's name, but he didn't answer. Thinking it was strange, she went to the front of the store to lock the front door before searching for Seth.

Stopping short of the front door, Lillian spotted her husband standing next to a large snowman similar to the one they'd made on their first date. Tears welled up in her eyes, and a lump formed in her throat. She opened the door and ran to him, jumping into his waiting arms. He spun her around before setting her down.

"I can't believe you did this for me. Are those the same rocks from the original snowman?"

Seth took off his gloves and cupped her face in his hands. "As a matter of fact, they are. I wanted you to know how much I love you…how much I will always love you."

Seth pressed his lips to hers and kissed her, gently sweeping his cold lips across her warm ones.

Lillian leaned into his kiss with a passion she hadn't felt for a while. "I love you too, Seth. Can we go to the B&B? I'm ready to meet Ellie."

Seth let out a whoop, and picked her up and twirled her around again. He hadn't felt this happy in a while, and it felt *gut.*

CHAPTER 24

Abby hung up her coat on the peg in Jonah's kitchen. She could hear faint voices from upstairs, and decided to place the cookies on a plate and bring a pitcher of milk with her before going up to greet the three of them. She dreaded having to tell Jonah she wouldn't be able to go to Florida with him right now, but hoped he would wait for her to straighten things out here with her family first. She hoped he would understand and be willing to wait for her.

As she neared the top step, Abby heard her siblings laughing. That was a *gut* sign. She stood in the doorway and waited for a break in the laughter.

Caleb held his hand out to her. "Abby, *kume.* We need to talk."

Abby walked timidly toward them, noting that Jonah was sitting upright and looking like the color had returned to his face. She sat in the chair that her brother had gotten up from, and waited for him to have his say.

Caleb sat on the edge of the windowsill. "I've had a couple of hours for your news to sink in, and I just want to say I'm sorry for the way I reacted—or didn't react. I'm also sorry for our little talk we had the other day in the barn. Why didn't you tell me the truth then?"

"It wasn't my truth to tell. It doesn't matter anyway. It's not like it would have made any difference. There isn't anything any of us can do about it."

She turned to Jonah then. "I'm sorry, Jonah, but I can't go with you to Florida right now. I know I'm grown up, but that doesn't mean I can run away from my *familye* again. I did it once, and it was the biggest mistake I've ever made. The longer I was away, the easier it was to stay away, and I don't want to do that again. I've missed too much time with my little *schweschder* already."

Rachel walked over and placed her hand on Abby's shoulder. "I want you to go to Florida."

Abby's heart sank. Did her sister want to be rid of her?

"Why, Rachel?"

"You're my *schweschder,* and I love you. I'll miss you terribly, but you must go so you can be happy. You can't do that if you stay here. Seeing you here taking care of Jonah is the happiest I've ever seen you."

Caleb stood up. "Rachel's right. I'd be honored if you'd marry my cousin. I can't think of a better *mann* for you. Go. Be happy in Florida."

Tears filled Abby's eyes as she looked over at Jonah. "Are you sure we can't try to stay here?"

Jonah had a mixture of emotion showing in his eyes. "I don't see any other way for us to be together. If you go with me, I promise to make you happy."

Abby reached over and placed her hand in his.

"You already do."

Caleb walked over to the tray of cookies and milk and started pouring the milk into the glasses. "Then let's celebrate. The smell of these cookies has been making my mouth water since you walked into the room with them."

Abby wiped a tear from the corner of her eye.

"How am I going to break the news to *Mamm* and *Daed?"*

Caleb handed her a glass of milk and a cookie on a napkin. "I'll help you. I think it might be easier if they know I support your decision. I'm curious about something though. Did *Daed* know about this all along?"

Abby gulped down the milk in her mouth. "I'm afraid so. In all fairness to him, he went along with it to protect *Mamm's* honor. His heart was in the right place, but neither of them had time to think it through. Bishop Troyer was a lot more strict back then. He pressed for the marriage more than either of them."

"I suppose it was what was best for everyone at the time, given the circumstances. That doesn't make it right for *your* situation. I stand by what I said. I think your best chance of happiness is to start over in the community in Florida."

Abby smiled. "*Denki,* Caleb. As far as I'm concerned, no matter what the truth is, you'll always be my *bruder,* and Jacob will always be my *daed.*"

Caleb hugged her lightly. "In my heart, you'll always be my *schweschder.*"

Caleb offered Jonah a cookie and he turned it down. "I'm not sure my stomach can handle any solid food yet, no matter how *gut* they are."

Caleb stepped back over to the window and leaned against the sill again. "There's one more issue we need to address."

He looked at Abby sternly. "I'll stay here with Jonah overnight while he's recovering, and you can take care of him during the day. That is, if Rachel is in agreement to act as chaperone."

Rachel and Abby nodded in agreement.

"Doctor Davis should be here soon. While he's here, we can go home and talk to *Mamm* and *Daed.* I've had Rachel pack your things. You can come back in the morning."

Abby was happy for her sibling's help with Jonah. While she couldn't wait to start her life with Jonah in Florida, she dreaded having to tell her parents.

CHAPTER 25

Abby pulled the buggy into Becca's yard. After the heart-wrenching talk she'd had with her family the night before, she was ready for something cheerful. She couldn't wait to see the new *boppli,* and give her the news of Jonah's recovery. Levi let her in and led her to the bedroom where Becca was cuddling her new bundle.

She approached Becca quietly, making sure she didn't wake the *boppli.* *"Gudemariye, wie gehts?"*

Becca sighed. "Still pretty tired, but I'm happy. How's my *bruder?* Is he giving you a hard time, or is he being a *gut* patient?"

Abby's cheeks heated. "He's doing much better, but I didn't stay with him last night. My *bruder* took over watching him at night, and I'll be watching over him for the next few days until the doctor gives him permission to be out of bed."

"Would you like to hold the *boppli?"*

Abby eagerly held out her arms and reached for little Adam. She cradled him close, enjoying the new *boppli* smell. *Boppli's* always had such a sweet scent that nothing could compare to.

Becca straightened herself in the bed, trying to get comfortable. "I hear your *Aenti* Lillian is adopting a *boppli."*

Abby cooed at little Adam. "They haven't decided for certain I think. But I'm hoping they will. I think it will be *gut* for them—and for the *boppli."*

Concern furrowed Becca's brow. "I'll be honest with you; when I heard what happened to your *aenti,* I told Levi I wanted the doctor in attendance for Adam's birth. I wasn't comfortable having just the midwife here. And it's nothing against Miriam. I just wanted everything to go smoothly."

"From what Doctor Davis tells me, you aren't the only one who feels that way. He's had several requests for deliveries in the past month."

Abby handed the baby back to Becca, and sat in the chair by her bedside. "There's something I need to tell you before you hear it from someone else."

Alarm crossed Becca's face faster than a lightning strike. "Is there something you haven't told me about my *bruder?*"

Abby held up a hand to stop her grief. "No, he's going to be sore for a few days, but doc says he'll recover. But this does have to do with Jonah—and me."

Becca let a gasp escape her lips. "Did the two of you kiss again? Oh no; by the look on your face, I'd say you did. Abby, don't you know the two of you are going to get yourselves excommunicated."

Abby couldn't help but fan her heated cheeks. "I'm not your cousin. I'm not Jonah's cousin. And Jacob Yoder isn't my real *daed."* She'd spoken it all so fast she didn't even stop to take a breath.

"Slow down, Abby. You're telling me you're not related to me or my *bruder?"*

Abby swallowed down the lump that tried to bring tears to her eyes. "It's a long story, and I don't really want to reveal the details right now, but it's true."

"What do you plan on doing? Will you go to the Bishop and tell him?"

Abby felt a tear roll down her cheek. "It's not that simple. If I go to the Bishop, it will bring shame to my *mamm* and *daed.* It could get *them* excommunicated. They are getting older, and they need the community. But Jonah and I can start over in another community. He suggested Florida since your *mamm's bruder* is there and he could help us."

Tears filled Becca's eyes. "Florida is so far away. Jonah is the only *familye* I have left. How long have the two of you been planning this?"

Abby suddenly wished she would have waited for Jonah to have this conversation with Becca. They'd been friends for fifteen years, but she and Jonah had been family for a lot longer. She couldn't bear to see Becca hurt, but she didn't think she could wait until the end of the week and surprise her with the news at the last minute.

"Jonah has been planning it for a week now. I thought he would have told you by now."

Becca sniffled. "He mentioned he'd like to go, but I thought he was only thinking about it. I never imagined he'd consider really going. I want little Adam to grow up knowing his *Onkel* Jonah. It breaks my heart that they haven't even met yet."

"The Doctor practically had to strap him to his bed to keep him from getting up and coming to see you. He feels just awful that he can't be here. And I'm sorry for telling you all of this; I thought you knew Jonah was leaving at the end of next week."

Becca placed the baby over her shoulder to burp him. "Will you be going with him?"

Abby paused before answering, hoping to gain some composure. "He asked me to go. At first, I told him I couldn't go with him, but Caleb and Rachel talked me into it. And when I talked to my *mamm* last night, it was apparent that she had no intention of going to the Bishop on my behalf, so I've decided to go. It's the only chance we have for having a normal life together. We plan to marry when we arrive in Florida."

"I'm going to miss your wedding?"

Abby managed a weak smile. "I suppose it's only fair since I missed your wedding. We'll want you to visit once we've settled into the new community."

Becca sniffled some more. "All this time I thought you were my cousin, and now you're going to be my *schweschder*-in-law. It's funny how things work out."

Abby was glad Becca was taking the news as well as she was. Deep down, Abby hoped they didn't have to go. Was it too unreasonable for her to hope that her *mamm* would save her from having to leave her family and her best friend again?

Please Gott, we're going to need a miracle.

CHAPTER 26

Lizzie took hot coffee out to the barn to Jacob, who had been making slow progress with the morning chores in Caleb's absence. As she trudged through the deep snow, she pulled her coat close to guard against the wind, wondering if spring would ever come.

Opening the barn door, she searched for her husband, dreading the moment when their eyes would meet, for he would surely know her mood just by looking at her.

Jacob reached for the coffee, "Is something weighing on your mind? You've been quiet since last night just after Caleb left for Jonah's *haus.*"

Lizzie knew it was time to discuss this with her husband, so why was it so difficult for her to say the words? Perhaps it was because she already knew what she needed to do, and she needed Jacob's approval.

"The *kinner* had a talk with me yesterday late afternoon, and I need to discuss it with you. I wanted them to include you in the conversation, but they thought it was best if they spoke to me alone first."

Jacob leaned against the pitchfork he'd been using to clean out the stalls. "This sounds serious."

Lizzie lowered herself onto a milking stool and cupped her forehead in her hands, pausing for a deep breath. "I've made a mess of my life from the very day I left this community when I was eighteen, and it's still affecting my *dochder* negatively. I made a mistake in judgment by trusting a young, *Englisch buwe* and I'm still paying for it all these years later."

Jacob set the pitchfork against the stall and went to his wife's side. "Lizzie, we've talked about this before, and you know that *Gott* brought forth the miracle of Abby when you strayed from His path. *Gott* always has a way of turning the bad things we do into *gut*—especially since He knows your heart is in Him. We might stray from the path, but He always brings us back to Him."

Lizzie began to get choked up. "I know that, but because of my sin, *Gott* has taken her from me once already. And now, it's happening again."

"What are you talking about?"

Lizzie began to cry. "Our *dochder* is planning on leaving the community again and I have the power to stop her, but I don't know if I have the strength to do it."

Jacob felt suddenly weak, lowering himself onto a fresh bale of hay across from Lizzie. "Why is she leaving? Is it because of Jonah?"

Lizzie wiped her tear-dampened face. "They're planning to go to Florida together so they can marry there."

If Jacob hadn't already been sitting, he'd have fallen over from the shock of it. "They plan to get married? Why didn't she come to me? Do you think she's never really felt I was her *daed?"*

Lizzie shrugged. "If I would have waited to tell her the truth back then until you could be there to help me break the news to her, I believe we could have spared all of us the pain of her leaving the first time. It's a regret I have to live with. But this time, I want to do the right thing so I don't keep living with regret. I have to go to the Bishop and accept whatever consequences there are—for the sake of my *dochder's* happiness."

"I think that's wise. But I shoulder the blame for how far this has gotten out of control. I should have spoken up from the very beginning." He turned to Lizzie. "Don't misunderstand me. I still would have married you, but I would have never gone along with this lie that has been eating away at our *familye* all these years."

Lizzie looked at her husband sorrowfully. Her lie to protect her daughter had been the very thing that hurt her most. And her husband still loved her in spite of it all. She didn't feel she deserved that love, but she intended to earn it. And if Abby would ever consider forgiving her, she had to make it right, and she had to do it immediately.

"Maybe we should break the news to the rest of the *kinner* before we go to the Bishop."

Lizzie shook her head. "Caleb and Rachel already know, and they're taking it better than I expected they would. They actually support Abby's decision to go to Florida. I don't think Samuel knows, but he's always off somewhere with his cousins and friends. He would be gone from sun-up to sun-down if we let him. I guess we need to track him down and have a *familye* discussion about all of this. If we can keep Abby here, and make it so she and Jonah can be married here, then I'm willing to accept whatever my fate is here in the community. But Abby deserves to stay here if that's what she wants."

Lizzie wondered how such an innocent lie could have gotten so far out of control that it had nearly torn her family apart. Her intentions in the beginning were to hide her daughter from the man who had taken advantage of her in her youth and stolen her innocence. A man who was a dangerous drug addict and a criminal for all she knew. She should have told Abby the truth after Eddie's death. Instead, she had allowed her own selfish desires to cloud her judgment of what was right. She had put her own wants before those of her daughter, and it was Abby who was paying for her mistakes.

All of that was about to change.

Lizzie could not let another day go by without bringing the truth forward once and for all. She would stand before the Bishop and confess, even if meant she would be excommunicated.

CHAPTER 27

By the time Abby reached Jonah's house, she was emotionally drained. Rachel had been fairly quiet the entire trip. She was grateful her sister had agreed to stay outside at Becca's house, and play with the kittens in the barn while she talked with her in private. It wasn't that she'd said anything Rachel didn't already know, but she didn't want her sister to hear any unpleasant conversation if there should be any. Thankfully, Becca had taken the news well. Abby suspected she was far too happy with her new *boppli* for much of anything to bother her for the time-being, but she welcomed the distraction nonetheless.

Abby left her horse outside in the yard at Jonah's house, knowing Caleb would tend to the mare before he left. She was eager to see how Jonah was feeling after not being able to stay with him during the night. When she entered the kitchen, Jonah was sitting at the table, fully dressed and wearing the grin that she loved so much.

"*Gudemariye,* Jonah. You look a lot better. Should you be out of bed though?"

Jonah smiled from ear to ear, but Abby could see he still fought back pain.

"Don't worry so much about me. I'm strong. And the doc gave me permission to be up. As a matter of fact, he even gave me permission to get a little fresh air."

Abby smiled. "That's *gut* to hear."

Jonah reached for Abby's hand. "We haven't taken a buggy ride for a long time. What do you say we do that now, while I still have the energy?"

Abby furrowed her brow. "Are you sure the jostling of the buggy won't hurt your head? Maybe we should just take a little walk instead."

Jonah squeezed her hand and smiled. "Where I want to go is a little too far to walk. If we go slowly I'll be fine."

Abby's pulse raced, and she smiled knowingly. She knew where he wanted to take her, and she was eager to go.

Abby's heart skipped a beat when the familiar set of mulberry trees came into view. Jonah had insisted on driving, and she'd cuddled next to him to stay warm. They'd taken many forbidden buggy rides together, but this one seemed more special than all the rest. This one seemed more like an official date.

Jonah stepped down carefully from the buggy, and then held out his hand to assist Abby. She thought he had never looked more handsome than he did now. His smile showed the slightest of dimples at each side of his cheeks, his blue eyes sparkled in the bright sunshine. With the bandage on his head covered by his hat, it was easy to pretend everything was alright—especially since he didn't let his pain wipe the smile from his face.

They walked over and stood beneath the mulberry tree where they'd shared their first kiss. Jonah pulled her into his arms and kissed her temples. He knew he shouldn't risk holding her and kissing her out in the open, but the school was vacant, and there was no one around but the two of them. She felt comfortable in his arms, like she had always meant to be there. He breathed in the scent of fresh lilac soap; a hint of cinnamon that lingered on the collar of her coat. The lonely void he'd felt for so many years all melted away in this one embrace. He never knew love could feel this freeing. He unbuttoned his coat, wrapping it around Abby as he held her close. Her warm breath seeped through his shirt as she rested her head against his chest. He didn't want to let her go, but he'd brought her here for a reason, and he needed to speak his mind before his energy drained.

"You know I always hoped we'd be married here beneath these trees. But since we can't, I figured at the very least, you deserved a proper proposal. And what better place than right here where it all began."

Abby wasn't willing to lift her head from his chest just yet. She needed to hear the soothing beat of his heart to validate the moment—to ensure the reality of it. Jonah's hand held her there at the base of her neck, his fingers gently raking through the loose strands of her hair. It sent twinges of desire through her, making her momentarily forget the riskiness of their actions.

Jonah tucked his hand under Abby's chin and lifted until her lips met his. The warmth of her mouth on his, and the sweetness of her shallow breaths made him wish they were already married. He gently held her away from him, and knelt before her. Taking her hands in his, he looked up into her glistening eyes.

"Abby, I've loved you since the day we first met, but I fell in love with you the first time I kissed you under this very tree. Marry me so I can enjoy your love and your sweet kisses I can't live without. Continue to be my best friend, and become my helpmate until death parts us."

Abby's lower lip quivered with joy, tears filling her eyes.

"I will marry you, but only if we're married here, under the mulberry tree."

Jonah stood up abruptly, the pain in his head causing him to groan under his breath. "That's not possible, Abby and we both know it. There's no way Bishop Troyer is going to marry us when he thinks we're first cousins. If we were second cousins, we wouldn't have a problem, but since your *familye's* lie is preventing us from marrying in the community, we must wait until we go to Florida."

Abby took Jonah's hands in hers. "Just the other day you said that even *Gott* Himself couldn't make us so we weren't cousins, but He did! Let's not be hasty and give up on that miracle we've been hoping for. *Gott* will make this right for us, and we *will* be married here."

Abby was right, but Jonah still found it difficult to trust in what he wanted most—to have her as his *fraa,* and to be able to live in this community with her.

Abby felt a mixture of sadness and elation as they left the mulberry tree. She was engaged, but her heart ached at the thought of not being able to marry Jonah under their tree.

CHAPTER 28

Seth steered the horse into the curved driveway in front of the B&B. It would be their second meeting with Ellie, and he was hopeful that she was going to grant them adoption rights for her baby.

Seth squeezed Lillian's hand. "Are you ready to go ask her if she's made up her mind?"

Lillian looked at her husband through tearful eyes. "What if she says no? I'm not sure I can handle that."

Seth pulled her into his arms. "We prayed about it, and now it's up to *Gott*. I believe He put Ellie in our path for a reason. We have to trust that."

Lillian wiped her tears. "You're right. If it's *Gotte's wille,* we'll be that *boppli's familye.*"

Seth kissed his wife full on the mouth. "I love you."

Lillian kissed him back and couldn't help but smile. "I love you too."

"*Denki* for opening your heart to Ellie. You're going to be a *gut mamm.*"

"And you're going to be a *gut daed.* I'm really happy *Gott* brought Ellie into our lives. I know *Gott* can't bring back our little *buwe*, but maybe He's giving us the opportunity to help a *boppli* who needs a *familye* just as much as we want to be his or her *familye.*"

Seth and Lillian stomped their feet on the porch of the B&B so they wouldn't track snow in on *Aenti* Bess's hardwood floors. She worked hard to keep the country charm atmosphere in the B&B, and the freshly polished floors were difficult to maintain in the winter.

Bess suddenly rushed down the stairs pretty fast for a woman her age. "I need your help up there, Lillian. Ellie's in labor. *Boppli's* coming fast. I'm not sure the doctor is going to get here in time."

Lillian's pulse raced at the thought of it. What could she do? She wasn't a midwife. Fear coursed through her when another thought crossed her mind. If Ellie was having the *boppli* now, then it was possible she was about to become a new *mamm.*

Please Gott, let Ellie bless me and Seth with this boppli. It's my heart's desire to be this boppli's familye.

Upstairs, Lillian felt awkward and out of place. She didn't know what she was doing there, except that *Aenti* Bess had told her on the way up to the room that Ellie had voiced that she wanted her to be there when she had the *boppli.* Lillian hoped her nervousness wouldn't be misinterpreted by Ellie as not wanting to adopt the *boppli.*

"What do you want me to do, *Aenti?*"

Bess took charge of the room. She was no stranger to delivering *bopplies,* even though she'd never established herself as an official midwife.

"Do you remember the breathing I taught you so you could give birth to your own *boppli?*"

The mention of Lillian's *boppli* didn't make her cry this time because she was too preoccupied with helping Ellie. "*Jah.*"

Bess prepared clean towels and a small quilt. "Stay near her head and help her breathe through this, just like I showed you."

Lillian turned to Ellie and panted with her through a long contraction. When it was over, Ellie whined a little and asked for a cool cloth on her forehead. Lillian went to the other side of the room where a basin had been set up along with a large pitcher full of fresh water. She dampened a cloth and quickly returned to Ellie's side, who'd begun another strong contraction.

"Where's Melanie? Why isn't she here?"

Bess draped fresh linens over Ellie in preparation for the birth. "She went into town for some things about an hour ago. Ellie's water broke and the labor has progressed very quickly for a first *boppli*. She's nearly ready to start pushing."

Ellie pushed the pillow out of the way and propped herself on her elbows. "I think I've been having these contractions for a few hours. They were so light earlier that I just thought it was regular aches and pains the same I've had for the last few months. It didn't start to really get strong until my water broke. Oh...here comes another one."

Ellie braced herself, finding it difficult to follow Lillian's lead with the breathing. She felt a strong urge to push, and began to bear down a little.

"Don't push yet, Ellie. It's not quite time yet. Breathe through the contraction."

Ellie threw her head back. "I can't do this anymore. It hurts."

Ellie let out a scream. "Make it stop. Please."

Lillian tried to get her to focus, but it wasn't easy.

"Try to breathe with me, Ellie. You're almost there. You can do this."

Lillian took Ellie's hand, and felt her squeeze it, as she fell into the rhythm of breathing with her.

"On the next contraction, Ellie, I want you to push with all your strength." Bess had taken charge and decided it was time.

Lillian's heart pounded as she held Ellie's hand through the long push. She could see the *boppli's* head, and felt like her own head was being squeezed just as hard from the fear that tried to grip her.

The next push revealed a very pink little girl. She let out the sweetest little cry, almost breaking Lillian's heart for her. Bess cut the cord and placed her on the quilt, and then handed her over to Lillian.

"Take her over there and get her cleaned up, Lillian."

Instinctively, Lillian carried the squirming, crying *boppli* to the bureau and set her down to examine the perfection as she dipped a cloth in the water to wash her off.

She'd held newborns before, but this one was special. This one could possibly be hers. Was it too bold to hope? She was possibly the most beautiful *boppli* Lillian had ever seen, and it scared her to think about how much she wanted to be her *mamm.*

She finished washing the perfect little newborn and wrapped her in a clean quilt, and then she walked over to the side of the bed where Bess was finishing up with the delivery. Lillian held her out to Ellie. "Do you want to hold her?"

Ellie put up a hand. "No. She's so small, I'm afraid I would break her. Besides, she's yours and Seth's. I signed the papers yesterday. You can take her home with you after you sign the papers. The lawyer is still here waiting on your signature."

Lillian's knees nearly gave out, and she stepped backward to sit in the chair in the corner of the room. She couldn't believe her ears. She cradled the *boppli* close to her and caressed her head. She was asleep from all the excitement.

Ellie smiled at her. "What are you going to name her?"

Lillian admired her new *boppli.* "I'm sure my husband would agree with me; I'd like to name her Ellie, if that's alright with you."

Ellie smiled again. "I'd like that very much."

CHAPTER 29

Lizzie was shaking as Jacob knocked on the Bishop's door. Was it too late to change her mind? It didn't matter because she knew she couldn't keep hurting her family. The truth had been long overdue to come out into the open, and she was prepared to face it.

Gott, give me strength, and soften the Bishop's heart toward me and Jacob. Please don't let us be excommunicated.

Mrs. Troyer greeted them with a smile. "This is an unexpected surprise. Please *kume*. I will let my husband know we have company."

Jacob stopped her. "We aren't here for a visit. We need to see the Bishop for a confession."

Mrs. Troyer looked confused, but politely excused herself to get her husband.

Lizzie wrung her hands, despite the constant prayers that she repeated in her head.

Jacob felt unusually calm as Bishop Troyer entered the room. "We're here for a confession."

The Bishop's eyes darted back and forth between Jacob and Lizzie. "Both of you?"

Jacob and Lizzie nodded in unison.

Bishop Troyer motioned them toward the shaker furniture in the sitting room. "I've been wondering when you were going to come to me. Since it's been so many years, I wasn't sure if you were ever going to come forward."

Jacob and Lizzie looked at each other quizzically.

"You know why we're here?"

Bishop Troyer suppressed a grin. "You're here to tell me about Abby, and why I performed an impromptu wedding when it wasn't necessary. Am I right?"

Lizzie cleared her throat. "That's part of it. How much do you know?"

Bishop Troyer leaned forward in his chair. "Not much gets by me in my community. I knew the timing wasn't right for the two of you to have conceived Abby given how long you'd been gone from the community. And I knew your relationship had been a pure one from the amount of time you'd been allowed away from your *daed's* strict hold on you, Miss Elizabeth. Is that what the two of you came to tell me?"

The color drained from Lizzie's face as she nodded her answer to the Bishop's question. He'd known all along. "If you knew, why did you marry us that day?"

"I didn't see any reason not to. The fact that Hiram was pressing the issue didn't help either of you gather enough courage to tell the truth. I didn't think it would ever be a problem, but having both of you in the same community and widowed, well…I thought it was best to have you married once and for all."

Jacob felt both relief and annoyance with the situation. "There's a problem that has arisen out of this. Something neither of us could have foreseen."

Bishop Troyer put up a hand to stop Jacob from saying anymore. "Like I said. Not much gets by me unnoticed. I know about the situation with Abby and Jonah. I understand they're planning on going to Florida to be married, and you want them to be married here."

Lizzie shook her head. "*Jah.* We don't want her to have to leave the community. But we don't see how the community will accept a marriage between them since they know them as first cousins, even though they're not."

The Bishop gave them a serious look. "Are the two of you prepared to make a public announcement about this? You don't have to divulge personal information, but you'll have to openly admit to the community that Abby is not related by blood to Jacob—that she isn't his *dochder.*"

Jacob answered for both of them. "We're prepared to do that for our *dochder's* happiness."

Bishop Troyer stood. "You can make the announcement at the services tomorrow, and then I'll agree to marry them."

Lizzie's eyes filled with tears. *Gott* had answered her prayers despite her sinful actions.

CHAPTER 30

Abby smiled as she stood before the Bishop, who'd positioned himself between the mulberry trees in the school yard, waiting for him to perform the marriage ceremony for her and Jonah. Snowflakes touched her pink cheeks, but she didn't care. She was finally marrying the only *mann* she could ever love. If it was possible, Jonah looked more handsome than ever on this snowy, February day. Wasn't this the month of love? Even if it wasn't for anyone else, it *was* for her.

Abby momentarily caught her *mamm's* loving glance. With that one look, Abby tried to convey all the love and gratitude she felt because of her *mamm's* brave confession. Abby knew it was because of God's love, and her *mamm's* strength, that she was standing here today, able to marry Jonah.

After a long talk with her *mamm* regarding the circumstances surrounding her conception, Abby finally understood why her *mamm* had felt the need to protect her in the manner in which she did. It was at that point that Abby stopped seeing her *mamm* as a liar, but as a strong woman who had endured a great hardship to protect her daughter. Abby admired her *mamm* for the strength it took for her to raise her alone in the *Englisch* world for the first ten years of her life. And for the courage it took for her *mamm* to return to the Amish community and face the consequences.

Abby quickly glanced at Jacob, who sat protectively at her *mamm's* side. She had a new respect for him, too. For accepting the responsibility of becoming her *daed,* and for protecting her from the harshness of her *Englisch* heritage.

Abby's eyes returned to Jonah, her love, and her future. She hoped that God would continue to bless her, and that she would be a strong wife for Jonah, strong like her *mamm.*

Abby shivered a bit from the wind, but she was too excited to be here to care. There was no denying that a Florida wedding would have been warmer, but nothing could have warmed her heart more than being married to Jonah under the mulberry tree.

THE END

Please continue to the next page to read BOOK 4 in this series

Amish Winter of Promises
BOOK FOUR

Samantha Jillian Bayarr
Copyright © 2012 by Samantha Jillian Bayarr

CHAPTER 1

"Help me! They're after me!"

The jingling of the bells on the front door of the bakery, and the frantic, female voice were enough to give Caleb's heart a jump start. From the spot under the kitchen sink, where he'd been trying to fix the leak, the noise startled him enough to make him hit his head on the copper pipe. Grabbing a rag to wipe his hands, he rushed to the front of the store to see what the urgency was.

As he rounded the corner of the kitchen, he could hear the dogs barking and snarling. They jumped at the front door, teeth exposed, as though they were after a prowler. From the corner of his eye, Caleb spotted the young woman, her arms full of books, a lunch pail dangling carelessly from her wrist. Her eyes were wide, her mouth agape, her ashen face glistening with a mist of perspiration. Caleb couldn't help but stare as he watched her gasp for breath as though she had been running for her life. Though she was safe inside the bakery, the dogs continued to make her jump every time they charged at the door.

Caleb turned fully toward her, a smile twisting up at the corners of his mouth. "Well that's your problem. I'd say they're after the salami and cheese in your lunch pail."

Katie Graber pushed her nose in the air. "I hardly see the humor in this. They tore the bottom of my dress, and nearly bit my leg off." She turned to the side to reveal the tear at the hem of her dress. "And how did you know what I have in my lunch pail?"

Caleb admired her as she pushed blonde hair behind her ear. "Because I'm in a bakery, but I can smell your lunch from way over here."

Katie straightened her disheveled coat and sighed at the torn hem of her dress. Her face was flush, and the blue of her eyes held a hint of fire in them. Agitation showed in her expression, and suspense hung in the air.

Was she Nettie Graber's replacement at the school? From the look of it, Caleb didn't guess she was beginning her first day on the best of terms. If he wasn't so enamored by her pure beauty, he would have reveled in her agitation over the stray dogs.

Katie stiffened her chin. "I believe if I hadn't come in here those mongrels would have made a meal out of me!"

Caleb suppressed a smile. "Those mutts are harmless. They're hungry is all, and they could smell that salami in your lunch pail."

Katie looked toward the door, where the dogs continued to pace and whine. "It's none of your business what my lunch pail contains."

Rachel came in from the storeroom wiping her hands on her apron. "What's all the commotion out here?" She looked up at Katie and smiled. "Where are my manners? You must be the new school teacher. I'm Rachel Yoder. I run this bakery for my *aenti.*"

Katie's look softened. "*Jah.* I'm Katie Graber. But if those dogs don't leave, I'm going to be late for my first day."

Rachel frowned at her brother, who seemed to be enjoying poor Katie's distress. "Caleb, take her out the back door and get her to your buggy before those dogs come after her again. You'll have to take her to school."

Caleb scowled at his sister. "What about the leak you wanted me to fix?"

Rachel shooed him with her hand. "It'll keep until you get back. You can put a bucket back under the sink." Her attention turned to Katie, who looked helplessly shaken from the experience. "She can't be late for her first day. What kind of impression would that make on her students?"

Rachel reached for the books in Katie's hands and set them on the counter. "You'll probably want to straighten your hair and fix your *kapp.* It's nearly off your head. I'll get you a few pins to tack the hem of your dress back together."

Caleb sighed in defeat. Rachel had always bossed him around even though she was his younger sister, but Rachel had an authoritative influence about her that Caleb found tough to match. He went to put the bucket back under the leaky sink and wiped down the grime from his face, hands, and arms. He wasn't sure why he cared what the snobby school teacher thought of him. But she was beautiful and educated, and he didn't want to appear unkempt in her sparkling blue eyes. But even if he was cleaned up, would it matter? Would Katie Graber ever look at him the way he wanted her to?

CHAPTER 2

Caleb offered his hand to Katie to assist her into his buggy, but she refused, her nose lifted in disdain. He felt self-conscious, wondering if he smelled like the dirty pipes he'd been trying to clean and repair. He didn't know much about the district she'd come from, but he was certain all districts frowned on prideful discord among the people. Maybe she was simply shy. Or she felt uneasy being in strange territory, rather than being snooty, which was his first impression of her.

Once he settled into the seat next to her, he grabbed the reins and clucked to his gelding to urge him out of the snowy rut the wheels had settled in while he'd been at the bakery.

"I'm Caleb. How long will you be teaching here?"

Katie kept her face forward and her chin tipped upward. "I'll be teaching until the end of the school year while my *aenti* recovers from her injuries from her fall. And I caught your name from your new *fraa* at the bakery."

Caleb chuckled. "Rachel is not my *fraa.* She's my younger *schweschder.* I'm not married.*"*

Katie let her eyes drift to Caleb. "You don't look anything alike. And since she seemed to have the upper hand on you, I assumed you were newly married. That, and the lack of beard."

Caleb smiled. "We don't look alike because we have different *mamms.* She can be bossy, but I guess I'm a pushover."

Katie's nose tipped even higher. "That's not a commendable trait for a *mann* to have. I suppose that's probably why you aren't married. A *mann* is supposed to be in charge—be the head of the household."

Caleb smiled. "I'm not married because I haven't found a woman bossy enough to turn my head. I guess I need a strong woman who'll keep me in line." His eyes drifted to Katie. "You seem like a strong woman."

Katie sighed with disdain. "I'm not bossy, but perhaps I'm too strong for *you.* But it's no matter because I'm betrothed to Jessup King."

Caleb raised an eyebrow. "Wedding season has just passed. Why didn't you marry then?"

Katie was clearly agitated by his question, but it was obvious he was getting a kick out of irritating her.

"Not that it's any of your concern, but I wasn't ready. I asked for a long engagement."

Caleb chuckled. "Sounds to me like you don't want to marry the *mann.*"

Katie pursed her lips. "That is none of your concern, and I'd appreciate it if you would not discuss my personal life."

Caleb's mouth turned up at the corners. "You started it."

Katie turned to him, her brow creased in a deep furrow. Caleb thought she looked even prettier when she was angry.

She glared at him. "Are you twelve?"

Caleb laughed heartily. "I'm twenty-five. How old are you?"

"Not that it's any of your concern, but I'm twenty-three."

Caleb snorted. "That's kind of old not to be married yet."

Katie cleared her throat. "You're one to talk. At least I'm engaged to be married. You don't even appear to have any prospects."

"I told you I haven't found a woman feisty enough to handle me. But you—how long have you been engaged?"

"You're getting awfully personal."

"Are you refusing to answer the question?"

Katie shook her head impatiently. "It's been just over two years."

Caleb muttered under his breath.

Katie leered at him. "What did you say?"

"I just said that I wouldn't wait that long for you."

Katie's face heated with excitement over her handsome driver's forward statement. She suddenly regretted telling him of her parents' arrangement with the King family for her to be married to Jessup. She didn't love him enough to marry him, but her parents had called it a *good match*. Who was she to argue?

At the time, there were no other prospects for her, and it was certainly better than becoming a spinster. But marrying only to avoid becoming a spinster was not a reason to marry. She'd hoped that time would put love in her heart for Jessup, but it hadn't. She knew there was only so much time she could keep the engagement going. Eventually, Jessup would expect to marry her. What then?

Katie couldn't see herself entering into a loveless marriage with the older widower any more than she could see herself as a *mamm* to his two *kinner*. She'd tried to break it off with him several times, but he just wouldn't accept it, and neither would her parents. She'd even avoided him for the past two weeks, making excuses to avoid taking buggy rides with him, but he was not one to take no for an answer.

The thought of marriage to a *mann* like Caleb excited her. If only there was a way out of her situation. Perhaps her absence from the community in Nappanee would change Jessup's mind about her—especially since she hadn't even told him she was leaving. She'd prayed about that very thing when she was offered the opportunity to take over teaching for her aunt. Was it possible that God was answering her prayers? Discouragement set in as she thought of her betrothed. There was no way another man would consider her as long as she was promised to Jessup. Now if she could only find a way to keep her attraction to Caleb Yoder in check.

Caleb steered the gelding toward the school house, enjoying Katie's company despite her snobby exterior. The fact that she was betrothed bothered him, even though they'd just met. But perhaps it didn't bother him as much as it should because he thought she was just the kind of woman he could see himself marrying.

CHAPTER 3

Caleb held out his hand to help the lovely school teacher down from his buggy, and this time she reluctantly took his hand. Even through her thick gloves, he could feel the warmth of her delicate hand that fit perfectly in his. He knew he had no right to think such a thought, but he couldn't help himself. He couldn't even be sure she knew how beautiful she was, even though her confidence and attitude might suggest otherwise.

He watched her walk into the school without even turning back. She'd not thanked him for the ride, nor had she acknowledged him once they reached her destination. Was she really that much of a snob, or was it all an act? Either way, Caleb was determined not to help her again. Next time, he would let the dogs have their way. He'd had a run-in with the stray dogs plenty of times, and their bark seemed to be all they had in them. He knew they would never attack her to cause her harm; they only wanted her lunch—but she didn't know that.

Feeling discouraged over such a dramatic meeting with the beautiful school teacher, Caleb steered his horse back toward the bakery and the work that waited for him there. Rachel had made a list so long for him that it would take him nearly a month to make all the necessary repairs to get the bakery up and running to full service again. Now that his aunt Lillian had a new baby, she was too preoccupied to pay any mind to the bakery that she'd never wanted in the first place. There had been discussion of Rachel taking over her interest in the property, but for now, she was merely running the place into the ground. She was an excellent baker, but she was too busy keeping up with orders, and had neglected repairs that would have been minor if she'd taken care of them immediately. Now, Caleb had his work cut out for him between fixing leaks in the sink, to broken slats on the porch and the doors on the display case.

Katie rushed into the school-house knowing she was late. She hung up her coat and bonnet as she stared out into the classroom full of impressionable faces. There was no time for her to dwell on the warmth that had emanated from Caleb's hand, or his kind smile that sent sparks of fire through her. Thankfully, she had what looked to be an eager class full of students ready for their first lesson from her.

One of the older boys had lit the stove and was stoking the blazing fire that brought warmth to the small building. From outside, the wind whistled through the frosted windows, threatening to bring the snow inside with it. She would have to remember to talk to the Elders about getting someone to make the windows a little more weather-proof so they wouldn't go through so much wood. She even made a mental note to check the wood pile after school to be sure they wouldn't run out. The school in the city where she'd taught adult education classes had a gas heater for the large building. She had only been a teacher's aide in the city, but as she looked at the hopeful faces of young students, Katie felt like a real teacher for the first time.

One of the younger girls suddenly raised her hand. Katie nodded her consent for her to ask her question.

"Are you our new teacher?"

Katie nodded and smiled cordially. "*Jah,* I'm Miss Graber."

The girl tipped her head sideways and scrunched her brow. "But that's our other teacher's name."

Katie nodded again. "That's because she's my *aenti.*"

Another girl shot her hand high above her head, wiggling her fingers impatiently. "When will she be back?"

Katie breathed deeply and then let out the breath. This was not going to be anything like teaching adults. These children seemed much more inquisitive, and they lacked the control to wait to speak until given permission. Perhaps that was something she would have to work on with them while she was here.

"I'm afraid your teacher won't be able to return this school year. She'll need that time and the entire summer to recuperate from the spill she took on the icy steps of the school-*haus*. Let that be a reminder to all of you to be extra careful when entering and leaving the building."

The boy who had stoked the fire put up his hand. Katie fumbled with the books she'd set on the desk looking for the student roster so she could learn their names. Her aunt had drawn out a seating chart from memory that listed each of the children's names.

When she found it, she perused the chart until she came to the end of the fifth row. "Henry...is that your name?"

He nodded. "It's my chore to keep the stairs shoveled, but I wasn't here the day that Miss Graber fell. I feel awful about it."

Katie smiled warmly, feeling sorry for the boy. "It isn't your fault, Henry. But for the future, perhaps we should have an alternate person to do the shoveling in case someone is absent. Do I have any volunteers?"

Three hands shot up quickly.

Katie looked at the seating chart again. Calling each one by his name, and the girl that also volunteered, Katie told them they could take turns each week. Going to the chalk board, she placed Samuel's name on the board and declared it *his* week to fill in as the back-up for shoveling. She further explained he would need to arrive a few minutes early to school every day to be sure the chore was taken care of.

The next order of business would be to establish where each of the children was in their lessons. Her aunt had written that out for her too, but she preferred to interact with the students and get their input, hoping it would help her learn their names along the way.

Before Katie realized, her first day as a real teacher had come to a close. She was exhausted, to say the least, and she still had papers to grade. A quick stop at the Miller's place on her way home was necessary in order to find out who would be responsible for insulating the school's windows. She had met Elder Miller at the long row of mailboxes at the end of her aunt's road when she'd gone out to gather the mail for her on the first day she'd arrived in the community. Katie had only been here for a few days, but already she could tell he was concerned for her aunt.

Hiram Miller lived across the road from her *Aenti* Nettie, and he'd introduced himself, letting her know that if she or *Nettie* needed anything to let him know. She couldn't be sure, but it seemed the widower had a crush on her aunt. He'd already made it a point to come over early that morning and shovel the steps and walkway to the barn. He'd offered to hitch up the mare to the buggy for her, but she'd declined. She wasn't keen on the idea of driving an unfamiliar horse on the busy road. Although after the dog incident, she'd decided to rethink a way to avoid giving the dogs another opportunity to attack her.

Pride over a good first day filled her as she left the school, but she would keep that to herself. No sense in borrowing trouble in a new community.

CHAPTER 4

"How long has the buggy wheel been broken, *Aenti?*"

The older woman adjusted herself on the kitchen chair, her broken leg propped up on the chair beside her. She'd insisted on getting a walking cast so she could hobble around her small house without any assistance. She held a potato with the hand of her arm that rested in a sling, while she peeled with her good hand. She was a tough old bird, determined not to let a broken leg and a sprained wrist keep her bed-ridden.

"It's been like that since last spring, so, going on a year."

Katie picked up another potato and began to peel. "Why haven't you had it fixed?"

"I enjoy walking. It keeps me young. The school isn't that far, and I don't have much need to go anywhere else. When I do, I have friends that I go with. A woman my age doesn't like going into town alone anyway."

Katie looked up from her work. "I'm sure Mr. Miller would be happy to fix it for you. He's offered his assistance if you should need anything. He offered again when I inquired about help from the church to fix the windows of the school. The wind blows right through them."

Nettie looked up from her work. "I wouldn't let that *mann* help me if he was the last Amish *mann* on earth."

Katie put the last potato down and look up into the anger showing in her aunt's eyes to be sure she heard her correctly. She wasn't sure if she dared ask why, but she couldn't resist.

"I know I haven't seen much of you in the last few years, but haven't you lived across from him for a long time?"

"Your *daed* moved away from this community when he met your *mamm.* I was the youngest of the seven children, and so I was still pretty young when he married. No one in the *familye* knew that I was once sweet on Hiram Miller."

Katie leaned in closer as though she wouldn't be able to hear her *aenti* otherwise. "What happened?"

Nettie cast her eyes downward, but Katie could still see the pain in her eyes.

"He married my best friend, Rachel. That's what happened. The two of them were sneaking around behind my back, and then they announced their marriage real sudden-like. I was certain she was with child, but they didn't have their first *boppli* until almost two years later. She passed away when her youngest was only ten years old. I was still not speaking to her at the time, and didn't even know she was ill until it was too late."

Katie gulped. "It's not too late to patch things up with Mr. Miller."

Nettie looked up sharply, disgust twisting her expression. "It *is* too late! He has a *familye—kinner* and *grandkinner*. Why do you think I never let my own *familye* visit me here? I don't want my own *familye* to see me like this, and I don't want Hiram Miller being reminded of what I didn't have because of what he did."

Katie was unsure of what to say to her *aenti*. Was it possible the woman was still holding a grudge after all these years?

"His wife, Rachel, was my best friend," Nettie continued. "And I never got to say goodbye to her."

Katie cleared her throat, wondering how bold she could get with her *aenti*. "Mr. Miller seemed like he wants to make it up to you. I saw the same sadness in his eyes when he spoke of you as I see in yours now."

Nettie tossed the half-peeled potato into the colander, seemingly disgusted at the difficulty she had with peeling it. "It *is* too late. I've spent my entire life being mad at the two of them for taking away what should have been mine, and I'm not about to stop now. Hiram Miller can keep his guilt to himself."

Katie picked up the potato her *aenti* tossed aside and finished peeling it. "If you ask me, it sounds as though you've *wasted* your whole life over this grudge, and it's time you started living."

Nettie leered at her niece. "And I'll thank you need to start minding your manners. I can send you packing back to Nappanee."

Katie was beginning to understand why her family hadn't seen much of her aunt over the years, but she could also see the very real hurt in the eyes of this woman who was practically a stranger to her.

"If you sent me home, who would teach your students until you're back on your feet?"

Tears welled up in Nettie's eyes. "I wanted to keep teaching even after the accident, but the Elders thought it was best if I retired. The job will be up for grabs next year. I've got nothing left. My whole life is gone, and I'm an old shell waiting for my time to end on this earth."

This was more serious than Katie thought. Her aunt was obviously depressed, and she needed to take drastic measures to bring her life back to life. It was even more obvious that the buggy was never fixed because her aunt hadn't gone anywhere other than to school in a very long time. Katie was determined to change that.

"Well, you can't get rid of me that easily, *Aenti.* I'm asking someone to help fix that buggy wheel. I can't keep walking to school every day when there's a pack of wild dogs loose in the county." She held her dress hem up to show Nettie. "They would have killed me if it weren't for the saving grace of two new friends I met today."

Nettie scrunched up her brow. "How did you manage to make friends while you were at school? And what does that have to do with stray dogs? I know the ones you're talking about—they wouldn't hurt a flea."

"That's what Caleb tried to tell me, but I wouldn't listen."

Nettie pursed her lips, anger welling up in her.

"Are you talking about Caleb Yoder?"

Katie could see the fire in her *aenti's* eyes.

"Yes. He and his *schweschder,* Rachel, helped me this morning when I ran into the bakery. They're very nice. Caleb gave me ride to school since the dogs wouldn't leave. They wanted my lunch."

Nettie struggled to rise to her feet. Leaning over the table, the look of intimidation on her *aenti's* face scared Katie.

"You will stay away from Rachel and Caleb. They are no *gut.* Do you hear me?"

Katie started to ask why, but Nettie shot her down.

"Those two are Hiram Miller's *grandkinner,* and I won't have my niece running around this community with the likes of that *familye.* And you had better remember that you're betrothed, and will give yourself a bad name in these parts if you're seen taking a buggy ride from another *mann."*

Katie couldn't believe what she was hearing from her *aenti.* Her engagement was nothing less than a joke, and she was determined to find a way out of it while she was here. But the fact that she was now forbidden to see Caleb made him somehow even more appealing to her.

CHAPTER 5

Caleb pushed his horse just a little bit, hoping he could catch up with Katie before she turned down the road to the school. He'd seen the dogs almost a mile back tearing apart her lunch pail, and he wanted to be sure she was alright. When he pulled up alongside of her, she tipped her head in his direction. Pursing her lips, she swiped angrily at a tear that stained the side of her rosy cheek. He couldn't help but feel sorry for her, but her pouty-mouth was enough to drive him to throwing himself into a pack of wolves to defend her.

Caleb pushed open the buggy door. "Get in. I'll drive you the rest of the way."

Katie shook her head, stubbornness tipping her jaw upward. "I don't have much further to go. Besides, I'm not supposed to take rides from strangers."

"I saw you running from the dogs and tried to catch up with you, but the snow is too deep for my old horse to trudge through. Besides, we aren't strangers anymore since you took a ride from me yesterday, and you look cold. You're shivering."

Katie had to admit she was pretty cold, and her legs were sore from running in the slippery snow. She accepted the ride figuring there was little to no chance of her *aenti* finding out.

"What are you doing out this way? There isn't anything out here except the school."

Caleb pointed to the supplies in the back of the buggy. "I came to fix the windows. *Mei grossdaddi* told me you needed someone to fix the whistling windows."

Katie frowned. "I hope you didn't come on my account."

Caleb smiled. "Don't flatter yourself. It's my job. I fix things for people in the community."

"Aren't you still needed at your *schweschder's* bakery?"

He nodded with a smile. Katie thought his smile could melt the icy chill from her.

"I still need to fix the leak in the roof of the porch, and make new doors for the display case, but those can wait a couple of hours. I figured I could take the morning and put up some plastic on the windows to keep out the wind."

"I'd appreciate not shivering while I'm trying to teach. I brought an extra sweater, but I'm afraid I dropped it a ways back when the dogs attacked me and stole my lunch."

Caleb reached under the buggy seat and pulled out her ragged, soaking sweater and held it out to her. "I tried to save it for you, but I'm afraid the smaller one thought it would make a nice chew-toy."

Katie turned from it, scrunching up her nose.

Caleb put it back under the seat. "I didn't figure you'd still want it with dog slobber in it, but I thought it was worth a chance. I'm sure if you washed it and sewed it a little, it would be *gut* as new."

The corners of Katie's mouth turned up slightly. "Or we could throw it in the fire at the school and burn it. I doubt I'll wear it again."

Caleb smirked. "*Jah,* but what sort of message would that send to your students?"

Katie drew a sincere look across her brow.

"The message that dog slobber will not be tolerated."

"I may be wrong, but I think you'll have a tough time convincing your students you're a not a teacher to be messed with because of your *zero tolerance policy for dog slobber.*"

Katie sighed. "Maybe not, but it might make a *gut* ice-breaker. I'm afraid things didn't go as well as I'd hoped with my students yesterday—especially since I got off on the wrong foot by being late the first day."

Caleb steered his horse into the school yard and pulled back a little on the reins.

Katie opened the buggy door and quickly hopped out. "If I don't hurry, I'll be late again. Maybe today I'll have to tell my students why. *Denki* for the ride—again. And for fixing the windows."

Before Caleb had a chance to think of something amusing to say back to her, Katie was half-way across the school yard and running up the stairs. He could only assume all the students had already arrived since none were outside, and the stairs were freshly shoveled. Maybe she hadn't been able to make a good impression on her students, but she'd definitely made a memorable impression on him.

CHAPTER 6

Katie found it difficult to concentrate on her students while Caleb worked at each window. After he finished putting plastic on each window, he would come inside the building and stand near the wood stove to warm up. Each time, he seemed to linger longer and longer. Several times, she caught him watching her give a reading lesson to the younger children, and she wondered why he seemed so interested in her teaching. She couldn't even be certain she had the attention of her students, but there was Caleb, watching her every move.

Feeling scrutinized, she found it hard to keep her mind on task. Several times she forgot what she was saying and stumbled over her words. Between Caleb and her students, she worried they would all think she was incapable of teaching. She was conflicted. Part of her wanted Caleb to leave so she could teach without mistakes, but having him near invigorated her senses in a way no other man had.

She knew it was wrong for her to feel so strongly for Caleb when she was promised to another man, but she couldn't stop herself from having those feelings. Not when she felt more alive than she'd felt with Jessup. Her betrothed was too old for her, and she wasn't ready to be a *mamm* to his *kinner*. She wanted children of her own. But the guilt she felt over those poor children not having a *mamm* had been one of the reasons that caused her to give in to her parents' arrangement. It saddened her that her parents seemed so eager to have her out of their house. Being the youngest of nine children, Katie often felt her parents were too old to be raising her. They already had twelve *grandkinner,* and she supposed they were looking forward to adding Jessup and his *kinner* to the family—even if meant their daughter was miserable.

Even though Caleb's constant watchful eyes were on her, the attention from him made her feel alive again. In seven short weeks, she would be back in her own community at the close of the school year, and that meant returning to her boring life with Jessup. In the meantime, she intended to enjoy Caleb's attention toward her. It wasn't hurting anything, and it would be the last fun she'd have before settling into her loveless marriage.

Katie reasoned with herself that if her parents were going to force her into a loveless marriage for the sake of keeping her from being underfoot any longer, then she was justified in her whimsical indulgence. Who would it hurt if she dreamed a little? No one could fault her for wanting something better for her future. Could they?

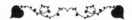

Caleb busied himself calking around the window casings from the inside of the building. It wasn't enough to watch Katie's lessons while he warmed himself by the fire. Every time he went back out to put plastic on the next window, he missed valuable information within her lesson—information that might finally help him to be able to read. He'd missed several of the letters she reviewed with her young students every time he had to return to the outdoors. Surely she would get suspicious if he spent too much time near the stove. He could tell his presence was making her uncomfortable, but he was more concerned with learning the letters and the sounds they made, than about the lovely teacher at the moment.

It was times like this that Caleb chided himself for not going to school. Right now, he wished his *daed* had forced him to go instead of letting him stay home and work the farm with him from the time he was a young boy. Although a few of his cousins had also stayed home to work the farm with their *daed,* they also were fortunate to have a *mamm* to teach them to read and write. All Caleb knew how to do was add and subtract, and that was only what applied to farming. He'd never had a need to learn to read, but suddenly, in this sophisticated woman's presence, he felt like a *dummkopf.*

There were a lot of things Caleb had missed out on by not having a *mamm* when he was growing up. Since she'd died giving birth to him, he'd never had the chance to become attached to her, but that didn't mean he didn't miss having her in his life. He remembered how excited he was when he got a new *mamm* after Abby's *mamm* had married his *daed.* Even when Abby began to attend school, his *daed* didn't press him to go with her. He'd gone a few times here and there just to get out of doing extra chores, but he'd found that he was too far behind to catch up. After that first year when their twin siblings were born, even Abby had left school, and the two of them lived their lives centered around their family and the farm.

Caleb looked around at the students listening intently to their teacher, suddenly realizing what he'd missed out on the most—a normal childhood.

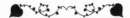

Katie's eyes followed Caleb as he walked out the door of the school to put plastic on the last window. Maybe now she would be able to concentrate enough to teach her class without stumbling over ever word. With very little time before she would have to break for the lunch hour, she wanted to finish her lesson so she could move on to the math in the afternoon in keeping with her *aenti's* schedule for her students.

After only a few minutes, her students became restless, and she knew a break was needed. She dismissed them, watching them scramble to the back room where a long table was set up for them to eat. In the warmer months, she figured they ate outside, but the snow would be around for another month at least. Occasionally, they wouldn't have so much snow in March, but this winter season had been nothing but non-stop snow. Lost in thought, Katie didn't even realize Caleb standing in front of her desk, wearing the sweetest smile.

"Would you like to share my lunch?"

CHAPTER 7

Katie was so stunned by Caleb's offer that she stared at him for a small eternity.

Caleb cleared his throat. "I figured since those mutts stole your lunch this morning you might be hungry."

Katie pushed her chin in the air. "I appreciate the offer, but I don't want to put you out. You've worked very hard today."

Why does she act so prideful? Or is it embarrassment? I don't understand women.

Caleb handed her a treat from the bakery wrapped in pink tissue paper. "At least take the cookies my *schweschder* sent with me for you. When I told her I was weatherproofing the windows at the school today, she asked me to give them to you."

Katie took the cookies. Truth be told, she was very hungry, and it would be a long afternoon with an empty stomach.

"*Danki.* I'll have to stop by there on my way home and thank her."

Caleb smiled. "I'm sure she would like that. Are you sure you don't want some of my sandwich? It's ham and cheese."

Katie couldn't resist ham and cheese; it was one of her favorites. She held out her hand and took the half sandwich from Caleb, wondering what he was thinking. He'd worked hard, and probably was very hungry himself. Yet here he was, sharing his lunch with her. Jessup wasn't the kind of man to do such a thing, was he? She'd never had the occasion to see. They'd eaten together during family gatherings, but they sat separately. But here was Caleb pulling up one of the students chairs to sit with her at her desk. Her face heated, and she found it difficult to swallow the small bite of sandwich she'd already chewed to a soupy consistency. Her nerves prevented her from taking another bite.

Caleb looked at her as she set her sandwich on the napkin he'd given her.

"You don't like the sandwich?"

Katie looked into his kind blue eyes that held a genuine sweetness. Jessup's eyes were tired and stressful.

"*Jah,* I do. I'm not used to having a *mann* sit with me while I eat. In my community, when there is a gathering, the *menner* sit separately from the women, and they are served first."

Caleb chuckled. "They do that here too. Not really sure I like that. If it bothers you, I can sit with the *kinner.*"

Katie smiled. "*Nee.* I don't mind if you sit with me. It's a nice change."

She picked up the sandwich and took another bite. It was a good sandwich and good company. And she liked it.

After school, Katie walked to the bakery to thank Rachel for the cookies Caleb had brought for her. She had never tasted anything like them; they were the best cookies she'd ever had, and there were a lot of recipes floating around her community. When she reached the small bakery, Caleb was on the porch fixing the railing. She felt suddenly shy around him, and said a quick "hello" before walking inside. She didn't dare say any more than that for fear her admiration of him would show in the pink tinge of her cheeks. To her, there was nothing more appealing than watching a man work, and she didn't trust herself not to linger over a conversation with him while he worked.

As Katie entered the bakery, the bells jingled against the top of the door announcing her presence. Rachel came from the kitchen, flour dusting her face, but a smile softened her expression, making her look less flustered from an obviously busy day.

"Hello, Katie," she said cheerfully. "Are you here for more cookies?"

Katie stomped the snow off her boots onto the rug in front of the door. "*Nee,* I better not take any back to my *aenti's haus,* but I wanted to say *danki* for the ones you sent with your *bruder.* Those dogs stole my lunch from me on the way to school today, and I would have had to go without if it hadn't been for the generosity of you and your *bruder.*"

Rachel looked at her as if she was trying to process her entire statement. "But why is it that you don't want to take anymore sweets home? Is your *aenti* trying to stay away from sweets?"

Katie wished she hadn't said anything, but she owed Rachel an explanation now that she had. "*Nee,* it's more like your *familye* she's trying to stay away from. I'm sorry, Rachel. I want you to know I don't share her feelings."

Rachel couldn't help but smile. "Everyone in the community knows of your *aenti's* past with my *grossdaddi.*"

"I'm certain my *familye* knows about it too since she's my *daed's schweschder,* but I only learned of it yesterday. It seems that no one ever tells me anything. My *daed* could have at least warned me not to bring up your *grossdaddi* to her. He offered to fix her buggy wheel, and I thought she was going to declare war."

Rachel giggled. "If it's a buggy wheel you need fixing, my *schweschder's* husband, Jonah Beiler, is the one to ask. He's the buggy-maker in the community. I can let you know tomorrow if you'll stop by after school."

Katie slipped her knitted gloves back on her hands, preparing to battle the snow and wind for the rest of her walk home. "*Danki.* Would you mind if I came by in the morning to pick up some more cookies? I've never tasted anything like them."

"Of course you can. They are an old *familye* recipe—probably why you've never encountered them before. You won't find them anywhere except this bakery. Are you sure you don't want to take a few home? I have some left over from today's sales."

Katie thought about it for a minute. "I better not. I'll never hear the end of it if I do. As tempting as they are, I'll have to wait until the morning."

Rachel waved to Katie as she stepped onto the porch. Standing in the doorway for a minute, Rachel observed the interaction between Katie and her brother. If she didn't know any better, she'd have to say the two of them were sweet on each other. But she'd have given almost anything to know what they were saying to one another.

CHAPTER 8

Katie pulled her knitted scarf over her nose to shelter her face from the wind and icy snow that pelted her cheeks. She hadn't seen the dogs yet, but she was close enough to the bakery that they could jump out from behind a tree at any time. Today, however, she was armed with an extra few slices of salami and cheese to keep them busy while she could get away with her lunch intact. So far, not a dog in sight. Perhaps the weather had forced them to find shelter. Suddenly, Katie felt sorry for the dogs, who didn't seem to have anyone to care for them.

No sooner had she thought it, than one of the dogs crawled out from under a large span of evergreen bushes. Katie didn't dare move as she sized up the snarling dog with his teeth showing. The wind and snow swirled around his head, but he shook and growled as if it made him even angrier.

Remembering the salami and cheese, Katie slowly reached into her bag, her eyes fixed on the animal with its threatening stance. She tossed a chunk of salami toward the dog and he caught it midair. She threw another piece, and the dog did the same thing, and wagged his tale. A whine escaped his throat as he tipped his head to the side and blinked, a hopeful look in his eyes.

"Caleb was right," she said.

"What was I right about?"

Katie gasped as she turned around swiftly to find Caleb so close behind her, she bumped into him.

She pulled the scarf down from her nose and mouth so she could talk easily. "The dogs. I think they're just hungry. Perhaps with a proper home and regular meals they wouldn't be so *mean.*"

"Now hold on there. You still haven't seen his brother this morning. This is the nicer of the two. You can't just take an animal home with you because he ate from you without biting off your hand. What if he has rabies?"

"He doesn't have rabies. He's just hungry. I'd be angry too if my owner put me out in the cold. Where do you suppose they came from?"

Caleb stared her down as she tossed a piece of cheese to the dog. "You are not the same person I met two days ago."

Katie smirked. "Living with a cranky *aenti* will change a person right quick."

The other dog sauntered out from under the evergreens, teeth showing, a low growl stopping Katie and Caleb from moving.

"You still think you can just take them home with you? Maybe I was wrong about them." Caleb wasn't so sure they should be standing so close to the meaner of the two. "Throw him some food before he bites us."

Katie looked over her shoulder at him. "I thought you said they were harmless?"

Caleb chuckled nervously. "That was before that one started looking at me like I was dinner."

Katie tossed the dog a handful of cheese and salami chunks, and watched him gobble it up. She tossed another few pieces to the first dog, who was sitting patiently on his haunches for another bite. "Animals understand kindness. They were just hungry. The big one has stopped growling."

Caleb raised an eyebrow at her. "This coming from the same girl who came screaming into the bakery two days ago thinking they were after you!"

The wind had died down and the snow had let up a little, making it easier to talk. "I'll admit I was afraid that first day. And the second day. But today, I decided I was going to shower them with kindness and make friends with them since we'll be seeing each other every morning on my way to school. At least until I get my *aenti's* buggy wheel fixed. Even then I've decided to bring them food so they won't terrorize anyone else. How long have they been around here?"

Caleb stood beside her now that the dogs were happily eating the last of the treat Katie had brought them. "I've been seeing them hanging around for about three months now—just after Christmas. I'm amazed they never bothered your *aenti* all those mornings she walked to school."

Katie flashed him a smile. "My *aenti* is too ornery to let a couple of dogs get the better of her. They're probably afraid of her."

Caleb laughed. "Ornery, huh? My *grossdaddi* seems to think awful highly of her."

Katie's eyes widened at his words. "If he thinks so highly of her, why did he leave her when they were young and marry another woman?"

Caleb held up a hand in defense. "I don't know the details, but I've heard it was your *aenti* who turned my *grossdaddi* away. Not the other way around."

Katie had forgotten all about the dogs, who had gone back under the evergreen bushes to get out of the cold. "The way I heard it, your *grossdaddi* married her best friend."

Caleb held up both his hands. "This isn't our argument. I never had a chance to meet my *grossmammi*, because she had passed away before we even met my *grossdaddi*. But I do know that my *schweschder,* Rachel was named after her."

Katie was confused. "You aren't blood-related to Hiram Miller?"

"*Nee.* But he's been my *grossdaddi* since I was ten years old. He's my new *mamm's daed,* and he's a *gut mann.*"

Katie conceded. "He was very nice when he offered help to my *aenti.* Maybe he wants to make amends with her. She was pretty clear that she wanted nothing to do with him, but I think it's a front. I could see the hurt in her eyes."

Caleb smiled. "Maybe we should help them."

Katie wasn't sure she should be spending so much time in Caleb's company since she was promised to Jessup, but that wasn't what she wanted, and no one, not even her own parents seemed to care about what *she* wanted. For now, it was her decision what she would do with her time, and helping Caleb mend fences between his *grossdaddi* and her *aenti* might be the last thing she did of her own free will.

CHAPTER 9

Katie happily accepted a ride to school after getting her cookies from Rachel, who wanted to help with the plan to reconcile things between their families. Caleb had been asked by the Elders of the church to chop wood for the school, and so he would be spending the morning getting under Katie's skin like he had the day before. She knew it was wrong to feel attraction toward Caleb since she would probably end up marrying Jessup when she returned to Nappanee, but that didn't stop her from wishing things could be different. That she could hope for a different future for herself—one where she could do her own choosing of a husband.

Caleb enjoyed the closeness with Katie as he urged his horse to walk a little faster through the deep snow. He wished they could get to know one another better, but the fact she was betrothed stood in the way of anything more than friendship between them. It bothered Caleb that he felt he'd finally met his match, but she was promised to another man. It didn't matter that she didn't seem happy about the arrangement because a promise was a promise—and it was one to be honored.

When they reached the school yard, Katie jumped out of the buggy before Caleb could say anything to her. Because of all the excitement over the dogs, she was a few minutes late—again. He knew it would not look *gut* for her to continue to be late, and he knew the Elders would give report of her tardiness to her *aenti*. He also knew that it would be reported that he had driven her to school each day, and her *aenti* would surely discipline her for such unacceptable actions. Caleb didn't want to be in the middle of the old squabble between his *grossdaddi* and Katie's *aenti*, but it was a little late to think about that now. Right now, his biggest concern was chopping the wood without freezing, and getting a peek at Katie's reading lessons while he warmed himself by the fire.

Once again, Katie found it difficult to keep from stumbling over her words as Caleb stood by the fire to warm himself after chopping a considerable amount of wood. She could feel his stare on the back of her neck as if the fire from the stove was close enough to overheat her. She tried to keep her eyes on the chalkboard and the letters she was reviewing with the young students. The older students worked quietly on an assignment while she worked with the younger group.

Unable to resist his stare any longer, she glanced at Caleb, realizing it was her lesson he was watching so intently and not her. His eyes didn't leave the chalkboard as she scribbled a few more letters on the board. From the corner of her eye, she could see his lips forming the letter sounds with her students as they repeated them.

Was it possible that Caleb couldn't read? It wasn't unheard of in the community—and for any community, for that matter. After all, her job in her own city was to assist in teaching the adults at the adult center how to read. There were many adults that didn't know how to read. But why would Caleb not have learned that from his *aenti* when he attended school? Her *aenti,* she knew, had been teaching in the community for almost forty years, so Caleb surely would have been one of her students. She didn't dare inquire about it to her *aenti,* or the woman would know she'd been talking to one of Hiram Miller's relatives. But she could ask Rachel when she visited with her after school.

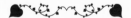

Caleb tried really hard to keep up with Katie's lesson, but found it difficult to follow along when he'd had to continuously return to the outdoors to chop more wood. He tried to be as discrete as possible, but he feared he'd gotten caught mouthing the letter sounds more than once. If she was aware that he was paying attention to her lesson, she didn't let on. He would be embarrassed if she knew his secret. But why should he care so much what she thought of him? After all, she would be leaving in a few weeks to return to her own community, and she would be marrying one Jessup King.

Katie's afternoon seemed to drag on slowly after Caleb finished stacking the wood pile. He hadn't even stayed for lunch, much to her disappointment. Though she was eager to find out from Rachel if what she suspected about Caleb's inability to read was true, she also wondered if it would be impolite for her to even ask such a thing. Knowing she could never take such a concern to her *aenti* without raising a red flag, she decided that Rachel would be the best one to approach about the subject. She told herself that her interest in knowing was simply out of concern as a teacher, but she also couldn't quite admit that her interest was purely selfish.

Am I really such a snob that I would judge a mann simply because he couldn't read? He doesn't seem dumm by any means, but my familye would consider him an unsuitable match because of his lack of education. Not that I care what they think...

CHAPTER 10

Katie thought about her reasons for wanting to know Caleb's personal business as she trudged along in the deep snow. The path from the school to the bakery had been well-defined by buggy tracks, making it a little easier for her walk. She both dreaded and eagerly awaited spring. Dreading it because it meant she would be going back to Nappanee and back to Jessup. But eagerly awaiting the flowers and the sound of birds chirping.

Spring planting was something she always looked forward to, but this year she was supposed to begin a kitchen garden at the King house in preparation of her wedding. How could she have let things get this far out of control? Maybe if she made nice with her *aenti,* the ornery woman would let her stay. And with the teaching position open, perhaps she would be chosen to be the permanent replacement. But that wouldn't make *Aenti* Nettie happy. In fact, it would probably prompt her to insist on Katie's immediate departure.

The only thing Katie could see in her future was being the wife of a thirty-three-year-old widower she didn't love, and being a *mamm* to his *kinner.*

Walking into the bakery, Katie's ears were assaulted with the sound of large dishes clanging on the floor. She rushed to the kitchen when she heard Rachel squeal.

"Do you need some help?"

Rachel stared up at her from where she sat on her haunches gathering utensils into a cake pan.

"*Ach,* I knocked the whole pan of clean utensils off the counter, and now I have to wash them again. I'm never going to finish all these dishes before tomorrow."

Katie looked at the counters that were filled with dirty pans, flour dusting every surface, including the floor. Grabbing an apron from a nearby hook, she removed her coat and pulled the apron over her head, ready to dive in and help.

Rachel saw her new friend donning that apron and put up her hands. "*Ach,* you don't have to help me. I'm the *dummkopf* who isn't domesticated enough to clean a kitchen. I'm *gut* at the baking part, but not so *gut* at the cleaning."

Katie smiled as she bent down to help pick up the mess. "Well then you're in for a treat because I'm an expert at cleaning up messes. But not so *gut* at baking. I'd say we'd make a *gut* team. We should have this mess cleaned up in no time at all."

Rachel giggled. "You are already such a *gut* friend, Katie. And perhaps someday you might be more."

Katie put the dirty utensils back into the dishwater. "What do you mean?"

Rachel smiled. "Perhaps we will one day be *schweschders.* I see the way you look at my *bruder.*"

Katie's heart kicked up into high speed at such a forward statement. "*Ach,* he's handsome, but you have it all wrong."

"I don't think I have anything wrong. I've seen the way he looks at you."

Katie couldn't help but laugh. "Now I know you're seeing things. Your *bruder* isn't interested in me. I thought he was at first, but then I realized he was more interested in my reading lessons to my students than he was in me."

She flashed Rachel a knowing look.

"*Ach,* you know that he can't read?"

Katie's heart beat faster. "I suspected."

"*Ach,* I'm such a *blabbermaul.* Caleb will never forgive me if he finds out I told his secret. Promise me you won't tell him."

She was practically begging.

"*Nee,* I won't tell him you told me. But I think it's only fair he knows that I know. I can help him. In Nappanee, I used to teach at the adult education center. I taught adults how to read. There are a lot of adults who don't know how to read. There is no shame in that. The real shame is when their pride keeps them from ever learning."

"It wasn't pride that kept Caleb from learning. It was the responsibility of *familye*. I have a lot of respect for my *bruder*, but he lacks the confidence he will need to ask for help. Maybe if he doesn't know you're helping him it would be the best way to help."

Katie was confused. "What do you mean?"

Rachel thought about it for a minute. "Is there anything else at the school that needs fixing?"

Katie could see where she was going with this line of thinking. "*Jah*, the entire building is practically falling apart. I'm not sure my *aenti* ever asked for a single thing to be fixed."

Rachel nodded knowingly. "That's because she would have had to ask my *grossdaddi* for help."

The two of them giggled.

Rachel handed Katie the washed utensils for her to dry. "Make a list of things that need repairing and drop them in my *grossdaddi's* mailbox on your way home. That way your *aenti* won't see you talking to him. I'll make sure that Caleb goes straight to the school in the morning instead of coming here to finish the porch. While he's there, make sure you plan your lessons so he can pay attention. Before he finishes all the repairs, he should have enough lessons in him to be able to start reading."

Katie liked the idea of helping Caleb while keeping his secret safe. Admittedly, she didn't think any less of him. In fact, she had more respect for him for being able to make a living for himself despite his adversities. She would try her best to keep his secret even if it meant sneaking around behind her *aenti's* back. She loved her *aenti*, but the woman had a few too many rules. It wasn't that Katie was rebellious, but she was beginning to think she could be. Maybe she could even get up enough nerve to call off her engagement to the Widower King once and for all. But how was she going to do that when every other time she tried she'd failed?

CHAPTER 11

Caleb was caught between watching the beautiful school teacher and paying attention to her reading lessons. Her face would light up with a sparkling smile each time one of her students answered a question correctly, but she never let disappointment show when they got one wrong.

Trying really hard to pay attention to what he was doing, his concentration was too involved with Katie's lesson, as he teetered on the ladder patching holes in the ceiling with plaster. He smoothed over the same spot with the trowel as he paid close attention to the lesson on vowel sounds. If he learned this, he would be able to spell his own name, and that was something that was suddenly very important to him. He'd never really given reading much thought. Occasionally it would become an issue if he was in town buying supplies for his job, but most of the workers in the lumber yard knew his standard orders, which made it easy. Half the time he didn't even have to talk much.

Something felt different about this situation. He knew he didn't stand a chance with the school teacher since she was betrothed, and he wasn't one to break up a couple. But something about meeting her made him hopeful that he could have a future with someone, though he'd like it if it could be Katie. He was already smitten. He liked her feisty attitude, and even the snobbish front she put up. He knew already from talking to her that she had a sweet side to her. But for some reason, the snobbishness was a distraction from something that seemed to be bothering her deep down where she wouldn't let anyone in. He hoped that even if only as a friend, he could break down that wall she'd built around herself.

Katie couldn't help but notice Caleb patching the same hole in the ceiling for the past twenty minutes as he watched her lesson intently. She held a soft spot in her heart for him, knowing how difficult it must be for him to function in his every-day life without being able to read. He was a good, responsible man, and wondered if his inability to read had kept him from pursuing marriage and a family.

She knew she'd be honored if a man like Caleb would want to marry her. She often wondered if there was something wrong with her that would cause her parents to think she needed to be promised to a man instead of allowing her to find her own match. It saddened her to think that her future could be so final, especially when there was a handsome man staring her right in the face.

Katie chided herself for wishing for things that could never be. It was obvious that he was only interested in learning to read, and not in her personally. But she wasn't going to let that keep her from admiring his trim build, or the muscles she could see through his royal blue shirt. It was her favorite, she decided, since it brought out the blue in his eyes.

Deciding it was time to break for lunch, she dismissed the squirming children to the back room. The sun was shining today, and they would probably want the chance to play outside for a few minutes before returning to their work. When she announced it, they all cheered in unison. She would welcome a few moments of quiet time to go over the afternoon lessons while they played.

"Aren't you hungry today?"

Katie looked up from her daydream to see Caleb standing in front of her desk. His brown hair was pushed back off his forehead; his chiseled jaw formed a friendly smile.

"I was just trying to decide if I should use this break to grade some papers. I didn't really have time to pack much for myself since I was so worried about making sure I had enough to give the dogs."

His smile grew wider. "I have fried chicken if you'd like to share with me."

"I'm afraid I owe you for the ham and cheese already. I don't want to get too far indebted to you."

He raised an eyebrow to match his crooked smile. "I'll be working here for a while. Perhaps you can bring enough to share with me tomorrow."

Katie couldn't help but smile in his company. "I could do that. But I'm afraid I'm not much of a cook."

Caleb puffed out his muscular chest. "It just so happens that I'm an excellent cook. I made this fried chicken."

Katie's mouth watered as he pulled the chicken out of his insulated carrier. The aroma made her stomach growl, reminding her that she was very hungry. She accepted one of the five pieces he'd packed. Did it really take that much to feed a man like Caleb?

Biting into the boneless chunk of breaded meat, her taste-buds did a little summersault.

He's handy at fixing things, he can cook, and he certainly is nice to look at. He's the perfect man for me.

"Mmm…this is the best chicken I've ever tasted."

Caleb's face heated from her compliment.

"You should taste it when it's fresh out of the frying pan."

"I'd like that." Now it was Katie's turn to wear pink cheeks.

"Would you like to have dinner with my *familye* on Sunday? I could make a fresh batch of fried chicken, my famous potatoes, and Rachel could make biscuits and a sweet treat to go with the meal."

"It sounds very tempting, but I should probably check with my *aenti* to be sure it would be alright."

Caleb smiled. "Invite her too. I'll invite my *grossdaddi.*"

Katie nudged him playfully. "That isn't funny. You know she would never agree to share a meal with your *grossdaddi.*"

"*Jah,* but I thought we were going to try to get them together?"

Katie agreed with him. "All I can do is ask."

She knew exactly what her *aenti* would say, but she prayed that God would soften her heart and convince her to say yes.

CHAPTER 12

Katie tried to remind herself that dinner with Caleb's family was not a date—no matter how much she wished it could be. She would have to settle for being just friends with Caleb. But anytime people say they're *just* friends with someone, it usually means it is more than friendship, or that they *want* it to be more. Katie couldn't deny Caleb interested her and made her wish she was free to pursue more than friendship, but it was looking like he didn't see her that way.

Caleb wished the invitation for dinner he'd extended to Katie could be a date with only him, but for now, he would have to settle for time spent with her in the company of others. He hoped that in time, she would reveal what he already suspected about her relationship with Jessup King. It wasn't uncommon for parents to promise their daughter to someone if she was getting older and had no prospects, and he hoped that might be the case with Katie. At least then his suspicions that she didn't want to marry Jessup would be true, and he might have a chance with her. But until he knew for certain, he would play it safe and pursue only friendship with her.

When they finished their lunch, Caleb invited her outside for a few minutes so they could get some fresh air. The students had been out playing for a few minutes already, and Caleb was eager for Katie to see the fun side of him.

Caleb reached for her hand to help her down the steps of the school house, but she declined. He could only assume it was because when they stepped out the door, all eyes were on them. It was as if they had never seen the two of them before, the way the students stared. But Caleb refused to let it rattle him. He was determined to play in the snow with the lovely school teacher, and the watchful eyes of her students would not interrupt his fun.

Reaching down and grabbing a handful of snow, Caleb determined the snow was perfect for packing.

Katie eyed the snow in his hand. "If you throw that at me, I will be forced to defend myself. I'm warning you, I have five brothers, so I'm guessing I can dish it out better than you."

Caleb laughed at her statement. How could he take someone as cute as her seriously?

Katie didn't waste any time. Before he realized, she had a handful of snow aimed at him.

Caleb held up his hands, mocking her. "I wasn't going to throw it. I was going to make a snowman is all."

Katie watched him carefully as he bent down and started rolling the snowball along the deep snow. Bending down to do the same with the chunk of snow in her own hand, she decided she would make her own snowman—or snow-woman.

The students had gone back to their own snow-filled fun, leaving Katie and Caleb to compete for who had the best snowman built.

"Mine is taller," Caleb boasted.

"That's because mine is a girl."

Caleb chuckled. "Are you sure? That kind of looks like a short boy to me."

Katie pulled off her light green knitted scarf and wrapped it around the neck of her snowman. "Is that better?"

Caleb unraveled his navy blue scarf and wrapped it around his snowman's neck. Then he removed his black hat and placed it on top of the snow head.

Leaning his arm on the edge of his snowman, Caleb whispered in its *ear*. "I'll need that hat back before I leave, but I have a feeling your head will be cold even with it on."

Katie let a short giggle escape her lips as she watched Caleb talking to his snowman.

He smiled at her as he continued. "You see this beautiful girl next to you? She might want to go for a buggy ride later. Don't you be a fool and let her get away."

Katie giggled again, this time allowing her head to tip back with delight over the *conversation.*

She looked at Caleb. "What if she isn't ready to take a buggy ride with him? After all, they hardly know one another."

Caleb pushed out his lower lip. "Look at him. How could she turn him down when he's so obviously smitten with her?"

Katie raised an eyebrow at him. "Smitten? How could he be smitten so quickly?"

Caleb poked his head between the snowmen and put an arm around each of them. "Love at first sight is the best kind of love there is."

"You really believe in love at first sight?"

Caleb winked at her. "I didn't used to, but I'm beginning to think I could believe in such a thing."

Katie scowled. "I'm not sure I believe in it, and neither does she."

Caleb frowned. "How can you say such a thing? These two were meant for each other. Maybe she just doesn't know it yet."

Katie had to wonder why he was pulling her into such a conversation. If he was trying to make a point, he was confusing her more than she was before. Was he talking about the two of them? Or was he simply playing a game involving the snowmen?

Caleb tipped his hat sideways on his snowman's head. "Either way, he'll be patient with her. But in the meantime, she's stuck with him."

"What if she isn't ready to be stuck with him yet?"

Caleb smiled, revealing dimples that made Katie swoon.

"I suppose he'll have to wait for her to become ready. But you might want to tell her to hurry because he really likes her."

Katie hoped he was talking about the two of them and not the snowmen. If only there was a way she could be sure.

CHAPTER 13

Katie paused before knocking on the Yoder's door. "Be nice, *Aenti* Nettie. The Yoder's were kind enough to extend the invitation to us, and the Bishop would not permit such discord if he knew the sour feelings you harbored for this *familye*. Bishop Troyer will be joining us, so you need to mind your manners."

Katie had thought her *aenti's* attitude had changed a little since she'd allowed Jonah Beiler to fix the buggy wheel yesterday. Today, it seemed the ornery woman was full of renewed anger. Katie and Caleb had decided to invite the Bishop and his wife to dinner with them, knowing that her *aenti* would not be able to turn down the invitation. Katie secretly hoped that having the Bishop in attendance would open her *aenti* up to the idea of socializing more.

Nettie scowled at her niece, but decided to paste on a smile before entering the house.

Rachel answered the door with a smile. "*Kume,* Katie, I'd like you to meet *mei mamm.*"

Lizzie Yoder stood by her husband, Jacob's side. She extended a hand to Katie, while her husband nodded.

"Welcome. You must be Katie, the new teacher. Miss Graber, it's so nice to see you up and about so soon after your fall."

Nettie smiled, trying to keep her aggravation in check. She didn't miss the look that passed between her niece and Caleb when he entered the large kitchen. She'd seen that same look in Hiram Miller's eyes when they were young, and she wasn't going to let her niece fall prey to the likes of Hiram's *grandkinner.* She knew her niece was betrothed, and wondered why she was even getting involved with that boy.

When Hiram stepped into the already crowded kitchen, Nettie wanted to bolt from the room. The walking cast on her right leg would slow her down too much to even attempt it. She wished she'd not been so easily convinced to attend this dinner. If not for the Bishop's wife standing between them, Nettie might have been tempted to have an unpleasant word with Hiram right there in front of everyone. Truth be told, a look from the man still sent shivers up her spine, and it angered her that he could still have such an effect on her after so many years.

Feeling suddenly very vulnerable when he offered to pull out a chair for her, she knew she couldn't do anything except succumb to feelings of defeat. Unable to turn down the offer under the watchful eye of Mary Troyer, Nettie swallowed her anger and graciously accepted the chair. It didn't matter that everyone else was still standing; the walk from the buggy to the house had worn her out.

Mary sat next to her. "I think I'll sit down too. All these young people in the room tend to make me feel tired."

Nettie didn't utter a word. She was fuming inside and worried she might say something she shouldn't.

Before long, the *menner* sat across the table from Nettie and Mary, while the rest of the women brought food to the table.

"Rachel and Caleb made dinner tonight," Lizzie said as she placed a large platter of fried chicken on the table in front of Nettie.

She turned to Katie. "How long will you be visiting in our community?"

Katie flashed a look toward Caleb that Nettie didn't miss.

"I was thinking of staying through the summer."

Nettie cleared her throat. "Is that alright with Jessup King? I would think your betrothed would miss you if you stayed here that long."

Katie's heart slammed against her chest wall at the mention of her estranged betrothed.

Rachel touched Katie's arm and flashed an uncertain smile. "I didn't know you were engaged to be married. How exciting for you."

Katie forced a smile that was too weak to convince anyone of her happiness. Suddenly, all eyes were on her. She felt she might faint if she couldn't distract them somehow.

"I love weddings. I hope you will invite all of us," Mary Troyer said.

Katie's face drained of all color, and she worried she might vomit in front of everyone. It was Rachel who saved her by spilling the pitcher of tea down the front of her.

"I'm so sorry, Katie. *Kume*, I'll get you a clean dress to wear."

Lizzie jumped up to mop up the puddle on the floor.

Before Katie realized, Rachel had whisked her upstairs to her bedroom. Once they were inside, Rachel shut the door and turned to Katie.

"Why didn't you tell me you were being forced into an arranged marriage with Jessup King?"

Katie hadn't yet caught her breath. "How did you know the marriage was arranged?"

"I could see it on your face. No wonder you didn't want to tell me about it. Does Caleb know?"

Katie sighed. "I told him the first day I met him that I was betrothed. He was irritating me. How was I to know I would end up…"

Rachel took hold of Katie's arms. "You are in love with Caleb!"

Katie's legs began to wobble, forcing her to collapse onto the bed. "Promise me you won't tell him."

Rachel smiled. "I guess we both have secrets we're keeping from my *bruder*. The first thing we have to do is find a way to get you out of that marriage. And then we'll work on getting you together with Caleb."

Katie didn't want to go back downstairs and face everyone. "Is it too late to get out of the dinner invitation?"

CHAPTER 14

Caleb couldn't believe his eyes when he saw Rachel pour the pitcher of tea down the front of Katie. Knowing Rachel, she had a reason, but that didn't make it right. He hadn't missed the look of pure terror on Katie's face at the mention her betrothed. Did Rachel know the circumstances surrounding Katie's engagement? He squirmed in his seat, trying to think of an excuse to go upstairs to find out what was taking the two of them so long. He pushed back his chair, avoiding eye-contact with his *mamm,* who would be the one to call him out.

Thankfully, she was too engaged in conversation with Bishop Troyer's wife to pay him any mind. Katie's *aenti,* however, flashed him a scowl as he left the table.

Upstairs, he could hear Katie and Rachel laughing about something. He knocked lightly on the door.

"*Kume,*" Rachel said.

Caleb opened the door cautiously, not wanting to interrupt. He poked his head inside. "Everything alright in here?"

Rachel flashed Katie a mischievous smile.

"Caleb, would you mind taking Katie home?"

Caleb frowned at his *schweschder.* "Didn't you bring your *aenti's* buggy?"

Rachel answered for her. "*Jah,* she did. But I can't find anything of mine that will fit Katie. She is so much taller than I am, that none of my dresses will be the appropriate length for her to wear. She can't go downstairs wearing a short dress in front of the Bishop. And she can't stay in that soaking wet dress the entire night."

"*Jah,* I suppose I can take you home. But what about your *aenti?*"

"Don't disturb their dinner," Rachel said. "Slip out the front door. I'll get her coat and meet you out at the barn."

"Could you wrap up some chicken for Katie? I promised her fresh fried chicken, and I don't want to go back on my promise." He shot a quick smile toward Katie.

Rachel nodded. "*Jah.* Now go, before *mamm* and *daed* start looking for us."

Caleb grabbed Katie's hand and led her down the stairs. He was surprised when she didn't try to pull her hand away. It was warm, and it fit perfectly—almost like a missing piece to a puzzle. When they reached the bottom of the stairs, Caleb reached for the doorknob, but his *daed's* voice stopped him.

"Where are the two of you going?"

Caleb turned around to face his *daed,* still clutching Katie's hand. "Rachel doesn't have anything that will fit her properly. I'm taking her home so she can avoid further embarrassment. I didn't want to disturb everyone's meal, so I thought we could leave quietly through the front door."

Jacob's eyes drifted to their hands that still intertwined. He forced his gaze back to Caleb. "I'll let your *mamm* know. It was nice to meet you, Katie. Perhaps next time we can finish the meal together."

"*Danki,*" Katie managed with downcast eyes.

Before she could say another thing, Caleb pulled her gently onto the porch and closed the door. He continued to hold her hand until they reached the barn, where he reluctantly let go.

Katie turned to him. "I can't believe your *daed* just let us go like that. My *daed* is so strict, he would never let me get away with leaving in the middle of dinner—especially not with the Bishop as a guest."

She was smiling so much her cheeks ached.

"That was the most fun I've had in a while."

Caleb raised an eyebrow. "If that was the most fun you've had in a while, you need to hang out with me and my *schweschder* more often."

Katie smiled as he grabbed an extra quilt and draped it across her shoulders. "I'd like that."

Caleb pushed the buggy out of the barn, and then threw a blanket over his horse before leading him outside.

Katie stood in the shelter of the barn while he hitched up the horse. Within minutes, Rachel entered the barn, slightly out of breath.

She pushed the chicken into Katie's hands. "Do you want to just hold your cloak so you don't get it wet? You should be warm enough with the quilt around you."

Katie shook her head. "*Danki*, Rachel. I don't know when I'll be able to repay the favor since my *aenti* will probably ground me until I leave here."

The two of them giggled.

"You're a grown woman, Katie. If she grounds you, I'll have to sneak you out."

Katie hugged her. "If I had a friend like you back in Nappanee, I might not be in the predicament I'm in."

"My parents are very liberal. They remember what it's like to be young. It helps that they made a few mistakes along the way and don't judge us harshly."

Katie smiled. "I wish I could take you home with me at the end of the school year so you can help me talk to my parents about Jessup. I really don't want to marry him."

Rachel suddenly looked very serious. "You shouldn't have to. My *daed* would never make me marry someone I didn't love. I'm going to do everything I can to help you so you can be my new *schweschder*-in-law."

Katie's face turned several shades of red. "I don't know if you should be planning that far ahead. He isn't going to even ask me for a buggy ride until I'm free from my engagement with Jessup. It wouldn't be proper."

Rachel giggled. "I think it's a little too late for that. You're about to take a buggy ride with him right now."

CHAPTER 15

"Are you warm enough?"

Katie smiled as Caleb piled yet another quilt on top of her. "*Jah,* I think that will do it. I'm almost *too* warm."

Caleb looked out the front window of the buggy at the thick snow that fell from the heavens. It was nearly dark, and he was glad he didn't have far to go to take her home.

"Do you mind if we stop up the road a ways and eat this chicken before it gets cold? You promised me fresh chicken hot out of the griddle, remember?"

"*Jah,* I did. We can pull off the road at the schoolhouse if you'd like."

Katie smiled her acceptance of his plan.

They rode in silence until they reached the school yard, where Caleb pulled the buggy under the shelter of two trees.

"My older *schweschder,* Abby, was married here recently."

"In the school yard?"

"Under these trees to be exact. They'd shared their first kiss here when they were very young. So this is where they wanted to be married."

Katie's face heated at the thought of it. Why had he brought her to such a sentimental place?

"It must be a popular spot. I've already seen two of my older students sneaking a kiss under these trees."

Caleb chuckled. "They start kissing pretty young these days."

Katie giggled at his statement. "You sound like an old *mann* saying such a thing."

Putting his hand to his chin, he scraped his hand across the whiskers Katie estimated to be two day's growth.

"I'm at least eleven years older than your oldest students. That's a lot of years when you think about it. That makes me *feel* kind of old."

Katie reflected on the number of years between her and Jessup, and wondered if Caleb would say it was too many. Ten years was a lot. There would come a time in the future when the age difference would seem far greater than it does now. He would become old and gray long before she would, and the difference in their ages would make them look even more mismatched than they do already. It embarrassed her to be seen in public with such an older man now; how would she feel ten years from now?

"Shall we eat before it gets cold?"

Katie opened the plastic container filled with chicken, allowing the steam to reach her. The aroma alone was enough to make her stomach growl. She'd saved her appetite all day in anticipation for this meal, and she was finally about to get a taste of it. Caleb bowed his head in silent prayer, and Katie paused to join him. Before she opened her eyes, she could feel the weight of his hand reaching into the plastic container she held on her lap.

"Dig in before it gets cold," he said around a mouthful of chicken.

Katie sunk her teeth into the juicy chicken. She had to admit it was much better fresh, but she imagined it would have been even better if it had been eaten immediately after it was cooked.

"So what do you think?"

Katie nodded. "It's even better than the first time. "

Caleb chuckled. "I have a feeling it might not have tasted this *gut* if we had eaten it in the company of your *aenti*. Will you be in trouble when she returns home?"

Katie's appetite suddenly soured at the thought of it. "*Jah,* I told Rachel she'll probably forbid me to leave the *haus* until it's time for her to send me packing at the conclusion of the school year—if not sooner."

Caleb smiled warmly, taking her hand in his. "If she does, my *Aenti* Bess runs the B&B a few miles from here, and she'll let you stay there."

Katie felt discouraged thinking about the animosity between her and *Aenti* Nettie. "I would hate to have to spend a portion of my salary on room and board. I should probably apologize to her first thing when she returns from dinner with your *familye.*"

Caleb squeezed her hand gently, sending shivers of delight through her.

"I hate the thought of you getting on her bad side because of me."

Katie squeezed back. "I was on her bad side the moment I asked her to dinner. She's compiled a long list of offenses against me, starting with tricking her into a dinner with your *grossdaddi.*"

Caleb looked into her eyes. He suddenly didn't care that she was betrothed. He wanted to pull her into his arms and kiss her. He wouldn't do such a forward thing. He cared for her, and would never engage her in unwanted affection. Still, he found it increasingly difficult to keep his thoughts pure. He twirled his fingers across the palm of her hand, not caring how flirtatious this action was. He intended to convey his feelings toward her—even if he couldn't kiss her.

Katie felt a surge of desire course through her as Caleb lightly tickled the palm of her hand with his fingers. Was this the kind of behavior friends engaged in? She had never gotten this close with Jessup. He'd kissed her a few times on the cheek or the forehead. But never once had she sat in his buggy and delighted in his touch. She doubted his touch would have the same effect on her as Caleb's touch did now. She wanted Caleb to throw his arms around her and pull her into a deep kiss—her first. She could feel the pull of desire like a magnet, causing her to lean into him. She had never been this close to a man. Her breath came in shallow puffs as she leaned even further until their cheeks touched. His warm breath tickled her cheek, drawing her closer still. His lips swept across her temple and down to her ear, causing her head to tilt back and her eyes to close.

CHAPTER 16

Katie pulled away suddenly. What was she doing? Surely she didn't want to give him the impression that she was a free woman. Not only was it not fair to encourage him, but it was improper and could soil her reputation. It didn't matter that she did not love her betrothed, or that he had been forced upon her by her parents. The fact still remained that she was engaged to be married.

Caleb straightened, apologized, and then picked up the reins. He clucked at his horse. "I better get you home."

How could he have acted so rashly? And why had she let him get so close to her? Was it a moment of weakness after being absent from her betrothed? He didn't dare say another word to her for fear of saying the wrong thing and alienating her. He wondered if things would be awkward between them now, and if it would be too difficult to see her at the school.

Panic surged through him at the thought of not being able to sit in on her reading lessons anymore because of his actions. He'd made such progress this past week that he hated the thought of not being able to finish the lessons. Was there a way to recover from this mistake in judgment?

"I'm sorry, Katie," he whispered.

She didn't respond.

Caleb sighed inwardly. Had he just cost himself any chance he may have had at winning Katie's heart?

Katie's insides were tied up in knots. She was shaking uncontrollably, not from the cold, but from what had almost happened between her and Caleb. What would have happened if she hadn't stopped it? Would he have kissed her? And if he had, would it have changed his opinion of her? Now she was worried that their near mistake may have cost her his respect, or worse, his friendship.

Nettie tried to turn down Hiram's offer to drive her home, but just couldn't do it gracefully under the watchful eye of the Bishop.

How is it that this mann still manages to get under my skin?

So she conceded with a heart full of anger toward her niece.

When I see Katie again, she's going to get an earful.

Hiram assisted Nettie inside, being careful of her injuries. She was healing nicely and could get around quite well without assistance, but she was playing on Hiram's sympathy.

Might as well milk it for all it's worth...

Hiram handed Nettie a lap quilt and she snatched it from him. He was trying too hard to get on her *gut* side, and it suddenly angered her.

"Stop fussing over me. The Bishop can't see us anymore. They went back inside the *haus.* "

Hiram's mouth formed a grim line. "Is that what you think? That I'm helping you to score points with the Bishop? Let me remind you I'm an Elder of this church district, and I don't need to impress anyone."

Nettie snorted. "You don't impress me."

"Nettie, why do you still carry a grudge for me? Is it because you never had a *familye* of your own?"

Nettie snatched the reins from Hiram and halted her old mare. "Get out of my buggy Hiram Miller before I throw you out!"

"You ornery old woman. You can't throw me out of here."

Nettie pursed her lips. "Old? Who are you calling old? You're still a year older than me—*alt mann.* And I *can* throw you out. If you'd like, I can prove it to you. "

Hiram turned to her. "I'm sorry. I should not have said such mean-spirited things to you. It's my fault you didn't have a *familye.* I took that option away from you when

I married Rachel. I won't apologize for having a *gut* life with her, but I *am* sorry for hurting you."

Nettie chuckled. "That has got to be the worst apology I have ever heard. And let's get one thing straight. You were *not* my only option. I had other offers for courting, but I had my heart set on being a teacher."

"Is that why you refused my proposal? Because you would rather teach?"

His question caught her off guard. She hadn't thought about it from that angle before now. Maybe all this time she'd been blaming him for a decision she had made on her own. No one had talked her out of marrying Hiram—except herself. She'd been the one to choose teaching over his proposal.

Nettie looked Hiram in the eye for the first time in nearly forty years. "I think that's exactly what I'm saying. I was the one to choose my teaching career over you—not the other way around. I guess my feelings got stepped on when you married Rachel so soon and forgot all about me. It stung pretty bad watching you have a life with her over the years."

Hiram took a chance and pulled Nettie's hand into his. She didn't pull away. That was a good sign.

"I never forgot about you. There will always be a special place in my heart for you, Nettie. You were my first love. I could no sooner forget you than I could forget how to breathe."

Nettie's heart did a somersault. His hand was warm in hers, just the way she remembered. Was he declaring love for her after all these years?

"I have had a full life, Hiram. My students were my *kinner*. I have been happy for the most part, but I've always felt that nudge for what was missing."

Hiram smiled. "It's never too late to have what's missing."

Nettie blushed. "What are you talking about? I'm too old to have *kinner* of my own."

Hiram's smile widened. "You're not too old to be married. We're only sixty. Rachel has been gone for close to thirty years. I've been waiting a long time for you to let me back into your heart."

Nettie snorted. "That's *narrish.*"

Hiram pulled her close. "It's no more crazy than spending the rest of your life lonely and unhappy. As for *kinner,* I can share mine with you."

Nettie's heart beat double-time. "What are you suggesting, Hiram Miller?"

"Marry me, Nettie. I still love you."

Nettie leaned into him and kissed him gently.

It was just the answer he was hoping for.

CHAPTER 17

Katie tossed and turned all night, unable to sleep after the confusing mishap between her and Caleb. She'd managed to slip into the house before her *aenti* returned from dinner at the Yoder's. She'd gone straight to her room to avoid any conversation between the two of them. She'd even pretended to be asleep when the light knock sounded at her door an hour later. After the evening she'd had, she only wanted to sleep, but sleep eluded her. She knew she would be tired during school the next day, but she had too much on her mind.

Rolling over toward the window, Katie peered out at the full moon.

Maybe you're to blame! I've heard people act strange during a full moon.

Katie sighed. She couldn't blame her mistake in judgment on the moon. That was *narrish.* She dreaded having to face Caleb tomorrow at school. They'd ridden in silence the rest of the way home. He'd uttered a faint *guten nacht* to her, but she'd ignored him out of embarrassment. Why didn't she just tell him how she felt?

Because I'm engaged. If only I could love Jessup. Then I wouldn't be in this predicament. But maybe nothing could change the way I feel about Caleb.

Sometime in the wee hours of the morning, Katie had finally drifted off to sleep. She'd still tossed about in her sleep, making for a very tough time getting up on time. Knowing she'd be late again, she readied herself quickly and ran down the stairs, taking them two at a time. In the kitchen, her *aenti* sat at the small table sipping her morning cup of coffee. She wasn't prepared for the inevitable confrontation from the woman. Grabbing a few things out of the refrigerator, she threw her cloak over her shoulder and started for the kitchen door.

Her *aenti's* voice stopped her.

"Katie, can you spare me a minute? I'd like to talk to you about something."

Katie didn't dare turn around and look her in the eye. "I know we need to talk, *Aenti.* But it's going to have to wait until after school. I'm late."

With that, she closed the door behind her. She was sure she would be in for an even bigger lecture once she returned from school at the end of the day, but for now, she had managed to avoid what was sure to be a heated conversation. If only she could avoid the same with Caleb.

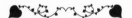

Nettie heard a light knock at the kitchen door.

"*Kume.* It's unlocked."

Hiram poked his head in the door. "I just stopped by to make sure you haven't changed your mind about marrying me."

Nettie chuckled. "What if I have?"

Hiram didn't let her teasing rattle him. He walked over to the stove and poured himself a cup of coffee from the pot.

"I guess I would have to say maybe I beat you to it and changed *my* mind."

Nettie lurched forward in her chair almost spilling the coffee down the front of her.

Hiram picked up her hand. "Relax, Nettie. I haven't changed my mind. I would never want to hurt you again."

Nettie smiled nervously. "I knew that."

Hiram suppressed a smile. "Is that why you practically fell off your chair just now?"

He pulled her hand to his lips and kissed the back softly. Sitting down across from her, he leaned forward, a serious look on his face.

"I want to marry you soon—before you change your mind, Nettie."

She smiled thoughtfully. "There's no chance of that. How about as soon as the doctor removes my cast?"

Nettie crossed her arms over her ample chest waiting for Hiram to answer. He simply nodded, causing her heart to do another somersault.

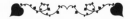

Katie threw leftover chicken from the previous night to the hounds before they had a chance to bark at her. She was determined to make her day go more smoothly than the day before. Despite the fact she was late, she tried to keep in good spirits. If she were to let one thing disturb her, it might ruin her entire day.

Before she even opened the door, she could hear the students laughing heartily. Upon entering the back room of the school, Katie could see Caleb at the front of the classroom. He was telling them a story of two children falling into Goose Pond while trying to catch pollywogs. It was a story about him and his cousin. Katie admired the way he held the attention of the entire class that ranged in ages between six and fourteen. He was a natural with the *kinner,* and Katie wondered why he didn't have any of his own.

When he saw her, he smiled, putting Katie at ease. Maybe things wouldn't be so awkward between them after all—she could only hope.

Neither of them said a word to each other, but went to work on the things they needed to do. Caleb climbed the ladder to finish plastering the holes in the ceiling, while Katie took over at the front of the classroom. Once again, Caleb stared as she gave the reading lesson to the younger students. He'd learned the first half of the alphabet before they broke for lunch.

The students gathered in the back room without any effort, while Katie remained at her desk grading the spelling lesson for the older students.

"I have to admit, I was a little worried about seeing you today. I wasn't sure if you'd even speak to me after last night."

Katie searched her words carefully, not wanting to mess things up between them. "I'm sorry for allowing things to get weird between us. The last thing I would want to do is lose your friendship."

"Nothing you can do would cause me to stop being your friend."

She smiled, unaware that the door to the school had swung open.

"Katie Graber." A familiar voice startled her.

"Jessup!"

CHAPTER 18

Katie's heart nearly jumped from her ribcage. Caleb quickly excused himself, though she'd wanted him to stay. She wasn't ready to face Jessup, and certainly didn't want to do it alone. But here she was, looking into his disapproving eyes, and wishing she'd stayed in bed today.

"May I have a word with you?"

Katie allowed her eyes to drift over to Caleb, who had joined the students in the back room. When their eyes met, he looked away, seemingly disgusted. Her heart fluttered haphazardly as she wondered how to get out of talking to Jessup.

"What are you doing here?"

Jessup narrowed his eyes. "I should ask you the same thing, but you never bothered to ask me if you could come here."

Ask you? I don't have to ask your permission to live my life the way I want to!

"We'll have to talk later," she said firmly. "I'm teaching, and I can't leave my students to have a personal conversation."

Jessup looked back at Caleb. "You didn't seem to mind having a personal conversation with *him*."

Katie fumed as she pointed to the holes in the plaster. "He's making repairs to the school."

Jessup's brow creased with irritation. "I've taken a room at the Miller Bed & Breakfast. I'd appreciate you joining me for dinner this evening."

"I don't understand why you came all this way, Jessup. I really cannot meet with you this evening. I have some things to take care of with my *aenti*. It will have to be another time."

Jessup pursed his lips. "I wasn't asking, Katie. I will expect to see you precisely at six-thirty."

He leaned in to kiss her on the cheek, and she froze. She didn't respond as he turned sharply and left the building. In fact, she didn't move for several minutes. She swallowed the lump in her throat and pushed back tears that threatened to spill if she blinked.

Caleb hadn't missed her comment about him. Was that all he was to her? Just the man who fixes things around here? Or was she too frightened of her betrothed to stand up for herself? He also hadn't missed the look of fear that shrouded Katie, or the control Jessup seemed to have over her.

"He's kind of old for you, don't you think?"

Caleb's teasing startled Katie out of her state of shock.

"Please excuse me."

Katie ran to the bathroom, closed the door behind her, and began to weep.

How could she marry such a controlling man? Especially when she would rather have Caleb, who was so gentle and caring. She hadn't realized until Caleb said it just how old Jessup looked. His beard had bits of gray—a beard he'd grown for his first marriage. Did she really want to marry a man who still wore the badge from his deceased wife? She wanted to court a young man with a clean-shaven face—one with no past to remind her she wasn't his first love.

She wanted Caleb.

There had to be a way out of this mess. She couldn't talk to her *aenti,* who would surely side with her parents. She could never ask Caleb to help her—it would make her sound desperate in his eyes. Rachel was the only one who might be able to give her sound advice—except that she was only around sixteen, and didn't seem to have a beau of her own for comparison.

It's hopeless. I have no one to turn to.

Wiping her eyes on the corner of her apron, Katie cleared her throat, pushed up her chin, and walked out of the bathroom prepared to teach.

Caleb was gone.

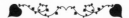

Caleb could hear Katie crying in the bathroom as he packed up his things and prepared to leave. He'd felt bad for teasing her and making her cry, but he didn't know how to help her either. He could apologize, but he had the feeling their friendship was not strong enough yet to withstand this kind of setback so early. Not to mention, he felt it was a waste of time to pursue a woman who had given her heart to another. He wanted to be the only one she wanted—the only one she loved.

When he reached the bakery, he went straight to work finishing the porch. He was already cold, and nothing, it seemed, would warm him.

Rachel opened the door and handed him a cup of hot coffee. "You looked like you could use something to warm you up. But I'm afraid I don't have anything to help that long face of yours. What's wrong?"

Caleb thought about it for a minute. "I don't want to talk about it. Don't you have something burning in the kitchen?"

Rachel smirked. "I just took the last batch of cookies out of the oven, so I've got plenty of time. It must be something serious if you're trying to get rid of me."

Caleb sighed. "It's something serious alright. Jessup King showed up at the school."

Rachel's eyes widened. "Katie's Jessup?"

Caleb wished she hadn't said that. He nodded sadly.

She reached inside the door and grabbed her coat off the hook. "I've got to borrow your buggy. Stay here and hand out the last five orders for the day. I won't be long."

Rachel was in his buggy before he had a chance to say anything. Was she going to help Katie? He hoped so, because he didn't know what to do.

CHAPTER 19

Katie's head hurt. She found it difficult to concentrate and didn't feel like going over the same lessons, reviewing what her students already knew. She felt as though she'd been repeating herself for the past hour, and all she wanted to do was go home and forget about what had just happened.

"I'm dismissing class early today so I can get caught up on grading your homework."

The student's shouted all at once.

Katie put up a hand to quiet them. "I'm giving you homework, though."

"Awww," her class said in unison.

She put up her hand again. "Your assignment is to come up with an idea for our spring festival."

Smiles abounded as they rushed to the back of the classroom to gather their things.

Katie knew the festival was more than a month away, but she didn't have the heart to pile homework on them when she knew most of them had an abundance of chores waiting for them when they returned home.

As she was wiping off the chalkboard, Rachel walked in the door. The students had all left, and she was just beginning to feel sorry for herself all over again.

She rushed to Rachel and hugged her. "I'm so glad you're here. I need someone to talk to."

Rachel showed genuine concern. "Caleb told me about your visitor. Did you tell him it's over between the two of you?"

Tears pooled in Katie's eyes. "I didn't get the chance. My parents must have told him where I was. He's angry with me. He demanded that I have dinner with him tonight at six-thirty. I can't go. I will crumble under his authority and probably agree to marry him now. I don't have the strength to stand up to him."

Rachel smiled. "Yes you do. You are stronger than you think you are, Katie Graber."

Katie shook her head. "He's angry with me for not telling him—no, asking him—if I could come here to teach. If I'd mentioned it to him, he'd have forbidden it. The only reason my parents consented was because of something my *Aenti* Nettie said to them. I'll probably never know what she said because she's probably never going to speak to me again. *Ach,* I've made such a mess of things. What am I going to do?"

Fresh tears ran down Katie's cheeks.

"I'll tell you what you shouldn't do, and that is to show up to dinner tonight. You're in no shape to have dinner with that *mann.* Especially if he's going to order you around like you're one of his *kinner.* You're a grown woman, Katie, and you have to learn to stand up for yourself."

A hiccup escaped Katie's lips. "I was in such a state of shock over seeing him here that I didn't even introduce Caleb as my friend. I told Jessup he was only here to fix the holes in the ceiling. I'm sure your *bruder* hates me now."

Rachel put a comforting hand on Katie's shoulder. "He doesn't hate you, but I can see how that might upset him. But probably not more than seeing your betrothed show up here unannounced."

Katie sniffled. "I don't know why I let my parents push me into this marriage with Jessup in the first place. My *schweschder,* Rose, would never put up with such a thing. She's a year older than I am. She's stronger and more independent. She would never let my parents force her to marry Jessup. I wish I could be more like her."

"Is Rose married?"

"*Nee,* Jessup chose me over Rose because he thinks my *schweschder* is strange. She's smart is all, and he knew he wanted a *fraa* that he could boss around. I'm the weak one, and he knew that when he chose me."

They had slowly made their way to the back room where they sat down at the lunch table.

"I think you're selling yourself short. You have a lot more to offer a *mann* than being his weaker half. My *bruder* would never make you feel like that, and I think you two are made for each other. If it is *Gott's wille*, then it will be so. But it can't happen as long as Jessup thinks you are to marry him. We have to find a way to break it to him so he will finally accept it."

"I believe any woman *dumm* enough to marry Jessup will be nothing more to him than a *mamm* to his *kinner*. I don't want to be that woman."

Rachel needed to understand something. "Why did you agree to the arrangement in the first place?"

Katie cried even harder. "Because *mei daed* threatened to put me out of his *haus*. That's when I decided to ask for a long engagement. I thought that if I had time to save money from my teaching salary, then I could eventually be able to support myself, and I wouldn't have to marry Jessup. If I know Jessup, he's here to force me to go back to Nappanee so he can marry me immediately."

Rachel crossed her arms over her chest. "Well, he'll have to go through me to get to you, and I won't let him take you back. I'm sure when Caleb knows the whole story, he will help too."

Katie jumped out of her chair. "*Nee*, don't tell him about this. It's embarrassing enough just to have *you* know about it. It would lower his opinion of me if he knew how *dumm* I've acted."

Rachel took Katie's hand and guided her back to her chair. "You're not *dumm*. What you've done is very smart. You did what you had to, and no one can blame you for that. I will keep your secret if that's what you want, but we need to think of a plan to get Jessup to go back home—without *you.*"

"I could tell him I'm in love with Caleb!"

"Katie, that's a brilliant idea!"

CHAPTER 20

Katie dreaded going home and facing *Aenti* Nettie. Jessup was sure to have already made his appearance to the ornery woman, and she probably directed him to the school. How else would he have known where to look for her? She supposed it was well-deserved since she'd ambushed her *aenti* by forcing her to go to a dinner with Hiram Miller— her biggest enemy.

As she approached the house, she wondered what her *aenti* would say when she heard of her feelings for Caleb. In a community this tightly-knit together it wouldn't stay a secret for long. But hopefully she would be long gone from her *aenti's* house by that time.

There was no way her *aenti* would permit her to marry Caleb any more than her parents were going to permit her to get out of marrying Jessup. She was stuck. There was probably nothing more she could do but to leave her *aenti's* house and spend her salary on room and board. Thankfully she'd had the presence of mind to bring her box of earnings with her when she left home. But even with that money, she would only have enough to get her through the summer. She would need to find another job since the teaching position would end in just a few short weeks. And given her tardiness all week, it was unlikely that the Elders would offer her the job on a permanent basis.

Ach, I'll worry about that when the time comes. For now, I need to worry about what I'm going to say to Aenti Nettie so she won't put me out by my ear. The longer I can stay here, the better it will be for my savings.

Before she approached the kitchen door, she could smell fresh-baked bread and several other delightful aromas coming from the kitchen. Taking the cowardly approach, Katie decided she would try to sneak in through the front door to avoid her *aenti,* who was obviously in the kitchen cooking a feast of a meal. Glancing at the pendulum clock over the hearth, she realized that she'd spent so much time talking to Rachel that she had gotten home half an hour later than usual.

As she closed the front door quietly behind her, Katie could hear her *aenti* in the kitchen humming, and the house smelled delightful. Something was amiss. She didn't know her *aenti* very well, but humming and cooking anything that wasn't simple seemed out of character for her. The ornery woman didn't hum, and she had already made it clear to Katie that she hated to cook. So why the sudden change? Was it possible that this was Katie's last meal with her, and she'd cooked it as a means of breaking the news to her that she'd be kicking her out?

Katie's heart raced as she went to the kitchen to get their unavoidable talk over with before she lost her nerve. She rounded the corner toward the kitchen and noticed three place settings on the table. It wasn't the regular plastic plates she'd been eating off since she'd arrived. This was pretty china plates like her *mamm* used for special occasions. She stood at the doorway panic-stricken.

Aenti must have invited Jessup over here for dinner, and the two of them are going to ambush me! She's humming because she's going to be rid of me, and she will probably get her teaching job back.

Nettie looked up from the stove, where she was happily preparing a light gravy to go with the steaming mashed potatoes that sat on the table in a glass, covered bowl. A loaf of bread nestled in a basket, sat at the center of the table, while a large platter of lemon-pepper chicken crowded the setting.

It was too late for Katie to make a run for it.

She'd been spotted.

She could hear someone whistling an unfamiliar tune in the small bathroom off to the side of the kitchen, and knew it had to be Jessup. Only *menner* whistled while they were in the bathroom. There was no way out of this dinner. This would be pay-back for making *Aenti* Nettie endure a dinner with Hiram Miller the night before. Now she would have to endure an uncomfortable dinner with Jessup. She supposed she deserved it after what she'd done. She just hadn't expected her punishment to fit the crime.

"Katie, I'm so glad you're home. I wasn't sure if you would make it time. Sit. We're about to eat."

Katie did as she was told. Tension built in her as her *aenti* bustled happily about the kitchen bringing things to the already crowded table. Her eyes ran over the table settings once again. All three of them. The back door was so close to her, she was tempted to bolt. But she was not a child. She was a grown woman, and it was time she faced her inevitable future with Jessup. There would be no tolerance of a confession about loving Caleb. There would only be a demand for her immediate hand in marriage, and she would consent.

It was the grownup thing to do.

A new wave of panic hit Katie as she heard the squeak of the bathroom door. This was it, whether she was ready for it or not. Her future was sealed. There was no turning back. No getting out of it. Her love for Caleb would have to be pushed down. She was about to marry her betrothed and become a *mamm* to his *kinner*. It no longer mattered what she wanted. She would succumb to the demands of her family. In time, she would be able to get over Caleb…wouldn't she?

Her heart pounded with each footfall, as they seemed to move in slow motion toward the kitchen. Her eyes drifted upward as she spotted a male figure rounding the corner.

She looked up into the face of…*Hiram Miller?*

CHAPTER 21

What was Hiram Miller doing at her *aenti's* house—for dinner, no less? Katie watched him sit down at the table across from her like he had been coming to dinner for years. There was something different about him and her *aenti*. They were acting like they were in love—with each other. Was it possible that they'd talked after she'd left the Yoder's dinner last night, and they'd made amends? Or was this some sort of intervention trick, and Jessup would come from somewhere else in the house to ambush her? She stared at the place settings again—still only three, which meant that Hiram Miller was their only dinner guest.

He was all smiles, and he hadn't even noticed her. He only had eyes for *Aenti* Nettie, and she for him. Then it dawned on her. Her hand clamped over her mouth to avoid saying it out loud.

They ARE in love!

Nettie put the last of the fixings on the table and sat down next to Katie.

"Stop looking like a spooked horse, Katie, and welcome our guest."

Katie couldn't help but breathe a sigh of relief. Jessup wasn't here to take her back to Nappanee and force her into a loveless marriage. Her *aenti* no longer seemed upset with her, and she and Hiram Miller had made amends. Maybe there was hope for her and Caleb after all.

Katie smiled at their guest. "Welcome, Elder Miller."

She was truly happy to see him. Not just because it meant she was off the hook with her *aenti,* but because she could see how happy her *aenti* was for the first time since she'd known her.

Nettie smiled at her niece. "You're going to have to get used to calling him *Onkel* Hiram. We are to be married next Thursday after I get this cast off my leg."

Katie squealed with delight. But then her expression turned serious. "Why so soon?"

Hiram took Nettie's hand and smiled into her eyes. "At our age, Katie, we don't have any reason to wait. We've waited long enough already."

Katie stood up and hugged her *aenti.* "I'm so happy for you. Can I help with the wedding plans?"

Nettie was surprised at Katie's willingness to help. "It's only going to be *familye,* but that's quite a few. Your *mamm* and *daed* will probably be here. But we aren't announcing it until Sunday after services. You're the only one who knows so far, so keep quiet until we make our announcement."

Katie simply nodded. She couldn't promise such a thing because she couldn't wait to tell Rachel and Caleb. Hiram bowed his head for the silent prayer and then they started eating the feast fit for such a special occasion.

"I want to talk to you about a few things, Katie."

Now she was nervous.

Nettie set down her fork and perched her elbows on the table—a very big offense back home. Katie and Rose had often gotten a fork poked in their elbow by their *daed* for displaying such terrible manners. But here was her *aenti* casting her cares to the wind. It was nice to see this relaxed side to her *aenti.* It almost made her seem like a different woman.

"After the wedding, I'll be moving into Hiram's *haus.* I haven't decided what to do with my *haus* yet, but I want you to know you can stay here until the school year is over and you have to go back home."

Katie didn't want to think about having to go back home. She had never had an entire *haus* to herself before. She didn't have her own room back home, so this was going to be a very freeing experience.

"*Danki, Aenti. Das gut* and generous of you to offer to let me stay in your *haus* when you aren't living here."

Nettie clutched Katie's hand and gave it a quick squeeze. "Your parents might not agree, but you're a grown woman. I will talk to your *daed* about it. I know how strict he can be. But I lived alone in this *haus* when I was your age. I don't see why you can't live here. You have shown me that you're a responsible person with a *gut* head on your shoulders."

"*Danki.*"

Katie didn't know what else to say. She liked this new *aenti,* right down to the fact that she would let her stay in her *haus* alone. Maybe God was beginning to answer her prayers after all. She didn't need to bow down to Jessup's demands. She was on her way to being independent just like her sister, Rose.

Glancing at the clock on the kitchen wall, Katie realized she'd missed dinner with Jessup. What a liberating feeling it was to let go of that obligation. Her *aenti* had just given her hope for a better future, and she wasn't going to waste a single moment of it worrying about disappointing Jessup King—or her *daed.*

After dinner, Katie offered to wash the dishes for her *aenti.* It was the least she could do after her generosity. She whispered a quick prayer asking for forgiveness for referring to her *aenti* as *ornery.*

Since it was too cold to take a buggy ride, Nettie and Hiram settled into the sitting room by the fire where they could talk and make plans for their future.

Hiram kissed Nettie on the cheek. "You make me feel like a young boy again."

Nettie chuckled. "I'm not sure I would go that far. Maybe closer to ten or fifteen years younger. But definitely younger. I wish *mei mamm* was still around to see this. She'd be happy that I'm finally getting married."

Hiram looked at her seriously. "Are *you* happy that you're finally getting married?"

"*Jah.* I've spent too many years rattling around this *haus* alone. I'm a little worried the same fate might befall Katie."

Hiram tugged on his gray beard. "I thought she was betrothed?"

Nettie slighted her smile. "I have a feeling that's about to change."

CHAPTER 22

As much as Katie tried, she just couldn't make it to school on time. She didn't like being tardy, but it seemed that no matter how early of a start she got, something always got in her way of making it on time. This morning it was the deep snowfall that had covered everything in a thick blanket of white. She was beginning to wonder if spring was ever going to arrive, or if it was going to snow indefinitely.

By the time she reached the school, Caleb was already hard at work, while her students worked quietly on assignments. She'd wanted to share the news about her *aenti* and his *grossdaddi,* but it would have to wait until they broke for lunch.

Though the morning seemed to drag on, Katie managed to catch Caleb sneaking a glance at her more than once. He'd even flashed her a quick smile a few times, causing her heart to flutter. She couldn't wait for the break when she could talk to him. She had so much more to say to him than the news of their relatives getting married in just over a week. Katie wasn't sure if she would have the nerve to tell Caleb how she felt about him, but she was willing to try.

When she finished the reading lesson, which she masterfully geared toward Caleb, she was tempted to call the lunch break early. She knew if she did that, the students would have a tough time getting through the long afternoon, and truthfully, so would she. Instead, she called on them to give suggestions for the spring festival. Some of them voiced discouragement over the recent snowfall, while others gave some odd suggestions.

When they'd all settled down, she cleared her throat and gave her opinion on the subject. "I thought we could set up booths with games like at the county fair. We could raise money for new books for the school's library, and maybe a new chalkboard. This one here has so many cracks in it that it's tough to write on."

She figured it was a long-shot, but the students seemed to be receptive to the games. By the time they finished their discussion, they had several game suggestions ranging from drop the clothespin in the milk bottle, to setting up a fish pond using a horse trough. For the most part, the games wouldn't cost much if anything to put together as long as Katie could count on donations from the community, but she didn't think that would be a problem.

Feeling satisfied with her morning, she finally broke for lunch, watching the students scatter to the back room for their much-needed break. Caleb eventually made his way over to her desk and perched on the edge. He watched over her shoulder as she marked off the assignments in her grading book. She decided not to grade this particular assignment, but merely to give them credit for having done it. She would read the essays later at home and give them extra credit accordingly. For now, all she cared about was whether or not the assignment had been done.

Caleb watched Katie writing things in her grade book, and amazingly, was able to catch some of the words on the pages that the students had written. Her lessons were paying off for him whether she realized it or not. Before long, he would be able to read important instructions on products that he used every day in his business. He had learned most of it by asking for advice at the hardware store in town, but now he would have the knowledge to read them for himself instead of depending on others for help. He felt empowered with his new knowledge, and that was important to him.

He admired Katie's intelligence, and her ability to teach her students—and him—with ease and confidence. He hoped one day he would be that confident when it came to reading. She had given him a precious gift, even if she wasn't aware of it. He would have to think of a way to thank her when the school year was over. For now, he would continue to admire her work *and* her beauty.

She finished what she was doing and pushed the papers aside, and then stood up to retrieve her lunch from the back room.

"I have some news to tell you. Do you plan to stick around for lunch?"

Caleb stood up from his spot on the corner of her desk. "I don't want to hear it unless it's *gut* news."

Katie smiled. "It's very *gut* news, but I'm not supposed to tell anyone."

Caleb raised his eyebrows over his blue eyes. "Now you have to tell me. It irritates me when people say they have to tell you something, but they can't tell you. My *schweschders* do that to me all the time."

Katie giggled. "I made certain I didn't promise, but I wish Rachel was here so I could tell her too."

Caleb sighed. "Do I have to wait until after school so you can tell us both at the same time?"

Did all girls act like this, or was it only the ones he cared about? Did he really care that much about Katie even after he'd seen her betrothed with his own eyes? Maybe he cared more for her after seeing the way he treated her.

Katie couldn't wait any longer. "Your *grossdaddi* and my *aenti* Nettie are getting married next week on Thursday!"

Caleb's brow scrunched together. "What? How do you know?"

Katie couldn't wipe the smile from her face. "I had dinner with them last night at my *aenti's haus.*"

Caleb scooped her up into his arms as he let out a whoop. He twirled her around as she giggled with delight. When he set her down, neither of them moved to break apart. The electrical energy passing between them was enough to light up an entire town.

"Katie Graber."

Was Jessup's voice only in her head, or had she really heard it? Caleb pulled away from her, and she stood there, stunned at Jessup's presence.

Caleb held up his hands in defense. "I'm sorry Mr. King, this isn't what it looks like."

Katie moved back to Caleb's side and hooked her arm in his. "No, Mr. King. This is *exactly* what it looks like. I'm in love with Caleb!"

CHAPTER 23

Caleb stole a glance at Katie. Had he heard what he thought he'd heard come out of her mouth? A quick glance at Jessup King let him know he had heard exactly what he thought he'd heard. But why had she said it? Was she using him as a human shield to get out of marrying Jessup? The thought of it angered him. He would not be used by her for any reason. He cared about her, and he thought she felt the same. But he also didn't need a fight with her betrothed over this misunderstanding.

Still in shock, Caleb moved away from Katie. "I'm going to go. I think the two of you need to talk. I'll talk to you later, Katie."

Jessup sized him up. "I think it would be a *gut* idea if you left us alone, but I want you to stay away from my Katie."

Katie stood in front of Caleb, blocking him from leaving. "I don't have anything else to say to you, Jessup. I believe I've just said it all. And I'm not yours. I belong to Caleb now."

Caleb wasn't going to stand there any longer and let Katie use him to make Jessup jealous. It was humiliating enough that she was making a fool out of herself. He wasn't going to stand by and let her do the same to him. He did not like confrontation, and that's exactly what this was. He moved aside, intending to bolt, when he caught the look on Katie's face. Maybe she had a *gut* reason for what she was doing. Was it possible?

Jessup's brow formed a deep crease, making him look old and angry. "If you refuse to listen to reason, perhaps you will listen to the Bishop."

Katie pushed her chin up defiantly. "I won't go back to Nappanee with you."

"Then I will speak to the Bishop here. And I will put a call out to your *daed's* barn first thing in the morning. Doesn't he go out for milking around six o'clock?"

Katie laughed heartily. "You can talk to my *daed* all you want to. I live here now with my *aenti,* and I'm not going back."

Jessup narrowed his eyes. "Then you leave me no choice but to marry your *schweschder,* Rose."

Katie laughed even harder, slapping her hand on her knee. "Rose wouldn't marry you if you were the last *mann* on earth."

Caleb couldn't believe the sudden change in Katie. She was being disrespectful and downright mean to this man. Granted, he was dishing it out too, but Caleb couldn't understand the reasoning behind Katie's actions. He hoped she had a good reason for engaging in a public confrontation with Jessup. But the students didn't need to hear any of this.

"Mr. King, I think you and I should leave, and let Katie finish her day of teaching her students. This is not the time or the place for such a conversation."

Jessup moved to kiss Katie, and she turned her back to him. "I asked you to leave, Mr. King," she said over her shoulder.

She didn't say a word to Caleb.

Standing outside in the snow, Caleb thought about the past few days. He stood beneath the mulberry trees remembering his near-kiss with Katie. Had she mistaken his actions as an unspoken commitment between them? He certainly hadn't done anything since he'd met her to discourage her thinking they were involved on some level beyond friendship.

He was partly to blame.

If she needed to use him to get out of an obviously wrong-suited match with Jessup King, he would help her. But only on *his* terms would he agree to such an absurd plan. He would have to make it seem more like a business deal than a commitment between them. He didn't want any more confusion, and he certainly didn't want her caught in the middle of anymore confrontations with such an unreasonable man as Jessup King.

Gott, forgive me for what I'm about to do if it is not right and just in your eyes.

Caleb shook as he entered the school. He was about to confess to her that he couldn't read, and ask for her help in exchange for helping her out of her marriage with Jessup. He pushed down his insecurities, knowing this was the only way to keep from falling in love with her when it was obvious she didn't return his feelings.

Katie looked up from her lesson when Caleb entered the school, and he motioned her to meet him in the back room. The look on her face as she walked toward him was fearful. The last thing he wanted to do was add to her worry.

"I won't take up much of your time, but I can't help but feel partially responsible for what happened with Mr. King," he lowered his voice. "I want you to know that I will help you by pretending to be your beau, but as long as there is an even exchange. There has to be something in it for me."

Pretend?

Katie was furious. She couldn't believe he was trying to gain something from her pain. He didn't care about her at all, which meant he had tried to kiss her with no feeling in his heart for her whatsoever.

"*Ach,* you want to know what's in it for you? How about in exchange for helping me, I'll teach you how to read!"

CHAPTER 24

Caleb wasn't sure he would ever get over the smug look on Katie's face. She had been so sure of herself, but ended up shaming him in the process. Was she really the snob that he had originally thought her to be? If she was, he wanted no part of her, and was glad he would only have to pretend for as long as it took to finish learning how to read. He almost wished he'd had never gone back into the school. He wished he'd never made that deal with her, but it was too late to take it back now. Before long, the news would spread across the community of his *relationship* with Katie. He knew that a meeting with the Bishop was unavoidable, whether Jessup went to him or not.

As far as Katie was concerned, if she wanted a fake beau, he intended to give her just that. He would be the best fake beau she could ever hope for. Especially since he intended to earn every reading lesson she gave him.

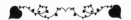

Katie couldn't stop thinking about the hurt look that crossed Caleb's face when she blurted out his secret. Why had she let her own selfish wants cloud her ability to decide between right and wrong? She loved him, and the last thing she wanted to do was hurt him. But she had also broken a confidence with Rachel. She had made a promise not to tell Caleb she knew he couldn't read, and she had broken that promise. How could she have let this situation get so far out of control that she'd hurt her friends just to get her way? She felt like the worst person in the world. How would either of them ever forgive her? She would lose the respect of the community and her *aenti* when they found out her relationship with Caleb had all been a lie.

She was glad her school day was finally over, but her pain wasn't. As she pulled the buggy into the parking lot of the bakery, her heart raced at the thought of what she knew she had to do. She had to apologize to Caleb and Rachel and hope they would forgive her. She had made a complete mess of everything, and it was up to her to start putting the pieces back together.

Katie stepped nervously out of her buggy after seeing Caleb on the front porch finishing the repairs. She hadn't expected to run into him again so soon, but she supposed they would have to get past the initial awkwardness if they were to keep to their deal.

Caleb unexpectedly greeted Katie with a smile. Then he did something that completely threw Katie off guard. He pulled her into his arms and planted a kiss on her cheek. Lingering over his embrace, she wondered what he was thinking. Amish didn't allow such public displays of affection.

She pushed gently at his strong chest. "What are you doing? Do you want Rachel to see us in an embrace?"

Caleb smirked. "If we are to pull off this charade, then *everyone* has to think we are a real couple, and that includes our *familye.*"

He pulled her back in his arms. He was enjoying watching her squirm.

She tried to push him away, but he was too strong. "Why can't I tell Rachel the truth? She's my friend."

Caleb put his mouth to her ear and whispered, sending tingles down her spine. "We can't tell *anyone* the truth or this will never work. And I don't want anything to keep you from teaching me how to read."

Was he trying to provoke her, or was he still hurt because she exposed his secret? She would go along with whatever he thought was best since she didn't want anything to ruin her chances of getting away from Jessup once and for all.

"I'm sorry for the way I exposed you about not being able to read. I didn't mean to hurt you."

"I'm fine. Just keep to our deal and everything will be fine."

Katie finally managed to squeeze out of his grasp. "I came here to talk to Rachel about all of this, but I can't leave now without talking to her. What do you suppose I should say to her?"

Caleb pulled five dollars out of his pocket and shoved it in her hand. "Tell her you came here to buy cookies. She'll accept that."

Katie tried to give him back the money but he wouldn't take it. "I don't need your money, I have my own. And I don't need to buy any cookies from her. I could tell her the news about *mei aenti.*"

He snatched the money from her hands and turned to pick up his tools. "Suit yourself. But don't leave here without telling me *guten nacht,* or my feelings will be hurt."

Was he serious? He was going to take this as far as he could stretch it. Katie was certain of that.

Inside the warmth of the bakery, Katie suddenly didn't feel like sharing the happy news of the upcoming wedding for her *aenti.* She was confused and scared at the same time. She couldn't believe what she'd gotten herself into. Had she traded one overbearing man for another? Thankfully, the relationship with Caleb was a ruse, and she would be able to get out of it easier than it was going to be with Jessup.

Rachel greeted her with a smile. "What brings you in here this time of day?"

Katie cleared her throat to hide her nervousness. "I decided to bring home some cookies after all."

Rachel winked at her. "I'm glad to see you stand up for yourself to your *aenti.*"

Rachel packed up the cookies and handed them across the counter to Katie. "Is there something you want to talk about, Katie? You look kind of pale."

Katie shook her head. "I've just had a long day is all. I should probably get home so I can get to bed early."

"It's closing time for me, too. I'm eager to get home myself."

Katie paid for the cookies. *"Danki."*

Rachel stepped to the door to switch the sign over to *Closed,* and then twisted the lock, noting her brother was putting his tools away for the evening.

Katie stepped onto the porch and looked at Caleb, her nerves on edge. "*Guten nacht,* Caleb."

He closed the space between them, pulling her into his arms and pressing his cold lips gently against hers. Katie closed her eyes for a split second, allowing herself to enjoy the moment, until the sound of bells jingling against the door of the bakery broke the spell between them. Katie rushed down the stairs without looking back. Climbing in her buggy, she clicked to the old mare urging her away from the bakery, and the prying eyes of her friend. Her friend who had no idea of her deception.

Rachel pulled on Caleb's jacket. "Did I just see you kissing Katie?"

Caleb smiled, still stunned from the feel of Katie's warm lips against his. "*Jah,* we are courting."

He wished with all of his heart it wasn't a lie.

Rachel pulled her brother into a hug. "I'm so glad Katie finally told you she's in love with you."

CHAPTER 25

Caleb fought hard to keep his eyes on the road as he drove his buggy toward the school. He'd stayed up half the night trying to figure a way out of the mess that he and Katie had made.

If Katie was really in love with him, then she had told the truth when she blurted it out to Jessup. Why hadn't she just told him how she felt about him? Why did she have to say it to Jessup instead of him? More importantly, why would she agree to have a fake relationship with him if she really loved him?

Was it possible she didn't think he would return those feelings? He had to find a way to reverse the damage of this deal they'd made before it destroyed any possibility of them having a real relationship.

How was he going to carry on with her in this charade, knowing she really loved him? One thing was certain; he couldn't let on that he knew the truth because for some reason she hadn't told him yet. Perhaps he would have to devise a new plan to pull the truth from her.

Caleb entered the school with his tools in tow, prepared to work while he listened to Katie's lessons the same as he'd been doing for the past two weeks. But she had a different idea in mind, it would seem.

Katie beckoned him to the last row and offered him the chair before turning to her class to get their attention. "Mr. Yoder will be observing the morning portion of our classes for the remainder of the school year. He will also be evaluating my lessons. Please be considerate of his work here as you go about your own lessons."

With that, she handed him a tablet and a pencil and urged him to sit in the chair in the last row. It was vacant, so there was no chance that another student would see him writing anything. He appreciated her care where his privacy was concerned.

The morning went by quickly—too quickly. He was just getting the feel for forming some of the letters in his tablet after Katie's instruction, and the lesson was over. He closed the cover of the tablet and walked over to his toolbox and stuffed it to the bottom. He was going to have long days for the next few weeks learning to read in the mornings and then making repairs to the school in the afternoons. But he didn't mind; he was happy to be in the presence of the lovely woman he was falling deeply in love with.

The two of them sat with the students during lunch, trying to keep some semblance of normalcy to his presence there. But that was ruined the minute the door swung open and Jessup stepped inside, Katie and Caleb jumped from their seats.

Katie turned to the students. "Would everyone like to have recess today?"

They all shouted acceptance as they jumped up to pull on their coats. Katie was grateful it was a reasonably warm day for the end of March and the snow had begun to melt.

Once the students had gone outside in the school yard, Caleb asked Jessup to sit down at the table in the back. He hoped this would be the end to his visits, but only if Caleb was able to convince him to go back to Nappanee and forget about Katie.

Jessup looked at Katie, who sat close to Caleb's side. His arm was sprawled out across the back of her chair, and that disturbed Jessup.

"I came here hoping to talk some sense into Katie and bring her back home with me."

Katie sighed. "I already told you yesterday. I'm not going back to Nappanee. My home is here now," she turned to Caleb and pushed her hand in his. "With Caleb."

Jessup's face twisted with anger. "I didn't want to have to go the Bishop, but it appears that I must."

Caleb clung to Katie's hand. Knowing she loved him, gave him the strength to sit there and endure the unforgiving stares from Jessup. "I think Katie has made her choice clear. Going to the Bishop isn't going to change her mind."

Jessup stood up abruptly and slammed his fist on the table. "I will not leave here without Katie as my *fraa.*"

CHAPTER 26

Katie jumped, and Caleb held tight to her hand even as he stood to face Jessup. He leaned across the table, looking Jessup in the eye.

"I'm sorry that Katie made you believe the two of you were going to be married, but she's changed her mind. I think it would be best if you were on your way, or I'll go to the Bishop myself."

Jessup's mouth twisted. "I would appreciate it if you would allow Katie to speak for herself."

Caleb was losing patience with this man. He could see why Katie wanted to get away from him.

"She's said all she has to say on the matter. I'll be speaking on her behalf now. If you have something to say to her, say it me instead. I'm her betrothed, and I will not permit you to speak to her anymore."

Katie's pulse raced. Was Caleb taking this a bit too far? Although she liked the idea of marrying Caleb, she didn't welcome the thought of having her heart toyed with because of Caleb's outrageous stretching of their story.

Katie held up her hands to the men. "If you neither of you mind, I have something to say."

The two of them sat back down, impatience hanging thick in the air as all eyes were on Katie.

"I owe you an apology, Jessup. I've been lying to you."

Caleb squeezed a warning against her hand, pleading with her not to continue. If she told Jessup their relationship was a lie, Caleb feared he would lose all chance to keep her in his life—even if it was just for show.

"The only reason I agreed to accept your request to marry me was to buy myself enough time to earn money to be out on my own."

Jessup tried to put his hand over her hands that now rested on the table in front of her, but she pulled away from him. Caleb claimed her hand in his own, reassuring her of his support.

"*Mei daed* threatened to put me out of his *haus* if I didn't accept your proposal, so I accepted and asked for a long engagement. I hoped it would buy me the sort of time I needed to save money to be on my own. I was frightened I would have nowhere to go. But I was wrong. I have my *aenti*."

Caleb squeezed her hand. "And she has me now. I'm not going to let anything bad happen to her. That includes anything from you or her *dead*. It's my job to take care of her for the rest of her life. You can go back home. I wish you well, and I pray that you find a *gut* woman who wants to be your *fraa,* but that woman is not going to be Katie."

He meant it, and he hoped Katie knew that.

She looked up at Jessup. "I'm sorry, Jessup. I shouldn't have hurt you like that."

Anger narrowed Jessup's eyes as he stood to leave. "This is not over. I plan to speak to the Bishop and make certain the two of you are excommunicated for your actions."

Panic claimed Katie as she watched Jessup leave the school. Fresh tears pooled in her eyes, and she couldn't stop them from running down her face.

"Maybe this was a bad idea," she sobbed.

Caleb pulled her into his arms. He loved the feeling of her close to his heart as she rested her head against his chest. It was all he knew to do at the moment. He couldn't stand by and watch her cry; he loved her too much to be that cruel. He couldn't bring himself to tell her how he felt about her. In her emotional state, he feared she would reject him.

He smoothed her hair, tempted to draw it into the clutches of his hand and bring her mouth to his, but this was not the time or the place for that.

"I'm sure he's just angry. Once he calms down, he will see reason, and hopefully, he will decide against going to the Bishop. The odds are in our favor since he hasn't gone already. I'm sure they're empty threats fueled by his anger and humiliation. I'd be upset too if you told me that."

Katie lifted her head from his chest and swiped angrily at a tear. "Are you defending him?"

He took her hands in his. "I'm not defending him. I'm simply trying to see this from his point of view. You apologized to him, but maybe it wasn't enough."

Katie's face distorted at his comment. "What do you suggest I do? Marry him out of pity?"

"*Nee.* I'm only suggesting you seek his forgiveness. It might go further than a simple apology."

Katie threw her arms up in disgust. "There was *nothing* simple about that apology. That humiliated me to admit my own *vadder* doesn't want me living in his *haus* because I am a burden to him. To have you know that my parents arranged a marriage for me so I wouldn't become a spinster is hard enough. Then to admit that I used that *mann* for my own personal gain makes me sound like some sort of monster."

"You're not a monster for doing what you had to do in order to survive. Your own *daed* treated you harshly, whether he knows it or not. And Jessup was never the supportive person he should have been if he intended to marry you. To put you in a position where you would have to go to such extremes in order that you would not become homeless is wrong. I admire your strength for what you did, even if you went about it the wrong way. It may not have been the right thing to do, but it was what you *had* to do. But you have to know; if you had done to me what you did to Jessup, I'd be hurt."

Katie pursed her lips. "Jessup isn't hurt because he doesn't love me. He's angry for losing. And *our* relationship is just as fake as my relationship with Jessup was. Does that hurt you?"

"*Jah,* it does."

CHAPTER 27

Katie couldn't wait to go home. School had become so stressful. Not because of her students, but because of the visits from Jessup. And now, the complications from her fake relationship with Caleb were starting to wear her down.

After he'd walked away from her this afternoon, she wasn't sure what to think of him anymore. What had he meant by telling her he was hurt by their relationship? Was it possible that he cared for her more than he'd admitted?

When she entered the back door through the kitchen, she collapsed into a chair at the table, unable to push herself any further. The kitchen was filled with delectable aromas and the table was set for three again, but her *aenti* was nowhere to be found. She forced herself out of the chair and walked toward the sitting room where Hiram was stoking the fire in the hearth.

He looked up when Katie entered the room. "Would you like me to put away the horse for you?"

"*Danki,* but I already took care of her. Where's *Aenti?*"

Nettie walked into the room wiping wet hands on her apron. "I was in the bathroom. Are you hungry? I made a big meal."

Katie shook her head and walked toward the stairs. "I'm not hungry. I think I'll just turn in."

"That's *narrish.* I'm not going to let you go to bed on an empty stomach. You don't have to tell me what's bothering you, but I won't take no for an answer about dinner."

Katie continued to walk toward the stairs. "Don't the two of you want to eat alone? This is your courting period."

Nettie grabbed Katie by the hand and gently guided her toward the kitchen. "We will have plenty of time to be alone when we're married. Right now, I want to hear how your day went. From the look on your face, I'd say you had a rough time of it. Are my students giving you trouble?"

"*Nee,* the students are *gut.* But I do have something that is worrying me…but I'm not sure I should talk about it in front of company. Can we talk later?"

After the silent prayer, Hiram smiled sympathetically toward Katie. "We are practically *familye.* You don't have to be shy around me."

Katie flashed Hiram an unsure look. "Even if it involves Caleb?"

He raised an eyebrow. "Especially if it's about Caleb. Has he done something to upset you? He isn't too old for a trip out to the barn with a switch."

Katie almost laughed at the thought of Hiram trying to take a switch to Caleb. She imagined he would have a tough time of it. She couldn't imagine Caleb sitting still for such a thing.

"*Nee,* I'm the one who did something to hurt *him,* and I'm not sure I understand what."

Nettie patted her hand. "Why don't you start from the beginning, and we'll see if we can help you figure it out."

She wasn't hungry anyway, so she began to tell the story while they ate. Katie worried what her *aenti* would think when she described the harshness with which her *daed* had treated her, but the woman seemed to take it all in stride. Then she explained her plan to save money so she would have a place to stay, but since she'd come here, she wanted to stay with her *aenti*.

Nettie looked at Katie sternly. "You don't have to marry anyone you don't want to. I already told you that you can stay in my *haus* for as you need a place to stay."

Hiram interrupted. "What does any of this have to do with Caleb?"

Katie cleared her throat nervously. "I'm getting to that part. When Jessup came to the school, he saw me and Caleb in an embrace, and…"

Hiram's eyes grew wide. "Why were the two of you embracing? Has he been improper with you?"

"*Nee,* I had shared your news of the wedding with him and he hugged me. I know I promised to keep it quiet so you could make the announcement, but I have become quite the *blabbermaul* lately, and I'm sorry, but I keep breaking promises to people and I don't know why. Maybe I just can't be trusted with a secret."

Nettie and Hiram laughed. "We've already told a few people too. We couldn't keep it to ourselves any more than you could. But breaking promises is another thing. Who else have you hurt?"

Tears pooled in Katie's eyes, and she swallowed them down. "I promised Rachel I wouldn't tell Caleb I knew he couldn't read. And I promised Caleb I wouldn't tell anyone that we've been faking a courtship to get me out of having to marry Jessup, but I can't keep this stuff inside anymore. It's giving me a stomach ache."

Nettie patted Katie's hand again. "I knew Caleb couldn't read. He came to school a few times, but got discouraged when he couldn't keep up with the other students. He made the decision to stay home with his *daed* and work the farm. There's no shame in that."

"I know *aenti,* and I don't have a low opinion of him for it. In fact, I tried to help him in exchange for pretending to be my beau so Jessup would go back to Nappanee."

Hiram sat back in his chair and wiped a spot of gravy from his beard. "That doesn't sound like my Caleb. Either he's fallen off his horse and hit his head, or he's fallen for *you*, Katie."

Katie's heart fluttered. "He told me that the fake relationship was hurting him. I don't want to hurt him. I love him, but I'm too afraid to tell him. I don't think I could bear it if he rejected me."

Hiram nodded to Nettie as if to say he'd answer this one. "I could tell him for you, but it wouldn't mean the same coming from me. He deserves to know the truth about how you feel. If you don't ever tell him, how will you ever know how he feels about you? I held back telling your *aenti* how I felt because I was afraid she would reject me. She did the same thing to me. Look how many years we wasted? Don't make the same mistake we did. Tell him, and tell him soon. Or you might lose him."

CHAPTER 28

Caleb was determined to tell Katie how he really felt about her—even if it meant she would reject him. He pulled up to the school and noticed her buggy was already there. He pulled his timepiece from the pocket of his trousers and noted that she was early. He smiled, feeling proud that she'd finally made it on time after two full weeks of being late.

When he entered the school, Henry was tending the fire, and Katie was busy grading papers. Several students were already seated and busy preparing for their day. He sunk into his place at the back of the room and pulled out his own writing tablet. He was eager to talk to her, but it would probably have to wait until the lunch hour. For now, he would enjoy his reading lesson and the opportunity to learn from the woman he loved.

Within minutes, the last of the students arrived, and Caleb settled in for his lesson. The morning went by quickly, and before he knew it, Caleb was faced with an opportunity to talk to Katie. He approached her, but one of the students interrupted them asking about the spring festival. Katie whisked the little girl to the front of the room so she could show her a few plans she'd drawn up for the various booths. The child whined, asking if she could run the fish pond, but Katie told her she would have to have her sister's help. The little girl didn't like that answer, but Caleb admired the grace with which Katie handled the girl's tantrum.

Watching her diversion tactics with the young student made him think how patient she might be with *kinner* of her own—*their kinner*. Without realizing, Caleb's face heated at the thought of having *kinner* with Katie. He was in love with her; there was no denying that. He only wished he could be sure she wouldn't break his heart.

The door to the school suddenly swung open, and Caleb braced himself for another confrontation with Jessup. When he turned around, it was Bishop Troyer that he faced instead. Assuming Jessup had followed through with his threat to expose his relationship with Katie, he found himself grasping onto the words he might use to satisfy the Bishop's inquisition.

The two of them shook hands, while Katie looked up, feeling suddenly very intimidated. She had only met the Bishop briefly at the Yoder's before she and Caleb had left without saying a word to anyone. She wondered if her actions that night would make it difficult for the Bishop to have compassion for their situation. Knowing it was inevitable they talk; she excused herself from her student and went to the back of the school to greet Bishop Troyer with the most convincing smile she could manage.

"Bishop Troyer, it's *gut* to see you again. What brings you out this way?"

His look was somber, and Katie didn't find that encouraging in the least.

"I was wondering if I might have a word with the two of you. Could you drop by my *haus* after school so we can have a brief talk?"

"*Jah*, we'll be there at four o'clock." Caleb shook his hand again, and Katie nodded agreement to the meeting time.

Bishop Troyer left just as swiftly as he'd come in, leaving Katie's stomach in knots.

"I'll get Henry to take my buggy home. He lives just past my farm, so I'm sure he won't mind. We can take your buggy since you don't know the way. There isn't any sense in taking two buggies."

Katie frowned. "Do you think that's wise for us to show up together in the same buggy?"

"Katie, he asked to speak to both of us together. What difference does it make for us to arrive in the same buggy? Besides, it will help show the validity of our relationship."

Katie leaned in close and lowered her voice.

"But it's not valid."

It was for him, and he aimed to make her understand it somehow.

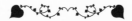

By the time the school day was over, Katie was exhausted. She was so nervous about talking to the Bishop, she could barely think. She'd prayed a couple of times, asking God to make things right for her and Caleb.

She climbed in her buggy and let Caleb take the reins. She didn't even trust herself to drive. Despite the cold wind that blew into the buggy, Katie could feel little beads of sweat forming on her forehead, and her palms were clammy inside her gloves.

Caleb started to pull away from the school, and then he stopped.

"What are you doing? We told him we'd be there at four o'clock. We're going to be late."

Caleb let go of the reins and turned to Katie. "I can't lie to the Bishop."

Katie began to shake. "I don't want to lie either, but we got ourselves into this mess, and now we can't back out of it. We have to stick together, or I'll have to marry Jessup."

Caleb said a silent prayer asking for courage to tell her what he need to. "I won't lie to the Bishop."

Before he could say another word, Katie looked up at him with watery eyes. He couldn't hurt her. Pulling her into his arms, he felt her frame turn rigid. He knew he needed to show her what he was too afraid to say. He cupped her face in his hands and drew her lips to his, kissing her gently at first. His hunger for her drove him to deepen the kiss, and she pressed her lips to his in response.

"I love you, Katie," he whispered. "I truly love you, and I don't want to pretend anymore."

Katie giggled. "I love you too."

CHAPTER 29

The meeting with Bishop Troyer had gone better than Katie could have hoped for. Katie felt like they were out of the woods, but there was one more thing she had to take care of.

She snuggled in close to Caleb. "Will you take me to the B&B so I can speak to Jessup? I need to try to make things right with him."

"Are you sure you don't want to wait for the Bishop to have his talk with him? He said he would handle it."

Katie sighed. "*Jah,* I know. But you were right about the apology not being enough. I need to at least try to fix the mess I've caused."

Caleb kissed the top of her head that rested on his shoulder. "Alright. But keep it brief. He seems like the sort of *mann* that tends to get heated easily, and we don't need another confrontation with him. I know my *Aenti* Bess won't stand for any discord at her place of business."

Katie hadn't even met his *aenti* yet, and suddenly felt a little uneasy about the circumstances with which they would meet for the first time. She hadn't made a very *gut* impression on his *mamm* and *daed* either after running off at the dinner they'd hosted. Hopefully, the fact that his *grossdaddi* would now be married to her *aenti* would make a difference. Hiram certainly didn't have any ill opinion of her.

Suddenly feeling very unsure, she asked Caleb to turn the buggy around. "I changed my mind. I'll write him a letter explaining everything. I don't want your *Aenti* Bess to think ill of me."

Caleb chuckled. "Trust me, she won't. If nothing else, she'll have as much respect for you as I do for facing your wrongs and trying to make them right. The members of my *familye* are not like yours seem to be. They are very understanding and never judgmental. They've all made so many mistakes, that they have nothing but acceptance for everyone."

Katie couldn't imagine such an accepting bunch, but she was open-minded enough to accept Caleb's word for it. As they pulled into the curved driveway of the B&B, Katie's stomach clenched.

Caleb turned to her and placed a quick kiss on her forehead. "Everything is going to be fine. I won't leave your side. I'm proud of you for doing this."

"*Danki.*"

Caleb assisted her out of the buggy, and they started up the porch. Jessup was sitting on one of the rocking chairs, a suitcase at his feet.

He stood up to greet them. "I'm waiting for a taxi. I'm going back to Nappanee."

Katie looked him in the eye. She was shaking, but she needed to clear the air between them.

"Jessup, I never meant to hurt you. I came here asking for forgiveness. Do you think you could forgive me for treating you like you didn't matter?"

Jessup's look softened. "You aren't the only one who is at fault here, Katie. I was only wanting to marry you so my *kinner* would have a *mamm*. I don't love you, Katie. I still love my *fraa*, Elizabeth. But she has gone to be with *Gott*. I don't think anyone could ever replace her. I'm sorry, Katie, for not considering your feelings. It was selfish of me. Please forgive me."

Katie suddenly saw a side to Jessup that she hadn't seen before—a kinder, more caring side. She knew that he had only been a widower for six months before he began to pursue her hand. She hadn't realized he needed her more than she had needed him.

"Of course I forgive you, Jessup. You will find someone to love again. It might take a little more time, but I'm certain *Gott* does not intend for you to be alone and your *kinner* to be without a *mamm* indefinitely. Keep your eyes and your heart open, Jessup, and *Gott* will surely bless you greatly. You're a *gut mann,* and I wish you well."

Jessup smiled. It was the first time she had ever seen him smile in the two years she had known him.

"*Danki.* I forgive you, Katie. Go and have a *gut* life. I wish you and Caleb well."

Katie couldn't help but smile. *"Danki."*

Caleb and Jessup shook hands. Katie felt the burden of her sin against Jessup lift away. They had mistreated each other without meaning to, but now they were both forgiven.

Katie was finally free to have a life with the man she loved.

CHAPTER 30

Katie couldn't believe she was actually looking forward to seeing her family. They would arrive in the morning in anticipation for the wedding. *Aenti* had gotten her cast off, and the doctor had given her hope that her bones were strong and had healed perfectly.

Katie was happy that things had gone well with the Bishop, and he had accepted her relationship with Caleb. It helped that the relationship was finally real. Caleb had offered to help smooth things over with her *daed,* but it didn't matter to Katie if he accepted Caleb as a suitable replacement for Jessup. The only thing that mattered to her was that she was courting the man she loved, and she would continue to live in this community since Bishop Troyer had given her his blessing.

As she put on her cloak to go out to the barn to collect the eggs for breakfast, Katie heard whining. Peering through the window of the kitchen door, she could see the stray dogs pacing on the porch.

"So you found out where I live, huh?" she said aloud. "Let me get you a couple of ham steaks so I can get around you."

After finding the meat left over from dinner the night before, Katie tossed it out to the dogs and slammed the door. She watched from the safety of the window as they gnawed on the large slabs of ham. Feeling confident that they were preoccupied enough that she could slip out to the barn unnoticed, she opened the door cautiously.

She stepped out onto the porch feeling brave until the larger of the two stopped what he was doing and eyed her. Reaching behind her, she felt for the doorknob, unsure if trying to run back inside was the best course of action. She knew it was too far to the barn to try to make a run for it. But this dog was so close, he could rip her leg off before she managed to get back in the door.

Gott please help me. Let these dogs know I wish them no harm.

A whine escaped the larger dog, and his tail lifted in a slow, cautious wag. He lowered his head, bobbing it a couple of times and then dropped to Katie's feet, resting his chin on the toe of her boot. He let out another whine, looking up at her with hopeful eyes.

"I was wrong," she said to the dog. "You're not just hungry, you're lonely."

She bent down slowly and cautiously and put the back of her hand out to the dog. His nose lifted enough to give her hand a sniff. His tongue jutted out of his mouth and he licked the back of her hand. Then he nudged her with his nose. She slowly placed her other hand on the top of his head and began to pet him. He scooted closer to her, keeping his belly to the cold ground, and she allowed both hands to rub his fur. Before long, the other dog inched his way over to her, begging for attention.

Tears dripped down Katie's cheeks. She was happy because it seemed that the three of them had found a new home.

THE END

Chasing Fireflies
Book Five

Samantha Jillian Bayarr
Copyright © 2012 by Samantha Jillian Bayarr

Chapter 1

I'm drowning!
Help me!

Rose Graber couldn't say the words she longed to scream. She knew that even if she *could* scream them, there was no one around to hear her, and she had sunk too far to the bottom of the pond for any sound to escape her lips.

Panic seized her as she tried to free her foot from the entanglement of the thick plant roots at the bottom of the murky water.

Blackness surrounded her.

Her conscience had warned her not to borrow the paddle boat, but the temptation had been too strong to resist. The moon was full, and with only a few sparse clouds in the sky, it was the perfect night for a quick boat ride. She'd been careful to place the Mason jar filled with fireflies at the end of the dock to guide her way to a safe return. But even the fireflies couldn't help her now.

Rose tugged, but the plants had a strong hold on her foot. She twisted every which way, unable to break free. Instinct tried desperately to bring air into her lungs, but there was only water. Hopelessness shrouded her as she surrendered to the pull of her fate.

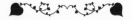

Noah Beiler skipped a stone across the large pond, trying to mask his feelings. Even after more than a year, he could not put that day out of his mind. That day changed his life forever; it was the end to his future—his life. Picking up another stone, he leaned sideways and tossed it across the surface of the pond, his anger propelling it further. His eyes followed the smooth, flat stone as it skipped seven times before sinking below the murky depths of the pond in which he despised.

Following the ripples the stone had created on the surface of the water, Noah fixed his eyes on a small paddle boat making its way toward him. Even from that distance, he could see that it was a young woman pedaling the boat that he knew belonged to the Miller B&B. The boat was reserved for guests, and Noah thought it strange that the driver was not an *Englischer*. He continued to watch her for a few minutes from behind the tall willow reeds that grew along the bank.

Intending to avoid being seen, he turned and pointed himself toward home. A loud splash suddenly echoed from behind him. Heart pounding, he turned around, racing back to the water's edge. Straining his eyes to see movement on the water, he caught only the slow-moving wake from the disturbance the splash had caused. Had she fallen in? She was no longer on the boat, and he heard no other sound indicating she was swimming or even struggling.

He scanned the pond one more time.

Nothing.

A paralyzing silence consumed him as he contemplated having to go into the water. His heart was racing and his breathing heaved as he robotically removed his shoes. Tossing them to the ground with shaky hands, he attempted to yell out to her, but no sound escaped him. Fear circulated through him as he stepped off the shore and into the cool water. He waded quickly through the muck on the bottom until he was out far enough to begin swimming. Each stroke he took toward the young woman reminded him of that night—that cold night in November when his whole world fell apart.

Chapter 2

Reaching the boat quickly, Noah grabbed onto the edge and scanned the water's surface for any sign of the young woman. Just as he'd feared, he would have to dive down in the murky depths with only the light of the moon to guide him to her whereabouts.

Taking in a deep breath, Noah pushed aside his fear and said a quick prayer as he dove down head first. Moonlight filtered through the water making his journey easier, but he couldn't see the bottom. A rush of bubbles floated up past him from just below where he was, and he knew they had come from the young woman. They may have been her last breath.

Running out of air himself, he surfaced long enough to take another deep breath, then plunged himself toward the bottom of the pond where the young woman awaited his rescue. The further down he swam, the more difficult it was to see, but it was just light enough that he was able to locate her.

Grabbing hold of her limp body, he tried to pull her toward the surface but she was stuck. Knowing he was risking his own air supply, he pushed himself further down to where her foot was tangled. With only his hands to guide him, he separated the plant's roots that imprisoned her, setting her foot free. Cupping his hand under her dainty arm, he pushed off from the bottom of the pond, hoping to surface before his own lungs collapsed.

It seemed a small eternity as he kicked and fluttered his free arm to get to the surface.

Gott help me to hold on just a little longer. The light is getting brighter. I can see the moon.

Noah exploded to the surface, gasping for air as he continued to kick his weary legs to stay afloat. Leaning on his side with the young woman against him above the water, he heaved air into his lungs and kicked a little harder until he closed the short distance between him and the paddle boat. Reaching up with his free arm, he grabbed hold of the side of the boat. He pulled himself up until his arm hung over the side, and then he hoisted her small, water-soaked frame into the boat. Pulling himself up, he climbed on the edge and pushed the young woman onto her side. He thumped his open hand across her back the same as he had over a year ago.

Why wasn't she breathing?

Emma please don't die.

Placing a finger to her throat, he felt a weak pulse. Fighting back tears, he pulled her into his arms and kissed her gently on the cheek before applying light pressure to her ribcage. He knew he had to expel the water from her lungs quickly or he would lose her forever. He'd endured that once already, and he would not let it happen again.

Chapter 3

Rose convulsed, spewing a rush of water from her lungs. She gasped for air; coughing each time she tried to draw air into her lungs. Her eyes fluttered open and closed several times before remaining closed. Noah positioned himself on the opposite seat and began to pedal the small watercraft as fast as his wobbly legs would work. The shore, where he'd been just a short time ago, seemed like it had somehow stretched to double the length it had been when he swam out to rescue the young woman.

Hold on, Emma, don't let go this time.

Rose groaned, tossing her head back and forth a few times, but didn't open her eyes.

Noah grabbed her hand. "Stay with me, Emma. We're almost there."

As soon as the boat hit the bottom of the pond, Noah jumped out and yanked it ashore. Then he reached in and pulled Rose into his arms and carried her up the bank.

She wriggled in his grasp. "Put me down."

Noah looked at her, shock in his eyes as she began to smack at his chest with her open hand.

"I said, put me down!"

He attempted to set her down and she stumbled backward, landing in the grass.

"I'm sorry," he said. "I didn't mean to drop you, but you were wiggling so much I couldn't hold onto you."

Rose examined her soaking wet dress, and then looked up into Noah's eyes. She studied him for a minute. His hair was long and wavy, and rested on his shoulders. His jaw line was covered in a line of neatly-trimmed whiskers, yet he wore traditional Amish clothing.

"Did I hear you call me Emma?"

Noah's face drained of all color. He hadn't realized he'd said it.

"You fell into the water. You were stuck down in the muck at the bottom of the pond, but I pulled your leg free. I'm sorry if I called you Emma. I guess I was a little disoriented and thought you were someone else."

Rose's eyes grew wide. "The boat! I have to take it back to the B&B."

She jumped up from the ground and started to walk, but collapsed in the grass again, her legs too weak to hold her up so soon.

Noah took a step toward her, but she verbalized a warning.

"If you come any closer, I'll scream. My *schweschder* will hear you and so will her beau. He's strong."

Noah stood his ground. "I don't want to hurt you. I pulled you out of the pond. If I hadn't, you would have drowned. Are you alright?"

"I'm a little dizzy, and I feel like I can't get enough air."

Noah crouched down on his haunches so he wouldn't tower over her any longer. He hoped the gesture would make her feel safe.

"You need to cough up the rest of the water that got into your lungs. If you don't, pneumonia could set in."

Rose leered at him. "Are you a doctor?"

"*Nee,* but *mei grossdaddi* is. He taught me a lot until…" his voice trailed off, and Rose didn't care to press him for more information.

Rose pushed her damp hair off her face; her *kapp* hanging precariously from her neck by the ribbons. "I need to go home before my *familye* starts to look for me."

Noah held a hand out to her and she took it, allowing him to assist her to a wobbly standing position. Her teeth were chattering, and water dripped from her dress.

"Can I get you a blanket?" he pointed behind her. "My *haus* is right there.

Rose turned around and looked at the dilapidated home. Overgrown weeds covered most of the yard, except for a narrow path leading to the embankment. The shutters were crooked, and she could see by the moonlight that it was in desperate need of a *gut* white-wash.

Noah could see the apprehension in her eyes. Who could blame her? He hadn't done anything to preserve the home for the past year and one half. He'd merely existed there—a shell of a man.

He took a step toward the path and called over his shoulder. "It'll only take a minute. I'll be right back."

Rose watched him disappear into the thick weeds, and couldn't decide whether to wait or make a run for it. But she was cold, and the thought of having a blanket would buy her enough time to dry off before returning home to Katie and all her inquisitiveness.

Noah returned quickly, offering her a wool blanket one might use for a horse. Didn't the man own any soft quilts?

She shied away from him when he tried to drape it over her shoulders, so he handed it to her.

"*Danki,*" she said as she ran toward the boat.

"Wait," he called after her.

It was too late for him to stop her. She had already pushed the craft into the water and hopped in. She pedaled away quickly, and Noah wasn't willing to go back into the unyielding water.

Chapter 4

Noah set out on foot, walking along the pond's edge, keeping track of the young woman's course.

He feared for her safety, and prayed that he wouldn't have to go in and rescue her a second time. It was the second time he had said a prayer on the young woman's behalf. Praying had become strange to him—a thing of the past, as he had not uttered a single prayer since the night Emma had left him.

When Rose pulled up to the dock at the B&B, the light from the jar of fireflies had become dim, and Noah was waiting for her there. Grabbing the rope, he towed her to the edge and tied up the boat without saying a word to her.

She looked at him, moonlight accentuating her milky smooth skin. He longed to reach out and touch her, but suppressed the notion, wondering why he felt such a pull toward the young woman.

"Why are you following me?"

Noah gulped. "I'm not. I only wanted to make certain you would make it back safely."

"I'm here now so you can go. *Danki* for pulling me out of the water, but I think we should both go back home."

She brushed past him, pulling the itchy wool blanket around her shoulders.

"Wait," he called after her a second time. "I don't even know your name."

She hesitated, considering telling him, but then decided against it. She walked away without saying a word. She knew it wasn't polite, but she couldn't have him knowing who she was or he'd go straight to Caleb's *aenti* and tell her she'd taken the boat without permission. It was better to stay away from the strange man whom she couldn't even be sure was Amish.

Noah dragged his bare feet through the cool grass as he trudged back toward his house. The moon shone brightly, lighting the way, but he knew the path well. The humidity level had prevented his clothing from drying even a little bit, and so he still dripped and sloshed as he walked. When he reached the spot where he'd carelessly tossed aside his shoes, he collapsed in the grass beside them. He looked out across the smooth, glassy surface of the water that reflected the moonlight, and let out a long sigh. He'd managed to save her—the young woman he'd mistakenly called *Emma*. Had he gone mad after all this time? Or had the stress of the event brought him too close to his own reality?

Noah cupped his hands over his face and began to weep as he prayed.

Danki, dear Gott, for helping me save her.

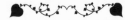

Rose felt the shock of what happened to her as she slipped under the warm quilt in her *Aenti* Nettie's old room.

After *Aenti's* marriage to Hiram Miller, the woman offered to let her come back and stay for the summer with her sister, Katie, whom she'd given the house to as an early present for her upcoming wedding. Since her *aenti* moved into Elder Miller's house, she and her sister had the whole place to themselves.

But tonight, Rose wasn't happy to be all alone in this strange room. She had avoided Katie, who'd sat on the porch swing with her beau, Caleb. Rose had sneaked in through the kitchen so she wouldn't have to explain how her clothes had gotten all wet.

If God was teaching her a lesson for borrowing the boat without permission, she felt it rather harsh for a punishment that she should nearly drown. Or it was possible that she shouldn't have leaned over so far to get a closer look at the frogs on the lily pads. Either way, whether it was a lesson or her own fault, she had to make it right.

I'll put the money for the boat rental in a jar and leave it tomorrow if that will bring redemption. Forgive me dear Gott. And please bless the mann who saved me. If I didn't know better, I'd think he was the one who needed saving just as much as I did. Danki for sparing my life. I am your servant. Please direct me to do your will.

Rose drifted off into a restless sleep, filled with dreams of being trapped beneath the surface of the murky pond water—until her handsome rescuer took her into his arms and—kissed her? Rose rolled over and groaned as she opened her eyes to the little bit of sunshine filtering in through the sheer curtains on her window. How had morning come so quickly? And why had she dreamed that the man who pulled her from pond had kissed her?

Chapter 5

Rose dressed quickly and straightened her hair, pinning on a clean *kapp* and tying the ribbons at her neckline. She wanted to get a head-start on morning chores so she would have time to explore the surrounding area before it turned too warm.

Once outside, the chickens clucked impatiently for their grain. When she exited the barn with a full bucket of grain for the hungry yard-birds, Caleb pulled his buggy into the drive near the kitchen door. Rose stood back and watched her sister run to him and kiss him full on the mouth. Rose had never had a kiss from a man and wasn't sure if she ever would. She was older than Katie, who would be married in November.

She held back near the barn for a minute and waited for the two of them to notice she was standing there and stop with their mushiness. When it became obvious they were not going to notice her anytime soon, Rose cleared her throat as she approached the happy couple, who seemed oblivious to the world around them.

Katie backed away from Caleb, her cheeks turning pink. "*Gudemariye,* Rose. Did you sleep well? I didn't hear you come in last night."

Rose pursed her lips. "That's because you were too busy with Caleb. Doesn't he ever stay home?"

Katie raised an eyebrow at her older sister.

"That's not a very kind thing to say."

Rose began to toss feed to the chickens who were clucking relentlessly at her feet.

"I came here to spend the summer with my *schweschder,* and I've been here almost a month already and have had to entertain myself because you're too busy with Caleb. I thought you wanted me here to help you plan the wedding. We've barely gotten anything done, and there is still so much to do before I go back home."

Caleb was busy retrieving tools from the back of his buggy and could not hear their conversation. Still, Katie felt unnerved that Rose was voicing dislike for her betrothed so openly.

"Why do you dislike Caleb?"

Rose's look softened. "I don't dislike him. I only dislike the amount of time you spend with him. I haven't had a single moment with you since I've been here."

"I'm here now. What would you like to do today?"

Rose bristled. "Why is he here?"

"He's here to fix the barn door so it latches correctly, and the hole in the side where the wood has decayed. *Aenti* hired him to take care of these things before the foxes come and make a meal of our chickens."

Rose suddenly felt selfish. What right did she have to demand her sister's time away from her betrothed? They had overcome some great obstacles to be together, and they deserved to be happy.

"I'm sorry, Katie, for sounding like a selfish *boppli.*"

Katie hugged Rose. "You're right about me neglecting you since you've been here. You came here to help me before I have to go back to teaching in the fall, and I've already wasted your first few weeks here."

"I know you want to spend as much time with him as possible. I'd probably be the same way if I had a beau. But since that isn't likely, I'm taking it out on you."

Katie felt badly for her sister. "Don't say such things, Rose. You never know what God has in store for your life. And here I was envying you for being so independent."

"Why would you envy me? Independent is a kinder word for lonely spinster with no prospects."

Katie fought the lump forming in her throat.

"You will find someone; I just know it."

Rose hated to admit it, but she may have already stumbled upon someone who had caught her interest. He was a little rough around the edges, and perhaps a little unkempt, but with the right woman in his life, he could change. Couldn't he?

Rose chided herself for thinking such things about the man who had—saved her life. Rose sank to the grass, the reality of what happened last night hitting her suddenly.

Katie crouched down beside her. "Rose, is something wrong?"

The hens swarmed to the feed bucket that had tipped out its contents onto the ground when Rose collapsed.

Rose waved off her sister's concerns. "I think I got a little dizzy for a minute. I'm *gut.*"

"You don't look very *gut.* You look pale. Are you ill?"

Rose was trying to sort out how she felt about nearly drowning the night before. She'd come very close until the handsome stranger had rescued her. She'd run off without even catching his name. He'd asked for hers, but she'd ignored him. Why had she acted so rashly? Was she in shock? Was she still in shock now?

"Maybe I should have had more than a glass of milk before coming out in the hot sun. I can't believe how warm it is already. Usually it doesn't get this warm until the middle of July."

Katie called for Caleb who was only a few feet from them.

"Help me get Rose over to the shade of the tree."

A hand-crafted wooden bench sat beneath the tree that held two birdhouses. A set of birds twittered overhead while Katie and Caleb assisted Rose to the waiting bench.

Rose looked out over the expanse of the yard toward Goose Pond. From this distance, she could scarcely see the disheveled house at the opposite end of the water's edge.

Rose looked to Caleb. "Who's the *mann* who lives across the pond in the *haus* with all the overgrown brush?"

Caleb sat next to Katie at the opposite end of the bench. "That *haus* has been abandoned for over a year now. The brush is so overgrown you can barely see the barn anymore."

Rose squinted her eyes. "Are you sure?"

"*Jah,* I'm sure. My cousin, Noah, bought it two years ago. But he's gone now. Did you see someone there?"

"I thought I did, but maybe I was wrong."

Caleb rubbed his hands together thoughtfully.

"It's a tragic story, really. Noah bought that *haus* for his betrothed as a surprise for their wedding. But she never got to live there."

Rose leaned in so she wouldn't miss a single bit of the story. "What happened?"

"The night before their wedding, they went out skating on the pond. The ice was too thin and she drowned. He couldn't save her. It destroyed him—especially since her *familye* blamed Noah for letting her go out onto the thin ice. He left the community with no word."

Rose's heart nearly leaped from her ribcage.

"No one has seen him since then?"

"*Jah.* The *haus* has remained vacant out of respect. We have all hoped he would someday return to the community. His *daed,* my *onkel,* has been so worried about him this whole time. Especially since Noah's *mamm* died just a couple of years before he lost his betrothed. This has been very difficult for his *daed* to first lose my *aenti,* and now my cousin. But no one has seen Noah since the funeral."

"What was the name of his betrothed?" Rose asked slowly.

Caleb looked up at her. "Her name was Emma."

Rose felt the blood drain from her face.

"What's wrong?" Katie asked. "You look like you've seen a ghost."

Rose jumped up and tested her legs for stability before she took off. "I *may* have."

Chapter 6

Rose stepped into the yard of the disheveled house looking for any sign that the man who had rescued her was real. Feeling a little unnerved about being in his yard, she considered if she should wade through the tall grass and weeds to gain access to the door. She wasn't sure how brave she felt at the moment, especially since the reality of her near-drowning had just hit her full-on. Katie had tried to run after her, but Rose had always been a fast runner. She'd called over her shoulder for her sister not to worry, but she couldn't be sure Katie had heard her. It was too late to worry about it now. She was standing on the edge of a property that belonged to a man who might very well be dead—the man who'd saved her from drowning last night.

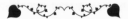

Noah sat at his kitchen table drinking a cup of coffee when he noticed the young woman whom he'd rescued the night before enter his yard. Why had she come here? He'd managed to keep himself hidden away from the entire community all this time, and now she was about to expose him. He still didn't feel ready to face them after failing to save his beloved Emma. He'd managed to cut himself off from the community and remain secluded in the fortress he'd allowed to grow around him, and he wasn't about to let a pretty woman ruin it for him.

He considered remaining in the house, but he worried she might try to peer into the windows. She would surely see him then since his Emma had never had the chance to adorn the windows or any other part of the house with her talent for sewing.

He'd had his moment of weakness last night when he'd kissed the young woman's cheek and held her in his arms. But it was time to put his feelings back on the shelf where they belonged. He had no right to any kind of happiness as long as Emma lay cold in the ground.

Rose wandered around toward the pond, noting the deep grooves in the mud where the paddle boat had been pushed aground. It was evident that she had been here, but there was no sign of the man whom Caleb had called Noah. Had she imagined him? Was he gone like Caleb said, or had he meant that Noah was also dead? If she'd imagined him, then how had she gotten out of the lake?

Standing at the edge of the pond, she looked out over the water. This pond had taken a life, and had almost taken hers. Was it her own carelessness that had caused the accident, or had it been God who'd orchestrated the events as a way of opening her eyes to something?

Show me what you want from me, Gott. If this is all part of your plan, please give me the courage to endure your will for the sake of your purpose.

A rustling sound from behind startled her out of her reverie.

As she turned around, she saw *Noah.* The sun was directly behind him, but she could see that it was him. She held up a hand to shield her eyes from the bright sun.

Rose took a step toward him. "Are you Noah?"

Noah couldn't help but feel drawn to her, but he pushed his feelings down. She was even prettier than he'd thought last night. Her dark blond hair was pinned back neatly, but little wisps of hair fluttered across her cheeks in the gentle breeze. He had no right to delight in the depths of her hazel eyes that sparkled when she smiled.

Why is she smiling at me? She shouldn't be here. I can't be trusted. I let my poor Emma down, and it's only a matter of time before this lovely creature finds out that I failed to save her. And then she will despise me like Emma's familye.

"Why are you here?"

"I came to see if you're real. Or if I imagined you last night."

Noah was not prepared for such a question, and had to admit he'd begun to wonder the same thing himself lately. He'd kept himself secluded for so long, that it was strange hearing his name spoken.

"I think you imagined me," he surprised himself by saying.

Rose stepped forward and placed her hand on his forearm. "I'm not imaging that. Are you?"

Noah shook his head. The feel of her warm hand on his arm sent a shiver of longing through him. He had denied himself of all contact with any others in the community for too long. He'd been punishing himself for not being able to save Emma. He knew she would not want him to deprive himself the way he'd been doing for more than a year, but it was what he felt he deserved for being the one to live when she had died.

Noah flicked his arm away from her grasp.

"You should go. And don't tell anyone you saw me here."

"What about your *familye?* They would be happy to see you haven't left the community. I know your cousin, Caleb, would. He said so just a few minutes ago."

Anger showed in Noah's eyes. "You told him I was here?"

"Nee, but you should. He's worried about you."

Noah scowled. "No one is worried about me. If you didn't tell him I was here, how is it that you know my name?"

Rose jutted out her chin. "I only asked who lived here."

Noah's expression turned dark. "No one is to know I am here, do you understand? I am dead to them."

Rose left the stubborn man, determined never to talk to him again. What had she been thinking when she saw him as kind and handsome? She'd been a fool to see him as anything more than a coward who refused to face his biggest enemy—fear.

Chapter 7

Noah felt empty and alone as he watched the young woman leave his property. He still hadn't learned her name, but it was probably for the best. If he knew her name, it would make things personal between them, and that's the last thing he wanted.

Wasn't it?

He didn't need any complications in his life. His life was just fine before she came along. No one bothered him. He didn't have to answer to anyone. But most of all, there was nothing to remind him of what he'd been missing.

Until now.

Noah had done all he could to remain focused on avoiding his community. So why did this young woman suddenly make him want to change his mind? Loneliness was not a *gut* enough reason; there had to be more to it than that. Was God prompting him to help her beyond pulling her out of the pond? Whatever it was, he decided he would keep a look-out for her—just in case.

"Where were you?" Katie demanded. "I've been worried about you."

Rose dabbed at the sweat on her brow with her apron. "I had to clear something up in my head, but I'm fine now. I'm sorry to have worried you. But really, you can see that I am fine."

Katie narrowed her eyes. "If you're really *fine,* why do you keep saying it? Is there something you don't want to tell me?"

Rose forced a smile. "I am the older *schweschder,* and I'm telling you everything is fine. Why don't we get a little *kaffi* so we can begin planning your wedding?"

Katie's face lit up. "I have a better idea. Let's go to the bakery and sit with Rachel. She will make us *kaffi,* and we can discuss everything over a fresh batch of the best cookies I have ever tasted. Now that I'm going to be part of the *familye,* Rachel has agreed to give me the recipe as a wedding gift."

Rose shook her head. "Nothing is better than *mamm's* snickerdoodles."

"You will take back that statement when you taste these cookies. But never tell *mamm* there is a better cookie out there than hers."

They both giggled as they walked toward the barn to hitch up the buggy.

Lillian's Bakery was abuzz with plenty of customers, both Amish and *Englisch.* Rose was impressed with Caleb's sister's ability to handle each and every one of them so quickly and efficiently. Rose had given some serious consideration to the summer job at the B&B, and watching Rachel move about the bakery enjoying her work was enough to convince her. Caleb's *aenti* was in need of help since her current employee had to go back to Lancaster for the rest of the summer to be with a sick relative, and so she had offered the position to Rose first thing. Rose hoped it wouldn't be too late to accept the offer.

When the last customer was served and happily on her way, Rachel motioned for Katie and Rose to sit at one of the tables along the front wall of the lobby. She brought coffee and three cups, and then sat down across from Rose.

"I'm so happy to see you made it back, Rose. I'm sorry I've been stuck here and haven't had a chance to visit yet. Caleb tells me you might be working at the B&B for the remainder of the summer."

Rose smiled. *"Jah,* I just now decided to take the position. After watching you bustle around here helping customers, I figure I can clean rooms and wash linens. It should be fun and a lot easier than your job, *nee?"*

"*Jah,* it does get a little busy in here sometimes, but I've finally gotten used to it. I felt like a *dummkopf* when I first started here. Ask Katie how many times she had to help me clean up the kitchen. All it took was a little organization, and I was in business with a full customer load. I really like this job, and it may be my own business soon."

Rose took a sip of her coffee. "*Das gut.* But Katie promised me you bake the best cookies I could ever taste."

Rachel laughed. "Katie is the best form of advertisement I could ever have. She tells so many people about my cookies I can scarcely keep up with the orders sometimes."

Rachel disappeared into the kitchen and returned quickly with a plateful of frosted cookies and set them on the table in front of Rose, offering her the first one.

Rose sank her teeth into the moist sugar cookie, enjoying a burst of flavor. "Oh my, I *have* to know what you put in this frosting to make it so *gut.*"

Rachel winked at Katie. "I'm sorry but that is privileged information. I can't give out such an old *familye* recipe to everyone who asks. If I did, it would put me out of business because everyone would be able to make them for themselves. Keeping it a secret is what keeps my customers coming back."

Rose giggled. I suppose you're right, but that doesn't mean I like it. You can count on me as a regular customer."

Rachel smiled. "And that is how I keep customers wanting more. But because you're Katie's *schweschder,* I'll give you a discount."

Rose laughed. "I suppose that's fair enough. *Danki,* Rachel."

Katie set down her empty cup. "We didn't come here just for the cookies. We also want to discuss plans for my wedding to your *bruder.*"

Rachel poured herself a second cup of coffee.

"I won't be able to help with weeding the celery patch or anything else that requires me to leave the bakery. But I am more than happy to help with sewing and list-making in-between serving customers."

"I can let you know what my work schedule will be at B&B as soon as I talk to Bess Miller. But I'd enjoy keeping up the celery patch since I prefer being outdoors."

Rose had already noticed Katie's celery patch overlooked Noah's place across the pond, and she was just as interested in keeping an eye on him as she was in keeping the celery free from weeds.

Chapter 8

Rose swallowed hard, determined to get this over with before she lost her nerve.

"There's something I need to confess before I take the job, Miss Miller. You may not want to hire me after you hear what I have to say."

Bess narrowed her brow. "If you are going to work for me, you're going to have to start calling me by my first name. I'm too old to be called *Miss* anymore, and I was never a *Missus,* so Bess will do just fine. And I already know you borrowed my boat last night. And I know that you nearly got yourself drowned. If it weren't for Noah pulling you out of the water, we wouldn't be having this conversation."

Rose felt weak in the knees. "But how…"

"Awhile back I had a critter getting into my garden, and I didn't know how to defend myself against the damage it was causing. So I borrowed a pair of binoculars from *mei bruder,* and that's how I saw everything…right down to the kiss he placed on your cheek."

Rose could feel her cheeks heat up.

He really did kiss me! The nerve of him!

"You know he's here, instead of gone like everyone thinks?"

"I saw you go over there again this morning. I've known he was here all this time. I've been waiting for something or someone to bring him out of that *haus* and make him want to start living again. I saw the way he looked at you this morning. You haven't seen the last of him."

"What if I don't want to see him anymore?"

Bess placed her hands on her broadened hips. "I think it'd be a shame if you never talked to him again. He hasn't had an interest in talking to anyone in over a year. He needs help, and it seems *Gott* has already placed you in Noah's path."

Rose was too embarrassed to speak.

"The job is yours if you want it. I'll even let you take the paddle boat out anytime you like. But only on the condition that you wear the life vest I keep under the seat."

Rose couldn't resist such an offer. If she'd known there was a floatation device on the boat last night, she would have used it. But maybe things were just as Bess had said, and she was meant to fall in the pond—for Noah's sake.

Bess gave Rose a tour of the B&B, and pointed out her duties. She would have two days off per week, which was the perfect amount of time she needed to keep up with the celery patch for Katie's wedding.

Noah looked around at the mess that was his yard. When he'd purchased the house, he'd envisioned the beautiful flowers and over-sized garden Emma would have here. There would be white linen curtains flapping in the breeze from open windows, and there would be bed linens drying on the clothesline. Chickens would hover around her as she threw feed to them every morning, and even their milking cow would greet her happily for the morning milking. He would gracefully tell her to let him do the milking, and she would gently encourage him to spend his time instead on building a cradle for their firstborn. But none of that would happen now. She was gone, and there was no getting her back.

Noah's thoughts took a sudden turn to the young woman, whose life he'd saved. Was it possible that God had sent her to him for a reason? It had always come naturally for him to accept that everything happened for a reason, but now he found that he second-guessed every decision he made.

Except for last night.

He hadn't thought twice about diving into the water of the pond to save her. He did what needed to be done without any consideration for his own worries. They'd been there on the surface, but he'd done what was needed to do for *her* sake.

Using the sickle he'd brought from the barn, he began to clear the top layer of the thick brush that masked the property. As he made his way toward the pond, he realized that if he cleared all of it, someone might notice. Not yet ready for the community to know he was here, he stopped a few feet short of the edge of the pond.

After working for more than an hour in the warm afternoon sun, Noah had cleared a fair portion of the thick grass and weeds to the point that he could see over the tops of them. He knew it would take several more hours of work before he would have it trimmed to a reasonable length that was suitable for a yard. He'd made some progress. Not nearly enough, but that would come in time. For now, he was satisfied with the improvement that such a seemingly insignificant change had brought.

Knowing it was already late in the season, he decided he'd spend the day tomorrow breaking ground for a garden. With a lot of care, he would still be able to grow tomatoes, peas and potatoes. His root cellar was nearly empty, and he would need to go after food if he didn't grow some. He'd caught a few rabbits and made stew with the root vegetables he had, but even those stores were thinning. The strawberries and raspberries that grew wild alongside the barn were blooming, and he knew that no matter what, he was resourceful enough to keep from going hungry. But would he be able to do that much longer without having to mingle among the community?

Chapter 9

Rose pushed her arms into the life vest and tied the straps. Some might consider her a *dummkopf* for going back out onto the water so soon after nearly drowning, but she had always been one to face her fears directly. Her heart raced a little at the thought of being vulnerable out on the water alone, but she would not let the fear paralyze her. With shaky hands, Rose placed the jar full of freshly-caught fireflies onto the end of the dock, and then slipped the rope off the post. Taking a deep breath, she uttered a quick prayer before stepping into the paddle boat. She sat there for several minutes working up the nerve to pedal out into the open water.

"Are you going to just sit there, or are you planning on leaving the dock?"

Startled by the voice, Rose looked up to see Noah standing at the end of the dock. Eyeing his bare feet let her know why she hadn't heard him approach. His presence was enough to convince her to start pedaling.

Noah lifted his foot and placed it against the side of the paddle boat, giving it a gentle shove.

Rose pursed her lips as she pedaled backward until she was clear from the end of the dock. She moved the lever to turn the rudder, and began to pedal forward. She moved slowly out into the open water, moonlight illuminating the way. Though she was a little frightened, she was glad to be away from Noah, who seemed to have a way of getting under her skin with one simple question—a question she answered only by her actions.

Resisting the urge to look back toward the dock to see if Noah was still standing there, Rose kept her eyes focused on the opposite end of the pond, which was her goal. She wasn't sure if she thought it was odd that Noah should sneak up on her the way he did, or if he was somehow looking out for her.

Rose forced herself to follow the same path she had the night before. She hoped that if she could get all the way across the pond and back, she would be rid of the fear that gripped her.

Gott, please bless me with enough courage to make this journey across the pond and back without falling apart.

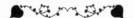

Noah wasn't sure if he should follow along the edge of the pond to keep a better eye on the young woman, or if he should stay where he was. As he watched her leave the dock, he realized she seemed to be heading straight out into the middle of the pond toward the opposite bank. If he set out on foot, he could meet her at the other end, but from this vantage point, he could more easily see her.

Gott, please place a hedge of protection around her. Bring her back to the dock safely.

Realizing that praying was all he could do for her frustrated him. It was hard for him to trust in God's will for himself. He'd trusted his entire life, and it seemed his biggest prayer had gone unanswered. Or had it? He'd had the opportunity to love and be loved, but he never got the chance to have a family of his own. Could it be that God had other plans for his life? Plans that he'd been too consumed with grief to see? Was it time to put his past behind him and move forward in God's will for his life? He'd certainly been ignoring the gentle prompting up until last night when he'd jumped into the pond and saved the young woman.

What was God trying to tell him now? And why was he following the young woman's every move as though she was now his responsibility?

Noah lowered himself onto the end of the dock and let his bare feet dangle over the edge, his toes lightly touching the cool water. Listening to the gentle swish of the boat as the blades pushed through the water, he looked up to see that the young woman was already pedaling back toward the dock. He lifted the jar of fireflies from beside him and examined it. The lid was screwed on tightly, and the insects inside seemed to be slowing down from lack of air. Their glowing ends began to dim, and he felt sorry for them. They no longer floated around the jar. Instead, they piled on top of each other at the bottom fighting for space.

Noah looked out across the pond, noting how close the young woman was to the dock already. Opening the lid, he gave the jar a gentle shake, releasing the fireflies out over the water. Their tails lit up as they flew out over the expanse of open water.

He'd freed them just in time.

The young woman pedaled the boat up to the dock, bumping it as she tried to navigate it gracefully back into its spot. Noah stood up and took hold of the rope, tying it around the post. The young woman exited the small water craft, and then stood on the end of the dock, her fists planted firmly on her narrow hips.

"Why did you let my fireflies go?"

Noah took a step backward, wondering if she wanted to take a swing at him. "They were dying."

Rose fumed. "I was going to let them go when I got back to the dock. You could have waited five minutes longer."

Noah couldn't help but smile at her fury. She was cute when she was mad.

"I wasn't certain they would last another second in that jar. Besides, you were close enough to the dock that you could see your way safely."

"And what if I hadn't been? Are you going to follow me around making sure I don't fall in the pond again? I wore a life vest so you can go home and stop spying on me."

Noah turned to go, but then turned back toward her. "Will you at least tell me your name?"

"*Nee,*" she blurted out. "You have no use for knowing my name. I appreciate you being there to save me last night, but now I want you to leave me alone and stop following me."

She brushed past Noah, storming off the dock, and didn't look back.

Chapter 10

Noah knew exactly what he was risking when he drove his buggy into town to purchase some chickens from the feed store, but he kept his hat pulled down over his face and didn't intend on making eye contact with anyone if he could help it. It was time to start bringing his small farm back to life, and the chickens would be a nice start. Not to mention the fact that his stomach would appreciate having eggs on a regular basis, and eventually, a plateful of fried chicken.

The last time he'd gone into town, he'd purchased several bales of hay for his horse along with enough bags of feed to get him through the winter. He knew it was time to pick up a few things for Silo, who'd been his only companion since he'd closed himself off from the community. Truth be told, he'd missed his family, and simple conversation. But he still wasn't sure if he was ready for all of that yet. It was tough enough talking to the young woman. Getting out the few sentences he'd said to her was one of the most difficult things he'd had to do in a long time. He could only imagine how much harder it would be on the day when he finally faced his family.

Given the length of his hair and the trim of his whiskers, he doubted anyone would converse with him. They might assume he was a Mennonite convert, or worse, that he'd been shunned. For all he knew, he *had* been shunned—especially since he hadn't attended church service for more than a year. It wasn't as though he hadn't thought about it; he'd wanted to go and reach out to family and friends, but the longer he stayed away, the easier it was to remain hidden.

After selecting a half-dozen Rhode Island Reds, Noah placed his order for chicken feed and horse chow. It would be all he would be able to carry this trip to town. Already in his head, he was planning a second trip, which really surprised him. But for some reason, *Gott* seemed to be pushing him to make some changes.

As he steered his buggy away from the feed store, he thought he heard someone calling his name.

Rose tossed the sheet over the top of the bed at the B&B, letting it rise above the mattress and fall in a puff of slow-motion freshness. She reveled in the fresh aroma of the line-dried linens, as she made the beds for the incoming guests. She'd already beaten the braided rugs and scrubbed the planked, wooden floors. A little light dusting, and she would be finished with this portion of her duties. Bess had advised her that her days off would depend on the schedule of guests, rather than on specific days. She was agreeable to such a flexible schedule, knowing it would afford her the time she needed to spend with Katie and Rachel planning the wedding.

Her thoughts drifted to Noah, and she wondered if he would show up again this evening when she took her boat ride. Part of her wanted him to be there and was even eager to see him, but another part warned her not to get too friendly with the man, who seemed to be running from God. Although he'd been kind and even patient with her, he'd closed himself off from the community for a very long time. She couldn't even be sure he was ready to reach out to anyone other than her, and that felt like a very heavy burden for her to carry.

She'd prayed about the situation for some time before finally falling asleep last night, and she was still waiting on an answer. It concerned her that she found him attractive, especially since she did not think he would find her attractive. Katie had always been the pretty sister. She didn't consider herself unattractive, but she knew she was plain in comparison to most other women. She saw herself as having no striking features or special talents that would make her a smart choice for a man.

Rose wasn't especially talented in the kitchen, and her gardening skills were lacking. It surprised her when Katie had agreed to allow her to tend the celery patch. The real reason she could see was that her younger sister looked up to her. It made her feel better knowing that Katie trusted her with such an important task, but she couldn't help but wonder how it would feel to prepare for a wedding of her own.

Allowing her thoughts to drift back to Noah, Rose wondered what marriage to such a handsome man would be like. The thought of it brought heat to her cheeks. She chided herself when reality reminded her that he had loved Emma so deeply that he'd abandoned everything to mourn her. She wondered if any man would ever love *her* that deeply.

Chapter 11

"I'm telling you, Katie, it was him. I know it was."

Rose sat down at the table, placing the freshly-baked biscuits in front of her. "Who are you talking about, Caleb?"

He grabbed a biscuit and dropped it on his plate. "My cousin, Noah. I saw him in town at the feed store. When I called out to him, he took off so fast, I couldn't catch up to him."

Rose didn't know much about the man but she knew enough about Noah to realize he didn't want anyone knowing he was still in the area. He'd made that very clear to her. She'd never known the depth of grief he'd experienced, so she couldn't judge whether it was normal for him to want to be so secluded. For whatever his reasons were, she felt they should be honored until he was ready. It dawned on her that he had tried several times to reach out to her, and she'd rejected his company.

Suddenly feeling shame for her actions, she felt the need to keep his secret. "I'm certain you *think* you saw him because we were talking about him yesterday. Maybe part of you *wanted* for it to be him. But you said yourself; no one has seen him since the funeral. Wherever he is, when he's ready, he will come home."

Caleb let his face drop. "I suppose you're right. I just wish I knew if he was alright. His *daed* is worried about him."

Rose ignored the rest of the conversation, nodding occasionally to make it look like she was participating. She finished her dinner quickly, eager to go the dock at the B&B—eager to see Noah.

After the dishes were washed, she counted on Katie being preoccupied with Caleb. It was such a warm night, they might even take a buggy ride. With the two of them out of the way, Rose was free to go.

Noah was unsure of himself. Unsure if he should leave the small token with a note, or if he should wait for the young woman to show up so he could give it to her in person. She'd made it clear that she wanted him to leave her alone, but he felt drawn to her in a way he could not explain. As he turned to leave, she wandered up to the dock.

"Noah."

All she said was his name, but it was enough to make him smile. "I brought something for you."

He handed her the square of cheesecloth, and she looked at him with confusion.

"If you put it on the top of the Mason jar in place of the lid, you can still twist the ring over the opening. This way, the fireflies will be able to last long enough for you to pedal the boat from one end of the pond and back again. When you return, their glow will still be very strong, and you will be able to release them unharmed."

Rose looked down at the cheesecloth in her hands. It was the most thoughtful gift anyone had ever given her.

"*Danki,*"she said softly.

Noah looked into her eyes and the sparkle that reflected more than just the moonlight. She had such a natural beauty to her that showed humility. He was sure he wasn't meant to see beyond the tough exterior she tried very hard to keep up, but he could see her meek spirit in the reflection of her eyes. It drew him to her like a moth to a flame, burning brighter the closer he came. He wanted to draw her into his arms and kiss her soft cheek the way he had a few nights before, but he was sure she would reject such an advance. After all, she still hadn't told him her name, which showed him she didn't trust him.

Rose walked to the end of the dock to retrieve the Mason jar so she could collect enough fireflies to make a small beacon for her safe return to the dock at the conclusion of her nightly boat ride.

Noah sat in the grass on the embankment watching Rose chasing after the fireflies. He couldn't help but chuckle at her frustration when she leapt for a handful, only to come up empty-handed. In a span of several minutes, she had only caught two.

"How did you ever manage to catch an entire jar-full chasing after them like that?"

Noah's question surprised her.

"It takes a while to get a full jar. It takes patience."

Noah chuckled. "Or it requires a different method. When you chase them, it makes them scatter and fly away from you. It's almost as though they're taunting you."

Rose bristled. How did this man manage to get under her skin so quickly and efficiently. It was almost as though he delighted in aggravating her.

"If you think you can do better, I challenge you to see how many you can get. They are very fast, and hard to catch."

Noah stood up, a smile slowly curving up the corners of his mouth. Rose felt herself momentarily mesmerized by his mouth, but quickly cast her eyes to the ground, grateful it was dark enough he could not see the blush that she could feel heating her cheeks.

"Pick up the jar and have it ready for me," he demanded.

Rose picked up the jar from the grass and held it out to him with fake enthusiasm, mocking him.

Noah ignored her as he planted his feet firmly in the grass and held out his hands. The fireflies swarmed around him, seemingly surrendering themselves to his open hands that he quickly cupped around them. He reached over and deposited his first handful into the jar, leaving Rose feeling like a *dummkopf* for doubting him.

Handful after handful went into the jar until he was satisfied there were enough to light her way properly. She looked at him, almost no expression on her face, that it was hard for him to detect the admiration in her eyes—but it was there.

"The trick is to let them come to you. When you chase them, they scatter, but when you stand still, they float right by you."

Rose smiled, taking the jar from him after he twisted the ring around the rim, his square of cheesecloth covering the opening. She walked slowly up the dock, Noah on her heels. She set the jar of fireflies down at the end of the dock and stepped into the boat. Noah stayed on the dock, but she could see in his eyes that he had no intention of asking to ride along with her. She could see sudden sorrow in his eyes, but beyond that, a little bit of fear.

Noah untied the rope as she slipped on her life-vest. As before, he pushed her off from shore with his foot and she began to pedal backward until she was clear from the edge of the dock. Before she left him, she looked into his face once more. He was so handsome and so vulnerable she wanted to hug him, but she knew such an advance was unacceptable. She turned the rudder and set her feet in forward motion.

"My name is Rose."

Chapter 12

Noah's heart fluttered as he watched Rose pedal away from the dock. Knowing her name seemed like such a simple gesture, but to him, it meant that she trusted him— even if only a small measure. He lowered himself onto the end of the dock intending to wait for her to return. Would she be happy to see him when came back, or would it annoy her that he was still here? Torn between what to do, he began to pray.

Gott, breathe life back into me. I want to live for you again. Forgive me for turning my back on you and my familye. Bless me with the return of my faith. And bless me with enough courage to face my familye and Emma's familye.

Noah looked out onto the water with a renewed sense of peace that could only come from God. He let his toes dip into the cool water as he listened to the gentle lapping of water against the underside of the dock. Looking up across the pond, he could see that Rose was already on her way back. Was there a reason she only went to one end and then back? Was it possible that she was still frightened from the near-drowning she experienced?

Gott, please bless Rose with peace and courage.

The prayer surprised him. It was the third time he'd prayed on her behalf. He was beginning to like the feeling of unselfishness that praying for others brought him. He had to admit that it was a little strange for him to be praying for another woman who wasn't his betrothed, but Emma was gone, and Rose was here and very much in need of prayer.

As Rose neared the dock, his heart began to flutter again. It was a feeling he hadn't felt in so long, he knew it was one to be treasured. He stood up and took the rope, tying it around the post without saying a word to her. Then he held out his hand to assist her out of the boat, and surprisingly, she took it. Her hand was warm, and fit his perfectly—so perfect he didn't want to let it go, but he did for the sake of not causing her any reason to worry about his intentions for her.

Truth be told, he was attracted to her beauty and humility, but he would not risk saying that to her. The fact that the feelings were still a little foreign to him weighed on his mind, but he tried not to let it show on his face.

"*Danki,*" she said as he released her hand. "I wasn't certain you would still be here when I finished my trip across the pond. I pray that after I do that a few more times I will be able to put the fear of drowning behind me for *gut.*"

Noah stood beside her on the dock. He was so close he could smell the sunshine that still lingered on her. "I prayed that *Gott* would give you peace and courage about what happened."

Rose's heart felt like it skipped a beat. The thought of a man praying for her in such a way was a blessing in itself.

"*Danki,*" she whispered.

She continued to stand close to him, her breathing coming out in intermittent wisps. Noah could feel the heaving of his own chest in anticipation of having her closer still. She looked up at him with dreamy eyes that begged him to pull her into his arms. He wanted to respond. To hold her like it would be the last time he would ever see her.

Crickets sang loudly in the grass nearby, and fireflies fluttered and glowed magically around them. He watched her as she tipped back the *kapp* from her head and pulled the pins from her dark blond hair. She didn't take her eyes off him as she tucked the pins in her apron pocket. He couldn't resist her any longer; the pull was too strong.

Noah closed the space between him and Rose, pulling her into his arms with the sort of desperation one would expect from a heart-wrenching farewell. Then he scooped her loose hair into his fists, using it to draw her head upward. His lips touched hers and she responded with a hunger for him and the love he would give her.

Then it hit him.

He didn't know her well enough to love her.

Did he?

Was he so selfish still that he would engage her in a kiss so filled with passion, but lacking in the love it needed to back it up?

He let go of her, gazing into her eyes that were filled with hope. "I'm sorry. I shouldn't have done that. Please forgive me."

He didn't wait for a response. He left her side before he lost his nerve to do the right thing.

Chapter 13

"Noah, don't go," she begged him.

It was too late. He disappeared quickly into the darkness of the night, leaving Rose all alone. Now she understood what Katie had meant when she had told her that *menner* can be complicated. Why had Noah suddenly run off? Why had he apologized for kissing her? It was a beautiful kiss—her first.

Could it be that he wasn't ready to kiss me or any woman? Did it frighten him to let his guard down with me?

Please, Gott, if it be your wille, please let Noah love me.

Rose reached down and opened the lid to the Mason jar, letting the fireflies escape into the darkness. They glowed happily as they flitted about lighting her path to the base of the dock. Dragging her bare feet in the soft grass along the perimeter of the pond, Rose directed her reluctant steps toward the small *haus* she shared with Katie. She resisted the urge to cry, even though she really wanted to. Kissing Noah had been like a dream-come-true, and her lips still tingled from it.

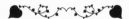

Noah called out to *Gott* as he hurried to get home. He had made a big mistake in judgment when he kissed Rose, and he had no idea how to fix it. He'd acted selfishly without any regard to her feelings.

She'd kissed him back. Hadn't she?

He hadn't been able to resist her once she pulled her hair down. Had she done that for him, or because she was uncomfortable? He'd remembered Emma telling him on many occasions how uncomfortable the head dressing could be, especially in the heat of summer. She'd enjoyed letting the breeze float through her hair many times when they were together. After all, they were to be married, and she showed her hair to him as a gift.

Had Rose offered herself to him for marriage? Panic filled him as he thought about marrying a woman other than Emma. Was he ready to consider such a thing? Was it possible she was falling for him only because he rescued her? He'd heard that those things can happen, and he needed to be sure of her feelings. Before that, he needed to keep his distance from her long enough to figure out why he'd acted so impulsively toward her.

Rose was glad she had the day off from the B&B. She knew Bess had probably seen the kiss exchanged between her and Noah the night before, and she wasn't up for discussing it with the woman. She knew Bess meant well, only having her best interest in mind, but she would probably offer her some unwanted advice on the matter, and Rose was in no mood for it.

After breakfast, Katie rode into town with Caleb for a few supplies, promising to pick up the material for their dresses. Rose was happy for the time alone, giving her word to her *schweschder* that she would have the celery patch weeded by the time she got back. As she waved to Katie, she felt a sense of relief at having gotten through the morning meal without having to engage in anything other than talk of the wedding. Thankfully, her *schweschder* was too preoccupied to notice anything different about Rose. The fact remained she *had* changed. The kiss from Noah had changed her in a way she didn't quite understand, but she knew she couldn't wait to see him again.

Rose dragged the garden tools from the barn and headed toward Katie's celery patch which ran alongside of the large kitchen garden. She picked a ripe tomato off the vine and rubbed it on her apron to remove any dirt. As she bit into the sun-warmed fruit her gaze drifted across the pond toward Noah's *haus*. Spotting Noah on a ladder adjusting one of the crooked shutters, she wished she could see him better. As she stared with a hand over her eyes to shield them from the bright sun, it appeared that Noah was working only in a pair of trousers.

What I wouldn't give to get my hands on those binoculars that Bess uses to keep an eye on us.

Rose giggled at her own thoughts as she reluctantly turned around to till up the rows with the garden hoe. The sun was already burning the back of her neck, and she wished she had put on her bigger bonnet. With her hands already dirty, she decided to wait until she took a water break. She intended to get two rows finished and out of the way before taking a break, but the humidity level was almost unbearable. Turning around for a brief moment to check on Noah, she was sad to see he was no longer in her line of vision. Thankfully his house rested on the bank of the narrow end of the pond so it wasn't too far for her to see him if he should get back on the ladder he'd left against the side of house.

Before moving onto the next row, Rose looked up again in the direction of Noah's house and spotted him watching her. She waved at him, but he looked away and went back to work. Had he seen her and ignored her? She hoped it was only that he hadn't seen her wave, instead of what she feared—that he'd changed his mind about her. If he no longer wanted anything to do with her after kissing her the way he had, then she would be glad to be rid of a man who would take advantage like that. On the other hand, he'd given her a beautiful kiss that she wouldn't soon forget.

Chapter 14

Rose took her time catching fireflies the way Noah had shown her the night before. She was surprised when he wasn't waiting for her at the dock the way he had for the past few nights. She hoped that if she took her time gathering fireflies, he would soon show up. But she was getting tired, and he still had not arrived. Tears stung the back of her eyes at the thought that he could be so inconsiderate.

I should have known it was too gut to be true. A mann like that would never fall in love with a woman like me. I'm too plain, and he's very handsome, ain't it so?

Suddenly, she didn't feel like going for a boat ride. She lowered herself to the end of the dock and looked at the fireflies glowing in the Mason jar. Noah had been right about them lasting longer with the cheese cloth at the top of the jar to let in air. But she was guessing he'd thought it wrong to kiss her, and that's why he wasn't here to greet her at the pond tonight.

I was right about him ignoring me when I waved to him. Why would he kiss me if he didn't like me? Does he think it too soon to fall in love again after losing his betrothed? If he did, then he should have never kissed me. Shame on him.

Rose fought the tears that stung the backs of her eyes. She swallowed hard the pain of rejection as she released the fireflies from their temporary captivity. Sadness consumed her as she stood up from the dock to find she was still alone. She knew Bess would probably have something to say about it when she arrived at work in the morning, and was not looking forward to it.

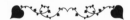

Several times Noah set out to meet Rose at the dock at the B&B, but every time, his feet would not take him past his own yard. It wasn't that he didn't care for her—he did, and that's what scared him so much. He just wasn't ready to face her until he had sorted out the end to his grieving. He needed to end the mourning period, but he just didn't know how to let go of something he'd held onto for so long—even if he *was* ready. It wasn't fair to Rose if he were to move forward with her when he hadn't yet closed the door on his past. He knew the only way to close that door was to face her family and his own once and for all.

Having not spoken to anyone since Emma's funeral, he worried that they would reject him. He also worried he may have been shunned, and figured a visit to Bishop Troyer would be his first order of business. He intended to pursue his interest in Rose so he could get to know her better, but there were a few things he had to take care of first. He prayed she would understand, and not form a low opinion of him because of his actions.

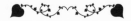

"If there's one thing I do know about *menner,* they get spooked easily like horses," Bess said as she helped Rose set out the place settings at the dining room table. "If you ask me, I think he's feeling guilty for kissing you."

Rose sucked in her bottom lip. "Because of Emma?"

"*Jah,* but don't worry. Noah is an honorable *mann.* He wouldn't kiss you unless he really liked you. He just needs some time to sort out his feelings."

Rose's heart quickened at the thought of Noah liking her.

"I have to say something else to you. I noticed you took your hair down from your prayer *kapp.*"

Rose couldn't look Bess in the eye. "I have seen Katie do the same for Caleb. I only wanted Noah to think I was pretty like my *schweschder.*"

Bess placed cutlery at each place setting. "That sort of thing will make a *mann* think you are interested in marriage."

Rose smiled. "*Jah,* that's why I did it. To see if he would receive me. I thought he had, but now I can't be certain. His absence from the pond last night has made me worry I acted in haste."

Bess smiled knowingly. "Love always makes people act in haste. There is no way around it. But it is worth it if you can work through all the ups and downs of relationships. They take a lot of work."

Rose looked at Bess shyly. "I wouldn't say that Noah and I have a relationship."

Bess put down the linens she was folding into swan-shaped napkins. "*Jah,* you do. Even if it's only a friendship. You have a relationship with him now, a bond that cannot be broken."

"But he's already broken it." Rose collapsed into one of the dining room chairs.

Bess crossed the room and sat across from Rose. "It's not broken. It's just getting started. And new relationships can take the most time. So much time, in fact, that it might seem that they're moving backward, but I assure you it's not broken."

"How can you be sure?"

"He just needs some time to digest it like a heavy meal. That kiss might have come a little too soon, but it did happen. It happened because he obviously is interested in you. A *mann* doesn't kiss a woman like that if isn't interested in her becoming part of his future."

Rose blushed at her comments.

"Noah has lost at love once already, and he's probably afraid he could lose you too. Loving another can be scary. There is always risk in loving someone, but the risk is always worth it. When he realizes that, he will come back around."

Rose hoped Bess was right about Noah and his potential interest in her. If she wasn't, Rose wasn't sure she could survive such a heartbreak.

Chapter 15

Noah stood in front of the small mirror at the bathroom sink for some time, staring at his reflection. Even with the scissors in hand, he found it difficult to part with his shoulder-length hair. He hadn't cut it since Emma had died. In some ways, it was a symbol of his loss—his outward sign of mourning. Was he truly ready to put it behind him and let go of Emma forever?

An image of Rose entered his mind. Her natural beauty and humbleness pulled him toward her like a magnetic force. He had thought he would never be able to love again, but here he was, feeling very strongly for Rose, and he couldn't ignore it much longer. He wanted to know everything about her. He wanted to catch fireflies with her and hold her in his arms.

But he couldn't.

Not yet.

First, he had to cut his hair and his ties to Emma. Then he would go to see the Bishop. Rose would certainly be more eager to accept him if he made his commitment to the community and the church known. Was he already considering marriage with Rose? How could he not? She was the angel who had pulled him from the darkness that was his life until only a few days ago.

Noah lifted the scissors to his hair and snipped the first piece. Regulation stated that he was to have his bangs trimmed straight across. He'd never really liked the look, to be truthful, but his long hair would not go over well with the community or the Bishop. If he wanted to remain and have a chance to pursue Rose he must cut it straight across.

Noah sighed as he snipped another chunk from the front of his hair. He had been in a state of rebellion against the community for so long that suddenly he questioned the rules he had adhered to his entire life.

It was only hair.

Was it really that important?

The humble style established conformity, and that was important within the community. But that didn't mean Noah liked the look. Such thoughts would be considered prideful, but he'd seen the admiration in Rose's eyes when she looked at his hair. He'd felt her fingers glide through it when he'd kissed her. Shivers ran through him at the thought of having Rose's fingers tangled up in his hair.

It didn't matter that he wanted to keep his hair.

Cut it, he must.

It was the only way to remain in the community.

Snipping the last section in the front, Noah had set the precedent for rest of the hair to go. But as he did, he realized it was no longer Emma that he clung to; it was Rose and her fingers playing delightfully in his long hair.

Another few snips to the sides, and he was almost there. He could feel the rebellion leaving him with each snip. And as the hair fell to the floor, so did his ties with Emma. Through his prayers, Noah had resolved that Emma was not meant to stay with him; she was destined to be with God.

This would be a new start, and his hair was still long enough that Rose could run her fingers through it freely. Did he want her to? The answer was a resounding *yes*.

Unable to see the back, Noah wasn't certain if he'd managed to cut a straight line, but it was now short enough that the imperfections would be hidden beneath his hat.

Next, he would tackle the scruff of whiskers that he'd kept trimmed in more of an *Englisch* style. After rinsing the bone-handled shaving brush, he swished the horse-hair bristles against the cake of peppermint soap at the bottom of the old coffee cup he kept it in. Thick, soapy lather formed on the end of the brush, and he lifted it to the chiseled angle of his jaw. The cooling soap spread smoothly across his face, creating a white beard.

He paused for a minute, thinking it funny that he could one day have a white beard, but not until after he and Rose had had a full life together. No matter what, he couldn't keep his mind off her. It seemed that every plan that came to his mind lately involved her somehow. One question weighed on his mind though; was she thinking the same things?

Lifting the straight razor that he'd sharpened on the leather strap, he scraped it across his chin carefully. He was careful to take small strokes and rinse the blade after each stroke to avoid cutting himself. The whiskers were tough, and would require a second pass with the blade, but slow progress was changing his look in ways he was no longer used to.

Would Rose like his new look? Most women, it seemed, preferred the clean-shaven look. But he had also noticed admiration in Rose's eyes every time he rubbed his chin in her presence. Her eyes had followed his hand as he'd swiped it across his whiskers; it had not gone unnoticed.

With the majority of his whiskers now gone, Noah rinsed his face and began the process all over again, this time pulling the blade a little tighter against his skin. His skin felt bare and vulnerable the way it always did after a clean shave. A final rinse of his face and shaving supplies, and Noah was finally done.

He stood there for a moment, examining his new look, and feeling unsure about it. He hoped Rose would approve of his new look since she'd not met him looking this way.

Certainly now he would be presentable to the Bishop and the community, and that was what he wanted.

Chapter 16

Rose dragged the hose over to the celery patch so she could set the sprinkler on it. The soil was getting dry, and she didn't want the plants she'd been entrusted with to wilt in the hot sun. She'd made sure that the gas-powered generator in the shed was running so it would power the sump-pump to bring water up from the well. Everything at her parent's house was a little easier since it was all solar-powered, but *Aenti* Nettie's small farm was still surviving on more primitive means.

She stood watching the track of the sprinkler to make sure it was reaching all the way to the end of the celery patch. When she was satisfied every last stalk was getting its fill of water, she turned to leave. She'd purposely kept her back to the pond; the temptation to look for Noah was too great. It had been three long days since their kiss, and she'd sat at the end of the dock each night waiting for him, only to return home each night disappointed. Not only had he not shown up to meet her, there was no indication he'd even been there since the night they'd kissed. He'd also made no attempt to see her in any way, and that had instilled deep feelings of discouragement in her.

A faint splash from behind her forced her gaze toward the pond, where Noah stood on the other side skipping a rock across half the expanse. Was he trying to get her attention?

He certainly had it now.

She couldn't resist watching as he tossed another. Her gaze followed the stone as it skipped across the surface five times before sinking. Looking up from the pond, Noah made eye contact with her even from that distance. He stood there for a few moments, staring across the water at her, and then removed his hat and held it in his hands. Rose nearly gasped as her hand instinctively clamped across her mouth.

He's gone and cut his hair. And he shaved too!

Rose remembered the feel of his long, silky hair entwined in her fingers the night the two of them kissed. The tickle of his whiskers had given her goose-flesh when his lips had swept over hers. What would a kiss be like with him now? Would she ever get the chance to see?

From across the pond, Noah lifted his hat in a salutatory wave before placing it back on his head. Then he turned and walked toward his house without looking back.

Rose's heart thumped against her ribcage. He'd waved—sort of. It wasn't much, but it was something. She wished she knew what was going on with him, but he had cut his hair and shaved his face clean. Though he now looked *Amish,* Rose would not soon forget the sultry look in Noah that had attracted her to him in the first place. At least now, with the changes he'd made, she felt confident that she had a chance to have a life with him in the community. Unless it was too late, and he'd already been shunned.

Please, Gott, allow Noah to remain in the community. I think I've fallen in love with him. Please, Gott, make it so.

Rose couldn't wait to get to work so she could discuss Noah's changes with Bess. Katie would never understand such a dilemma, and if she confided in her, she ran the risk that Caleb would discover his cousin was living there. Noah had warned her that he wanted his presence kept secret, but she hoped his change in appearance meant he had changed his mind. Was it too much to hope that he was getting himself ready to rejoin the community? She certainly hoped it was so.

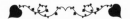

Noah hitched up his buggy as he rehearsed what he planned on saying to the Bishop. He disliked showing up unannounced, but he hadn't been to church services in so long, there wasn't a chance to prearrange a meeting with him. He was nervous, that was for certain, but he knew if he let it show, it would put him at a disadvantage with the Bishop. Bishop Troyer encouraged confidence among the men in the community. At the moment, Noah could only feel numbness mixed with a bit of apprehension. His prayers had left him confident that he was doing the right thing—that he was finally ready to move forward out of his mourning period and get on with his life. He hoped it wasn't too late to be welcomed back into the community where he knew he belonged.

As he pulled his buggy in front of the Bishop's house, Noah was confident that he would have the right words to make things right for his return to the community.

Bishop Troyer stepped out of his barn at the sound of an approaching buggy. He tipped his hat forward to shield his eyes from the sun so he could see who had come to visit. His heart leapt for joy when he saw that it was Noah Beiler. He quickened his steps to greet the young man, who had fallen away from his flock too long ago.

Noah stepped out of the buggy, still feeling a little unsure of himself, until he saw the look in Bishop Troyer's eyes as he approached him. The older man threw his arms around him, welcoming him, making Noah's apprehension slip away.

"Noah, it's so *gut* to see you. I've prayed that *Gott* would bring you back to us, and here you are. *Kume,* we will go inside and see if there is any lemonade left. I could use a refreshing drink on such a warm day as this."

Noah followed Bishop Troyer into the house, thinking that a sip of *Frau* Troyer's tart lemonade was just what he needed.

Chapter 17

Rose fidgeted on the backless bench during church service. It was too warm to sit there for so long, and her legs and back ached from working so much in the celery patch and the B&B over the last week. She was not looking forward to wash-day tomorrow, as she would be doing her own wash as well as all the linens for the B&B. The best thing about her job was having Bess to confide her worries to over Noah.

Since the men sat on one side of the room, she was stuck sitting next to Katie, who wasn't paying any more attention to the service than she was. The big difference between she and Katie, was that her sister was confident of her relationship with the man who sat across the row from where they were. Caleb was making sheep-eyes at his betrothed when he thought Rose was not looking. Noah, who was at the front of the large room, sat wedged between two of the Elders, as though they guarded him.

With the windows open, the aroma of honeysuckle blooms floated in on the warm breeze. Rose took a deep breath of the sweet flowery air as it wafted by her. It reminded her of the night she and Noah had shared their one and only kiss. She had smelled the flowers that warm evening from the bushes that grew to each side of the dock at the B&B. The aroma had contributed to the romantic feel of the night, and Rose couldn't let go of that feeling—even now.

Katie nudged her in the arm. "Get up, Rose, the service is over."

Rose blinked.

The room was emptying of the community, and she was the only one still sitting. Feeling her cheeks heat up, she had to wonder how long she'd been sitting there staring unresponsively. Had Noah seen her when he'd walked past her?

"What's wrong with you, Rose?" Katie asked impatiently.

"I...I was reflecting on some things," Rose stammered. It wasn't a lie, but it also wasn't the sort of thing she should have been thinking about during church.

Pushing down embarrassment, Rose stood and followed Katie into the kitchen where most of the women had gathered. Most of the men had already gathered in the yard with the children, except for the few that had already begun to take the benches outside for the meal. Rose glanced out the kitchen window and spotted Noah helping Caleb and a few others set up tables in a long line under the shade of the many trees.

She paused to admire the smile that played along his lips every time one of the men spoke to him. He seemed genuinely happy to be back in the community, and the men had obviously welcomed him back—except for one, who seemed to keep his distance. She watched the strain crease Noah's brow as the older man approached him.

Noah felt his chest tighten as Emma's father approached him in the yard after church. He'd both dreaded this moment and eagerly anticipated it ever since his meeting with Bishop Troyer. Greeting him with apprehension, Noah took a deep breath and tried to remember the words of wisdom the Bishop had shared with him.

"Abraham, it's *gut* to see you. You and Mary look well. I've missed you both very much." Noah stammered over his words hoping they would be well-received, but he couldn't be sure from the older man's expression.

Abraham paused. "Mary and I have been concerned for you, Noah. How long have you been back in the community?"

Noah felt his heart thump against his ribcage.

"I've been here all along. I never left. I'm sorry for not coming to see you sooner, but I just couldn't bring myself to face the two of you."

Abraham placed a hand on Noah's shoulder.

"You were like a son to us. That hasn't changed. We know you did everything you could to save our Emma, including diving into the icy pond to pull her out. She is with *Gott,* and remaining closed off from your *familye* would not have brought her back to us."

"I know that now that I've spent the past year and a half rejecting the community. It means a lot to me that you and Mary are so willing to accept me now that I'm back."

Abraham swallowed the sorrow that formed in his throat. "We love you like one of our own. We want you to be happy and to feel free to move on with your life. You're too young to be alone. You deserve to find a *fraa* and have *kinner.*"

Noah was happy to hear Abraham's words, but he wondered if he would still feel the same if he knew he'd already developed strong feelings for Rose. The very thought of her sent delightful shivers through him. He only hoped that his delay in seeing her hadn't ruined his chances with her. But he was still not done putting his life back in order.

His own father still hadn't received him, and he worried that if he took too long to mend fences with him it could hinder the relationship he desired with Rose. Even though his *daed* and Rose each stood only a few feet from him, he could not go to either of them. His *daed* needed time, and Rose was just out of his reach because of his unsettled life. He would not hurt her more than he may already have.

Rose set a casserole dish on the table in front of Noah. He didn't smell the food; he only smelled honeysuckle, even if just from memory of the night they'd shared such a beautiful kiss. How would he be able to bear it if he had to continue to put a life with her on hold until he set things right with his *daed?*

Was it possible for him to do both?

Chapter 18

Rose lingered at the table near Noah, hoping he would speak to her, but so far he hadn't. There was only so much rearranging of the stacks of plates left on the table that she could do near him without making herself look desperate for his attention. When she'd finished laying out all the place settings available, she slammed the last plate against the table hard enough to break it. Still, he did not acknowledge her. Was it possible he regretted kissing her? Perhaps it was a moment of weakness on his part, and he wished to take it back.

Choking down tears, Rose turned her back to him and walked out toward the edge of the property. She didn't want to be anywhere near him if he didn't like her. She'd prayed that the kiss had meant as much to him as it had to her, but now she wasn't so sure it had ever happened. At the time, she'd been stressed and emotional from nearly drowning. Was it possible she'd imagined the whole thing? His appearance now made her wonder if he had rejoined the community with another woman on his mind—a woman who was not her.

Rose collapsed at the base of a large oak tree. Who was she kidding? Noah was very handsome and could have his choice of any woman in the community. Why would he choose her? She was far too plain and had nothing to offer him.

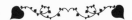

Noah couldn't help but follow Rose, who was obviously upset from his lack of acknowledgment of her. He wasn't trying to ignore her, but it was obvious she saw it that way. The last thing he wanted to do was hurt her. But no matter how hard he'd tried to spare her feelings, he'd managed to do the exact opposite. Now he would have to explain things to her, when he'd hoped he would be able to avoid this conversation with her.

He slowly approached the tree and leaned against it. "There's a nice breeze under this tree. I can see why you picked this spot. It's kind of crowded over there with the entire community trying to eat all at once."

Startled by his presence, Rose bit back the tears that threatened to spill from her eyes, and looked off into the distance. She allowed the rustling of the leaves to soothe her as she calmed herself enough to speak.

"Why are you following me? Don't you have other interests to pursue?"

Noah was baffled by her question. "*Mei daed* won't speak to me for not telling him where I was all this time."

Rose looked up into his blue eyes. "I'm sorry that your *daed* has shunned you. But what does that have to do with me?"

Noah kicked at acorns in the grass trying to quell his nervousness. "It doesn't, but I was hoping I could bend your ear a little. I thought we were friends."

Rose cringed at the word.

Friends.

So that was all she was to him? He'd made it clear by saying the word. She didn't want to be his friend. She wanted more from him than that. If all he wanted was friendship, she didn't think she could handle that— especially if he should decide to begin dating someone else. But he'd said it, and there was no ignoring it.

If he wants to be friends, I will be the best friend he's ever had. Gott, please let him see me as more than a friend.

"*Jah,* I suppose we are...*friends.*"

The word didn't come out as gracefully as she was trying for, and Noah noticed her strange tone.

Noah cleared his throat, feeling suddenly awkward with the silence between them. "Would you like to come back to the meal with me? I'm sure everyone is seated and eating by now."

Noah wished he could sit with her, but the rules stated they were to sit at opposite sides of the table. There were some rules he didn't agree with even though he'd followed them all his life. He'd wanted to sit with her during church service as well, but that was also not allowed.

"I'm not real hungry. I'd rather go home. I woke up with a headache, and it doesn't want to go away."

Noah kicked at the acorns nervously. "I rode with Caleb this morning, or I'd offer you a ride."

"I don't mind walking. It's not that far. I can't take our buggy or Katie will have to walk home, and she will have dishes to bring back with her."

"Would you mind if I walked with you? I don't really want to hang around there anymore with my *daed's* disapproving looks."

Rose took the hand Noah offered, stood up and dusted off the back of her dress. "You have to face him eventually."

They began to walk toward Goose pond where they both lived.

Noah sighed. "I tried to talk to him, but he doesn't understand. He thinks I turned my back on my *familye* and the community."

Rose looked at him as they walked slowly along the road. "I can see how he might think that. You said yourself that you were dead to them."

"Jah, I did, and I was wrong. I've spent a lot of time in prayer lately, and *Gott* has shown me that leaving the community and turning my back on my faith was the worst thing I could have done to help myself heal from what happened. I have to find a way to get *mei daed* to see that I'm truly repentant."

"Perhaps your constant presence in the community from here on out will let him see you are serious about your commitment, and he will accept it with time."

"He hasn't ever really approved of me. He always said I had a rebellious streak in me. I'm certain he's correct since I don't like some of the rules we live by."

Rose had always felt the same way, but had never dared voice the opinion to anyone. "My *familye* refers to me as *independent,* but what they really mean is rebellious. I'm the same way."

Noah smiled as he slipped his hand in hers, swinging her arm slightly as they walked along; the hot sun heating their backsides.

Chapter 19

By the time they reached her *Aenti* Nettie's small farmhouse, Rose had a better understanding of what Noah had gone through after Emma's death. She knew it was best to be a friend to Noah, and be patient about the rest of it. She feared that if she pressed him for more he may withdraw even further from her, and he was finally talking to her again.

Noah walked her to the back door. He wanted to pull her into his arms and hold her. He'd missed her this past week that he'd been busy working on his return to the community. But the truth was, he didn't trust himself not to get too caught up in her, and that wouldn't be fair to her as long as he still had personal issues to work out. Instead, he reached up and placed a kiss on her forehead, hoping it would convey his feelings to her without going overboard. She responded with a sigh, and he hoped that meant she understood his position.

Noah stepped away from her and turned to leave. He waved over his shoulder while she stood there with a stunned look on her face. He didn't want to leave her, but he had to—for both their sake.

Rose felt her heartbeat catch in her chest as his lips touched her forehead. She was sure he would give her more than that, but to her disappointment, he hadn't. She took that as his way of letting her know that they were indeed friends, and nothing more. When he'd held her hand as he walked her home, she'd hoped that it meant something, but it was obvious it didn't. How was she supposed to go from a kiss as passionate as they had shared to accepting kisses on her forehead? As she watched him walk away, she felt like a *dummkopf* for thinking he could ever be interested in her for more than friendship.

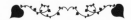

Rose stretched on her tiptoes to reach the clothesline at the B&B so she could help Bess hang the bed linens they had washed. Her last load of personal wash was still hanging on the line at home, where it would be waiting for her after she finished work for the day. It was only three o'clock, and she was already exhausted. She'd tossed about most of the night worrying about Noah, even though she knew worrying would not change the situation.

Bess pinned the other end of the queen-size sheet to the clothesline. "Are you going to tell me what happened when Noah walked you home yesterday, or do I have to pull it out of you?"

Rose sighed with frustration. "There isn't anything to tell."

"I saw the two of you holding hands as you walked down the road. That's something."

Rose's heart skipped a beat. "Did anyone else see?"

Bess picked up a pillow slip and pinned it to the line. "*Nee,* everyone had bowed their head for the prayer. By the time they lifted their heads, you were long down the road out of sight. Is that all you have to say about that?"

"There isn't anything to tell. He only wants to be friends. He said so."

Bess flashed her one of her unconvincing, crooked smiles. "Seems to me, a *mann* doesn't hold a woman's hand unless he likes her for more than friendship."

"That was my way of thinking too, but then he kissed me on the forehead before he left. And he actually asked if we were friends. All he wants is friendship."

Bess stopped what she was doing and peeked at Rose from behind the hanging linens. "And you want more than friendship?"

"Jah."

Bess walked around between the laundry to face her. "Then you have to show him what it would be like to have more than that."

Rose sighed again. "How am I supposed to do that?"

Bess smiled. "For starters, you need to give him an opportunity to miss you, and then you surprise him by doing something he wouldn't expect."

Rose was already feeling overwhelmed. "What do you mean?"

"Don't go to the dock tonight. He expects that, and if you're not there, he'll have the chance to miss you."

Rose hung up the last pillow slip. "He hasn't met me there all week, so that won't work."

Bess laughed. "Just because he didn't meet you doesn't mean he didn't know you were there. I saw him watching you. I could tell it was tearing him up not to meet you. But if you're not there, it will make him wonder why,"

Rose couldn't believe what Bess was saying. Was it possible that he was still interested in her?

"What is it that I can do that he won't expect? Or was that it?"

Bess tried not to smile. "Ever since the accident with Emma, I've taken food over to Noah once a week and left it on his doorstep. I'm pretty sure he knew it was me, but he never came out of the *haus* until after I left. What if you took him a basket of food in the morning instead of me taking it?"

Rose picked up the laundry hamper and walked toward the back door with it. "That doesn't sound like much."

"My point is, Rose, that Noah won't expect *you* to be delivering him a food basket. I haven't even dropped one off in two weeks, so he won't be expecting it at all. But when he sees that you've done this for him, it will soften his heart toward you, and might afford you the opportunity to talk to him."

It all sounded too simple, but Rose was willing to give it a try if it meant she would have the chance to see Noah again. Truth be told, she wasn't too keen on the idea of skipping her trip to the dock tonight, but she was of the mindset that she had nothing more to lose.

Chapter 20

Rose woke earlier than usual so she would have enough time to get over to the B&B to get the food basket from Bess so she could get it to Noah before he went about his day. She'd practically had to sit on her hands the night before so she wouldn't be tempted to go to the dock with the hope of seeing Noah. She hoped Bess's plan would work and Noah had noticed she wasn't there and had missed her. She supposed she would find out soon enough.

As she pulled on a clean, purple dress, Rose eyed the attending dress she had worked on last night while Katie and Caleb sat on the porch swing talking of wedding plans. She was glad in a way that she'd stayed home to work on the dress, especially since she had made a lot of progress. Katie had already inquired why there wasn't much done on the dress yet, and now she would be able to present her sister with a nearly finished product.

Rose tip-toed out of the house so she wouldn't disturb Katie. She wasn't up for any questions about what she was doing or where she was going. She was a little nervous about Bess's plan, but figured it might be the only way she could appeal to Noah's heart.

When she arrived at the B&B, Bess had the basket already prepared. She'd packed it with half a dozen fresh eggs, a loaf of freshly-baked bread, cinnamon rolls, a bag of oats, a small bag of ground coffee, a small bowl of freshly-picked strawberries, and a Mason jar filled with milk fresh from the morning milking. The basket was rather heavy, but Rose was determined to set out on foot to deliver it, despite Bess's offer to use her buggy. It didn't make sense when she could be half-way there in the time it would take to hitch up the buggy. Little did she know that she would end up feeling differently by the time she reached Noah's doorstep. Sweat rolled down her back beneath her dress, but thankfully, the slight breeze had kept her face dry.

Rose hefted the large basket from her hip, where she'd rested it like a baby, and set it on the porch step at the back of the house. She admired the fresh coat of paint on the clapboard siding and the neatness of the porch. A wooden, folding chair sat in the corner near the rail, and a galvanized watering can contained freshly-picked hydrangeas in a variety of hues. It seemed like an odd thing to see on the porch of a man's house, but she already knew him to be a sensitive, creative type. The yard had been cleared of debris and thick weeds to the point of resembling a roughly-cut lawn. It was apparent that Noah had been hard at work trying to resurrect his small farm house to the point Rose thought it was beginning to look like a home.

She turned to leave, her thoughts of what it would be like to live in the small house with Noah interrupted when the back door swung open.

"Won't you stay and join me for a little breakfast?"

Noah's deep voice caught Rose by surprise. She turned and searched his face for sincerity. Finding it, she smiled her answer, and then followed him into the small house. It was apparent by the scant furniture and bare windows that there was still a lot of work to be done inside to make it look more like the outside, but it was still a comfortable space.

Noah offered her a chair at the small, round table in the kitchen. She wouldn't admit to him that she'd left the house without her own breakfast so she could bring him the basket of food, but the aroma from the still-warm cinnamon rolls was making her mouth water. Setting two mismatched plates on the table, Noah urged her to help herself to the food she'd brought for him.

"I see *Aenti* Bess has you running her errands for her now."

All that time she'd been confiding in the older woman, and she'd not known the relationship between her and Noah. She felt her cheeks warm over embarrassment from going on like such a love-struck school-girl over Noah to his *aenti*. Why hadn't Bess told her Noah was her nephew?

"*Mei* own *vadder* won't speak to me, but *Aenti* has always been there for me. Even when I couldn't help myself."

Rose cleared her throat. "She told me that she'd been leaving baskets of food for you all this time, and when she asked me to do it for her this morning, I could hardly turn her down. But she didn't tell me she was your *aenti*."

"I'm not surprised. If I know *Aenti* Bess, she had ulterior motives for sending you over here. She probably has the notion if she throws us together we'll fall in love."

Rose's heart fluttered all the way to her toes. "I haven't known her long, but I enjoy working for her. She has a *gut* heart."

Was it possible that Bess's plan was working?

Noah served her a glass of milk and a cinnamon roll. She wondered what it would be like to be the one serving him a meal in this quaint little farm house. She felt terrible sitting there allowing a man to serve her, but he didn't seem to mind.

"*Aenti* Bess is *mei mamm's* youngest *schweschder.* *Mei daed* always tried to keep me at a distance from her, but she was always my favorite *aenti. Mei daed* always said that because *Aenti* Bess was the youngest of the twelve *kinner,* that by the time she came along, her parents were too old to raise her properly and it caused her to develop a rebellious streak. I think that's why I like her so much. She's never judged me, even when I turned my back on the community. She helped me and didn't pressure me to come back until I was ready, but she was there for me in the meantime. Knowing she was there for me is what kept me from slipping completely away from everyone. With *mei mamm* gone, I feel even closer to her."

Rose hadn't realized until now just how much loss Noah had endured in his life. She was grateful that Bess really loved her nephew. She felt suddenly right about her decision to confide in her, as it was obvious she did indeed have a very good heart.

Chapter 21

"Katie is NOT going to be happy when she finds out Jessup King is a guest here!"

Bess steered Rose to sit at the kitchen table and placed a glass of cool lemonade in front of her.

"That's why we will not be telling her. He is a paying guest and he has business in town. I expect you to respect the privacy of the guests here."

Rose gulped the tart lemonade. "I'm sorry, Bess. But what if Katie finds out he's in town?"

Bess sat down across from Rose and fanned her warm face with her apron. "His business with Katie is over and done with. I won't tolerate gossip about my guests."

Rose had never heard Bess talk so firmly, and she tried to understand the situation from the business side of things. But if she didn't know any better, it almost seemed that Bess was jumping to Jessup's defense. For the life of her, Rose couldn't think of a single reason other than for business that Bess would do such a thing. She knew the guest roster had slowed down a bit, but Bess had told her that was normal until July when folks usually started taking their vacations. Still, why would Bess be so defensive regarding Jessup King? From her experience in watching his relationship with her sister unfold, he had not been the kindest man.

Rose looked at Bess sheepishly. "I will keep my personal feelings regarding Jessup to myself. You have been very kind to me, and I would never want to be the cause of you losing business because I couldn't control my tongue."

Bess smiled. "*Danki*. Now tell me what happened over breakfast with Noah."

The eagerness in Bess's eyes helped Rose to relax. "Why didn't you tell me he was your nephew?"

"Noah was *mei schweschder's* only *boppli*. He's pretty special to me. I really miss his *mamm*. We were the only two girls in the *familye*. It was hard to grow up with ten bruders, but *mei schweschder* and I had a special bond."

"How long ago did you lose her?"

"It's been going on five years now. Poor Noah lost his *mamm* and Emma right close to each other. It's no wonder he needed so much time to get over it."

Rose pinched her eyebrows together in a deep furrow. "Do you think he's over her?"

Bess smiled and nodded. "Over Emma? *Jah*. Noah is an honorable young *mann*. He wouldn't have kissed you if he wasn't ready to move on with his life. He's put his past behind him."

Rose didn't feel too confident of Bess's answer even though she had no reason to doubt the woman's word. Still, she worried that her accident in the pond may have forced Noah out of hiding before he was ready. Even if all signs pointed toward his recovery, she had to wonder why he still held back his feelings for her after the single kiss they'd shared.

"I hope you're right, Bess. I'm glad you made me take the food to him. He shared it with me and we had a pleasant meal together. I learned a lot more about him, but I have to wonder if he has changed his mind about me. I don't think he wants anything more than friendship."

Bess got up and brought a plate of fresh cookies to the table to go with their lemonade. "What would make you think a thing like that? Did he say he only wanted friendship?"

"Not in so many words, but *jah,* he's made it clear with his actions that he doesn't want to take our relationship beyond friendship."

Bess bit into a sugar cookie. "Maybe he's trying to slow things down. You got a kiss out of him pretty soon after you met him. He might want to get to know you—the way you did this morning at breakfast."

Rose couldn't deny that he still seemed to want her in his life, but he had distanced himself physically from her. She'd enjoyed his company this morning, but she'd hoped for a kiss when they parted, but he hadn't even attempted it. She was comfortable with taking things slow, but she worried things had come to a complete stop with Noah.

"Are you planning on going for a boat ride this evening?"

Rose thought about it for a minute. She wanted the chance to run into Noah, but she was now fearful that if he didn't show, she would feel let down.

"Do you think I should?"

Bess smiled. "I saw him skipping rocks on the pond last night. He noticed you weren't there. I think it's safe to say he missed you. So I think you should go and see if he shows up. If he doesn't, don't take it personally. He may not be ready."

Don't take it personally? How can I take it any other way if he doesn't show up to meet me?

Rose agreed to go and to give Noah some space. She knew he might need more time, and she felt he would be well worth the wait.

Chapter 22

Rose walked to the end of the dock to retrieve the Mason jar so she could catch a jar-full of fireflies. She hadn't yet seen any sign of Noah, but she was a little earlier than usual. She was so eager for the possibility of seeing him that she had practically ran out of the house after the supper dishes had been done. Katie was too preoccupied with Caleb to pay her any mind, and for once, she was happy about that.

Crickets chirped and frogs croaked, bringing the humid, summer night to life. Clear skies boasted millions of stars, giving it a magical feel that Rose was never able to see beyond the bright lights of the city that was too close to where she had lived before.

Fireflies danced around her, daring her to capture them. Remaining still, just as Noah had shown her, she watched their lights blink on and off in tune with the symphony playing in her head. She'd hidden her love for classical music from her family, knowing it was forbidden in the Ordnung. Knowing this did not make her love for it any less. Rose hummed and twirled in the swarm of fireflies, lost in thought.

"Sounds like Mozart."

Noah's voice stopped Rose in her tracks and she looked into his smiling eyes. "You know the music of Mozart?"

"Jah, I listen to it on my battery-operated radio."

Noah couldn't help but admire her beauty. He'd caught her at a vulnerable moment, and it made her even more appealing to him. How could he possibly resist her? It wouldn't be easy, but he wouldn't rush to her either, for fear of scaring her away. Instead, he slowly closed the space between them, grabbing a handful of fireflies and pushing them into the jar she held. He took hold of the lid, placed the cheese cloth on top, and then twisted the lid in place before they could escape. All this he did without taking his eyes off Rose.

Mesmerized by her gaze, he stood close enough to her that he could hear her breath catch in her throat, his presence causing her to gasp. His heart beat in perfect tempo with the cricket's song as he leaned down and brushed a kiss against her temple. Her hair smelled like sweet strawberries ripened by warm sunshine.

"You are so beautiful," he whispered close to her ear.

Noah's warm breath sent shivers from her ear all the way to her toes. Had he called her beautiful? Such talk of vanity was forbidden, but it delighted her to hear it from his full lips that taunted her. She wanted to kiss him, but didn't dare make a move toward him, fearing he would run from her again. She remained still and allowed him to sweep kisses across her cheek until finally he reached her eager lips. Unable to hold back any longer, she deepened the kiss, reaching up and tangling her fingers in his silky hair. Oh how she'd longed for this moment. She'd dreamed of it over and over again, reliving that first kiss. But now she wouldn't have to. He was holding her close again, and unpinning her hair from her *kapp.* She delighted in the feel of his fingers in her hair as she continued to kiss him. She felt his arms tighten around her, pulling her close enough to warm her.

Noah couldn't help but pull Rose closer to him. He wanted her to be a part of him, but he had no right since she was not his wife—but he wanted her to be.

"Marry me, Rose," he whispered.

Rose gasped.

He hadn't meant to say it. He'd felt it in the heat of the moment, but he knew it was too soon. But that hadn't stopped him from feeling it.

Rose stepped away from him. It was much too soon to think about marrying Noah—wasn't it? She wanted it more than anything, but she didn't really think he was ready. Was it possible he'd gotten caught up in the moment? Surely he would feel differently tomorrow, and she would be left feeling like a *dummkopf* for blurting out the answer she longed to say. She wanted to marry him more than anything, but not if he wasn't ready. They hadn't known each other long enough for that sort of thing to be anything more than a fleeting thought. The stunned look on her face sent the message to him without her having to utter a word.

Noah stepped back, allowing Rose to fall from his grasp. The moment was gone. The look on her face told him he had made a big mistake in voicing his feelings aloud. Would she be the one to run from *him* this time? Her expression let him know he'd gone too far. There was no taking it back. What could he do? Would she even take him seriously after such a foolish statement? He was falling in love with her, that much he knew for certain. He couldn't help it. God, himself had placed her in his path, and he couldn't reject such a precious gift. But how could he make her understand he'd meant what he'd said without scaring her away?

"Rose, I'm sorry. I didn't mean for that to come out. I was caught up in the kiss. I feel like I keep messing things up without meaning to, and I'm sorry. I don't want to hurt you. I care about you."

There it was—his confession. He hadn't meant it at all. She'd been a fool to hope he had.

He cares about me, but he doesn't love me. How could I have allowed him to pull me into another passionate kiss without knowing how he felt about me first? I wish I could take it back. All of it. Maybe then I wouldn't feel like a dummkopf and this wouldn't hurt so much.

"I should go," she managed.

Rose couldn't face him. And she certainly couldn't come back to the pond ever again.

Chapter 23

Rose wept quietly into her pillow. She didn't want to risk having to explain her tears to Katie if she should hear her. How could she have been such a fool to let Noah use her to feed his own cravings for a replacement for Emma? Was he using her as a substitute to quench the pain of losing Emma?

Then it hit her. He'd said *her* name. He'd asked *her* to marry him. He hadn't mistakenly called her Emma like he had that first night when she'd nearly drowned. Was it possible he'd fallen in love with *her,* and he was truly over Emma?

Sitting up, Rose wiped her tear-soaked eyes on the sheet. She'd wasted what might possibly have been her only proposal of marriage, and she'd rejected him. Panic consumed her at the thought of losing Noah completely. Was it too late to tell him yes? Would he still want to marry her after the way she'd behaved?

Gott, please bless me with the strength to endure the heartache if Noah should decide he doesn't really want to marry me. I pray that he does, and that you will soften his heart toward me to forgive me for rejecting him. I didn't mean to. I love him, Gott. Please open his eyes to see the love I have for him.

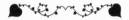

"Where are you going in such a hurry?"

Rose gulped the last sip of her coffee and set the cup in the sink. "I told you. I have to go to the B&B."

Katie was growing impatient with her sister's secrets. "I thought today was your day off?"

"It is, but I promised Bess I'd go into town with her. She wants to pick up some new fabric to make new drapes for one of the guest rooms, and I told her I'd go with her."

Katie walked over to the sink and stood beside Rose. "You were complaining to me about how I've neglected you since you gotten here. And now I haven't seen you a full day since. You're always running off somewhere. Is there something going on with you that I need to know about? Are you up to something?"

Rose placed a hand on her sister's shoulder. "*Nee.* Everything is fine. I have things to do, and you should be happy since that will allow you to spend more time with Caleb. I'm happy with my job. Bess has been very kind to me."

Katie scrunched up her face. "You call her by her first name? She'll be my *aenti* when I marry Caleb, and I don't even call her by her first name."

Rose smiled. "I suppose that's because we've become more like friends."

Katie nearly choked on her coffee. "Friends? She's so much older than you are, Rose."

"The age a person is has no bearing on whether they will make a *gut* friend. Besides, she's only turning fifty this year. That isn't so old."

Katie felt a little jealousy rise up in her. "I suppose not. When you get home, will you have time to work on the wedding dresses? I'd like to finish them so that is out of the way."

Rose smiled. "Of course we can. But you know the wedding is still several months away. You don't have to have everything done now."

"Come harvest season, everyone will be too busy with canning bees and the like, so I want all the big details taken care of now."

Rose hugged her sister, and then walked out the door. She understood wanting to ready everything for the wedding, but Rose hoped that she would be planning for her own wedding soon as well.

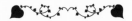

Rose wasn't keen on riding into town with Jessup driving, but Bess had trusted him with her mare. She didn't want to ride in the front of the buggy, but Bess had insisted she needed to sit in the back so she could stretch out to avoid getting queasy. Rose felt a little awkward around the man with which her own sister used to be betrothed, but Bess trusted him, so she didn't argue. Even though she knew it was a sham and that her parents had forced Katie into the engagement, it still felt odd being around Jessup. She didn't dislike him the way Katie had at the time, but there was something odd about his visits to the B&B. This was his second trip in three weeks, and Bess had told her he was here on business. But now Rose learned he would return at the end of the week with his *kinner*. If Rose didn't know any better, she'd think Jessup King was looking to move to the community.

When they reached the outskirts of town, Rose admired many shops that were run by the Amish. Everything from a bakery to a quilt shop, and even a shop that sold antiques and wares homemade by the Amish in the community graced the main road. Rose was mesmerized every time she caught a glimpse of the town-folk, and often wondered what their lives were like.

Jessup parked the buggy in front of the bank, claiming he had some business to take care of. He'd suggested they meet at the diner around the corner as soon as they'd finished getting fabric.

"I won't be long," Jessup called over his shoulder. "I'll meet you in twenty minutes."

Rose wondered what sort of business he might have at the bank, but it only furthered her assumption that he was planning to move to the community. Why would he want to live in the same community as Katie? Unless he had plans to try to win her back. Would he stoop so low as to try to break up Katie and Caleb after all this time had passed? He'd have to be a fool to try.

Chapter 24

Caleb pulled his buggy across Main Street and parked in front of the hardware store. He'd recognized his *aenti* Bess's buggy parked at the bank across the street and thought it odd. He walked across traffic and patted Buttercup on the head. She responded with a whinny and bobbed her head, nudging Caleb affectionately with her nose.

Caleb gave her nose another pat, and then walked around the corner to get an ice cream cone from the diner. The only time he indulged in the sweet treat was during his summertime trips to town, and it was warm enough today to make him crave the frozen treat. As he rounded the corner, he glanced inside and noticed Rose sitting at one of the tables. She was with a man, and giggled like someone who was on a date and flirting. When the waitress walked by the table, the man turned to get her attention. She tore a sheet off the pad of paper in her hand and handed it to *Jessup King!*

Even though the man Caleb now stared at was beardless, it was indeed Jessup King. Was he courting Rose? Was that the reason for shaving his beard? Katie had complained to him that Rose had been running off lately and spending a lot of time at the B&B—even on her days off. Why would his *aenti* allow the two of them to take her buggy into town for a date? He would get to the bottom of this, but Caleb would not engage in a public confrontation. He would wait and go over to the B&B to talk with his *aenti* later. Right now, he'd suddenly lost his appetite for that ice cream cone.

Noah waved to his cousin who had just crossed the street and walked toward the hardware store. Standing in front of the diner, he wondered what had caused Caleb to stare through the window so intently. As he peered inside, his heart skipped a beat at the realization of what had caught Caleb's attention. Rose sat in the middle of the diner at a small table with an older man—an un-bearded man. If the man wore no beard, he was unmarried. Who was he? Did his cousin know? Noah watched the two of them converse happily—almost as though they were on a date.

When he'd approached the diner from the feed store, Caleb's back had been to him and he'd been staring through the window of the diner. He hadn't gone in. He'd simply stood outside the window before jogging across the street to the hardware store. Caleb had seemed as unnerved as Noah was now, but he couldn't ask his cousin about it, or he would discover his feelings for Rose. His feelings that had obviously gone unrequited.

Noah walked away from the diner before Rose caught him staring through the window. He'd embarrassed himself enough by throwing himself on her twice, and now it seemed she was dating someone else. He wondered how long they'd been together, and why she hadn't mentioned it to him before they kissed? Was she unhappy with the man? Judging from her laughter, he'd have to say she was not unhappy with him. He didn't think Rose was the type of girl to date more than one man at a time, but it was possible he was wrong about that assumption.

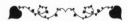

Bess returned from the bathroom and sat down at the table between Rose and Jessup.

"Jessup was just telling me the funniest story, Bess. You have to get him to tell you while I use the ladies' room. I'll be right back."

Jessup began to recount his story while Rose got up and went toward the back of the diner to reach the ladies' room. She wasn't real keen on using public restrooms, but she'd had too many refills of her soda-pop.

When she finished, she stood at the sink to wash her hands and examined herself in the large mirror as she did. She'd gotten a lot of sun lately while taking care of the celery patch for Katie, and she thought she was beginning to resemble the *Englisch* girls who wore a lot of makeup. She'd always tanned easily, and she thought she looked better with a little color on her face. It seemed to override the dullness that normally paled her.

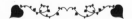

By the time they arrived back at the B&B, Rose felt like she'd put in a full day already. She wanted to stop by and visit with Noah, but she'd promised Katie she would work on sewing the wedding dresses when she returned. She'd had fun, which surprised her. She'd never thought she could actually have fun talking to Jessup, but he'd had some funny stories about the constant antics of his *kinner,* and it was quite entertaining listening to him. She could see that he genuinely loved his *kinner,* and Rose thought that was a *gut* quality—one she'd missed when he was engaged to Katie.

"We need to talk about something serious, Rose, and this can't wait."

"At least let me get my sewing. We can talk then."

Katie didn't wait for her to return with her sewing. She followed closely on Rose's heals as she clomped up the stairs, exhaustion apparent in each step. She turned around midway, frowning at her sister.

"Katie, why are you following me? I'll be right down."

Katie continued to follow, causing Rose a great deal of irritation. "What is so important that you had to follow me up the stairs?"

"I know why you've been disappearing all the time. Why didn't you tell me you were seeing *someone?*"

Rose's heart fluttered with dread. She didn't want to say anything about her relationship with Noah until she was certain where it stood.

Katie scowled at Rose. "Your silence tells me it's true! Well, I forbid you to date Jessup King!"

Chapter 25

"You forbid me?"

Rose decided to play along. She had no idea what had made Katie think she was seeing Jessup, but it was the perfect cover-up until she could figure things out with Noah without her sister getting into her affairs like she was now.

"Yes, I forbid you. I decided to follow you to the B&B to see what was *really* causing you to run off all the time, and that's when I saw you getting into the buggy with Jessup. I know he's changed, but he made me miserable when I was forcibly engaged to him. Besides, I find it a little creepy that you would decide to date him. You aren't serious are you?"

Rose pressed her lips into a grim line. "And if I am? What then? Would you forbid me to marry him if I chose to do so? Honestly, I find it *creepy* that my own sister thinks she has to spy on me!"

Katie fumed. "It's obvious *someone* needs to keep tabs on you. Why would you even think to marry Jessup? Has he proposed to you?"

Rose remembered the heated proposal she'd received from Noah. Her cheeks warmed at the thought of it.

"I've been proposed to."

It wasn't a complete lie. She'd been proposed to— just not from Jessup.

Katie's eyes bulged and her mouth gaped.

"He proposed to you? Please tell me you told him no!"

Rose was almost enjoying this. It angered her that her sister would accuse of her of such a thing in the first place. But to believe it to be true was another thing altogether. She wasn't sure how long she could keep this up, but certainly long enough to teach Katie a lesson to stay out of her business. Katie had always tried to boss her. She never understood why, but she assumed it had everything to do with the fact that their parents controlled her so closely. It still surprised her that her parents had allowed Katie to remain in this community, but she suspected *Aenti* Nettie had had a lot to do with winning that argument.

"I didn't give my answer."

It was still the truth…

Katie breathed a sigh of relief. The thought of Rose marrying Jessup was too much for Katie to accept. She *had* to stop it from happening—for Rose's sake—and for her own. It would be awkward, to say the least, to see her sister marry him.

"Then you still have time to break it off."

Rose bristled. "What if I don't want to break it off with him? What if I love him?"

"Do you love him?"

Rose thought about Noah. There was no denying her love for him.

"I do love him. Very much."

Katie drew in a quick breath. "Does he feel the same about you?"

With the way Rose had responded to Noah's proposal, she wasn't sure if he would still have her. It broke her heart to even think about it, but she had to face the fact that even though she loved him deeply, his proposal may not have been sincere. He'd practically taken it back afterward. She wished she could be sure of his feelings for her, but the truth was, she couldn't.

"I hope he does," Rose whispered.

Katie furrowed her brow. "What do you mean, you *hope* he does? You seem so sure of your own feelings. Why aren't you so sure of his?"

Rose was confused over Katie's sudden change of attitude toward her *relationship* with Jessup. It almost seemed she was being supportive of it.

"I really don't feel like discussing this anymore. Can we work on sewing the dresses for your wedding, and just forget about this other stuff?"

"No, Rose. It's obvious you're upset. I only want to help you."

Rose grabbed the wedding attendant dress from the peg in the corner of the room and headed back downstairs.

"Rose please let me help you," Katie said as she followed her sister down the steps.

Rose turned on her heels so quickly that Katie ran into her. "If you really want to help me, you'll drop it and forget I ever said anything."

Their conversation had gotten so out of control that Rose, herself, was becoming confused by it all. She no longer thought it amusing that Katie had mistaken her love for Noah and transferred it to her suspicion over Jessup. Truth be told, she was heartbroken at the moment, and she didn't know how to make it right. Only seeing Noah and being in his arms would make things right, and she didn't see that happening.

"How am I supposed to forget that my *schweschder* is in love with Jessup King?"

Rose fought tears, and turned her back to Katie so she could get control of her emotions. She busied herself at the sink making a fresh pot of coffee even though it was much too warm to drink it. She needed something to keep her hands busy and her mind off of Noah long enough to figure a way out this new mess she'd brought on herself.

Rose suddenly turned toward Katie, who'd sat at the kitchen table and had begun to pin the hem of her blue wedding dress.

"It no longer matters because I don't think he returns my feelings."

"Why would he propose if he didn't love you?"

Rose bit her lower lip. "He proposed to you when he didn't love you."

Katie stood up and walked over to the sink and placed her arm around Rose. "That was different because I didn't love him either."

Rose couldn't hold in her emotions any longer. With her sister's arms wrapped tightly around her, she began to weep softly. "Why do *menner* think it's alright to ask a woman to marry them when they don't really mean it? After he proposed, he practically took it back. He said he didn't mean for it to come out. That he had only said it because he was so caught up in our kiss that he hadn't thought it out."

Katie pushed Rose from her arms so she could look her in the eye. "He kissed you on the mouth?"

Rose remembered her kisses with Noah with a far-off look in her eyes. "*Jah.* And it was lovely.*"

Katie shook. Not once during her engagement to Jessup had he kissed her on the mouth.

Chapter 26

"I have something I have to tell you!" Katie was nearly out of breath when she ran out to meet Caleb after he pulled his buggy into the yard.

"I have something I have to tell you too, and it can't wait."

Katie climbed into the buggy and settled in next to Caleb. "My news first, please. I don't think I can wait another second to tell you."

"Jessup is back in town and I saw him at the diner with Rose," Caleb blurted out.

Katie's eyes grew wide. "Then it's true!"

Caleb dropped the reins. "What is true?"

Katie held back the tears that threatened to spill from her eyes. "He proposed marriage to her."

"Jessup King proposed marriage to your *schweschder,* Rose?"

Katie let loose the tears. "*Jah,* and he broke her heart. As soon as he proposed, he took it back. She really loves him."

"What do you mean he took back his proposal?"

"That's what she told me. She said that he proposed to her right after kissing her full on the mouth. He never once kissed me on the mouth. This is serious."

Caleb raised an eyebrow. "He never kissed you on the mouth? Really?"

Katie scowled. "Why do you say that like you're surprised?"

"I'm not as surprised as I am happy about it. It means I was your first real kiss, *jah?*"

"*Jah,* you were."

"*Das gut.*"

Katie wiped her tears and smiled at her betrothed. "Let's put our concentration back on my dear *schweschder.* What are we going to do about this?"

Caleb thought about it for a minute. "I think I need to have a talk with the Bishop again, but I'd like to give Jessup a chance to explain his side of the story."

"He has nothing to explain. He has gone and done what he threatened to do. I can't believe we thought he'd changed. He hasn't changed. He was biding his time until he could lure my *schweschder* into his plan of revenge. He gave us his word he would not pursue her, and he broke that promise. And now he's broken Rose's heart along with that promise. He's a horrible man, and you need to tell the Bishop of his actions right away."

Caleb put his arm around Katie to calm her.

"Is it possible that Rose misunderstood him?"

"You didn't see how upset she was. Rose has always been very level-headed. We've seen first-hand what Jessup King is capable of."

Caleb rubbed his hand across his smooth chin. "It doesn't make any sense to me. When I saw them at the diner earlier, they looked happy. Rose was laughing; Jessup was laughing. They were having a *gut* time. I don't understand what could have happened in the last hour to make him change his mind about her."

Katie sniffled. "He didn't change his mind about her. He never cared about her in the first place, just like with me. The only difference between the two is that I didn't fall in love with him, but Rose did. And he took advantage of her vulnerability. He should never have kissed her on the mouth. That sort of kiss should be saved for the *mann* you're to be married to. He has taken that special first-kiss from her and she can never get that back. He should suffer excommunication for his behavior."

Caleb was trying to see this from Katie's point of view, but there was still something that was nagging him about this. "That seems a little harsh, don't you think? Perhaps we should hear him out first. We talked to him last time, and his remorse seemed genuine."

Katie leered at Caleb. "An evil *mann* will let honey drip from his tongue."

"I don't think we should assume he's become evil until I have a talk with him first so we can get to the bottom of this. There *has* to be a logical explanation, and we owe it to Rose *and* to Jessup to find out what that is before we jump to conclusions."

Katie wiped her face on her apron. "What are you waiting for? Let's go find out why he did this to Rose."

Caleb pulled Katie's hands into his own and looked her in the eye. "I think you should stay here with Rose. She needs you. I'm going to go over and get Noah to help me. I don't want to approach Jessup alone, and I think Noah would be a *gut* person to take with me. He's always been very level-headed. I think it's best if I have another *mann* with me when I defend your *schweschder's* honor."

Katie sighed. "But Noah doesn't even know Rose *or* Jessup. How can he help if he doesn't know who he's up against?"

Caleb kissed Katie's hands. "I think it is better that Noah doesn't know either Rose or Jessup. That way he can be neutral in case I get a little too heated."

Katie cuddled him. "I think that's wise."

Caleb kissed Katie on the forehead, and then hugged her. "It's getting dark. I'm going to stop by Noah's place on the way home and fill him in on what's going on. We will probably go over to the B&B first thing in the morning and talk to Jessup. I'll come over after and let you know how it went. In the meantime, go spend some time with Rose."

"*Danki*. I don't know how I would have managed this without your help. I know I only met Noah briefly at the meal after church before he disappeared, but thank him for me. I appreciate whatever the two of you can do to fix this."

Katie waved to Caleb as he pulled the buggy out of the yard, and then she went in the house to comfort Rose. She called out to her, searching the upstairs, the yard and even the barn, but Rose was gone.

Chapter 27

Rose stood in the grass at the end of the dock and watched mindlessly as fireflies swarmed around her. The night air was humid and warm, only a slight breeze bringing relief as the draft floated up her dress. Every minute that ticked by was another minute that Noah was not with her. She didn't hold out much hope that he would show up, but it remained in the back of her mind, tucked away where she refused to acknowledge it.

Not feeling up to catching fireflies, Rose walked to the end of the dock and lowered herself into the spot in which Noah usually waited for her while she took a boat ride. She hadn't been out on the boat in nearly a week, and she found that she lacked the desire to do so even now. Sadly, it only held amusement as long as she knew Noah was sitting in this very spot waiting for her. Without him, everything paled in comparison.

Rose kicked at the water, sending ripples across the pond. It reminded her of how much Noah liked to skip stones across it. Would everything she did remind her of Noah, or would she eventually forget him just as he seemed to have forgotten her?

Perhaps it's time to go back home to Nappanee.

Noah was just getting ready to head out to the dock at the B&B when his cousin, Caleb, drove his buggy up the drive to his house. He'd planned to clear the air with Rose and tell her he loved her enough to marry her. Unsure of what he'd seen earlier in the diner, he decided to give her a chance to explain why she was with the older man. Perhaps there was a logical explanation, and he was a relative. Either way, he loved her, and he was ready to commit if she would have him. Now he would have to postpone that meeting, depending on how long his cousin planned to stay.

Caleb jumped down from the buggy and held a hand out to his cousin. "*Wie gehts,* Noah."

Noah took his hand. "What brings you out here this time of night? Shouldn't you be taking a buggy ride with your betrothed?"

Caleb chuckled. "I wish I was. Even going home and cleaning the horse-stalls would be more fun than what I have on my plate right now."

Noah gave his cousin a concerned pat on the back. "What could be troubling you so much? You are engaged; you should be happy all the time."

"I'm very happy with Katie. It's her *schweschder,* Rose, that is causing concern."

At the mention of Rose, Noah's heart fluttered.

"What did she do that has you so concerned?"

Caleb leaned up against the porch railing. "It's not so much what she did as what Jessup King did to upset her."

The thought of someone hurting Rose sent anger through Noah. He was almost afraid to ask the question he knew he needed to. "What did he do to her?"

Caleb shot a look of concern to his cousin. He'd never known him to talk through gritted teeth before. It was almost as though Noah had a vested interest in Rose's well-being, but that would be impossible since he didn't even know her.

"It seems he asked her to marry him and then took it back."

Noah collapsed against the porch-rail, and caught himself so he wouldn't fall back. "He asked her to marry him? When?"

Caleb looked at his cousin with concern. "Are you able to handle news of the community, Noah? Maybe I shouldn't have relied on you so soon."

Noah shook his head. "I lost my footing is all. Is this Jessup an older fellow?"

"Jah. How did you know?"

Noah clenched his jaw. "I saw them in the diner today. They looked happy to me."

Caleb did a double-take toward Noah. "How do you know what Rose looks like?"

Clearing his throat, Noah chose his words carefully. "I spoke to her after church on Sunday."

It wasn't a lie. But it wasn't the entire truth either.

Caleb ran his hand through his hair and replaced his hat. "I'm not sure when everything happened, but I saw them in the diner this afternoon too. They did look like they were having a pleasant conversation. So I suppose it happened between then and an hour ago. Either way, he took back his proposal, and it seems he broke her heart."

That statement hit Noah too close to home. *He'd* been the one to propose and retrieve it. Had *he* broken Rose's heart? Or had she been counting on the proposal from Jessup too? Did he even propose? Noah certainly was eager to find out.

"I came over here to see if you would go with me to talk with Jessup tomorrow so we could get some answers. I want to know what he's up to with Rose. He'd warned Katie and me a while back that he intended on pursuing Rose out of spite, and I want to know if that's what he's up to."

Noah wanted answers more than Caleb could possibly understand. He loved Rose, and he thought she loved him too. But after seeing her in the diner with Jessup, and now hearing he may have proposed to her, Noah was worried he may have misjudged her character. Was it possible that Caleb's visit tonight had spared him from going to Rose at the pond and making a fool of himself?

"*Jah,* I will go with you. Do you think there's much truth to this proposal from Jessup?"

Caleb shrugged. "I have no idea. But I hope not for her sake. What baffles me the most is why Rose would allow herself to get involved with him to the point he could break her heart. I don't understand how or when she could have fallen in love with the *mann.*"

"She said she was in love with him?"

Caleb nodded.

Noah shuddered. If Rose was in love with Jessup, then why had she kissed *him* the way she had when they were together?

Chapter 28

Noah shuffled to the kitchen for some coffee. After such a restless night, he needed something to perk him up. Because nothing could make him forget that the woman he loved had been proposed to by another man, he wished Caleb had never told him.

After several hours of tossing about trying to sleep, Noah had all but convinced himself it had been a mistake to re-enter the community. He felt he'd been better off staying hidden in the shadows of the community where nothing could hurt him. But he couldn't regret meeting Rose, or she might be dead and gone, consumed by Goose Pond just as Emma had been.

Striking a match, Noah lit the pilot light of the gas stove, turned on the burner and set the percolator over the flame. He leaned against the sink wondering how things had gotten so out of control in his life. Life was supposed to be simple for Amish, wasn't it? How then, was his life beginning to feel so tangled and complicated? At the end of the week, his *daed* was expecting him for dinner. Was he even ready for that? He'd realized he may not have been ready to fall in love with Rose either. Everything was happening so fast all of a sudden that his mind had not had the proper amount of time to process it all.

The clip-clop of a horse and the sound of turning buggy wheels brought Noah's gaze toward the small window above the sink. Caleb had arrived early. He could only assume he was eager to get some answers, but Noah was no longer certain he wanted to know.

Sometimes what you don't know can't hurt you.

Caleb gave a quick warning knock at the back door, and then entered. "I know it's early, but I wanted to get this over with. If I know Jessup King, he'll slip out of town and we will miss the chance to confront him about Rose."

The mere mention of her name sent prickles of agony coursing down his spine. Bubbles of dark coffee pushed up into the clear, glass percolator at the top of the tall pot on the stove. Noah turned off the burner, not caring that he'd be drinking weak brew. He was too tired to worry about steeping his morning beverage to perfection. He wanted to get this over with more than his cousin could ever know. His stomach roiled as he took his first sip. Would he be able to face Jessup without a physical confrontation? Right now he wasn't so sure about it.

Noah gulped the last of the still-hot coffee, not caring that it burned his tongue. "Let's go," he growled.

Caleb held the door for his cousin. "Why are you in such a bad mood this morning?"

Noah waved him off. "Nothing. Just didn't get much sleep last night. I have a lot on my mind."

Caleb turned before climbing into the buggy.

"I'm sorry. If you're not up to this, I can go alone."

Noah looked at him sternly. *"Nee.* I want to go. Why don't we walk over? We can go through the back, around the pond."

Caleb agreed it would be quicker to avoid the traffic on the main road just to get to what seemed like was just around the curve from Noah's place.

They walked in silence the short distance to the back of the B&B. Noah eyed the dock as they approached. His heart sank at the thought of the kisses he'd shared with Rose, the kisses that had meant everything to him.

As they neared the back door, Caleb spotted a taxi-cab coming up the side road toward the B&B.

Caleb sped up his walk. "Jessup must be leaving. We need to hurry and catch him."

They entered through the back door and made their way to the parlor. Caleb stopped in his tracks when he saw that Jessup's arms were wrapped tightly around a woman who was clearly not Rose. He was passionately kissing her full on the mouth.

A strangled gasp escaped Caleb's lips.

Startled, the couple broke apart, the faces of each of them turning bright red. But more shocking than the kiss was the fact that the woman he'd been passionately kissing was *Aenti* Bess.

Noah reacted before Caleb could process what he'd seen. Noah charged toward Jessup, pushing him against the wall near the front door.

Caleb watched it all as though in slow motion. His brain told him he'd seen Jessup kissing *Aenti* Bess—on the mouth—passionately. Had he imagined it? Watching Noah confronting Jessup, and hearing his *aenti* rushing to the man's defense told him he hadn't imagined it at all.

"How dare you take advantage of *mei aenti* after proposing to Rose! What kind of *mann* are you?"

Noah held Jessup against the wall with his forearm pressed against his chest. Bess tried to get between them. "Let him go, Noah."

Jessup fought to catch his breath. "I didn't ask Rose to marry me. I asked Bess to marry me."

Noah released him. His heart was beating so fast, he had to take a deep breath to calm himself.

Caleb stepped forward. "What are you talking about? We saw you yesterday at the diner in town with Rose. The two of you seemed pretty cozy. She told Katie you proposed to her and then took it back."

Bess cupped her arm in Jessup's and held a warning hand out to her nephews, letting them know to back off. "I was with them at the diner yesterday. I must have been in the bathroom when you walked by. I'm not sure why Rose would say that Jessup proposed to her, because he proposed to *me*."

Caleb reached out a hand to Jessup. "I guess congratulations would be in order here. Sorry for the misunderstanding, but what about..." he lowered his voice to a whisper. "The *age* difference between the two of you."

Bess pursed her lips, and eyed Noah who'd stood by without uttering a word.

Jessup cleared his throat. "I know that Katie thought I was in my mid-thirties, but I'm really in my mid-forties. I led her to believe I was younger than I am because I was embarrassed about the age difference between the two of us. But now I don't have to hide my age anymore. Bess is only a few years older than I am, but I find that comforting. We're happy, and I hope in time you will be able to accept our union. We are to be married at the end of the week when I return with my *kinner*. We'll be living at the B&B."

Caleb's heart softened at the look of love in his *aenti's* eyes. It was obvious she was happy, and he had no right to judge her for wanting what everyone wanted. It was her choice and he would respect it. "I hope you will extend us an invitation to the wedding."

"I was going to tell everyone at dinner on Friday at your *daed's haus.*" She aimed her statement at Noah.

Noah relaxed at the thought of his *daed* inviting him to a family dinner. That meant he was finally ready to mend the rift between them.

Caleb pulled off his hat and scratched his head as though deep in thought. "There's one thing I don't understand. If Jessup didn't propose to Rose, who did?"

Noah swallowed the lump of nerves constricting his throat and looked into his cousin's waiting eyes. "I did."

Chapter 29

"What?" everyone, including Jessup, asked in unison.

Caleb raised an eyebrow. "What do you mean? *You did*? You're the one that proposed to Rose and broke her heart? Why would you do such a thing? You don't even know her."

A honk sounded from outside. Jessup picked up his suitcase. "As much as I'd like to stay and hear all about this, I must go. I've got a lot of packing to do in the next two days before I return. *Gut daag,* I'll see the two of you later."

Caleb and Noah ignored Jessup as Bess walked him out to the waiting taxi-cab.

The two of them sat down on the landing of the wide stairwell, Noah on the upper riser.

"I do know Rose, and I love her. I don't know why she would think I took back my proposal. She's the one that walked away from me without giving me an answer. For the past two days I thought she didn't want anything to do with me. And after the fun we've had in each other's company, I've felt awful about not seeing her. Then when I saw her with Jessup yesterday at the diner, I thought it was over between us for certain."

Caleb shook his head, still trying to process this new turn of events. "How did the two of you meet? Have you been seeing her all summer?"

"We met at the pond one night. She fell in and I pulled her out of the water. She thinks I saved her life, but it was *my* life that was saved that night. If not for her, I'd still be wallowing in the self-destructive pity that took me from the community. I owe her my life."

"So you asked her to marry you?"

"I asked her to marry me because I fell in love with her. We have fun together, and we can talk about anything.

She understands me and accepts me with unconditional love."

"Noah, she thinks you took back your proposal."

Noah sighed. "I apologized for blurting it out. I think I told her I proposed to her because I was caught up in the moment of our kiss—that it spurred the proposal. She must think I didn't really mean it. I have to talk to her and get her to understand that I didn't take it back."

Noah jumped up and walked over to the check-in desk in the front parlor of the B&B and grabbed a notepad. He scribbled a quick note on the page, folded it and handed it to Caleb. "Will you make sure Rose gets this? I'm going to stay here and wait for *Aenti* Bess to come back in and talk to her. I think I have a way to make things right with Rose."

Caleb slapped his cousin on the back. "I'll do whatever I can to help. I will be praying for you. Don't mess it up this time. Rose is a *gut* match for you."

"*Danki*. That means a lot that you support me on this."

Caleb and Noah walked back to the kitchen. Caleb left, and Noah poured himself a fresh cup of coffee. It was going to be a long day.

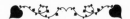

Caleb knocked on the back door and waited for Katie to answer. Instead, she hollered that it was open. As he entered the kitchen, Rose and Katie sat at the table eating breakfast.

"Won't you join us?" Katie asked him.

"*Nee*. Noah asked me to give this to you."

He handed the note to Rose. She opened it and read the contents, a smile forming on her lips.

Katie looked between Rose and Caleb. "Why is Noah sending notes to my *schweschder?*"

Rose jumped up from the table happily and bolted from the room. Katie cringed at the stomping she'd made as she ran up the stairs.

Katie turned to Caleb. "Are you going to tell me what's going on? What happened with Bess? And why is your cousin, Noah, sending notes to Rose? He doesn't even know her."

Caleb found it difficult to hide his smile.

"Jessup didn't propose to Rose. Noah did."

Chapter 30

Katie spit her coffee across the table. Choking and coughing, she tried to speak.

Caleb patted her on the back. "Are you alright?"

Katie nodded her head. "Why did Noah propose to her? What about Jessup? Why didn't she deny it when I asked her about Jessup?"

Caleb took the cup from Katie's hand and set it aside. "There's more. Are you ready for it?"

Katie nodded. How much more news could there be?

"Jessup asked *Aenti* Bess to marry him."

Katie pushed back her chair, scraping it against the wood floor. "We have to go to the Bishop. We can't let him take advantage of that poor woman. Doesn't Jessup King know how to prey on anyone his own age?"

Caleb suppressed a smile. "Turns out, he's only three years younger than my *aenti*. He led you to believe he was in his mid-thirties, but he's about eleven years older than he told you he was."

Katie couldn't breathe. If what Caleb said was true, she'd nearly been tricked into marrying a man twenty-one years her senior. Leaning over the sink, she turned on the faucet and splashed cold water over her face several times. Was it possible to wash off disgust?

She looked back at Caleb, her face dripping.

"Do you have anything else to tell me as long as I'm hanging my head over the sink? I think I'll stay here just in case I lose my breakfast."

Caleb stepped up to the sink and placed a comforting arm around his betrothed. He understood how she was feeling. He remembered how sick he felt when he found out she was promised to Jessup. But that seemed like a million years ago now. "I have no more shocking news to tell you. That was it."

Relieved, Katie wiped her face on the linen tea-towel hanging from the handle on the stove.

"Tell me about Rose and Noah."

Caleb pulled Katie into his arms and kissed her lightly on top of her head. "I will later. Right now, I just want to hold you."

Chapter 31

Rose lay across her bed staring at the words on the note from Noah. He'd requested a meeting with her on the dock at the B&B at nine o'clock. Several thoughts ran through her head; everything from Noah declaring his love for her all over again and asking her to marry him, to the possibility that he wanted to see her so he could break things off with her. At first, she'd thought the letter to be a positive one, but now she couldn't be sure. The only hint she had was his signature: *Love, Noah.*

Had it meant that he loved her, or was it simply a polite salutation? Either way, she would find out at the end of the day. Since today was her day off at the B&B, Rose decided to spend the time finishing her dress for Katie's wedding. She'd promised her sister she would have it done by the end of the week, and there would not be another day when she would have the entire day to fill. If she didn't keep herself busy today, it would drive her mad thinking about her meeting later with Noah. Whatever his intentions were, she would not let him go without telling him how much she loved him. She would risk everything on the chance that he truly loved her in return.

Noah lit the candles in the Mason jars he'd used to line the dock at the B&B. Bess had loaned them to him, stating it would create a romantic walkway for Rose to meet him at the end of the dock. Stars twinkled in the black, cloudless sky, and the thumbnail moon angled itself amidst of the canopy of stars. Noah couldn't have asked God to provide a more perfect setting for this special night with Rose.

Rose pulled her neatly-pressed, pink dress over her head. It was the prettiest color she owned. She didn't twist her hair up in the back, and she left her *kapp* on its hook. She looked into the oval mirror that hung from the back of her bureau admiring her long hair. She hoped Noah would approve of such boldness since he didn't seem to mind the previous times they'd spent together. For her, it was a way to relay the message that she was giving herself to him.

After learning of Jessup's proposal of marriage to Bess, Rose felt more confident than ever that love was in her own future as well. She was happy for her friend, and knowing that if even Bess could find love at such a late stage in life, surely Rose had an even better chance for the same in her own young life.

Rose tip-toed down the stairs in her bare feet. She didn't want Katie to stop her and reprimand her for not wearing her *kapp*. She knew her sister was getting ready to take a buggy ride with Caleb, but she couldn't wait for them to leave or she would be late for her special meeting with the man she loved.

Breathing a sigh of relief at having made it out of the house without being seen by Katie, Rose walked swiftly through the cool grass toward the B&B. The closer she came to the dock, she noticed the lighted jars along the edge of the dock. Her heart leapt with joy, for she knew that he loved her. He wouldn't have gone to the trouble to create something so romantic if he didn't want the night to be more special than the previous nights they'd spent at the dock.

Then she saw him standing at the end of the dock. His smile told her he'd been waiting for her. She walked between the candles that flickered in the Mason jars, keeping her focus on Noah, who stood patiently waiting for her. Neither of them spoke for fear of breaking the romantic spell between them.

Rose stood before him suddenly feeling shy and unsure of herself. Was she really bold enough to get what she wanted? She *had* to be. Even though she was scared of rejection, she couldn't let anything stand between them any longer or it would destroy her.

Closing the space between them, Rose coiled her fingers in his royal blue shirt and used it pull him low enough until his lips met hers. She deepened the kiss when she wrapped her arms around his neck. Noah held her close, lifting her slightly until she stood on her tip-toes.

"I love you, Rose," Noah said between kisses. "I want to marry you."

Happy tears formed in Rose's eyes. "I want to be your *fraa.*"

Noah let out a heavy sigh of relief. "I'm so glad. I've been here for more than an hour going over what I would say to convince you in case you said no."

"How could I say no to you? I love you."

Rose looked down at their feet where a jar of fireflies was glowing brightly. She reached down to pick it up and examine the contents.

"How did you manage to get so many?"

Noah chuckled. "Like I said, I've been here for over an hour."

"One is trying to escape. It looks like you twisted the lid on crooked. The cheesecloth is loose at the top."

Rose strained to untwist the lid, which seemed to be stuck, when her elbow knocked into Noah's chest with enough force to make him lose his balance. He teetered backward and then fell into the pond with a big splash.

Rose held her breath until he surfaced.

She reached a hand out to him, but he boosted himself up from the end of the dock.

"I'm so sorry. I didn't mean to push you in."

Noah laughed heartily. "Maybe I should throw you in and then we'd be even."

Rose squealed.

"You're lucky I'm a gentleman, or I would."

Not caring that he was dripping wet with pond water, Rose pulled Noah into another deep kiss, and his response to her was just what she'd hoped for. Magically, fireflies swarmed around them, but Rose noticed they'd come out from the jar she still held in her hand.

"Oh no. They got away. I didn't mean to let them go. You worked so hard to catch them."

Noah leaned in and kissed her ear and whispered to her. "It's alright, we can catch more. Don't you know, Rose, there is no place I'd rather be than here with you, chasing fireflies."

The End

Please turn the page to read BOOK 6 in this series

Amish Summer of Courage
Book Six

Samantha Jillian Bayarr
Copyright © 2012 by Samantha Jillian Bayarr

Chapter 1

"Don't scream!"

Rachel couldn't breathe.

The cold hand clenching her mouth was making it impossible for her to take in air. Panic seized her as she tried to wriggle free, but the man's grasp on her was too strong.

"If you scream, I'm gonna have to hurt you."

He was behind her, and she couldn't see his face, but she could smell his sour breath on the back of her neck. It was enough to make her want to vomit. His free hand worked quickly, winding thin rope around her wrists so tight her hands were going numb.

What's happening to me? Gott, please help me!

Tears filled Rachel's eyes as the stranger tied her wrists tightly behind her back. She couldn't move even if she wanted to; her legs felt like silos filled to the brim with thousands of pounds of grain.

The bakery had closed for the day, and she had stayed longer than she should have washing dishes that should have been done during her down-time after the noon rush. It was nearly dark, but even at this late hour, no one was expecting her at home. It was Saturday, and she always made deliveries on her way home, distributing leftover bread to members of the community who were struggling. By the time her deliveries were missed, it would be too late for anyone to help her. Was he going to kill her? Was he here to rob the cash drawer? She would gladly give him all the money she had if he would let her go. But how could she tell him this?

She tried talking around the hand that covered her mouth, but the words came out muffled and unrecognizable.

He tightened his grip on her. "I'll be taking the money you have here, but it's not enough. Your sister knows where there's more, and I aim to get it—in exchange for you."

His hand dug into the flesh on her cheeks, causing her pain. He let a mean-spirited chuckle escape his lips as he forced her down onto a chair. Keeping his hand over her mouth, he leaned down and wrapped the rope around her ankles, binding her tightly. Rachel watched with unseeing eyes as he masterfully bound her with only one hand.

He thinks my family has money to pay—a ransom? I'm being abducted! Gott, please make him let me go without hurting me!

After tying her ankles, he reached into his pocket and pulled out a roll of thick, gray tape. "I'm going to take my hand off your mouth for just a minute so I can put tape across your mouth. If you scream, I'm gonna have to hurt you. Do you understand that?"

Rachel nodded her head. He slowly moved in front of her, his head down. He was wearing Plain clothes and a straw hat. But no Amish man would do harm to another like this.

"Who are you? And what do you want?" Rachel managed before he clamped his hand back onto her mouth.

Slowly lifting his head, she looked into his bloodshot eyes. Either he was *not* Amish, or he wasn't from around here.

"I'm here for my million dollars and I ain't leaving until I get my money. You're my insurance policy. Now shut up or I'll have to get out my gun. I know you don't want that." He gritted deeply stained teeth at her.

Rachel shook her head, her breath heaving through the fingers that clenched her mouth. Tears had blurred her vision, but there was something almost familiar about this *mann* that threatened her.

Rachel watched in horror as he stretched out a piece of tape from the roll. The screeching sound it made sent shivers through her.

"Please don't put that on my mouth. I won't be able to breathe. I promise I'll be quiet." Rachel begged.

The stranger grinned, showing his yellowed teeth. "That's what they all say."

Rachel's heart slammed against her chest wall. Had he done this before? Did he let them go, or did they *die?* It was too scary to think about.

There has to be a way out of this.

He stretched the tape across her face and smoothed it over her mouth with his hand. There was no one around even if she *could* scream, and no one was expecting her home until later. She tried not to cry anymore, knowing her nose was already too stuffed up to breathe well. It was a task to pull air in and out of her swollen nostrils, and she felt dizzy from the effort.

The stranger left her in the chair while he went to the front of the bakery. If she stood up, would she make it to the back door and into her buggy before he could get back? But how would she drive? Before she had any more time to think about it, he was back and looking her right in the eye.

Rachel blurred her vision, not wanting to see the evil in his eyes. He yanked her to her feet, pulling her close to him. "Let's go. It's gonna take forever to get back into town with that horse of yours."

That was his plan? To abduct her using her own buggy? No wonder he wore Plain clothes. It was a disguise so no one would notice him even if they rode right past him.

He turned her around to face him. "I don't want you to make any noise when we leave here or I'll have to get out my gun."

Rachel's eyes bulged as she looked at him closely for the first time. The long scar on his cheek was familiar. With a rush of thought, she remembered where she'd seen this man before, and it made her sick to her stomach. She had been so foolish, so trusting. This man, her abductor, had been in the bakery last month—with Levi.

Chapter 2

One month earlier...

Rachel had just put the last loaves of bread into the oven when she heard the jingling of the bells on the front door to the bakery.

It's a little early for a customer.

As she rounded the corner, her heart fluttered at the sight of the handsome stranger. Though Amish, she could tell he wasn't from her community, even if she had known him.

He smiled brightly, exposing dimples in each cheek. He tipped his black hat, leaving it securely on his head that was full of thick, blond hair.

"Gudemariye. Wie gehts?" he almost seemed to struggle with the words, but Rachel was too busy admiring his amber eyes that seemed to twinkle when he smiled. His Plain suit was a little too big for him, but she'd seen that many times in the community when an older sibling passed on clothing to the younger ones. She guessed him to be around eighteen years old.

He held out a soft hand to Rachel and she took it. Most Amish men had calloused hands by the time they reached the age of five. Why didn't he?

"I'm Levi Schrock. I'm looking for Hiram Miller's place."

"You came to the right place. I'm Rachel, and he's *mei grossdaddi*. Are you the one he hired to help bring in the harvest?"

"Jah," he said.

Rachel tipped her head to one side. "He isn't expecting you for at least another month."

"Jah, mei daed sent me a little early, hoping I could earn some extra money. It's just the two of us, and we rent a little place in town with no land. I will send most of my

earnings back home to Ohio to cover the rent. He's getting on in years and can no longer work."

Again, his accent was off, and his story sounded almost rehearsed. Rachel ignored the gentle nagging in the back of her mind. He was handsome, and a stranger. What more could a girl who was bored with the locals ask for?

"I'm sorry to hear that. I'm sure there will be plenty of work to keep you busy until the harvest. You aren't far from his farm. If you go out of the bakery and walk across the road and down to the left, you will reach his farm."

For a fleeting moment, she thought she'd seen him in the bakery a few days before, but the man she'd seen had not been Amish.

Rachel sized him up. "You look familiar. Have I seen you in here before?"

"*Nee,* this is my first trip to your community."

Levi shifted the knapsack hanging from his shoulder, and pointed his nose toward the display case behind Rachel. "How about I get some of those cookies before I go? I could use something sweet."

He winked and Rachel blushed. She'd never been winked at before, but the Amish boys in the area weren't real big on flirting. She moved behind the counter and opened the display case.

She smiled at Levi. "How many would you like?"

"If they're half as sweet as you, Rachel, you better give me only a few. A fella can only handle so much sweet stuff until he gets addicted and wants more."

"I've been told my cookies are very addictive, so you come back for more any time you like."

Rachel was surprised by her own forwardness, but Levi didn't seem to mind. His smile told her he had enjoyed every flirtatious word.

Chapter 3

Rachel watched the handsome stranger walk out the door of the bakery and head in the direction she had sent him. Part of her wanted to close the bakery and go with him. She would definitely be taking an extra loaf of bread to her grandfather's house after work, and hopefully she would get an invite to have dinner with him, Nettie, and Levi.

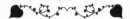

When he was clearly out of view of the bakery, Levi pulled a cell phone out of his knapsack to call Bruce, his *dad*. He knew Bruce would be pleased that he'd already made fast friends with Rachel Yoder. He wouldn't dare tell Bruce he'd found her attractive and would enjoy dating her without the deceit. If this job was going to be as easy as he now thought, he would be rid of his dad and all the abuse that came with him before too long. He would take his cut of the money Bruce promised him, and then he'd leave without looking back. The sooner he could get the information on the whereabouts of the money Uncle Eddie had stashed just before he died, the sooner he would be a free man. With his eighteenth birthday just around the corner, he was more eager than ever to pull off the last job he would ever do for his dad. He never liked the stealing or the lying, and very soon he wouldn't have to anymore.

Unlike Bruce, Levi had a conscience. That had to count for something, and he didn't plan on entering into adulthood following in his father's footsteps. At eighteen, he would no longer have to obey his dad, and he would be free to make his own choices…the choices of the righteous man he wanted more than anything to be.

Rachel looked at the clock for the hundredth time in the past hour. She'd been washing pans and bowls for the past forty-five minutes and hadn't had a single customer during that time. Tempted to lock the door and close for the day, Rachel forced herself to wash dishes until the last utensil was clean. After wiping down the surfaces, she hung up her apron, feeling a sense of accomplishment. She was almost too tired to pay a visit to her grandfather, but she was too eager to see Levi again to care.

Unable to wait any longer, Rachel locked the door to the bakery, two loaves of fresh bread tucked under her arm.

Heading toward her grandfather's farm, Rachel uttered a quick prayer that Levi was able to secure work the way she'd half-promised him he would. If he wasn't, and he'd had to leave, there was no telling if he'd return for a second trip later in the season. She didn't like the idea of not finding the handsome newcomer at the farm. But if he wasn't there, he'd be long-gone by this time, and she'd be lucky to ever lay eyes on him again.

Chapter 4

Nettie welcomed Rachel with a smile. "*Danki* for the bread. It will make a *gut* addition to the meal tonight. I was hoping to make something light this evening since it's so warm; now we can have cold meat sandwiches. Would you like to join us?"

"*Danki,* I'm very hungry after working all day. Where's *mei grossdaddi?*"

Nettie set the bread on the counter and began washing a few tomatoes. "He's in the barn with the new hired hand. He arrived early from Ohio hoping to find work sooner than the harvest. Hiram didn't waste any time putting him right to work."

Rachel was delighted to hear that Levi had indeed been hired on and would be spending the next few months in the community. She felt that would be plenty of time to get to know him better. Her heart fluttered at the possibility of courting Levi. Surely he wouldn't be here if he was betrothed back in his own community.

Nettie cut up lettuce and tomatoes for the sandwiches, while Rachel sliced cheese from the large block that her grandfather made. He sold the cheese to others in the community after curing it in the barn, but it was more of a hobby than a source of income, she thought.

"Go ahead and ring the bell. I'll finish putting out the pickled beets and cold potato salad I made earlier."

Suddenly feeling a little nervous, Rachel stepped outside and pulled the string, clanging the bell to alert her grandfather and Levi. She didn't stay outside to wait for them. Instead, she quickly returned to the kitchen to busy her hands with setting the table. Hopefully, they would take a few minutes to come in from the barn, allowing Rachel enough time to steady her nerves.

All too soon, Rachel heard the back door swing open, and the sound of male voices. She kept her back to them as she finished stirring up a pitcher of grape Kool-Aid.

She felt an arm go around her shoulder. "It's *gut* to see you, Rachel." Hiram said.

Rachel stopped what she was doing and hugged him back. "You smell like cheddar cheese, *grossdaddi.*"

"I've got two milk cows that give us more milk than we can possibly use. I'll be making some butter this week too, if you need some for the bakery."

"*Danki,* my supply is starting to run a little low."

Hiram chuckled. "I had a feeling it might be. Let's eat. I'm hungry as a horse."

Up until this point, Rachel had avoided seeing Levi, though she knew he was just a few feet behind her. Luckily, they sat very quickly and bowed their heads for the silent prayer. She hadn't dared look at him for fear her family would see the blush that already tried to creep up her neck.

Dear Gott, please keep my nerves steady, and don't let me make a dummkopf of myself in front of Levi. Oh, and please bless this food and my familye.

When she heard the clanging of silverware, Rachel lifted her eyes to Levi, who sat staring at her. Had he been watching her the whole time? She fidgeted a little in her chair until she noticed her grandfather slapping a hand on his shoulder.

"This is Levi Schrock. He'll be helping me until mid-October."

That long? That was nearly three months away. Rachel was pleased to hear it.

Levi felt funny being called by his friend's name from back in Ohio. When he'd stayed with the Schrock family over the previous summer while Bruce was in jail, he and Levi had become good friends. And now, here he was, using Levi's good name to deceive these people.

It's only for a little while so I can get away from Bruce. Then they will never see me again.

Levi nodded his head and smiled at Rachel, bringing heat to her cheeks. *"Jah,* we met this morning when I stopped at the bakery for directions."

Nettie nudged Rachel gently with her foot under the table, startling her. "Why didn't you tell me you already met him?"

Rachel's cheeks turned a deep shade of red at Nettie's question. What could she have said? That she'd met a really handsome, possible suitor, and she only came over to see *him?*

"I suppose it hadn't crossed my mind to mention it."

Nettie looked at her knowingly, leaving Rachel feeling as though she'd lied to the woman. In a way, she had lied by way of omission of information, but she was of the mindset that what they didn't know couldn't hurt *her.*

Hiram placed another slab of ham on his bread, making his sandwich almost too thick to bite into. "I'll be having Levi make deliveries for me to save time, so he'll bring the butter over to the bakery on Thursday. I think I'm going to like having a hired hand. We might just have to negotiate an extended stay for you, Levi. Already my mind is awhirl over everything from chopping wood and shoveling snow, to making candles and sheering the sheep. I don't know why I've been trying to do everything myself this year. Since Seth got married, I've been trying to shoulder all the work on my own." He slapped Levi on the shoulder. "Now I may not have to. We got more done today than I have in the last week."

Levi smiled, catching Rachel's eyes. She was happy to hear that it was working well for him to help—if it meant he might stay in the community. But then a thought hit her like a rock.

"What about your *daed,* Levi? Won't he miss you being gone all this time?"

How could he have a chance to miss me when he got himself a room in the motel in town so he could keep an eye on me until I get him the stolen money?

Levi shrugged. He shoved a forkful of potato salad into his mouth, keeping his eyes on his plate.

It was obvious to everyone at the table that Levi didn't want to answer that question. She knew firsthand that every family had its struggles, but Levi almost seemed like he was hiding something. Perhaps he was younger than she'd originally thought, and he'd run away from home. He hadn't mentioned his *mamm,* but spoke only of his *daed.* She noticed a sense of sadness about him that he was trying hard to cover. But his eyes gave him away; those sad, amber eyes.

Chapter 5

During the meal, Levi felt Rachel's eyes on him, but he tried to steer the conversation to his new duties at the Miller farm, hoping she wouldn't catch his mishaps. If he didn't start keeping track of his lies, he would blow his cover, and she would never trust him enough to confide in him. He also needed to keep her interest to allow him the opportunity to talk to her sister, Abby. Knowing Abby was married, he would not be able to talk to her unless in the company of Rachel, so she would be the perfect go-between. He hated the deception, especially since this family had already been so kind to him. And if he wasn't careful, he would end up falling for the beautiful Rachel, and that would interfere with his plan to be rid of his father once and for all.

The previous summer he'd spent at the Schrock farm had taught him a lot about the Amish culture. They were a kind and generous group of people, and he hated taking advantage of their pure goodness. He had learned that each community is different and has its own rules; however, one thing remained true in all of them—their kind and gentle nature. At the end of the summer, when Bruce had gotten out of jail, Levi hadn't wanted to leave the farm and return home.

His dad had been the one to suggest Levi pose as Amish to weave his way into their lives so he could get the information he needed to locate the stolen money. His dad had told him the money had sat long enough that the state of Ohio had probably forgotten all about it. He certainly hoped it was true since he didn't want to go to jail.

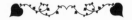

Rachel climbed reluctantly into her grandfather's buggy; she couldn't believe he'd suggested so casually that Levi drive her home. As she nestled in next to Levi, Rachel blushed at the closeness.

Levi picked up the reins with shaky hands.

"I'm not the best driver. I've only driven a few times last summer when I helped my cousins on their farm. Since *mei Daed* and I have lived in town most of my life, we don't even have a horse."

"I can teach you the way *mei Daed* taught me when I was just a wee little girl."

Rachel placed her hands over the top of Levi's hands, guiding the reins to maneuver the horse. It amazed her at how soft his hands were. She supposed living in town instead of on a working farm would do that to a man's hands. In time, she would see the callouses of a hard-working man—especially if he continued to work for her *grossdaddi*. Hiram Miller had worked hard all his life, and he expected the same from those around him. Rachel had always admired that about him, though she'd heard from her *mamm* and *Onkel* Seth that he could be quite stern.

As they let the mare trot down the main stretch of road past the bakery, Rachel let go of Levi's hands and allowed him control. "I think you're getting the hang of it. Will you be alright by yourself on the way back?"

Levi smiled at her. "I think I will. *Danki* for trusting me."

Rachel smiled. "If *mei grossdaddi* trusts you, then I do too."

Maybe this job will be easier than I thought. If she trusts me enough to drive her home, surely she will get her sister to trust me with the secret of where that money is hidden. The sooner I get it back to Bruce, the sooner I can get on with my life. All I want to do is finish this job for Bruce and get out of here before I become too attached to this beautiful girl.

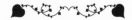

Rachel allowed herself to bump into Levi every time the buggy hit a rut in the shoulder of the road. She didn't mind the contact with the handsome stranger who intrigued her with every story he told about his life in Ohio. Though he was only making small-talk now, she picked up subtle traces of inconsistencies in his tales. Not that she doubted he was from Ohio, or that he lived in town with his *daed;* perhaps that was why he seemed more *Englisch* than Amish. She wondered if her grandfather had picked up the same clues in Levi's speech, or if he was so happy to have help that he didn't see past the strong pair of hands that eased his own workload.

"How long have you been without a *mamm?"*

Levi cleared his throat, pausing to choose his words carefully. "I honestly don't know. *Daed* told me a story, but I don't remember much about her. I haven't seen her since I was seven years old. She didn't live with us, but she visited. Then she stopped suddenly. I've not seen her since, and don't really remember her."

Rachel's heart thumped in her chest. She couldn't imagine not seeing her *mamm,* or knowing where she was. Her own sister had never seemed to display a void from losing her real father, but Levi held a cloud of sadness in his eyes when he spoke of his *mamm.* Was it possible that Abby felt the same at losing her *daed,* but pushed her feelings down? They'd never really talked about it. She knew he had been of undesirable character, but it was obvious that Levi's *mamm* was of questionable character as well.

"You should talk to my *schweschder.* She's had kind of the same problem in her life, except my *daed* became her *daed* when she was ten years old. I know it's too late for you to have a new *mamm,* but you both lost a parent around the same age. Maybe she could offer some advice on how she settled things in her heart."

Levi couldn't believe Rachel had just handed him the key to open the door of communication with her sister, Abby.

"*Jah,* it would be nice to speak to someone else who might understand what I've gone through. Losing a parent isn't easy, no matter what the circumstances. Did your *schweschder's daed* walk out on her too?"

"*Nee,* he died in a car accident. But he didn't know she was his *dochder.* They never knew each other.*"

Levi steered the buggy into the long drive leading to Rachel's house. "But if she never knew him, what was there for her to settle? How can you feel a loss for something you never had?"

Rachel scrunched her brow. "I'm not sure. I suppose you will have to ask her yourself. *Danki* for the ride. I hope I will see you again soon."

Levi smiled. "You can count on it."

Chapter 6

"Why are you telling complete strangers my personal business?"

Rachel looked at her sister across the counter of the bakery. Her arms were crossed over her chest and her eyes narrowed.

They exchanged Abby's order across the display case that was already emptying of the day's baking.

"He's not a complete stranger; he's living with Nettie and *Grossdaddi.*"

Abby rolled her eyes. "That's no testament of a *mann's* character. *Grossdaddi* would take in a dozen prisoners if he thought he could rehabilitate them. He told you he was from the community near where *mamm* and I used to live. How do we know that Eddie's friends aren't still out there somewhere hoping to collect on his debt? You know how quickly word gets around when people start wagging their tongues. If he wants to talk about loss in his life, that's one thing. But please don't talk about my past anymore. You know how hard *mamm* worked to keep all that a secret."

Rachel leaned across the counter. "Didn't her secrets almost destroy your chances of a normal life with Jonah?"

Abby scowled. "We are married now and that's all that matters. *Mamm* did what she thought she had to do in order to protect me. I know that now. I only hope that my connection with Eddie's *familye* hasn't jeopardized my future. I will always have that little bit of fear hanging over my head. Just be careful what you say to Levi. You never know what he could be putting in his letters back home."

Rachel agreed, though she didn't understand her sister's continued caution over the subject. Eddie had been gone since Abby was ten years old.

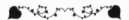

Hiram pulled the bucket up from the well and splashed the earth-cooled water on his face. He had gotten too warm again and run out of energy. His back ached, and his joints stiffened. Levi was a hard worker, so why was he still pushing himself as though he were still a young man? The doctor had told him to take it easy, but he feared if he sat around he would feel useless. His sons had farms of their own and had no use with his. Who would even inherit his property when he was gone? Hiram shook the thought from his mind; he wasn't ready for God to take him yet. He was newly married, and it had made him young at heart again—hadn't it?

Feeling over-heated and sick from the heat of the sun burning his backside, Hiram stumbled over to the large oak tree in the yard and collapsed at the base.

Dear Gott, please don't make my Nettie a widow so soon.

Levi hadn't noticed when Hiram disappeared from the field where they'd been turning up the soil between rows of vegetables. When he saw his boss fall against the tree in the yard, he took off running toward him. When he reached the tree, he leaned against it, trying to catch his breath.

"Are you hurt?"

Hiram looked up at him with weak eyes that squinted against the bright afternoon sun. "I think the heat got to me. Let me rest a spell, and I'll be back in the field to help you."

Levi crouched down and leaned on his haunches. "Your entire shirt is soaked with sweat, and your face is beet-red."

Hiram waved him off with his hand. "I spilled water down the front of me when I pulled the bucket from the well. I'm probably just sunburned. I should be alright in a few minutes."

Levi wasn't convinced. "You sound out of breath. Should I get a doctor?"

Hiram tried to stand, but his legs were too shaky, and nausea consumed him. "Maybe you better go call Doctor Davis. The number is on the wall in the barn near the phone."

Levi didn't want to leave Hiram alone too long, so he ran to the barn as fast as he could.

Lord, please don't let my new boss die. Spare his life, and let the doctor get here in time.

Levi rushed back to Hiram after begging the doctor to hurry. "The doc said to get you out of the heat. Do you think you can walk if I help you?"

Hiram nodded.

"C'mon, let's get you inside."

Levi bent down and tucked his arm under Hiram's and helped him to his feet. Steadying him, Levi walked slowly to get him in through the kitchen door and set him down at the table. Hearing the commotion, Nettie rushed into the room.

"What happened?" She held a hand to her throat, her face ashen.

Levi began to unlace Hiram's work boots. "He got overheated. The doc said to get him inside and take his shoes off to cool him down. Could you bring him a drink of water? Doc said only tap water—nothing cold or it could throw him into shock."

Nettie had already gotten a glass out of the cupboard before he finished his sentence.

"The doc said he'd be here in a few minutes."

When he finished with Hiram's shoes and socks, Levi pulled his hat off his head and fanned Hiram's face with it.

Hiram snatched the hat from Levi's hand playfully. "Don't fuss over me. I'll be fine as long as I sit here for a minute and catch my breath."

Nettie placed the glass of water in her husband's hand. "Don't be so stubborn, old *mann;* the boy was only doing what Doctor Davis told him to do. Now drink up."

Levi sat across from Hiram, feeling the danger of what could have happened to his boss if he hadn't noticed Hiram had left the field when he did. If anything had happened to his boss, he'd be out of a job and would have to go back home empty-handed.

Shame on me for thinking such selfish thoughts. Lord, forgive me for being so selfish. Please make Hiram well again; not for my sake, but for Nettie's.

Chapter 7

Doctor Davis put away his stethoscope and stood at the foot of the bed of his most stubborn patient.

"You rest now, Hiram. Heat stroke is no laughing matter." He turned to Nettie. "Don't let him out of that bed tomorrow."

Nettie smirked. "Now, Doc, you know that's not as easy as it sounds."

Hiram adjusted the pillow beneath his head. "I have to tend to my corn field."

Levi stepped in from the doorway where he'd remained while the doctor did his examination. "I can finish it. You get your rest."

Hiram shook his head in discouragement. "You know I can't afford to pay you more wages for doing my half of the work."

Levi looked at him sternly. "I can only work as fast as *one* man and can only do the work of *one* man. You will pay me the wages we already agreed upon; you can help when you're feeling better, or whenever the doc gives you the *okay*."

Hiram looked at Levi. He was an honest, hard-working young man, but for the first time, Hiram noticed Levi spoke like an *Englischer*.

Levi picked up the cell phone from the solar-powered charger he'd put in the window of his room at the Miller's house. Bruce had sent him several text messages asking for a progress report. He was tempted to ignore the messages, but he knew Bruce would come looking for him if he didn't stave him off with some sort of news. But what could he say without hurting Rachel or her family, and yet give his dad a sense of satisfaction that this trip was producing the results he'd sought?

"I got the job. Will meet the whole family at dinner on Saturday. Will know more then."

Levi hit *send* and turned off the phone before he could get a response. Levi wasn't in the mood for a confrontational text war with Bruce, and when he received his son's vague text message, it was sure to make him angry. Feeling the exhaustion from the long day he'd had in the field, he collapsed onto the soft bed and pulled the feather pillow under his weary head.

Lord, if you see fit to get me out of this mess somehow, I pray that you will rescue me from my own poor judgment. Please forgive me for deceiving these nice people.

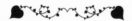

Because of Hiram's heat stroke, the butter did not get made the day before. Now it was up to Levi to take over. Sadly, he had to admit that he'd never churned butter before. After a few quick instructions from Hiram to get started, Levi headed for the root cellar where a ten-gallon bucket full of fresh cream waited for him. How hard could it be to slosh it around a churn for a few minutes? He'd seen Mrs. Schrock churning butter on the front porch of the farm where he'd worked the previous summer, so he felt he had a basic understanding of it from watching the process. So how hard could it be?

With a churn full of cold cream, Levi settled in on the front porch where he could enjoy the summer breeze while he worked on the first batch. After about twenty minutes, his arms started to ache. He opened the lid on the churn to see that the cream had begun to thicken and separate. Feeling confident the process was nearing its end, Levi pushed through the pain, taking very short breaks to rest his arms.

Hearing the screen door squeak, Levi looked up to see Hiram making his way toward him with two glasses of lemonade. He sat down in the chair beside Levi and offered him one of the glasses.

Levi took the glass and gulped the entire thing.

"*Danki*, that hit the spot."

Hiram cocked his brow. "I thought you could use a little break. How long have you been at it?"

Levi wiped sweat from his brow with the back of his hand. "Almost thirty minutes."

Hiram chuckled. "You're about halfway done. You want me to take a turn?"

Levi shook his head. "Doc said you were not to exert yourself. This is laborious work."

Hiram chuckle again. "Yes it is. It will give you some muscles."

Levi laughed. "I could stand to gain a bit of muscle."

"When you finish this part, I'll show you what the next step is."

Levi was grateful his boss was a patient man. He wished his own father could have been half as patient as Hiram, and a better example. Maybe then he wouldn't be here trying to deceive this man he admired. But maybe God wanted him here for a reason. Maybe he was meant to come here and learn to be a better man from this family. If anyone could teach him to be a better man, it was Hiram.

Then there was Rachel—beautiful Rachel, a girl he could see himself falling in love with. A girl he could see himself spending the rest of his life with. But who was he kidding? A girl like her would never want to be with him. Especially when she and her family discovered what kind of man he really was. He was a thief and a liar. Would they ever forgive him? Would God forgive him?

Chapter 8

By the time Levi finished straining and rinsing the last batch of butter, he wasn't sure his arms would ever work again. He had placed two pounds of the butter into wooden molds for the Millers to use; the rest was packed into plastic, reusable containers that would need to be delivered to the bakery immediately. Though Levi was much too tired to make the delivery, he was eager to see Rachel again.

He had never worked so hard in all his life. When he'd worked for the Schrock family the previous summer, they'd taken it easy on him, teasing him and saying that he was a soft *Englischer*. Today he didn't feel like that. Today, he felt he could pull his weight and more if needed, in order to prove his worth to his new employer—especially since Hiram believed him to be Amish. He had to put that *soft Englischer* behind him and tough it out. He knew the Amish worked hard, and he would pull his weight even if every muscle in his body protested.

Filling the back of the buggy with the tubs of butter, Levi set off on the short journey to the bakery before Rachel closed for the day. Hiram had told him that she would need the butter when she opened in the morning, and he didn't want to let either of them down. Steering the buggy down the main road, Levi remembered the softness of Rachel's hands when she'd wrapped them around his the other day. Using the method to give him a driving lesson had tickled his senses in a way no other female had ever come close to in his life. Driving was really a matter of a few simple commands, Levi had discovered, but the horse was so well-trained, the buggy practically drove itself. It still made him tingle at the thought of her hands resting on his.

When he pulled into the back of the bakery, he wasn't sure if he should go around to the front the way her customers did, or if he should risk frightening her by going in the back door. Stepping down, his body stiffened under the strain he'd put on his muscles. Moving was slow, and everything ached. Leaving the butter in the buggy, he decided it was best to go through the front door so he wouldn't startle her.

The jingling of the bells on the door rang in his ears as he opened the door, the strong smell of sweet baked goods filling the air. Levi's stomach gave a rumble, reminding him that he'd not eaten for many hours. He chuckled to himself knowing that hard work had made him that hungry.

Rachel was behind the counter and looked beyond the customer she was helping to flash Levi a smile. In that short moment of eye-contact with him, she'd thought he looked somehow different than he'd looked the day before. How had one day managed to change him? Truth be told, he looked more Amish than he had the first day she'd met him. Was it possible that living in the city instead of a farm had robbed him of his true heritage? Rachel could sense his eyes on her as she finished with the last customer for the day.

Levi stepped forward and managed a weak smile. "I have your butter in the back of Hiram's buggy. Shall I bring it in through the back door?"

Rachel nodded, noticing how worn out he looked. Her eyes followed him as he walked slowly out the door, his gait was that of a much older man. She giggled, knowing he was probably sore from churning the butter. She walked through the bakery and unlocked the back door, swinging it open for him.

She could see he was moving slowly, so she went to the buggy to help bring in the butter. Looking in the back at all the tubs, she gasped.

"You and *mei grossdaddi* have been hard at work today."

Levi cleared his throat. "Hiram suffered from a bit of heat-stroke yesterday when we were working in the fields. The doc told him to rest for the next few days and he'll be good as new."

"Did you churn all this butter by yourself?"

Levi looked at her with tired eyes.

"Yep—er—*jah,*" he said.

Rachel ignored his change in speech. She could see why he walked like he had been out plowing all day.

"I would not have been able to churn that much butter in one day."

Levi looked at her with one raised eyebrow and a crooked smile that she thought made him look very handsome. "It was the first time I'd ever churned butter before. Is it supposed to take that long?"

Rachel giggled. "*Jah,* it does." She opened one of the containers and peeked inside. "It looks and smells heavenly, so you must have done it right. *Danki,* you did a *gut* thing helping *mei grossdaddi.* May I ride back with you so I can check on him?"

"Of course you can," Levi managed.

Looking into her hazel eyes made Levi want to be a better man. If he could, and she would accept him, he would become Amish for her. He admired the closeness of her family and the unconditional love they all seemed to have for others. Was he capable of such love? He thought it was possible, especially with someone like Rachel to love him in return. Her lifestyle was something he'd craved ever since he left the Schrock farm at the end of the previous summer. He'd learned so much from the family—even how to pray. But when he'd returned home to his dad, his life was once again filled with hatred and despair to the point he'd made a promise to himself to find a way out. He would finish this job for Bruce, and then he would be free to love and be loved the way God wanted him to.

Chapter 9

Levi lay awake on top of the handmade quilt in his room at the Miller's house. He'd turned off the cell phone without checking the messages from Bruce. He was certain they were full of venom as usual, but tonight he didn't want to think about anything except Rachel. He would deal with his dad tomorrow morning when he went into town to give him most of his first week of pay. Levi wasn't looking forward to seeing the man, and all he wanted to do now was have a pleasant night of sleep after such a full day of hard work. His muscles ached more than they ever had before, but all he could think about was wrapping his tired and worn-out arms around Rachel.

A warm breeze fluttered the sheer curtains at the open window. It reminded him of the way Rachel's hair had danced across the side of her face when he drove her home in the open buggy. Hiram had offered the smaller buggy to save the tired horse from too much of a workout at the end of a long day. Levi thought it resembled the courting buggies he'd seen while staying with the Schrock's. Remembering how badly he'd felt at the end of the summer when Bruce got out of jail and he had to return to the careless ways of his father, he was grateful to be once again among the Amish and their gentle ways. If he could, he would stay here for the rest of his life. But even he knew that wasn't a realistic thought.

Levi rolled over toward the window, listening to the crickets and watching fireflies glow along the grass down below. His life had never been better than it was when he was among the Amish. Was it possible that he could take his share of the lost money and buy himself some land here and continue to live among the Amish? What would happen when they discovered he wasn't Amish? Would they shun him? If he was careful, maybe they would never know.

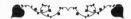

After the morning chores, Levi harnessed the small buggy and headed into town. He'd asked Hiram before he took the job if it would be okay for him to take his wages to the post office at the end of each week, and he'd consented after making a comment about how pleased he was that Levi was responsible enough to take care of his elderly father. If Hiram had known that he was taking the money to a greedy *Englischer,* he might not have been so impressed with him. Bruce wasn't so old that he couldn't earn an honest wage, but he had led a hard life being in and out of jail over the years and leaving his only son to fend for himself. Levi hadn't even stayed in school, and his peers were about to graduate high school without him.

Maybe I fit in here in more ways than one. The Amish rarely go to school past the eighth grade. At least none of them would ever call me dumb like my so-called friends did.

When he steered the horse onto the main road in town, his heart rate went into double-time as the small motel came into view at the end of the strip. This would be the first time he'd seen Bruce since he'd gone to live at the Miller's house, and he wasn't looking forward to seeing him.

No sooner did he pull the horse up in front of room 217, than Bruce came staggering out the door. He smelled of tobacco and whiskey, and looked like he was in need of a good bath. His peppered gray hair stood up on one end, and his clothing looked as if he'd slept in it.

Bruce rested his arm across the buggy and leaned in toward his son. "Well look at you, Blake. I almost didn't recognize my own boy in that get-up. You look like a real Amish."

"Be quiet or someone will hear you. My name is Levi, and you better remember that or you will blow our cover."

Bruce grabbed his son by the collar and pulled him close. "And you better remember to respect me, Boy, or you won't like what will happen to you."

Levi cringed under his dad's threat. The sour smell of whiskey on the man's breath made him sick to his stomach, and his heart raced remembering many such similar confrontations that didn't end well. He was too old to allow this man to bully him, but Bruce had turned him into a coward who cringed at the rise of his dad's voice alone.

Bruce tightened his grip on Levi's shirt. "You got some money for me, Boy?"

Levi jerked from Bruce's grasp and reached into his shirt pocket. He pulled out the bills and handed them to his father.

Bruce snatched them out of his hand and examined them momentarily. "Is this all that Amish farmer is paying you? You're not holding out on me are you, Boy?"

Levi gulped. Bruce would know if he was lying to him, but he needed to keep a little bit of money to himself so he could buy a few necessities. He couldn't let Hiram pay him wages and take care of his every need on top of that.

He took a step back. "I kept a few dollars for myself so I could buy a bottle of aspirin and a tube of toothpaste. They're working me pretty hard and I get sore."

Bruce shook the money at his son. "You're young. You'll bounce back without aspirin. This is barely enough to cover my expenses here. What am I supposed to use to buy food? I gotta eat. I bet those Amish folks are feeding you real good. Meanwhile, your old man is sitting here starving."

Levi wanted to yell at his dad. Tell him to stop wasting his money on whiskey and cigarettes, and to put in an honest day's work. But anything he could have said would have fallen on deaf ears. They'd argued it over many times before, and the outcome was always the same. He wouldn't give Bruce the opportunity to give him a sound lashing out here on the street. He hopped in the buggy and flicked the reins on the backside of the mare, pulling back a little to the left to get her to back up. Levi wished he'd driven a car to the motel so his get-away would be faster, but he'd managed to send a clear message to Bruce. All he wanted to do was leave this life behind and truly be Levi Schrock; he no longer wanted to be Blake Monroe.

If only it was that easy.

Chapter 10

When Levi returned to the Miller farm, Hiram was waiting for him in the barn.

"I decided I needed to work with you today since we will end our work day early to have a meal with my *dochder* and her *familye*. I was a little curious as to why you aren't doing things traditionally. I know each community does things a little differently, but some of the things you do seem a little off balance."

Levi's heart beat faster. Had he been found out before he was able to get any information for Bruce regarding the whereabouts of the money?

Think, Blake! How would Levi answer such a question?

"I've lived in town with my *daed* all my life. I only learned most of what I know from being around my cousins on their farm. Last summer, when my cousin broke his leg, I stayed with them and stepped in to do his chores. It wasn't easy since I'd never lived on a farm before. I'm sorry if I'm doing some of it wrong, but I've had very little instruction and had to learn most of it on my own. Since my *aenti* is a widow, my *onkel* wasn't there to work with me. Please show me what it is I've done wrong. I'd like to make it right."

Hiram put his hand to his beard and gave it a tug. There was something not quite right about Levi's story. He hated the idea of checking up on him, but perhaps a letter to the Bishop in Ohio was in order. He would send the letter as soon as possible and make sure there was not something that Levi was trying to hide. If he was hiding from an offense in his own community, he would not find refuge here. Bishop Troyer, though very lenient, would hold him accountable for whatever it was that Levi was hiding. Hiram hoped it was just his imagination and that there was nothing Levi was running from. It wasn't just his language, but his lack of skills over simple chores that made Hiram suspicious of him. As an Elder of the community, he had a duty to make sure Levi's story checked out.

"Why don't we start with you putting things back where you found them? Since you're obviously not used to working on a farm, I'll tell you that being organized is the best way to save time. I appreciate you making the butter in my absence yesterday, but now I can't even find the churn."

Levi gulped. "I left it on the side of the barn where I rinsed it off. I left it to dry and forgot to put it away. I'm sorry."

Hiram held up the milking stool and showed Levi its broken leg. "You left this in the stall after milking and she trampled it. I had to fix the leg before the morning milking. You must be more responsible, Levi."

"I will, Sir. I give you my word."

Hiram already thought Levi was a hard worker and admired his polite manners. But he couldn't shake the look on the young man's face when he'd talked to him just now. He could see fear in Levi's eyes. He had to wonder if he'd suffered a few too many lashings growing up. The sadness in his expression when he thought no one was looking was almost haunting.

Instructing Levi on the proper way to clean the horse stalls was the first priority on Hiram's list. Each taking a stall, Hiram gave Levi detailed instructions, which he followed to the letter. It did his heart good to see how dedicated the young man was. He certainly earned every penny of his wages. But there was still something not quite right about his young hired hand. If only Hiram could narrow it down.

Levi worked silently beside his boss. He knew the more he spoke, the more opportunity that left for him to make a mistake and say the wrong thing. He was already worried that Hiram suspected he was an imposter. Why had he thought he could pull off such a scam? Surely the Amish can recognize one of their own. He'd heard stories of people trying to hide among the Amish when they were in some sort of trouble, but he'd never heard of the outcome. Had it ever been successfully done? With few phones in the community and no internet access, how would they ever find out he was an impostor? Unless he made a mistake big enough to cause them alarm, he didn't see any reason his plan couldn't work. He'd already managed to fool them. He would work hard, keep his mouth shut as much as possible, and his ears open for any clues to the whereabouts of the money. The money that would free him from all of his problems.

Chapter 11

Levi was exhausted, and no longer feeling up to having dinner with Hiram's family. But knowing Rachel would be there made him eager to wash his face and put on a clean shirt and trousers. Knowing it might afford him the opportunity to talk to Abby made him both apprehensive *and* eager. He was all for getting the information he needed so he could get Bruce off his back once and for all. The sooner he could find out what Abby knew about the money, the sooner he could be rid of Bruce.

Levi paused, reflecting on the simplicity of the room he'd been staying in. No place had ever felt more like home to him. Never before had so much been at stake as it was now. His entire future was riding on this one piece of information. If he couldn't get it, he had no idea what his future would hold. He hated the thought of following in his father's path of petty crime. He wanted freedom—from a future life filled with sorrow, and freedom from Bruce. He could not let his fear get in the way of what he had to do. He would be bold and get answers, even if it caused suspicion.

Hiram called from the base of the stairs, asking if he was ready to go. Nettie had made a casserole to take with them. The smell filled the house, making Levi's stomach growl with anticipation. He'd worked so hard the past few days, he was hungry constantly.

Fresh air and hard work will do that.

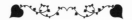

The drive to the Yoder farm was pleasant and scenic, as was all the area. He loved the sounds of cows and other animals from neighboring farms, chicken's clucking filling in the silence of the ride. It would have seemed awkward to ride in the back of the buggy, except that he enjoyed the secure, family feeling it gave him. He wished he could have been raised in such a serene place, but his reality was far from this. People had told him the Amish were a backward people, slow in everything they did. He'd seen the opposite since he arrived a week ago. They didn't have modern conveniences, but their lifestyle was anything but slow. Everything they did had a purpose: to serve their families and the community. If Levi could have his way, he would never leave.

When the buggy stopped, Levi jumped out of the back and assisted Nettie with her casserole. Rachel stood on the front porch wiping her brow with a tea-towel. She leaned against the rail and waved to everyone, sending a smile in Levi's direction. His heart sped up as he took in the wraparound porch with hand-carved scrollwork in the corners of the posts. Tall, grassy plants bordered the porch, purple flowers shooting up between the blades and thick stems.

Levi watched Rachel hug Hiram and Nettie while he lingered in the yard near the buggy. He listened to the pleasant exchange of words between family members, wishing he'd had such a loving family. Levi had known of his dad's half-sister, but she'd warned Bruce to stay away because of his criminal nature. His dad's only brother, Eddie, had been dead since Levi was too little to remember him well. He'd missed out on having cousins and family the way most kids had. But here he was about to enter into a house where his cousin Abby was, and all he could see was Rachel.

As Hiram and Nettie slowly made their way inside the house, Rachel looked up, flashed another smile, and waved her hand for Levi to go inside with her.

"*Kume,* everyone is hungry."

Everyone?

Levi looked behind him at the line of buggies filling the yard. Why hadn't he seen them before? Her entire extended family must be here for the meal. How many were there? Would he be able to get lost in the mix, or would he stand out as the one who didn't belong? Was it too late to back out?

Rachel seemed to sense his hesitation. "You will fit in with us just fine. We are easy to get along with. Just be yourself."

That's the last thing I can be.

He was having a tough enough time walking in there as Levi Schrock, but he could never walk in there as Blake Monroe. They would *never* accept him. He was not like them. He didn't have the support of a family to build him up. He only had Bruce, who took every opportunity to tear him down to his level. It was best if these people never saw who Blake Monroe really was—especially Rachel.

Her smile could melt all the ugliness off him. All the lies, the petty crimes and the deceit. All of it washed away from his thoughts with one smile from her. In her presence, he felt the courage to be something better than he'd been his entire life. The man he was raised to be was not the man he wished to be. He wanted to be a man of honor—a man worthy of Rachel's love. But she did not know the real him, and if he could help it, she never would. If she did, she would surely turn her back on him.

Levi hesitated. "That's a lot of folks to meet all at once. I'm not sure I can go in there."

Rachel hooked her arm in his, sending shivers through him.

"*Mei familye* will be *gut* to you."

Levi swallowed a lump in his throat. "They already have. I don't deserve to be accepted like I'm a member of your family. I don't belong here."

He was practically blowing his cover, but his conscience would not allow him to deceive Hiram or Rachel anymore. In the week since he'd arrived, he'd felt more love and acceptance than he'd had his entire life. It was not something he'd earned, and he'd had a sudden revelation that maybe it was time to come clean with the truth.

Chapter 12

The screen door squeaked open and out came a woman who was slightly older than Rachel. She and Rachel had the same kind eyes, but there was something even more familiar in the way she looked. Levi thought she looked a little like *him*.

"There you are. *Mamm* is looking for you."

Rachel smiled at the woman. "Abby, this is Levi. He's the one I told you about. He's visiting from Ohio, near where you grew up."

So this was his cousin. No wonder she looked like him. Did either of them see the resemblance?

Levi managed a nervous smile. "It's nice to meet you."

Rachel turned to her sister. "I'll go see what *mamm* wants. Will you please convince Levi to go inside? He's nervous about being around everyone."

Abby sat in one of the rocking chairs on the porch and invited Levi to take the rocker next to hers.

"No one in there is going to bite you! Surely you're used to being around a lot of *familye*."

"*N-nee*. My *d-daed* and I live in town and we don't see many others. We don't even have a buggy."

Levi tried to calm himself, hoping she wouldn't notice him stumbling over the Amish words.

"A big *familye* is nothing to be afraid of. In fact, sometimes there are so many of them you get lost and no one knows you're there unless you talk to them. Your *daed* is in Ohio alone?"

"*J-jah*. He hasn't been able to work for many years. He hurt his back. We've lived in town in a little rental house most of my life. I'll be sending most of my wages to him each week so he can pay the rent."

"Do you get help from the community?"

Levi thought about the things Bruce often *borrowed* from others in town. "*Jah*, sometimes."

Levi tried to change the subject. "Rachel tells me you lived in Barlow."

"*Jah.* Is that where you're from?"

"I live in Newport, along the Ohio River."

Abby wasn't sure what to think of him. "That's a long way to travel to look for work."

"I saw the advertisement in *The Budget.*"

Bruce had told him to look in the paper on the off-chance that there was a *Help Wanted* section, and to his surprise, this opportunity seemed to fall right into their laps.

Abby wasn't certain what it was about Levi, but she didn't trust him. "Normally *Englischers* answer those advertisements."

Levi smiled nervously. "The only *Englischer* I'm familiar with in those parts is Eddie Monroe."

Abby nearly choked on her own spit.

"He's famous in that area. There's claims that he buried a million dollars near the Ohio River. A lot of people have tried to find the money, but rumor has it he left a map to his only child."

Abby could feel the blood draining from her face. *She* was Eddie Monroe's only child—at least that's what she thought. But she didn't have any map leading her to a million dollars.

Levi hadn't missed the ashen look that crossed Abby's face at the mention of the map. Did she have it? Would she tell him even if she did?

"I've never heard such a tale. I lived there until I was ten years old and then again for a short time before I got married. I never once heard anything about that."

Levi smirked knowingly. "Maybe living in town has its advantages. You might not have heard it if you lived in the community away from the talk around town."

Abby shook her head. "*Nee,* I lived in town. I worked at *The Brick Oven* bakery. Surely I would have heard such a tale from one of the customers there. That's quite a wild notion. A million dollars is a lot of money. Why would the man have hidden the money instead of giving it to his daughter?"

Abby knew better than to open old wounds, but her curiosity was too strong to ignore.

Levi looked off in the distance somewhere in the yard, and focused on the line of family buggies that reminded him of why he was here. "They say he died just after he stole the money. And no one knows where his daughter is."

Abby gasped.

Eddie stole a million dollars and left her a map? Eddie's sister knew where she was. Her *aenti* had given her a book, *The Velveteen Rabbit,* that Eddie had with him the day he died. She'd received no map, and neither had her mother. The day he died they set in motion their plan to move back to the Amish community. Neither of them had attended Eddie's funeral. If anyone would know about the map, it would be his sister, wouldn't she? That is, if such a map even existed.

Abby giggled nervously. "That's quite a wild story you tell. Sorry I can't help you. I'd never heard such a wild tale before. I'd have remembered it if I'd heard something that outrageous."

Levi wondered why she was rambling. Did she know something? It was obvious by her tone and the way she fidgeted in her chair that she knew something. Would he get another chance to talk to her in order to gain her trust? Opportunities did not come along this easily. He figured he better take advantage of the fact she was talking and the conversation was already open to the subject. He needed information, and he needed it fast or he couldn't trust Bruce not to take matters into his own hands. He feared a visit from his dad. Bruce would force him to point out where Abby lived so he could search her house. He didn't trust the man not to hurt anyone that got in his way. The way he saw it, he had two choices. Press her for information and cause her to become suspicious; or he could let the matter drop and take his chances with Bruce.

Chapter 13

It was Rachel who made the decision for him when she poked her head out the screen door. "Are the two of you going to sit out here and gossip all night, or are you going to come in and join the *familye* for the meal?"

Her presence seemed to startle Abby, who hadn't said a word for several minutes. She stood up after shaking her head and walked into the house without saying a word.

Rachel turned to Levi. "What did you say to her? She seems a little rattled."

Levi wasn't sure if he should answer, but he knew she would probably find out anyway. Sisters confide in each other, don't they?

"I was telling her a story about a man and his stolen million dollars, and the map he left to his daughter. The guy is famous where I live. People are always caught digging around the Ohio River near my home and they get arrested for looking for the money. It's been hidden away almost as long as I've been alive, and not even the police can find it. Rumors have it that the money never existed, but that doesn't stop people from trying to find it."

Rachel leered at him. "Have *you* looked for the money?"

Levi wasn't expecting that question, and it caused his heart to thump.

"Of course not. I don't want that money, or anything it represents. It's stolen."

That part was now true. He knew how much that money had changed Bruce, and how bitter it had made him that his own brother had not told him where he hid the money before he died. That money was stolen and had been a source of pain throughout nearly his entire life. He no longer wanted anything to do with that money, even if it meant he would be poor his entire adulthood. He would not accept stolen money from Bruce, and he would never steal for him again. Since he'd been on the Miller farm, he'd learned the value of a hard day's work, and the wages he earned made him proud. Being here made him realize that he didn't need money or material possessions to be happy.

Rachel smiled and took his hand, leading him inside the house. Levi's heart did a somersault. Having her hand in his was all the confirmation he needed that it was time to turn his life around. Suddenly, he no longer cared about getting information out of Abby about the money. If he had anything to do with it, he would make sure Bruce would never lay eyes on that money. If he did manage to find the map, Bruce would have to get it without him.

Lord help me, I think I'm falling in love with Rachel.

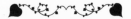

Dinner went better than Levi could have hoped for. Aside from a few odd looks from Hiram, Levi felt very comfortable with the extended family. They accepted him, and it felt good to be accepted for a change. He'd spent most of his life on the outside looking in at other families, and even envying them. But now, he almost felt like a part of this family. He listened to one story after another of good times they'd all shared, and he didn't feel left out even once. At the conclusion of the meal, the men went out into the barn while the women cleaned up the dishes. The men talked about their crops and horses and the proper style of suspender the Bishop had approved. Levi had never been happier to talk about so much *nothing* in all his life.

When they returned to the Miller farm, Levi rushed to complete the evening chores so he could sneak out and meet up with Rachel. She had asked him if he would meet her at the end of the dock at the B&B, which was the halfway point between them. Levi knew from staying at the Schrock farm that the youth of the community would often sneak out late at night to meet with a potential crush. He was certainly hoping that Rachel's invitation meant she was interested in him. If not, he still intended to enjoy her company.

The crickets disguised his footfalls as he neared the dock where Rachel was waiting for him. The warm summer breeze ruffled little wisps of her hair that had come out of her *kapp*. He walked slowly to the end of the dock, not wanting to disturb her. His hands felt sweaty, and he mentally reminded himself to stay calm. He'd never really had time to consider dating before, especially since he had to drop out of school to take care of Bruce.

Rachel turned around, her face looking lovely with the pale moonlight shimmering against her dainty features. Levi didn't think he had ever seen a more lovely young woman than Rachel. She smiled briefly and invited him to sit next to her on the end of the dock.

Rachel let her bare feet swish and splash in the pond water. "You can take your shoes off and join me if you'd like."

Levi hoped his feet smelled okay as he started to remove his boots. Just in case, he plunked his bare feet into the water just as soon as the socks came off.

"Ahhh. The cool water feels good on such a warm night."

"Whatever you said to *mei schweschder,* Abby, really upset her. She pulled me aside after dinner and told me to stay away from you."

Levi's heart felt like it skipped a beat or two. "I didn't mean to upset her. I was just making conversation. I guess I should know better than to repeat gossip. Tell her I'm sorry."

Levi seriously regretted every word. Talk like that could blow his cover. But what did he really need his disguise for anymore? Would Hiram keep him on as a farm hand the way the Schrock's had? Probably not once he learned of Levi's deceit. What could he do? There was no taking it back now. He worried he would probably be asked to leave, and that was the last thing he wanted.

Rachel nudged him with her elbow and smiled.

"I'll tell her. But for the record, I have no intention of taking her advice where you're concerned."

Levi smiled. He would have never thought that sitting on the end of a dock with his feet dangling in the water and staring at a pretty girl could make him feel so happy.

Chapter 14

Rachel tossed about trying to sleep, but all she could do was think of Levi. She would have to be up in just a few short hours to open the bakery, but none of that mattered at the moment. She'd had to sneak into the house after spending a little too much time out on the dock talking with Levi. She was certain that Rose and Noah had seen them out on the dock from across the pond at his house, but she knew her friend would keep her secret.

As the night wore on, she'd hoped Levi might try to kiss her at the conclusion of their time together, but much to her disappointment, he hadn't.

From the way he'd spoken, she'd gathered he and his *daed* had not spent much time if any at all in their own community. She didn't blame him for the lack of knowledge about farming. From what she understood, the only time he'd spent on a farm and doing chores had been sparse visits with his cousin. He'd even admitted to her that the only times he'd gone to Sunday services at the church was with his cousin the previous summer. He'd confided in her that it had sparked an interest in knowing God more closely.

Rachel rolled over and stared out her window at the moon. It had seemed almost magical sitting under the moonlight with Levi. The thought of it made her giddy. Was it possible that she was falling in love with Levi? Certainly Abby would scold her for thinking such things. After all, she barely knew him. What she had learned about him as they'd conversed on the dock late last night had made her feel a lot of compassion for him. It seemed he'd led a pretty sheltered life away from the community and more among the *Englisch.* He seemed more worldly than most Amish boys her age, but it attracted her to him even more than she was willing to admit to herself. She'd considered spending time among the *Englisch* the way her sister and her *mamm* had at her same age, but maybe now she wouldn't have to. With Levi there, it seemed the *Englisch* had come directly to her through *him.*

Levi couldn't sleep even though he would have to be up in a few hours to milk the cows and do the morning chores which would begin his busy day. His mind wandered to Rachel. It seemed he couldn't keep his mind off her since he'd met her that very first time when he'd come into the bakery with Bruce. It had been Bruce's idea to check out the community and the surrounding area. He said he needed to know where everything was—just in case. In case of what, Levi had no idea, and he wasn't sure he even wanted to know. But he'd hoped it was for reasons of helping him to get to know everyone he needed to get information from.

Now that he had met most of Rachel's family, he felt worse about the deception and what he was doing. If he told Rachel the truth, would she forgive him for lying to her? He needed the work, and if her grandfather found out about his deception, he could be fired. Then he would have no choice but to return to a life of crime with Bruce. How could he be honest with her and still protect his own interests?

Lord, help me to be honest. Help me to give up my selfish ways and think of other's needs instead of my own.

A peaceful calm warmed him to his very core. Was that God telling him it would work out if he told her the truth? He *had* to tell her. His conscience was eating away at him. She'd asked him to meet her again the following night at the dock and he would have to find a way to tell her then. In the meantime, would he be able to tell Hiram? Admittedly, he was afraid of losing his job, but not having the respect of his employer would feel worse to him.

The light on his cell phone blinked. Why was Bruce messaging him at this late hour? Levi scrolled through the twenty-plus messages that ranged from *"I want an update."* to *"Where are you?"*, and everything in-between. The newest was a demand to answer him immediately.

Levi sent a return text asking him what the problem was. He was sure he already knew. Bruce was more than likely drunk and had decided to do some thinking before he passed out. The phone lit up indicating Bruce had answered.

Levi read the text message. *"I want my money NOW!"*

What could he say to defuse his drunken father, and calm him enough to keep him from coming into the community and causing trouble? Could he tell him that he spoke to Abby? Bruce was not that dumb—even when heavily intoxicated. He would want a solid answer and to know that progress was being made to locate the money he intended to claim as his own. Bruce had taught him to lie. Should he use that against the man, and lie to him now? Levi told himself that it was only to protect Rachel and her family, but even that would not make it right.

Lord, please forgive me for lying to this man who is my earthly father, but I can't let him hurt the people I have grown to love.

Before he lost his nerve, Levi's fingers began to roll over the keys to form a message to Bruce. He hoped it would be enough to stave him off while giving him the illusion that he had a handle on the situation. He pushed *send* on his final text. *"I am very close to getting to the truth."*

Chapter 15

After a fairly sleepless night, Levi rose from the bed reluctantly so he could begin his day. The sun was just making its way over the edge of the horizon, boasting beautiful crimson, amber, and violet highlights across the sparse clouds gathered there. Chickens rallied in the yard for their feed, the roosters crowing relentlessly.

I thought you were only supposed to crow once when the sun came up? You haven't shut up for the past twenty minutes!

Hiram hadn't yet made it to the barn, and Levi was content with the animals to keep him company. With Hiram here, he might be tempted to spill his guts about why he was here. The light of day had changed his mind about such foolish thoughts. He was prepared to continue the charade in order to keep the weekly wages flowing to Bruce. At least until he could think of a way out of this mess.

Once he reached the fields, he would be out there alone for the entire day. Hiram, according to Nettie, was still too tired to work in the hot sun. Although he felt bad for his boss, he was determined to keep clear from him as much as possible and do a thorough job to really earn his wages. Being only his second week at the Miller's, he was determined to prove his worth and keep his job—even if that meant lying to his own father. Meeting this family had already taught him the value of others. His loyalties were beginning to take root in this family, and he would not let them down.

The breeze rustled the corn stalks that had grown tall enough that Levi could barely see over the tops of them. This was the life he desired; there was no doubt about it. The hard work didn't bother him. He suddenly found joy in working for his meals. How would he be able to provide for himself once this job ended? He had to start thinking of his future. He didn't want to end up like Bruce. He hated the thought of leaving, but he couldn't go on deceiving the people of the community. Was it possible for him to convert? Did the Amish even allow such a thing?

The clanging of the Miller's dinner bell rang in Levi's ears. He looked up at the sun that was still low in the eastern sky. It wasn't close enough to noon for him to return for a meal. His heart pounded in his chest. Something was wrong! Levi took off running toward the house, not thinking of anything but his friends and their well-being.

When he cleared the rows of corn, all he could see was Nettie crouched on the ground near the back porch. She was hovering over Hiram, who lay lifeless in the dirt.

Levi skidded to a stop just short of them and collapsed next to his boss. "What happened? Did he have another spell?"

Nettie's face was flush and she didn't take her eyes off her husband. "I don't know. I found him out here when I came out to empty the mop-bucket."

Levi was relieved when he could see that Hiram was still breathing. "Did you call the doctor?"

Nettie shook her head. "I don't know how to use the phone in the barn."

Levi scrambled to his feet and ran to the barn. It was the second time in a week that he would make the call for his boss and friend.

After hanging up with Dr. Davis, Levi ran out to tell Nettie he was on his way. The relief in her eyes put a lump in his throat.

"Let's get him inside and see if we can get him to drink some water."

Nettie nodded, not looking up from her husband, whose head was nestled in her lap. He seemed to go in and out of consciousness, and that worried Levi. Putting a hand under Hiram's arm, he and Nettie helped the man inside the house like they had the previous week. Was this going to be a regular thing? Levi hoped not.

"Help me upstairs," Hiram mumbled.

Levi was happy to hear him speaking coherently, even if he didn't seem to have any strength whatsoever. Wrapping Hiram's arm around his shoulder, Levi hung onto his wrist for leverage, and put his other arm around the man's torso to keep him snug at his side for the trip up the stairs. Nettie stayed behind her husband to help steady him, making the short journey a little more manageable. Once inside the small room, Levi steered his boss toward the bed. He pivoted the man with one quick movement, putting him square in the middle of the bed. Nettie rushed to his head, resting it gently on his pillow and smoothing back his hair.

"He feels a little warm like he did last time. I'll get a cool cloth for his forehead."

Levi went to the window and pushed it open to bring in the breeze that had kept him cool out in the field all morning. Storm clouds were rolling in, and Levi was grateful. They could use some rain.

Since when do I care if it rains?

He looked over at his boss lying helplessly on his bed.

I care because this man has been so good to me. Lord, bring the rain for this man's vegetables that he grows to feed his family. Please bring healing to Hiram. He's an honorable man, and I can't bear to lose him.

Levi turned from the window, but looked back out toward the road when he heard the thunderous footfalls of a horse being pushed to its limits to get the doctor here quickly. Nettie rushed back into the room with a wet cloth and a glass of water for her husband.

Levi tipped his hat. "I'm going out to take care of the doc's horse. I'll be back when the he's had a chance to examine Hiram."

Nettie looked up briefly, sending a smile of thanks to him. Levi walked out of the room feeling he didn't deserve her trust.

Chapter 16

"Do you want me to take you home?" Levi asked. "It won't take long to hitch up the pony cart."

Rachel sighed. "I'd rather walk. Will you walk with me?"

Levi nodded. The rest of the family had left Hiram's home an hour before, but Rachel had stayed behind to wash dishes and straighten the kitchen for Nettie so she could remain at her husband's side.

During his exam, it had come out that Hiram had been suffering for more than a year with a heart condition that the doctor had under control with medication. But now, it seemed his current dose was failing him. Doctor Davis had some concern that Hiram had suffered a mild heart attack, but the stubborn man would not agree to a trip to the hospital. After an increase in his medication, he was already starting to regain his coloring. That didn't stop Levi from worrying about him.

After walking some distance in total silence except for the occasional crunch of a rock under foot, Rachel nudged Levi. "Why are you so quiet tonight? Last night I could barely get in a single word. Now, I think I could talk for an hour, and I fear you might not hear a word of it."

"I'm worried. I know I shouldn't be, but I can't help it."

Rachel cupped her arm in Levi's, sending a wave of heat coursing through him.

"I always find that if I'm worried about something, distraction always works."

She was right. He was currently so distracted by her arm being intertwined with his, he could barely think of anything else. It was comforting to have her so near him, and that was a feeling he didn't think he could ever live without. In the short time since he'd come to work for Hiram, he'd never felt more accepted than he did right now. Was it possible she would still like him even if she knew the truth? The Amish seemed to give their love unconditionally, and that confused him. He'd always had to earn any attention, good or bad, from Bruce. It usually came with a price.

The cricket's song filled the warm summer air, while the gentle breeze rustled the leaves on the trees that lined the road. This was the most peaceful Levi had felt his entire life. How could he give this up? How could he give up Rachel when his job here was done? The truth was; he didn't think he could, even if he wanted to.

"Do you allow outsiders into your community?"

Rachel looked at him briefly. "You mean *Englischers?*"

"*Jah.*"

She smiled warmly. "We have had a few *Englischers,* and even a few from other communities join us. Our Bishop is very lenient. Isn't yours?"

Levi cleared his throat. "I don't know that much about him. I only met him a few times when I attended services with my cousin. My *daed* isn't exactly a church-going man."

Rachel tightened her grip on his arm. "How sad for you. Has your *daed* turned his back on the church?"

Levi shrugged. "Somehow I doubt he was ever a believer. But I am. I'm very new to my faith, though."

Rachel kicked at rocks along the road. "I can't imagine my life without my faith."

Levi swallowed hard. "I feel the same way. I don't know how I managed my entire life without it."

Rachel giggled. It was one of the most pleasant sounds Levi had ever heard. He couldn't remember the last time he *really* laughed.

"Now that you have it, you will never be without it. *Gott* is never far from us unless we turn our backs on Him. What about your *mamm?*"

That wasn't a question Levi cared to address. How could he tell her his mother had been a prostitute and that his father had been her regular companion? The way his dad told the story, his mother had dropped him off on Bruce's doorstep two days after he'd been born, and then went back to her profession. She'd visited sparsely until he was about seven years old, but he didn't remember her—not that he cared to.

"I don't know where she is. According to my *daed,* she dropped me off after I was born and only saw me a handful of times. I don't know her."

Rachel slowed her steps as they neared her farm. "Perhaps that was the turning point for your *daed* that made him turn his back on God. Maybe it hurt him too deeply to trust anymore. Grief will make a person question everything."

Was Rachel correct? Had his father loved his mother so much that it changed him when she chose to return to a life of prostitution over staying with him and raising their child? Was it possible Bruce was a better man before she left him? Probably not if he was frequently visiting with a prostitute. Still, it made him wonder why Bruce had made the choice to care for him instead of getting rid of him like his own mother had. Why had he raised him so harshly? Was it possible his father blamed him for his mother leaving?

"I suppose anything is possible. He is a bitter man. Has been as long as I can remember."

Rachel let her arm slip until her fingers met his. She slowly intertwined her fingers in his, sending tingling jitters through him.

"I'm so sorry you missed out on having your *mamm* raise you."

Levi turned to face her. "Nettie is so kind to me; she makes me wonder what it would have been like to grow up with two parents instead of one."

"She has been very *gut* for *mei grossdaddi*. That's how I know he will fight his weakness—to stay with her. They haven't been together very long, and I know he is not yet ready to leave her."

Levi pushed down the lump in his throat. Where had all this emotion suddenly come from? If Bruce would ever catch him as close to tears as he was now, he'd take a switch to him. His dad had always told him that crying made him look weak. Right now, he felt pretty weak, but he welcomed the strength God seemed to be offering him at the moment.

Chapter 17

The rest of the week was very busy for Levi as he took over the entire workload of Hiram's farm by himself. Hiram's sons and grandsons had all offered to help, but he told them he had complete confidence in his hired hand. That confidence filled Levi with the courage to face every new experience with enthusiasm. With only a few verbal instructions, Levi felt ready for each day. He was so busy, he'd neglected his contact with Bruce. He had saved his only free time to be spent with Rachel. He knew he couldn't ignore Bruce indefinitely, but he wished he could.

As he shuffled in from the fields alone for the third day in a row, Levi felt both exhaustion and exhilaration at having completed an honest day's work. His clothing was dusty, and he felt like he had ten pounds of dirt on his skin. He lifted the straw hat from his head and fanned the back of his neck. Aside from keeping the sun off his face, he couldn't see what purpose the hat served. It made him too warm, but he wore it to prevent even more suspicion against him than he already felt. He didn't dare speak much to Nettie when she served him lunch, for fear he might say the wrong thing. When Hiram instructed him, he listened intently and didn't do much more than nod his answers.

He needed a shower, but he didn't want to go into the house just yet. He'd eyed the pond at the far end of the property several times, thinking it looked like a refreshing spot to take a dip. Walking toward the water, he could feel the temperature in the breeze shifting a few degrees cooler. Already he felt refreshed, but the anticipation of the cool water was too much temptation to resist as he began to unbutton his shirt. Pushing down his suspenders, he let them fall to his sides as he loosened the shirttails from his trousers. Pulling off his boots and socks brought even more relief.

Levi stepped toward the edge of the pond where frogs sunned themselves lazily on top of water-lily leaves. The water was clear in the bright sunlight, the dark, sandy bottom inviting his toes to burrow in the cool mud. From the house, he could hear the faint clang of the dinner bell, but he was too preoccupied with taking a quick swim to rinse off the dust and sweat of a hard day's work.

The moment his feet sank in the muddy bottom, dirt clouds swirled around his feet. He didn't care; the water brought instant relief to his overheated body. With the bottoms of his pant-legs now submerged, he wondered if it would be more practical to continue or remove the pants and swim in his boxers. Knowing how conservative the Amish were, he decided it was best to leave the pants on in case anyone should spot him swimming. With Hiram's sister, Bess, running the B&B that bordered the pond, he knew it was possible she could have guests that would be out on the water using the canoes or paddle-boats she rented out.

Wading out a little further past the lilies and croaking frogs, Levi dove under and swam a good stretch in the sparkling water. To him, this was better than taking a shower, and much more refreshing. As his head broke the surface of the still water, he could see Rachel standing on the shore looking out at him. While treading water, he watched as she pulled of her shoes and stockings and stepped into the edge of the water.

She cupped her hand over her mouth and shouted out to him. "Are you going to come in and eat dinner? I rang the bell, but when you didn't come in, Nettie sent me to look for you."

He swam toward her, making ripples on the smooth surface of the water. When he reached shallow water, he stood, exposing his bare chest. He wasn't shy about his looks; he had always worked out and took pride in his six-pack abs. But the look of shock on Rachel's face told him he should hurry to the shore and put his shirt on. The strange thing was, she didn't look away even though he expected her to. Was it possible she was attracted to his physical side?

He stood in front of her, allowing her to look at him. Was it wrong that he wanted to pull her into his arms and kiss her? From the look on her face, he would guess she was thinking the same thing.

She blinked. "I brought left-over bread from the bakery—for dinner."

Rachel chided herself for blurting out such a random statement. But she couldn't take her eyes off Levi's muscular frame, and she had no idea what to do about it. His wet hair lay to one side, and his water-soaked pants clung to him. His bare chest glistening against the low-lying sun. If she wasn't so worried about him thinking ill of her, she would have kissed him right there. The temptation to reach out and touch his bare flesh surprised her.

She stumbled backward. "Do you want me to get you a towel so you can dry off before you come in for dinner?"

Levi smiled at her. He could see how much his presence made her nervous, and he found it cute. If he kissed her would she run off? Or would she let him?

Levi shook the inappropriate thoughts from his mind. "A towel would be very nice. *Danki.*"

Chapter 18

Levi rode into town, grateful the horse knew where she was going because he couldn't concentrate on the road at all. His thoughts were too preoccupied to notice the *Englischers* bustling around conducting business with the many Amish shops in town. He didn't even feel particularly nervous about his weekly visit with Bruce. He almost felt invincible as he steered the horse along the outskirts of town to the little motel in which Bruce had taken up residence.

His mind kept drifting to the night before and the look on Rachel's face when he'd stepped out of the pond shirtless and dripping wet. He reveled in the way she'd looked at him with a yearning in her eyes. They'd continued to eye one another throughout dinner, and when he walked her home, she'd let him hold her hand. He could almost feel the warmth of her hand even now.

As Levi stepped down from the pony cart, he felt a tight grip on the back of his collar catching him off guard.

"Boy, what took you so long?" Bruce dragged him by the arm into his motel room.

Levi nearly gagged from the smell. The drapes were pulled closed, but he could see the sheets on the double bed were stained with vomit. An old rotary-dial phone sat on the single night stand beside a digital clock radio. The numbers on the clock flipped to the hour and the radio blared out an oldies tune. Bruce lurched toward it and slammed the snooze button on the top.

"I don't know how to shut that thing off. I tried to set the alarm, but I can't get it to stop playing that loud music. I didn't want to unplug it because I need to know what time it is."

Levi could see that Bruce was hung-over and not thinking straight because of it, so he went over to the clock and adjusted the off button. "It should stay off now. You just push this button right here."

Levi didn't know why he was bothering to explain it to his father. He would only get drunk again and forget what he said. He stepped toward the doorway for some fresh air as he reached into his pocket and pulled out his weekly wages. As expected, Bruce snatched the money from his fingers and counted out the bills.

Bruce snarled. "I don't think that Amish farmer is paying you enough. You look tired from all the work. And this ain't enough for me to live on." He waved the bills at him.

Levi walked out the door, and then turned to face his father. "Then I suggest you get your own job." Levi tossed the cell phone at Bruce. "And stop calling me and texting me. You take the phone. I don't want it, and I won't hide it anymore. I'll see you next Saturday."

Levi hopped in the pony cart and clicked to the horse. He knew it wasn't right the way he spoke to Bruce, but he didn't feel there was any other way to communicate with him.

"What about my money?" Bruce called after him.

"I'm working on it," Levi hollered as he pushed the horse to a fast trot.

The real Levi Schrock had told him over the past summer that he was to honor his mother and his father. How could he honor a mother who left him and a father who abused him? Bruce didn't understand his son's kindness— he never had. Maybe it was time for a little tough love.

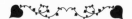

Rachel turned over the sign on the bakery door to let her customers know it was open for the day. She'd spent most of the morning making flower-shaped cookies and daydreaming about Levi. As she frosted the last batch of cookies with the variety of pastel-colored frosting, she heard the jingling of the bell on the front door. She poked her head around the side of the kitchen, surprised to see Levi entering the bakery. Her heart fluttered until she caught the expression on his face. He looked distraught; perhaps he'd received bad news from back home. She hoped whatever it was wouldn't lead him away from the community so soon. Not when she had only begun to get to know him.

She came around the side of the kitchen, towel in hand, as she tried to wipe frosting from her fingertips. "*Gudemariye,* Levi. What brings you here?"

He looked at her cheerful face and her beautiful, smiling green eyes. That was all he needed to bring his spirit up.

"I missed my breakfast this morning since I drove into town early. I was hoping you might have some fresh biscuits and honey. I'm starving."

Rachel giggled. "I hardly think you're starving, but I'd be happy to get you something. Would you like *kaffi?*"

"*Jah, danki.*" Levi felt awkward using the words he'd learned from the Schrock's, but he already felt like his world was falling apart. He didn't need to add losing Rachel too. He had to keep her suspicion of him to a minimum.

Rachel motioned for him to sit at one of the small tables along the windows while she went into the kitchen to get the items for a small breakfast for Levi. As she poured his coffee, she wondered what it would be like to serve him breakfast every morning as his wife someday. Her cheeks heated. She tried to look down, but Levi had already noticed.

He smiled. "I could get used to this."

His comment took her by surprise, causing her cheeks to burn with embarrassment. He took her hand in his and gave it a squeeze. A shy giggle escaped her lips, but she quickly straightened and leveled her expression.

Rachel cleared her throat. "I don't have any biscuits, but I have banana nut muffins. Would you like one?"

Levi shook his head while he sipped the hot beverage. He let her hand slip from his grasp, but she allowed it to linger there. He cupped his fingers around hers again and asked her to sit with him. At her touch, his worries suddenly seemed to slip away.

Chapter 19

Levi felt funny sitting on the backless wooden bench during church services. It was his first one in this community, but not his first ever. Hiram had insisted Levi and Nettie bring him to the Yoder home for service, despite the doctor's orders for him to remain in bed for another few days. Hiram had stated his case to the two of them, saying that he would take it easy after they went back home.

Levi would never forget the day that the Schrock's had hosted the service in their home while he was staying with them. It had intrigued him, and given him a hunger for God's word. He'd sat on the stairs and looked over the service, witnessing how God had brought the families and friends together, and he had craved that unconditional love the Amish shared with their community.

Now, as Levi sat among them, he felt as though he was betraying their trust. They had taken him at his word that he was who he said he was. Would his word mean nothing to them if they found out his true identity? He had been welcomed with open arms with no questions asked. Did he deserve their trust? Did he deserve *Rachel's* trust? How would she react if she knew the truth? Would she reject his feelings for her?

Levi glanced over at Rachel, who was sitting across the set of benches from him. She locked eyes with Levi, fluttering her long, auburn lashes in a flirtatious manner. He enjoyed the attention, sending her a smile of appreciation. His heart yearned to belong here, but who was he kidding? Being deceitful was not from God.

Lord, help me to find a way to tell these people who I really am. Help me to have the courage to be myself, even if they turn their backs on me.

Rachel couldn't keep her attention on the service. Thankfully, Katie, Rose, and Abby all faced forward, and had no idea what Rachel was up to. If they had, she would surely have gotten a scolding from each of them—even though they had done the same thing when they had new love interests. Rachel, however, wanted to keep her relationship with Levi a secret since he lived with her *grossdaddi*. Keeping her relationship a secret the way all the youth did made her feel very grown up. Since her sixteenth birthday a few weeks ago, she'd felt no difference, but the possibility of having a beau made all the difference in the world.

Rachel fidgeted in her seat, determined to face forward and pay attention to the service. She could see out of the corner of her eye every time Levi stole a glance in her direction, and it caused her to smile. Did he like her as much as she liked him? Since she'd turned sixteen, she'd been invited to youth singings by two of the local young *menner,* but those dates never amounted to anything. Levi was a different story. They hadn't attended any of the usual youth gatherings, yet they had already developed a deep friendship in such a short time.

At the conclusion of the service, Rachel signaled Levi with her eyes so he would follow her. She ran out of the house before her *mamm* could ask her to help with the meal. Her *mamm* had Abby and the others to help. The kitchen was always too crowded anyway, and Rachel doubted she would be missed. She entered the barn and retreated to the loft, where she often went to think. Sometimes she would sit at the pond, but she was usually spotted by someone. Today, she wanted seclusion.

Levi climbed the ladder to the loft and sat beside her, his feet dangling over the edge. "So this is where you live?"

"*Jah,* it was our turn to host services. I'm supposed to be inside "hosting", but my *familye* can handle it. Was our service the same as in your community?"

"I've only been a few times with my cousin, but it seemed like it was the same."

Levi pulled her hand into his. "Will you have time to meet me at the dock tonight? Hiram is getting better, so Nettie won't need me after I finish the evening chores."

Rachel smiled. "I will need to help Abby and *mamm* after everyone leaves, but I'm certain I will be done in time. Should we meet at dusk?"

Levi pulled her hand to his lips and kissed the back of it. "Sounds like a plan. Should we get back before someone comes looking for us?"

Rachel stared at him. "Can't we stay here until everyone leaves? I'm not up for visiting today."

Levi rubbed her hand across his whiskery chin and then kissed it again. "I would love to stay here all day with you, but I don't want to get you into trouble."

Rachel smiled. "If I didn't know better, I'd think that's exactly what you wanted to do."

Smiling, Levi kissed her hand once again.

"Maybe, but we are young. We have our whole lives ahead of us. Let's go hang out with the old people. It's their time now."

Rachel wasn't sure what he meant by that, but she had an idea he was talking about her *grossdaddi's* health. She hadn't allowed herself to think about it much for fear that she would have to face life without him. She was not ready for that. She had made light of his poor health for a while, unwilling to think about him as old and most likely nearing his end.

Rachel tightened her grip on Levi's hand. "I suppose you're right. We will have plenty of time to talk at the dock later on."

"And I can do this." Levi kissed her hand again.

Having Levi so near gave Rachel a sense of security she liked. She could be herself with him, and he understood her without much explanation. That was something she could see in her future, and it was enough encouragement to join the others—for now.

Chapter 20

After the shared meal following church services, Rachel was eager to get the dishes done so she could meet Levi at the dock. She hoped her *aenti* Bess, who'd left an hour ago would be asleep by the time she and Levi met. Her *aenti* had complained of a stomach ache before her husband, Jessup took her home. She claimed she intended to go to bed early, and Rachel hoped she would. Tomorrow being wash day, most of the women in the community went to bed early on Sunday evenings, but it was barely dusk and Rachel hoped the woman would be fast asleep by the time she reached the dock, especially since there weren't currently any guests staying at the B&B.

"Why are you in such a hurry tonight? I've never seen you wash dishes so fast," Abby said.

Rachel didn't stop to look at her sister.

"I was thinking of all I have to do tomorrow. We have a lot of wash to do before I have to go to the bakery to start Tuesday's baking."

Abby snickered. "It's going to be an even longer day if you stay out too late with Levi tonight."

Rachel felt her heart slam against her ribcage.

"Levi and I are just friends."

"Any time someone says they are *just* friends with someone it means they are more than *just friends.*"

Rachel pursed her lips. "That's not always true. We are *just* friends."

Abby struggled to wipe the dishes as fast as Rachel washed them. "That's how it started with me and Jonah."

Rachel broke her momentum long enough to stare her sister down. "That's different. You and Jonah grew up together. Me and Levi only just met a few weeks ago."

Abby put the dishtowel down. "I see the way the two of you look at each other, and the way your eyes light up when he's near."

Rachel narrowed her eyes. "Alright, I'll admit I like him. But please don't tell. Can we just keep it a secret between us?"

Abby hugged her younger sister. "No one knows more than I do how important it is to keep a relationship quiet. Rumors and gossip nearly kept me and Jonah apart. I will keep your secret, if you will keep mine."

Rachel's eyes widened. "What secret?"

Abby smiled. "Jonah and I are expecting a *boppli.*"

Rachel squealed.

Abby shushed her.

"Go and meet Levi, I'll finish up these dishes."

Rachel squealed again and hugged Abby.

"*Danki.* I'm happy for you and Jonah."

Abby smiled. "I know you are. Now go, before I change my mind."

"Why are you keeping the news a secret? *Mamm* and *daed* would be so happy to hear they are going to have *grandkinner.*"

"We wanted to wait until the end of harvest to tell everyone so the *familye* won't stop everything they're doing to make quilts and furniture and clothes. You understand what big news this is."

"*Jah.* You're right. *Mamm* won't get any canning done because she will be too eager to start sewing. *Onkel* Seth will insist on making a cradle and rocking chair instead of helping with the harvest. I see what you mean. I will be happy to keep your secret, but even after you tell everyone, you still have to keep mine."

Abby smiled. "Of course I will."

Rachel wiped her hands on the dishtowel and kissed Abby on the cheek. "*Danki.* See you later."

Rachel ran upstairs to put on a clean dress and comb out her waist-length hair. The sun had lightened her auburn hair to a dark blond, and she really liked the lighter color. She was tempted to leave her hair down, but wasn't sure she should risk getting caught with her *kapp* off. She knew that other girls in the community had done such a thing in private with their beaus, but she was still unsure of Levi or the rules of his community—or if he even belonged to one.

Rachel crept down the stairs quietly, being careful to avoid the squeaky step. The sitting room was devoid of all family, so she slipped out the front door, closing it quietly behind her. Once outside on the porch, she breathed a little easier. How did her friends manage to sneak out every night to meet their beaus? She figured they must have gotten pretty *gut* at it since she hadn't seen any of them except at Sunday services all summer.

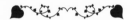

Levi's palms became sweaty as he paced the length of the dock over and again. What was he thinking getting involved with Rachel while he was there to do a job and get out of the community? The last thing he wanted to do was hurt her, and if she learned why he was really there, it might ruin things between them. He wondered if he should just do his job, get on with his life, and leave her behind where she would always be safe, or if he should take his chances and tell her the truth.

Either way, she's going to get hurt. So why not stick it out and try to help her through it—if she'll let me.

Rachel stepped onto the dock with bare feet. The smell of honeysuckle filled the humid air, and the crickets quieted their song at her presence. Fireflies hovered around the large oak tree beside the dock, and an occasional mosquito buzzed her ear. She must have missed that spot with *Mamm's* herbal repellant. She'd been in too big a hurry to get out of the house before she was caught to worry about getting every prime spot that the annoying bugs like to attack. Now she wished she'd taken the time to douse every inch. She hated the thought of swatting at bugs while trying to have what she hoped would be a romantic evening.

Levi approached her. "Mosquitoes bothering you?"

Rachel sighed. *"Jah.* I neglected to put *Mamm's* herbal repellant everywhere. I was in a hurry and must have missed a few spots."

Levi chuckled. "I may have a little too much on. Come here and I will hide you from them for a minute until they get the hint and fly away."

Rachel wasn't sure what his meaning was, but she stepped closer to him anyway. Suddenly, he scooped her up in his arms and buried his face in the crook of her neck. Instinctively, she wrapped her arms around his waist. It was nice being in his arms. She felt safe and *loved.*

Levi sucked in a deep breath. "You smell very nice."

"That's *Mamm's* herbs from her garden." With her face buried in his chest, her words came out muffled.

Levi snuggled her closer. "I don't smell any herbs; I think it's just the way you smell. It's beautiful—like you."

Rachel's heart fluttered. Was she falling in love with Levi already?

Chapter 21

There was no telling how long Levi had held Rachel in his arms before a sudden splash in the water broke the spell between them. Levi looked out toward the water in time to see a family of ducks swimming into the center of the pond.

Rachel giggled. "That scared me. I thought there was someone out here."

Levi took her hand and led her to the end of the dock. "Maybe we shouldn't stand here like this in case someone does come along. I wouldn't want anyone to misunderstand."

Rachel allowed him to steer her like a horse to the end of the dock, where they sat down, letting their feet dangle in the water. What had he meant by his statement? Had she been the only one enjoying their embrace?

Once they were settled, Levi lifted her hand in his and pressed the back of it to his lips. "Don't get me wrong; I would love to stand there and hold you for the rest of the night, but I wouldn't want to get you into any trouble."

Rachel nudged him with her hip. "We're in our *rumspringa,* Levi; we won't be accountable until we are baptized."

Levi cleared his throat. "I-uh-I know that."

"Has it been hard for you not being part of the community while you were growing up?"

How could he answer her without giving himself away for the fraud he was?

"I don't know as much as I should about the rules of the ordnung. I only know what my cousin has told me while I visited him."

Rachel looked at him. "That might explain a few things."

Levi raised an eyebrow. "Such as?"

Rachel's eyes softened. "Why you stumble over your words, and why you don't know how to do some things that most of us as Amish take for granted."

Levi nodded agreement.

Rachel rested her head on his shoulder. "Your *mamm*...she was an *Englischer?*"

"Jah."

It wasn't exactly a lie. Just because he and Bruce were *Englischers* too, didn't mean he wasn't telling her the truth.

"That might explain why she didn't stay with you. She might not have wanted to adhere to the ordnung. Many *Englischers* can't. They say they want to at first, but they find it is too difficult to give up the modern conveniences of the world."

Levi thought he could give up everything except air and food to be with Rachel. He wanted no part of the world he'd been raised in or the harshness that came with it.

"I've thought about it most of my life and I can't make any sense of it. If there's anything I can take from my childhood, it would be to do the exact opposite with my children than the way I was brought up. My children will never have to wonder if I love them."

Rachel felt heat rise in her cheeks. "Abby says the same thing sometimes. I wonder if it's because her biological father abandoned her. She doesn't talk about it much, but when I was younger, I would hear her praying about it."

Levi kicked at the water, his legs swinging over the edge of the dock. "I can't imagine not wanting to watch my child grow up. What kind of a person abandons their own child?"

"Sometimes it's what is best for the child. My *onkel* and *aenti* adopted a little girl because the birth mother couldn't raise her on her own. I think, in that case, she did a very *gut* thing for her daughter. But then there are times when a parent acts selfishly, as in my *schweschder's* case, and maybe yours too. But even though Abby's *daed* was selfish for leaving her, it was still what was best for her. Do you think that could be the case for you too?"

Levi sighed, swallowing the lump in his throat.

"I honestly think I would have been better off if they *both* would have abandoned me. Neither of them was prepared to be the kind of parent a child needs."

"Is your *daed* harsh with you?" Rachel wasn't sure if she should pry, but it seemed Levi wanted to confide in her. She admired his openness and honesty about his life, and she felt honored that he would trust *her* with his most private thoughts.

Levi wasn't sure if he should open that can of worms or not. He wanted to tell her everything about his life—to tell her the truth about why he was here, but something still held him back. Was it fear? If he had to be honest with himself, he would say he feared rejection from her. The Amish had been the only people to ever love and care for him the way he needed. Now, Rachel was one of the few really good relationships in his life, and he didn't want to risk losing her.

"He has always been harsh for as long as I can remember. He hasn't been a good example, or even a good person."

Rachel allowed herself to snuggle closer to Levi, and he put his arm around her.

"I'm sorry you have to live with that. But you will be old enough to be on your own soon. Have you given any thought to what your future holds?"

He gave her shoulder a squeeze. "I do every day."

Chapter 22

Levi couldn't concentrate on poor Lulu's milking. He'd almost told Rachel the truth about himself the night before. What a relief that would have been. But he also knew that now was not the time to reveal his true identity. He needed to keep it a secret just a little longer until he could go to Bruce at the end of the week and tell him he was out of the deal he'd made with him. Rachel had encouraged him to separate himself from his dad and to stand on his own. He would be eighteen soon, and that meant he needed to stand up for himself and become a man—the man *he* wanted to be instead of the man Bruce had taught him to be.

Levi patted the Holstein cow on her side, apologizing for being so distracted. She wagged her tail and nodded at him as if to accept. Things were so much simpler here. Telling Bruce he no longer intended to hand over his pay was not going to be easy. But he had to stand up to the man once and for all—to stand up for what was right.

Levi decided that if he had any chance at making it on his own, he would need the pay he would earn through the harvest to start his own life away from Bruce. He was grateful that his job came with room and board along with a generous wage. He'd done the math, and at the end of the harvest, he would have enough to get himself a small apartment in town. Then he could get another job and maybe think about going back to school. He would love to be like the Amish and live off the land, but he wasn't in any position to acquire any land at this time. Levi had made up his mind that if Bruce ever got his hands on the stolen money, he wanted no part of it. Even if it meant he would struggle, he would earn his money honestly.

Levi exited the barn with a pail of milk for the house. Nettie was already hanging wash on the line, and from the look of the horizon, she probably wouldn't get much done before it rained. Levi said a quick prayer for the community that it would be a slow-moving storm so the women would get their wash hung and dried first.

"Levi," Nettie called to him. "Would you mind going into town when you finish the morning chores? Hiram has a list of things that need to be bought from the hardware store, and I could use a few kitchen staples from the grocery store."

"*Jah,* I'll be happy to."

Nettie picked up the laundry basket and followed him inside the house. "Will you drop off these dishes to Rachel at the bakery on your way out? She left them here after the meal yesterday, and she'll probably need them."

Levi nodded, trying not to seem too eager for the opportunity to see Rachel again so soon.

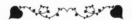

Levi steered the open buggy into the parking area behind the bakery. Rachel opened the back door and pushed a pile of dirt out the door with a homemade corn broom. She waved to him and smiled as thunder rumbled from a distance. Levi hoped he could get his errands finished before it rained—especially since he had taken the open buggy to save time. It was smaller and easier for the mare to pull. Not to mention easier for Levi to maneuver. His driving skills were improving, but he preferred the smaller buggy.

Levi stepped out of the buggy and gathered the dishes in his hands. He walked toward the back door that Rachel had left open for him. He found her standing at the sink filling a mop bucket with soapy water. She looked so beautiful—even with a dark blue scarf on her head. She wore an old, brown work dress, and her cheeks were a little pink from the heat. But Levi even found the light mist of sweat on her brow to be cute. She turned off the water and went to lift the over-sized bucket from the sink.

Levi rushed up beside her. "Let me get that for you."

Rachel took the dishes from him and stood back, watching with amusement showing on her up-turned lips as Levi struggled with the large pail of water. "Do you usually use this much water to mop the floors?"

He set the bucket down with a small splash.

"*Nee.* I have to mop both the front of the bakery and the kitchen. I thought it might be easier if I filled the bucket to the top rather than filling it twice. I don't like having to change the water."

Levi stood up straight, and then leaned back with a hand at the small of his back to stretch it. "I don't think you should try that on your own. That ten-gallon pail is very heavy when it's full."

Rachel giggled. "Why do you think I let you lift it out of the sink? The last time I tried that on my own, it sloshed all over the kitchen floor and it took me over an hour to mop it all up."

Levi put a hand to his chin. "I would have used that broom to push all the water out the back door."

Rachel narrowed her eyes. "You think you're so smart, don't you?"

"Mmm-hmm." Levi couldn't help but let out a hardy laugh.

"Are you going to stand there and laugh at me, or are you going to help me as long as you're here?"

Levi held his hand in front of his mouth to hide the snicker that threatened to escape. She looked so adorable with her hands on her hips, trying to act tough.

"I can for a few minutes, but then I'll have to go. I need to go into town to pick up a few things before it rains."

Rachel's eyes lit up. "Do you mind if I tag along? I'm out of a few spices and I need fifty pounds of sugar."

"I brought the open buggy. What if it rains? All your sugar will melt."

"I have a plastic tub with a lid we can take to carry it in."

Levi nodded toward the mop bucket. "Is this something you can do when we get back, or can you mop quickly?"

Rachel grabbed the mop. "I can make faster work of it if you'll move the tables and chairs up front."

Levi moved to the front of the bakery and did what Rachel needed. He thought he would probably do almost anything for her.

Chapter 23

Bruce Monroe stood outside his motel room leaning against the doorway smoking a cigarette. He looked up the road at the sound of horses hooves against the wet pavement. Laughter filled the stagnant air that hung thick with humidity from the short-lived down-pour. The rain hadn't lasted more than a minute, but that had been long enough to irritate Bruce. The sound of the rain pelting the tin roof of the motel had sufficiently disturbed his sleep so that he couldn't return to the dream he'd been having. Too bad his dream of finding the million dollars had only been a dream. It was enough to put him in the sourest of moods.

Bruce wiped the sleep from his eyes, trying to focus on the young Amish couple running into the hardware store down the road. If he didn't know any better, he'd say that Amish boy was his son. He'd been holding hands with the girl as they ran into the store. Flicking the cigarette onto the pavement, Bruce snuffed it out with his shoe and took off toward the hardware store to see for himself.

As he neared the hardware store, he tried to think of an excuse to enter the store. Luckily, he didn't need one. The couple ran out of the store laughing and holding hands. It was his son alright.

So my boy has found himself a girl. That might come in handy later. If he decides to back out of our little arrangement, I'll threaten to tell the girl everything.

Bruce ducked into the doorway of the business next to the hardware store so he wouldn't be seen. Not that his boy was paying any attention to anything other than *his* girl. Bruce watched his son pull the buggy away from the building and head in the opposite direction. He wondered where they were going next, but it didn't matter. It was obvious to him that he'd forgotten all about the deal they'd made.

I might just have to give him a reminder when I see him on Saturday. I'm not waiting around anymore while he plays house with that girl.

Rachel opened the umbrella and held it over the top of her and Levi as they left the outskirts of town. What started off as a little bit of drizzle had turned into heavy down-pour. Levi didn't want to push the horse to go faster on the slippery shoulder of the main road.

"Maybe taking the open buggy wasn't the best idea I've had." Levi apologized.

Rachel giggled, causing the umbrella to fall away from their heads briefly. "Where is your sense of adventure, Levi Schrock?"

Hearing the name from her lips sounded wonderful. If only there was a way to make it his true identity. Being here with her in the rain was like a dream come true. If only it could last.

"I think I left my sense of humor back at the hardware store. Should we go back and get it?"

Rachel laughed even harder. Levi joined her. He hadn't played in the rain since he was a child, but he had to admit it was more fun with Rachel. He pulled the buggy over into the abandoned schoolyard. He steered the horse toward a set of trees hoping to give the mare a little rest from the heavy rain.

"We don't have much further to go, are you sure you want to stop?"

Levi turned to her and took her hand, leading her out of the buggy. "I want to play in the rain. You can stay under the umbrella where it's safe if you want to, but I'm going to get soaked."

Rachel tossed the open umbrella into the back of the buggy over the plastic tub full of sugar and joined Levi out in the open field. She twirled with her arms outstretched and her face pointed toward the heavens. Levi stopped to watch her. If it was possible, she was even more beautiful with her hair soaked and sticking to the side of her face. Her *kapp* had come loose from her head and hung down her back by the small bow that was tied at the end of the ribbons. She pulled the pins loose and shook her head from side to side until her long hair flopped against her cheeks with a wet slap.

Rachel stopped suddenly and faced Levi. "Why are you staring at me?"

Levi closed the space between them, raindrops forcing him to blink frequently. "Because you're beautiful."

Rachel blinked away raindrops and smiled. Levi pulled her into his arms and pressed his lips to hers. She responded with a quiet moan as he deepened the kiss. With his free hand he ran his fingers through her wet hair, holding her head in place as he continued to kiss her. Rachel folded her arms around his neck, pulling him closer to her. Her breathing was heavy, and she felt light-headed. It was exhilarating. If she wasn't already falling in love with him, she certainly was now.

Levi couldn't believe his luck. Not only was he holding and kissing the girl he had learned to love, she was kissing him back. Was it possible she loved him too? Or was he only dreaming?

Chapter 24

Levi lurched forward in his bed, his arms tangled in the freshly laundered linens. His heart raced as he forced himself away from the pull that the nightmare had on him. Rachel had ridiculed him in the dream, telling him she never wanted to see him again. She'd called him a liar.

Taking a deep breath to calm himself, Levi looked out his window at the moon that still hung high in the sky. He couldn't have been asleep very long.

What was I thinking, kissing Rachel this afternoon? She is going to hate me when she finds out I've lied to her. And Hiram will surely fire me!

Levi pressed his weary head back against his pillow. He faced the window, looking out at the moon and wondering how he was going to break the news to Rachel. He would certainly have to wait until after his visit with Bruce on Saturday. He needed closure with his dad before he could move forward with the life he intended for himself. A life that would be free from lies and petty crimes.

Levi sighed, wondering if his life could ever be that simple. He had a feeling Bruce wouldn't let him go without a fight. The man needed him to steal for him or get odd jobs to support him. But maybe if Bruce had the million dollars he would leave him alone forever. He could only hope.

The trouble was, how could he get his hands on a map that might not exist? Did he dare press Abby further for more information? Or worse; did he have the guts to ramshackle thru her house when she wasn't home? No, he could never do anything that disrespectful to his own family.

Stealing small things here and there, or pick-pocketing was a lot different from breaking into someone's house. Not only was the risk greater, he was determined to put his stealing days behind him. He'd spent many hours praying over the last few weeks, asking forgiveness for past crimes and begging God for a way to put an end to any future crimes his earthly father would expect him to commit. If he was to truly change, he had to turn his back on anything and anyone who would threaten his redemption—and that meant his own father.

Levi was afraid to be on his own. Especially if he lost his job with the Miller's.

Lord, I don't have a high school diploma or even any money to go out on my own. Bless me with the tools to change my life even without those things. Please soften Hiram's heart for me and keep him from firing me. Bless my relationship with Rachel to honor you in every way. I love her, and I don't want to lose her. Give me the courage to tell her and Hiram the truth about who I am. Give them understanding hearts for me, Lord. Heal Hiram and make him strong again. Bless him with long life.

Levi closed his eyes intending to continue his prayer, but he fell back asleep. When he woke again, it was morning. He could hear the rooster crowing out near the barn. Levi's stomach growled, telling him he was just as hungry as that rooster must be. He pushed his aching body from the bed and stretched for a minute. He could smell coffee, which meant Nettie had been up for a while already. He had tried to rise before her nearly every day since he'd arrived, but it seemed she awoke earlier each morning. He dressed quickly so he could get to the milking before Nettie or Hiram went out there after tiring of waiting for him. The sun was barely up, but he'd already learned that the day began when the farm was ready—not when the farmer decided.

As he trailed down the stairs, the smell of cooking bacon made his mouth water. He knew he had at least thirty minutes worth of chores to do before he could get any breakfast. He would get the milk for the house first before he did anything to ensure Hiram would have some fresh milk when he sat down to eat with Nettie. They had been so good to him, and he would miss them when he had to leave, which might be sooner than he'd originally anticipated if he went through with his plan to tell the truth at the close of the week.

"*Gudemariye,* Levi. Would you like some *kaffi* to take with you before you head out to the barn?"

"*Danki*," he said as he took the steaming mug from her hands. "I'll be back with the milk before Hiram comes down for breakfast."

Nettie smiled and nodded as she went back to stirring a large iron skillet full of eggs.

Levi left the kitchen before his hunger made him forget his manners. He was tempted to snitch a piece of bacon off the plate, but he forced himself out the door into the humid morning air.

His walk to the barn was filled with the sound of birds chirping and flitting about the trees. Nettie had put out some fresh bird seed in the feeder, and the rain had filled the bird bath with fresh water for their morning routine. He would have loved to spend a few minutes watching them, but he had a job to do. His strong back was the only thing he had going for him for the time-being, and he wasn't about to waste time on bird-watching. If he wanted a chance to keep his job after he told Hiram the truth, he would have to prove to the man that his services were indispensable. Hopefully, his hard work would speak for itself when the time came.

Chapter 25

Rachel woke with a stiff neck, most likely from playing in the rain. *Mamm* had always told her to keep dry and warm or she would catch a cold. She felt awful and she ached all over. But she felt her time with Levi was worth every ache. Perhaps some of *Mamm's* herb tea would help ease her muscles back into shape. She hadn't slept well, but most of that was because of the giddiness that filled her from head to toe. She'd decided hours ago that she was definitely in love with Levi. When she entered the large kitchen, her *mamm* was busy at the stove making a fresh pot of coffee. Rachel cleared her throat and corralled her emotions so as not to give away her feelings to her *mamm's* watchful eye.

She shuffled up next to her *mamm* and put the tea kettle on, ignoring the cup in front of her. "I need tea this morning, *Mamm*. I feel a little stiff from being caught in the rain yesterday when Levi took me into town to get sugar for the bakery."

She'd dried off for the most part before reaching home for the day, but she was certain her *mamm* had noticed her rumpled clothing and disheveled hair.

Lizzie looked at her daughter and smiled. "I sort of noticed something was different, but I didn't want to offend you. You've been spending quite a bit of time with Levi."

She'd been waiting for such a comment from someone in her family, but she expected it more from her grandfather. But since he was recuperating from a possible heart attack, she'd thought she was in the clear.

"We've become friends. I've spent more time with *Grossdaddi* and Nettie since he's been ill, and Levi is always there. He offered to give me a ride into town since he had to run errands for Nettie. But since he took the open buggy, we got pretty soaked in the rain."

Concern showed on Lizzie's face. "I hope you were able to salvage the sugar from melting."

That was all she was concerned about? Rachel knew her *mamm* trusted her to make smart decisions, but would it really be that easy to participate in her *rumspringa* without her *mamm* looking over her shoulder? She'd never given her parents any reason to worry or question her judgment, but this was a first time a boy had entered the equation.

"*Jah,* I brought a plastic tub with a lid just in case."

The tea kettle began to whistle, and Rachel took some tea out of the glass jar and put it in the small steeping basket. Dropping it into her cup, she removed the kettle from the flame and poured the hot water over the tea, using the little chain to bob the aluminum basket up and down in the water. She sat down at the kitchen table and spooned two teaspoons of sugar into the cup and held the steaming beverage to her lips to blow on it.

Lizzie sat down across from Rachel. "I hope you don't get a cold from playing out in the rain like that."

Rachel nearly spit her tea across the table at her *mamm.* "Who said I was playing in the rain?"

Lizzie smiled knowingly. "You did. Since I just took you on Saturday to pick up sugar, I'd say you wanted to go into town because of the company."

Her *mamm* knew her all too well. But she was smiling. Was it possible she didn't care that her youngest *dochder* was taking a beau? Rachel's cheeks heated at the thought of it. She couldn't look at her *mamm,* so she kept her face down blowing and sipping on her tea.

"We've become friends."

Lizzie smiled wider. "You already said that."

Rachel pursed her lips. "I wasn't certain that you heard me."

"He seems like a nice young *mann.* Your *grossdaddi* and Nettie tell us he's a hard worker."

It delighted Rachel that her family liked her new beau. She would never admit to them her interest in Levi beyond friendship, but she suspected her *mamm* already knew.

The hot tea began to work on relaxing Rachel's stiff muscles. She could no more regret the stiffness any more than she could regret her time with Levi the day before. She had a long day ahead of her, but one look out the window at the myriad of colors painted across the sunrise, and she knew the day held promises that would come with no regrets.

Rachel tipped the cup and emptied the last drops down her throat. They felt soothing going down, and would help her to do her chores before work. She had to gather eggs and milk Daisy before she could go. She needed the ingredients for her day, and her *mamm* needed them to start breakfast for the family.

She brought the eggs in quickly and rushed out to the barn to get enough milk to fill a few Mason jars. While her *mamm* made breakfast, she would feed the chickens and then rush inside to change her dress for the day ahead of her. Thankfully, her *daed* and brother would finish the rest of the chores.

As she scattered chicken feed along the ground for the pecking hens, her mind drifted to Levi and the kisses they'd shared in the rain. It was her first experience with a real kiss, and it had left her wanting more of the same. She wanted to kiss Levi every day, but she wasn't sure if he would want to after the way he suddenly pulled away from her at the end of their time together. He'd made an excuse that he didn't want her to catch a cold, but there had been something in the way he'd looked at her that told her there was more to it than that. What had he wanted to say to her that he'd kept to himself?

Chapter 26

By the end of the week, Levi knew without a doubt that Rachel loved him and that he returned her feelings for him. They had met each night at the dock of the B&B, and had talked and kissed late into the night. Rachel had voiced a desire to explore the *Englisch* world during her *rumspringa*. Levi hoped it would work out for them when she discovered he was an *Englischer*. He decided that tonight would be the night to tell her the truth. Then in the morning, instead of taking Bruce his weekly wages, he would sever his ties with him, and he would be a free man.

Levi patted Lulu's side as he sat down on the small stool to prepare for the morning milking. When the large pail was full, he patted Lulu once again, thanking her for cooperating with him.

A noise from the loft of the barn drew his head automatically toward the rustling sound. Bruce staggered toward the edge of the loft, kicking alfalfa hay to the floor of the barn below him. Levi's heart lurched in his chest as he stood abruptly, knocking over the small stool and causing Lulu to let out a nervous *moo*.

Levi rushed to the edge of the loft and looked up at Bruce, who was standing dangerously close to the edge. "What are you doing here?"

Bruce waved his half-empty bottle of whiskey in one hand and held the other arm out in mock-balance. "I've been here a couple of days, but now my food is gone and my last bottle is half empty. I need some breakfast. Be a good boy and get your dad something to eat."

Levi's lips formed a grim line. "What happened to the motel room I paid for?"

Bruce plopped down on the edge of the loft and let his legs dangle precariously over the edge. "They kicked me out when I ran out of money to pay for the room. I told you that money you gave me wasn't enough to pay the bills."

Levi stood under his father, prepared to catch him if he toppled over the edge of the loft. "It would have been enough if you would have budgeted the money instead of spending so much on cigarettes and whiskey."

Taking a swig from the whiskey bottle in his hand, Bruce leaned over the edge of the loft, making Levi very nervous. If the man fell, he might break a few bones in the best-case scenario, and then he would have a tough time convincing Hiram of his worth as a farm-hand. He would have a hard time explaining Bruce's presence to his boss.

"Why don't you come down from there and we'll talk. I'll get you something to eat, and then I'll take you back into town and get you back into the motel."

Levi didn't want to spend his hard-earned money on this man anymore since all he did was waste it on booze and cigarettes. But if it would buy him the time he needed until he could explain things to Rachel and Hiram in his own way, it might be worth it.

Bruce pushed himself to his feet and teetered for just a second, causing Levi to feel a rush of adrenaline course through his veins.

Taking a step back, Bruce waved the bottle at his son again. "My things are up here. I'll go sit with them. Bring me something to eat, and then we'll talk."

Levi wrung his hands. "It might be a while before I can sneak any food out of the house without the Millers knowing. They'll be sitting down to eat in just a few minutes. I can't just walk in there and take a plateful of food out of the house when they're sitting right there."

Bruce frowned. "Well you better hurry up Boy, or I'll come in there after it. I'm hungry."

Levi felt like a kid again, cowering under his dad's authority. The last thing he needed was to have Bruce barge into the Miller's house and frighten them. There would be no time for a plausible explanation then.

"I'll get you the food, but I need you to be patient. Promise me you'll stay put until I get back."

Bruce raised his upper lip, exposing his teeth like a rabid dog. "I ain't promising you nothing, Boy. You hurry on into that house and fetch me some breakfast, or I'll be coming in after it. And while I'm in there I might just tell your boss exactly who you are."

Levi found it difficult to pull enough air into his lungs. Was he having a panic attack? If he was, he couldn't let Bruce see his weakness. The cruel man would play off of it, and he would be on the losing end of the game.

Levi clenched his jaw. "I'll be back just as soon as I can. There's no need to threaten me."

Bruce whipped his head around toward Levi so fast, he nearly fell over. "Don't you EVER think you can tell me what to do, Boy. I'm the boss of you, and don't you ever forget that."

Levi leered up at Bruce. "I already have a boss. I need a dad."

He knew he was pushing his luck speaking out of turn the way he was, but he had reached his limit for tolerance of this man.

Bruce waved a hand behind him as he walked toward the back of the loft away from the edge. "Go on. Get out of here. And don't come back without some food for your old man."

Levi took the pail of milk and exited the barn. Hiram's presence just outside the entry surprised him. His heart lurched again, and he wondered if he was too young to suffer a heart attack.

Hiram nodded. "I was just coming out to see if you'd fallen asleep milking Lulu. Nettie has breakfast ready. Might as well eat it while it's hot. The rest of the chores will keep until you finish."

Levi nodded to his boss, fearful the man had overheard his conversation with Bruce.

Chapter 27

If Hiram had heard him conversing with Bruce in the barn, his expression didn't show it. Aside from the clanking of a fork on a plate, the room was silent. It wasn't like either of them to be this quiet during breakfast, but Hiram had his nose in the latest issue of *The Budget,* and Nettie was busy eating. Levi picked at his breakfast, moving the eggs around the plate. His melancholy went unnoticed this morning, and he was grateful.

When Nettie rose from the table to get a second cup of coffee, Levi took the opportunity to stuff a biscuit and a few pieces of bacon into his napkin and push it back onto his lap. The tricky part would be to get out of the door with it. Perhaps if he took his time eating, Nettie would start the dishes before he finished, and Hiram would remain glued to his newspaper. With any luck, he would be able to slip out without either of them being the wiser.

Just as he'd hoped, Nettie started to clear the table while he finished his eggs. He grabbed another biscuit and a few more strips of bacon off the plates before she removed them, and poured himself another glass of milk. He was hungry, but he was nervous. Paranoid was probably more likely. He took Hiram to be the type of man to say outright if there was something on his mind. But his silence this morning was a little unnerving.

Levi quickly gobbled down his breakfast, and then picked up his napkin full of food and went for the back door while Nettie's back was turned. He'd already thanked her for the meal, so there would be no reason to linger. As his hand went for the door handle, Hiram called his name. He tried to turn around without showing the napkin he held close to him.

"How's the corn looking this week?"

Levi smiled with pride, knowing he had helped the plants grow by tending to them. "The ears are getting mighty thick. We should be ready to start picking the first few rows this week."

"I'd like you to take a bushel of tomatoes and squash up to the roadside stand today. There is a *gut* breeze to keep you cool today. Should be a *gut* day to sell to *Englischers* passing by the main road. If that corn is as thick as you say, then take a bushel of that up there and sell it too. The prices for vegetables and the change jar are on the shelf in the tack room. I'll walk up there in a little while and sit with you if you want me to."

Levi could feel the heat rising to his cheeks.

"That isn't necessary. I wouldn't want you to strain yourself too soon."

Hiram waved a hand at him. "Doctor Davis said I need to start walking every day. The end of the road is a *gut* start, don't you think?"

"*Jah.* I'll see you in a little while then."

Levi rushed to the barn. He had to act fast if he was going to get his dad out of the barn and get the vegetables picked and hauled to the roadside stand under the big oak tree on the main road before Hiram took his walk out there to meet him.

First things first; he climbed the ladder to the loft, and thankfully, found his dad asleep in the alfalfa hay. How long would he sleep? Levi hoped it would be long enough to pick the vegetables and get them back to the barn. He intended on using the enclosed buggy to smuggle Bruce out of the barn. He would put the vegetables in back with the man, and then take him as far as the main road. Bruce would have to walk the rest of the way back to town, which Levi guessed he'd already done when he came here. He set the napkin full of food next to his dad's head and slid down the ladder. Gathering the bushel-baskets, he headed out to the field.

Once there, he picked as quickly as his hands would work, pushing the basket along with his foot while he used both hands to check each ear before removing them from the stalk. In his frantic state, he knew he couldn't keep up this lie any longer. It was eating away at his peace and stealing his joy. Joy that he should be feeling about his love for Rachel. Instead, he was anxious and full of regret. Would this feeling ever go away? He hoped so, or he would surely make a mistake, and at this point, he couldn't afford to do such thing.

With Bruce safely in the back of the buggy with the produce, Levi steered the mare to the end of the road. He parked the buggy under the tree behind the stand to give the horse relief from the sun. He would ask Hiram to take the buggy back with him when he arrived.

Tying the horse to the oak tree, Levi opened the back door and ushered Bruce out. He handed him fifty-seven dollars and grabbed his duffel bag from the back. "This should get you back into the room at the motel for the night. You can use the rest to get yourself some dinner. After that, you're on your own."

Bruce gritted his teeth and growled. "What do you mean *I'm on my own?*"

Levi took in a deep breath. "I mean, I'm out. I can't do this anymore. These people have been very kind to me, and I won't continue to work with you. They don't know where the stolen money is. That is, even if it exists. The authorities haven't been able to find that money all these years. What makes you think you can find it? I won't hurt these people, and I won't let you hurt them either."

Chapter 28

Bruce caught Levi off guard and pushed him up against the tree by his neck. His fingers dug into the flesh of Levi's neck, and he struggled to bring in air.

"What are you gonna do, Boy? You aren't gonna threaten me. I'm the boss of you. I already told you that." Bruce tightened his grip on his son's neck and knocked his head against the tree. "I'm gonna tell you how it is and you're gonna listen or you're gonna get what's coming to you. I'm gonna give you until tomorrow to deliver that map to me, or I'm gonna take matters into my own hands, and you're not gonna like that. I've been watching you and that pretty little brunette. I'd say by the way she kisses you she likes you a lot. If you don't get me that map, we'll see how much she still likes you when I tell her what kind of a man you really are—a thief and a criminal just like me."

Levi had only stolen under his dad's instruction, and by his way of thinking, he'd been a victim of poor parenting. He'd hated it when Bruce made him steal. The very clothes on his body had been stolen off the clothesline of an Amish farm in Ohio. He knew he would be held accountable for what he'd taken, but he would not put Rachel in harm's way because of his sins. He was nothing like Bruce, and he wanted nothing more to do with him.

"Now, do we understand each other?"

Levi nodded.

Bruce let him go, and Levi coughed and held his sore neck. He had no intention of helping Bruce. His plans had now changed. He would tell Rachel the truth when they met for their date this evening. Then he would tell Hiram after he finished his work for the day. He would leave the community of his own accord and hope that his final week of pay would be enough to get him as far away from Bruce and all the hurt of losing Rachel. He didn't want to tell her or Hiram the truth, but he owed them that much. He could go away quietly and neither would be the wiser, but that was not the kind of man he wanted to be. If being honest and honorable would come with the price of losing his job and the girl he loved, then that's the price he was willing to pay.

Hiram pulled his straw hat down over his eyes to shield the sun so he could get a better look at what was going on with Levi and the older gentleman. They seemed to be having some sort of scuffle. Hiram didn't know whether to holler at them to make his presence known, or just continue walking toward them at a slow pace. He wished he had the energy to walk faster or even run, especially since it appeared that Levi was in some sort of trouble with the *Englischer*. Had the man been so unsatisfied with the quality of the produce, or did Levi know him? Hiram supposed it was possible that the man was attempting to rob Levi, but there wouldn't have been enough time for the boy to have made enough sales to accumulate the money that would make a robbery a worthy attempt.

He was still too far away to know for certain what the apparent argument was about, and it wasn't possible for him to hear their conversation. Hiram remained hidden from their view, thanks to the many trees that lined the long driveway that led out to the main road. Before he was able to get any closer, the *Englischer* picked up a bag from the back of Hiram's buggy and took off walking down the road.

Hiram held back for a moment now that Levi was no longer in any immediate danger. He watched the young man unload the remaining produce onto the stand as though nothing had happened. Had the *Englischer* been the same man that Hiram had heard talking to Levi earlier that morning in the barn? He decided to slow his pace more than was necessary to allow the *Englischer* time to walk down the road and out of sight, and to allow Levi a little space before he approached him.

Levi picked up the cell phone that Bruce had tossed at his feet. Bruce had warned him to answer it when he called tomorrow, but Levi had no intention of doing that. Levi intended only to carry out his own plans for a change. A plan that would put him on a Greyhound bus back to Ohio in search of the aunt he'd never known. Rachel had told him about her, explaining to him that Abby had found the woman a few years ago when she visited the area. Levi knew the woman's name and general location, and that was good enough for him. He prayed that she would take him in like she'd done for Abby until she got a job and her own place. If he had a relative that kind, he would do everything he had to in order to make his life right. He was prepared to do whatever it took to turn his back on the life of crime his dad had forced him into. With the fact that he was about to turn eighteen, he knew that he could be put in jail the way Bruce had so many times. Levi's belief was that there wasn't anything in this world worth going to jail for.

Levi shoved the cell phone in his pocket as Hiram came into view. He was still several yards away, but he instinctively looked up the road to be sure Bruce was no longer visible. Relived at not seeing him, he greeted Hiram cheerfully.

Chapter 29

Hiram decided to give Levi time to tell him about the strange visit from the *Englischer* when he was ready. He'd suspected something was amiss, but when he'd gotten confirmation that there was indeed a Levi Schrock from the Ohio community, he'd thought the young man had told him the truth. But after overhearing part of a disturbing conversation between Levi and the *Englischer* earlier, Hiram decided to take a second look at the records he'd received from the Bishop in Ohio. He'd noticed inconsistencies with Levi's story, and now, his confrontation with the *Englischer* confused Hiram. So had the part of Levi's story about living in town with only his *daed,* and having no *mamm* or siblings. According to the records from that community, Levi Schrock was one of the youngest of nine *kinner,* and both his parents resided in the house.

Hiram trusted Levi to come to him with the truth in his own time, and so he let the matter drop for the time being. He'd watched Levi from the window since he'd become ill, and he was a hard worker. He'd always proved he could be trusted. But there was one thing that nagged at the back of Hiram's mind.

Was Levi an *Englischer?*

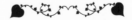

Levi cleared his throat nervously several times, pacing the length of the dock, waiting for Rachel. His palms were drenched with nervous sweat, and his heart raced to the rhythm of the cricket's fast song. He'd rehearsed his speech several times on the way to his meeting with her, so he knew exactly what he wanted to say. It would be those first few words that would be the toughest to speak, but he was determined to see it through, even if it meant he would lose her. He would rather lose her in the truth than keep her in his web of lies.

"Do you always pace nervously when you're waiting on me, Levi?"

His heart sped up at the sight of her. She'd left her hair down, and she'd never been more beautiful than she was now. Rachel closed the space between them and lifted her head to press her lips to his. He tasted the sweetness of her lips. Did he have the right to kiss her one last time? Or should he stop her before they got lost in the moment? He would give almost anything right now if he didn't have to break the news to her, but he'd prayed all afternoon that his announcement would not break her heart. He wasn't certain he could live with himself if he hurt her in any way. He loved her, that he knew, and holding her was only going to make things harder on both of them.

Rachel dropped her arms to her sides and stopped kissing him. "You're doing it again."

Levi looked at her quizzically.

"The other day I felt you pulling away from me, and now I feel it again. Is there something wrong? Have you changed your mind about me?"

Levi swallowed the lump in his throat. This was going to be harder than he thought. He didn't want her thinking he was rejecting her. There was no turning back now. She'd given him the out, and now he had to take it.

"Levi, what's wrong? You can tell me."

He took a deep breath and let it out, turning toward the pond and looking out over the expanse of the calm water. The surface was so smooth it looked like glass in the reflection of the moonlight.

"That's part of what's wrong."

"What's part of it?" Rachel interrupted.

She is not going to make this easy, is she?

"My name is not Levi Schrock, and I'm not Amish."

Rachel smiled, thinking she'd play along with his joke. "Then who are you?"

He cleared his throat. "My real name is Blake Monroe and I'm English—an *Englischer.*"

Tears filled Rachel's eyes and she backed away from him. "If you're an *Englischer,* why did you come here pretending to be Amish? Did you think that was the only way you would be hired to work on the farm? We have plenty of *Englischers* who work with us during harvest season and they assist with barn-raisings. Are you mocking us?"

She was not going to make this easy for him. He'd expected nothing less, so he pressed on. He was shaking, but he needed to press through before he lost his nerve.

"Bruce, my dad, sent me here to get something from your sister Abby, my cousin."

Rachel's eyes grew wide. "You're Abby's cousin? I kissed you!"

Blake tried to comfort her, but she pulled away.

"You and I are not related. Only Abby and I are because our dads were brothers. She is your half-sister."

Rachel moved to the end of the dock and sat down, inviting Blake to join her. "I don't understand. Why wouldn't you just ask your cousin for help instead of going through all this trouble to try and fool us? I feel humiliated. Do you even like me, or is that a lie too?"

Blake turned to her. He wanted to kiss her pouty mouth so badly. He wished he could wipe her tears away. Knowing he'd caused them made his heart sink.

"Of course my feelings for you are real. I love you, Rachel. Nothing will ever change that."

She looked over at him. She could see the sincerity in his eyes. She loved him too, and she owed it to him to listen to his reasons. Rachel leaned her head on his shoulder. He let out a sigh of relief and continued his story.

"Bruce had the idea that if I could come here and work as a hired-hand, that I could keep him at the local motel while I worked on getting information out of Abby. He thought she might be more inclined to spill her guts to a total stranger before talking to someone who was related to her real dad. We'd heard she never knew him and that her mother—your mother—had run from him before she gave birth to your sister."

"*Jah,* that's all true, as far as I know. But since she never met her real dad before he died, why is it so important for you to get information about your *daed's* brother from Abby? She never knew him."

Blake put his arm around Rachel. "I thought as much and told Bruce that was probably the case, but he gets all riled up when he drinks. He's not been a good parent to me. He's been a poor example—teaching me to lie and to steal since I was real little. I've prayed a lot and asked forgiveness, but I need to know that you forgive me too."

"That depends."

Blake held his breath for a moment. "On what?"

"Do you want to become Amish? Do you plan on joining the church?'

Blake sighed loudly. "I'd like nothing more, but I don't think Bruce is going to be too willing to just let me stay here. What happens when your grandfather and the rest of the community finds out I've been lying to them?"

Rachel smiled warmly. "I told you. We are a peaceful and forgiving people. Occasionally we have a trouble-maker in the bunch, but that is true with any group of people. They will forgive you and welcome you the same as they do now."

Chapter 30

Rachel sat quietly next to Blake. She hadn't really answered him, and she knew he was waiting. Part of her was hurt that he'd not trusted her with the truth. Another part was angry over being lied to and made a fool of. But most of her loved him.

"It is the way of our people to forgive. But that doesn't mean I will stand by and let you lie to me again."

Blake's heart fluttered happily. He was forgiven, but he would do everything to earn back her trust.

"Thank you. It means everything to me that you forgive me."

"I'm curious about something. Is your *daed* mean to you, Lev--*Blake*?"

His real name sounded strange coming from her lips. Blake swallowed hard as he nodded. He was embarrassed by his answer, but Rachel deserved to know the whole story. "He forced me to steal and threatened me that if I didn't get his important papers from Abby, I was going to pay. How can I go back to him empty-handed? I'm afraid my only choice is to leave here and find a safe place where he won't know where I am. I will have to start a new life there, but at least I won't have to live a life of crime anymore."

"What if you make him *think* you're leaving here? Then you can stay here after telling him some odd destination. Would he fall for such a trick?"

Blake played with her hair that hung down her back. "He might. But he threatened to come here and tell you and your grandfather everything if I don't bring him what he wants."

"What does he want?"

"It's not important. Your sister obviously never knew anything about Eddie Monroe."

Rachel looked up at him. "Is that the only reason you're telling me the truth now? Because your *daed* threatened to tell me?"

"No!" Blake bravely touched his lips to hers.

"I've wanted to tell you since the first time I met you at the bakery. All this lying has given me an ulcer."

Blake found no reason to tell her about the money. It was not an issue and would only worry her. He'd told her the most important thing, and that was his true identity. He'd already made the mistake of saying too much to Abby the first time he'd met her at dinner a month ago. Had he only been in the community a month? It had felt like a lifetime.

"It seems like a lot of trouble to go through just for some papers about his own brother. Was it his Will?"

Blake shook his head. "Something like that. Eddie supposedly left some important papers behind, and Bruce thought he might have given them to Abby before he died."

"The only thing he had with him when he died was a copy of a children's book. *The Velveteen Rabbit.* Eddie's half-sister was given his personal effects when he died. She gave the book to Abby a while back when she visited her in Ohio."

Blake sighed. "Well I guess that settles it then. Bruce will have to go back to Ohio empty-handed. A children's book would be of no use to him. He isn't going to be happy about this. I'm going to have to be very convincing if I want to make him think I'm leaving Indiana too. I like the idea of staying here, but only if your grandfather will let me continue to work for him."

"I'm sure you won't have to worry about that. I must say, *mei grossdaddi* is really quite a clever *mann,* and I have to wonder why he hasn't already figured all of this out for himself. Must be because he's been ill."

Blake shook a little. "Do you really think he might suspect me? I wondered if he'd overheard my conversation with Bruce this morning in the barn."

Rachel gasped. "Bruce was here? He was in *mei grossdaddi's* barn?"

"He spent the night in there last night. Quite possibly more than one night. He's lucky he didn't get caught. Would your grandfather be the type to call the police?"

Rachel giggled. *"Nee.* He would probably invite him in the *haus* for a glass of lemonade."

Blake shook at the thought of it. "That wouldn't be a wise thing to do. Bruce can get a little rough when he's been drinking."

"He wouldn't hurt him would he?" Rachel sounded worried.

"He's bloodied up my lip a few times, but I don't think he's capable of violence. At least I would hope not. But there is no telling what a man is capable of when his thinking is altered with whiskey."

The two of them stood up, and Blake pulled her into his arms. He was happier than he'd ever been, but there was still a big hurdle he had to clear before his life would be at peace.

Chapter 31

Bruce struggled to get Rachel into the back of the buggy. It wasn't easy with her hands and feet bound. Her whimpering was getting on his nerves.

"I guess your boyfriend didn't tell you he had a daddy, did he?"

Rachel leered at him with tear-filled eyes. She was angry. Bruce could see it in her eyes. He closed the buggy door and sat in the driver's seat. He pulled on the reins, surprised at how easily the horse obeyed. When he pulled onto the main road, he looked back at Rachel to make sure she was paying attention to him.

"That's right. Your boyfriend came here pretending to be Amish so he could get his hands on the map my brother left to your sister, so we could be rich. You see, right before my brother died, we stole the largest amount of money we'd ever stolen. He was going to stash the money away, and we were going to sit for a while and let the heat cool down before we went back and collected it so we could start spending it. But he crashed your mom's car and died before he could get back with the map. My brother promised me he'd make a map that would mark the money's hiding place. Did my son tell you about the million dollars?"

Rachel's heart sank. Levi—Blake had not told her about a map or a million dollars of stolen money. She'd been such a fool to think he loved her. He only wanted the money—the money he expected Abby to find for him. If she'd had a map from Eddie, she would have said so before now.

Unless she doesn't know she has it! What if it's in the book somewhere? It could be hidden. But how can I tell this mann with tape on my mouth?

Bruce steered the horse down Main Street toward the motel. "I bet you didn't know your boyfriend is a thief *and* a liar. He's quite good at it. He stole the Amish clothes so he could fool all of you into thinking he was just like you. Of course, it was my idea to make him go in under-cover. He wanted to go and meet his cousin like a fool, but I warned him she wouldn't talk to him about it unless she thought she could trust him. That's when I came up with the plan to dress him up like the Amish. He didn't want to because he can be stubborn. But after I gave him a good "talking to", if you know what I mean, he was all for it."

Rachel had an idea she knew exactly what he was talking about. It was obvious this man was far more violent than Blake had let on. Was he even aware that his father was capable of such an act as this? Was it *his* fault she was in danger now? Or was Blake a victim in all of this too? How would she ever be able to trust him again? Or would nothing matter since she would be dead soon?

"How does it feel knowing that your boyfriend fooled you? You didn't really think he actually liked you, did you? His goal was to get his hands on the money the whole time. As soon as your family gets the ransom note, me and my son will be rich. He won't think twice about you when he's counting all his money."

Rachel wept quietly. Her heart was broken and she didn't think she would ever live to see her *familye* again. She knew too much already, and he kept telling her more. He would have no reason to let her go when she could identify him.

Dear Gott, please spare my life. Soften this mann's heart toward me and make him let me go. Give me the courage to forgive him if he should decide to end my life.

Blake packed his things in the knapsack he'd carried with him when he first came to live with the Miller's. He knew that Bruce would not be convinced that he was leaving Indiana unless he had his things with him, and he knew that man would check his bag. Blake had considered drawing a fake map that would lead his dad on a wild goose chase looking for the money, but Bruce would never believe it. There was no way Blake could make a map to look almost as old as he was. It would take too much time and planning, and he didn't have that kind of time.

Sneaking out of the house with his things, Blake knew it would be easier to get away once it turned dark. The Miller's would be in the sitting room reading from the Bible at this time, just as they had every Saturday night. The sun rested just above the horizon and it was sinking fast. If he didn't get away now while they were preoccupied, he might not get another chance. The walk into town to the motel would take him at least forty-five minutes, and by then, the sky would be pitch-black.

He quickly passed by the bakery and was slightly disappointed to see that Rachel had already left for the day. He'd hoped he could get one last bit of encouragement from her before he faced his father, just in case he walked away with a black eye. He drew comfort from knowing Rachel was safe at home for the night.

Chapter 32

"Rachel's been abducted!"

Abby ran through her parent's *haus* looking for Caleb and her *daed*. This was all her fault. If she'd paid closer attention to Rachel, she wouldn't be in jeopardy. She had thought there was something strange about Rachel's new beau asking so many questions, but she'd dismissed it. She'd been too busy with her own life to pay attention to what was going on in her dear sister's life.

No one was in the house. Odd. Where was everyone? The barn? Abby raced to the barn and threw open the door.

"*Daed,* where are you? I need your help."

"In here, Abby. *Kume.* We have a new foal."

The sound of her *daed's* voice brought little comfort as she ran to the inner part of the barn where her family sat watching the miracle of life unfold before their eyes. She hated to ruin such a beautiful moment with such tragic news, but it couldn't be helped.

Abby pushed the note she'd found at the bakery into her *daed's* hand. She was out of breath from running, and her face was drenched with tears.

"This note says Rachel's been abducted. The kidnapper is demanding one million dollars, and he thinks I have the map that leads to it. He says I'm to bring him the map or we'll never see her again. Does that mean he plans to...?" Abby couldn't push the unspeakable from her lips.

She didn't want to think about the possibility that her sister could be harmed.

She should have known something was wrong when Levi seemed to know things about Abby's past. Things about Eddie, her real father. She wrote it off as gossip when Levi had said he heard that Eddie had buried a million dollars and left the map to its whereabouts to his only child. That would be her, and she had no such map. She'd not even admitted to Levi that Eddie was her real father.

"*Daed,* I think Levi knows something about this, or he could be in on it. We have to get over to *Grossdaddi's haus* to see what he knows about this. He was asking all sorts of strange questions about Eddie and a million dollars he supposedly hid before he died. Levi said there were rumors around town that he'd left me a map to its whereabouts. I don't have a map to any stolen money."

Caleb jumped into action readying the buggy.

Jacob showed the strain in his eyes. "Why didn't you tell us about this sooner, Abby?"

Abby began to cry all over again. "I didn't think it meant anything. You know how small-town rumors can be. I just didn't think. I'm sorry, *Daed.*"

Lizzie hugged her daughter as she wept. "Abby, this isn't your fault. It's mine. If I'd done a better job covering our trail, none of this would have happened. I also knew that she'd been sneaking out late to meet Levi. I didn't think it was a problem since it's her time of *rumspringa.* I was trying to give her some space so she wouldn't leave the community like you and I did, Abby."

"*Mamm,* what if they know about us because I stayed in Ohio all that time? I can't believe it took them this long to catch up to us."

Jacob fought back tears. "We don't know for certain that the two are connected, but if they are, we might have to call the local police to help us find her if we can't get any answers out of Levi."

Hearing that her *daed* thought the police should be called suddenly made it real, and that frightened Abby to her very core. "I'm going with you, *Daed.* This has something to do with me, I just know it."

Jacob didn't argue with his daughter. He could see she was determined to go, and she would find a way if he didn't give his consent.

Abby couldn't help but feel guilty for not heeding the warning signs as she climbed into the back of the buggy. Levi had come from a small Amish community in Ohio, just outside of the small town where Abby had grown up. He'd come early for harvest season, and no one had questioned him. He looked Amish, and his story had seemed realistic enough. Her grandfather had no reason not to bring him on as a hired hand. He was one of their own. Wasn't he?

Chapter 33

Blake feared he was probably walking into a beehive at the motel. Bruce was already angry and what he was about to say to him was going to add fuel to the fire. He spent the better part of the walk into town praying and practicing his speech. His legs were sore from all the walking after a long day of farm work, and he wished he'd had a water bottle. The night was balmy, and the Amish clothing was very warm. The only relief he felt was from the slight breeze that cooled his sweaty neck. He pulled off the straw hat and used it to fan his face. If Bruce hadn't given him an ultimatum, he'd have waited until the morning to make this trip into town.

Eager to see Main Street, Blake picked up his pace, kicking up stones along the side of the road. He wished he'd thought to take the buggy and park it on the far end of Main Street because now he would have to walk all the way back, and he was already tired. He hoped that Bruce would take the bait and leave town, but he would have to put on his best poker face to fool the man.

As he approached Main Street, Blake was happy for the street lamps to light his path. All of the stores were closed, and the only traffic was further down where all the fast-food places could be found. The smells coming from them were making him hungry after such a long walk, and he was tempted to keep walking and get himself a burger. It had been a month since he'd had any fast-food. Part of him missed it, but he had to admit Nettie was a fine cook. He had not left the table hungry since he'd been there. He'd suffered hunger too many times with Bruce. As a child, his only saving grace had been the free lunch he got at school.

Blake passed the hardware store, and as he fixed his gaze forward, he saw something that looked out of place. An Amish buggy was parked in front of the motel. Did the Amish ever take a room in a motel, or would they stay with someone in the neighboring community if they were traveling? His heart beat faster as he realized the horse looked a lot like Rachel's.

Blake took off running toward the mare. She recognized him, tipping her head when he approached. He opened the door of the buggy and discovered it was empty. Placing his bag on the seat, he wondered if Rachel had decided to take matters into her own hands and confront Bruce. Not knowing what he would find when he walked into his father's motel room, he walked slowly toward the door. He listened at the door, thinking he heard muffled cries.

"Shut up," he heard Bruce yell.

Shaking, Blake slid over to the window and peered through a small slit in the drapes. His heart slammed to his feet when he saw Rachel bound and gagged. She had been tied to a chair and Bruce had a bottle of whiskey in one hand and a *gun* in the other.

Blake backed away from the window, fearing he would be seen. Then he remembered he'd put the cell phone in the knapsack when he'd packed his things at the Miller's house. He ran over to the buggy, grabbed the phone, dialed three numbers, and then held it to his ear with a shaky hand.

"911, What's your emergency?" the operator on the other end asked.

"My d-dad," Blake stammered. "H-he's kidnapped my girlfriend. He has her tied up in his motel room, and he has a gun! You have to send someone right away."

Chapter 34

"What's this all about?" Hiram asked his son-in-law and *grandkinner*.

"We came to see Levi," Jacob said. "Rachel's been kidnapped, and we think he might know where she is."

Hiram nearly fell over at the news. Jacob and Caleb assisted him into the nearest chair.

"Levi went out a little while ago. I thought I heard the door close, so I went upstairs to check on him, he was gone and so were all his things. I looked out the second-story window and saw him walking up toward the main road carrying the same knapsack he showed up here with. I don't know where he could have gone."

"Caleb, go out to the barn and call the police," Jacob ordered his son. "He couldn't have gotten far if he was on foot. Hopefully, they will catch up to him."

"Tell them he was headed toward town," Hiram called after him.

Jacob turned to Hiram. "Will you be alright then? I think we're going to ride toward town to look for Levi. The kidnapper left a note saying that we were to wait for further instructions, but I don't think we can wait. I have to find my *dochder*. When the police get here, give them this note from the kidnapper and tell them we went to look for Levi."

When they left, Hiram took to praying for Rachel's safety. He found it hard to believe that Levi would be involved with kidnapping her.

Blake hung up the phone after being assured by the operator that there was an officer already in the area they could send. Knowing the police were probably around the corner, Blake decided he would make an attempt to reason with Bruce. He went to the door of his room and tried the doorknob. It was locked, so he knocked with a shaky hand.

He heard Bruce tell Rachel to shut up again, and then he heard him lean against the door to look through the peephole. The door swung open quickly, and Bruce stood with the gun pointed at his son.

"Well, look who decided to join the party! Get in here before I shoot your girlfriend."

Blake rushed to Rachel's side and knelt down beside her, smoothing her hair. "Are you okay? He didn't hurt you, did he?"

Bruce went over to Blake, picked him up by the back of his shirt, and shoved him across the room.

"Where's my money, Boy?"

Blake held his hands up in surrender. "I don't have it and neither do they. There is no map. There never was one. My cousin never knew her real dad, so there was never an opportunity for him to give her anything."

Bruce cocked the gun in his hand and pointed it toward Rachel. "Don't lie to me Boy, or I'll shoot your girlfriend."

Rachel squealed around the tape that was coming loose on her mouth.

Blake took a few steps closer to Rachel. "I promise you I'm not lying."

Bruce staggered closer, waving the gun carelessly. "I think the two of you planned to run off with my money. I've waited a long time for that money, and I ain't leaving here without *my* money. If I don't get it, I'll shoot the girl."

Blake took another step toward Rachel, keeping his eyes locked on Bruce. "I wish I could give it to you so you'd go away and leave me alone. I don't want to be your son anymore. I haven't for a long time. The truth is, the money doesn't exist, so why don't you just go back to Ohio and let her go."

Bruce gritted his teeth. "You leave me no choice, Son. I have to shoot her."

Bruce aimed the gun at Rachel's head, and Blake dove across her, pushing them both to the ground. The gun went off with a deafening crack, and Blake could feel the hot sting of the bullet piercing his shoulder. Agonizing pain assaulted him just before the room went black...

Chapter 35

Blake's ears were ringing, and noises seemed muffled as though he was under water. He blinked a few times, meeting Rachel's eyes as they both lay on the floor. They were face-to-face until someone picked her up, chair and all. His eyes closed uncontrollably. Someone had taken her away from him.

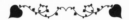

Rachel looked at Blake, trying to get him to keep his eyes open, but he wouldn't. She wanted to yell his name and tell him to hold on, but her mouth was still taped shut. She could hear Bruce laughing on the other side of the room until the door burst open.

Police officers took the gun from Bruce, handcuffed him and hauled him out of the room in one quick movement. One of the officers called for an ambulance from his two-way radio and then approached her.

"Are you okay, Miss?" he asked her.

Rachel looked at Blake lying on the floor, blood pooling around them. He closed his eyes just as the officer lifted her from the floor. She watched as another officer pressed a hotel towel against Blake's wound, while the other removed the tape and ropes that bound her.

As soon as she was free, Rachel collapsed onto the floor beside Blake. She picked up his hand in hers, held it to her lips and kissed it.

Please, Gott, let him live.

Sirens drew near, and as she looked into Blake's face, she feared he was already dying. He had saved her life, and she might never get the chance to thank him or tell him how much she loved him.

The officer moved Rachel aside as the paramedics lifted Blake onto a stretcher.

"I want to go with him," Rachel said slowly.

The paramedics motioned her to come along.

The officer stopped her. "We'll need a statement from you about what happened here."

"Can it wait? I'm all he has. I need to be with him."

The officer shook his head. "I can give you a ride to the hospital after I get your statement. They'll be taking him directly to surgery, so he won't know you're there."

"He'll know I'm there." Rachel stepped away from the officer and followed the paramedics. She turned her head over her shoulder. "You can meet me at the hospital and take my statement while I wait for him."

As Rachel climbed into the back of the ambulance, her family rode up in their buggy.

Abby jumped out and ran to the back of the ambulance. "Rachel, what happened? Is Levi alright?"

"Get the book, Abby. *The Velveteen Rabbit*. Give it to the police. I think the map is hidden in it somewhere."

* * *

Blake groaned, trying to open his eyes, but his lids felt like they were glued shut.

"Blake, can you hear me?" a sweet, angelic voice asked him.

It sounded like Rachel. If only he could open his eyes. Was he dreaming? Or was he dead? He tried to move, but felt a burning pain in his shoulder that radiated down his arm and across his back.

Dead people don't feel pain, do they?

Blake groaned with pain that seemed to pulsate through his whole upper body. His lips felt dry and his mouth felt pasty. A beeping noise blipped steadily, and the smell of fresh, clean air roused him to wakefulness. Something pinched his nostrils, but he couldn't move his arms to see what it was. A swooshing sound mixed with the beeping. What was that noise? He was sure he'd heard such noises before.

"Blake, are you awake?" the dreamy voice asked again.

Blake fluttered his eyelids. Light peered in through the narrow slit, but he just couldn't seem to pull them open any more than that.

Lord help me. I think I'm dying. Please don't let me die. I have to save Rachel.

Blake moved his head slightly from side to side, testing his eyelids once more. Gradually the light brightened, and the grogginess lifted a little more. A shadow stood over him. It looked like Rachel.

"Rachel," he struggled to say.

He felt the warmth of her hand in his. "I'm here."

Her voice sounded shaky, and he heard her sniffle. Had she been crying?

"Where—am—I?" he managed around the pain.

"You're in Elkhart General Hospital. Can you open your eyes?"

Blake tried his eyes again. They fluttered several times until they focused on Rachel. He blinked, wondering if he was dreaming.

"What happened? I hurt."

Rachel smiled sympathetically. "Your *daed* shot you. Don't you remember?"

"Where—is he?" the struggle to speak sent waves of pain through him.

Rachel looked away. "They took him to jail."

Blake pursed his lips. "Good."

Rachel squeezed his hand lightly. "I'm so sorry."

"It's not—your fault." Blake reached up slowly and grabbed at the nose clasp that fed oxygen through his nose and tried to remove it.

Rachel reached up and replaced it. "Leave this on until the doctor tells you that you can take it off. You just got out of surgery a few hours ago, and I'm sure you need it."

A nurse walked into the room just then. "I see you're awake. You are one brave young man taking a bullet for this young lady. How are you feeling?"

Blake tried to smile, but gave up. "Not—so—brave anymore."

"You had a bullet wedged in your shoulder. I imagine it will be a few weeks before you'll be ready to save any more damsels in distress." The nurse turned to Rachel. "Be careful. He won't be there to save you if you get yourself into any more trouble."

Rachel smiled at the nurse, hoping she was kidding. "When can he have visitors? *Mei familye* has been here all night waiting to see him."

Blake became nervous. Were they going to reprimand him for lying to them? Or would they be so pleased that Rachel was now safe that they would welcome him? Were they really as forgiving as Rachel had told him when they'd sat on the dock together?

"They can come in one at a time." The nurse said.

"Danki," Rachel answered.

Rachel left the room and came back with Abby.

"My *schweschder* tells me we are cousins. I'm very pleased to meet you, Blake. *Danki* for saving Rachel."

Blake nodded. "I'm sorry."

Abby looked at him with tears in her eyes. "I know. I'm more sorry that we didn't get to grow up together. We're *familye,* and since you just lost part of yours, we'll be your *familye*, if that is what you want."

Blake felt a tear roll down his cheek. "Yes."

Abby looked at Rachel. "Should we tell him now, or wait?"

Blake strained to look at the two of them. "Tell me—what?"

Abby smiled. "The map was in the inside flap of the book Eddie left me. The police found the money an hour ago. All one million dollars of it. The best part is, they sent an officer here to tell me there is a reward. We each get fifty-thousand dollars, cousin."

Blake tried to shake his head. "You can—have it."

"I won't hear of it, dear cousin. I hear you plan on staying in the community. You'll need to buy a piece of land if you plan to be an Amish farmer."

With that, she left the room.

Blake didn't know what he'd done to deserve such a nice cousin. She was the only family he had now, and she had welcomed him as his real self. Not to mention, she'd thought of *him* with regard to the reward money. Though a part of him felt he didn't deserve it, he would welcome it if it meant he would be able to own a piece of God's green earth and work it as his own. God had truly answered his prayer.

A few minutes later, Hiram entered the room and stood next to his bed.

"How long before they let you out of here, Blake?" he asked.

Hearing his real name from Hiram made Blake a little more than nervous. Did the man want him to get well so he could take him out to the barn and have good "talk" with him?

"I—don't know." Blake answered.

"I hope it's soon because we need you for the harvest. That's what I hired you for, and I need a *gut* strong *mann* to help me. I hope you're still willing to help me even though I hear you're a wealthy *mann* now."

Blake couldn't believe his ears.

"I'm not—fired?"

Hiram laughed. It was probably the only time Blake had heard him *really* laugh. "*Nee*, you can't get out of this by getting shot. We know that your *daed* was the one that forced you into this life. You were a victim more than we were."

Blake swallowed the lump in his throat. "I'm sorry."

"I know you are, Son. I forgive you for lying about being Amish, but Rachel tells us you'd like to join the church."

"Yes, I—would."

"Get your rest then, and we'll talk to the Bishop about getting you into the classes as soon as you get out of here. You can take the Baptism after the harvest."

Hiram patted Blake's hand and then left the room. A few minutes later, Rachel returned.

"*Grossdaddi* says you're to take the Baptism in the fall."

Blake chuckled, but the pain stopped him.

"*Jah*. Imagine. Me—Blake Monroe—Amish!"

"It doesn't matter if your name is Blake Monroe, Levi Schrock, or something else. *Gott* knows your heart, and just so long as it belongs to Him…and me…" Rachel kissed him lightly on the lips.

Blake closed his eyes, feeling overwhelmed with thankfulness. "Always."

Danki, Lord.

THE END

Under the Harvest Moon
Book 7 Jacob's Daughter series

Samantha Jillian Bayarr

Chapter 1

"Come quick!" Rachel pleaded with Doctor Davis from the phone at her *Aenti* Bess's B&B. "*Mei aenti's* rolling on the floor holding her stomach. Something's really wrong with her! I can't get her to stop crying long enough to ask her what happened!"

Rachel wasn't sure what the doctor could do for her *Aenti,* but Bess had given her a strict warning not to call for an ambulance—even if her appendix burst. She wouldn't tell the woman that the doc insisted on sending an ambulance anyway.

For a moment, Rachel considered whether she should leave Bess to look for her husband, Jessup, but his horse and buggy wasn't in the barn when she'd arrived, and Bess's screams had prompted her into the house. Taking a deep breath, Rachel ran back to tend to her crying *aenti*, whose screams became louder the closer she came to the kitchen entrance. Right where she'd left her, Bess lay sprawled across the floor in a puddle of water. Her deep blue dress was soaked and clung to her skin as the poor woman doubled over, groaning from the pain.

Rachel scanned the kitchen for a possible source of the water, but realized the puddle was only under Bess. It hadn't been there when she'd gone into the parlor to call for the doctor.

She'd seen this before!

"*Aenti,* can you get up so I can move you to the sofa? I think you might be more comfortable there until the doctor gets here."

"*Nee,*" she groaned before doubling at her ample waistline.

Bess had always been a thick woman, and Rachel knew there was no way she could get her to the sofa without some cooperation from the woman.

Rachel gulped. "*Aenti,* I don't mean to pry, but when was your last cycle?"

Bess suddenly opened her eyes and glared at her niece. "I went through the change about the same time I married Jessup," she grunted. "*Ach,* am I hemorrhaging? It feels like my insides are trying to come outside of me." She reached down and felt the dampness of her dress, and then brought her hand to her face for examination. Confused at the lack of what she thought would be blood on her dampened hand, Bess looked to Rachel quizzically.

"You're not bleeding, but I suspect you might be— having a *boppli!*

"*Nee,* that's impossible," she grunted and bore down. "I'm old and already went through the change. Doctor Davis even said it was so."

It wasn't impossible. Bess was only in her early fifties. Many of the women in the community had *bopplies* well into their fifties.

Bess grunted again and cried out. "I have to go to the washroom."

Rachel had no idea how she would get her there, but she suspected Bess was feeling a need to bear down. Bess and Jessup had been married for more than a year now, and the woman had always been so plump that she could easily disguise a pregnancy in the folds of her girth. But how could she have gone this long without knowing she was pregnant? Was it even possible? Rachel supposed at her age, Bess and Doctor Davis both would have assumed the change before a pregnancy. Since her *Aenti* had never been pregnant before, she wouldn't have known to look for it. But how was it that none of her family had even suspected?

"Can you get up?" Rachel asked in-between the woman's cries.

Bess shook her head frantically as she held her breath and grunted. "I'm sorry for the mess I'm about to make. I can't make this urge stop."

Suddenly Bess's face turned pale. "I think my womb just fell out. Maybe—you should call for that ambulance." She began to cry and Rachel soothed her.

Rachel approached her next statement with care, hoping she wouldn't offend her *aenti*. "I should make certain you are not bleeding."

"Hurry," Bess cried. "If I'm dying and you can save me, then do what you have to."

Rachel could hear the sudden panic in Bess's voice, and wondered if she should reassure her by admitting that an ambulance was on its way. Reluctantly, Rachel lifted the water-soaked dress to see what was happening. Both joy and anxiety filled her as she spotted the crown of a baby's head.

Rachel looked at Bess sternly. "I need you to push as hard as you can when the pain seizes you again. I can see the *boppli's* head."

There was no time for either of them to think about it. Within seconds Bess grunted and pushed with a loud screech. Rachel eased out one shoulder, cradling the head just before the wee one slipped from her *aenti's* womb. Tears filled Rachel's eyes, emotion constricting her throat as Bess rested her head on the linoleum from pure exhaustion, the pains finally subsiding.

Rachel used the corner of her apron to wipe the baby's mouth, causing him to let out a wail. Bess's head popped up from the floor and stared at the wiggling infant in Rachel's hands.

Immediately, Rachel handed him to his *mamm* as she watched her *aenti's* expression turn from shock to sheer joy as she reached for her baby. Bess cradled the infant in her arms while Rachel pulled a pillow and lap quilt from the sofa to make her *aenti* more comfortable until help arrived. After tucking the pillow under her head, she reached up onto the table and grabbed yarn and a pair of sheers where Bess had been crocheting before the pains had consumed her. Rachel tied the length of yarn in two spots onto the cord and snipped it with the sewing sheers.

Bess hadn't taken her eyes off her new son and hadn't paid any attention to Rachel's bustling about her kitchen. By the dreamy look in her *aenti's* eyes, Rachel could tell she was enamored with her unexpected gift.

Chapter 2

Jessup burst in the back door of the B&B, shock paling his face. He looked at his *fraa* lying on the kitchen floor, a *boppli* in her arms, while Rachel sopped up water from the floor around her.

Rachel looked up from the chore. *"Onkel* Jessup, I think *aenti* has something to tell you."

Bess looked up from the wiggling bundle in her arms long enough to beckon her husband to her side. *"Kume,* meet your new son."

Jessup nearly fell over. He stepped back and caught himself against a kitchen chair as he stared at his *fraa*. His heart raced, but strangely, no pain existed there. He put his hand to his chest. Was he having a heart attack, but was in too much shock to notice the pain?

Jessup looked at the baby in Bess's arms, and at the expression on her face. He'd seen that look before from his deceased wife when she'd borne him his older children. Now he was a new *daed* again. Was he ready for this? Would his aging body hold out long enough to watch the wee one grow to be a man?

A thrilling fear gripped Jessup, but he swallowed it as he knelt close to his *fraa's* head to place a kiss on her forehead. He placed a hand over the baby's head and smoothed his dark hair. Tears welled up in his eyes as he felt pure love for his wife and new son.

"He's really ours?" Jessup asked with a shaky voice.

"He is a miracle, *jah?*" Bess asked.

"I suppose the doc was wrong about you going through the change," Jessup chuckled.

They both laughed and cried at the same time, as Jessup cradled his family in his arms. To start over with his wife was truly a miracle.

Rachel entered the room, holding another quilt she'd taken from the spare room upstairs, and handed it to her uncle.

"If we wrap the *boppli,* then we can get *Aenti* into her own bed where she might be more comfortable while we wait for Doctor Davis."

As Rachel wrapped the baby in the quilt, Doctor Davis walked in through the kitchen. With the door open, they could hear the siren from the ambulance nearing the B&B.

Doctor Davis looked to each of the faces, and then focused on the bundle in Rachel's arms. "What happened here? Bess, are you alright?"

Bess let out an unusual giggle none of them had ever heard before. "I had a *boppli!* I wasn't going through the change after all. I was pregnant!"

Doctor Davis smiled. "It's not the first time I've been wrong."

Jessup shook the doctor's hand. "I'm mighty glad you were wrong *this* time. He's a handsome fella, ain't so?"

They shook hands vigorously. "Yes, he is. Let's get momma into her own bed if we can, so I can examine her. How are you feeling, Bess?"

"I couldn't be better. Did you call for an ambulance?"

Doctor Davis nodded. "I was worried it was something serious, so I called for one as a precaution. Do you want them to stand by until I make sure everything is alright?"

Bess shook her head as she admired her newborn son. "Everything is fine. Send them away."

Rachel followed the two men into the bedroom, her new little cousin resting peacefully in her arms. It seemed strange and natural at the same time for Rachel to recognize who the baby was in connection to her.

Once Bess was safely in her own room, she asked Rachel to help her into her nightgown. Rachel handed the baby to Doctor Davis, and then went to the bureau to get fresh linen bedclothes for her *aenti*. Doctor Davis busied himself examining the new arrival while Rachel fussed with Bess to get her settled. Jessup quickly left the room to meet the ambulance and to send them on their way.

Doctor Davis pulled the stethoscope from his ears. "That's one strong boy you have there."

Rachel excused herself to make some tea for her *aenti*. When she entered the kitchen, she realized she'd almost forgotten about the mess on the floor. *Aenti* would be in no condition to take on her house chores for at least a week, depending on what the doc said to her. But given her age, Rachel imagined her *aenti* would be bound to bed-rest for at least that long.

Inside the mudroom, Rachel found a bucket, a stack of clean rags, and a scrub brush she knew she could use to clean the floor. She filled the bucket and set to work after putting on the kettle for tea.

Blake entered the kitchen while Rachel was finishing up the floor. He looked at her a little strangely.

"Why is the doc's buggy here?"

Rachel emptied the bucket of dirty water out the back door and wrung out the rags she'd used beneath her feet to "mop" the floor. "Doctor Davis is here for *Aenti*."

Blake looked around at the disheveled kitchen.

"What happened here?"

The tea kettle whistled and Rachel wiped her hands on her apron so she could remove it before it lost all its water through the steam cap. Rachel looked back at Blake, her eyes gleaming. "*Aenti* Bess had a *boppli.*"

Blake chuckled. "A baby? I didn't know she was expecting."

Rachel laughed. "Neither did poor *Aenti*. She had an awful time of it. No one was here, so I had to deliver him."

"Him? She has a boy? Jessup has to be beside himself."

"*Mei onkel* is quite beside himself indeed." Rachel laughed at the sound of her own statement. "I can't believe those two didn't know she was expecting. *Aenti* assumed it was the change she was going through, but this is such a blessing."

Blake pulled Rachel into his arms and nuzzled her neck. "By this time next year, we could have a *boppli* of our own."

Rachel felt heat rise in her cheeks at the thought of having Blake's *kinner*. "Maybe we should concentrate on getting married first. I can't believe we are to be married in less than two weeks! This past year has gone by so fast."

Blake pulled away from her and drew a letter from his pocket. "I finally got a letter from Bruce."

Rachel's ears perked up at the sound of her kidnapper's name. It was hard for Rachel to believe that it had been more than a year since her ordeal with Blake's father, but she felt safe knowing he'd been in prison the entire time.

"By the look on your face, it must be *gut* news," Rachel said, trying not to worry.

Chapter 3

Blake held the letter up in front of his face, a faint smile forming on his lips. "I'm guessing that having a year to sober up and reflect on his lifetime of mistakes has been good for him. His letter says he started attending the church services they have at the chapel in the prison."

"That is *gut* news. I suspect you still have cause for concern. You look a little stressed."

Blake pulled the straw hat from his head and placed it on a hook near the kitchen door. Looping his fingers in his suspenders, he let them snap against his muscular chest. "He doesn't understand why I took the baptism to become Amish. He thinks I did it just for you. I've tried explaining to him that because of my baptism I was able to forgive him for kidnapping you and shooting me. I'm hoping that the church-going will open his eyes. It's obviously bringing him around a little bit or he wouldn't have written back to me after all this time."

"We can continue to keep him in our prayers," Rachel offered. "Surely *Gott* will soften his heart."

Blake let out a breath in a whoosh. "I pray that it is so. But his letter didn't sound as remorseful as I'd hoped."

Rachel wrapped her arms around Blake and placed a soft kiss on his neck. "You've done your part by forgiving him. The rest is up to him. Perhaps in time."

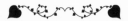

Jessup couldn't take his eyes off his new son. He cradled the wee one in his arms while Doctor Davis finished his examination of Bess. He couldn't wait to show him off to his older children and the rest of his family.

For now, he would savor this moment and cherish it, remembering how quickly babies grow. His immediate thought was to get the cradle he'd made for his first-born, but it had been left behind in Nappanee along with most of their belongings when they'd moved to the B&B. Their mother could never part with the cradle or quilts and such, saying they could someday be used for *grandkinner*. But after her death, Jessup couldn't bear to see them. As far as he knew, the items had remained undisturbed in the attic of his farm that his eldest brother had moved into after Jessup had left Nappanee. Surely Bess would want to make new things for the baby in the meantime, but he aimed to get that cradle somehow.

When the doctor finished with Bess, Jessup pulled the ladder-back chair next to the bed, his new son tucked in his other arm. He looked up into his wife's dreamy face and smiled.

"What shall we call him?"

Bess managed a weak smile. "I was thinking since he's my first, and probably my last *boppli*, that I should give him the name Adam."

Jessup smiled. "*Das gut.* It's a strong name for such a strong boy."

Jessup couldn't help but feel a swell of pride as he gazed lovingly upon his newborn son. The wee one represented a new start for him. He'd been feeling his age recently as his other children continued to grow older. His oldest would be out on his own in just a few short years, but with a new brother in the family, perhaps the boy wouldn't seem so eager to grow up.

Bess closed her eyes, feeling too sleepy to resist a little nap. With Jessup and her new baby securely next to her, she yielded to her body's prompting to let sleep overtake her. Jessup slipped out of the room with Adam in his arms. Once he was in the kitchen, he handed the *boppli* over to Rachel.

"I need to call Hiram to give him the news of his *schweschder's boppli*. Won't he be surprised? I suppose I will make calls to the rest of our *familye*. If Bess wakes up, let her know where I am."

Blake winked at Rachel as he followed Jessup into the front parlor of the B&B. She knew they would most likely be preoccupied for a while, so she took the baby into the private sitting room to relax in the rocking chair. It had been a long day, and she hadn't made it back to bakery to reopen for the afternoon.

"I don't care if my customers missed me this afternoon," she cooed at little Adam. "I wouldn't have passed up the opportunity to help bring you into this world for all the customers in Elkhart County."

If Rachel hadn't come over early to have lunch with *Aenti* Bess, the woman would have been on her own. The thought made Rachel shudder. The thing she was most grateful for was that there were presently no guests staying at the B&B. One thing was certain, though, they would either have to close down temporarily, or hire someone to run the place until *Aenti* Bess was back on her feet.

She peered down at little Adam sleeping trustfully in her arms.

Danki, Gott for this little miracle.

Chapter 4

Lila King looked out across the room of the crowded bus station. Most everyone was being greeted or sent off by a loved-one, but not her. She was waiting for a stranger to pick her up. She felt foreign among a sea of *Englischers* as she leaned against *Onkel* Jessup's handmade cradle. It was large and heavy, and she'd had to have assistance from the driver to haul the cradle into the waiting area of the bus station.

The musty air of the station was stifling and almost nauseating when coupled with the smell of diesel fuel exhaust that drifted in through the open doors from where the busses sat in the holding area just outside with their motors running.

Lila's attention suddenly wavered to the doorway where a handsome Amish man entered. It was as if she had somehow sensed his presence. She could see the blue in his eyes from where she sat, and the dimples that formed at his instant smile when his gaze met hers were enough to unseat her. She wondered—no hoped—it wasn't Samuel Yoder, *Onkel* Jessup's new nephew to come for her. Her uncle had sent for her after the news of a baby that had shocked the entire family. With no other relatives to take care of the B&B, while the new parents tended to their unexpected blessing, Lila was the logical choice to provide her services to the family. Besides, it had been urgent for her to get the handmade cradle to her *onkel* to use for his new baby. Now, Lila was certain she would have to endure the discomfort of riding with this handsome stranger.

The young man approached her with the sort of confidence Lila would deem to be somewhat prideful, but still charming. "Are you Lila?" he asked.

"*Jah.* You must be Samuel." Her voice shook nervously.

Samuel bent down to pick up her bag and the wooden cradle, and then he walked toward the door without another word to her. Would the ride to her *onkel's haus* be filled with the same reserve? She was fairly certain she didn't want to engage in conversation with Samuel, but neither was she fond of awkward silence. She forced herself to believe that awkward silence was better than letting this man's alluring smile distract her from the pact she'd made with herself to not become caught up with marriage and having children the way her friends had. Since her *mamm* had died minutes after giving birth to her, she had determined, even at a young age that she would not risk bringing children into the world only to leave them without a *mamm* the way she'd grown up.

Lila sighed, knowing that the ride in close-quarters with such a handsome man would not be an easy test of her willpower. But she'd been able to resist the advances of every suitor for the past few years who had come to ask her to take buggy rides with them. She could handle a short buggy ride with Samuel, especially since she would most likely not see him again.

Lila tried not to show her discomfort as Samuel's leg rested so close to hers she could feel his body heat. Never mind that it was a chilly day, and there didn't seem to be a lap-quilt in the buggy.

Samuel slapped the reins against the gelding's muscular flank. "I hope the weather stays cool without freezing for the next couple of weeks so it will be nice for the wedding."

Be polite, but not encouraging. He doesn't have to know I would rather not talk to him.

"*Mei schweschder,* Rachel, is marrying Blake Monroe," he continued. "There is much to be done to prepare. It's *gut* timing for your visit so you can help with preparations at the B&B since that is where the wedding is to take place. The *familye* was concerned that with the arrival of the new *boppli,* that it would slow the progress, but you will be a *gut* addition. I'm certain Rachel will be grateful for the extra help."

That's just great, Lila groaned inwardly. *I didn't realize that Onkel was volunteering me to help with a wedding!*

Lila didn't allow herself to swoon over babies or weddings the way her friends and cousins did. She was against all of it, and would just as soon steer clear of any part of it. Unfortunately, her *daed* had put her into a tight spot, where both situations would be clearly unavoidable.

"I imagine you're eager to see the new *boppli. Mei schweschders* and *mamm* have already spoiled him. Most women are *narrish* when they learn of a new *boppli,* and they all have to visit and make clothes and quilts."

She wasn't crazy over the presence of a new baby, but she would not admit that to this handsome stranger.

She smiled politely. *"Onkel* Jessup said I was to take over the duties at the B&B to keep it running."

"Jah, but there are no reservations set until Christmas, so he will most likely ask you to help with wedding preparations or to help *Aenti* Bess with the baby.

Lila had no intention of helping with the infant, but the only alternative was to assist with preparing for something she did not believe in—a wedding. How could she help with something she was so much against? It would be the first time she would meet her new cousins, and she was not getting off to a very good start.

Samuel flashed her a sideways glance while keeping his eye on the busy road ahead. "You *do* like weddings, don't you?"

Chapter 5

When Samuel steered the gelding into the circle drive of the B&B, Lila could not get out of the buggy fast enough. Most girls would daydream about having Samuel pull them into an embrace, and wrapping his work-strong arms around them.

Not her.

She had spent nearly the entire buggy ride pushing such thoughts from her mind to avoid giving into something that could never be a part of her life. In her mind, it was best to be casual and cordial, but nothing more.

Lila didn't wait for Samuel to fetch her bag from the back of the buggy. While he tied his horse, she was nearly up the steps to the B&B with it, and didn't dare look back. It wasn't her intention to be rude, but when he brought in the cradle, she would thank him for the ride to her *aenti's* house in the presence of family. This way she could avoid any lingering conversation with him. The buggy ride had seemed excruciatingly lengthy because of the long silence between them, but she'd made it very clear to Samuel that she was not interested in being overly friendly. It was better that way. It was best not to give him any reason to ask to call on her company.

Samuel took his time with his horse, making certain there was fresh water in the trough. He patted the side of his gelding's nose. "Do you think that girl is a mite shy, or do you think she has a beau?"

The gelding nickered and bobbed his head.

"You're right. A girl that handsome probably has the *menner* lining up to visit with her at Sunday Singings."

Samuel moved to the open door of the buggy and retrieved the handmade cradle. He knew Jessup had been eager for it to arrive. And not a day too soon since the baby was already three days old. He'd overheard his *mamm* and sisters talking about Jessup's unhappiness over having to place his new son in a wicker laundry basket packed with a quilt. Samuel didn't see what the big deal was. In fact, he'd thought it was a pretty good idea. But what did he know? He wasn't married with *kinner* of his own. Even though his twin sister was about to get married, Samuel didn't have a sweetheart or even any prospects.

It wasn't until he met Lila just now that he'd even given it any thought before. What was it about her that prompted such thoughts in him? Perhaps it was her aloof behavior. He was used to the girls in the community paying a lot of attention to him, but he hadn't found one yet that he had any real interest in—until now. He could have his pick of any girl in the community, so why did he suddenly find himself wanting this one?

Samuel let himself in through the kitchen door of the B&B. He could smell the woodsy smell of the fireplace even before he heard the crackling and popping. It brought warmth to his bones from the chill of the late afternoon. Jessup greeted him before he made it to the small sitting room on the private side of the B&B.

Jessup's face lit up at the sight of the cradle tucked under Samuel's arm.

"When Lila didn't come in with it, I worried for a minute."

Jessup took the cradle and gazed upon it as though it was made from pure gold. "I never thought I would have to use this again unless it was for *grandkinner*. Isn't it funny how life changes sometimes? Just when you don't expect *Gott* could give you anymore, he blesses you one more time."

Tears welled up in his eyes as he walked to the back stairwell that led to the private living quarters.

Not knowing what to do with himself, Samuel walked back to the kitchen to make a pot of fresh coffee to keep him warm on his trip home. The sun had begun to sink below the tree-line, and it was starting to feel like the end of October out there. The first week of November would be a little colder, but Samuel prayed the weather would hold steady until his sister's wedding.

Lila entered the room and turned to leave when she saw Samuel. He looked up at her and beckoned her back into the room.

"You want some *kaffi?* The ride here was a little chilly. I'm sorry I forgot to put the lap quilts back in the buggy."

Lila nodded shyly and eyed the cupboards wondering which one contained the cups.

Samuel could see what she was asking without saying a word. He pointed to the cupboard to her right. "The cups are in that one."

He pulled on the utensil drawer. "Spoons are in here." Then pointed to the narrow cupboard beside her. "Sugar and honey are in there."

"Danki," she said almost too quiet for him to hear.

Samuel was used to the women in his life being outspoken. He had his work cut out for him if he was ever going to get this one to feel comfortable enough around him to talk. From the few words she'd spoken, he knew she had a lovely voice. It was gentle and angelic—one he could get used to listening to for the rest of his life.

Lila cleared her throat. "The *kaffi* is ready."

Samuel's face heated. Had she noticed him daydreaming? *"Danki,"* he muttered as he poured *kaffi* into the cups Lila had set beside him.

He looked into her angelic face as she sipped the hot beverage cautiously. He wanted to ask her to the Sunday Singing tomorrow evening, but he suddenly lost his nerve. What was wrong with him? He'd always been at ease when talking to women. Was his sudden inability to form more than two words because she appeared to not be interested in him?

Chapter 6

Lila scooped the pumpkin seeds and fleshy insides from the freshly-picked gourd. Now that she'd been at her *onkel's* house for three days, she'd settled into a routine. Her duties were a lot different than what she'd been expecting when she was asked to help, but she didn't mind. As long as she wasn't being asked to tend to the baby, Lila would be content with taking over the kitchen duties and assisting with wedding preparations for Rachel.

Mashing the pumpkin in the mixing bowl, she hoped her loaves of bread would be enough for the family dinner that Jessup had asked her to cook for. Lila intended to serve the dinner in the large dining area that was normally for guests, hoping the distance would keep her from contact with Samuel. She knew he would be attending, but what she didn't know was why it worried her the way it did. She refused to admit to herself that she could be attracted to his baritone voice or his lively blue eyes that seemed to dance with constant delight.

Lila mindlessly knocked the bowl with the pumpkin seeds onto the floor.

Oh no, they're ruined. Now I can't roast them! I better stop daydreaming and concentrate on what I'm doing so I don't shame onkel with my carelessness.

Bending down to clean the mess, she wondered if she would always be happy working in someone else's kitchen. It hadn't struck her until just now that she could be tending her *mamm's* kitchen in the deceased woman's absence for the rest of her life—as a spinster.

"Do you need some help?"

The strong baritone voice startled her, causing her to bump her head on the underside of the table. Lila rested on her haunches, rubbing the sore spot on the top of her head as she glared at Samuel.

He reached a hand to assist her, but she refused, scooping up the last of the spilled pumpkin and placing it back in its bowl.

"I didn't mean to startle you. Sounds like you hit your head pretty hard. I think it's bleeding on the top." He reached out toward the back of her head, but she flinched away from him.

"At least sit down for a minute and let me get you a wet towel so we can make sure you don't need the doc to come and stitch you up."

She reluctantly obeyed his gentle urging, but only because her scalp stung and her head wouldn't stop pounding. She reached up and touched the tender spot, and then instinctively drew her hand in front of her face. She dizzied at the sight of blood on her fingers.

Samuel rushed to her side with a wet dishrag, pressing it to the wound. "Hold this for a minute. Put pressure on it. Head wounds always bleed a lot."

She replaced her hand on the dishrag, wincing at the pressure she placed on the injury. Samuel unpinned her *kapp,* causing her to gasp. She automatically reached up with her other hand and tried to stop him.

Samuel gazed into her eyes, momentarily hypnotizing her with the blue depths that pleaded with her to trust him.

Lila allowed him to unpin her hair to better reach the abrasion on her scalp that suddenly didn't hurt anymore.

Samuel ran his fingers through the tresses of Lila's sun-streaked chestnut hair, trying desperately to focus on assessing the severity of the laceration. He had never had his fingers in a woman's hair before, and the sensation drew him to her in a loving way.

Lila couldn't help but be mesmerized by the feel of Samuel's fingers trolling across her scalp. Until now, she had remained untouched by any man. How would she ever be able to resist such an awareness of his touch for the remainder of her stay here? Out of necessity, she steeled her emotions against him, suddenly becoming rigid.

Lila jumped from her chair suddenly. "Does it need stitches?"

Samuel, caught off guard by her sudden change of demeanor, shook his head. *"Nee."*

Lila narrowed her mouth. "Then please leave me alone to finish making the meal. It's getting late, and I don't have time to worry about a little scrape on my head when I have to prepare a meal for the entire *familye.*"

Until she suddenly changed her tone to reflect harshness, Samuel had been tempted to meet Lila's full lips with his. He conceded, knowing his sisters would arrive any moment to assist her with the meal. He looked into her steely hazel eyes once more before exiting the room. He'd seen vulnerability in those eyes just moments before, and he couldn't bear to gaze upon the indifference he saw there now. What had imprinted such hardness of her heart that it should reflect in her eyes?

Samuel left the room, his exposed heart feeling the twinge of pain from her steely gaze. Had it been his imagination that he'd felt her respond to him? He was certain he hadn't mistaken the dreamy look in her eyes at his touch that was quickly replaced with such melancholy he could hardly bear it. Why did he feel such a strong desire to be the one to break through the sadness in her heart? He barely knew her, but yet he wanted to be the one to shelter her and bring joy to her heart.

Lila chided herself for letting her guard down long enough to let Samuel affect her the way he had, as she twisted her hair back into a tight bun at the back of her head. She had no desire to become romantically involved with any man. Her lifelong stance had been never to wed and never to bring a baby into the world full of the sort of emptiness she had endured from growing up without a *mamm*. No relative had been able to fill the gap that her *mamm* had left in her heart when she'd died moments after giving birth to her. She would not risk doing the same thing to a child of her own.

Chapter 7

Samuel couldn't help but stare at Lila as she placed the plate in front of him. She had not made eye-contact with him at all as she moved about the room making certain everything was in place. Her reluctance to sit with the family during the meal did not go unnoticed. She seemed friendly enough with his sisters, causing him to wonder if it was not the world she loathed, but him. But when Rachel tried to pass little Adam to Lila, Samuel saw Lila's reaction and couldn't help but wonder at the look of fear in her eyes. Had she never held a baby before? She'd looked upon Adam as though he was a poisonous snake rather than an innocent baby, and that concerned Samuel.

In the kitchen, Lila placed a second batch of yeast rolls in the basket and covered them with the linen towel to keep them warm.

Rachel entered the kitchen and watched her for a moment. "Are you alright, Lila? You seem to be a little nervous. Was it too much for you to prepare the meal for this many people? I know you're not used to this much cooking."

"*Nee,* we don't have this much *familye* back in Nappanee. Most of them are scattered in other communities."

Rachel felt compassion tug at her heart. "I'm certain your *onkel* would enjoy it if you stayed on here at the B&B for a while."

"I will be settling here, it seems. A letter arrived today with the details. *Mei daed* has finally managed to sell *Onkel* Jessup's farm for him, and he'll be here in three weeks. We'll live in the *dawdi haus*. *Onkel* has asked me to clean and paint it to prepare for his arrival."

Rachel pulled Lila into an unexpected hug.

"That's *gut* news*!*"

Lila turned serious. "I promise it won't interfere with the wedding preparations you've asked for my help with."

"I'm not so much worried about that as I am with you taking on another project on your own. You seem so stressed as it is."

Lila waved her off. "I will be able to get everything done as long as there are no guests at the B&B."

Rachel smiled thoughtfully. "I'll ask Samuel to help you. He enjoys painting."

"*Nee,*" Lila said with an urgency that alarmed Rachel.

She patted Lila's arm. "I know you aren't used to *familye* helping, but my *familye* does nothing but help each other. I'm certain it will be no trouble at all for Samuel to help you get the *dawdi haus* ready for your *daed.*"

Lila smiled nervously as she thanked Rachel. How was she going to endure being alone with Samuel while they painted the *dawdi haus?* She would just have to spend more time in prayer asking God for strength to resist the temptation that Samuel posed.

Lila returned to the dining room and took her place across from Samuel. She could feel his eyes on her, and it made her too nervous to finish her meal. Pushing the potatoes and asparagus around on her plate, Lila decided to focus on the banter around the long table.

"We must finish the fitting of your dress," Lizzie said to her daughter. "You have to take a little time off from the bakery to let me sew it, or it will not be finished in time for the wedding."

Katie nudged her. "I'd be more than happy to take over for a day if you need me to. We can't have the bride showing up to her own wedding in an old work dress."

Rachel's eyebrows furrowed. "That's *narrish,* Katie. You're too close to term. I can't have you giving birth to *mei bruder's boppli* in the bakery."

"If *Onkel* can do without me for the day," Lila said cautiously. "I'd be more than happy to step in for you."

"I thought you were going to spend the day painting the *dawdi haus*, Lila," Bess interjected.

"I'd be more than happy to help you paint, Lila," Samuel offered.

Rachel smirked at her brother. "I already volunteered you for the job, Samuel."

Lila's cheeks heated up, and she could feel Samuel's gaze upon her once more. She resisted the urge to make eye-contact with him, no matter how tempting it was to get lost in the sea of blue in his eyes that lured her in like a fish. It was best if she not give him any reason to hope they could be anything more than distant acquaintances. She was not the one for him. She was certain he deserved more than she could offer even if she was interested—which she was not. That's the way it would remain as long as she had control over guarding her heart.

After the meal, all the women crowded into the kitchen to help with the cleanup, with the exception of Bess, who needed to nurse Adam and get him to sleep for a while. Lila could tell the *boppli* was draining the woman of her energy, but Bess remained smitten with her infant.

Katie sat at the small table in the kitchen, rolling her hand lovingly over her large belly as though her *boppli* were already born. Lizzie, Rachel, and Abby worked like machines to scrape plates, stack them, and put away all the messes Lila had made while she was cooking. Each worked, leaving Lila to put on a fresh pot of *kaffi* for the *menner,* who waited in the other room for shoofly pie. Lillian sat across from Katie at the table, bouncing one-year-old Ellie on her knee to keep her from fussing.

Lizzie handed her a wet dishcloth. "Let her chew on this. She needs something to bring those molars in. Poor thing must be in pain."

Lila felt a little out of sorts being in such an enclosed setting with Samuel's *familye.* They were *her familye* by marriage, but that didn't make her feel any closer to them. She hoped that in time she would get used to being around them. Since all her friends back home were married, she hadn't seen much of them and wasn't used to being around this many women all at once. They seemed to be enjoyable, and if it was possible, she might even become friends with them—but not with Samuel—definitely not with Samuel.

Chapter 8

Before long, Lila began to relax as she fell in step with the women in the kitchen. They all seemed to work in sync with one another, and Lila soon found her place wiping the dishes dry and replacing them in the cupboards. She was still learning her way around Bess's kitchen, and putting away dishes was a *gut* way to learn.

Rachel knocked elbows with Lila. "What do you think of *mei bruder,* Samuel?"

Lila nearly dropped the glass plate she was drying. What exactly was it that Rachel was asking her? "I don't know him," she answered simply.

Rachel smirked. "You don't know any of us yet, but it seems like you were avoiding Samuel most of the night. He was trying hard to get your attention."

Lila didn't dare say a word as she took the next clean plate from Lizzie to dry. She didn't want to discuss what she thought of Samuel in front of his *mamm.*

"Rachel, don't embarrass the poor girl," Lizzie said over her shoulder.

"We have been trying to get Samuel matched up with someone for a while, and he keeps turning them away," Katie said from where she sat at the table with Lillian.

"It seems he wants to be a bachelor for the rest of his life," Lillian added.

What did all of this have to do with her? Lila didn't want to be part of this conversation. She didn't want to paired-up with Samuel, and if that's what these women were up to, she didn't want anything to do with them.

"There is nothing wrong with a *mann* wanting to be a bachelor," Lila stated nervously.

Rachel took the next plate, leaving Lila with nothing to busy her nervous hands. "I think he wants to be married, but he just hasn't found the right girl yet."

"I noticed him watching you several times throughout the meal, Lila" Katie interjected.

Lillian smiled. "I noticed the same thing."

"I think we all did," Abby said.

Lila didn't find anything too amusing about this conversation, but Samuel's family seemed to be having fun at her expense.

She stiffened her upper lip. "I hadn't noticed him watching me, and if I had, I probably would have politely asked him to stop."

Rachel giggled. "You could tell him to stop, but I doubt he would. He was swooning over you."

The women in the room all laughed, and Lila pasted on a smile to keep from letting them know the subject of Samuel was not one she cared to talk about.

"If he was swooning, he was alone in it, because I have no interest in him." Lila tried to keep an even tone to prevent them from seeing how disturbed she was by the conversation.

"Not even a little?" Katie asked. "He's a handsome young *mann.*"

"And thoughtful, too," Abby chimed in. "And I'm not just saying that because he's *mei bruder.*"

"And he's available," Lillian added.

Lila's lips narrowed to a grim line. "Well I'm not—available."

The women looked at each other and turned serious. Had she ended the conversation, or had she merely insulted them and their efforts to help her?

"So you have a beau back in Nappanee?" Katie finally asked.

"*Nee,* I don't have a beau," Lila said quietly.

Lizzie turned around from the sink after washing the last dish. "Are you married, then?"

Lila was getting tired of all the personal questions. "*Nee,* I'm not married, and I don't intend to ever marry."

Abby placed a comforting hand on Lila's shoulder. "You poor thing; you've had your heart broken."

If having your *mamm* die just after giving birth to you, and growing up without a *mamm* while everyone around you has one, then, yes, her heart had been broken beyond repair. But she was certain they were talking about heartbreak from a beau.

"*Nee,* I've never even dated before," Lila said, her face heating from the confession.

She didn't want them to know her deepest secrets, but they were prying them out of her.

Lizzie suddenly shooed the other women from the room.

"Why do *we* have to leave?" Abby asked. "What did we do? We were just trying to get to know Lila a little better!"

Lizzie looked at Lila, who was shaking.

"I think you've asked enough questions for now. Give us a minute to talk. *Git* on out of here—all of you," Lizzie said with an authoritative tone.

After they shuffled from the kitchen one-by-one, Lizzie invited Lila to sit at the table with her. She placed a hand on Lila's from across the table.

"I understand from Jessup that you grew up without a *mamm*. I'm sure that's been tough on you, since most girls see an older sibling dating, or they talk to their *mamm* about such things. If you ever want to talk, you can talk to me or *mei Aenti* Bess, or any of these women. We are *familye* now, and we want you to feel like you can come to us if you need to."

Lila appreciated Lizzie's kindness, but she didn't think the woman understood her situation.

"*Mei mamm* died a few minutes after giving birth to me, I don't want to put a child through that. So I made a choice not to marry or have any *kinner.*"

Lizzie became serious. "I grew up without a *mamm* too. It wasn't like your situation; she was with me until I was ten years old. But sometimes I think that was harder on me because I got the chance to become attached to her. That may sound like a harsh thing to say, but it's sometimes easier to deal with a loss we never knew than to love someone that long and lose them. But you can't let that situation rule your entire life. You're young and full of life. I understand your fear, but that doesn't mean you should be alone for the rest of your life. Nothing in this world is guaranteed, but that doesn't mean we should close ourselves off to the possibilities *Gott* has in store for us."

Lila felt the need to make Lizzie understand, hoping she would let the matter drop. "I'm afraid the same thing will happen to me, and I will leave a *boppli* without a *mamm*. I know *mei mamm* didn't do it on purpose to me, but she still did it." Lila knew that was a harsh thing to say, but it was how she felt.

Lizzie smiled warmly. "Don't let your fear of the unknown cause you to miss *Gott's* calling in your life—even if that calling involves marrying and having *kinner*."

Chapter 9

•

Lila was eager to begin painting the *dawdi haus,* but it was Sunday and everyone was out visiting. She felt anxious with nothing to do, but she knew better than to take on such a laborious task on the day of rest. She'd prepared the meal ahead of time in anticipation for Jessup and Bess to return, but even that hadn't occupied enough of her day. *Onkel* had invited her to go with them, but she didn't want to chance running into Samuel. She'd had enough of his charm last night at dinner, and she wasn't certain she could continue to reject him if she didn't try to avoid him altogether. Lila had never felt such temptation from any other before Samuel, and she wasn't sure what made him so different from the others.

Lila pulled her cloak around her shoulders to shelter her from the wind and walked out to the dock out back of the B&B. The sun peaked around from the clouds, but it wasn't enough to warm her. A cold wind blew across the large pond, rippling the surface. Except for the wind, it was quiet, lacking the usual sounds that summer provided. It had turned too cold for the frogs and crickets. Even the fireflies and mosquitoes had long-since gone for the season. The trees clung to the last of their leaves of autumn-rich hues, a tell-tale sign that winter was on its way.

Lowering herself at the end of the dock, she folded her legs under her rather than dangling them over the edge. She wished it was warmer so she could dip her feet in the water, but the icy wind coming off the oversized pond was enough to discourage the temptation. Despite the cold that tried to chill her bones, it was a very peaceful, pleasant afternoon. She was grateful for the day away from everyone so she could finally take some time to think.

"I see you found my favorite thinking spot," a now-familiar baritone voice interrupted her reverie.

Looking up into the sinking sun, she spotted Samuel making his way to end of the dock. Her heart tumbled behind her ribcage as she admired the way the sun lit up his strong features. His broad shoulders looked somehow wider with the sun behind him, and the chisel of his jaw peppered by a day's growth of whiskers, gave him a more rugged look. Why couldn't he just leave her alone? Why did he have to stir feelings in her that she was trying to push down?

Lila lifted slightly off the end of the dock and looked at the worn planks of wood beneath her. "I don't see your name on this spot."

She didn't mean to react in such a snotty tone, but she wanted him to leave—or did she? The depth of his dimples as he smiled when he sat down beside her was enough to snatch the air from her lungs.

"I actually wrote it here when I was younger, but it has worn off since then," he said smoothly. "But everyone knows this is my spot."

He smiled again, bringing heat to her cheeks.

"It's surprisingly cold today, but I suppose that is to be expected now that it's the end of October. Are you warm enough?"

A gust of wind caused her teeth to chatter. "*Jah,*" she said through clenched teeth.

Before she realized, Samuel had shrugged off his wool coat and was placing it around her shoulders. His warm hands brought shivers to her as they brushed her neck. What was happening to her? His charming pull was interrupting her every thought; every reasonable argument she had for getting up and leaving immediately was thwarted by the lingering warmth of his touch.

Attempting to summon the strength to leave, she tried to wriggle from his coat, but she couldn't help but breathe in the smell of straw and horses, along with the rugged smell of shaving soap that clung to the collar. How would she be able to resist this man if she didn't stop acting so foolishly? She was normally so strong-willed, but his kindness had broken through the barrier of her heart, and it seemed to take up residence there.

"Perhaps since I will be living here from now on, I should put *my* name at the end of the dock so there will be no more confusion," Lila said lightly.

She was surprised she was even able to form a coherent sentence with the smell of this handsome man filling her senses.

Samuel plucked a pen from his shirt pocket and wrote her name beside her before she even had a chance to stop him.

"I was kidding," she said, trying not make to eye contact with him.

Then he wrote *his* name beside his leg, causing Lila to roll her eyes. Was he trying to impose on her space on purpose?

"Now it's *both* of our spot," he said as he replaced the pen in his pocket.

Lila met Samuel's gaze, and it was enough to warn her she did not have the strength to resist him. The blue in his eyes reflected the glint of the sinking sun over the water, and it was almost hypnotizing. If she didn't move quickly, she would be lost forever in their depths.

Chapter 10

Lila stood abruptly, easing Samuel's warm, masculine-scented coat from her shoulders. She tossed the coat in his lap, and a wind gust stole his scent from her, sending it floating across the pond.

"*Danki* for your kindness, but I have a meal to prepare for *Onkel's* return."

She did not dare meet his gaze, nor did she give him time to stop her, for her feet padded across the dock as swiftly as they could in a lady-like manner.

When she reached the back door to the B&B, she stopped to catch her breath.

I have a plan for my life, and it does not include a husband or kinner. I will not give in to that mann's temptation to change my mind.

Lila knew she could tell herself that all day long and it was not going to matter. Samuel had already breached the wall that surrounded her heart, and that frightened her.

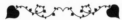

Samuel lifted his coat to his face, breathing in the lingering scent of homemade banana bread and coconut oil she probably used to smooth her hair back. He knew his sisters used it, but the scent of it never affected him like it did now, knowing it belonged to Lila. He was beside himself with worry over why she resisted his attempts to befriend her.

Lift the burden that rests on Lila's shoulders, Gott, and shelter her under your wing.

Samuel's gaze fell upon the ripples in the water that moved across the pond. Was it possible that he already loved Lila? If he did, he feared she would never love him in return. He thought he'd seen a flicker of hope in her startling green eyes, but it left as soon as he'd recognized it. What was she hiding from him that held such defenses against her heart? Had another man broken her heart by ending an engagement to her? He couldn't imagine any man doing such a thing to her. He could only hope that there was an easier explanation.

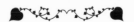

At the evening meal, Lila was not surprised to see Samuel at the table with Bess and *Onkel* Jessup. Samuel had agreed to help *Onkel* put up storm windows on the B&B to prepare for winter, and Lila had overheard her *onkel* invite him to partake in the meal with them. She didn't want to sit with Samuel through another meal, but she was grateful that Bess and Jessup would be there to filter his interaction with her.

Lila stood at the stove pouring brown gravy into a serving bowl when she heard the back door open. Samuel's masculine scent drifted to her nose with the gust of wind that entered the door with him. She immediately felt her stomach tighten anxiously. Samuel was early, and *Onkel* was busy helping Bess put Adam down so she could eat with them. She didn't dare turn around when he greeted her; she knew that if she looked into his sparkling blue eyes she might not survive the temptation to get lost there.

Be strong. It's only one meal. Resist him until Onkel and Bess finish, and there will be nothing to worry about.

Lila could hear Adam fussing from the other room, as his parents tried to soothe him. If they couldn't get him to settle down, she feared she would be forced to entertain Samuel until they finished with the *boppli*. Lila continued to busy herself preparing the meal and completely ignored Samuel.

Before long, Adam's fussing turned to wailing. Lila glanced at Samuel looking for a sign that the crying was normal. She'd never heard a baby cry so hard, but she'd never spent too much time around any to fully compare.

Just when Lila didn't think she could stand the screaming any longer, *Onkel* entered the kitchen, desperation showing in the lines of his face.

"Samuel, please call the doctor. I think something is wrong with *mei* boy. "

"I saw his buggy at the Beiler farm on my way over here," Samuel said. "I'll fetch him at once."

With that, Samuel was out the door, and Jessup disappeared. Lila heard the bedroom door open and close, muffling Adam's screams once again. Lila returned the food to the stove, placing it back in the pots and pans to keep it warm. Filling the sink with sudsy water, Lila began to wash the dirtied dishes to keep her hands busy.

Dear Gott, please spare the boppli from whatever pain he's in. Bring the doctor swiftly, and bless him with the ability to assess Adam's condition. Heal that innocent boppli, and don't take him away from his mamm and daed.

Lila tried to keep her mind off the cries that did not subside from the upstairs room. She tried not to think about what could happen, but she knew it was another reason she did not want to bring a *boppli* into the world. Too many things could go wrong that could take a *mamm* away from a *boppli,* or the other way around. Panic raced through her at the thought of Bess losing her *boppli.*

Tears fell unchecked from Lila's chin, dropping into the dishwater. She mindlessly washed the dishes until Samuel threw open the kitchen door. Startled, Lila pulled her apron to her face and wiped away evidence of her distress over the situation. It was too late. Doctor Davis followed the sound of Adam's screams while Samuel approached Lila, laying a comforting hand on her shoulder.

"He's going to be fine," Samuel said, his smooth baritone voice sending shivers through her.

His nearness paralyzed, her and his scent charmed her into submission. She felt a strong pull toward him, feeling like she couldn't resist him if he were to pull her into his strong arms and hold her captive against the strong plane of his chest. Could it really be that simple to let him comfort her?

Gott, give me the strength to resist this mann.

It was no use; she allowed herself to drift toward him as he encompassed her in the safety of his embrace.

Chapter 11

Lila flinched away from Samuel. She had to be stronger than the pull she felt from this man. It would take extreme measures to guard her heart from him, but she would not let him pull her into a dream that could never be hers. How could she have given in to such a moment of weakness? She didn't want him to think she was interested in him. The feel of his embrace haunted her, enticing her to allow more of the same.

"You don't always have to be so strong and independent," Samuel said.

It would be too easy for her drift back into his arms, but she'd made a choice for her life, and she had no intention of changing her mind.

"Maybe I do."

Lila suddenly realized the baby had stopped crying. Alarm caught in her throat where it nearly choked her with emotion. Samuel drew her back to him, and she didn't resist the peaceful retreat his strong arms offered. She breathed him in, wishing she could shut out the world and all the hurt that came with it. Blinking away fresh tears, Lila felt safe in the clutches of Samuel's arms. She reasoned with herself that she would bask in the safety of his affections, but she would not allow herself to lose herself in him.

An upstairs door opened and Lila pulled away at the sound of footfalls padding down the steps. She couldn't read the doctor's face to discover the outcome of the visit with Bess's *boppli.*

Gott, please let him be alright.

Doctor Davis sighed. "Just a bad case of colic." He sniffed toward the food warming on the stove. "Do you have enough to spare this old man some supper? I'm afraid by the time I reach home the missus will have already eaten."

Lila snapped into action. "*Jah.* Sit. I'll make you a plate."

Out of the corner of her eye, Lila could see Samuel sit down across from the doctor at the table in the kitchen. Now she would have to serve him as well. Otherwise the doctor might find her impertinent. She readied two plates and served the *menner* who sat making small-talk about the weather.

"Thank you, dear child," Doctor Davis said with a worn smile on his aging face. "Won't you sit down and join us?"

Samuel nodded, his dimples showing as he winked at her.

Lila's heart thumped an extra beat. "*Nee,* I should wait for *Onkel* and Bess."

The doctor put his fork down and wiped his mouth. "You might want to eat without them. That baby wore them out. They thought it was best if they rested now that he's settled down. I don't think they'll be joining us anytime soon."

Samuel jutted his chin out toward the food on the stove. "Get a plate and join us."

"Might as well eat it while it's hot," the doctor said. "You should be the one enjoying your cooking. It's very good. You'll make some young man a good wife with cooking this good."

The doctor's comment struck a nerve, and it didn't help that Samuel smiled at her as if to say he'd like to have her as his wife.

"Will you excuse me, please?"

Lila dashed to the back door, grabbed her cloak off the peg on the wall, and shouldered her way out into the cold night. She padded across the back yard to the dock and didn't stop until she reached the end. Her breath created a mist that showed bright against the moonlight. It was cold, and her teeth chattered, but she didn't care. Anything was better than being paired off like cattle. Lila didn't like being teased, especially about something she was so much against. Did everyone really expect her to get married? Why did it seem that was her only choice?

In the crisp, stillness of the night, Lila could hear the back door to the B&B open. She hoped it was only the doctor leaving to go back home, but she knew the old man would stay until he finished his meal. That only left one other person that would walk out that door; Samuel.

Lila turned around to face him as he sauntered up the dock toward her. His chiseled features were illuminated in the moonlight, the depth of his dimples looking like the dark side of the moon. He was too handsome to resist, and his confidence made him even more appealing. How was she to resist Samuel if he was always around? It almost seemed that everyone expected them to pair up, and she would have no say in the matter. It wasn't fair that as an Amish woman, it was assumed she would marry and have lots of *kinner*. What about what *she* wanted? Didn't that matter?

Samuel closed the space between them and placed his wool coat around her shoulders. The sweet memory of his arms around her when they were in the kitchen taunted her. Was there somewhere deep in her subconscious that wanted what he offered? She had enjoyed the closeness between them so much it frightened her. She had a plan for her life, and now she felt confused all because of one embrace. An embrace that left her wanting something she thought she would never want.

Why did he have to be so wonderful and irresistible? Why couldn't he be more like Henry Hochstetler from back home? Then she could just be content with being his friend. It was because Samuel was nothing like Henry. Samuel was handsome and kind the same as Henry, but Samuel was just a little bit too confident. That smooth confidence both scared *and* angered her.

"I don't want to marry you," Lila blurted out.

Samuel smirked at her. "I don't remember asking you!"

Chapter 12

Lila glared at Samuel, but he could see in her eyes that she was upset by his comment.

"So you don't want to marry me?" she asked through pursed lips.

Samuel found it hard to keep from laughing. Lila was on his hook, and she didn't even realize it. How long would he keep her dangling there before cutting her loose or reeling her in?

"I didn't say I didn't want to marry you, but I didn't ask you, either."

He smiled so brightly, the moon was pale in comparison. Lila turned her gaze toward the pond to keep from falling prey to the lure of his charming arrogance.

"Did you want me to ask you?" Samuel quipped.

Lila hesitated.

What was she waiting for? The anticipation rolling through Samuel's veins was enough to set his nerves ablaze. Did she want to marry him? He knew he already liked her, but was he ready to ask her to marry him?

Pursing her lips, Lila jutted her chin out. What was wrong with her? She knew the answer to that question just as sure as she knew her own name. But for the first time, she was unsure of the decision she'd made so long ago. Now that the question was actually being posed, she didn't have the heart to turn Samuel away. What was happening to her?

"I don't want you to ask me," she said soberly.

Lila slipped out of the warmth of Samuel's coat and handed it to him. She tried to walk past him, but he stopped her and pulled her into his arms. Caught off guard, Lila didn't fight him when he lowered his lips to hers. His warm breath quieted the echoes of reason her mind stirred to the surface.

Heat radiated off Samuel, scorching her with desire for him. Lila deepened the kiss like a woman who was ready to commit her heart and soul to him. But was she really prepared to marry him simply because of his magnetic pull on her heart? Lila was falling for him, no doubt, but her mind told her to back away before it was too late—if it wasn't already.

Samuel curled his fingers around the nape of Lila's neck, drawing her closer still. He couldn't help himself. He wanted to drink her in like she was the last drop of water in an acrid desert. His heart was already bestowed to her whether she was ready for it or not. Her mouth had said she didn't want him, but her lips against his told him she did.

"Marry me," he whispered at her temple.

"I can't," she whispered as her lips dragged across his rugged cheek until they met his once more.

Samuel cupped her cheeks in his hands and deepened the kiss. He would either wear her down with his fervent kisses, or he would enjoy it as long as she would allow it. Either way, he wasn't willing to let her go without giving it everything he had. Something about her made him want her for his wife when he'd never even given marriage a single thought before.

"Marry me, Lila" he whispered again.

Lila's heart did a flip flop in her chest. Why did Samuel have to be so handsome and such a good kisser? If he wasn't so wonderful, she would have no trouble resisting him at all, but she had to do it. Her fear of the future wouldn't let go of the stronghold it had on her.

Lila broke away from Samuel and gazed into his eyes that reflected the harvest moon. How could she say no to him? She wanted to kiss him for the rest of her life, but she didn't want to make babies with him—or with any man. He would expect to have *kinner,* and she wouldn't give them to him. It would break his heart more than if she let him go now while his feelings for her were still so new.

"I can't marry you, Samuel." She nearly choked on the words.

Lila watched Samuel's expression twist with sorrow, his eyes glazed over with emotion. Her stomach clenched with immediate regret.

"Why did you kiss me like that, then?"

"I could kiss you for the rest of my life, but that doesn't mean I can marry you."

Tension claimed Samuel's jaw. "Did I do something wrong? Was this too fast for you?"

"You did nothing wrong. I enjoyed kissing you, but you could wait a year and it wouldn't matter. I don't want to get married."

Samuel tried to pull her back into his arms, but the spell between them had broken. "I'll wait however long I have to."

Lila's eyes filled with tears. "Don't wait. It wouldn't be fair to you because I will never say yes."

He nodded grimly.

Lila knew she'd hurt him, but it was better to do it now than to wait until he'd vested too much of his heart. The cold no longer affected her, for her emotions numbed her from the inside out. She hated to leave him, but she knew that if she didn't leave now she never would. Staying would only hurt him more in the end.

Samuel let go of Lila. It was no use trying to keep her close to him if she didn't want to be there. She glanced at him once more before walking away slowly. He could see she hadn't wanted to leave any more than he wanted her to go. Was this the part where he was supposed to go after her? He couldn't help but hope it was worth a try.

Sprinting across the wet grass, Samuel captured her up into his arms, catching her off guard. He pressed his lips to hers again, hoping she wouldn't resist him.

She didn't.

Pausing between kisses, he gazed into her fiery green eyes. "Don't marry me."

"What are you talking about?" she asked.

His look turned serious. "Don't marry me, then. Just kiss me every day for the rest of your life."

Chapter 13

"*Nee*, Katie, please wait until the doctor gets here!"

"I trust you," Katie said breathlessly. "You did a *gut* job of helping Bess to birth Adam."

Katie let out a scream from the pain. She pulled on the sleeve of Rachel's dress. "Please don't leave me. I'm scared. What if Caleb doesn't make it here in time?"

I've got to stop visiting pregnant women!

Rachel was trying not to show concern, not wanting to alert her brother's wife. "Let's concentrate of getting you comfortable first. Then we'll worry about Caleb. The important thing is help you relax so that maybe you can keep from pushing until the doctor gets here."

Rachel had no idea why she was so nervous. She'd just been through this with Bess. But that day she'd had no time to think about it. Now that she'd had time to think about it, she didn't want to be in this situation again—especially not with her brother's *boppli*.

"I called the doc from the barn, and he should be here soon. Please try to wait until he gets here."

Katie was not listening. Rachel could see that the woman was already bearing down. She let out another scream. Bess had not made this much fuss, and Rachel feared something could be wrong.

Mopping up sweat from Katie's hair, Rachel soothed her through a difficult, long contraction.

"It's getting worse," Katie cried. "I have to get up. I can't lie in this bed anymore. It hurts my back too much."

Rachel assisted Katie out of the bed and helped her lean over the mattress. She rubbed her lower back during the next contraction, and that seemed to ease the pains. Rachel hoped that meant it was Katie's position on the bed that had made her so uncomfortable.

Grabbing a pillow and hugging it to her chest, Katie leaned into the mattress during the next contraction. They were coming faster and lasting longer, and Rachel knew that meant it wouldn't be long before she was ready.

With a sudden gush, Katie's water broke, causing her to let out a scream with the pain of the contraction. Rachel grabbed a few towels she'd brought into the room with her and placed them around Katie's feet.

"I think I better get back in bed now," Katie said breathlessly.

Rachel agreed, helping her. She placed a clean towel beneath her and propped the pillows up behind her head just in time for the next contraction.

"I think you better catch *mei boppli,* Rachel."

. A quick glance out the bedroom window showed no sign of the doctor or her brother, so Rachel braced herself to catch Katie's *boppli.* One more contraction later the *boppli* was crowing.

"Push slowly, Katie, on the next contraction," Rachel urged her.

"I'll try," Katie squeezed out before pushing.

"It's a boy!" Rachel said around the lump in her throat.

Katie's eyes welled up with emotion as she reached for her new *boppli.* "Your *daed* will be so happy to see you," she cooed to him.

Rachel brought the quilt across Katie's lap to wait for the doctor to finish. "Where can I find a pair of scissors to cut the cord?"

Katie pointed to a sewing box in the corner of the room, her eyes not leaving her new son.

Rachel worked fast to tie and cut the cord.

"He's beautiful."

Katie looked up for only a moment. "*Danki*. For being here and helping me. I could not have done this without your help."

Rachel placed a warm hand on Katie's shoulder as she gazed upon the new life she'd helped bring into her brother's family.

"Do you have a quilt made for him?"

"*Jah*, it's in the cedar chest at the end of the bed." Katie pointed to a hand-carved piece of furniture she could see had been made by her brother.

She lifted the lid and retrieved a small blue and yellow quilt and brought it to Katie so she could wrap her new *boppli* in it. Hearing faint buggy wheels, Rachel was relieved when she peered out the window at Caleb's buggy coming up the lane followed by Doctor Davis.

Rachel busied herself mopping up the floor, tossing the wet towels over the edge of the bathtub in the bathroom down the hall. When she returned to the room, Caleb was taking the stairs two at a time to get to Katie.

Joy filled his face as Caleb rushed to Katie's side. "Why didn't you wait for me?"

"Your son had other plans for his day," Katie said proudly.

Caleb's face lit with emotion. "It's a boy*?*"

"*Jah*, and your *schweschder* helped deliver him."

Caleb looked at Rachel, who readied a pan of water and linens on the bureau across the room. His *thank you* showed in his misty expression without even saying a word to her. She smiled at her older brother, feeling equally happy.

Doctor Davis entered the room and looked directly at Rachel. "Did you deliver this one, too?"

Rachel beamed. "*Jah,* but I didn't do it on purpose any more than I did with Bess."

"I'm glad you were here," Caleb said.

"I am too," Katie said, not looking up from her son.

"That makes three of us," Doctor Davis agreed.

Rachel offered a silent prayer for the miraculous outcome for the second time in the span of a week. If this kept up, she'd be known as the midwife of the community, and she wasn't certain she wanted the women in the community to start asking for her when they were birthing. She was more than happy to leave that task to the doctor. He was older and had more experience. Rachel only wanted to concentrate on her wedding for now.

Doctor Davis busied himself with examining the new *boppli.*

"He's healthy and strong, Caleb. Have you picked out a name?"

A few whispers later, and Caleb announced his new son, Isaac.

Chapter 14

Lila opened the windows to the *dawdi haus,* hoping it would air out quickly. After being closed up for several years without occupancy, the house needed a thorough cleaning, painting, and some airing out before it would be livable again. Once upon a time, Bess had used it as living space until she had the private living quarters sectioned off in the B&B. It seemed a shame to Lila that Bess had let the house sit for so long as she looked around at the quaint little bungalow. It would be just the right size for her and her *daed.*

"It's a little stuffy in here."

Samuel's familiar baritone voice startled her. He advanced toward her and placed a quick kiss upon her cheek before setting down a bucket full of paint supplies. She watched him move about the small rooms assessing the needed repairs.

"It won't take much to get this place in order before your *daed* arrives."

Samuel's smile warmed her in the chilly house. Had she made the right decision about their relationship? She wondered how long he would *really* be satisfied with things the way they were; sooner or later he would most likely want to marry her. Today, she decided, was not the day to think about that. She had work to do to prepare for her *daed's* arrival, and she was not about to let him down.

Lila surveyed the workspace. "I figured we should leave the linens on the furniture until we get the walls painted. I figured I could help with the painting since I can't do a lot of cleaning until it's finished."

Samuel smiled, his dimples tempting her to forget the painting and spend the day kissing him. But that would be neither practical nor advisable since she still wasn't certain if that was one of her best decisions.

"I'm just happy that today is a little warmer than it was yesterday so we can leave the windows open. It'll make the paint dry faster."

Lila pulled on the sleeves of her sweater. "It's still cold."

Samuel closed the space between them and drew her into his arms. "Is that better?"

Lila had to admit it was, but it wasn't going to get the work done. "*Jah,* but we have work to get done."

She pushed him away playfully. If she wasn't careful, she was going to fall in love with Samuel, and that was the last thing Lila planned on doing.

"*Mei bruder,* Caleb, and his *fraa,* Katie, had their *boppli* yesterday. Would you like to go with me to visit them?"

Lila's heart did a flip-flop. Forget her worry over falling in love with Samuel; seeing another baby was the last thing she planned to do.

"*Nee,* I have too much to do. Besides, what if Bess needs my help." Lila knew it was an excuse, but Samuel didn't need to know she would never help Bess with her new baby. But how long could she expect to keep such a secret from him?

Samuel pulled on Lila playfully, keeping her close to him. "So wouldn't you want a little place like this of your own someday?"

"I couldn't live on my own, Silly," Lila said.

Samuel pulled her into his arms again. "I meant with me."

Lila pushed him away again. "I already told you I'm not marrying you."

Samuel knelt down beside a can of white paint and used a key to open it. "I was hoping you might change your mind."

Lila was afraid of that. He was going to keep hoping until he either gave up or spent every day trying to wear her down. Either way, all she saw was heartbreak waiting at the end for both of them. How long could they be content with just kissing before they wanted more? She already wanted more, and her stomach was in knots just thinking about it.

"I can't, Samuel, and if you are going to continue to ask me, then the agreement we already have between us will never work."

Samuel poured paint in a plastic pan and closed the lid on the can. "Don't you think people will expect something to come of our relationship? What will we tell them?"

Lila picked up a paintbrush, dipped it in the paint, and brushed against the wall. "We will tell them it's none of their business. In my opinion, people are way too nosey as it is. They think they need to know everything about you. Maybe some things are too private for everyone else to know."

Samuel stroked the paintbrush along the opposite wall. "You won't hear any argument out of me there. *Mei schweschders* talk about a lot of stuff that I don't think is any of their business."

Lila giggled. It was the first time Samuel had heard her laugh and he liked it.

"Does this mean we are keeping our friendship a secret?"

"We're more than friends, and I think you know that." Samuel threatened to dab his paintbrush on her nose, but she backed away and squealed.

"I know nothing of the sort." Lila swiped her paintbrush across Samuel's cheek in jest.

Shaking his paintbrush toward Lila, Samuel watched her expression twist as paint splattered across the front of her, some on her face. Lila charged at him with her dripping brush, but he caught her in his clutches. She struggled to swipe at him with the paintbrush until he managed to take it from her and toss it on the drop-cloth on the floor.

"You don't play fair," Lila squealed. "You're stronger than I am."

"Just remember that when you keep turning down my proposals. I can hold out longer than you can."

"Sounds like you're challenging me," she giggled.

Samuel drank in the sound of her laughter.

"You won't turn me down forever."

His mouth captured hers as he pulled her closer. Samuel could get used to kissing her every day; that he was certain of.

Chapter 15

"Blake Monroe, where are you taking me?"

Rachel knew he was surprising her with a first look at the completed farm in which they would live once they wed, but she allowed him to think she hadn't a clue of his surprise. She would play along until the last minute, knowing how important this day was to her betrothed.

Blake had worked hard over the past year trying to prepare for their future together. He'd used the reward money he'd shared with Abby to build a home for the two of them to share after their wedding.

After going through the baptismal classes and taking the baptism, Blake had become Amish and very much a part of the community. Most of the *menner* has assisted him at one time or another in building the house, but he'd wanted to do the inside work on his own. Rachel had to admit she was indeed very excited to see what the finished product looked like.

Eagerness filled Rachel as they approached a fair-sized farm house complete with a large barn.

"I had no idea you were going to build this much *haus*," Rachel said with surprise.

"I used the majority of the reward money, but I saved aside enough to get us through two years. I figured that would give us enough time to make the farm operational where we could pull in a reasonable profit and yield enough of a crop to support us too. Your grandfather was very generous to sell me all thirty acres of his land, and I want to put it to good use."

Rachel couldn't help but feel a swell of pride for Blake. "You thought of everything. You have a sound business sense."

Blake chuckled. "I can't take credit for that. If not for Hiram's guidance, along with several of the men in the community, I would have probably spent the entire thing on just the house alone. I had visions of living in a mansion!"

Rachel sighed at the beauty of *grossdaddi's* property that had become theirs, and the house and barn that she would soon call her own. "We don't need a mansion. This is perfect for us."

Blake nudged her playfully. "It has a few extra bedrooms for *bopplies.*"

Rachel felt her cheeks warm as Blake helped her out of the buggy. Already, Rachel envisioned flowerbeds filled with colorful, fragrant blooms and the kitchen garden she would have out back between the house and the barn. A fenced corral beside the barn was set up for the horses, and she could already hear the chickens that would cluck as they roamed the yard. She could almost taste the fresh eggs that she would cook in her own kitchen—her own kitchen. She liked the thought of that.

"Are we going to look inside today, or do you want to save that for after our wedding?"

Rachel looked at him quizzically. "You don't want me to see the inside? I thought you said it was finished."

Blake scooped her into his arms to shield her from the chilly wind. "I can't wait for you to see the inside of the house, but *Englisch* tradition dictates that I am to carry you over the threshold the night of our wedding."

Rachel giggled as she nuzzled Blake's neck to warm herself. "That sounds very romantic."

Blake smothered her cheek with kisses until his lips met hers. "Does this mean you want to observe an *Englisch* tradition and wait to see the inside until I can carry you over the threshold?"

Rachel didn't have to think about the sacrifices Blake had made for her. The *haus* and his baptism had been more than she could have ever asked for. And so for him, she would gladly wait and share an *Englisch* tradition with the man she loved.

Chapter 16

"Lila, could I trouble you to watch Adam for me while I get cleaned up?" Bess asked. "I feel like I haven't had but one bath in the week since I've had him."

Lila's voice caught in her throat, and before she could make a reasonable excuse as to why she couldn't watch him, the woman had disappeared into the washroom. Panic seized Lila as she crept near the cradle where little Adam slept soundly. She'd only entered the room the change the bed linens, and now she wished she hadn't.

What would she do if the baby stirred from his peaceful slumber? She'd never held a baby, and she didn't know the first thing about how to pick him up without breaking him or dropping him. She'd watched Rachel flop him around like a kitten, and she didn't think she could ever handle a baby with such ease. Not to mention the fact that she wanted nothing to do with babies.

Still, his little gurgling noises enticed her to draw close to the cradle and observe him sleep. His tiny little fists rested above the top edge of the quilt that was tucked snuggly around his tiny frame. He seemed so perfect in every way as he let little wisps of air escape his tiny rosebud mouth. The magnetic pull to watch Adam sleep was more than Lila thought possible. She'd never been this close to a baby, and she had to admit, it was easy to see how others might be so enamored with the wee one.

Lila tiptoed around the room, cringing every time a floorboard creaked. Setting about the task of stripping the bed, Lila was extra careful not to make any noise. She carefully tucked in the bottom sheet and placed the pillow slips onto the feather pillows. After partially unfolding the top sheet, she flicked it to spread across the surface of the double bed. The crack of the linen as it floated above the bed startled Adam, causing him to let out a loud cry.

"*Nee, nee,*" Lila said to the baby. "I didn't mean to wake you. I promise I'll be quieter if you stop crying."

Adam wailed so loudly, he could not have heard Lila's pleas—even if he *could* understand her. She rocked the cradle, hoping it would quiet him, but it was no use. Panic nearly seized her at the thought of having to pick him up. If Bess returned from her shower and saw that Lila had not tended to Adam, she would be angry.

Gott please make him stop crying. I'm too afraid to pick him up. What if I accidently drop him?

Peace filled Lila as soon as she breathed the prayer. Instinctively, she placed a hand under the baby, cradling his head and bottom, and lifted him carefully from the cradle. He was much lighter than she'd anticipated—no heavier than the Miller's puppies.

Drawing him into the crook of her arms, Lila delighted in his sweet smell. She lifted his tiny head to her nose and breathed in the most heavenly scent she'd ever come across. How could something she'd feared all her life be so delightful?

Little Adam looked up at her with big blue eyes that broke through the hardness over Lila's heart. She nestled him closer, surprised at the emotions that put a lump in her throat. How could she have thought to deprive herself of such a feeling? Had her own *mamm* felt this way about her just before she'd died? Lila's *daed* had described the look on her *mamm's* face when she'd held her for the first time after giving birth—just minutes before she'd hemorrhaged and passed away. Suddenly, thoughts of her *mamm* didn't bring pain and anger to the surface of her emotions, for they were too overcrowded with the simple joy of having a baby in her arms.

Lila breathed a silent prayer, thankful for the opportunity to experience such joy in something that had paralyzed her with fear for so many years. Even though Adam was not her *boppli,* her heart filled with love toward him—an emotion she never would have thought was possible. She hugged her little cousin close and kissed the top of his sweet smelling head. Laughter filled her at the delight that poured over her. For the first time in her life, she felt free from the bondage of fear that had held her captive for too long. It was a liberating feeling to let go of something that had nearly ruined her future. She prayed that it wasn't too late for her to change this part of her life around.

Tears filled Lila's eyes as she suddenly realized how much she desired marrying Samuel and having as many *bopplies* as *Gott* would bless them with. Eagerness to tell Samuel she'd marry him occupied her immediate thoughts. It would be tough waiting for him to propose again— especially since she'd begged him not to ask her again.

Nervousness crowded her sudden joy, overwhelming her with worry that he would never say the words again.

Lila looked down into Adam's innocent face.

"I think I've made a mess of things," she cooed to him. "What will I do if he never asks me again?"

Fresh tears filled Lila's eyes turning her joy to sorrow.

Chapter 17

Rachel's hands trembled as she fingered the letter she pulled from the mailbox. The return address told her it had come from the prison, and she wondered why Bruce would write to her. She was aware of the recent letter Blake had received from his *daed,* but she wasn't certain she could stomach the words of the man who had kidnapped her just over a year ago. She'd worked so hard to put the incident behind her, and now, as she held the letter penned by the man who had nearly killed her betrothed, Rachel felt the old wounds breaking open again.

Walking up the lane from the main road where the line of mailboxes invited the *Englisch* world to invade the peacefulness of their seclusion, Rachel felt secure in the protection her family provided and in knowing Bruce would not likely get out of prison until he was a very old man. Still, the letter set her nerves on edge, and she contemplated disposing of the letter without opening it. Knowing it wouldn't be right to keep the letter from Blake, Rachel tucked the letter in her apron pocket and walked up to the house.

Not yet ready to go inside, Rachel pulled her cloak tightly around her and sat in one of the rockers on the front porch. She looked out onto the lawn and the large oak tree with its long branches that canopied the circle driveway. Sunlight glinted off the orange and red leaves. The crisp, afternoon sky boasted fluffy clouds teased with a silver lining of rain, and Lila wondered if it would bring the season's first snow flurries. If not for the chill from the breeze, Rachel could easily snuggle up on the porch swing and take a catnap. She was exhausted from endless preparations for her upcoming wedding, but her emotions now caved with heaviness from the letter tucked away in her apron pocket.

Why had Bruce chosen now to reach out to her? She wished he'd waited to contact her until after they'd put the wedding and its business behind them. But would there ever be a *gut* time to receive news from the man who'd caused her and Blake so much grief? If only she hadn't seen the letter. It was too late now, and she would not be able to hide her melancholy from Blake.

Gott, renew the forgiveness I have in my heart for Bruce Monroe. Prepare my heart to receive whatever is in his letter, and bless me with the strength to be able to endure it.

A warm breeze brushed Rachel's cheeks, making her shiver—not from the cold day, but from the unusual warmth her prayer brought. Still shaking, Rachel lifted the letter from her apron pocket and opened it. She was ready to face the words of the man who had kidnapped her—with a heart full of forgiveness.

Dear Rachel,

It is with a heavy heart that I write this letter to you. I know I don't have any right to be asking any favors of you, but I need to know that you forgive me for what I did to hurt you last summer. I never meant to cause any harm to anyone. At the time, I was consumed with alcohol, and that can make a man do terrible things. I've had more than a year to sober up in jail, and I even started going to Bible study with the preacher and a few other inmates.

I am truly sorry for what happened. I don't know if I will ever be able to forgive myself for shooting my own flesh and blood, but I thank God every day he didn't die because of the hate I carried in my heart. Blake is everything to me, and I'm just sorry it took me so long to realize it.

I still don't really know how this forgiveness thing works, but my boy told me the Amish people are true forgivers. I have prayed that is true. I only wish I can someday experience the unconditional love that the two of you have for each other, and my son seems to have for me. He's told me he forgives me, but I have a hard time wrapping my head around such a thing—especially since I don't think I will ever be able to forgive myself for almost killing him and putting you in so much danger. I'm sorry for scaring you half to death that day.

Because of my actions, I will miss out on seeing the two of you get married, and seeing my grandchildren grow up. Truthfully, that hardly seems punishment enough for what I put the two of you through. Know that I will pray for you, and spend the rest of my days in repentance for what I've done.

Yours Truly,
Bruce Monroe

Tears dripped from Rachel's eyes onto the page. How could she begrudge the man for his apology—especially if it was from his heart? The letter seemed genuine enough, but she still held a little distrust for him. She breathed a quick prayer asking for guidance. Then her answer came to her.

Rushing up the stairs to her room, Rachel grabbed a few sheets of paper and began to pen a letter to Bruce.

Mr. Monroe,

Although I cannot speak for my betrothed (your son), I forgive you for everything. I am happy to hear you have an interest in the Bible, for the words will guide you on learning to forgive yourself. I believe it is important to do that, not for us, but for your own peace of mind. I wish you well. Feel free to stay in touch. Blake and I will keep you up to date on the developments in our familye throughout the years.

Sincerely,
Rachel Yoder (soon to be Monroe)

Rachel folded the letter, feeling light of heart, and finally ready to marry Blake. Now there would be no hindrance to their future happiness. She was finally free of the past, and it felt liberating.

Chapter 18

"I'd be more than happy to give you a ride over there to help *mei schweschder,* Rachel, with the pumpkin rolls. I know how important they are to her, and if you're late, which I suspect you will be if you walk, she will not be happy with you."

Lila looked into Samuel's serious, blue eyes.

"I appreciate the offer, but didn't you just come from there? I don't want to make you take the trip all over again."

Samuel smiled as he pulled her into his arms and placed a kiss across her cold lips. "You're already freezing. Think of how cold you'll be by the time you get there. I think today is colder than it was yesterday."

Lila was already shivering, and the shelter of his arms had warmed her more than it should. She'd been looking for the opportunity to allow Samuel to propose to her again, and the close quarters of his buggy and the time it would take to drive her to meet Rachel might be the perfect setting.

"I am running a little late since I've been helping Bess with the *boppli* all morning. *Danki.* I promised Rachel I'd get there a little early to help her pick the pumpkins."

Samuel pulled her into a tight squeeze and kissed her again just before helping her into his buggy. It would be her first buggy ride with a man, and she had to admit she was a little nervous. She loved him, but she feared he would give up on her since they'd made a deal *not* to marry. Why had she acted in haste? She should have never said anything to him about it. But at the time, she had no intention of marrying him. How could she convey to him, without being too bold, that she was now ready?

Samuel grabbed the reins, slapped them gently across his gelding, and clicked his tongue to signal a command. The buggy lurched forward, causing Lila to grab onto Samuel for stability.

He tucked his arm around her, pulling her closer to his side. "I'll hold onto to you so you don't slosh around."

"*Danki,* I'm certain your *schweschder* would appreciate it if I showed up to help her with the wedding in one piece."

Samuel chuckled. "Is this your first wedding?"

"*Nee,* I've attended a couple of other weddings."

"Well, as much against weddings as you are, I thought you might have avoided them until now."

Lila's heart sank. How could she tell Samuel she was no longer against marriage—that she wanted to marry— him? He would think she was *narrish* for sure and for certain. She couldn't seem too eager and blurt it out or he would lose respect for her. Perhaps she could ease into the conversation and keep him there until he made another attempt to propose. The only problem was that he'd made a promise to her that he wouldn't ask her again.

"I'm warming up to the idea," Lila said. "Your *schweschder* seems to be happy about getting married."

"Well, you don't have to worry about that since you'll never get married. And don't worry about me asking you again. I promised you I wouldn't, and I won't." Samuel teased her, hoping it would change her mind, and from the look on her face, it was working.

Lila sighed hopelessly. What had she done? Was there no undoing her mistake? Now he would never ask her. An entire lifetime of being a childless spinster stretched out before her as she envisioned her life without Samuel.

"Stop the buggy," Lila said abruptly.

Samuel pulled over to the side of the country lane near his *familye* home. "What's wrong?"

Lila was shaking. "I'm feeling a little too warm, and I think I want to walk the rest of the way."

She jumped from the buggy, and Samuel followed her. "At least kiss me before you go."

"You already got your kiss for the day," Lila said, choking back tears. "You kissed me before I got into the buggy."

Samuel closed the space between them. "That one didn't count. Your lips were cold. Now that you're warmed up, I'd like a *real* kiss."

Lila couldn't resist him, even if kissing him was all she would ever have with him. There would be no marriage or *bopplies* in her future because she had broken her own heart with her hasty decision. Now, it seemed, there would no undoing it.

Samuel pressed his lips to hers, his hunger for her more apparent with every sweep of his mouth across hers.

"I love you," she whispered in-between kisses.

Panic seized her when she realized she'd let the words slip from her tongue.

Samuel pulled away and looked at her, his eyes glazed over with emotion. "I love you too!"

Lila smiled delightfully as she pressed her lips to Samuel's. It wasn't a marriage proposal, but it was progress.

Chapter 19

Rachel stood at the edge of her *mamm's* kitchen garden surveying the last bits of vegetation. Except for a few squash, it had been pretty well picked over, and the stores of canned vegetables she and her *mamm* had put up for winter filled their pantry.

A sense of accomplishment filled her as she realized she was bringing a great deal more to her marriage than she'd originally thought. She knew Blake expected nothing from her other than her love for him, but she wanted to be able to provide for him just as much as he was doing for her. Come spring, she would be planting her own kitchen garden at her own house, and she hoped they would be blessed with their first baby within their first year of marriage. It was going to be a *gut* year; she could just feel it in the air. The letter from Bruce had freed her in a way she never thought possible; his letter could not have come at a more perfect time.

The pumpkin patch was another thing altogether. Six long rows boasted enough pumpkins to make the pumpkin rolls for her wedding meal. Her sister, Abby, *Aenti* Lillian, and Lila would arrive soon to help make pumpkin rolls. Rachel intended to get the pumpkins picked and cleaned before they arrived so she would be ready since time was running low.

With only three more days until her wedding, Rachel was more anxious than ever to complete as many tasks as possible ahead of time. She hadn't spent more than five minutes alone with Blake in the past two days, and she was ready to be married.

Pushing the wheelbarrow down the row, Rachel selected each pumpkin carefully, knowing the ones that were the most ripe would be the easiest to work with, and the tastiest. She left several on the vines that were still a little green. Rachel knew they would use them to make pies later, but they would need to be picked before the first frost and stored in the cellar. Her *mamm* had already promised her she could have most of the remaining pumpkins to make pies for her first Christmas with Blake. She had so many firsts to look forward to she found it difficult to concentrate on what she was doing.

Pushing the full wheelbarrow toward the kitchen door, Rachel was surprised to see Lila show up with her brother, Samuel. She'd thought they would make a good match, but Lila seemed very apprehensive around him the last time she'd seen them together. Rachel wondered what had changed as she watched the two of them smile and converse as though they'd known each other all their lives. But there was something else she couldn't quite understand. They almost acted like they were courting. Was it possible they'd begun courting in secret?

Rachel approached her brother's buggy carefully watching the interaction between him and Lila. "Why did you bring her so late, Samuel?"

Lila stepped forward, eyeing the wheelbarrow full of pumpkins near the back door to the house. She couldn't detect from Rachel's mood if she was angry that she was too late to help with the picking. "I'm sorry, Rachel. It was my fault we were late."

Rachel planted her fists on her hips and eyed Samuel for an explanation.

Samuel tried to divert his sister's obvious annoyance with him. "Don't look at me like that. For a change, it wasn't any of my doing."

Lila leered at Samuel. "You don't have to blame it *all* on me!"

Samuel nudged her playfully. "I'm not the one who jumped out of the buggy."

Rachel's eyes grew wide. "You jumped out of his buggy?"

Samuel held up a hand. "It wasn't moving!"

Lila was suddenly angry at the blame Samuel was letting her take responsibility for. "I might have jumped out of the buggy, but you're the one who..." she suddenly realized what she was about to say, and stopped herself abruptly. She could feel the heat rising up her cheeks in a tell-tale hue.

Rachel gasped. "You kissed her!"

Samuel chuckled. "She kissed me back!"

Lila felt her face heat up, and anger took over her emotions. "It won't happen again!" she stormed off, leaving the two of them while she grabbed a pumpkin in each hand and walked inside the kitchen.

She was too angry with herself for nearly telling hers and Samuel's secret, but she was even more angry with him for actually revealing something so intimate between them. How would she ever be able to face Rachel again? Worse, how would she get through an afternoon of making pumpkin rolls with Samuel's relatives without being teased?

Before Lila could get her cloak off and hang it on a peg near the kitchen door, Rachel came bustling in the door toting a pair of pumpkins.

She looked at Lila sincerely. "I'm sorry for blurting that out. I was just so excited that *mei bruder* finally has someone. We've all been praying for him that he would find someone he could marry, but he hasn't even courted anyone yet."

Lila narrowed her mouth into a serious line.

"We aren't getting married."

Rachel's look softened. "Of course not right away, but I'm certain he will ask you."

Lila took the pumpkins from Rachel and put them on the table. "He already did—more than once."

Rachel tipped her head to the side quizzically.

"You don't want to marry Samuel?"

Emotions surfaced, bringing tears to Lila's eyes. "I do, but I told him I didn't."

Rachel looked at Lila affectionately. "Why?"

Lila felt unsure if she could confide something so personal with a woman she barely knew. But Rachel was not a stranger; she was Samuel's sister. Surely she could trust someone so close to the man she loved.

"I didn't even tell Samuel the reason." Lila said quietly.

Rachel placed a comforting hand on Lila's shoulder. "You don't have to tell me if it's too personal. But I would encourage you to share it with *mei bruder*. I could see the love in his eyes for you already. I'd hate for his heart to get broken."

Lila felt the sting of reality hit her. She didn't want to break Samuel's heart any more than she wanted her own heart to break. Is that why he hadn't asked her again? Had she broken his heart a little? She hoped her declaration of love had smoothed that over and would open the door for a future proposal from him.

"Would you mind if I practice on you before I have to tell Samuel? I do owe him that, but I'm afraid."

Rachel offered an accepting smile. "Whatever it is, you can be certain he is a very understanding *mann*. I see in his eyes how much he loves you, and that will not change. But you need to be able to trust him with whatever is holding you back."

"I decided a long time ago that I didn't want to marry and have *kinner* because *mei mamm* died a few minutes after I was born. She only got to hold me for a minute, and then she hemorrhaged. The doctor was not there, and *mei daed* couldn't save her. I've spent my entire life being afraid of the same thing happening to me."

"But you said you changed your mind?" Rachel interrupted.

"*Jah,* when I held little Adam yesterday, I realized that the risk is worth the reward."

Rachel pulled Lila into a hug. "Then you need to share your change of heart with Samuel. He will ask you again—I'm certain of it."

Lila prayed she was right.

Chapter 20

Abby and Lizzie entered in through the already crowded kitchen at the Yoder home.

"Lillian isn't coming," Lizzie said. "Ellie had a stomach ache and she doesn't want you getting sick before the wedding."

Rachel felt disappointment at her *aenti's* absence, and worry for her cousin. But they had too much work to finish for her to spend time dwelling on something she had no control over. She whispered a prayer for her family and then went back to work carving the meat from the pumpkins.

Lila placed a stew pot on the stove in preparation for cooking the pumpkin. She busied herself away from the others, feeling a little intimidated since they were all family.

Rachel put her arm around Lila and pulled her back toward the table. "If we are to be *familye,*" she whispered. "You better get used to talking to us."

Lila felt her pulse quicken and her cheeks heat up with worry that the others had overheard Rachel's whispers. She smiled, putting her best face forward, and bit down her anxiety for Samuel's sake. Rachel was right about her needing to draw closer to his family. It would give the probability of their future together a little push in the right direction. If she could get closer to these women, Samuel would be more likely to propose. Lila had not had the advantage of having family around her. She usually avoided community gatherings since she and her *daed* had mostly closed themselves off from everyone. Her *daed* had never gotten over losing her *mamm,* and Lila shied away from social events for the same reason.

Maybe Rachel's advice was for her own good, especially since she had never taken advantage of community events to draw her into the security and love they offered. Why *had* she closed herself off from everyone all these years? Now that she'd been exposed to the kindness and sense of belonging that *familye* offered, she was grateful for her *daed's* decision to send her here to stay with *Onkel* Jessup and her new *Aenti* Bess. Her new cousin, Adam, was going to grow up knowing he had family that loved him; Lila would make sure of it.

Lila moved about the kitchen, aware of the closeness of these women, and couldn't help but want to be a part of Samuel's family. He had declared his love for her only a few short moments before, and she was giddy with her love for him. It amazed her how much her life had changed since she'd come to stay in this community. Would her *daed* recognize the changes in her and want to change himself too? She hoped the move to be near his brother would help him to be more social. They had both spent a lifetime of being lonely and cut off from loved-ones. It was time to put the past to rest along with her *mamm,* and move on with their lives.

"Let me help you with that," Lila said bravely as she took two pumpkins from Abby's arms. "You shouldn't be lifting these in your condition."

Abby giggled. "I'm hoping a little hard work will bring this *boppli* into the world. I feel like I've been pregnant for too long. But I know it is all in *Gott's* timing."

Lila placed a comforting hand on her shoulder as she offered her a chair at the table. "How much longer do you have?"

Abby blew out a breath as she sat down with difficulty. "It should be any day now. I can't believe *mei bruder,* Caleb and his *fraa,* Katie, had their *boppli* before I did. I've been married longer than they have."

Lila smiled. "Like you said; it's all in *Gott's* timing."

Abby patted Lila's hand. "You'll make a *gut fraa* for *mei bruder,* Samuel."

Lila looked at Rachel. "Does everyone know?"

Lizzie crossed the room and pulled Lila into a hug. "I didn't know until just now. Why am I always the last to know what my *kinner* is up to?"

Lila swallowed hard. "I'm sorry you had to find out this way, but I'm not even certain I will be marrying Samuel. I'm waiting for him to ask me—again."

Lizzie pulled her coat off the peg near the door.

"I'm not sure I want to know what that is all about. I think you can let me know when it's official." She smiled at Lila. "Right now, I'm late to go meet *mei* new *grandkinner.*"

When she closed the door, Abby and Rachel giggled. "*Mamm* always thinks we keep things from her," Abby said.

"We do sometimes," Rachel said. "But she should expect that. It's the way *kinner* is. Our own *kinner* will do the same to us one day."

Abby rolled a hand over her large stomach.

"This *boppli* better not keep secrets from me."

Lila went to the stove and stirred the cooking pumpkin. She couldn't help but think that if she'd been fortunate enough to grow up with her *mamm* that she would have told her everything. She'd longed her entire life to tell her every little thing that happened to her. It was an especially large void now that she was in love and wanted to marry. It saddened her that her *mamm* would never have the chance to meet her *grandkinner*. Perhaps it was time she started sharing the things in her life with her *daed*. After all, he probably needed that closeness just as much as she did.

Chapter 21

Lizzie took the hand her husband offered as he assisted her into the buggy. Jacob tucked the lap quilt around her, being protective and considerate as always. She looked into his eyes lovingly, thinking he was more handsome than the day she fell in love with him. And to think that they had come full-circle with that love, and were now grandparents.

Jacob squeezed Lizzie's hand. "I still remember the first ride we took in this buggy. I was so nervous."

Lizzie smiled. "I was too. Things were so uncertain then. But now—well, now they are exactly as I imagined they would be in our future."

Jacob tugged on his beard that was peppered with gray. "Do you ever wonder what your life would have been like if you hadn't returned to the community? If we hadn't gotten married?"

"I think about it all the time," Lizzie said cautiously.

"I've never regretted the decision to marry you."

Lizzie nudged Jacob playfully. "I have a couple of regrets."

"You have?" Jacob said nervously as he slapped the reins against his gelding just lightly enough to move him forward. "You don't regret marrying me, do you?"

Lizzie sighed. "*Nee.* I just wish I could take back all the mistakes I've made in my life."

Jacob tucked his arm around his wife. "Those mistakes are what define who you are today. Without the little mistakes we've made, you and I would not be on our way to see our first *grandkinner.*"

Emotion caught up in Lizzie's throat. "I know that, but I would have preferred to have done everything right."

Jacob steered the gelding down the country lane. "If everyone did everything right all the time, then *Gott* wouldn't know our true heart. We have to endure these trials in life to make us stronger and to prepare us for eternity in Heaven."

"You're saying this was all in *Gott's* plan for us?"

Jacob nodded. *"Gott* knew every step we were going to take, every stumble, every fall—just to get to this place in our lives right at this very moment. He orchestrated every aspect of our lives to bring us to this very spot at this very time so that when we got here, it would be to drive over to see that new *boppli.*"

Lizzie adjusted the lap quilt a little more snuggly around her. "Why do you suppose *Gott* doesn't try to stop us from making the mistakes we do?"

"He gives us our own will, and when we walk from the path He has laid out for us, He's always at the end of that path waiting for us to turn from our mistakes and return to Him."

Lizzie looked up into her husband's aging eyes that could still put a song in her heart. "How did you get to be so wise?"

Jacob smirked. "I'm not so wise, I'm just old."

Lizzie clicked her tongue on her teeth. "If you're old, that makes me old. I'm not certain I'm ready to be old just yet."

Smiling, Jacob placed a loving arm around his wife. "I'm a *grossdaddi.*"

"Jah, and I'm a *grossmammi.* But I'm happy about it."

Jacob gave Lizzie a quick squeeze. "I am too. I wouldn't have it any other way."

"I hate to think what my life would have been like if I hadn't come back here."

Jacob brushed her cheek with a tender kiss.

"The important thing is that you did."

Lizzie looked up into the crisp, blue sky watching her breath form a fog in the cold air. "It seems like just yesterday when I'd first met Caleb. Now he's a grown *mann* with a *fraa* and a new *boppli*. Where has the time gone?"

Jacob let a chuckle escape him. "Do you remember the first thing he said to you?"

Lizzie's eyes filled with happy tears. "He put his little hand in mine and introduced himself to me, and then told me how happy he was that I was going to be his new *mamm*."

Jacob placed another kiss on Lizzie's cheek. "I'm so glad you put my name on Abby's birth certificate. But I'm even happier I had the opportunity to be her *daed*. I wouldn't have had our lives be any different."

Lizzie wiped her face with her apron. "I wouldn't either. I guess *Gott* knew what he was doing when He told me to put your name on that birth certificate."

Jacob craned his neck to look at his *fraa*. "You never told me that before."

"*Jah*," Lizzie said. "I prayed about it, and that was the first thing that came to me. It was like a bright light went off in my mind. I couldn't put Eddie's name on there since I was too afraid he'd find us and take her from me. So I prayed asking for guidance. I really believe that *Gott* put your name in my mind at that time. I didn't think twice about it. I just put it on there and never thought about it again until Abby was old enough to start asking about her father."

Jacob chuckled. "She's always been a curious little one."

"I'm certain that little *boppli* she's carrying is going to be just like her—the way it kicks day and night. That's the same way Abby was. Rachel and Samuel didn't kick me that much, and there were two of them! I hope she's prepared to have her hands full with that one."

Jacob turned the horse into the driveway of Caleb's *haus* and parked near the large oak tree. "She'll be just fine because she will have you to help her."

Lizzie turned to her husband and looked into his blue-green eyes. "*Danki* for marrying me that day."

Jacob leaned in until his lips met Lizzie's. "*Danki* you married me, too."

Lizzie gazed lovingly upon her husband. He was her past, her present, and her future, and she couldn't be more grateful to God for orchestrating it that way.

Chapter 22

Lila had to remind herself as she readied for Rachel's wedding that she was not just a guest. She was to be a server, and that meant she would be warm and sweaty from the heat in the kitchen. And so, she chose her lightest dress and apron. Though it was quite cold for the first day of November, Lila didn't want to overheat in the kitchen. Samuel would be watching her today, she was certain, and she didn't want to look flustered and washed out. She wanted to look like she was able to handle serving his entire family and the community with ease—she wanted to look like marriage material.

Downstairs, the B&B was already bustling with activity as the *menner* were busy setting up the benches for the wedding. All the furniture had been removed the day before and placed in the barn, making it easier for Lila to scrub the floors. It had taken her hours, but when she finished, it was so clean you could have eaten off the floor. Not that she would do such a thing, but the thought had crossed her mind, amusing her at the end of a very tiring chore.

Straightening her apron, Lila was satisfied she'd picked the right dress. It was already the second time she'd changed her clothes this morning, and she feared it wouldn't be her last before the day was through. Lila hurried down the stairs, worried she'd already been absent from the activities too long. If Rachel should need her for something, she wanted to be certain she would be available to her. To think that Rachel could someday be her sister-in-law made her somehow want to work even harder at making certain this wedding was perfect.

Katie's sister, Rose, had been the most help to Lila this morning. Together, they had managed to clean and prepare about fifty pounds of celery. The kitchen still lingered with the aroma of it as Lila entered.

"Now that you have a dry dress, maybe we can finish the table arrangements," Rose said to her.

"*Jah,* I think that is the last thing we have to do before the guests begin to arrive."

Half the community was already there, but they were each working on some aspect of the preparations. It had been a long morning, and Lila found herself looking forward to being able to sit through most of the three-hour ceremony.

She'd seen Samuel a few times from a distance, but she was certain he hadn't seen her. He was busy with Rose's husband, Noah, and the other men putting in the benches in the front parlor and large dining area so all the guests would fit. She wished today was *her* wedding day, but Samuel still had not asked her. Would he ever? Today, Lila determined, she would keep her mind on task, and keep her eyes where they belonged—on her work.

Samuel couldn't keep his mind on task. All he could do was search out Lila, hoping to catch little glimpses of her as they each worked to finish the wedding preparations. He wished today could be *his* wedding day. But the fact remained he hadn't dared to ask Lila even once more. Too afraid of being rejected every time he asked, he wasn't certain if he would ever be able to ask her again. Though he was certain she didn't realize it, her rejection had humiliated him.

Perhaps she will let me know when she's ready to be asked. After all, she did declare her love first.

Samuel let his mind fill with the memory of the sweet words that had rolled off Lila's tongue. He'd never heard sweeter words. He wanted more than anything to marry her, but he feared she may never be ready. Of course, he didn't think she'd ever tell him she loved him either, so maybe there was still hope.

Trying to get Lila's attention, Samuel nearly tripped over one of his small cousins. Why wouldn't she look at him? Had she changed her mind? How would he convince her to change it back?

Please, Gott, give me the strength to get through this day, and to be supportive of mei schweschder on her special day. Help me to keep my mind on the needs of mei familye so I don't wander from your path.

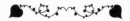

Near the conclusion of the ceremony, Lila and a few other women rose from their seats to ready the feast that had been prepared in honor of the wedding couple. Lila knew that Samuel would be busy moving the benches and setting up tables for everyone to eat. A long table had already been placed in the large kitchen, and Lila was busy uncovering dishes of food, and arranged the plates on the counters for easy access to all the guests. Several pitchers of sweet tea were being prepared, and rolls were being warmed in the oven.

Samuel suddenly burst into the kitchen, stopping abruptly when all eyes fell on him. "I need to see you outside for a minute, Lila."

Lila momentarily searched the faces of Samuel's family, looking for approval of Samuel's request, but none came. "Can't this wait?" Lila said through a gritted-toothed smile. "We have to tend to the wedding guests."

Lizzie shooed her son with a linen dishtowel.

"You can talk to her when everyone has been served, Samuel. Now get out of this kitchen."

"But *mamm,*" Samuel pleaded. "I'm not sure I can wait that long."

Lizzie looked at him sternly. "Then you'll have to keep those idle hands busy until Lila can talk to you later. Now go back and help the *menner,* and get out of this kitchen."

Samuel walked away feeling embarrassed by the giggles behind his back. He needed to ask Lila to marry him before he lost his nerve.

Chapter 23

Lila couldn't think straight. Was Samuel going to end things with her? She loved him, and he'd said the same to her. He'd kissed her like a man in love, but was it enough for him? Was he finally going to end it simply because she had turned down his proposals, or was he prepared to give her another chance and propose again? She prayed it was so.

Lila gazed upon Rachel and Blake, feeling somewhat envious of their commitment to one another. They knew exactly what they wanted, and they'd sealed their future together with marriage. Why couldn't she and Samuel be that happy?

Gott, free me from my stubbornness. Give me the courage to face my fears about marriage and having bopplies. The desire for those things is not enough. I need courage beyond my comprehension, Gott.

Lila worked in silence beside Samuel's *mamm*. Was the woman angry with her? She didn't think Lizzie was the type of woman to anger easily, but somehow, Lila wondered if maybe deep down, she disapproved of the blossoming relationship between Samuel and herself. When all was finished, Lila excused herself and went outside to look for Samuel. She had caught a glimpse of him out on the lawn setting up tables for the youth to have their meal.

As her feet padded across the dock, Lila remembered the sweetness of the kiss she'd shared with Samuel on this very spot. Gazing out across the pond, she had to admit that it was indeed a very romantic spot. Had he only gotten caught up in the moment of their kiss instead of falling in love with her the way he'd claimed? She prayed it wasn't so.

Behind her, she could hear the sound of a man's shoes padding across the dock toward her. She didn't dare turn around for fear it wasn't Samuel.

"I was hoping to find you out here so we could talk."

The familiar smooth baritone of Samuel's voice sent shivers through Lila. As he neared, she sensed his presence like a warm breath on the back of her neck. He leaned in and kissed the top of her head.

Lila whipped her head around. "Don't do that here. Half the community is only a short distance from us. What if someone sees?"

Samuel curled his fingers around hers. "Then they'll see a couple of people who are in love."

Lila felt giddiness overtake her, but she braced herself for Samuel's rejection. Though he loved her, would he refuse to move forward with a relationship since during their last conversation she'd informed him she didn't want to marry him? How could she tell him she changed her mind without seeming desperate? She *was* desperate for him to know of her change of heart.

"I know you were eager to talk to me earlier. Are you still as eager to tell me whatever it was you felt couldn't wait? Or have you changed your mind?"

Samuel held tight both her hands in his, pulling them to his mouth to blow his warm breath on them.

"Your fingers are like ice."

"I was hoping it would be a warmer day for your *schweschder's* wedding, but I'm grateful the sun is warm at least."

Samuel gazed into her eyes lovingly. "I wish we were alone so I could collect on my daily kiss."

Lila wasn't certain how much more small talk she could handle. "I want to marry you," she blurted out.

Samuel's eyes narrowed. "I haven't asked you. Why do you keep doing that to me?"

Lila's eyes misted. "I'm sorry. I understand if you don't want to marry me."

Samuel lifted Lila's chin and kissed her lips gently, not caring who would see their intimate moment. "I *do* want to marry you, but I want to be the one to do the asking."

Lila's lower lip quivered. "You said you wouldn't ask me again."

Samuel smiled. "Only because you said not to. But I was prepared to do just that earlier when I wanted to talk to you—when *mei mamm* kicked me out of the kitchen like I was still one of her wee *kinner.*"

Lila's face brightened as Samuel took a knee in front of her. Still holding her hands tightly, he looked up at her, his blue eyes sparkling in the afternoon sun.

"Will you marry me, Lila?"

Lila nodded. "*Jah*, I will. I will marry you and kiss you every day for the rest of our lives."

Samuel stood abruptly and pulled her into his arms, not caring who might witness their embrace.

"When did you change your mind?"

Lila kissed him full on the mouth.

"It was when you kissed me right here in this very spot, under the harvest moon."

The End

If you enjoy Amish Fiction, join me on Facebook

"Like" the page to be among the first to know about all future giveaways and contests.

Printed in Great Britain
by Amazon